EMERGING FRONTIERS

RENEWAL IN THE LIFE OF WOMEN RELIGIOUS

Sisters of Charity of Leavenworth, 1955–2005

EMERGING FRONTIERS

RENEWAL IN THE LIFE OF WOMEN RELIGIOUS

Sisters of Charity of Leavenworth, 1955–2005

Marie Brinkman, SCL

*Barb—
thank you for your thoughtful and insightful response
Marie*

Paulist Press
New York/ Mahwah, NJ

Scripture extracts are taken from the *New Revised Standard Version, Catholic Edition* Copyright © 1993 and 1989, by the Division of Christian Education of the National Council of the Churches of Christ in the United States of America and reprinted by permission of the publisher.

Unless otherwise identified, archival sources of photographs are the Sisters of Charity of Leavenworth Archives, individual hospital and clinic archives, and the University of Saint Mary Archives, used by permission.

Cover design by Lynn Else

Book design by Celine Allen

Copyright © 2008 by the Sisters of Charity of Leavenworth

All rights reserved. No part of this book may be reproduced or transmitted in any form or by any means, electronic or mechanical, including photocopying, recording, or by any information storage and retrieval system without permission in writing from the Publisher.

Library of Congress Cataloging-in-Publication Data

Brinkman, M. Jean (Marie Jean), 1932–
   Emerging frontiers : renewal in the life of women religious : Sisters of Charity of Leavenworth, 1955–2005 / Marie Brinkman.
      p.   cm.
   Includes bibliographical references and index.
   ISBN-13: 978-0-8091-4540-9 (alk. paper)
   1. Sisters of Charity of Leavenworth (Kan.)—History. I. Title.
   BX4454.B75 2008
   271'.91073—dc22

                                                   2008014259

Published by Paulist Press
997 Macarthur Boulevard
Mahwah, New Jersey 07430

www.paulistpress.com

Printed and bound in the
United States of America

*To my parents who gave me my brothers and all that belongs to life,
and to my sisters in community who challenge me daily*

Contents

Preface ix

Acknowledgments xi

Introduction 1

Part I
As We Were...

1. Reading the Signs 15
2. Responses of Head and Heart 29
3. Heeding Many Voices 41
4. Untold Stories 63

Part II
As We Struggled to Become...

5. Unfolding of a Drama 83
6. Experimentation: An Interval of Learning 104
7. Drama of Renewal, Continued 120
8. Getting from Here to There 139
9. A Heritage of Care: Children and the Aging 159
10. The Care of Teaching 178
11. Teaching an Investment 200
12. The Maturing of a College 222

13. A Heritage of Healing 247
14. Expanding Frontiers of Healing 267
15. Ministry in a Post–Vatican II World 289
16. Mission Unlimited 310
17. "The beginning and the end of our coming together…" 329
18. Seeking a Common Voice 343
19. Seeking a Common Vision 357

Part III
As We Are Becoming…

20. Re-envisioning the Charism 371
21. Crossing Borders 388
22. Jubilee: "Year of Favor from the Lord" 401
23. Motto for Community: "Choose Life" 424
24. Teaching: A Heritage Firm and at Risk 445
25. Health Care in New Hands 464
26. Emerging Frontiers 484

Epilogue 507

Notes 511

Appendix 575
    Living Sisters of Charity of Leavenworth, 1955–2005
    Deceased Sisters of Charity of Leavenworth, 1955–2005

Index 603

Preface

In general, three principles govern the telling of this story. The account of any religious community's life for the last half-century is particularly dependent on context, or the world of its unfolding. Renewal enjoined by the Vatican II Ecumenical Council required change that touched every nerve of that life. For two decades the rhythm of continuity and interruption, necessary to growth, became tension insistent enough to endanger the very continuance of that life as it had been known and cherished. The society served by such a community was itself changing in radical ways. The meaning of faith and authority, of sacred and secular, figured in questions being asked by the Church of itself and by all with moral responsibility.

Before Vatican II, however, women religious had been responding to calls for renewal of their life and ministry from both the Church and their own national leadership. Even a limited account of such a context is necessary, not as cause for effects but as the condition for a story that evolves on its own terms. Archival research that positions the Sisters of Charity of Leavenworth in early renewal among religious communities of women in the United States suggested comparisons. Data from National Sisters' Surveys commissioned by the Leadership Conference of Women Religious and from a study by the National Sisters Vocation Conference found significant parallels in other kinds of evidence from the Community archives. The story told here in its context is a heartening image of the Church in this country for the past fifty years.

A second guiding principle for telling the story was that it should draw on individual memory of experience, personal and communal, and reflection on change as it had developed. This occasioned the construction of surveys and analysis of responses, all in consultation with colleagues in behavioral and social science and, for graphics, information technology. Respondents to four surveys were the Sisters of Charity of Leavenworth, women who had lived in the Community and left it during the period, and a cross-section of associates, colleagues, and friends. Interviews and conversations complemented the surveys and archival research.

Chapters that integrate survey response into the history offer a new perspective on phenomena that drew attention through the 1970s and

1980s from religious and public media. Departures from religious community in startling numbers and radical change that perplexed many, both familiar with and strangers to the way of life, continue to provoke speculation. Chapter 4 uncovers patterns in extended reflections from former members of the Community that substantiate and personalize conclusions drawn from documents. Other surveys record individual impressions of change and reflection on central values that clarify the experience of the Sisters of Charity. In the process of integrating survey responses into the narrative, the recent past of hundreds of American religious congregations gains credibility. Personal accounts of discernment and ministry image the growth of a community expanding beyond institutional boundaries. From interpretation of recorded discussion, documented action, and reflective memory emerges a living history. (See Appendix for names of Sisters of Charity of Leavenworth who lived during the period of this history.)

A third principle invites the reader's understanding and, where it is needed, thoughtful critique. From the beginning of the task, the writer sought and prayed to see what is true and to say what is just. This cannot eliminate error or bias. Judgment of the outcome must rest with others wiser, better informed, and curious about what lies ahead. That the story is not simply a record of the Community's activities, achievements, and members may disappoint many. That story would take even a larger volume and would exceed the capacity of the author. If this account in some fashion mirrors the life of women religious serving the people of God in a crucial half-century of the history of the Church, it is perhaps a contribution to that developing story.

Notes on Terminology

At this point, I would like to explain certain stylistic aspects of the text.
- Because of frequent mention of religious communities and for the sake of clear distinctions, the term *Community* in reference to the subject of this history is capitalized.
- To distinguish the *Church* as the Body of Christ, born of his life, death, and resurrection, is to acknowledge the gift of his life to all as the way of eternal salvation. So, far from suggesting exclusive claims, capitalization of the term signals the universality of Christ's gift.
- To speak of the *people of God* is to recognize the freedom with which God is present and calls to every human being as open to truth and capable of redeeming grace.

Acknowledgments

Were it not for a request from my Community director, Sister Sue Miller, in the fall of 1999, this debt of gratitude would not have mounted over the past five years. I thank her first for a task that has brought me to know my Community as nothing else could, and for the freedom she gave to its realization.

For the thanks I owe three magnanimous, relentless, and discerning readers, I lack words. From the start, Sister Peter Parry provided insight beyond my ken and good counsel beyond my courage. Her assistance began with early planning and recommendations for interviews and continued for five years of reading and advice, all the way through the minute tasks of indexing. With an innate sense of style and rare certitude, Sister Maureen Craig distinguished between what worked in the manuscript and what did not. Her advice was perceptive, invaluable, and a pleasure to follow. My colleague, Sister Susan Rieke, edited the text with the linguistic precision and structural instinct only a poet and professor of English enjoys. She prevented more than a few disasters; those that remain are mine. For all this aid and more from these generous counselors, I am deeply grateful.

An editorial board of some thirty-five sisters piloted the surveys and offered valuable suggestions. They included Sisters Madelon Burns, Kathleen Coman, Marie de Paul Combo, Rosalie Curtin, Jean Martin Dawson, Georgeanne Desch, Mary Jo Downey, Peg Driscoll, Mary Sarah Fasenmeyer, LaVonne Guidoni, Agnes Virginia Hamm, Bernadette Helfert, Eileen Hurley, Mildred Marie Irwin, Paulette Krick, Ann Louis LaLonde, Ann Loendorf, Mary Lenore Martin, Mary Janet McGilley, Perpetua McGrath, Mary Helen McInerney, Rose Carmel McKenna, Mary Beth Minges, Jean Anne Panisko, Victoria Perkins, Peter Parry, Mary Hilaria Phipps, Susan Rieke, Linda Suzanne Roth, Frances Russell, Barbara Schrader, Daniel Stefani, Mary Kathleen Stefani, Anita Sullivan, and Mary Andrew Talle.

Sister Mary Kevin Hollow and Sister Mary Kathleen Stefani, former Community directors; Sister Mary Janet McGilley, late president emerita of Saint Mary College; and Sister Rose Dolores Hoffelmeyer, author of the Community's Latin American mission history, graciously provided clarifying information. Without the professional consultation and oversight of

Dr. Nancy King, I could not have created valid, useful surveys of members, former members, and Associates and friends of the Community. Her counsel and her reading of the manuscript were invariably honest and reassuring. Rick Silvey constructed precise charts and graphs to accompany my analyses. To these colleagues on the faculty of the University of Saint Mary I owe many thanks.

The daily presence and instantaneous support of the Community treasurer, Sister Katherine Franchett, and Sister Dorothy Marie Rilinger made travel and accounting easy. Margaret Anne Kearns gave me technical assistance of every kind from computerization of data analyses to the loan of her laptop, with no limits on time spent saving me from PC fatalities. Dean Stith generously assisted my halting computer operations, made my tables look good, and burned countless CDs for me. At my hand daily, Evelyn Lange made my computer do whatever I could not manage. For charting an appendix, scanning innumerable photographs, creating sample pages—and much more—I am grateful to Sister Paulette Krick. Sister Kathleen Mary Connelly was an invaluable resource for photographs, creating composites where these were not available. She made me a partner in the enterprise.

Throughout the work, Sister Ann Louise Eble guided me through the vast territory of Community archives, assisting my searches, identifying needed files, and resolving difficulties. Sisters Rose Marie Catudal, Perpetua McGrath, and Vincent Clare McDonald, of the archival staff, helped me in specific ways. Sister Mary Lenore Martin opened university archives to me; Sister Barbara Sellers, Community archivist, pointed out files of great benefit. Both kindly researched historical records and data. Former Community secretary Sister Helen Forge assisted me with vital information regarding membership and other records necessary for Chapter reports. Sister Margaret Ellen Johnson, Community secretary, never failed to answer vital questions. Her assistants, Janet Seber and Stephanie Balock, tirelessly researched and ordered Community statistics in useful and accessible formats.

Recording data and verbal entries from surveys was a demanding task. I am grateful for the care and skill with which Sister Mary Erwin Baker and Sister Kathy Atkins devised computer formats for complex survey responses. Sister Mary Hilaria Phipps recorded extensive verbal accounts with necessary attention and accuracy. Meeting other needs, she cheerfully searched many essential websites for me.

For painstaking work with records, I am grateful to Sister Kathleen Coman, who died with the labor almost finished, and to Sister Delia

Lawless, who completed it. With characteristic ingenuity, Sister Ann Barton was always on call to provide necessary information. Sister Regina Mary Link, Mother House librarian, secured books with economy and dispatch. Sister Donna Jean Hanson replied to requests for supplies that she frequently delivered. Environmental, maintenance, and administrative staffs met innumerable and unpredictable needs with professional competence and unfailing courtesy.

The welcome extended on visits to the Sisters of Charity Health System hospitals in Billings, Butte, Grand Junction, and Denver and to St. Vincent's Home deepened the familial dimension of the work. Sisters opened their homes and made available their staffs, offices, and archives. Thanks to the sisters and resources there, Saint John's Health Center in Santa Monica became a second worksite and—more important—community family. Innumerable conversations turned research in these cities into personal encounters; informal interviews provided valuable material. The price of such generous collaboration is my inability to include more of the result in this history. The same applies to countless conversations with sisters at home in Leavenworth, Kansas City, and Topeka. Responses to the necessity of reducing an hour's visit to a sentence or paragraph have been repeatedly magnanimous.

I am indebted to William Kevin Cawley, archivist and curator, University of Notre Dame Archives, for access to documents of the LCWR Sisters' Surveys and review of their use in my text. Sister Barbara Kraemer, OSF, then director of the Center for the Study of Religious Life in Chicago, was helpful in my early research.

Without the professional guidance and technological proficiency of former publisher Tom Turkle, the work would not have been completed. Pertinent questions and good counsel were only the preface to essential communication with Paulist Press and preparation of the manuscript in required formats for final submission. Sister Mary Ann Theisen's meticulous work made possible the final proofing on time. Sisters Linda Roth and Kathleen Mary Connelly and Sandi Crisp and Evelyn Lange gave invaluable assistance.

For their energetic collaboration in the task of publishing the book and their unfailing professionalism, I am deeply thankful to Paulist Press editors Paul McMahon, Kevin di Camillo, and Celine Allen. Celine's editing was singularly helpful and perceptive.

For the considerable time and attention they gave to two demanding surveys, I thank my sisters across the Community. For all manner of quiet support and assistance from the sisters of my local community in Mead and my office floor in Cantwell, I am more grateful than actions tell. Sisters of the Mother House and Ross Hall have been a steady resource of prayer and encouragement. The personal presence, sensible humor, and spiritual strength of all these friends nourish the Community whose story follows. For what it lacks of anything, I ask the reader's cheerful tolerance.

Introduction

The altar boys were young and newly trained, proud to be serving the bishop's Mass at their parish church in Kansas City, Missouri, one Sunday in the 1970s. At the offertory these neophytes were, by some miscalculation, offering the water and towel a second time to the bishop, who waved them away. But the youngster holding the water stood his ground and cautioned His Excellency in the clear and certain tones only the very young can manage, "You better. Sister said you'd do it."[1]

With no more than a smile, the bishop washed his fingers a second time.

Whatever else it recalls, the incident is a reminder of the aura of competence, order, and authority that surrounded Catholic sisters at midcentury and a decade or two beyond. It was a reputation earned, not assumed, in service to a Church that needed such competence in its schools, hospitals, and homes for children and aging persons in need. The authority, moreover, was limited to a sphere and range of competence assigned by others—ecclesiastical superiors responsible for the institutions staffed by sisters. Nonetheless, they were women more often than not respected by parents, students, patients, pastors, bishops, and altar boys.

These sisters, including missionaries and social workers ministering beyond diocesan and national borders, numbered 158,069 in 1954, members of some 250 religious communities,[2] a few indigenous to the United States, most in extension from European foundations. They had been, for upwards of a century and a half, pioneers of Catholic education, health care, and manifold works of mercy in a country of immigrants, a nation shaped by advancing frontiers. Their story has not yet been—may never be—adequately told. The account of a given religious community can be but a portion of what is so far a fragmentary record.

The story of the Sisters of Charity of Leavenworth, from their founding on the western banks of the Missouri River through their growth into ten middle western and far western states, has been told by one of its early members, Sister Mary Buckner; it has been retold, in a biography of the Community's founder, Mother Xavier Ross, and in an account of its first century of growth, two works by Sister Julia Gilmore. The story reaches back to the prelude of a civil war that rent the young nation, and forward to the end of a world war that thrust that same nation into global leadership. Within that framework of violence, the lives of these women religious represented a continuity of purpose and commitment that became a bulwark of faith for the people they served, a public symbol of transcendent values, and a sign to many of the presence of God.

This new chapter of the story carries it forward through a half-century of change that for many diminished, if it did not destroy, that image—change that threatened the very unity of the Community itself. Contrary to the impression that all change in the contemporary Church began with Vatican II, some women religious in the 1950s were asking themselves questions that anticipated new frontiers in their way of life. They were asking if the competence, so evident in the conduct of countless schools and in the care of countless patients and children, was adequate for rapidly advancing standards. They were wondering if the valuable order maintained in religious institutions had been bought at the price of individual freedom and initiative. They were pondering the authority assumed to be theirs by parishioners, coworkers, and patients, and measuring it against new and demanding goals. They were contemplating their own capacities, their own limited knowledge, their own spiritual shortcomings, and looking with faith to what lay ahead. The Sisters of Charity of Leavenworth were no exception to this spirit of inquiry, not yet strong enough to suggest a need for profound change. We know this from documents and decisions not meant to be prophetic.

Significantly, it was Pope Pius XII who called for national congresses of religious in every country to examine their way of life and apostolic works in the light of contemporary culture and the needs of its people. Mother Mary Francesca O'Shea, her councilors, Sisters Mary Ancilla Spoor, Mary Immaculata Desmond, Agnes Vincent Bauman, Mary Lorian Degan, and the novice mistress, Sister Laurentia Sullivan, participated in the first congress of its kind in the United States, held at Notre Dame University in 1951. In that same year, Social Security was taken out for all employees of the Community's institutions who wished it. Ending its ninety years' history, St. Mary's Academy closed in 1950 to allow for the inauguration of a Graduate Division of Saint Mary College that would award the master's degree in education needed by administrators of schools in Kansas staffed by religious communities. Four Sisters of Charity were awarded the Community's first degrees in pharmacy, earned at Creighton University and the University of Missouri in Kansas City.[3]

Other precursors of change were more explicit. Replies to correspondence with women under temporary or perpetual vows who left the Community between 1960 and 1968 revealed conditions that needed close attention. The letter sent to them sought honest evaluation to illuminate possible causes of less than a decade's departures. Patterns of response emphasized contrasts between "beautifully human and sensitive" sisters and superiors and those who assumed "mothering" roles or controlling oversight; between concentration on perfect observance of the rule and a desirable and healthier stress on its purpose; between priority placed on the "job" or on the living of community that "is the heart of religious life." After six and a half years in the Community and four months since departure, one woman reflected on a life that now seemed unnecessarily complicated, unrealistic, relatively ineffective, and self-centered, while another found it a sound preparation for motherhood and service to the Church.

Such contrasts—natural to most human experience of a phenomenon—take on significance in the light of the renewal to come. Some of the concerns expressed were almost prophetic—for more stress on personal relationship with Christ and the significance of other people, for more open association with lay people, and for more attention to the individuality and maturity of candidates and to personal qualifications of superiors. Concerns focused on better professional preparation and acquaintance with world events, on mature spiritual direction, and on personal values as the foundation of conscience and responsible choice. All such pleas presaged change to come. One of the most touching and unconsciously profound appeals was that the "smallest voice should be heard at all times."[4]

The centennial celebration of 1958 betrayed, however, neither an excess nor a lack of confidence in the future. In her syllabus for a course in Community history, marking the event, Sister Mary Paul Fitzgerald began with a statement significant for any future account: "To know whence we are, why we are, what we are would seem to be the very minimum required by our dignity as religious women." Observing that the Community is "a grass roots foundation springing from a local spiritual need on the frontier...," she wrote of the founding sisters that "they pioneered wherever they went." She said serenity marked their spirit, and no little humor.[5] Their story must reflect the spirit of their deeds.

The first Sisters of Charity came to the land known as "bleeding Kansas" in November 1858, at the request of John Baptist Miege, SJ, Vicar Apostolic of the Indian Territory. Recommended to him by the missionary, Peter De Smet, SJ, Mother Xavier first met the bishop in St. Louis, then visited Leavenworth to get the lay of the land and to see what sort of service to Indians and settlers she and her sisters were being asked to give. Enthusiastic about prospects, the first to come were five professed, a novice, two postulants or young applicants to the Community, and an orphan. Six more sisters and three orphans joined them in December.

Mother Xavier and Sister Joanna Brunner arrived in February, having settled all the business of closing the academy in Nashville, Tennessee, paying debtors, and thanking friends. Their young diocesan community had separated from the original foundation of Sisters of Charity at Nazareth, Kentucky, and found themselves under a bishop ultimately unable to sponsor them. They now came west, to a frontier that needed their ministry but could offer little material support.

Leavenworth was the first city and the military outpost of a territory that wanted schools, hospitals, and—it was soon discovered—orphanages. That Mother Xavier had a predilection for orphans was no disadvantage. Within a week after their arrival, the sisters accepted responsibility for the boys then being taught by a Jesuit brother in a cottage near the bishop's rectory. Shortly after this they opened a school for girls in a frame building across the street from their small convent cottage. In a larger house, St. Mary's Academy opened for boarders in the spring of 1859. Parentless children of the area were welcomed to the Academy and boys' school from 1861, and five years later to the new St. Vincent's Orphan Asylum. The territory's first civilian hospital, St. John, with the territory's first registered nurse, Sister Joanna, in charge, was opened in 1864 when immigrant families were pouring into the frontier. Little more than five years later, the growing Community sent five sisters to Montana in response to the repeated requests of Father De Smet, their first benefactor in the West.[6]

There they opened a hospital, academies, parish schools, and an orphanage. A similar sequence of building and staffing occurred in Colorado, when the Community was able to respond to entreaties for sisters from pastors or bishops or laymen. But resources were few. The school or hospital the sisters were to staff was yet to be built; living quarters were scant or temporary. Food and fuel for patients and children were the priority; the sisters considered their own needs deferrable. Sewing towels and bedding by hand or on borrowed machines; getting coal from army surplus at thirty-five cents a ton—when the market price was eleven dollars; securing monthly subscriptions of seventy-five cents from Anaconda Copper Mining employees were stratagems of ingenuity and a little luck.[7] This did not prevent sisters, in school and hospital convents, from serving "St. Joseph boys," the homeless who could count on one good meal on a jobless day. Convents were the precursors of soup kitchens.

"Vincent had a passion for simplicity," wrote Sister Mary Paul, "and his chief preoccupation...was the salvation...of the average Christian, above all the despised and neglected." These pioneer sisters and their successors had no trouble finding such people. In Kansas they opened the first school for Negroes; in Wyoming a school for Indian girls; in California, without support from the Board of Pediatrics Service, a clinic for children in need. In their first stage of development, 1864–98, the Community's hospitals commonly received the chronically ill, the injured, the homeless, and the insane. Consistently, they would give the same care and accommodation to the indigent as to the paying patient.[8]

Initial growth of the Community in the rapidly expanding city it served led Bishop Miege to recommend in 1869 the building of a Mother House on a wooded plot of land south of Leavenworth. In anticipation of its cost, Mother Xavier sent two sisters eastward, across the Mississippi to the coast, from Maryland up to Massachusetts, soliciting contributions from the faithful wherever bishops gave them leave. Both sisters were natives of Ireland, one of them nineteen years old. This simple begging, carried on with dignity and courage, open to rebuff and occasional humiliation, became the pattern wherever the Community opened institutions. In the West, it became a venture worthy of film or fiction. Accounts of the begging tours in letters written home are material for many a tale— of miners and bartenders, loggers and railroad workers, not a little astonished at these women coming to request a portion of their wages for children or the afflicted.[9]

By the turn of the century, the sisters numbered 280. The sixteen who had founded the Community had attracted 411 young women to their way of life. Seventy-eight of these had died in its service; fifty-three had found themselves unsuited to religious life. They had established and still maintained twenty schools, ten hospitals, a school of nursing, and three homes for children, in six states. The Community and Academy were housed in two Victorian buildings, Italianate in style; a third, attached to these, and the Chapel of the Annunciation, a replica of a Renaissance basilica, were dedicated fourteen years later.[10]

Brought into being at no little cost, such foundations are the story of every religious community serving on the successive frontiers of the burgeoning nation. During these decades and early in the twentieth century, six congregations put down stakes in Kansas: Benedictines, Dominicans, Ursulines, Sisters of St. Joseph, Sister Adorers of the Precious Blood, and Sisters of Charity.[11] They supported themselves and their apostolic works by living much of the time in dire poverty; by appealing to the charity of residents in the communities they served; and by begging for contributions from people of good will. They had no lay or ecclesiastical organizations, as did missionaries of other faiths, to provide regular financial support.

The archives of the Sisters of Charity of Leavenworth witness to an invincible trust in the Providence of God, a trust without presumption. They were ministering not only in frontier territories, but in a missionary country. When they saw that their numbers, though growing, were not sufficient to maintain the institutions they were called on to staff, they turned to a land replete with young women eager or willing to experience life in America. Two sisters traveled to Ireland in 1895 to bring back a group of thirty-eight young women to begin their novitiate in Kansas; a second group of thirty-six arrived in 1903. Between the two dates, thirty-eight more entered the Community, besides the dozens of Irish women who came before and after.[12]

The hallmark of this first half-century of the Sisters of Charity of Leavenworth was a spirit that would carry them through the next fifty years: the abiding love of neighbor that sees a need only to meet it, whatever the cost; imagination and courage that finds a way through unpredictable difficulty; and a serene and contagious zeal that attracts collaborators in the venture. No one of these sisters would lay claim to such a spirit but as a gift of God, to whom they had vowed their lives, to whose care they had entrusted their daily endeavors, and whose Son was the beginning and end of their charity. The spirit and rule of Vincent de Paul and his associate, Louise de Marillac, were being adapted to the needs of nineteenth-century American frontiers.

Within two decades after Mother Xavier's death in 1895, the ninth head of the Community, Mother Mary Berchmans Cannan, undertook the process of gaining papal approval, which would put the sisters under the auspices of the Congregation for Religious in Rome. This would free them to serve in whatever area of the Church they were needed. With the decree of the Third Plenary Council of Baltimore in 1884 that parochial schools be established in all parishes to educate Catholic children, dozens of communities of women religious across the country were summoned to staff those schools. By 1910, more than 4,800 elementary schools, enrolling more than 1,237,200 students, claimed the services of more than 40,000 women religious. Adequate education for the teachers was an overwhelming necessity.[13]

Social and political conditions complicated the task. The mechanization of society, a European conflagration that had drawn the United States into the first of two world wars, and the most severe economic depression in the nation's history were the harsh context of the Community's growth in the first half of the twentieth century. As standards of production, distribution, labor, and wages were developing in the industrial and commercial world, so standards of service in both private and governmental agencies imposed necessary controls and tested the resources of non-profit providers.

Religious communities governed by women led the way in establishing standards of performance in education, child care, and nursing. Diocesan certification of teachers in Kansas' Catholic schools pre-dated the Baltimore ruling. Sister Mary Olive Mead received the first certificate in 1888; thirty-eight more Sisters of Charity of Leavenworth were certified at the same time, twenty-one of them for life. The Community's standards were no less stringent: a 1902 Revised Course of Study for Use in Schools of the Sisters of Charity of Leavenworth was succeeded in 1915 by Directives for Teachers and Outlines of School Management.[14]

It was Mother Berchmans's insight into the needs of educating and certifying religious teachers that led to the opening in 1923 of a junior college in St. Mary's facilities. It shortly became a four-year liberal arts institution, equipped to prepare with baccalaureate degrees teaching religious and lay women for service to the Church and American society. For the first two decades of the college's existence, laymen filled the office of president, assisted by Sisters of Charity as deans or later vice president. Growth depended in large part on the quality of its early faculties: lay women and men recommended by their teaching experience and sisters assigned to earn advanced degrees from both Catholic and leading state universities.

Those assigned to hospitals received their training in nursing schools and in hospitals, mentored by professionals on the job. By the 1940s, a year's college courses preceded two years of clinical training. National associations of medicine and nursing further standardized training in three years of college and clinical experience. Progress in health care followed patterns originating both in research laboratories and in battlefield conditions. From treatment of shrapnel wounds, effects of poison gas, and the flu epidemic of World War I came new clinical practice and research in vaccinations, diagnostic radiology, and antibiotics. From the very weaponry of World War II came the promises of nuclear medicine; field surgery initiated advances in anesthesiology, use of blood plasma, and early ambulation of patients. Modern "miracles" of open-heart surgery and joint replacement developed from life-or-death decisions in field hospitals. Hospitals staffed by the Sisters of Charity of Leavenworth in Kansas, Colorado, Montana, and Wyoming looked to such advances in their strategic planning. Departments of cardiopulmonary medicine and technology, orthopedic surgery, radiation, and immunotherapy required entire staffs of specialized physicians and nurses. In anticipation of wartime and postwar needs on the West Coast, civic and religious leaders of Santa Monica, California, had sought the Community's sponsorship of their thirteenth hospital, dedicated as Saint John's in 1942.[15]

Traditionally havens for foundlings and unwed mothers, the Community's hospitals gave impetus to nursery homes. Attached to St. John's in Helena from 1881, St. Ambrose's Orphans Home enlarged to St. Joseph's Home twelve years later. A baby annex at St. Joseph's Hospital in Denver, from 1902 accepted infants from hospitals and nursery homes in the city until its necessary expansion led to the opening, in 1917, of the

Holy Child Nursery. St. Vincent's Orthopedic Hospital School in Billings, Montana, served children from four western states and inspired movement of the work into the Middle West. In the turbulent decades that spawned the Second World War, social agencies favored foster homes for children without parents; the Social Services Act of 1935 provided financial aid for them. After the war, increasing numbers of children of wartime marriages, broken homes, or dysfunctional families crowded established institutions and overburdened the foster home system.[16] Counselors and the courts saw the need to create new systems of child care, as well as new formats for special and individualized education.

Delinquency and drop-out rates were distressing a system struggling to handle postwar revolutions in both the advancement of knowledge and the science of teaching. The education department of Saint Mary College was gaining a reputation in the public school system for the quality of its graduates and student teachers. Located in the vicinity of the Command and General Staff College of the United States Army, Saint Mary enrolled "boot-strappers," World War II veterans whose college education was funded by the G.I. Bill of 1944. The faculty was challenged to offer learning experiences as significant, if not as dramatic, as those of daily living in harm's way.

Bishops in the region, aware of developing needs, sought sisters to staff new facilities. Bishop Paul C. Schulte's building program for orphans, the aging, and the homeless led to the opening of Mount Saint Joseph Home for the aging in Kansas City, Kansas, in 1946. As early as 1920, Bishop Edwin Vincent O'Hara had initiated the idea of religious education for Catholic rural youth; it would generate thousands of religious vacation schools under the umbrella of the Confraternity of Christian Doctrine. The sisters assigned to schools taught Saturday and Sunday classes and in summer vacation schools. From the beginning, however, in the summer of 1929, the sisters had shown a "missionary enthusiasm, long dormant, or never evoked.... Many volunteered for the work...."[17] CCD correspondence courses, monitored by students, were organized out of Saint Mary College. Students knew too that some of their teachers visited inmates in the federal and state prisons north and south of Leavenworth, in a tradition of ministry that had begun with the coming of the Sisters of Charity to Kansas. Home of the sisters who served in these ministries, the present Mother House was dedicated in 1940, an imposing neoclassical structure built with vision toward a future dependent on a diligent faith.

In 1958 the Community celebrated its centenary with the opportunity to look back at the winding paths by which it had come to all of its mid-century frontiers. The nation had outgrown—if it had ever rightly claimed—its Manifest Destiny, looking now to potential statehood for ocean-bound territories, to explorations of space and nuclear fission, and to international tensions that could thrust the world into a third and fatal conflagration. Its postwar frontiers were those of science and technology, security and prosperity, and tenuous balances of power. In contrast, a religious community, never really isolated from the world it served, symbolized a peaceful daily existence founded on common beliefs, purposes, and customs, faithful to a charism, or spirit, defined by a specific and concrete rule, and faithful as well to its apostolic commitments.

In the first century of their life on a frontier that had moved westward from Leavenworth at a dizzying pace, the Sisters of Charity had proved themselves genuine pioneers, breaking new ground and establishing institutions with a sense of permanence. The sisters now numbered 873, staffing sixty-one elementary schools, eleven secondary schools, fourteen hospitals, and four homes for children and the elderly.[18] By dint of a broad base of support and their reputation as professional religious educators and caregivers, they were part of a network that spanned the country; their foundations soon stretched from Chicago to Los Angeles. But statistics and professionalism were not the ultimate measure of their worth.

That lay in their fidelity to their origins, in the mission of Vincent and Louise to the poor; in their fidelity to the Church, serving her people under the aegis of their pastors and bishops; in their fidelity to Jesus Christ through the daily living of their vows in community. Their distinction was a way of life marked by simplicity, realistic self-appraisal, undiscriminating hospitality, and readiness to perform any service for anyone in distress—in the words of their Constitutions: a spirit of simplicity, humility, and charity. That they had lived as individual members or as community leaders with exceptional, even heroic, courage was not how they would describe their experience. They did not often think of themselves as pioneers. That they were what a recent social historian would call Americanist in their loyalties[19] was perfectly natural, philosophically and practically. By reason of their place in history, their education and culture, they found little if any contradiction between the teachings of Catholicism and the political and economic order of their country.

Theirs was an age of breaking ground, of building the institutions that a progressive frontier needed, in the name of a faith that a frontier could not of itself sustain. They had achieved what explorers made way for, stabilized what missionaries had died for. And they had developed a quality of service respected by professional peers and sought out by clients of every religious persuasion, in fields essential to family and community life: healing the sick, caring for children, teaching the young, comforting the aging and the dying. There had been little time and little demand for critical reflection on the way of life that nurtured them. That was soon to change.

Over the course of the next fifty years, the Sisters of Charity of Leavenworth were to examine the ways they observed their commitment to the Gospel of Jesus by vows of poverty, chastity, and obedience; the ways they celebrated the Eucharist and prayed together; the ways they daily lived in community; the ways they ministered to the needs of God's people; and—not quite incidentally—the way they dressed. They were about to extend their ministry to South America and, through individual sisters supported by the Community, very nearly around the globe. They were soon to minister to victims of AIDS and to advocate for victims of systemic urban poverty. Their convents would soon include houses situated in deprived areas, open to women of all classes who need some quiet space for themselves and a sense of belonging to a community beyond their family. Clinics designed to meet medical needs of the uninsured and new ways of sheltering children were in the making. In coalitions with other communities of women and men, religious and lay, through membership on boards and lobbying in legislatures, they were to act vigorously for justice and for peace. They were soon to welcome lay Associates in a shared reverence for the spirit of their founders.

Again, such things were accomplished at no small cost. Chapters, elective bodies representing the Community's members, agonized every six years over issues that first divided and ultimately united them. Experiments in community and ministry both strengthened and weakened common life, extended the services of existing institutions, developed into new missions. All occurred in the face of diminishing numbers, aging members, and fewer applicants to succeed them. If the test of every innovation was fidelity to the Gospel and to the charism of their founders, the binding force of the sisters during the next half-century was the charity they professed. But discernment of what justice, renewal, and charity required was not easy; it required a trust and openness to the Spirit that would transform their patient endurance into lively hope.

The story we begin here, then, is one of change in the past fifty years of the life of the Sisters of Charity of Leavenworth, but of change ratified in continuity: continuity of the pioneer spirit and determination that moved their founders, continuity of their very identity. The frontiers, having outstripped geography, now defy imagination. Leadership and heroism are daily redefined. By now the most thoughtful of the world's inhabitants recognize that the needs of the human spirit will not be denied. Religious leaders are reaching across ancient barriers to arrive at mutual respect, if not yet reunion. The spirit of Vatican II informs whatever identity we may seek to clarify and continue. A Church defined by its mission to realize the reign of God, scriptures that record a story of salvation wrought with leading roles assigned to women invite us to understand our vocation ever more deeply. Lay people ask our collaboration in service that does not depend on our numbers. That we have not yet realized the potential of our teaching, the manifold forms of our healing, ways of meeting the range of needs in children and aging populations is reason for hope, not discouragement.

The story falls into three parts that aim at our knowing a little better "whence we are," or who we were in 1955; "why we are," or how we struggled to remain who we were within transforming change; and "what we are," or who we have become since then, to ourselves and to the people of God. It aims to be the story not so much of events and achievements as of all the members of the Community who lived it. A possible aid to the reader who seeks particular facts is identification of chapters by content and focus. The account of what life in Community was like and what renewal effected develops in chapters 1–4, 5–8, and 17–19. Institutional ministries have their own stories in chapters 9–16, with diversity of ministry growing from these experiences as well as from freedom to change. An honest struggle to renew the Community's charism and mission in the Church with recovered unity and common purpose underlies the story of chapters 20–26.

Principles learned first from teachers at Saint Mary College are guides in this attempt to tell the story of fifty years with justice: principles that say one must, to understand effects, distinguish causes from conditions; find significance and look at events in their context; and trust many perspectives from a broad range of view. A contemporary religious historian, Thomas Tweed, has said that "historical narratives...are *ordered* chronicles ...that construct meaning out of the human past."[20] Insofar as such a statement describes the task at hand, the maker of such a narrative must select evidence from the mass available and call on "ordering elements" for shaping the story. Because the narrative aims to be a living history, evidence is both recorded fact and remembered experience.

The overarching ordering element of this narrative, however, is the living presence to the people of God of a community of women whose heritage is a life of charity, in the spirit of Vincent and Louise, as it has been lived by their founders and predecessors for a century and a half; and whose future will continue that heritage in ways still being shaped by a half-century of inquiry, renewal, and developing vision. How they will pioneer in the world of this third millennium is the challenge. That women religious, in their unique communal character and in their unity with other lay women of the Church, will be a recognizable and effective power in the global community of God's people is the promise of this and every similar story.

I

AS WE WERE...

CHAPTER 1

Reading the Signs

When the New Madrid earthquake changed the course of the Mississippi River at St. Louis in 1812, many thought that by divine intervention the American people were being given a prolonged chance to reform their dissolute ways and save their souls. The Great Awakening of religious fervor that had begun early in the eighteenth century and its evolution into the Revivalist movement of the nineteenth gained new impetus from such events as signs of God's displeasure with a people who had clearly been chosen for an immortal destiny and stood in danger of forfeiting it.[1]

Ann Ross's father was a fundamentalist Methodist minister who believed with all his heart that renewal of a religious spirit and moral regeneration were the only hope of the new nation moving westward; he preached that message to his congregation in Cincinnati on the Ohio River. The grief of his soul was Ann's conversion to Catholicism in 1829 and—an act of further and deeper rebellion—her entrance into religious life as a Sister of Charity of Nazareth, Kentucky. Though her mother in the end blessed Ann's decisions, her father's last words to her were written in severe reproach sometime in 1836. Severance from all she had known and loved was to become the pattern of Xavier Ross's early religious life, which led her from Nazareth to Nashville and then to the frontier beyond the Missouri River. Her companions had in 1851 elected her Mother Xavier, their first superior to be recorded in the Catholic directory of the time.[2]

Mother Xavier Ross

With such pioneer foundations by women religious, the shifting of a mighty river's course would become sign and symbol of a different kind. The Community these sisters founded in 1858 was, a century later, about to experience change of seismic proportions. But like the great rivers they crossed on their way to the Indian Territory, that Community shifted its course without losing its identity or drying up its rich bottom lands. It had sent its roots deep into middle-western soil and nurtured them with unwavering purpose and daily sacrifice, not to speak of the suffering that attends human limitations. Forty years after their centenary, the sisters gathered on the Mother House grounds in Leavenworth to journey a few miles to the bank of the Missouri River near the spot where their founders had disembarked. There they placed a marker that informs passersby of women who came west to minister to the needs of a frontier people.

A century after their coming, the nation fronted oceans that no longer protected its shores. The 1950s manifested national strength recently nourished by victory over powerful foes. Yet the price of victory was the threat of unprecedented atomic destruction as well as a Cold War and an arms race that were to consume resources and human lives for four decades. After World War II, the Berlin Wall rose as an effective symbol of the world's separation into armed camps. At home, anti-Communism reached fever pitch, bred McCarthyite hysteria that afflicted even Congress, and perverted national policy. The United States supported dictators, immune to the needs of their people, in the name of Soviet containment and helped to suppress Third World revolutions as inimical to national security. Defense of vulnerable new nations in Africa ran parallel to exploitation of natural and human resources by American firms in Latin America, where an Alliance for Progress floundered for lack of U.S. funding. Seen as prey to Asian forms of Communism, Vietnam became the battleground of East and West, bloodied by the deaths of Buddhist villagers, Ho Chi Minh's warriors, and fifty-eight thousand American soldiers. Three presidents governed a nation rent by grief, protest, and the opposing convictions tolerated by a democracy.

In American streets, riots and bloodshed attended enforcement of laws made necessary to uphold the Fourteenth Amendment. Topeka, Kansas—capital of the state where blood had first been shed in the legal conflict over slavery—was site of the 1954 lawsuit, *Brown v. Board of Education*, that culminated in the civil rights legislation of the 1960s. Throughout that decade many acts of heroic defiance, on the part of both African and Caucasian Americans, countered methodical resistance to racial integration. After her son's brutal murder in Mississippi, Mamie Moxley Till insisted that his mutilated body be visible to all who came to

1950's
1960's

mourn. Fifty thousand Chicagoans saw what blind prejudice had done; the domestic and foreign press made Emmett Till's death and the acquittal of his attackers a national shame. Rosa Parks's resistance to state segregation laws initiated nonviolent sit-ins and protests. At the same time, in the name of socio-economic equality, women invoked the law, seeking protection under an Equal Rights Amendment. Yet with the sanction of the Supreme Court, women could claim rights over their bodies in legalized abortion. A president who had launched a Peace Corps of passionate young Americans was assassinated before he could prove the truth of his belief that there was not "anything this country cannot do." A War on Poverty, undertaken by the president who succeeded him, proved in the light of growing gaps between the excessively wealthy and the wretchedly poor to have been no more than a skirmish. This in spite of a new Office of Economic Opportunity and the introduction of Medicare and Medicaid.[3]

Such paradoxes were born of attempts by those of good will to combat evil and to relieve suffering. And in that irony lies the relevance of these events for the story of a religious community living through them. The sixties were a decade of radical change—in attitudes, critical understanding, priorities, even values. But the framework of religious life that had held steady for a century of challenges from frontier conditions and growth, in a nation now the arbiter of world affairs, did not allow for serious stresses in its structure. The Community could not readily embrace change that threatened to undermine the principles of its service.

The very Rule of common life and the vows that committed young women to it were to come into question, not in their essence but in the way they were lived. The institutions the Community had founded were to suffer losses of staff and, in the case of Catholic schools, doubts about their relevance. Concepts of authority and criteria for those exercising it were developing, with profound effects on the appointment and election of sisters to positions of responsibility. Loss as well as gain of potential leadership in the Community was one long-lasting result of diminishing trust in conventional judgments. It was later estimated by students of the period that the middle generation of religious, women and men, were in large part passed over. Change came for some with passionate conviction, for others as a dubious promise. What is clear in hindsight—that change for the Sisters of Charity depended on loyal continuity—was perceived by many in the 1950s and 1960s as delay born of reluctance and fear or, on the contrary, as an abandonment of sacred tradition. Few would have found prophets among those over fifty; few would have credited those under fifty with wisdom.

Need for Spiritual Depth

The coming deliberations of Vatican II were volcanic only in the accumulating force, among the faithful, of conflicting experience and the needs of the spirit. Such needs as expressed in communal religious life were certainly not revolutionary; initiatives for meeting them came from those in authority responding to their subjects' deepest concerns. With perceptive and forceful leadership, the structure allowed for much. In her five-year report to the Congregation for Religious in 1955, Mother Mary Ancilla Spoor wrote that "more Sisters [than before] manifested a greater concern for their spiritual growth ... especially evidenced in their desire for an increase in their mental prayer life." She cited summer theology courses, a reading program for sisters under temporary vows, summer conferences and Christmas institutes to assist spiritual development, workshops by a canonist for superiors, and a tertian program for those preparing to take perpetual vows. Progress in religious observance she attributed to such opportunities and to the vigilance of local and higher superiors.[4] Emphasis on fidelity to the Rule and authority for maintaining it was significant to many.

The tertianship had been established in 1948 by Mother Mary Francesca O'Shea as a summer program of prayer, conferences, reading, some manual labor, and an eight-day retreat before final profession. Directed by Jesuit priests, the tertians led a full community life under a carefully selected superior. Afternoons were often spent visiting the sick, checking out the local terrain, and creating symbolic objects for liturgies or bulletin boards.[5] Faculty and later directors of the program included knowledgeable and experienced Sisters of Charity. Sister Mary Serena Sheehy's lectures in 1966, one tertian wrote, offered a welcome "woman's view" that "focused the issues [on] what is reality for us." In succeeding summers others helped direct the groups, which numbered twenty participants in the beginning; later as many as thirty-seven; by 1970, thirteen.

Tertians experienced early changes. The 1966 group received "the smashing news," a tertian later reported, that Mother Leo Frances had given them leave to make vows in their home parishes. On hearing from his daughter, a father called Sister Mary Camilla Montgomery, the tertian mistress, from Wyoming to say, "Why, nothing like this has ever happened to Greybull before." A later group formulated for their vow ceremony on St. Vincent's Day, July 19, a commitment to the Community, with a congregational response. In 1957, the first Spiritual Life Institute for Silver Tertians extended this spiritual renewal program to sisters in the Community for twenty to twenty-five years. It was a time away from professional ministry and class work, an opportunity for "experience of the contemplative life."[6]

Progress in religious discipline, Mother Ancilla reported to Rome in 1960, was due to "an earnest desire to accomplish the purpose for which each Sister entered the Institute (her sanctification by the observance of the three simple vows and her desire to honor our Lord Jesus Christ, in the person of her neighbor)."[7] During the five years from 1955 to 1960, an annual average of two fewer sisters than in the previous period applied for admission—hardly an alarming decrease. Among the reasons given for seeking the life were the good example of priests and religious, understanding and encouraging parents, and seeing novices in action. The last was possible because of the proximity of the college; during the forties and fifties, 159 young women entered the Community from Saint Mary, after graduation or before. Ninety-three of them entered in the seven years between 1948 and 1954, an average of thirteen a year from the college alone.[8]

In introducing the General Chapter of 1956, Mother Ancilla reported that 820 professed members now made up the Community, 757 of them in active ministry and 191 under temporary vows. The novitiate numbered sixty-six novices and four postulants. Since the 1950 Chapter, 217 candidates had entered, 88 percent of whom persevered to first vows. In July, the Community boasted seventy-three living golden jubilarians and forty-nine more who had been Sisters of Charity for sixty years. Concern for the sisters' spiritual growth had inspired not only required reading for those under temporary vows but also the opening of what came to be called Mother's Loan Library, reference to excellent articles for table reading, and a rotation of books for spiritual reading—seventeen sets of them—to all houses.[9]

Such initiatives and response to expressed need on the part of Mother Ancilla and her Council were prophetic. Without explicit reference, they manifested the principle that growth and ministry depend absolutely on a deepening spiritual life. It was a truth the Community was to continue to realize in renewal, study, and action over the next fifty years. Significantly too, apostolic works reported in 1956 were flourishing. The annual average patient load for fourteen hospitals was nearly 124,000; about 200 RNs were graduated from three nursing schools each year. Just under 200 children were being cared for in three orphanages; St. Joseph's Infant Home in Denver saw about sixty adoptions a year. Fifty-seven grade schools enrolled an annual average of 13,000 youngsters; ten high schools enrolled more than 3,000. From 1950 to 1956, about 1,750 Catholic students in forty-four public schools had been instructed in religion by 83 sisters; 4,000 students had enrolled in vacation schools taught by 166 sisters. At home, the college housed more than 400 students on campus and educated more than 300 by extension.[10]

Sister Rosella Mary Hehn instructs altar boys at a parish church in Leavenworth.

To prepare students for parish life, Saint Mary established a unit of the Confraternity of Christian Doctrine; in 1945 Sister Leo Gonzaga Erbacher, assisted by a corps of students, directed a correspondence course in religion for 169 students enrolled in public high schools. By 1958, Sister Mary Seraphia McGinty was managing the course for 809 pupils in fifty-four parishes; 507 completed the year's work. Weekend classes in religion were conducted at Haskell Institute, the Kansas State Industrial School, and the Kansas State Hospital. Each Sunday, Sister Constantia Towle and Sister Mary Caroline Caffrey taught eighteen blind children at the home of Mrs. Nora Coyle, of St. Peter's parish in Kansas City, Kansas. Needs knew no limit. Since 1950, requests for sisters had come to the Council from fifty-two dioceses in the United States and from missions in Canada, Puerto Rico, Panama, Chile, Hawaii, Japan, India, East Africa, and Norway.[11]

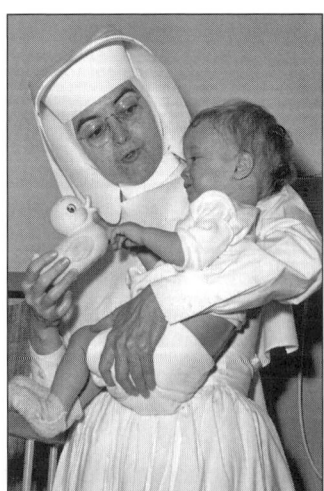

Sister Rose Orchard comforts an infant at Saint John's Hospital, Santa Monica, California.

The Church depended, as ever, on women religious for its sustenance and missionary growth. Their contributed services bolstered institutional budgets as well. Salaries in all parochial schools were actually stipends supplementary to the parish's provision of convent accommodations. For the Sisters of Charity of Leavenworth, these stipends ranged from $45 monthly for ten months to $60 monthly for twelve months, for each sister. Sisters in the children's homes received none. This assumption by a religious community of personnel costs could not long continue, especially if numbers were to decline even while the number of schools to be staffed kept rising. By 1958, the Community's centennial, approximately 375 sisters were ministering in sixty-one elementary schools. The numbers would hold, with some fluctuation, for the next eight years.[12]

Reflecting on women's presence as substantive for American religious history, a contemporary historian credits Catholic sisters with the very existence of the parochial school system as its "labor force whose subsistence wages constituted a massive economic subsidy.... Without the women who felt a vocation to the religious life, the Third Plenary Council [of Bishops] could not have made parochial education the hallmark of preconsilliar [sic] American Catholicism."[13] This is only one instance of the hidden power for good exercised by women religious for the first century and a half of American history.

By 1956, the hospitals—a traditional source of income for the Community by dint of professional salaries sent home—anticipated more lay assistance for personnel needs. At the same time, individual sister nurses were sent by their administrators to national conferences for operating room nurses, to learn what they could of advances in surgery. In 1954, Sister Mary Lillian Landauer, OR Supervisor at St. Vincent's in Billings, with Sister Raphaella Currie, assigned at St. Joseph's, had traveled to New York City; Sister Rose Orchard went from St. John's to St. Louis the following year. A harbinger of what was to come in terms of support and collaboration, the Marian Mothers Guild, established in 1954, had as its purpose to strengthen the bond uniting the sisters' families and the Community; to familiarize them with the history, apostolates, and needs of the Community; and to extend its works in a common endeavor.[14]

The General Chapter of 1956 elected Mother Mary Ancilla for a second term as mother superior. Sister Leo Frances Ryan was elected her first assistant; other councilors were Sister Mary Immaculata Desmond; Sister Mary Cornelia Donnelly for oversight of hospitals; Sister Mary Baptista Ward; Sister Marie Kelly, Community secretary; and Sister Ann Elizabeth Shea, Community treasurer. During that summer, the Council welcomed some eighty sisters to the first Institute for Superiors, an action significant in its potential for change in the exercise of authority, if not in immediate results. That fall, Mother Ancilla and a companion attended the first meeting of the Conference of Major Superiors of Women in Chicago. It was the consequence of Pope Pius XII's call in 1950 for national associations of the heads of religious communities.[15]

Mother Mary Ancilla Spoor, term in office, 1950–1962

Community Council 1956–1962: (seated) Sister Leo Frances Ryan, Mother Mary Ancilla, Sister Mary Immaculata Desmond; (standing) Sister Agnes Vincent Bauman, Secretary General; Sister Cornelia Donnelly, Sister Mary Louise Sullivan, and Sister Mary Florentia Schouten, who succeeded Sister Ann Elizabeth Shea as Treasurer

It is doubtful that cardinals in Rome realized the complexities of internal governance in religious communities; it was difficult enough for governing Councils to deal with its challenges. Reflecting on her experience in community during the eighteen years before she left, a former Sister of Charity, who had "loved being a Sister" and saluted the Community's "truly special and wonderful women," questioned reluctance on the part of the mother general to remove sisters from positions of authority when there was need. Recognized by another respondent as "good, holy women," some superiors were nevertheless not very approachable.[16] The difficulty of finding replacements for sisters who had clearly not been prepared for administration or religious governance, much less for both, was one result of a larger problem: lack of appropriate and adequate screening of candidates for religious life in the face of the numbers entering it in the middle decades of the century. It was the endemic problem of all rapid growth, exceeding means and methods of discernment and education. An Institute for Superiors was one small step to address problems of a large number of people who included the experienced and inexperienced, those talented for leadership and those for whom it was an extraordinary burden.

Another aspect of governance that was adversely affecting both individuals and the Community was a traditional interpretation of obedience and conventional structures of authority common to the religious life of women and men at the time. That women could have altered such structures and seriously reflected together on their life of religious obedience, influencing theological development and change to come, was not evident or even much thought of at mid-century. A young sister who entered in 1952 and left the Community eight years later wrote that "we were 'seen and not heard from'—especially if we were a 'sprout' (a young sister). We had no input, no feedback, [were] never involved in any decision making process—even if we were being [a]ffected by these changes or advancements."[17] Again, hindsight makes of such experience a sign of needed change.

Before Thanksgiving of 1956, Mother Mary Berchmans died. On Founders Day during a conversation with Sister Mary Paul Fitzgerald, she had said, "As near as we could do the job, we did it. We have gone as far as our faculties can go...." The words reflect the spirit of those who had gone before her, pioneers to the bone. Educator that she was, she undoubtedly approved of the Council's action that year asking Sister Rose Dominic Gabisch to conduct a survey of the Community's high schools. In 1957, the Council granted Sister Mary Paul a sabbatical from the college to do research for her book on the correspondence of Bishop Miege and appointed her chair of a steering committee to plan the next year's centennial celebration. Mother Francesca's death on May 19, 1958, occurred six months before the formal opening of the centennial year on November 11, 1958.[18]

Observing the centennial of the Sisters of Charity of Leavenworth in 1958, Saint Mary College and Academy students, alumni, friends, and clergy joined the Community, its novices and postulants in Annunciation Chapel.

The solemn high Mass of that Founders Day was celebrated in the Old Cathedral, the Church of the Immaculate Conception, by James Cardinal MacIntyre of the Archdiocese of Los Angeles. Clergy and faculty from thirteen SCL schools in the Archdiocese of Kansas City, Kansas, and the Diocese of Kansas City, Missouri, as well as administrators and staffs of hospitals and homes attended, along with hundreds of lay friends and families of the Sisters of Charity. At the end of Mass, Mother Mary Ancilla walked out of the church with Mother Mary Bertrand, head of the Sisters of Charity of Nazareth; Sister Leo Frances and Sister Mary Aline, SCN, followed. The centennial annalist wrote, "The old and the new, the mother and daughter, were united." This was the last formal event the Community celebrated in the cathedral that had been dedicated by Bishop Miege in 1868.[19]

A centennial is a time for taking stock. By reason of its celebration of a past, honoring forebears, and recounting accomplishments, it becomes the hinge and latch of a door opening onto the future. What it does not do, however, is assess the state of things or evaluate the costs of so much admirable progress. Celebration does not call for that. More to the point, the questions to be asked were only beginning to take shape in the Church and in religious communities. For that reason, events that immediately followed in the Community's life are the more remarkable for their intimations or signals of a need for change. The years 1959–1962 were a time of uncertain vision that nevertheless required action, of looking to a future that, given growing dissatisfactions, would not much resemble the past. Coincidentally, they were the years between Pope John XXIII's announcement that he would soon convene an ecumenical council, Vatican II, and the council's opening in October of 1962.

Educating Young Sisters

After a decision taken by the Community Council in 1959, the juniorate opened in 1960. This was a two-year program of spiritual and professional training to follow immediately after novitiate and first vows. It was developed along guidelines proposed by the Sister Formation Movement, a national organization created as a result of repeated injunctions of Pope Pius XII to provide adequate training of religious for their ministry in the modern world. The movement originated in 1953 from a survey conducted by the National Catholic Education Association that revealed a serious lack of professional preparation for teaching sisters. Its fundamental purpose was to enable sisters to complete baccalaureate degrees before they began teaching and to integrate professional education with their spiritual

Sister Mary Liguori Horvat tends plants behind Miege for use in teaching. Heralding renewal, Sister coordinated the Sister Formation Program for the Community.

growth. Under the leadership of Mary Emil Penet, IHM, the program aimed to incorporate into the formation of young sisters the study of theology and the social and behavioral sciences. From the Everett Conference of 1956, funded by the Ford Foundation, there emerged the draft of a model undergraduate curriculum for women religious that integrated the spiritual, intellectual, and professional disciplines.[20]

Sister Mary Liguori Horvat was assigned by Mother Mary Ancilla and her Council to participate in the summer institutes of Sister Formation in order to direct the Community's implementation of the program. Guided by the fruits of Sister Mary Liguori's study, a team of formation and college personnel, named in 1962, designed the program for the junior sisters of the Community.[21] They were responsible for considering the abilities and aptitudes of the individual sisters and the needs of the Community in schools and other apostolates, and then for recommending special fields of study for each. Those working for a degree took the basic liberal arts curriculum before declaring a major; those with professional degrees took further theology and philosophy as well as enrichment courses in the humanities, arts, and sciences. Those preparing for non-professional work in the Community took liberal arts and special courses, supplemented by practical experience. With varying degrees of success in individual programs, the movement's impact, according to recorded data, was deep and broad, evident in shifts in concepts of theology and spirituality, in worldview, and in thinking about experience of religious life. Such effects amounted to a growing readiness for renewal.[22]

Ironies attended the Community's Juniorate Program, a solid one as experienced by more than 180 young Sisters of Charity. Their last directress, Sister Gregory (Eileen) Sheehy, affirmed in retrospect her view of its effects over the six years of its operation before the Community undertook a thorough study of the entire formation program. As the juniorate developed in the light of succeeding groups' experience, the junior sisters, Sister Eileen said, "grew to have a feeling for each other," enjoyed broader exchange with older professed sisters than would otherwise have been possible, and gained confidence as well as competence from finishing their preparation for apostolic assignments. By 1966, however, change was taking hold: numbers of candidates for religious life were in decline, Catholic schools were beginning to close, hospitals were reorganizing personnel with lessening opportunity for sisters in direct nursing care. The program was "too little too late," Sister said, but in ways no one could have foreseen.[23]

In the Community at large, the need for shared information, for updating of skills in swiftly changing professional fields, for collaboration with support groups and public agencies, and for immediate acquaintance with a changing world motivated important initiatives. Innovations in curriculum and pedagogy preoccupied educators. Sisters learned new methods of teaching science and mathematics, as well as reading and literature. Students had to change gears and parents wanted to understand how they were learning. At St. Charles School in North Kansas City, with an enrollment at one thousand, sisters taught upwards of four hundred parents how their children were now learning math.[24]

The year 1960 saw the first *SCL Newsletter*. Mother Mary Ancilla urged it to "lessen the distance between our many houses and help to enlarge that family spirit so dear to all of us." It launched a twenty-year succession of publications designed to strengthen connections. Sisters Genevieve Tebedo and Agnes Vincent Bauman disseminated news from home, writing to sisters on the missions and at school. *Mother House*

Music-lovers lead a summer sing-along from the front steps of the Mother House.

Moments covered topics ranging from feast days to funerals, from book reviews to an account of tutoring Prince Khaled of Saudi Arabia. Sister Agnes Vincent's letters were as chatty as telephone calls, running a full gamut of events, commentaries, and advice.[25]

In 1960 a sister nurse was assigned to study operating room techniques at St. Michael's Hospital, Toronto; and St. John's of Leavenworth named Erwin Baker president of the Community's first board of trustees. Sister Joseph Cecilia Gausz was the first to be appointed school supervisor in the Kansas City, Missouri diocese. Sisters in the West were allowed for the first time to take classes at Carroll College in Helena, Montana. The Kennedy Child Care Center opened at Saint John's in Santa Monica; St. James Hospital in Butte combined with Community Hospital, the first "merger" in SCL health care. President Harry S. Truman spoke in Xavier Auditorium, at an event in the college's lecture series; the Honors Colloquium took students and faculty vicariously abroad.[26]

Growth continued as well. In 1960 fifty-two postulants came to the novitiate, the largest group to enter at one time; the total Community numbered 905. Ground was blessed and broken for a new powerhouse, kitchen, and science hall in the college, the beginning of a ten-year building program. On a different scale, in 1961 sister students and college faculty were given permission to study until 10 PM, a change less significant than astonishing for its delayed arrival. The short form of the Breviary was sent to all houses of the Community, for trial. The first survey on the habit

Picnic supper on the lawn south of the Mother House was a welcome Saturday custom.

was circulated, with less than dramatic results. The events themselves are not as significant as their indication of change to come.

Perhaps nothing so succinctly verbalizes the contrasts that shaped the decade of the 1950s in the experience of women religious as the terms used by two successive pontiffs in referring to their way of life. Pius XII, taking the first step toward national associations of religious, had called for a First General Congress of the States of Perfection; Paul VI, in promulgating *Perfectae Caritatis*, the Vatican II document on religious life, indicated its ongoing task—the perfecting of charity in service to others—and declared it not a "privileged state," nor a special preserve of Christian commitment, nor a middle way between clerical and lay states.[27] What it was or was to become was not so clear as what it was not. But that in itself opened the door, as he wished it to do, to what women religious would continue to determine for themselves.

CHAPTER 2

Responses of Head and Heart

However many the signs of upheaval ahead, the Sisters of Charity of Leavenworth were to change slowly, and only with sufficient reason. The Chapter of Affairs in 1962 rejected revisions in the Constitutions concerning discipline: the monthly chapter of faults, or communal confession of external transgressions; and governance: re-election of Community councilors. Delegates turned away suggestions that the Generalate be separated from the Mother House and that the mother general be limited to one term of six years. Changes closer to daily life were accepted: introduction of the Divine Office to replace the Community manual of prayers; flexibility in the order of the day, as approved for a given house; private spiritual reading and freedom of choice in meditation material; and, the most difficult to pace, some change in the habit. A selected committee was to draw up sketches and recommendations for attire with help from modeled options. Voting by sisters under perpetual vows would determine the outcome.

Directives from Rome were a guide for the use of radio and television; monthly permissions were to continue, as was the practice of traveling with a companion. A new exception was that, in necessity, the companion might be a lay woman. Charity or need was to be the guide for home visits. A meal might now be taken out of the house, with local permission; an overnight stay needed the permission of the mother general. Permission for photographs continued. To stress the value of healthy recreation, the Chapter recommended an hour a day for everyone and physical exercise in general, as well as an annual week's vacation, with vacation houses to be provided. Adaptations only emphasized the gradual pace of change in a closely regulated way of life. New freedom to use table reading of a professional kind, to sit by choice of companions in the dining room instead of by Community order, to take occasional meals with externs (those outside the Community) was occasion for rejoicing. A slight expansion of the weekly letter-writing permission was welcome, as was extension of the schedule for teaching sisters' evening study. The kind of customs retained as well as the modest relaxation of rule or custom reveal the order of life to which women religious had grown accustomed and for the most part took for granted.

To lend a degree of stability in apostolic service, mission assignments were now to be for three years. Most significant, perhaps, was change in the mode of electing delegates to Chapter, which was now to be composed of a total of forty delegates—as opposed to the previous ninety-eight. Thirty-three individuals were to be selected from assigned groups, assuring representation of both large and small houses. The General Council of seven was to make up the complement of forty. Traditional images of leadership had brought to earlier Chapters many of the same women, out of a common community experience. Broader representation of the membership and greater diversity of views and experience were anticipated outcomes of the changes. No one yet knew that six years later the first Chapter of Renewal would be summoned in response to Vatican II.[1]

The Chapter—representing 919 sisters, 854 of them in active ministry—elected Mother Leo Frances Ryan to lead the Community through what were to be its most turbulent years; and her Council, Sister Mary Seraphine Sheehan, first assistant; Sister Mary Ancilla; Sister Cornelia; Sister Mary Ellenice Colvin; Sister Mary Anselm Towle, treasurer; and Sister Marie Kelly, secretary. Proposals from the Community reported to the Chapter suggest visionary thinking and a desire to seek new frontiers in the Third World. Professional training of sisters had been the subject of annual recommendations; the proposal asked for a committee to study immediate and long-range needs in all apostolates and to consult authorities in each field. No committee was appointed at this time. Another proposal sought consultants or a committee to study problems of administration in the hospitals, specifically nursing service, office procedures, construction, and education. The proposal for a foreign mission met no opposition; the only problem was finding sisters to send. Urging of a new infirmary for aged and infirm sisters only awaited funds for building.[2]

Progress and expansion were hallmarks of both Community and college. In the next two years on campus, St. Joseph's Dining Hall, Miege Science Hall, and Maria Hall for resident students were dedicated; a fully equipped kitchen opened, serving both college and Community. On the north end of the Community's property, the old St. Vincent Home was razed and the land leased to the City

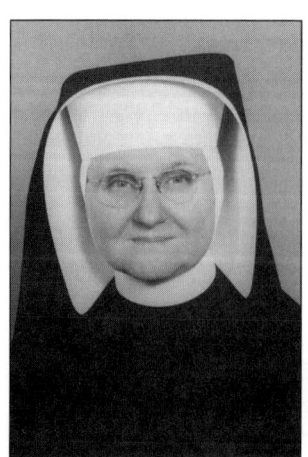

Mother Leo Frances Ryan, term in office, 1962–1974

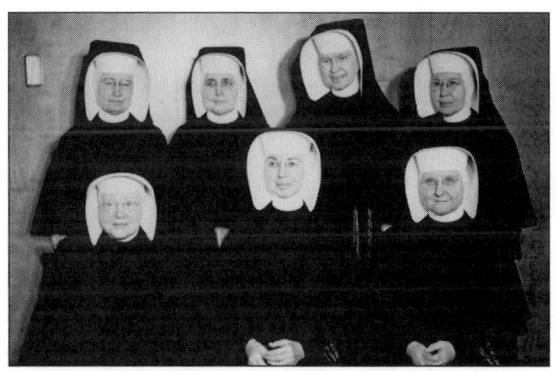

Community Council, 1962–1968: (seated) Sister Mary Ancilla Spoor, Sister Mary Seraphine Sheehan, and Mother Leo Frances; (standing) Sister Mary Anselm Towle, Community Treasurer, Sister Mary Ellenice Colvin, Sister Cornelia Donnelly, and Sister Agnes Vincent Bauman, Community Secretary

of Leavenworth for a much needed shopping plaza that proved a handy neighbor to the college and Mother House. Having served Leavenworth since 1864, St. John Hospital was built anew on Community grounds and blessed in May 1964; the Twin Towers of St. Joseph's in Denver were dedicated the same month. In nearby Kansas City, Kansas, a retreat was held at the new residence for nursing students, Marian Hall, attached to Providence Hospital.

New avenues of service opened as well. In the summer of 1963 sisters traveled the few miles on Highway 5 to Wolcott, where migrant workers, harvesting the sugar beet crops, lodged their families in abandoned railroad cars. Sisters visited them to ascertain immediate needs and to offer instruction to the children. The year 1964 saw other beginnings. Sister Mary Janet McGilley was appointed president of Saint Mary College, the first Sister of Charity to hold that position. Her twenty-five year tenure was to inaugurate significant change. An appropriate signal of dramatic growth in relationships with the civic community was Leavenworth's expansion of its city limits southward, to include the college and Mother House grounds. The commencement speaker that year was Irene Dunne Griffin. Sister Rose Dominic Gabisch, dean of the Graduate Division until it closed, was appointed executive secretary of the Sister Formation office in Washington, DC.[3]

Meanwhile, a turning point in the life of the Church was profoundly affecting American religious and clergy. In 1959, three years before the opening of the Second Vatican Council, Pope John XXIII had called them to come to the aid of Latin America. A shortage of priests and teachers, coupled with pervasive poverty and political turmoil, had left a people with an unbroken heritage of faith destitute of religious instruction and hungering for the nourishment of sacramental life. Many were turning to evangelical churches for spiritual support. Early in 1963, an urgent request for sisters from Father Thomas Reilly, pastor of Santa Rosa de Lima parish in Talara, Peru, prompted the Council to act in response to Pope John's plea.[4]

Mission on New Frontiers

Missionary Sisters (left to right) Mary Clementine (Rosalie) Mahoney, Blanche Marie Remington, Marie Columbiere (Irene) Skeehan, Ann Denise Shea, and Dennis Marie (Agnes) Klein are ready to board the plane for Peru with Sister Mary Seraphine Sheehan (far right). Mother Leo Frances (left) traveled with them as far as Miami.

Responding to a Community letter about the goal of a mission abroad, 197 volunteered. In May of 1963, Mother Leo Frances and Sister Mary Seraphine visited the proposed site for the first Latin American mission, the coastal town of Talara, diocese of Piura, in a country whose annual per capita income was between $100 and $200. On September 30, the Community's first missionaries, Sisters Dennis Marie (Agnes) Klein, Mary Clementine (Rosalie) Mahoney, Ann Denise Shea, Blanche Marie Remington, and Marie Columbiere (Irene) Skeehan left for Peru. Sister Mary Seraphine and Sister Mary Baptista accompanied them. October 3 was a Community day of fast for their safe journey and God's blessing on the enterprise. Only two years later, five new missionaries left Leavenworth: Sister Mary Anselma (Josephine) Bustos, for the school in Talara; and Sisters Mary Cabrini (Charlotte) Swain, Mary Martel (Joan) Kilker, Ann Louise Turk, and John Francis (Lucille) Harrington, for study at the Center for Intercultural Formation in Mexico City, preparing for work in Peru or Bolivia. Sister Cornelia and Sister Mary Anselm

Sister Lucille Harrington is welcomed to Bolivia by parishioners and pastor.

had visited the new mission site in Coripata, Bolivia several months earlier.[5]

A turning-point in the life of the nation, the assassination of President John Fitzgerald Kennedy, brought the Community to solemn observance of the national day of mourning, November 25, 1963, proclaimed by his successor, President Lyndon Johnson. His proclamation on the day of the president's death was a call to all peoples to join the citizens of the United States in their grief: "A man of wisdom, strength, and peace, he molded and moved the power of our nation in the service of a world of growing liberty and order. All who love freedom will mourn his death."[6]

In the face of cataclysmic changes in Church and civic life, the Community maintained its course of willing response to the Spirit and prudent provision for an unknown future. In keeping with liturgical renewal, the first burial Mass in English was celebrated for Sister Bernard Mary Knipsher in January 1965. That June, the sisters of the newly dedicated Ross Hall were welcomed to the first anointing of the sick in Ross Hall chapel; nineteen participated in the sacrament. For the first time postulants resided in convents for professional mission experience. Two sisters were assigned to full-time CCD work in Helena. In that year too Sister Mary Anselm recommended to the Council that the Community apply for Social Security. This foresight and careful implementation were an incalculable blessing. The college convent opened in Mead Hall in the fall of 1965, allowing some fifty sisters assigned to staff and faculty to achieve greater unity in their apostolate. They formed a local community led by Sister Mary Janet, who was named local superior.[7]

Early moves of collaboration in ministry can be attributed to individual initiatives and extraordinary diligence. The first Medical Staff Conference, undertaken by Thomas E. Havel, MD, chief of staff at Saint John's Hospital in Santa Monica, with full approval of the Council, brought to the Mother House physicians and board members from thirteen hospitals of the Community. In 1965 Sister Mary Pauline Degan was named the Community's first full-time CCD director and assistant to the archdiocesan director. Then considered by some to be working "outside" the Community, she was one of those who saw needs of the future Church and moved to meet them.[8] Prophetic voices, from within and without, could not be marked as such until a future was to confirm them.

Development of traditional ministries and unpredictable prophetic actions marked the tumultuous decade for many women religious. The Sisters of Charity of Leavenworth were no exception. An informal ministry to prisoners that the sisters had undertaken from their arrival in Kansas developed in many directions. In April 1965, ten sisters joined the women's choir of the Kansas State Industrial Farm in Lansing to sing High Mass on Holy Thursday. They sang with the men's choir on Easter Sunday. Each Sunday for some time three sisters had been teaching catechetics and hymns for the Mass celebrated at the Farm on Thursdays. Within a decade, the ministry was to take public academic form with Saint Mary's granting college degrees to both state and federal prisoners.

One of the first to undertake public action of solidarity and protest in the cause of civil rights was Sister Gregory Sheehy, school superintendent in the Kansas City–St. Joseph Diocese. She joined eighteen other women religious in a journey to Selma, Alabama to take part in African American voter registration demonstrations. Many Sisters of Charity of Leavenworth participated in communal memorial services March 14 and 15 at the Municipal Auditorium in Kansas City, Missouri, and at St. Joseph's Church in Leavenworth for Rev. James Reed, a white minister active in the civil rights movement, who died from wounds suffered in a beating by several white men.[9]

Dozens of Saint Mary students benefited from Sister Frances Therese Shea's "Summer of Hope" in 1965. Chair of the sociology department, Sister spent seven weeks at Marillac Settlement House in Chicago, working among the poor. The Daughters of Charity and their staff of African American young people administered the program. Sister's fieldwork with her students at the college had engaged more than one hundred of them weekly in projects of community service. Visits to juvenile court, the Ozanam Home for Boys, the Osawatomie State Hospital, and projects in Kansas City and Chicago fueled continuous weekend hours devoted to Leavenworth's Bain City School; to Neighborhood House, a day care center for handicapped children; and to Brown's Center, locale of an interracial dialogue they organized with Rockhurst students in Kansas City, Missouri.[10]

In her report to the Congregation for Religious for the years 1961–1965, Mother Leo Frances wrote of the Community-wide study of the Vatican II documents, planned throughout 1965 and implemented with personal and material resources from the college. Semi-weekly meetings during the summer of 1966 in multi-age groups aimed at comparison of ideas and the raising of questions. In a general assembly at the end of summer, a summary of the conversations offered some common ground for continuing them on mission and with hospital sisters throughout the year. In retrospect, Mother wrote that thanks to this initial study of the documents, "there is a greater spirit of unity than heretofore. All are endeavoring to recapture our original spirit and to live lives of religious as encouraged" by the decree on renewal. "We realize," she said, that "this has to be done slowly and will be a continuous process."[11] Mother's interpretation of this study was indicative of her habitual hope for a Community that would remain faithful to its heritage in shaping its future.

That seven professed sisters during a five-year period, 1960–1965, had requested and received dispensation from perpetual vows was a troubling sign that soon became urgent. In a letter dated January 1, 1968, professed sisters dispensed from their vows during the decade were asked to speak freely of their experience in community. Though no figures are recorded for this informal survey, the number of all those who left between 1960 and 1968, including sisters with temporary vows, is sixty-seven; sixteen replied to the letter, roughly 24 percent of the whole. The respondents' candor and good will make of their testimony an invaluable witness to the questioning spirit growing among women religious of the decade.

To account for a significant drop in the number of candidates, Mother listed in her report unrest in the world, material in the Catholic press that brought religious life into question, luxuries of the modern home, salaried jobs for women, reluctance on the part of young Catholic women to break ties and make sacrifices, and concern about acceptance should they choose to return home. To a reader now, implicit in such reasons were the beginnings of doubt about permanent commitment that would become characteristic of a new generation. Among factors mentioned by candidates then as influential in their decisions, the example of sisters they knew or observed was primary, for good or for ill. That was to be a constant factor cited as influential in the responses of former Sisters of Charity to a survey thirty years later.

Mother Leo Frances was not unaware of tremors beneath a relatively calm surface. She emphasized in her report a questioning of canon law, religious rules, Constitutions as now written, and developing ideas on obedience and freedom. "We should expect a sort of upheaval in the minds of religious," she wrote, "especially the young religious of today. Yet, apparently because of grace of vocation their zeal for...furthering the Kingdom of God on earth has been enriched....We are encouraged that great good will evolve from all this scrutiny and study." Observing that some had given up religious life, she said that "others have been strengthened and show signs of being more genuinely dedicated to their consecrated way of life than they were in former years and...of having a deeper appreciation of [it]."[12]

Her consciousness of both loss and gain was sound. But what lies unspoken in reports and records are the injustices suffered with rapid growth. Evidence must be anecdotal. Two young grade-school teachers, for example, assigned over a summer to teach in high school, were panic-stricken. Previous performance, demonstrated intelligence, their record in college coursework meant little to them: they did not know how they would fare with classrooms full of adolescents, high school class schedules, and the texts handed them for use.[13] Contingencies of staffing wrought other effects. A first-grade teacher was caught between acts, so to speak, of a seventh-grade teacher's transfer and a replacement's arrival. Two and a half months of managing—and managing to teach—one hundred pre-adolescent youngsters, moving from one group of fifty to the other in a given day, made her long for the young beginners. Dismay at their limited preparation troubled nursing sisters as well. Excellent performance as a surgical nurse, for example, with a swift shuttling from one hospital to another for experience in every department, was preparation for advancement to a supervisory position in surgery for one young sister. Like others of her time, she learned fast.[14]

Call for Change from Within

Allowing for exceptions, unavoidable crises, and no time for necessary study, assignments without adequate preparation were not singular, unless in timing and scale. Yet the quality of teaching and of health care maintained in spite of what would otherwise have been intolerable conditions is attested to by thousands of Catholic school graduates and thousands of former patients and their families. They remember the effects of altogether personal attention, responsibility for the job, and an invincible faith that this one *could* learn, that one could be healed in body and spirit. The inadequacy of preparation and lack of consultation in assigning sisters were systemic faults recognized by supervisors and administrators who witnessed the effects as well as by some bishops—faults that begged for correction or, better, systemic change.

Steps to remedy the situation were multiplying. Professional training for individual health care workers increased as the sixties progressed and collaboration beyond the Community began in formal ways. In 1966 sisters were assigned for the first time to secular institutions.[15] The first lay board met with sister administrators of St. Vincent's Hospital in Billings, Montana. The following year Sister Mary James Harrington taught remedial reading at Emporia State University. That change had to extend to all the structures of decision-making in the Church was not yet apparent. By 1965, women religious were staffing 13,292 elementary and secondary Catholic schools.[16] Despite a recognized need for teacher preparation, the continuing response to pastors' and bishops' requests allowed little time for training school sisters beyond what they had acquired by experience and what the state and the Community required for beginning teachers. The Sister Formation Program was the first systemic attempt to address the problem.

Change in Community structures and practices was beginning with long-range effects in view. In light of Vatican II mandates, a fundamental revision of the Community's formation program was undertaken in 1966. An appointed group examined all aspects of the program by these criteria:

- the Gospel experience of initiation into Christian community
- elements of psychological stability
- apostolic needs of the time
- Vatican documents on renewal of religious life and preparation of the clergy
- the history of religious formation to discern what was no longer relevant, and
- essentials for mature and responsible development for the woman religious.

Norms established for entrance into the Community included age and college or professional preparation for teaching, nursing, or social service. Enlarging the Sister Formation team, the Council now charged the renamed Formation Planning Committee with planning and implementing all facets of religious formation—spiritual, intellectual, apostolic, and professional. The task led to evaluation of the college's role in assisting that formation.[17] Directors were to bring two years of apprenticeship to their responsibilities, with a six-year limit on years in the office and the possibility of reappointment.

On recommendation of the Habit Committee, sisters began to wear a modified headdress and street-length skirts. The first paraliturgical Bible service introduced entering postulants to religious life.

As novices, Sisters Judith Jackson and Ann Staley serve a welcome snack to children.

In 1967, the first sisters who wished to do so returned to their baptismal names. Experimental adjustments of the horarium, or daily schedule, began. A Community health insurance program was undertaken, and personnel policies for all employees were drawn up. Sisters at the Mother House and on the missions met to determine their form of government and to elect, if they chose, a superior and local council. For the first time the sisters chose nominees for delegates to the approaching Chapter. The question of area supervisors, advisory to the General Council, became a major item for the Chapter agenda. These supervisors were to assist communication, attend to individual sisters' potential and interests in ministry, and advise on assignment to missions.[18]

Even before that Chapter began, renewal in concrete forms was under way. Precisely because a long-range view guided such changes, however, their fundamental effects would be a long time coming. Meanwhile, departures continued to mount. A former sister who entered the Community in 1952 and left eight years later wrote about her experience: "I believe I had waited to be more a part of [a community that] made decisions and plans for the Community. I was not a part of this process—on committees, etc."[19] Reasons for an individual's feeling excluded from a process can be manifold; the experience described, however, was not unique.

Other former sisters who responded to the letter of 1968, though few in number, cited experiences relative to structures and exercise of authority, inadequate training for the job, a lack of opportunity to discuss ideas and feelings, to be personally known to superiors. On the other hand, respondents' valuable insights into religious life invite respect: that community is the heart of that life, that flexibility and human values must be placed above routine procedures, that personal participation in one's own development and growth from within are necessary, that personal relationship with Christ and the significance of other people are the essentials. Gratitude for the time in community took many forms—admiration for magnanimous women, for their friendliness and kindness, for the unique spirit of the Sisters of Charity; the sense of being a

A novice entertains Ross Hall residents, Sisters Lucia Whelan and Diomede Sack.

better Catholic, a better wife and mother and lay worker in the Church for having spent years in community. One said of the place, "[I] left a little of my heart there."[20]

The truth of such a story of growth and suffering lies not between apparent contradictions but within the paradox of human endeavor. Charity knows no limit to what it will attempt, for another or for vast numbers; justice requires discernment that needs knowledge and time, even while it must act now. The mystery of the human heart, hidden within obedience and relationships and expectations, allows no ready answers, few generalizations. Both those who had left and would leave and those who stayed the course remember things larger than pain, things that preceded and transcended renewal. Perhaps the individual sister's capacity for compassion is the ultimate measure of an institution's effectiveness or a ministry's worth.

Sister Mary Bernice Mulcahy, who died in 1967, was teaching first graders at St. Rose of Lima's in Kansas City, Kansas, when a six-year-old boy, who had just lost his father to bone cancer, became totally mute. She knew the man had suffered screaming pain before death but did not know how much the child had experienced. One morning, at recess, she beckoned the silent boy to stay, and sat him on her lap. "Is it your daddy?" she asked. He nodded. For fifteen minutes each day after that, she sat with him and talked gently about losing someone we love, about his father's care for him, about how much he had to learn. She let him take his time. Gradually he relaxed and began again to talk. The sisters, as well as the children, loved Sister Bernice. She had ways of her own. Each fall she would cut pieces of old-fashioned corn candy into three parts, at the color lines, and distribute them, one apiece, to her pupils. Each color was significant. No one refused the offering.[21]

It is impossible to record the wit and the laughter, the poignant humor and patience that sustained communities of twelve, twenty, and thirty women, living together in a proximity they had taken for granted since novitiate days. Sharp retorts, even face-offs, eccentricities, and ineradicable habits reminded them periodically of one another's limits, but affection and genuine love nourished their community and reflected their love of God. Poverty in those days was not called and, in most cases, not felt as such. It was a way of life to which one was committed. Each house was expected to send in to the General Fund what remained of their salaries over and above moderate living expenses. The Community had real need of these contributions.

Orphanages, however, were always short of funds. It is said that Sister Mary Emilda Gleason, at St. Joseph Home in Helena, used to curl up near the heater in the dormitory, her blanket given to a child who needed two. With memories of her days at St. Vincent's Home in Denver, Sister

Hyacintha Marksman, retired to Nazareth, the Community infirmary, would frequently at night collect blankets from the sleeping sisters and carry them down the hall, muttering, "A shame the sisters sleep in blankets the children need." The night nurse would catch up with her, return her to bed and the blankets to their owners.[22]

Ingenuity made a good companion to need and compassion. St. Joseph's Hospital in Denver was demolishing a wing to rebuild, in that same decade. Sister Ann Raymond, administrator of St. Anthony's hospital in Las Vegas, New Mexico, had called Sister Mary Asella, St. Joseph's administrator, to arrange for Joe Pete Martinez, maintenance manager at St. Anthony's, to drive up to Denver, load salvaged tiles and bathroom fixtures, and bring them back to Las Vegas to remodel "the barracks," where some twenty patients had to share one bathroom. Result: tiled floors and a bath between every two rooms at St. Anthony's.[23]

Musicians always did their considerable bit toward Community expenses. In school convents, piano teachers and their superiors were responsible to keep the "music money" intact to bring home in person at the end of the school term to the mother general. The system worked well, with some unexpected consequences. At St. Laurence School in Laramie, Wyoming, Sister Mary Sarah Fasenmeyer, principal and superior, had no funds with which to send a sister, transferred in the middle of the year, to her new mission. She borrowed enough from the music money for a railroad ticket. When she reported this at home the next summer, Mother Mary Ancilla asked, "Why didn't you call me first?" Sister simply replied, "I didn't think you'd say 'yes.'" She was never questioned about any expenditure again.[24]

The incident speaks for the two of them, and many others. As well as for humor and lightheartedness, often under duress; as well as for a keen sense of justice, administered or suffered in the breach, the Sisters of Charity of Leavenworth were known by people and pastors for a good deal of common sense. That and other qualities served them admirably in crisis. A certain pioneer spirit, bred in the bone it seemed, prevailed throughout their first century and into the crucial decades that followed. More than a few foresaw, in many ways, deep change beyond the horizon of the 1960s.

Sister Mildred Marie (Mary David) reflected many years later, "My impression was that even before Vatican II or renewal there was a...sense among the sisters that we were not doing enough for the Church, too hemmed in by rules to do all we could. So when Vatican II came along we were ready to move...to less sheltered life, to life with more responsibility, whether for prayers or for ministry."[25]

CHAPTER 3

Heeding Many Voices

While readiness for renewal was indisputable, readiness for change of the magnitude needed was relative—to influence from the past, to conditions of the present, and to the urgency of calls to act. Those calls were coming with growing insistence from Rome, from the superiors of religious congregations, and from individual members. Many voices that pressed for change were responding to needs in a culture itself undergoing radical change. To characterize religious life in renewal as *response to needs of the world* is to voice a point of view, something a narrator of the past cannot escape. The point of view here is taken some forty years after the events recalled, interpreting the import of what makes up the story. As one religious historian says about such writing, "It is precisely because we stand in a particular location that we are able to see, to know, and to narrate." And this sighting tells the reader not only about the "site" but also about "what can be seen from there."[1]

In the call by Pope Pius XII in 1950 of religious superiors to a General Assembly in Rome, to consider the renewal and adaptation of religious life, few had recognized a revolutionary initiative. Nor did an International Congress of Teaching Sisters in 1951 draw much public notice. Nevertheless, repeated congresses of religious superiors, insistent papal decrees, and actions by the Congregation for Religious led to historic innovations. The Holy Father asked teaching communities to adapt their horarium, or order of the day, to apostolic duties and their dress and customs to the service of modern youth. He urged for teachers preparation that would meet and excel professional standards. The Regina Mundi pontifical institute in Rome offered training in the sciences and other academic disciplines for women religious.

In the United States, religious educators who had studied such needs throughout the 1940s pioneered the Sister Formation movement, which aimed at the education of young sisters through integration of their learning in the liberal arts and professional disciplines with their spiritual formation. This and a National Congress of Religious held at the University of Notre Dame in 1951 were immediate responses to the Church's call for renewal. From its beginnings, the Notre Dame Institute of Spirituality published presenters' papers for a broad readership. Summer institutes in essential elements of religious life introduced formation directors and local superiors to developing theology of the vows and the spiritual life. Not yet household names, Thomas Dubay, Yves Congar, Bernard Häring, Karl Rahner, and Elio Gambari were among the writers accessible through Sister Formation publications and religious journals.[2] But much depended on how far such exposure reached into a given community's life.

In 1956 the leaders of 235 communities met in Chicago to form themselves into the Conference of Major Superiors of Women (CMSW). Five years later, twelve hundred women religious gathered in a Second National Congress of Religious where they heard the appeal of the Holy Father for their united response to the crucial situation of the Church in Latin America.[3] *Aggiornamento*, or adaptation to the needs of their world, now meant personal and communal sacrifice of a new order. Then, with prophetic vision, the newly elected Pope John XXIII invoked a New Pentecost for the whole Church, calling the Second Vatican Council to convene in 1962. Out of this council came the mandate for renewal of religious life decreed in 1965 by his successor, Paul VI, in *Perfectae Caritatis*.

Such calls were then and are even now too comprehensive for all the members of a universal Church to grasp with one accord. The very condition of the poorest and most oppressed of the world was only in the 1960s becoming known as an immediate problem to those who governed the wealth and power of the world. What the poor had to teach women and men religious at close range would take yet more decades to realize from working with them on missions, at home and abroad, as partners and collaborators. The very diversity of a universal Church, growing in time and place, had to give rise to conflicting views of peace and justice, of authority and religious obedience, and of the Church itself.

Yet these congresses, councils, and documents stood in a long tradition of papal summonses to the Church to act prophetically in the world. The social encyclicals, beginning in 1891 with *Rerum Novarum*, "On the Conditions of the Working Class," were, in the words of Marie Augusta Neal, SNDdeN, "a call to biblically grounded action for the transformation of the unjust structures of modern society in privileged and unprivileged nations." Papal letters extended into the 1960s with *Mater et Magistra*, "Christianity and Social Progress," that called the Latin American Church to account for its alignment with power and wealth and urged its affiliation with workers and farmers. Every two years, from 1963 to 1967, Pope John XXIII and then Pope Paul VI called the whole church to account: *Pacem in Terris* made peace, poverty, and human rights its central mission; the Pastoral Constitution on the Church in the Modern World (*Gaudium et Spes*) warned that sinful social structures must be purged; and *Populorum Progressio* declared the rights of all peoples to self-determination.[4]

In his apostolic exhortation on renewal of religious life, Pope Paul VI spoke with passion of the ills religious were called to address:

> You hear rising up, more pressing than ever, from their personal distress and collective misery, "the cry of the poor." Was it not in order to respond to their appeal as God's privileged ones that Christ came, even going as far as to identify Himself with them? In a world experiencing the full flood of development this persistence of poverty-stricken masses and individuals constitutes a pressing call for "a conversion of minds and attitudes...."[5]

This glance backward suggests that what seemed to begin in the 1960s had deep roots. The structures of civil society and of the Church, including those of religious life, were products of centuries, hardly to be challenged and changed in a decade or two. Nevertheless, in the persons of leaders both in and out of elected office, women religious were not slow to respond to these calls of their Church. Wanting more facts than rhetoric, they resorted to the hard work of concrete research on existing conditions. In 1966 the CMSW commissioned a group of sisters led by Sister Marie Augusta Neal, of the Sisters of Notre Dame de Namur, on the faculty of Emmanuel College, Boston, to conduct a survey of its member congregations to determine their readiness in personal and material resources for renewal. Part I of the first survey recorded data from 301 congregations in all of their units or provinces. Mother Leo Frances Ryan responded for the Sisters of Charity of Leavenworth. The second part was sent in 1967 to all sisters in the member congregations of CMSW. These initial surveys requested by CMSW extended into follow-up surveys of selected populations in 1980 and 1989, with a summary report dated 1991 and revised in 1992.[6]

COMMUNITY IN A NATIONAL CONTEXT

Selected data are significant for what was happening in the Community at the time. Entrance trends for all the congregations responding to Part I of the 1966–1967 survey, marked at five-year intervals from 1948 to 1962, showed an increase of 17 to 19 percent for each period until 1963, when a decline to almost 6 percent was projected for the next five years. Though total membership held steady, there was a dramatic decline from 70 to 25 percent of the entrants in these years who persevered to final vows. Most departures occurred in the temporary-vow period. The trends of departures for all reporting congregations moved in even graver proportions. Marked at five-year intervals, the rate of departures doubled from 1950 to 1965, amounting to 30 percent of the total population by 1966. In 1950, in 54 percent of the congregations responding, no one under vows, temporary or perpetual, was leaving her community; in 1965 that was true for only 15 percent of the same congregations. In a matter of sixteen years, departures from women's religious communities in the United States had risen to almost a third of the reporting population.[7]

The Sisters of Charity of Leavenworth were to learn firsthand the kind of losses that send shock waves through a community. Candidates entered from 1950 through 1965 in numbers averaging approximately thirty a year, maintaining the Community's population of novices and professed sisters between approximately 900 and 1,000. Beginning in 1966, however, the number of entrants declined by slightly more than 50 percent annually for three years (i.e., 1965=21 entrants, 1966=11, 1967=6) and then averaged about two entrants a year for the next decade and beyond. Equally serious was the rising number of professed sisters leaving the community. For fifteen years from 1950, the rate of departures moved at five-year intervals from only 1.2 percent to 2.4 percent. Beginning in 1965 the numbers almost doubled every two years. In 1969, during the first Chapter of Renewal, departures for the previous four years were more than 12 percent of the Community's population. By 1970 they had reached almost 18 per-

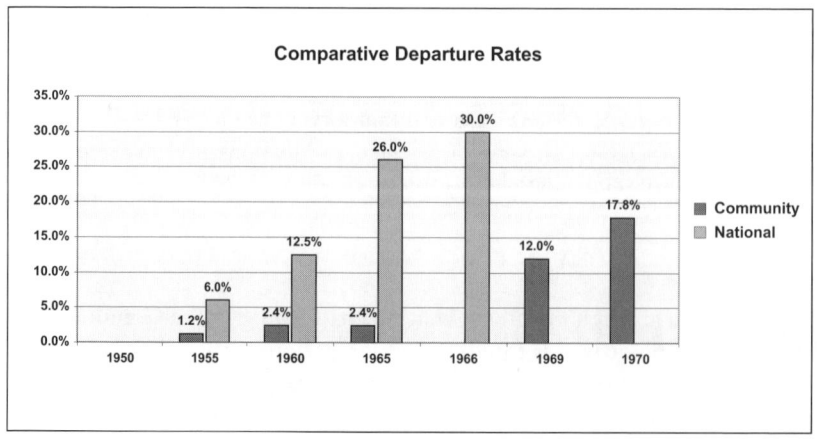

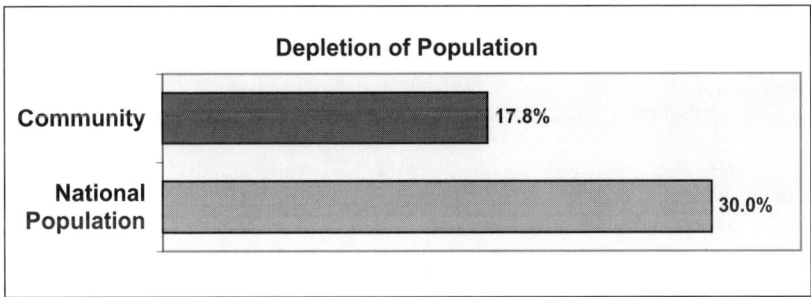

cent before they began to decline in the next five years.[8] While the national population of women religious had been depleted by almost a third, the Community's loss was nearer a fifth; both were of great consequence. Reasons for the alarming departures were to be of primary concern for the Community as it continued renewal.

To find causes for such numbers in the ongoing work and current thinking of individual sisters was imperative for all religious communities experiencing decline. The congregational survey revealed concentrations in the preparation and assignment of sisters needed for the vast school system that they themselves had made possible. Now these concentrations were something of a paradox. By 1966, across the country, 31 percent of the sisters with advanced degrees held them in education. Yet for engagement with the world and its problems, trained competence in theology and the social sciences was necessary.

This disproportion was natural, considering that 72 percent of the responding congregations' members were in the Catholic school system. Fewer than 10 percent of the total were in health care; fewer than 5 percent were in social welfare ministries. Five percent were in foreign missions and catechetics combined, the majority of the latter part-time. A smaller number were catechists of various kinds. Eighty percent of the major superiors responded that these were appropriate works for their sisters. As for new works, just 1 percent of the sisters represented in the survey were engaged in them, the majority in special education; a few others in calculable numbers: .13 of 1 percent assigned to adult education; .31 of 1 percent to poverty programs; and .06 of 1 percent to education of immigrants.[9]

In 1965 Sisters of Charity of Leavenworth paralleled the national scene in institutional ministries of Catholic education and social welfare, with about 70 percent of their number assigned to teaching and administration and more than 3 percent to homes for children and the aging. A separate ministry of religious education had not yet developed. It may be, however,

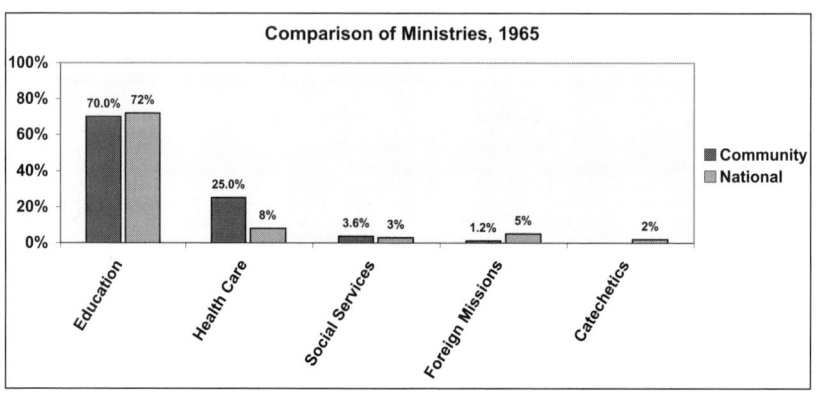

that the founders' legacy and midwestern roots made a difference. Sisters of Charity of Leavenworth first served on a frontier that included vast farm and ranch lands from Kansas to Montana and California, with large relative distances between metropolitan centers. Across that territory in 1965, almost 25 percent of the active membership, 852 sisters, ministered in health care. Ten sisters worked in the Latin American missions—in classroom, clinic, and the countryside—as catechists. As reported in their centennial year 1958, religious education was an additional ministry for 250 teachers in more than a hundred rural vacation schools; and about 160 of these gave weekly religious instruction to public school students. These sisters, more than 40 percent of the teachers in the schools, had an early start on the growing commitment to religious education that marked the 1960s and 1970s.[10]

Students' participation in such ministry was a natural evolution. Coordinated by Mother House and Saint Mary College sisters, with the help of students, a correspondence course sponsored by the Confraternity of Christian Doctrine reached eight hundred youth and adults in some fifty-five Kansas and Missouri parishes. Annually, in their steady round of visits to the sick or homebound, to state institutions and nursing homes, to federal and state prisoners, the sisters engaged high school and college students in apostolic work that became an important part of their education. It was natural, too, for novices in their first year of formation to engage in apostolic works, including assistance in the CCD religious education program.[11] For effective renewal, however, more information about what needed to change and what needed to be preserved in the life of the Community was crucial.

One more piece of the profile that the congregational survey provided suggests some directions for the inquiry. Responses about governance yielded relevant facts: 66 percent of the major superiors were planning wider participation in decision-making for their communities; 75 percent were planning to structure Chapters for it. On the other hand, 81 percent of the congregations had no training of superiors for their jobs; 41 percent had no program for training elementary school principals; 47 percent provided no training for high school supervisors. Only 5 percent had committees for planning and assessing community resources. In 77 percent of the communities, no one was working with poverty programs or immigrants. Yet the call of Pope John to renewal spoke of a world filled with desperately poor and oppressed people.[12] What no one could foresee in 1966 was the ultimate impact of broad participation by women religious in governance of their communities.

One of the most powerful influences at this time on the thinking of many Sisters of Charity of Leavenworth was the Community's common undertaking of renewal. In the summer of 1966, Sister Mary Liguori Horvat introduced the semi-weekly group discussions, emphasizing ultimate norms of renewal: the life of Jesus Christ and his apostles, the prototypical religious community; and the search for basic principles in the purpose and spirit of religious founders. Concluding syntheses were material for continuing discussion into the following year in seventeen designated geographical areas, with 390 sisters participating.[13]

Early on, Sister Rose Dominic struck a keynote: "The old hostile world was in some ways an insulation against loss of faith; today's religious pluralism demands a degree of courage and sophistication dependent far more than in the past on a higher level of education." As executive secretary of the Sister Formation Program, Sister well knew that "religious communities of women began their *aggiornamento* long before the word became current." She also touched on an issue not mentioned in the *Imperatives in Education* published by the American Association of School Administrators: the need to combat racial segregation and foster integration—the "permeating concept" of the formation of the religious teacher.[14]

In the light of work to come, certain insights from these syntheses were relevant for early goals of renewal. One group reported a yearning for further study of the Vatican II documents and of modern theologians, with application to life as a Sister of Charity of Leavenworth; a conviction that each sister must keep herself informed of changes and trends in the Church; and agreement that self-fulfillment is not an end in itself but comes with surrender to God in Jesus and in union with fellow human beings in Christ.

Three groups studied the vows. One asserted that "we must re-think the vow of poverty as it is practiced in an affluent society" and raised questions about whether the professed poverty of the sisters was a true witness to the world, or whether middle-class standards were simply accepted as a means of aiding service. Another pointed to the paradox that observing the vow of chastity can make a religious seem cold and unapproachable, withdrawn into herself. They affirmed the value of friendship as a basic human need and the benefit of understanding woman's nature. A third group emphasized that religious obedience springs from mutual trust, thoughtfulness, and maturity; that authority's decisions and sisters' cooperation must be informed acts; that a superior's first responsibility is to her sisters, not to their works; and that community is not a family, but a loving solidarity of adult persons.

A group discussing apostolic works spoke of the apostolate as sacramental, a sharing in Christ's priesthood, and as a participation in all the works done by all members of the Community. They emphasized the need to examine apostolates in the light of needs of the times—the need for adult education, clinics, service centers for families, collaboration with lay teachers, care for migrants and young mothers, contribution to Headstart, special education, retreats, CCD. Dominant questions raised by a group studying community touched on loneliness, communication, and recreation; on growing old gracefully; on reaching out to parish and community, working together and sharing interests, sensitivity and a sense of humor. For more than one, the group's talk made it imperative to continue the conversations.

Comments from the group on rules and regulations focused on dialogue as the avenue to change on the local level in managing the house and adapting the daily schedule; on principles of subsidiarity and collegiality as ways to unity and shared responsibility; on charity, not regularity, as the cornerstone of religious life. The summer schedule was cited as an example of liberty with personal responsibility. Many suggestions for summer study and for changes in the Constitutions and Book of Customs were accompanied by a caution: that intolerance of all discipline must yield to sacrifice for the common good and that those holding extreme viewpoints must unite in deep love for the Community and a spirit of gratitude.

That such a spirit prevailed overall was evident in overheard comments that expressed a heightened sense of community, a deeper appreciation of the religious vocation, new respect for others as persons and for their opinions, better knowledge of other sisters, freedom to voice opinions on Community affairs. The distance to be traveled and depths to be plumbed for genuine renewal were suggested by a range of recommendations. They emphasized evaluation of the Community's apostolic roles in the light of the Church's contemporary needs, an intensive study of community life and experimental programs in community living, and in-service formation for sisters. They asked for reflection on the Constitutions, efforts to reach consensus in interpretation of rules and customs, and study of Vincentian spirituality and of the vows as positive expressions of responsibility and mutual love.[15]

Correspondence between questions raised by the Sisters of Charity in their intensive preparation for renewal and questions posed by Sister Marie Augusta Neal to the assembled CMSW concerning the Sisters' Surveys is more than significant. Correspondence of dates—Neal's first report was made in late September 1967 and the deadline for the completion of the SCL Study Commissions' schemata was February 15, 1968—places the Community's grass-roots work in a national setting. Sister Marie Augusta's report and the commissions' eight schemata—each of them produced by a chairperson in constant communication with her commission—were being written almost simultaneously.

The creator and interpreter of the Sisters' Surveys asked the heads of congregations: "Are we doing the work the Lord intends and in his style? If yes, how do we make this work relevant so that the world...can receive and recognize it?" In the spirit of founders and in the face of the world's needs, "How do we distribute ourselves in service so all the needs of the suffering are assuaged?" and "How ecumenical are we capable of becoming?"[16]

Discerning the Mission

During the in-depth study that followed the summer discussions of 1966, many Sisters of Charity of Leavenworth were asking such questions and more of themselves and their Community. Each sister had the opportunity to approve or reject every recommendation of the commission members and to add recommendations of her own. Freedom of thought and expression was a priority. Considered imperative for the study was mutual respect for divergent views and attitudes in an atmosphere of openness as well as a steady flow of communication between commission members, directors, and the steering committee representative. Topics were derived from the work of a preparatory committee and the previous summer's discussions. A steering committee and members of a special commission on "Constitutions and Customs" were elected at large.

Each commission's final document included a list of sources studied, key concepts and principles agreed upon, differing points of view on the topic in question, and the commission's recommendations to the Chapter. The documents were supported by reading of extraordinary range and depth. Start to finish, the study was a typical Community undertaking: thorough, well planned and executed, and an effective means to its end, involving every sister who wanted to be involved, to each one's capacity. The challenge lay in transforming 276 recommendations into a Chapter agenda.

Recognizing the complexity of "The Sister in the Church," the commission on the topic treated first the Church and its mission and the sacramental character of the lay vocation. Emphasis was placed on the innovation of Vincent's rule in its call to serve *with* the people of God and on self-examination in the face of immediate needs. Recommendations called for functioning with other communities in each diocese; experimentation in the exercise of local community authority; assignment of sisters to study scripture, theology, and liturgy; cooperation with clergy, laity, Protestant churches, and civic groups toward ends of social justice. Preparation of sisters to teach and nurse in inner city schools and clinics, to participate in adult religious education, and to minister on secular campuses was seen as a priority.

The commission on "Life of the Counsels" experienced sharp differences in members' interpretation of religious vows. Recommendations ranged from consideration of a single vow of community—a way of life according to the Gospel in service to the common good—to a post-experimentation re-commitment by each member to "pursue the work of the Church in this Community." The alternative would be dispensation from vows. The distance between these two recommendations is difficult to overemphasize. In one self-selected group of several dozen women, it represented theological orientations and experiences of Christian life that were in themselves irreconcilable.

A recommendation to eliminate the distinction between sisters under temporary and perpetual vows in electing Chapter delegates suggested that many more voices needed to be heard in community governance. Expressed desires to emphasize poverty as availability for service; to find new forms of witnessing poverty, corporately and individually; and to participate in budgeting house money indicated the necessity of honoring divergent views. Recommendations to study opportunities for sisters to live with the poor, the possibility of a plebiscite vote on new community ventures, and release of institutions to lay administration and ownership said that movement toward structural change required much more information and communication. Other recommendations emphasized preparation for perpetual profession in serious attention to the foundations of celibate life and to the sources of religious obedience. They reflected the deep influence of post–Vatican II theology.

Exploring the roots of "Community," the commission on that topic looked to profound personal renewal as the beginning of communal renewal. Recommendations referred to meaningful eucharistic celebration and participation in parish liturgy, to community prayer as the prayer of the Church, and to the psychological climate and collegial conduct of local communities. Attention to professional aspects of ministry brought recommendations of freedom to serve in civic associations, to participate in the life of the parish, and to take greater advantage of cultural resources. A comprehensive recommendation asked for structural change in assignment to missions.

The commission on "Person in Community" distinguished spiritual and theological needs; physiological, psychological, and emotional needs; intellectual and professional needs; and needs of retirement. A central recommendation concerned choice regarding one's local community, traditional or experimental, given proximity to apostolic assignment. Description of a community's way of living—prayer, government, recreation, hospitality, budgetary management—was to provide the option as opposed to choosing companions. The proposal aimed at forestalling certain risks to community life in new opportunities to live in small groups.

Freeing sisters to work with the neglected poor or to take jobs outside the Community, especially in deprived areas, and participation in government programs for the underprivileged was a priority with the commission. Recommendations for individual choice of apostolate or specialization called for adequate preparation, for contracting for jobs with market salaries, and for learning to live within a budget according to apostolic and professional needs. Continuing formation with an annual institute of post–Vatican II theology and a mental health program for the Community were uncontroversial recommendations. Those that drew deep disagreement concerned common prayer, choice of attire, an annual vacation, and the question of Community Councilors living outside the Mother House. One area suggested for experimentation was inter-faith religious education on public high school campuses.

The group closed its schema with words of Paul VI to religious of the world:

> There is more to be asked of you.... Now you will be plunged into the midst of the life of the citizens of the cities of the world.... The mission I point out... will make you even poorer than before. It will make you capable of a poverty that will be lived, not merely professed.... You have left the sinful world, only in order to come closer to it.... Try to understand this modern vocation of the religious state. And... prepare yourselves for it![17]

The commission on "Spirituality" emphasized the need to study post–Vatican II theology, to form a Community committee on the liturgy, to adopt Lauds and Vespers as daily communal prayer, to experiment with the annual retreat and days of recollection, and to study Marian theology in the spirit of Vatican II and Community founders.

Considering its origin and purpose, the commission on "The Apostolate" sought means of renewal in evaluating the personnel and ongoing experimentation in each of the Community's areas of ministry. A singular passage introduced the entire text: "It is better to concentrate the work of a great number of people outward from a specific central plan than to engage in a great variety of works that may be somewhat unrelated and tend to deplete forces."[18] Its significance for the continuing identity and developing mission of a religious community would not be realized for some time after years of experimentation and change. In a new-found freedom to pursue the Gospel mission as capability and discernment suggested, members of renewing communities were to diversify ministries in direct service to the poor and marginalized for the next two or three decades. The power of a unified mission of women religious gathering their diversity to a force was to show itself gradually.

Educators in the Apostolate Commission suggested better use of the media and public relations, guidance programs, and collaboration with public school officials. In their report, hospitals and health care members focused on expanded opportunities for service, the need to call on aptitudes of individual sisters for best utilization of personnel, and reassessment of the place of religious in collaboration with private and public institutions. Social workers had few but far-reaching recommendations. Argument for a study of needs by a team of religious, clerical, and lay people from communities where Sisters of Charity serve was the most demanding. Education to leadership, consultation with professionals for funding opportunities, and participation in national and international organizations were practical recommendations. The group studying religious education presented a comprehensive plan for re-evaluation of the Community's catechetical apostolate to include its purpose, qualities of the religious educator, and the role of fine arts, creativity, and communication in the mission of the Church. Recommendations reflected a broad vision of apostolic needs.

The commission on "Government" proposed a new body for the new spirit of religious life. It recommended recasting Chapter membership to include all age groups and apostolates. An open Chapter would admit observers and eliminate the aura of secrecy. The group requested standing commissions to continue research and the utilization of consultants in canon law, theology, and psychology. Making a statement on the role of the Community in a postconciliar world and finding a method for ratifying major legislation before adoption were more complex challenges.

The need for fundamental knowledge of Community finances informed suggestions for a lay advisory board, annual reporting to the Community, monthly reports of expenditures by local houses, and statements of costs of experimentations. Broader recommendations sought evaluation of the exercise of authority on all levels, role descriptions for local and regional superiors as well as for the Council, common patterns for local community experimentation, structures for participation in Community decision-making, and a consultative voice in appointment of superiors. Such recommendations were visionary in many respects.

Preparation for changes in the Constitutions began with the work of special commissions on the canonical codes and documents on religious life. Principles guiding revision aimed at a union of the spiritual and juridical aspects and a direct style of writing. Clear statements were wanted about the nature of an American community reflecting balances of authority, allowance for change, and means of redress. They were to affirm the value of person in community and provide for continuing renewal.[19]

The tone and direction of these schemata suggested renewal already under way in the convictions and lives of a majority of Community members. Most impressive is the consistency of principles that guided the work and the vast range of agreement in its conclusions. Anyone who lived in Community through the decades that followed could recognize in these documents the origins of most of the changes. Areas of dissent, if not dissension, were noticeably few in number and clearly drawn. Further, the differences focused on observable actions or behaviors. That does not mean they lay in "mere externals." Depth of difference was more significant than range and issued in polarities that did not immediately reveal their origins. The causes of difference in views, attitudes, and values had deep roots in upbringing, education, and theological orientation. The intensive pre-Chapter study of 1967–1968 demonstrated that the Sisters of Charity exemplified divisions that were developing in many other religious congregations.

But thousands of American women religious had lived in community with such differences and with great equanimity for dozens of years up till this time. The differences surfaced—with some loss of that equanimity—only with these early moves toward renewal. Moreover, whatever the causes of changing numbers in communities—increasing departures and diminishing applications—these could not yet at least be attributed primarily to differing views or values. Such differences resided among both those who were leaving and those who were staying. Rather, something was threatening stability, reaching to the very heart of their life together; something was happening to the heartbeat of that life.

Seeking Causes for Conditions

Part II of the Sisters' Survey was designed to discover what was happening. Most of the major superiors in the CMSW wanted all their members to participate and wanted to study their individual communities in the light of a national profile. The survey was mailed in April 1967 to approximately 158,000 sisters; more than 139,000 responded—88 percent of the participating population, 75 percent of all women religious in the United States. Each community financed the processing of its data and contributed to the total project. Many still recall the homework demanded by 649 questions—with answers strictly guarded for confidentiality—about family rearing, education, socio-economic class, parents' ethnic origins and professions; about reasons for coming to religious life or for staying, preferences in ministry, quality of community life, attitudes toward renewal and its pace; about habits of reading, convictions and beliefs, and hopes for the future of the Church and religious life.[20] Participating in the survey, one could begin to think that her opinions, not just facts, certainly must matter to someone. And they did.

These are some of the questions that governed the design of the survey:

- "Do we really know what the world needs of our sisters? Are we ready to give it? Does formation relate directly to the life we expect them to live?
- "What kinds of people choose to enter our order as distinct from those who enter other orders? Why are they entering? If they are leaving, why?
- "Do we have frustration tolerance [necessary] to do the research and the experimenting prior to decision and the trust of our sisters to let them share not just the results but the grass-root planning...?"[21]

In the cover letter, the research committee explained the purpose and importance of the survey for wise Chapter decisions in directing renewal. How to distinguish needs that continue in the Church, new needs that cry out in the world, and which needs a given community with its resources and its charism should take on: this was the enormous task the survey aimed to assist. To be told that each and all of those participating were the resources of their respective institutes was a sobering assurance.[22]

In response, approximately 870 Sisters of Charity of Leavenworth—89.8 percent—recorded their yeses and nos to questions designed to reveal belief orientations, attitudes, and values significant for guiding renewal. Very

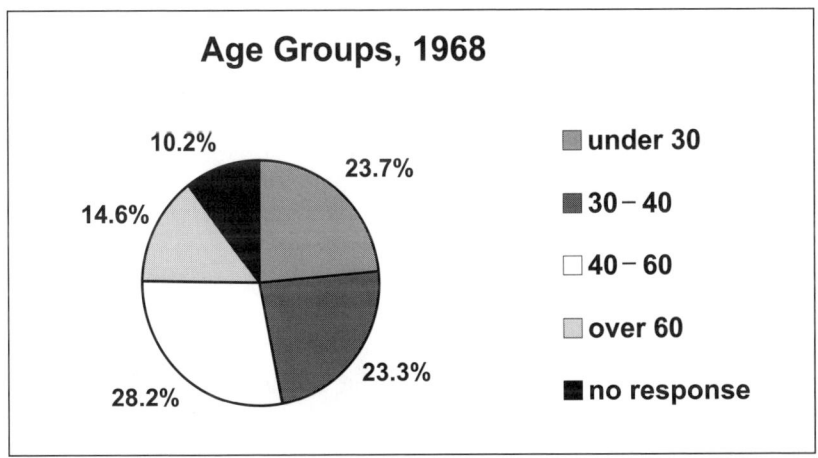

nearly half of the respondents were between twenty-one and forty years of age; somewhat under a third, between forty and sixty; and approximately 15 percent over sixty. Slightly more than 14 percent had been under perpetual vows for one to five years. The relative youth of the Community's membership was significant in view of Constitutional parameters of governance.

Between 20 and 24 percent of the Community, those under temporary vows and under thirty years of age, had only active voice in election of delegates to Chapter, that is, they could vote but could not be elected. In view of the desire expressed in the pre-Chapter study for greater participation in decision-making and better communication in convent life, this imbalance of representation in the primary governing body was significant. Equally important for results of Chapters to follow was continuity with the past and deep commitment to community implicit in the middle range in age of Chapter delegates. Other factors embedded in survey statistics had an indirect impact on renewal. Approximately 70 (69.5) percent of the respondents reported their religious upbringing as good and almost 60 (58.7) percent had a Catholic education through high school. It may be presumed that, for these, exposure to people of other faiths or value orientations in an educational setting was uncommon. Perhaps most significant of all, 38 percent of the respondents entered the Community from high school or earlier.[23]

This was a Community of individuals accustomed to working for whatever temporal advantages they might have enjoyed and responsible in large part for informing themselves about their world and their Church. Judging from the absence of clear patterns of response, their reading—important for influencing thought and ideas—was limited by reason of training, time, and accessibility. Though the Sister Formation Program was enlarging educational horizons for young members, most were earning college degrees in successive summers, largely for purposes of certification. These facts and others form a context for what the survey revealed of respondents' social and religious orientation. Questions addressed one's experience in community and apostolic work; one's beliefs, social attitudes, and values; one's views of community life and structure; and one's view of the future.

Taking Stock of the Situation

Responses about aspects of day-to-day living in community reflected varying experience, contrary to external appearances. With about 36 percent of the sisters reporting that they had worked at some time with the really poor, almost 39 percent thought the Community was sufficiently engaged in work for the poor, and very nearly 42 percent agreed that the founder, if alive today, would recommend the work the institute "is now doing in the way it is being done." In some contrast, a third of the respondents judged their local community's practice of poverty to be good; less than a third thought their house was effectively in touch with needs of local people. Sisters under temporary vows ranked significantly lower than the others in their estimate of the house's knowledge of local needs and service to the poor, as well as in their evaluation of their local community's practice of poverty.[24]

Nevertheless, respondents across all lines of age and community experience, roughly two-thirds, predicted basic changes in the style of religious life over the next ten years. Roughly half foresaw a new structure of religious life in adaptation to contemporary needs. Prediction of "radical change in the theological expression of religious thoughts about God and man" came from about 40 percent, while considerably fewer of young and older members expected that change, probably for different reasons.[25] It is difficult to judge but possible to speculate that these percentages reflect a relatively common experience of religious life, with deeply different responses to it dependent on reading, contacts beyond the Community, and interaction with like-minded sisters. The differences do not contradict but may rather reflect the convictions expressed in the pre-Chapter discussions and commission documents.

Though well over half the respondents found community governance too centralized, considerably less than half, and few superiors, saw local house governance as too centralized. And, given the necessity of higher superiors, almost 84 percent thought local communities should have superiors in charge. Less than a quarter of all respondents (but 31 percent of those under temporary vows) foresaw a *complete* restructuring of community life. The numbers reflected relative uncertainty about the degree of needed change and thinking that would affect decisions in forthcoming Chapters of renewal. Decisions for change, though bound to come, were not likely to be radical.

Indicators of community identity and sense of belonging were not altogether reassuring. Three-fourths of the respondents said they would recommend their way of life to others, though no clear pattern emerged about "a distinct spirit" that distinguished the institute. Only 56.4 percent of perpetually professed and about 62 percent of the temporally professed were certain they would choose to enter the Community given the choice again, though percentages rose for juniors and superiors. Reasons for staying in religious life focused, for about a third to half of the respondents, on its being a sure way of knowing God's will; fewer of the temporally vowed sisters cited this motive. For a quarter of the respondents, reasons included hope for renewal or living the Gospel in witness and service to the poor and suffering. Between 45 and 60 percent of the younger sisters had within the last two years seriously thought about leaving.

Good aspects of life in local communities—communication across age groups, openness of opinions, honesty with each other, appreciation of achievements, sensitivity to others, communication with superiors and general officers—were experienced unevenly within a range of 20 to 40 percent of the respondents. Nearly half found opportunity for friendships. In contrast, 60 percent of the respondents indicated that a change in the climate of communication was needed, especially by redefining the subject-superior relation. A desire for candid discussion of troubling or uplifting spiritual experiences was voiced by 64.4 percent of all the respondents—almost 80 percent of the temporally professed and more than 68 percent of the superiors. Such a clear need expressed across age groups called for serious attention.

Fewer than 20 percent of those under temporary or perpetual vows found the decision-making policy of the Community satisfactory. Little more than 20 percent felt informed about Community finances. Between 36 and 48 percent of all the respondents were satisfied with novitiate training; somewhat fewer of the younger sisters expressed satisfaction with juniorate education. Only a fifth of the respondents who had never been superiors could imagine themselves standing up for a sister's right in conscience to speak or demonstrate in conflict with a superior's wishes. Slightly more than a quarter of all respondents found their theology education to be adequate. About the same number thought renewal in the Church was too slow. Without clear ideas of how to act upon them, concerns about the Community were growing among the majority of the sisters, who were at the same time conscious of strong, though flawed, community life.

As reported, work relationships were less than satisfactory. Almost a third of the respondents found difficulties in the work itself. According to a quarter of the sisters under temporary vows, they felt deprived of independence of judgment and responsibility to carry out the work assigned. More than a third of all respondents felt little encouragement in their ministry. Though true only of a minority in each case, the kinds of experiences reported as frustrating were significant for the effectiveness of apostolic work. A clearer view of the apostolate comes from responses to questions about the Community's present and future works.

Between 50 and 60 percent of the sisters wanted to see basic changes in the parochial school system. Less than 12 percent considered the secondary school system to be effective. Half thought that sisters should be active in the public sector. Yet more than half the junior sisters (57 percent) and former superiors (52.4 percent) marked teaching in Catholic schools, foreign mission work, and catechetics for youth as traditional works to be expanded; somewhat less than half the others (45 to almost 49 percent) did so as well. Work with groups needing special care—including prisoners, adult learners, shut-ins, delinquents, racial minorities, public school and university students, inner-city families—was marked by 56 percent of the temporary vow sisters and half or nearly half of all perpetually vowed respondents. Radically new works were marked by less than 15 percent of any group except the junior sisters, a fifth of whom indicated they would protest against affluence.[26]

Of the scales used to assess beliefs, social attitudes, and attitudes toward change, the creator of the survey found the belief scales to be the most rewarding for predictive potential. A mixed orientation was quite possible and indicated diversity of a kind to make decisions on crucial points difficult and resolution of conflicts often painful. The national survey revealed that even while new theology—that of Vatican II—was affecting all members' beliefs in varying degrees, pre–Vatican II theology still provided a substantial element of a community's value structure. This was so although that very theology was outside the reflective belief of young religious and of growing numbers of seasoned members. All this was reflected in the responses Sisters of Charity made to given questions of the survey.

They ranked moderately close to the national profile in post–Vatican II theology, falling pretty consistently below average, however, on questions about the unity of all human beings in Jesus Christ, his presence and revelation in them; and rising above average on particular questions about revelation, grace, the laity, and the liturgy. On the other hand, they ranked appreciably below the national profile in pre–Vatican II theology—meaning their thinking veered toward Vatican II teaching—except for certain abstract concepts about God, prayer, religious life, sacraments, and heaven.

Thinking about the vows was uneven. Views of chastity were fairly consistent with developments in theology after Vatican II, with some lack of clarity about the purpose of the vow and relationships it fosters. Beliefs about poverty varied sharply—the nearest to post–Vatican II thinking in re-conceiving the vow as a way of life and work with the poor; the furthest from it in not conceiving a relationship of poverty to collective ownership and security. Views of obedience ranged wide: from a clear post–Vatican II understanding of personal freedom with responsibility for one's actions and communal decisions, to varying notions about the nature of authority as lodged in a person or in the community.[27]

Professionally designed and tested scales provided a measure of respondents' social attitudes. According to the design of the survey, high scores in political pessimism suggested a fear of the world in its present condition and a feeling that forces beyond control are responsible; low scores pointed to opposite attitudes. Prejudice, especially reflected indirectly in given responses, indicated uncritical over-submissiveness to authority and a tendency to project repressed hostilities onto unfamiliar groups. Again, low scores were desirable. Anomie, or withdrawal from the scene of action, brings on apathy deriving from loss of security or certitude in the face of changes in rules and sanctions. In the survey, its contrary was compatible with openness to change for value-oriented reasons.

Keeping in mind that responses to each question were recorded in percentages of a whole, a reader may find outcomes reflecting a basically healthy community climate among the Sisters of Charity of Leavenworth. On a five-point range, almost half their responses ranked very low or low

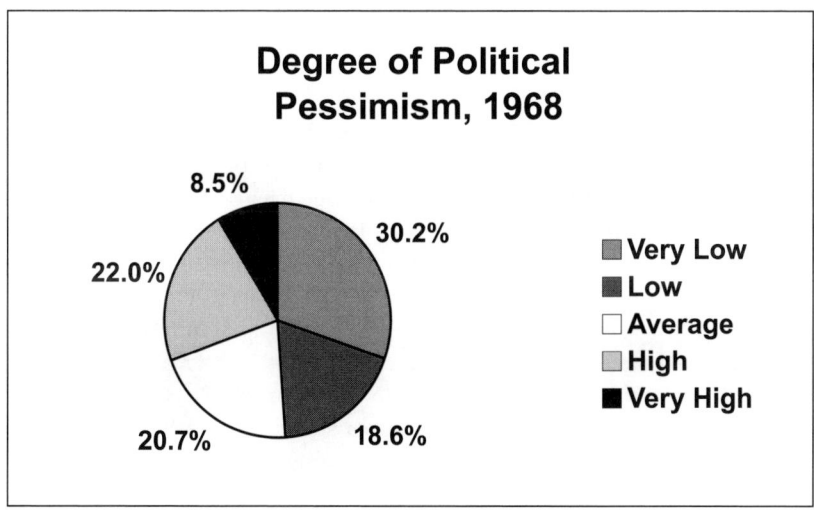

on political pessimism, anomie, and prejudice. Fewer than 10 percent of the responses showed a very high degree of these attitudes; somewhat more than a fifth, however, ranked high. This left only a fifth in the middle range, considerably fewer than the national average of 30 percent or more. Read as indicative, the results showed room for polarization.[28]

Authorities who studied effects of change in religious communities reported at the time that difficulties of a community experiencing life-changing renewal reside in two opposing cultures. These are fundamentally composed of mentalities and attitudes regarding authority, prayer, relationships, and vows. Resolution of such difficulties is commonly sought in synthesis and reorganization—not simply to prevent a final breach, but primarily to establish the best conditions for realizing the deepest values of each culture and its structure. Success depends on interpretation and acceptance of the fundamental meaning of religious life. Both methods may be necessary for success, or synthesis alone may suffice.

Synthesis is accomplished when points of mutual agreement outweigh differences, discussed with sufficient openness to discern the value inherent in the differences and with willingness to learn from one another. Reorganization leads to a community composed in such a way that all members are convinced they can shape their own outlook on religious life through communal experience, apostolic zeal, and personal and communal prayer. The fundamental religious view held in common will then be expressed in varying patterns of community life.[29] That fundamental meaning was to become the focus of the Chapter of Renewal that began in the summer of 1968.

Considering the crucial changes in the world the sisters inhabited, Sister Marie Augusta Neal's critical questions, posed in her report to the Congregation of Major Superiors of Women in 1967, were relevant for the members of that Chapter and are relevant still, forty years later.

- In an interdependent global society, where an economy of abundance leaves two-thirds of the world in real poverty, must we not ask ourselves how well our programs of health, education, and welfare affect the peoples of the world?[30]
- In a world whose population doubles every thirty-five years, where conflicting systems of value interact with violence, how visibly and effectively do "we teach, live and communicate ...the beliefs to which we are committed?"
- In a world where hunger for community runs parallel to the rise of corporate control and bureaucracy, can we live in ways that reveal the power of the love of God for each one and for all together?[31]

In 1967, the great majority of the Sisters of Charity of Leavenworth would have answered with a resounding "Yes! We serve as well as we know how as many people as we can reach through our seventy-two schools, our nine hospitals, and our three homes for parentless children or the aging. Furthermore, we're extending those services to two missions in Latin America, with hopes for more. We aren't perfect by a long shot, but we try to live together in communities that must reflect Christ one way or another, or why would thirty-odd young women join us, on the average, each August?"

Yet the dozens of recommendations that shaped the agenda for the first Chapter of Renewal said, in sum, that more than half the Community saw its government as too centralized, processes of decision-making unsatisfactory, and openness of communication in local houses seriously lacking. A sizeable majority desired revision of the parochial school system, development of religious education programs, broad expansion of social services, collaboration with private and public agencies, and freedom to serve the poor, especially in the inner city, in inventive new ways. Perhaps most significant of all, in the long run, was the absence of respondents' clear ideas about what distinguished their Community and its spirit, and the conviction of about 80 percent that their theological education was inadequate.

Sometimes the way others see us clears the lens. Asked years later what change or abiding character he saw in the Community's mission and spirit, Father John Stitz, former chaplain of Saint Mary College, said, "I would use the word resilient—a dogged determination to be consistent." Their greatest strength he named with no hesitation: "Their belief in themselves. Loyalty to their personal commitment. Even women who've left continue in that mode of believing in yourself. That's pretty strong."[32]

Loyalty to personal commitment and the determination to be consistent with a past of great value were at the bottom of the discernment that was to follow as the Community pursued its goals in the spirit of Vincent de Paul, Louise de Marillac, and its founders. The scope of preparation for the Chapter and the promise of change to come inspired hope in hundreds of sisters committed to staying the course and urging significant renewal. It should be clear from the volume of evidence contained in the detailed records of study groups and commission reports that the Sisters of Charity of Leavenworth were ready by 1968 for communal renewal. In 1967, about 870 sisters had responded to the national survey of women religious in the United States. While individual responses remained strictly confidential, percentages of replies reflected many of the concerns that were specifically recorded in the Community's pre-renewal study.

Such apparent readiness for change complicates rather than clarifies the phenomenon of departures from the Community, departures that continued through the Chapters of Renewal and beyond. Why 175 women under temporary vows chose to remain in religious life during the decade after 1964 while some 330 of their companions were leaving is a mystery that facts and figures cannot adequately explain.[33] Part of the answer may lie in the connection between individual commitment and varying perceptions of the Community's heritage and mission. In this connection, perhaps, is the clearest evidence of the mystery of grace—of that personal relationship that exists between the individual and God to whom she vows her life. It is one example, as well, of the strength those remaining had inherited from their forebears, symbolized in the trees they persisted in planting, "renewed...eager to rise...."[34]

CHAPTER 4

Untold Stories

Until 1965 little had appeared in statistics to diminish hope for the future. The Community's total membership was still strong at 889;[1] the number of sisters who left while under temporary vows had remained, on average, steady at one to five in a given year, and only five perpetually professed sisters had applied for dispensation from their vows. Within the next three years, however, even while preparation for the Chapter of Renewal was going forward, fifty sisters left the Community, twenty-three of them under perpetual vows. Those numbers were to increase for three years more. But neither numbers themselves nor the national parallel—the exodus of both women and men religious—revealed clear reasons for the rate and number of departures.[2]

Responses to a survey in the fall of 2001 addressed to all who had left the Community since 1955 are of some help in this regard, though a return of just 22.7 percent makes it, though valid, not impressive—at least at face value.[3] Several facets, however, heighten its worth. Anywhere from eight to forty-three years had intervened between the respondent's year of departure and the year of the survey, providing ample time for mature reflection. The open-ended questions about reasons for the decision to leave and about influence on the decision from societal unrest and from change in the Church asked for candid and thoughtful replies. The quality of the responses in this regard and the willingness to participate evoked both respect and confidence.

The fact that slightly more than a fifth of the respondents wrote of remembered anger or hurt or loss of respect for community policies or inconsistencies suggests that others with similar feelings did not respond. The number is impossible to determine. A third of those who did respond recorded that wounds suffered during their time in the Community had healed. Once analysis uncovered patterns in the responses, the correspondence of these to patterns revealed in Neal's 1967 national survey of women religious placed the Community's experience in a broad context. Further, the responses invite comparison with the schema prepared by the sisters before the Chapter of 1968–1969. Similarities are marked. Perhaps the most challenging parallels appear in particular responses or their patterns and in the reflections of aging sisters on this period of the Community's life.

Sister Mary Seraphine Sheehan, recalling those years three decades later, observed that as departures incrementally increased the impression was that of increasing speed—intensified no doubt by lack of perspective all around.[4] In her report on the national survey, Sister Marie Augusta Neal had remarked that "...willingness to let people go when they have difficulty adjusting to the system in its current forms is a factor in this accelerating trend."[5] In fact, in 1966, women religious had only begun to examine effects of the system on individual and communal living.

The 2001 survey of former members inquired into causes of the departure of 346 professed sisters from the Community over the forty years between 1955 and 1995. The largest number was concentrated in the decade beginning in 1965, when annual departures moved at a rapidly rising rate from twelve to forty-one in 1969 and back down to twelve by 1975; the rate increased and declined within the decade in almost equal proportion.[6] A cover letter explained the purpose of the survey: *to gain first-hand information from observations and perceptions of those closely associated with the Community for a considerable time during years of significant change, in order to clarify an account of the period.* The percentage of return was figured from the number still living—321—in 2001.[7] Analysis of the 73 responses, arranged in ascending order of entry dates, began with identification of topics mentioned in replies to the first three questions:

- Have the years led you to new insights into your reasons for leaving the Community?
- So far as you can judge, what effects did society and culture of the time have on your decision to leave?
- As you see it now, what effects did change in the life of the Church have on your decision to leave the Community?

Because of overlap in responses on a given form, no analysis of replies to each question was practicable. Listing topics and re-reading responses raised patterns that appeared in repetition or relationship of terms, reference to similar situations or experiences, conclusions about a given topic. Expressed attitudes and feelings might differ; this did not diminish significance. The number of times a pattern appeared in the responses determined its position on a frequency scale, not necessarily its importance. No attempt was made to identify a pattern with a given span of years; that would have required many more data points. Distinguishing major emphases and closely related observations and eliminating repetition made it possible to collapse roughly 240 items into twenty-one patterns that clarify reasons for leaving religious life.

Dominant patterns were expressed in various ways fourteen to twenty-one times:

- Impact of Vatican II documents on role of the laity and opportunities for service, desire to participate in renewal of the Church and society
- Impact of post–Vatican II theology in sense of enlarged freedom—from fear and for decision in spiritual development
- Conviction of a temporary vocation with call to another way of life, sense of Providence in decisions
- Difficulties in formation, initial and ongoing, with little individual counsel
- Emphasis in community life on outdated rules psychologically demeaning

Patterns expressed six to eleven times:

- Immaturity at entrance, from misguided religious education, sheltered early life
- "Growth pains" of change: new sense of too comfortable and secure a life, perceived self-interest in exercise of new freedom, laxity in religious commitments, difficulties of group living
- Tensions and inconsistencies in community, especially in exercise of authority
- Distrust, gossip, lack of charity
- Dissatisfaction with pace of change in religious life
- Lack of spiritual growth as experienced in community
- Lack of meaning in community life, confusion over Community's place in the Church
- Sense of isolation from God's people and from the world

Patterns expressed fewer than five times:

- Failure of recognition or encouragement of personal initiatives and gifts
- Unease or unhappiness in community

- Lack of theological vision from inadequate theological and sociological education
- Effects of personal models or the opposite in religious community
- Taboos on friendship with lack of guidance in sexuality
- Absence of voice or consultation in community governance
- Inconsistency of privilege or recognition in community
- Unapproachable or unqualified superiors

A singular comment pointed to emphasis on service in the Community, lacking encouragement of potential leadership. In about a dozen cases, personal reasons for departure had little or nothing to do with the patterns expressed; about fifteen saw no connection with Vatican II and subsequent change in the Church. If the climate of reassessment and discernment made the decision to leave easier for many, that was not a fundamental cause. Specific mention of Vatican II and its impact as an influence on their decision to leave came from half the respondents. The chief effect of studying the documents and observing the difference they were making in the life of the Church was the desire to participate in renewal through freely chosen service. Almost suddenly, for some, the service given in a Community apostolate was constrained or limited by comparison.

The invitation to re-examine one's convictions and choices, on the way to renewal of Catholic life, uncovered for others an earlier lack of self-knowledge and experience or an idealism in their decision to become a sister. For a few, the difficult ideals of collegiality and subsidiarity, to be sought in governance of the Church, its local churches, and religious congregations reflected the kind of community they had already in some way envisioned. A deeper understanding of the Church's teachings and their long development was for many a new realization of the Gospel they had embraced. Approximately thirty expressed in one way or another the sense that their calling now lay outside religious life.[8] Now and then direct reference clarified distinctions:

> The old dichotomy between sacred and profane, or the idea of being called to "a higher state"...no longer rang true for me. The Council document on the role of the laity in the Church made me realize I WAS the laity. I had a place in the world and it was part of my plan of life to be involved with it. (Kitty Goeters Bronec)

Varied experience in community brought them to this sense or conviction. For one the absence of challenge, for another the cultivation of dependence and consequent devaluation of self; for more than one, group formation in the novitiate, focusing on rules rather than on personal development, seemed a contradiction to what they were reading in the documents and post–Vatican II writing. "Spiritual development," wrote one, "needed an awareness of normal maturational stages and personal psychology. Sexuality seemed to be ignored or suppressed [rather than] openly discussed in a mature, straightforward fashion.... Personal and spiritual counseling on a 1:1 basis may have been very helpful" in understanding and processing personal struggles (Noella DeVolder McCray).

Need to Mature

Another concluded: "A community can create dependency, interdependency, or independence by its history, customs, philosophy, spirituality, and unspoken expectations. Although I came to community with dependency needs, I left community with a need for independence. My growing up with religious life was not supported as it could have been." With the caveat that encouragement of freedom was needed "especially for those not able to seek it on their own," the writer came to recognize "how tradition...can sometimes stand in the way of a person's growth as well as aid it" (Roseanne Maas Schmidt).

Still another confided: "I read and studied the Documents of Vatican II with religious fervor. It was as though each line gave me renewed life and hope.... Changes provided new depth and meaning to our spiritual life." She then added a mature insight:

> But integrating these changes on the level of each individual community was often a daunting task. Especially in large houses, difference of opinion and division by age groups sometimes separated us; this made living and sharing in community life more challenging. In retrospect I recognize what a difficult process it must have been for our superiors to discern how best to bring this renewal to their houses. (Ellen Corkle Viens)

One respondent expressed a deep conviction about the time of departures as providential in the history of the Church:

> I firmly believe that the Holy Spirit, through the Vatican Council, allowed the mass exodus from all religious communities, in order that its mandates be activated in response to the needs of the modern world. The exodus... permitted greater participation by the laity. They responded as partners, in education, medicine,

care of the elderly, etc., while religious communities could no longer depend on themselves to fill vacancies in the apostolates; they reached out to the people they themselves had trained, for new leaders, and made room for them as partners. (Mary Lorian Horvat)

Only six respondents directly or indirectly expressed an earlier desire for married or family life, although others spoke of their present happiness as wives and mothers. While respondents were not asked to indicate whether a prior association contributed to their leaving, a few did so. Influence from the movement for equality of women, its basic principles and effects, was a factor in the decision of half a dozen respondents. One acknowledged that "the recognition of women's place in the Church and in society were all changes that opened doors for me. I felt renewed and challenged and more mature and independent." A distanced view of her state of mind and heart at entrance from high school reflects the healthy self-knowledge she had even then begun to acquire: "I...was sure that I was meant to save the world. My brief idealistic idea was to be a martyr to great spiritual acts. I was sure that sainthood was my destiny" (Charlotte Smith Kelly).

Something of the same kind of growth was reflected in another's statement: "I idealized the Church, the convent and my influence on the world, and I thought I could become a saint by rigorously following what I was taught in the convent. Subsequently, I realize[d] that I need to know myself and be true to who I am as a person" (Rosemary Ziegler Banta). Evidence of the profound spirituality that sustains many of these women was clear in the words of another: "We are all women of the Church, the backbone, the silent significant others who, though denied ordination, yet sacramentalize our each and every particular milieu. All of us, of all kinds, of all ethnicities abide in the same steadfast love that is God's assurance to us" (Mary Rau).

Not all found themselves able or free to realize such a calling within religious community. As one observed:

> ...It is perhaps important that my vision of the church had changed dramatically. When I entered, and during my first few years, I believed in the total rightness of the decisions of the church...particularly in things like the authority and truth of pope and clergy. In living particularly the last five years of my community life, I had serious questions about the dogmatic approach, particularly in family life. As I saw abuse, poverty and real

questions that families dealt with particularly in the role of women and the attitude toward women...and the failure of the Church to recognize those needs, my need to leave was supported. (Jovanna Maronick Tanzey)

Another remarked that as an SMC '52 graduate, "I went from a sheltered environment to a more sheltered one. I knew there was a different world out there and I began to believe I belonged there" (Nancy Lyons).

Another, acknowledging that she "was blessed to be with women who helped me mature," said that the Community's increasing emphasis on the "essence of religious life rather than on the externals" led to "changes that had a profound effect on me, actually allowing me the courage to question and to look at myself. The process...was gradual and frightening, but the Community itself supported me through the great women with whom I lived and worked" (Marilyn Trudelle Krueger).

For others, changes were unsettling. "All I knew at the time of my leaving," said one, "was an unrest and absence of an inner peace. I loved the community....I received a good education and wonderful work ethics....My spiritual life...was certainly nurtured. It took a long time for me to realize that I did not really mature and was never challenged" (Judy Farley-Johnson). Gratitude for the time spent in Community as a foundation for spiritual development, service to the Church, and professional competence found expression in more than a third of the responses.

Growth in self-knowledge, as part of developing maturity, was an explicit theme of several responses. One wrote: "...Had I been a bit older, both chronologically and maturely, my decision to leave may not have ever occurred. There is no blame to be put anywhere for this, it happened." She added: "Giving women more freedom in the Church helped me....The priests and Sisters I worked with gave me the support and confidence I needed..." (Catherine Anzicek). Striking this double note, another acknowledged: "I had entered in 1952 as an idealistic adolescent. I left the community, an idealistic young woman of 31 years, searching for greater peace and eager to take on a new direction as a Christian woman, to be a part of the revolution that was brewing for real change in the Church and Society" (Patty Hughes Cole).

Clearly the times were a factor in many departures, as well as a sign that women religious were being asked by the Church to heed the call for necessary renewal. A thoughtful response referred to this:

> As a WWII child, [I was] taught the value of sacrifice. In the 60s I saw my contemporaries being socially active—especially in the

Extension Volunteers. Civil Rights activities also influenced me. I felt very isolated from the "action" as I was mainly in remote Wyoming. It seemed as if life was rushing by me, and I was being left behind. (Marcella A. Ishum)

Influences of social and religious change went deep into the spirit, as was evident in several responses. One wrote: "The culture of the time, which questioned all traditions and previously accepted ways of doing things, certainly was part of my decision process.... The changes in the Church allowed me to question my own life as the Church questioned her life" (Patricia Flanagan Petersen).

Another explained the impact of a priest's telling her that she had a religious vocation: "... I felt I was no longer free to make the decision." After Vatican II, however, "we were encouraged to take a good look at the Church, [and at] ourselves and make a judgment about past decisions. At this time I began to see that my decision to enter religious life was one imposed upon me rather than my own decision." Teaching in the novitiate and early religious life had reinforced early family training and community life became a burden affecting her health. "I loved the spiritual training and opportunity in religious life... but I gradually began to see that I mistook this for the spiritual life which I could have anywhere" (Doloris S. Vasquez).

Reading, dialogue, and coursework provided by the Community in early days of renewal had positive effects for many who left and many who stayed. One account noted specifics: "We were given the opportunity to take courses on the New Liturgies and I also remember a course on Teilhard de Chardin [that] gave a wonderful feeling of the vastness of God's presence." Remembered too was the opportunity for "more meaningful relationships with other Sisters in the community.... I think that Pope John XXIII's 'opening the windows' did have a loosening and expanding effect" (Charlotte Dillon-Moran).

Implicit in freedom to examine the past and to change was questioning of present experience:

> To look at rules and regulations in the light of what was going on in society, and the Church as part of that society, was a major shift in my response to religious life as it was at that time.... I felt free to look at basic principles upon which some of our customs and attitudes were based. As a result, I felt freer to act upon my thinking than I would have if the Church itself was not doing the same." (Lorraine T. Kroetch)

Explicit reference to the structures and exercise of authority in the Community came from relatively few, perhaps because these had not yet become the complex issue that Chapters of Renewal and subsequent experimentation would address. One respondent emphasized that "I was raised to think for myself and be willing to accept the responsibility for my actions.... My mother and father taught us to stand up for our beliefs. That was not possible in the situations [to which] I was assigned. I don't believe that was true of all situations, but I did not find anyone who was willing to listen to those of us in those situations" (Sammy Fratto).

Allied to this experience was another derived from the difficulties implicit in situations involving large numbers and increasing demands, as well as a conventional view of authority. A respondent wrote, "There is nothing I wanted more than to be a Sister for the rest of my life—but there was such total reluctance on the part of the Mother General to remove Sisters from the positions of Superior and Principal" (Darlene Erskine Merrifield).

Need for a Voice

Six years provided a limited experience of community, much less than the average time of all respondents, but it yielded this measured comment from one: "I had three superiors during the years I was in the community and while they were good, holy women none [was] very approachable" (Anna Mae McNeive Bishop). A contrasting experience—of forty-one years in community—brought a reflective response: "... As I became more educated and the more I read, the more I saw the lack of having a voice in Community. This lack was very painful for me." Her explanation reflected a long-range view: "I believe although the Community changed it was slower to develop a process (because of canon law partly) to have some inclusive decision making processes. I believe this is essential" (Dolores Sheehan).

Other aspects of community life troubled former members whose length of experience as a Sister of Charity of Leavenworth ranged from six to thirty-five years. (The time includes two years of novitiate before profession of vows.) One wrote:

> The community during the early 1960s seemed a remnant of the Middle Ages. It was not spiritually nor psychologically equipped to meet the needs of the young women in the mid 1900s. Psychologically, it fostered and developed deficiencies already present in my personality—fear, dependence, not seeing my value, a feeling of being condemned, and suppressing who I am.

The interpretation of obedience crystallized to a superior...and to laws. To survive I felt I had to leave.

Nor did discursive meditation satisfy, for her, a "yearning for a deep prayer life." Since that time, the grace of centering prayer has helped her to "a better understanding of spiritual growth and transformation" (Sharon Evers).

After nineteen years in the Community, one respondent wrote, "...I needed to go beyond the structure of community to realize my full potential." Referring to the "free-spiritedness" and the "prevailing feelings of that time," she observed, "I did not belong to any group, or associate with anyone," but admitted, "I do think that they [the feelings and spirit] played a small part." Then she added: "During this time, the church became...more a part of the world of the ordinary Christian person....I believe it was then that I came to realize, after much prayer and soul-searching, that I could be just as good a Christian outside the community. Maybe better—I wasn't sure. The hand of God is in all things—this I KNOW" (Joan Coupe Nelson).

Adding to "the turmoil within," said another, were "a lot of 'growth pains' throughout the community, and all religious communities, at that time....I left the community when I began to feel that I did not belong any more. At the time I blamed myself for not being able to reach out of my loneliness. At this time I feel it was a two-way street. Perhaps someone should have been able to reach out to me, too" (Mary J. O'Donnell).

Perhaps unacknowledged loneliness was a factor in other sisters' lives. One self-evaluation was starkly honest: "I was terribly tired after thirty-five years of seemingly endless work. I was lonely. There was very little community life for nursing nuns. I had not grown spiritually. I was caught up with worldly pleasures and community life was not there for me" (Frances Marie Friel). The significance of community life began to be realized in new ways during these years, yet with common strains. Because so much was invested in the common life, individual difficulties and desires could lie buried beneath the surface.

After years of expecting change from the renewal enjoined by Vatican II and of trying to contribute to its progress, one sister felt keenly both criticism and apparent indifference. Not even graduate study—however much it "opened up even more possibilities"—could erase the memory of no response or acknowledgement of initiatives from community members or those in leadership positions. The Red Carpet Reunion, a weekend celebration held in July 2001 to welcome 157 former sisters back to the Mother House and campus, helped put many of these feelings to rest (Ellen Burns).

Complex but related reasons informed one sister's leaving after five years: a sense of self not to be lost, not being "sold on what I was selling," feeling contented but not happy, and freely admitting immaturity—a sense of being "naïve and insecure." (Terry Sullivan Love). What another called "a unique living situation"—all eight years of professed life "in a one-house town"—contributed to a mature insight years after departure: "I'm not sure I had developed enough of a community spirit to keep me tied to the larger SCL Community" (Anne Martin Osdieck).

"A paradigm shift...that took place in the 60s left my 'religious life' irrelevant," wrote another respondent. In light of the shift on every level of society, change in the Church and Community were simply a part of it. "It was all very exciting to me and I was willing to let go of the old patterns and embrace the new.... My journey since leaving has been the journey back to myself." Yet looking back brought no regret: "I am grateful that I had clarity in my mind and heart" (Eve Hufnagel-Cone).

Admitting to a definite influence from society and the culture of the time, a respondent described the late sixties and seventies as "very exciting and challenging times." Teaching in an inner-city school, living in an apartment with two other sisters, working with other religious communities with many opportunities for service to others, and changes in the liturgy: all were experiences that led to a decision to leave. They contrasted with the years just past, when it had seemed "we were in a state of inertia, and yet sitting on an undefined powder-keg." After leaving, it was a new personal challenge to live singly with the support of a community of people she had come to know and within a new dimension of her professional field—teaching in the public school system. For her, it became "definitely a mission, increasingly filled with challenges and even risks" (Kathleen Anne Eraerts Stark).

Perceived distance from reality was a factor of uncertainty or discontent for more than a few. One wrote: "Teaching school I often felt it would be helpful to see the problem children in their home environments, but this was not allowed." After missions in Peru and Guatemala, such questions grew to conviction:

> [I] felt it was much more difficult to be a good Christian in the lay world than as a nun, where you were protected from so much, as opposed to the problems faced by the everyday Christian in the world.... My studies at the Intercultural Formation Center in Cuernavaca, Mexico, with Ivan Illich were a tremendous preparation for my work in the Hispanic culture, but at the same time made me much more aware of the serious problems in the world. (Frances Turk Granahan)

That early change and experimentation in the process of renewal had disturbing effects on many is common knowledge. Less well understood, perhaps, is the impact of some of those consequences on both young and older religious. One remembered it this way:

> There seemed to be a "rumble" developing in the community. The "let's leave things the way they are" group and the "we need to get out among the people more" group...caused division....For some of us, just beginning community life, it made it somewhat unsettling. I also saw that there were lay people in the parishes who were leading good Christian lives, giving of themselves,...and still having families, jobs and other responsibilities.

Nevertheless, her prayer life began in these years: "I learned that a relationship with God can mean just talking to Him, and relying on Him for help with all the things life sends us..." (Patricia Dotson).

Need for Stability with Freedom

Experimentation in the early years of renewal led to confusions and some abuses, along with necessary alternatives in house governance, living commitments, dress, and daily schedule. Effects on community were broad and deep. One respondent to the survey wrote of a certain dissonance between her reading—Vatican II documents and authors like Anthony Padavano—and daily life. What had been, for all, assignment to a convent convenient to her mission now carried the alternative of open housing, that is, the sister's freedom to choose a living group guided by criteria for house governance, common prayer, and hospitality. A respondent described her experience of being transferred with instruction to live at a given convent, only to learn that there was room somewhere else or possibly with the BVMs (Colleen Reardon La Porte).

The paradox of mature commitment to a way of life that after eighteen years became a temporary vocation was the experience of three respondents, whose reflections are instructive for those who remain in religious life and contemplate its future with serious questions. One of them wrote about the time from 1954 to 1972:

> Nothing had changed in religious life for years; now the Catholic Church became involved in major change. Bishops, clergy, religious and laity were challenged to understand and teach Vatican II theology and the philosophy behind drastic changes.... The

Sisters of Charity of Leavenworth, for the most part, accepted the challenge. It was an exciting time and I was given the opportunity to participate in new, updated religious education.... No longer did all Catholic teaching fit neatly in a box.... The comfort level of Catholics was upset and most didn't like it. In personal soul searching I began to explore my own motivation in living the religious life: the comfortable existence of being told to go here, do this, teach this grade, go here for summer school and always knowing there will be food on the table and a roof over my head. (Lucille B. Canjar Stanaway)

This kind of honesty merits respect. Equally self-revealing was the response of another who lived in community from 1956 to 1974. Admitting on reflection that greater delegation and fewer demands would have lessened the stress of her work, she wrote:

...Many were leaving, which was sort of contagious. I thought... that one could do the work one enjoyed, [with] purpose, [but] without the constraints of community. And yet I recall how deeply I was willing to give up my own will and do what was asked of me for the love of God. I enjoyed belonging to a community where we had such strong connections and where we shared like motives of living a life of prayer, understanding and love for God and one another. (Hilda Catherine Scharf)

Extraordinary consideration prompted the response of one who entered in 1951 and left in 1969. She wrote: "Today I know I was given a certain amount of time in the community to prepare me for a life of love, service and prayer in places and situations not then served by religious women." Observing that the 1960s were "a time of great ferment in the Catholic Church and in the health care field," she said that new ideas from Vatican II and the passage of Medicare legislation stimulated all, and moved her to embrace rapid change. Then she added:

In any change situation there are early adapters who have to go with the change idea regardless of the consequences, and there are stabilizers—the people who see the need for change and do it gradually, thereby bringing along people in a more orderly way. In the community during the 60s we had both types of people. I was an early adapter and probably an irritant to many who were stabilizers.... Our hospital administrators, more prudent about change management, wanted to move more slowly.... In my enthusiasm and lack of long view, I wanted to do everything now. (Barbara McCool)

Time and wide experience brought Barbara the long view. "My time under vows," she wrote, "allowed me to nurture the discipline necessary to give myself unselfishly to my clients, students, and patients. The life of prayer, started in Leavenworth, grew and developed over the years and is now as easy as breathing." The visit to the Mother House for the Red Carpet Reunion and learning of the many ways the sisters live their committed lives, of their liturgies and celebrations to honor members of the community, brought her to a new conviction: "As I listened to all these changes, I thought the SCLs are now the early adapters. The community is free to respond to the new challenges in the Church and the world. The transformation, which started in the 60s, is reaping many benefits. You, as a courageous group of women, have come full circle and this is good."

Appreciation for the support and good counsel offered during their years in Community, but especially at the difficult time of their decision to leave, was relayed both in general and particular terms. The process of discerning was not easy for most; friends and trusted colleagues helped one sister to decide. More specifically, another remembered Sister Mary Lucy Downey's saying to her in her dilemma: "Don't you think God wants you to be happy?"

Besides Sister Mary Lucy—mentioned more than a few times—respondents named women who, in the words of one, "influenced and blessed my life": Sister Mary Suzanne Braun, Sister Mary Camilla Montgomery, Sister Leo Catherine Horvat, Sister Mary Clarence (Madelon) Burns, Sister Laurentia Sullivan, Sister Mary Liguori Horvat, Mother Mary Ancilla, Mother Leo Frances, Sister Mary Baptista Ward, Sister Joseph Cecilia Gausz, and Sister Mary Janet McGilley.[9] These go far to suggest the list of unnamed sisters who listened, with care and compassion, to the untold stories of sisters struggling in myriad ways to find God's will.

Gratitude for Support

Almost all respondents saluted Sisters of Charity who, in both traditional and new ministries, are making a decided difference in the Church and society. A few named sisters they knew then, or know now: Sister Mary Laura Huddleston, Sister Joan Kilker, Sister Lucille Harrington, Sister Daniel Stefani, Sister Mary Arthel Cline, Sister Marie de Paul Combo, Sister Dominic Long, and mentioned—in addition to Pope John XXIII—Bishop

George Evans and Archbishop James V. Casey.[10] Whether as a source of counsel or inspiration or support, such individuals impressed these women for life.

One wrote that the sisters she lived with were "very special and good to me. Sister Mary Catherine Dougherty had...a sense of serenity that infected many of us" (Jovanna Marie Maronick Tanzey). Another remembered telling Mother Leo Frances that her years in community "were years of formation for the rest of my life..." (Mercedes Foster Craughwell). The witness to faith that informed many responses echoed in words that recall the Community Constitutions: "I always have had a deep inner communication with God who continues to lead me on the journey of 'becoming'" (Lois V. Wilde).

That in large part the respondents took to heart the Community's own journey of becoming was clear from responses to the fourth question put to them in the survey: "Have you thought of ways that women religious, in particular the Sisters of Charity of Leavenworth, might strengthen their contribution to the life of God's people?"

One of the ways already welcomed as a "great bridge to connect the present and former members" was the Red Carpet Reunion that took place July 7-8, 2001. The Associate Program and *Connecting* received high marks; one respondent recommended a page in *Connecting* that might serve as a "chat room" for keeping up connections among Community members of *all* kinds. Diversity of ministries met with approval, especially as these take sisters into the inner city, prisons, and the very lives of the poor. Their power there lies not in numbers but in their "ability to bring out the best in whoever they work with and serve"—power that comes from "solid spirituality" (Darlene Erskine Merrifield, Phyllis Gibbons, Noella DeVolder McCray).

Mary Carol Hogan, Mary Bodine, and Sister Susan Yerkich, novitiate group of 1963, reunite at the Red Carpet welcome.

"Vincent would be proud," said another, "of your visibility in the inner cities and with the poor wherever they are found"—not for the sake of being known, but because "you are leaders and leaven in all the fields where you work. You give life and lift others up." Her conviction rang true in a direct admonition: "Keep listening to the Spirit,

Mindful of their novitiate partner, Sue Wilmot, who could not attend the Red Carpet Reunion, Sylvia Lapke, Sister Lucille Degenhart, Judy Farley-Johnson, and Frances Granahan take a photo break.

each of you, and you will know where you are supposed to be and what you are supposed to do and what you are supposed to say" (Anne Martin Osdieck).

Vigorous emphasis on the life of the spirit marked many responses to the question. One urged "Christ-likeness" as the first contribution to the life of God's people—as strong as, another observed, "their prayer life and their loving relationship with God." The witness of simplicity, with charity and poverty and wisdom, is a "counter-cultural voice" needed now more than ever (Mary Lou Stein Buckholz, Doloris S. Peterson Vasquez, Kitty Bronec, Kathleen Anne Eraets Stark). But dissemination, through modern methods like the website, of information about what sisters are doing is necessary for witness, as urged by three respondents: "We need to flood cyberspace with stories of God's people fulfilling the reign of God." Peace and justice are "the hallmark of all Christians but especially of those who profess religion." As the Church needs your witness to social justice, so "the public needs to recognize your leadership and to hear your voice" (Lorraine T. Kroetch, Ellen Corkle Viens, Gertrude Greenhalgh Loqa).

Particularly the young need "a sense of God" and new knowledge of religious—"who they are, what they do, how they live their lives," wrote one concerned for a new generation. "They'll always be our future, and as dedicated people, you have something to give them in your value system of life...," said another. A respondent who welcomed new partnerships with the laity said of the traditional apostolates of education, medicine, care of the elderly and children: "The presence of the sisters in positions of leadership in these fields...is necessary, noticed, and appreciated" (Cleo M. Cardinal Stevens, Mary J. O'Donnell, Mary Lorian Horvat).

Likewise, in whatever forms it takes, "the witness of living in community is a significant one," wrote one. And another: religious community, opened to others for short periods or in particular ways, can help satisfy the "tremendous hunger for spirituality and prayer in our world. ...Certainly now more than at any other time in our history, we need leaders to show Americans how religious people of all faiths—Jews, Christians, and Muslims—must learn to live in harmony and love for all" (Ellen

Corkle Viens, Mary Lindenmeyer). Quoting a sister she knew, one respondent wrote that sisters are "no longer the foot soldiers of the Church, but are the Shock Troops.... The leadership of religious women has never been more important." Another urged: "Never fear to take risks; that prophetic stance will reap a great harvest" (Jovanna Marie Tanzey, Mercedes Foster Craughwell).

Even a cursory examination of the deepest concerns of the sisters recorded during preparation for the Renewal Chapter reveals experiences that parallel these of former members. Primary among them were a desire for further study of Vatican II documents and modern theologians and the need to be informed about changes in the Church and in society. Equally urgent were questions about the meaning of the vows as lived in the modern world. Governance, in the local and total community, was a far-reaching concern touching on the nature of authority in its exercise, a voice in Community affairs, and participation in decisions that affect individual and community life. Cries across the board for attention to individual needs begged for change in initial and continuing formation. Evaluation of apostolates, full use of individual abilities, and freeing sisters from institutional service to work with the poor were sought in the Study Commissions' recommendations.[11]

The national survey of approximately 135,000 American sisters uncovered trends and patterns that reflect similar concerns: relations between "subject and superior"; communication with the total community; the need for independence of judgment and responsibility to carry out tasks; reasons and readiness of young women for entering community; habits of reading; hopes for the future of the Church and religious life.

Judging from reports of fifty of the respondents, their lives and the lives of their counterparts contribute to God's people, the Church, in ways as varied as the individuals themselves, but also in identifiable directions of commitment and service. As single or married persons, they have continued in the professional fields in which they were launched in the Community; many have taught in and directed religious education programs or pursued nursing careers; several have earned master's degrees in these or in new areas. They have enriched family life—their own or that of aging parents, a deceased sister's or brother's children. Their ministries have developed in both traditional and new directions. More than a few have initiated programs of lasting benefit to parish, civic community, or profession. They have proved themselves quiet leaders and prophetic innovators.

More than a few wise women of the Community have reflected deeply on the very problems mentioned in the survey of these sisters in charity. Speaking of the early renewal experience, Sister Mildred Marie

Irwin remarked that we learned how troubled situations were generated by authoritative structures; the numbers admitted, relatively unscreened; the psychological immaturity that made life difficult for many. She observed that sound secular principles plus Gospel ideals were necessary for solid change, even though attended by pain and suffering.[12]

But these accounts do illuminate the potential and community spirit that so many carried away with them from their years as Sisters of Charity of Leavenworth. Even more significantly, they bring home the manifold roles of leadership open to women religious in a crucial century of the Church's life. So, far from leveling the experience and aspiration of those who stayed in religious life and of those who left, these responses clarify the absolute uniqueness of each individual's relationship to God. They represent a call to women religious to rediscover their inimitable and necessary role in the life of the Church. These reflections, generously shared, suggest that each community is bound to define its particular mission to God's people and to proclaim the Gospel of Jesus in ways known as yet only to the Spirit.

II

AS WE STRUGGLED TO BECOME...

CHAPTER 5

Unfolding of a Drama

The story of the nation in these years, beginning with Kennedy's brief term and ending with Ronald Reagan's election, offered the American people and the world a drama unlike any in the country's history. The story of a religious community's gradual renewal could hardly compare. Yet, the widespread renewal of religious communities produced unpredictable conflicts and outcomes that even in the public arena still raise perplexed and unanswered questions. What ultimately distinguishes them is a matter of means taken to achieve noble ends.

When Lyndon B. Johnson succeeded to the nation's highest office, he hoped to preside over the conclusion of the war in Vietnam and the dawn of a Great Society of better justice and equality at home, to be extended abroad. His hopes were dashed on the rocks of increasingly violent antiwar protests, an anti-establishment counter-culture, and a racially divided society. Fear of Soviet and Chinese Communism inspired deceitful accounts to Congress and the public about the Gulf of Tonkin threat and the uprising in Santo Domingo as well as concealment of peace feelers from the North Vietnamese. Though his Office of Economic Opportunity, education acts, broad-based medical care, and civil rights legislation were to have lasting effects, nothing could save his presidency.

The assassination of Martin Luther King Jr. in 1968 fueled fires already raging in the South and on the streets of major cities, ignited by implementation of the Voting Rights Act, school integration, and anti-discrimination laws. Instead of strengthening the non-violence King stood for, the tragedy of his death seemed to justify for a time the claims of "black power" for a community of African Americans deeply divided within itself. The same distance between reformers and radicals separated women who led the feminist movement. Opposing ranks of the National Organization for Women (NOW) pursued legislative action to eliminate sex discrimination in employment, the professions, and education by contrary methods: public protests and outrageous demands over against stubborn insistence on justice through law.

After a close election in 1968, Richard Nixon inspired hopes for a return to civic order at home and for economic supremacy abroad through a promising strategy of exploiting Chinese and Russian hostility and capturing foreign markets. Arms limitation treaties kept the East/West Cold War in wraps. But going it alone abroad with Secretary of State Henry Kissinger created illusions of power that ultimately undermined the "Nixon Doctrine." Repeated contradictions between formal pronouncements and broadcast facts about the war in Southeast Asia destroyed public confidence; a different sort of inflation threatened the economy. Success in the 1972 presidential election again blinded the victor, whose fear of political defeat had already done its work. The tale of break-ins conceived by a Committee to Re-elect the President, of doctored tapes and disgraced accomplices in high office, and the final drama of the threat of impeachment proceedings against a sitting President led to the end of an administration the more ignominious for its gratuitous deceits.

Vice President Gerald Ford finished the term without apparently significant effect except the issue of a presidential pardon to Nixon who had been brought, by Constitutional process and his own mistaken self-image, to resign. But in 1976 a relatively unknown Democratic governor from the Deep South made a covenant with the people for open, honest government and defeated the incumbent Ford. Before voters refused him a second term, President Jimmy Carter had attacked what he openly dubbed an alliance of money and political power but had unwisely surrounded himself with familiar rather than experienced advisers. Attempting to rescue a failing economy, he alienated liberals and conservatives alike with moderate social objectives. Ironically, his domestic and global programs for the betterment of all human beings' living conditions, the Camp David accords, and his return of Panama to Panamanians all backfired politically. Unable to support Central American rebellions, to counter OPEC's control of the oil market, or to protect agricultural markets abroad, Carter finally failed to secure the release of American hostages in Iran before an impatient public rejected him in 1980 for a clearly conservative and popular Ronald Reagan.[1]

Within the Church, dramas were unfolding with deeper and more lasting consequence. Attitudes among Catholics toward the Vietnam War, toward sexist and racial discrimination, and toward exclusion from decision-making paralleled secular views in a common ethical base, but provoked equally fierce polarities. Moral issues of poverty and peace, of respect for life in all its phases, and of every kind of discrimination were unifying people across racial and religious lines; doctrinal questions, on the other hand, about the status of divorced Catholics, about relationships with separated Christians, and about truths in non-Christian religions kept many of the people of God at loggerheads.[2] Study groups in parishes and beyond became sounding boards for questions, doubts, even disagreement in matters that had once been taken for granted as irrevocable and sure.

A living Church, the faithful were learning, must take on its role in a world where a vast majority of people were denied the means of achieving full human dignity. In a land where they had won full exercise of religious liberty, Catholics must respect all legal claims to its benefits by others. They must accept influences on their liturgy from traditions of diverse cultures, and at the same time learn the value of full participation in what had been a familiar mystery. Renewal of traditional teaching on the primacy of conscience and the development of doctrine put new demands on their personal moral judgments.

After John XXIII and the conclusion of Vatican II in the papacy of Paul VI, the Church found itself entering a new and different phase of growth, not to be measured by conversions but by new depths of spirituality, community, and openness to the world. If public statements are an indication, the world welcomed the change. But, within the Church, the invitation to radical renewal produced polarities of response among both hierarchy and laity. Fueled particularly by changes in celebration of the Eucharist, small groups of Catholics followed priests of like mind out of parishes into homes or churches where the Mass in Latin and traditional devotions might continue. A number of others gave voice to their frustration and sense of betrayal in the print media, at times rabid in their denunciation. Increasingly, Catholic unity in renewal depended on education of the young in Catholic schools, of congregations by their pastors, and of readers by first-rate Catholic publications and writers. A wide range of theologians produced volumes of varying merit, consumed by lay and professed religious readers. A decade after the close of the Second Vatican Council, its impact was both profound and uncertain.

The same might be said of the Special General Chapter of the Sisters of Charity of Leavenworth, 1968–1969, though it drew no public notice or acclaim. In the long-range view, moreover, it was only Act I of the continuing drama of four successive Chapters that marked the Community's renewal. Large hopes for renewal raised by the Community-wide conversations and commission work of the previous year were not to be satisfied in two summer sessions of approximately five weeks each. The work of the 1968 session followed five months of intensive study by the delegates. In four self-selected commissions they concentrated on questions about professed religious life guided by the Gospel, daily living in community, formation and development of individual religious, and the framework or governance structure of the common life they shared. The schema produced by the sisters in their self-study were the delegates' texts.

These had been fed not only by the commissions' intensive work but also by a Community-wide questionnaire and the monthly publication, *Perspective*, a vehicle that continued in print the intra-community dialogue begun in 1966–1967. Edited in turn by each commission, it summarized work in progress, surfaced questions, and ran excerpts from workshops conducted throughout the Community by theologians and published women religious examining issues of community, the vows, formation, and ministry. The stimulus of readers' responses to problems and questions facing the delegates was electric; never had a Chapter provoked such grass roots study, questioning, and exchange.[3] It became clear from results of apostolate reviews, special and common opinionnaires, and proposals prepared by each commission that the journey of renewal was to be a long one. What began in 1966 would not be completed until 1986 when each sister received her copy of the revised Constitutions, approved as canon law required by the Congregation for Religious Institutes.

Twenty years of study, experimentation, and evaluation, evoking at each stage prolonged discussion and sometimes sharp dissent, was not an extraordinary span of time for such fundamental reform. The changes it brought touched the daily spiritual and communal life of sisters as well as their individual and institutional apostolic works. They had pursued their ministries of education, medical services, and care of orphans in traditional institutional forms. They had done every conceivable kind of work in apparel that dated not only from their own origins in 1858, but also from the beginnings of visible social missions for women religious initiated in the seventeenth century by Vincent de Paul and Louise de Marillac. The anticipated depth of renewal was a phenomenon that Chapter delegates had little time to contemplate, though they knew many of the facts that made it necessary. Pioneers by heritage and instinct, they made their way through proposals and decisions with as much honesty and openness, conviction and compassion as they could muster.

The Chapter's make-up was one step toward renewal. For more than a year at the request of the General Council, a committee of eleven, chaired by Sister Rose Dominic Gabisch, had studied, by mandate of the 1962 Chapter, methods of electing delegates that would go further in making the body more representative of the entire Community. Accepted by 97.2 percent of the Community, their plan provided for a nomination ballot listing all the perpetually professed from whom each voter chose thirty-three nominees. The fifty receiving the highest number of votes appeared on an election ballot from which voting sisters, those under perpetual

Unfolding of a Drama 87

Community Council, 1968–1974: (seated) Sister Mary Margaret Shea, Mother Leo Frances, Sister Mary Seraphine Sheehan; (standing) Sisters Mary Serena Sheehy, Mary Kevin Hollow, and Mary Anselm Towle

vows, chose the thirty-three delegates. Eight general officers and former mothers general were *ex officio* members of the Chapter.

Responding to requests that temporary vowed sisters be allowed to vote for delegates, Mother Leo Frances had included the question in her letter to the Congregation for Religious seeking approval of the nomination plan. According to results of a Community-wide questionnaire, fifty-three percent of the sisters were in favor of extending the electorate. Hopeful for an exception from the two-thirds requirement, Mother asked for approval of the change. It was not granted. Mother's request that regional superiors be given *ex officio* status was also denied.[4] Duly respected structures of authority were difficult to change. Sisters under temporary vows were represented in the sessions by five observers elected from their number. The editor of the Chapter newsletter was an observer as well.[5]

In their first formal task, the delegates re-elected Mother Leo Frances for a second term, returned Sister Mary Seraphine as first councilor, and brought Sister Mary Dennis (Mary Margaret) Shea, Sister Mary Kevin Hollow, and Sister Mary Serena Sheehy to the Council. The delegates also re-elected Sister Mary Anselm Towle as Community treasurer and Sister Marie Kelly as Community secretary.[6] The day of prayer and deliberation was both climatic and energizing for work to come.

With children who live nearby, Sister Frances de Chantal Rodina takes a break from work during summer months at an inner-city housing project in Chicago, where she partnered with Sister Francis Therese Shea.

Forty-one women, representing more than nine hundred members of the Community, then met for two weeks in their four Chapter commissions to fine-tune their proposals for consideration by the whole Chapter. On July 11, Sister Francis Therese Shea addressed the delegates re-assembled for their common agenda. Her work as a delegate was especially valued for her dedication to the poor, her leadership in Christian social action, her influence on students as teacher and head of the sociology department for fifteen years, and her two-year battle with cancer now coming to an end. The next Sunday morning at 4:45 AM, she died.[7] A few days later, after the Mass of Resurrection for Sister Francis Therese, the full Chapter returned to receive proposals that carried now an even greater measure of hope for a renewed future.

Call for Renewal Growing Clear

Results of a pre-Chapter survey reveal much of the thinking within the Community at large that informed those proposals in their final drafts. A formal canvas of views and attitudes on every aspect of renewal drew 779 responses—a return of approximately 81 percent—to a questionnaire designed by Sister Rose Dominic and distributed in April 1968. Its purpose was to gain statistical evidence for clear and unambiguous answers to the question, "Who are we as Sisters of Charity of Leavenworth in the Church in the world?" A position paper drawn up from issues of the previous two-year study and the national Sisters' Survey produced questions for the sisters' response.[8] Recorded results became the basis of further position papers and the proposals presented by each of four Chapter commissions to the delegates in the first session of 1968 and brought to vote in the summer of 1969. Acceptance or rejection of proposals determined changes, deletions, and additions to be made in the Constitutions. The path from Community-wide study to fundamental questions to Chapter proposals was a clear and purposeful one.

No clear pattern had emerged in the national survey of 1967 about the Community's distinctive character and spirit. Almost 40 percent thought the sisters were sufficiently engaged with the poor; somewhat more thought that Mother Xavier, if alive, would commend the Community's work as it was then being done. Respondents to the 1968 Community survey were less sure: 30 percent thought the vision outward to needs of the world was sufficient, while 43.5 percent thought not, and a quarter were uncertain. Only 27.6 percent now thought the Community was sufficiently engaged in work for the poor, while nearly half disagreed. Even fewer, 20 percent, saw local convents in their material conveniences witnessing to the notion of evangelical poverty; almost a quarter were uncertain about it. Although 75 percent of the respondents were confident about the Community's distinct spirit as expressed in the position paper, a significant 22 percent were not at all, or else uncertain. No prophetic sign appeared to distinguish the Sisters of Charity of Leavenworth, but communal self-awareness was deepening.

Agreement was broad on responsibilities of women religious in today's world: for leadership and collaboration in the Church, for willing response to contemporary needs, for public witness to spiritual dedication and sacrifice, and for recognition of the impact of science and technology on modern life. It waited on renewal to forge the link between such responsibility and growth of knowledge. By their own estimation, between 8.5 and 19 percent of respondents in 1968 were very well informed about some dozen social issues of the day; most called themselves somewhat informed about all of them. Ironically, given the Community's foreign mission commitment, the topics least understood by the largest number were underdeveloped nations and the extent of the population problem in the world.

In answer to questions drawn from the position paper, respondents affirmed the identity of the Sisters of Charity as an apostolic community absolutely dependent on a life of deep unifying prayer, both communal and private. They declared further that such prayer is necessary for effective participation in the liturgy. A Chapter proposal that the sisters affirm celebration of the Eucharist as the focal point of their lives did not carry, however, not because delegates lacked conviction about its centrality, but because of differing assumptions about its daily celebration. Of the 779 sisters responding to the mid-Chapter survey, 748 thought that "the Eucharist should be a living, dynamic source of inspiration for our life in community," yet 462 sisters thought that the above proposal implied daily celebration as obligatory; 262 read it to mean optional. As many as 418 of the sisters only occasionally experienced the liturgy "in all its intended richness."[9]

With regard to governance structure, views remained somewhat ambivalent, as they had been in 1967. Although more than 60 percent of the respondents favored further decentralization, almost 90 percent wanted the

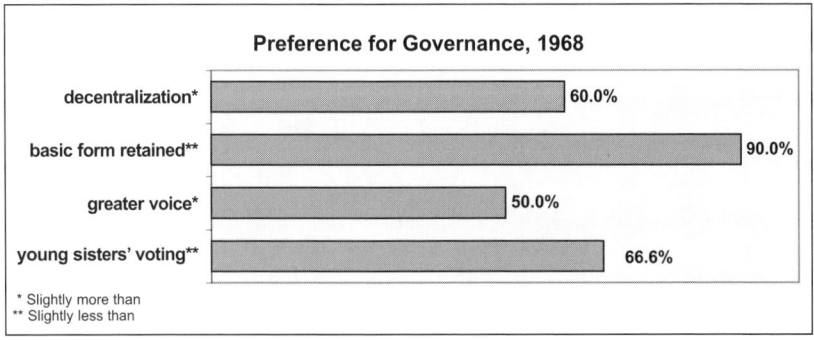

basic form of Community government to remain, without introducing regions or provinces. A desire for greater voice, however, emerged in a suggestion from more than half the respondents that a Chapter of Affairs every three years complement the six-year General Chapter and election of officers. A principle of participatory decision-making was gaining ground: more than two-thirds wanted to influence the choice of local coordinators through recommendations and 85 percent wanted sisters to be consulted before their appointment to the role. While almost a two-thirds majority favored temporary-vow-sisters' participation in election of Chapter delegates, only 53 percent thought they should serve as delegates.[10]

Attitudes toward the apostolate definitely reflected the desire for decentralization. Slightly more than a quarter of the respondents wanted the Generalate to determine apostolic priorities for the Community. Almost the same number wanted individual sisters' abilities and desires to govern them, while almost a third favored Chapter guidelines or an apostolic

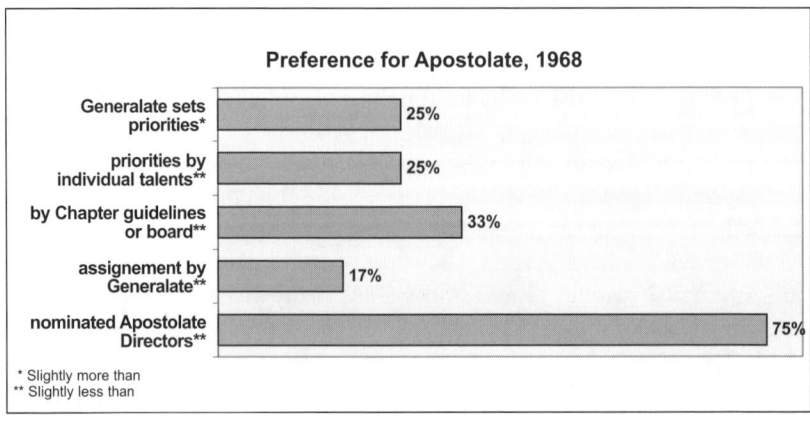

board. In choice of a method for apostolic assignments, however, support for any modified form of authoritative control shrunk to about 17 percent. The drift toward individual determination of ministry was clear. About three-quarters of the respondents wanted to nominate the directors of their apostolates, if not elect them as well. Confidence that an in-depth study of apostolates would be an adequate basis for directing the future of the Community's apostolic works was uneven and lowest among the school sisters, elementary and secondary.

A similar pattern took shape in responses to questions about formation. More than 70 percent thought the time before taking perpetual vows should depend on readiness of the individual sister, generally from three to nine years. More than 62 percent thought acceptance of a sister for annual renewal of vows should depend on consultation with the sisters of her house, her local coordinator, and her apostolic director. Responses to questions about community living confirmed a pattern of agreement on fundamental concepts and sharp division on some practical specifics. Large majorities assented to the idea that community is a deeper reality than the common life and that it gives public witness, nourishes and is nourished by the life of prayer and apostolic commitment. That so many affirmed community as compatible with diversity in individual ministry and response to the Spirit was a clear sign of developments to come.

In day-to-day living, a majority favored a practice of silence out of consideration for others rather than by rule. Only about a quarter of the respondents favored a traditional set time for general recreation. Almost three-fourths agreed that, with consideration of the sisters, guests were welcome in the convent. Fewer than half thought that choosing one's living companions was necessary. Certain other issues, however, foreshadowed conflict to come. Although opinions divided almost evenly on serving wine for special occasions, about 63 percent wished to retain the rule that "each sister in the spirit of poverty, self-denial, and reparation, continue to refrain from the use of alcoholic beverages," while about 31 percent did not. About 47 percent favored some sort of uniform dress; 59 percent did not. That the veil be worn at all times was the wish of 44.5 percent; 52 percent wanted circumstance and individual discretion to determine the practice.[11]

More important perhaps is the number of respondents—almost two-thirds—who felt certain that the Community would respond to the needs of the Church in the next ten years and the nearly 60 percent who were more optimistic about renewal than they had been a year ago. Though only a little more than 40 percent claimed very clear understanding of the changes taking place, almost all wished to continue experimentation. Some desired major revisions at a more expeditious pace; some no doubt hoped that experiment would ultimately yield to former wisdom. More surprising than any divisions evident in such a comprehensive survey is the solid ground of determination and fidelity of purpose it revealed. What was emerging was deep difference, not so much on issues as within a religious culture. But it is hindsight that tells us that. Much depended then on how much the agents of change—fellow sisters—would be able to articulate their thoughts and purposes and on how firm were the bonds that united them all. Much depended also on how women formed by a structured common life would handle unaccustomed freedoms in the pursuit of their ideals.

Reflecting a common priority, an initial focus of the Chapter agenda fell on aspects of spiritual life in community. After wide-ranging discussion in the 1968 session, by substantial majorities the following summer delegates affirmed daily celebration of the Eucharist as the focal point of community life; replaced daily communal prayers with Lauds and Vespers from the Office of the Church; and reserved for individual determination devotional prayers, spiritual reading, the form of one's annual retreat, and the manner of reflecting on scripture and Vatican II documents. With the Chapter's assent, one's baptismal name might now be resumed in place of the name assigned to symbolize the profession of religious vows. Ways of observing poverty as well as hospitality to visitors were to be part of each local community's giving shape to their life together at the beginning of the year.[12]

In reviewing the framework or governance structure of community life, Chapter delegates unanimously decided in 1968 that the General Council should include a sister qualified to fill the office of director of health care. By a near-unanimous vote, they approved experimentation in forms of local community government until the next Chapter. Any given form should embody principles of co-responsibility in making decisions, subsidiarity in solving problems at the local level, and individual accountability for living out communal commitments. Proposals to appoint a director of renewal and experimentation and to replace the terms "superior" and "subject" with "local coordinator" and "house members" passed with about two-thirds majorities. The vote possibly indicated divisions among delegates with regard to the locus of authority in community life.[13]

Initial Formation Crucial

Under the heading of development as Sisters of Charity in the Church, renewal of initial and ongoing formation showed effects of work by the Formation Planning Committee appointed in 1966. Accepted proposals provided, first, that entrants to the novitiate give promise of grasping the nature of a religious vocation and of contribution to apostolates of the Community; and, second, that they come with at least two years of college or work experience. A vocation director and Formation Committee were mandated, with latitude for experimentation with all phases of pre-service formation. Professional preparation was to precede apostolic assignment.

This and a parallel proposal, whose history dated from Sister Formation years, aimed at the quality of teaching in schools staffed by the Community. By Chapter mandate, all elementary teachers were to have completed work for the bachelor's degree by 1973, date of the next General Chapter. Pre-service formation requirements included complete professional preparation, if necessary after the juniorate year: the B.A. in theology for catechetics; the B.A. with a given major and certification for teaching; the B.A. in humanities for social services; and an appropriate degree for assignment in health fields.[14] These were accomplishments few could fully appreciate. They meant that preparation of the individual sister for her teaching mission took priority over filling all faculty positions in the schools each fall. Continuing education and in-service programs were to be provided for sisters engaged in ministry. These challenges were complemented by a mandate for systematic evaluation of each sister's development in her professional apostolic role.

Looking to development of the whole person, delegates approved proposals for a renewed summer tertianship in the spiritual life before final profession, and for an interim tertianship for all sisters fifteen years after their first profession of vows. They mandated a continuous Community-wide program of workshops in scripture, the sacramental life and liturgy, theology, the social mission of the church, missiology, and ecumenism. The local community was to encourage the sisters' social, cultural, and intellectual enrichment and participation in parish, professional, and civic organizations. An annual week of unstructured time—or vacation—and encouragement of a weekly day off were to aid personal well-being. If such changes sound like simple common sense, at the time they were signs of deep-seated need for renewal and updating of a valued way of life.

Proposals for the apostolate, or ministry of the sisters, were the fruit of examining how to express what and who women religious are in the church and the world. No fewer than fifty-five assumptions were brought to the assembly, emphasizing the particular needs of an age of increasing secularization, the interdependence of service and a life of prayer, and the characteristic virtues of Vincentian religious: simplicity, humility, and charity. Also assumed was the need to seek new frontiers of service in education, health care, and social service while continuing responsibility to dioceses and parishes where the Community then served. The realities of ministry in a middle-class American society were significant for sisters' responsibilities as citizens and their call to leadership in the Church. Final assumptions affirmed commitment to the people of Latin America and the priority of solidarity with the poor.[15]

In response to the sisters' desire to make principles of mature self-direction and co-responsibility effective in community life and apostolic assignments, the Chapter session of 1968 mandated an Advisory Board to maintain a two-way communication. On the one hand, it was to coordinate information for the Council, recommend action, and assist decisions; on the other, it was to take the pulse of sisters in the field, respond to new trends in the life of the Church and the Community, and keep attention turned primarily outward toward the world. Several members stressed the importance of consulting the experience of sisters on the missions and in the field.[16]

The board gave serious attention to various levels of evaluating experiments. Freedom to experiment in community living or to volunteer for new apostolic work was running into the complexity of meeting contractual obligations and assigning sisters in view of individual needs and compatibility of a given house. The need to respect personal choice, a priority of renewal, complicated experimentation in houses of sisters living together by dint of their ministry.[17] To determine the common good of several quite uncommon individuals who happened to be living together was no small task. What was becoming clear was that there were significant differences among some nine hundred sisters in the shape of their convictions, principles, and values even as they all shared a desire to serve God's people in a community identified by a life of charity.

Life between sessions radiated energy. In response to the urgency of hearing from sisters on the missions, delegates committed themselves to a series of Listening Sessions over the coming year to gauge effects first-hand now that substantial changes were in effect. Coverage was thorough: seven regional sessions were scheduled over three weekends for houses in Kansas Area I, Eastern Montana, Topeka/Oklahoma, Colorado/Wyoming, California/New Mexico, Kansas/Missouri II, and Western Montana. Delegates signed up for two sessions they would attend, making sure, on a ratio of one to every ten, that all sisters would have a "listener." Regional populations ranged from 62 (Eastern Montana) to 220 (Kansas Area I).[18] The delegates expected to hear contrary views about contrasting experiences in experimentation. That they did.

Directors of apostolates in education, health care, and social services personally interviewed sisters in their ministries during the winter of 1968–1969. Actions were perhaps more telling than words in the time between Chapter sessions. On their own throughout the interim year, sisters gathered in every city served by the Community for renewal sessions on community, the vows, local house governance, the apostolate, and principles of collegiality and subsidiarity as they figure in community living. Study guides and reading lists came from the Renewal and Experimentation Board, but the sisters themselves determined the topics and forms of their meetings. In Helena, Montana, they concentrated on social concerns, with emphasis on women's roles, Native Americans, intellectual currents of the modern world, and theological developments. An intercommunity group in Billings set up three-week sessions on group dynamics and liturgy. For some twenty convents in Kansas City, the sisters at St. Ann's enlisted a pastor and a clinical psychologist to examine with them "The Trilogy of Womanhood," or birth-to-death cycle, for its spiritual, psychological, and social potential. In Colorado, a group traveled to the Trappist monastery at Snowmass for a retreat weekend of praying, hiking, relaxing, and reflection on the Chapter statement.[19]

Renewal with Faces

Action with students for missions at home and abroad marked the year. More than seventy volunteers answered the call of Sisters Bernadette Marie Teasdale and Karen Louise Hennessy to join the Saint Mary College Community Action Program in the summer of 1968. Teaching and tutoring, visiting nursing homes and the Women's Industrial Farm occupied many in the Leavenworth area; others worked on Headstart programs in Falls City, Nebraska, and Joplin, Missouri. An inner city parish in Kansas City got extra help; others joined the Witness Program of the Home Mission Center in New Orleans. Two did catechetical work in Our Lady's Youth center in the Six Hells district in El Paso, Texas—dubbed such by residents of six tenements there.[20]

Students at Pius X High School in North Kansas City pledged personal sacrifices to raise $300 for the foreign missions during the 1968–1969 school year. A portion of the amount went to their sister school, La Escuela San Pio, at Trinidad Pampa in Bolivia. A Cuban national who had escaped to the United States, Teresa Simon, was inspiration for the students as she partnered with Sister John Agnes Bregin to sponsor the drive. Sister Angela Rose Barbieri's seventh-graders at St. Patrick's School caroled at Christmas for contributions that supplemented the amount. When Sister Lucille Harrington, home on leave from the SCL mission in Bolivia, visited the schools, told stories, showed pictures, and thanked them for their generosity, North American students suddenly felt like brothers and sisters to their South American counterparts.[21]

Thanks to *Relay*, the Community publication that had started up in 1964, renewal took on a face and came alive through articles rich with photographs and written with narrative skill. Launched by Sister Mary Seraphine Sheehan during her first term as Community councilor, with Sister Rose Anne Colvin as managing editor, the magazine was originally a way to inform others of the Community's mission apostolate. An editorial board of high school journalism teachers in the Kansas City area wrote most of the articles; other writers were enlisted or volunteered for particular pieces.[22] The Bartolacs—Stephen and Louise, parents of Sisters Virginia and Mary Ann, and their sister, Helen—handled circulation.

An "open forum" for the summer issue only confirmed what letters had already indicated: "There is no level on which the *Relay* does not influence thought and action." This was evident in the requests for more information that came from distant religious communities and educators about the Community's formation program, renewal projects, and modular scheduling in the high schools. After the latter story was featured in the *NCEA Quarterly*, requests from high schools and academies all over the United States made reprints necessary. Stories for the summer evaluation issue came in from Sisters of Charity and lay teachers across the Midwest.[23]

On June 16, 1969, after Vespers of the Holy Spirit, Mother Leo Frances opened the second session of the Chapter, addressing approximately 550 sisters by teleconference. She emphasized one major concern, that they become "a faith community serving the Church," and recalled the commitment they had made seventy, fifty, twenty, or two years before. "It was a heroic response," she said. "Do not be less than heroic now." She acknowledged the misunderstanding, doubts, and fears as well a growing love, tolerance, and gratitude that had marked preceding months. "Our history and our traditions are dear to us; yet we must be willing to enter into what is new and good."[24] Her words foreshadowed conflicts of experimentation that would not be resolved for another six years and enjoined a strength of unity to be sought for almost two decades.

Reports from the mother general and Community treasurer provided the delegates with a comprehensive overview of the Community's vital statistics and developments since the Chapter of 1962. Two sets of numbers suggested stability and strong potential in the face of mounting losses. In her report, Mother Leo Frances numbered Community membership at 964; of these, 817 sisters were in active ministry and 147 were retired and in the ministry of prayer. To estimate personnel changes in ministries, the General Council had issued work preference cards to the sisters in active ministry. Results revealed that more than 460 sisters were presently assigned in the area of their first preference. Of the seventy-three who were not, expressed preferences were for religious education, foreign missions, or social work.[25] In this Community at least, institutional ministries were not threatened by any imminent flight of the sisters from their assigned missions.

A favorite first-grade teacher, Sister Agnes Rita O'Neill, reassures her charges at recess.

Nevertheless, numbers were not adequate for the demand.

A study of the apostolate of education made in preparation for this second session revealed a paradoxical situation of enrollment growth on various school levels as well as uncertainty of resources. Factors that influenced planning for the future included the nation's per capita income, the possibility of limited federal financing, rising costs per pupil, and teachers' salaries. Already in the fall semester of 1969 in fifty-four schools staffed by the Sisters of Charity of Leavenworth, there were fifty-one fewer elementary teachers than in the previous fall due to withdrawals from the Community and assignment of sisters to full-time study, to religious education, or to Saint Mary College; to individual choices of ministry in social work and child care; and to retirement. At the high school level, ten sisters were being reassigned: three to the college, one to the public high school in Helena, another to a high school serving low-income families in Denver, one to a house of prayer, and one to religious education. Three were retiring. Interests indicated by junior sisters under temporary vows included all levels of education and special education, but also health care, foreign missions, social work, counseling and study in psychology, and support staffing.[26]

Demands on the Community were growing, especially in institutional staffing obligations, in professional preparation of the sisters, and in financing education for new apostolates. From these reports, questions rose about school closings, roles of principal and faculty under newly formed parish boards, ways of attaining quality education in all schools, and the most effective means of religious education. An overarching question was whether the Community was spreading itself too thin. However complex the situation was becoming on the surface, the roots of such problems lay deep within traditional roles, relationships, and commitments coming under scrutiny on every front. Questions of renewal were larger than amassed facts could encompass. What troubled the sisters concerning present responsibilities were, in the long run, signs of inevitable and radical change. The Catholic educational system was feeling the first tremors of shifting plates under the ground of its sturdy century-old structure.

The initial proposal for an in-depth study of the Community's apostolates, looking to strengths and weaknesses and long-range plans backed by research into personnel and material resources, passed unanimously. Further proposals emphasized an increased sense of professional competence, retaining the traditional comprehensive vision of the SCL apostolate, and discernment in choosing an individual apostolate. This required attention to the morale of local houses and limited workloads for sisters over sixty-five. Expansion of social service apostolates, preparation for ecumenical work, and introduction of young sisters to the works of the Community opened doorways to individual preferences. Awareness of the world they live in was echoed in discussion of the sisters' responsibility to keep informed about social issues, to vote and volunteer their services in the local community, and to exert influence on social legislation.[27]

Turning to final directives for the apostolate, the Chapter asked that the Community expand its efforts to accept informed choice by individual sisters as evidence of the Spirit's call to urgent needs in new directions. They approved a five-year plan for developing the Latin American missions with a continuing program of preparation to serve there. A report on the study of the Community's hospitals conducted by the consulting firm of Cresak, McCormick, and Paget illuminated the need for coordination of planning and resources within a central unifying organization. Action on the report was to be initiated by the General Council with direction from the councilor for the health care apostolate.[28]

Equally complex was the impact of change on community living. For a few, daily celebration of the liturgy meant worshiping with another community. Freedom to experiment with other forms of communal prayer was welcome but potentially a source of separation among sisters of a house striving for unity in essentials. The heartbeat of a community of adult women religious, however, was the quality of relationships, each to the others and all to the one charged with responsibilities of a superior. Most hoping for renewal looked to change in this traditional form of house governance; few realized yet that a question of religious authority was the issue. Accepted proposals allowed each house to determine its form of experimentation in local community governance, choosing to live (1) under leadership of an elected coordinator or one appointed by the mother general; (2) with the management of an elected team; or (3) by group government.

Whatever the form of governance, Chapter delegates agreed that it should derive from the concepts stated in Vatican II documents. These clarified the meaning of religious obedience to an authority that

- calls forth a response of loving service in support of individual freedom and with respect for personal charisms;

Unfolding of a Drama 99

- is a reconciliatory power moving the community to respond to the Spirit;
- is a unifying factor in community decisions, encouraging personal initiative
- with concern for the common good;
- is exercised in a spirit of loving correction; and
- is the source of obligatory action.[29]

In common practice of religious authority, the latter two notions had dominated. The other characteristics were seen as not so much a matter of principle as simply the qualities of given individuals in their exercise of authority. Another note now appeared in the Council's reflection on communal authority, which duly acknowledged the Church's right to direct activities of religious communities but without detriment to the charism, or founding spirit, of an individual congregation. This was to prove significant in the revision of religious Constitutions.

Accepting proposals that related to practice of the vows, the Chapter voted to change norms in the Community Constitutions that emphasized the juridical aspects of these promises rather than their essential meaning. Because chastity is a virtue to be practiced in all walks of life, the delegates acknowledged that the vow properly refers to consecrated celibacy and love that frees a person to embrace all in the charity of Jesus Christ. Likewise they reasoned that by vow a sister manifests an active and responsible obedience by faithful cooperation with all those who represent the authority of Christ in the Church and in the Community. Looking to its end, delegates saw the vow of poverty as obliging the individual sister with her local community to work out ways of using things not independently but in responsibility to the common good.[30] This was only a first stage in exploration of the vows for their full significance. Women religious were to pursue their meaning for the next several decades through theological reflection, writing, and workshops on life in community.

The approach to proposals for change in the habit or wearing apparel of the sisters came in a report on returns of a questionnaire that had been addressed to 1,000 lay persons and priests, individuals within and outside the Community's hospitals and schools, relatives of the sisters, and others. Of the 772 responses, 681 thought revision of the habit was needed, 507 wanted the veil retained, and 611 thought that dress suitable for professional women should be adopted. In reply to other questions, 234 indicated that change would make the sisters more approachable.

Throughout the Community since the fall of 1965, a rather startling stage of experiment with apparel had surprised co-workers and friends of the sisters. Early on, a spirit of poverty dictated for some an adaptation of the black serge habit to a two-piece black suit with white blouse. Others aiming at a professional appearance bought black material for the same basic skirt and jacket. Veils, if worn, were small and of varying lengths, falling from a white band set off from the forehead. With the Renewal Chapter came a limited choice of colors and variety of patterns. Though the sign value of dress guided the experiment, uniformity was not a priority. Emphasis fell on the habit as witness to a consecrated life, on good taste and grooming, and on a relationship between clothing and a profession of poverty.[31]

In an attempt to respond to concerns about unsatisfactory relationships with superiors and communication with the Community's officers, the General Council early in 1968 had inaugurated a plan for area superiors, named by the mother general and charged, in effect, with building bridges. Sisters Mary Camilla Montgomery, Mildred (Marie) Irwin, and Mary Clarence (Madelon) Burns made up the intermediate team. After the interim year's sessions with local superiors in their respective areas, followed by detailed reports, the area superiors recommended:

- a formation program to lend confidence and security to local superiors,
- improved communication between superiors and sisters through personal conversations, and
- separation of the offices of religious superior and apostolic administrator.

Though not equally precise, the last two recommendations were relevant to widespread concerns. Further observations suggested a clearer rationale for an intermediate level of governance. Experiments in house government showed the need for balance between the merits of group decision-making and respect for individual rights. Tensions were apparent between the exercise of personal freedom and the assumption of responsibility. The area superiors saw a general lack of clarity about sources of authority, applications of subsidiarity, and the meaning of community and mission.[32] Their concerns were taken seriously. Causes of such problems, however, lay deeper than structural moves could reach.

New Channels of Communication

As mandated by the Chapter, in the fall of 1969 the Community undertook an experiment in governance intended to meet the needs of better communication between the General Council and individual sisters and provide a channel for action on grass roots concerns. Full-time regional coordinators residing in five geographical regions were to be nominated

Unfolding of a Drama 101

by the members of each region and appointed by the mother general and her Council. Entrusted with what was chiefly an intermediate and pastoral role, the coordinators were to meet at least quarterly with the Generalate at the Mother House. With no reference to decision-making, their responsibilities took them into the center of community life:

- to foster living in community toward unity of heart and purpose,
- to encourage the sisters in personal and corporate renewal,
- to assist local houses in implementation of Chapter directives,
- to be available to houses for consultation in a problematic situation,
- to coordinate renewal programs and workshops with other regional coordinators,
- to serve as a representative of Community governance in the region, and
- to collaborate with apostolic consultants and administrators.

Regional coordinators were to approve of changes in the placement of sisters after appropriate recommendations by apostolic consultants. Conferences with individuals being changed and with institutional administrators were part of the attempt to bring those immediately affected into the assignment process. A field assistant for the Latin American missionaries was to be appointed for a two-year term, after which the sisters would select their own regional coordinator.[33] The system was comprehensive and depended for the most part on far-flung collaboration rather than delegation of authority.

A Personnel Board of eighteen members, appointed for two years by the mother general and her Council, was to act with the personnel officer as resource for the Generalate and regional coordinators in making or recommending assignments. The office was to channel information about openings, conduct aptitude tests, and collect individual professional and educational records—an enormous task at the time since such records were frequently incomplete. For the next Chapter of 1973–1974, the Renewal and Experimentation Board was to report on implementation of Chapter decrees and personal and apostolic evaluations.[34] Again, large aims reflected hope for renewal through organization and dependence on proven leadership rather than trust in untested change.

Members of the 1969 General Chapter changed rules for the next two-year Renewal Chapter. To enlarge representation and to increase the sisters' discretionary voting power, the list of nominees was to include ninety-nine names. The Chapter also made a significant addition to the role of the mother general as described in the Constitutions: "Intrinsic to this service is her availability to the individual sister." A small committee had been appointed the previous year to revise the Community's Constitutions, guided by the changes mandated by the 1968 Chapter. The writers now reported that the text of the final document would appear in December in a dual form: Book I, *A Life of Charity* and Book II, *Community Living*. The first would identify the Community by its spirit, heritage, and purpose in response to the call of the Gospel; the second would specify the sisters' commitments to their religious vows, their life in community, and apostolic works of service to the Church of Jesus Christ.[35]

Experimentation with communal prayer led to variations on Lauds or Vespers, to shared prayer in groups within the house, and to prayer with groups of lay persons and priests. These associations continued during the years before the Chapter of 1973–1974, supporting community life for some and bringing others to consider alternatives for serving the Church. Houses experimenting with various forms of local government had been designated first in 1967 in Kansas City, Missouri, then in Denver, Santa Monica, Billings, Helena, and on the college campus. Subsequent years brought many more. Group government was the common mode for such houses, with decisions made together on schedules for common prayer and meals, on hospitality, and on common undertakings. Other houses experimented with teams of two or three responsible for the efficient functioning of the house.

Memories of such experiments are rich with stories. A sister recalls living in a neighborhood of very poor people of ethnic minority groups in Kansas City, Missouri, in the fall of 1968. Members of the house worked in various ministries—in juvenile court, at a public school, as a school nurse with Catholic Charities, and in a satellite clinic for the uninsured that required daily commuting to Cameron, Missouri. One of their local community goals was "to bring about hopeful change in people's lives by showing concern for them and willingness to be of assistance to those in need."

Another sister worked with African Americans in parish ministry at St. Augustine's in Kansas City, later with Hispanics at Our Lady of Guadalupe parish in Topeka, and finally with Anglo-American ranchers in Miles City, Montana. Each mission was a new world for her. She had thought that growing up on a farm had surely prepared her for the Far West, but it took several cattle drives, bull shows, western parades, and bucking horse sales for her to realize "the difference between farmers and ranchers. The people of Eastern Montana were fiercely independent" and "proud inheritors and practitioners of the 'Cowboy Culture.'"[36]

As their predecessors had done on real frontiers, sisters were teaching themselves how to learn from those they served, how to turn naïveté into empathy, and how to act like natives in the territory. One of the most telling developments in this time of experimentation was learning and practicing discernment in making important decisions. A workshop clarified the Jesuits' adaptation of the day of election in the Ignatian retreat, a day of choice in the following of Christ that would make a significant difference in the retreatant's spiritual life. Such choice reflected the determination and generosity of spirit that infused one's vocation in any walk of life. The sisters began to call on the method of discernment communally in choosing their form of government at the beginning of the year and individually when they faced a difficult decision about ministry or some other change.

The interval of experimentation was four to five years, with evaluations to facilitate decisions by the Chapter of 1973–1974. It was a time of many initiatives, uneven communication about progress and problems throughout the Community, attitudes formed in consequence without sufficient knowledge, and relative degrees of suspense as to outcomes. Contrasts of impatience for significant change with fear of its impact threatened to divide a Community of sisters who had devoted anywhere from six to sixty years of their lives to the common life as Sisters of Charity. The ultimate test of their unity was yet to come. Contemplating the changes from a distance of decades, sisters speak with sensitivity of conflicting goods in principle and practice.

For example, trust in Providence under a vow of obedience that brought assigned ministry and local community stood in tension with prayerful discernment of necessary service to the poor with the support of a community of like-minded sisters. Each way of living might be self-selected, equally free, and psychologically sound. Sister Maureen Craig, of an age that gave her a foot in each terrain—of vividly remembered past and rapidly forming future—observed that community generated by sound secular principles lived out with Gospel ideals could be as genuine as that born of authoritative structures and unscreened numbers. In practice, however, even a short supply of psychological immaturity could plague either sort of house.[37]

Ultimate results of the pain and suffering that attended change were mature insights and decisions of women religious determined to renew their lives in community. What remained clear and certain was an invincible purpose and willing heart. No community could have worked with greater collective effort or imagination to prepare for and undertake renewal of their life together and their service to the people of God. The work ahead was that of distinguishing accidentals from essentials of religious vows, community, and witness; of integrating spiritual ideals with external manifestations; and of plumbing the depths of what truly united the Sisters of Charity of Leavenworth.

CHAPTER 6

Experimentation: An Interval of Learning

The time between the Chapters of Renewal was like a lease without option to purchase. Experiments multiplied, raising hopes for permanent change; because they were only experiments, hopes for a return to "normal" were equally strong. Relationships could not but be affected. As the number of experimental houses increased, sisters found themselves living apart from many whose companionship they had enjoyed. New ministries were on trial in parishes, a few social agencies, and new religious education centers; gaps in school rosters, once filled by sisters, were growing wider. Years later a retired secondary school teacher described her feelings at the time: those "left behind, plowing the West 40," saw friends turning to other apostolates, studying for new ministries, and leading change. Their sense of loss and real pain merged with honest praise and support of these pioneers.[1]

That the pioneers were blazing permanent trails was apparent only to those who were striking out—though they were not all that certain of the outcome—and to the farsighted who understood their initiatives. Sister Mary Seraphine Sheehan, a general councilor at the time, spoke later about change in the Church that impacted religious life and about consequences of changes in community. Better use of the sisters' talents resulted from freedom to apply for positions; freedom to express one's inability to do an assigned task and the desire to undertake another was healthy. But the span of interpretation both of Chapter enactments and the council documents was broad. Genuine freedom, as opposed to license, with a care for responding to the call for renewal in a responsible way was a demanding goal.[2]

Besides reviews and evaluations of the various experiments with community living, prayer, governance, ministry, attire, and recreation, preparation for the next General Chapter took other forms. Not the least of these was a study of withdrawals from the Community during the four-year period from April 1968 to April 1972. A letter mailed in January 1973 to each of 148 former sisters sought their participation in a survey designed to elicit their estimation of influences on or causes for their withdrawal. Of the total, 103 (70 percent) replied that they were willing to take part. Response to the survey came from 82 (55.4 percent) of the initial 148.[3]

From 59 to 65 percent marked *No* to the influence on their withdrawal of factors like age, experience, psychological difficulties, contemporary social values, and rapidity of change in the Church and society. Living in community with women religious who appeared judgmental, intolerant, or unconcerned was the factor marked as contributing to the withdrawal decision of 55 to 59 percent of the respondents. Approximately half said *No* to de-emphasis on religious life as an exclusive state of perfection, opportunities for service within the secular sphere, and social acceptance of withdrawal from religious life. Disenchantment with the institutional Church was cited by about a third. Unanimously, respondents discredited loss of faith and reverence for the sacred as an influence on their leaving.

Paraphrased responses to open-ended questions in Part II of the survey are perhaps more telling. They emphasized realization of a temporary vocation, or none at all; experience of a lack of community and meaningful relationships; loneliness, a sense of rejection, or lack of personal happiness. Some respondents were disturbed by the Community's apparent concern with non-issues and dissonance between generations. For others, changes in the Church and in community made the life seem irrelevant. Perceived lack of community leadership in meeting social needs, lack of a voice in community affairs, and isolating rules contributed to unrest. Respondents cited mental health principles incompatible with community life, novitiate training that contributed to immaturity, difficulties with superiors, and their own unreachable ideals. What they saw as failure in the spiritual life and lack of balance with academic expectations emerged from their self-examination. However scattered, these were serious concerns.

Comments on experience of living the vows paralleled the complexity of the issues and reflected insights comparable to those expressed in Renewal Chapters. That the vows were a commitment to live as a Sister of Charity in order to build up the total Christian community was a firm theological statement. Specific problems, however, attended their practice: a lifestyle better than that of most middle-class people and ignorance of true poverty; risks of increased contacts and strong relationships with men; difficulties of the celibate life and need of better preparation for it; the need for encouragement to strong friendship in community; and obedience as a way of absolving one from personal responsibility and discouraging mature behavior. Such problems demonstrated the gap between traditional views of the vows and the teachings of Vatican II.

That community was the heart of religious life for many of these women was clear from their comments. Community living for some had lost its full value because of changes that disrupted peace, institutional living that seemed expedient and too secure, lack of regard for persons and of responsive communication, need for skills of listening and problem-solving, and the too-sudden lifting of restraints. Life in common became more meaningful as more active participation grew. For thoughtful respondents, community was central to religious witness and a valid way of living; it was the key to active religious life, an alliance of mind and heart.

So too prayer was a crucial factor in decisions to stay or go. Insisting on its necessity for apostolic work and personal holiness, respondents said prayer should be free from legislation and realistically oriented, based on scripture, practiced in both traditional and new forms, and conducive to community living. Comments became forceful: "No one can stay in religious life and put anything... before prayer." At the time, one could write: "I fear for the Church if religious communities fail to emphasize prayer and I believe there is a tendency."

The subject of government drew a wide range of comment. That government is service to others, that it stands in need of qualified leadership and re-structuring, that it should not intrude on daily life but facilitate the working of community was common enough knowledge. That it had improved much in the spirit of Vatican II and was becoming more meaningful was a view probably shared by many in the Community. Availability of general officers to the sisters was a concern that was to issue in a major experiment after the next Chapter. The practice of collegiality to a greater degree was to become common on the local level and modified forms of participation were to develop regionally and in the whole. Government as a flexible vehicle for developing maturity or as an outgrowth of community living was a less clear goal but a challenging notion.

Ideas, rather than complaints, about apostolic work were also forthcoming. Greater presence to lay persons, apostolate as unlocking enormous potential, teaching as "Christ's basic labor," concentration on spiritual works, temporary commitments to work with the Community, professional excellence combined with holiness—all were to find their place in Chapters and initiatives to come. That sisters should select their own work without explicit mention of communal priorities; that older apostolates were no longer appropriate to meet contemporary needs; that everyone should get a job were more questionable suggestions because unqualified. An expressed sense that the Community had no vision and that no one was planning for the sisters was blatantly misguided.

Experimentation: An Interval of Learning

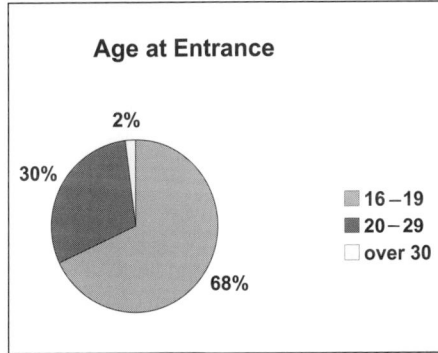

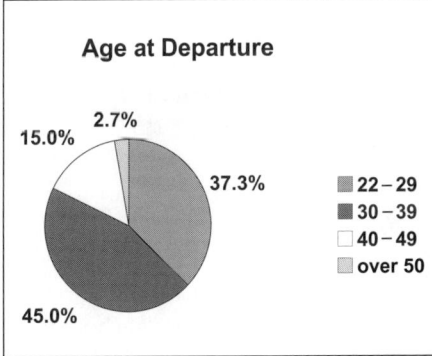

Nevertheless, the survey uncovered sources of discontent that Chapter delegates of 1973–1974 needed to examine. Though few were unknown, this did not diminish the effect of seeing them spelled out by dozens of women who had only recently left the Community. Both the youth of so many entering and the maturity of almost as many at departure are significant statistics. The median age of entering postulants was nineteen; the median age of sisters leaving was thirty-two. Equally significant, the 148 sisters who left had spent an average of more than thirteen and a half years in the Community. Their loss was grievous.

A few more facts about the 82 respondents to the survey round out the picture. Slightly more than 62 percent of them had finished in Catholic elementary school; 71 percent had four years of Catholic secondary education; 63.5 percent had not attended college; and 70.7 percent had had no work experience. Of the 148 who withdrew, 48 percent had been in the elementary education apostolate; just over 20 percent in health care; almost 13 percent in the secondary schools; and 11.55 percent in social work and religious education–pastoral work combined.[4]

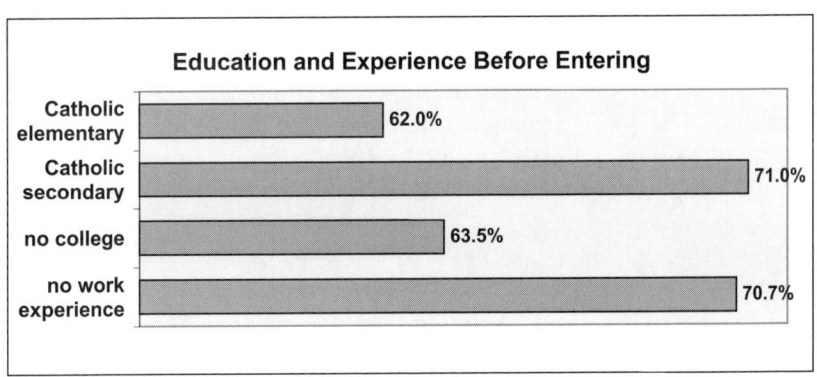

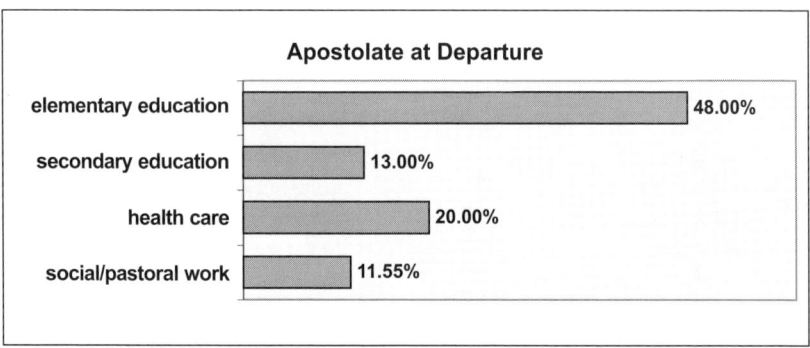

Study of women's withdrawals from religious life that began with Neal's national surveys for the Conference of Major Superiors of Women in 1966 and 1967 continued with increasing intensity though with less public attention than that generated by the clergy crises. A 1974 report on research supported by the National Sisters Vocation Conference and conducted by a sister and a layman, both sociologists in Catholic universities,[5] does much to clarify the reasons for so many withdrawals. Their analysis of 1,402 replies, a 70-percent return, depended on their view of the effects of stress on persons and institutions in times of social change as it relates to religion and religious roles. The roles of women religious who voluntarily commit themselves to a community come into grave question when that community, as part of the larger community of the Church, takes on the duty of examining and renewing its structures, its practices, and its priorities. The researchers wrote:

> The winds of social change within the institutionalized Catholic Church... have swept into the very core of the church and, most significantly, influenced the very lives of that army of individuals (men and women religious) upon whose shoulders the institutional edifice has rested for so many generations.... Catholic women religious are going through a multi-leveled stressful transition. They occupy changing statuses in changing religious communities, in a changing institutional church—that is also changing its relationship to a changing host culture.[6]

Causes of Serious Stress

Respondents to the survey identified twenty-seven items as possible influences on their decisions to leave their communities. The most important of these, emphasized by two-thirds of the respondents, dealt with the quality of interpersonal relations; the second, cited as important by more than half, dealt with the respondent's relationship with and commitment to her religious community. The first group of reasons for stress included inability to be oneself, too much tension in relationships, loneliness, personal insecurity, and lack of support; the second group included lack of ability to make adult decisions, slow pace of change, lack of social awareness in the community, and conflict with religious superiors.

Next most important were issues bearing on lack of personal intimacy in relationships, emphasized by nearly 40 percent of the respondents, and issues of work and career, cited by nearly a third. Almost a quarter of the respondents reported spiritual stress because traditional forms of prayer no longer nourished their lives, or because they could no longer represent the institutional Church. There were those who referred to a personal loss of faith. Eighty-five percent cited two or more sources of stress pervasive and intense enough to lead to departure. For most, this point was not easily reached.

More significant, perhaps, than many realized at the time—those remaining or leaving, in authority or not—was the fact that underlying each of the predominant themes of stress were questions of the meaning of the vows, in particular the vows of obedience and chastity.[7] Developing theology of the vows was accessible fragmentarily in formation programs and in relatively few first-rate books and publications. This source and foundation of community rested on little common ground for generations of women religious experiencing tensions and division.

More than once, Modde and Koval, authors of the report, referred to the legitimacy of an institutional and communal structure that offered total identity in exchange for the total commitment of its members. Moreover, that structure enriched by the lives of millions of women over centuries and developed under diverse charisms enjoyed the sanction and blessing of the Church. Now that very Church had legitimized—more, mandated—a review and renewal of an entire way of life. Fidelity to the relationship with God deepened by religious vows within a community dedicated to the people of God—that fidelity was the crux of the stresses of renewal for those who left and, above all, for those who continued together. Theirs was the task of speaking from experiences just as traumatic as anyone's, of articulating needs for change considered by many to be radical if not rebellious, and of evaluating experiments in renewal in ways that were true to a heritage of charity treasured by all.

A major effort to prepare for the second Chapter of Renewal and to meet voiced concerns was the work of regional coordinators nominated by the sisters and appointed by the Council: Sisters Dorothy Hanly, Regina DeCoursey, Marie Celeste Bride, Marie de Paul Combo, and Ann Jean (Edna) Hunthausen. The five were charged with the authority and responsibility to guide and evaluate community life within their respective regions, to encourage individual sisters and local houses in efforts of renewal, to lead implementation of Chapter directives from the mother general, and to implement in-service programs. In turn, they were to represent to the Council the Community as experienced in their regions; to collaborate with apostolate consultants, administrators, and other regional coordinators in placement of the individual sisters; and to promote community through visits, meetings, and regional assemblies.[8] Such a range of initiatives represented growing concern about pressures to change structures of apostolic assignment and community living. The coordinators lacked the authority, however, to effect such change.

Sisters in the five regions numbered 232 in Leavenworth; 181 in Kansas City; 103 in Topeka, Lawrence, Falls City, Chicago, and Oklahoma City; 131 in Colorado, New Mexico, and Wyoming; and 165 in Montana and California. Clearly, problems of travel, personal contacts, and common gatherings varied from region to region. Matters subject to a regional coordinator's confirmation or approval included models selected for local governments and financial plans. Very few decisions, however, were to be made by the regional coordinator. According to the principles of subsidiarity and co-responsibility, affirmed by the Chapter session of 1968, the individual sister was accountable for living out both personal and communal commitments; problems were to be solved on the local level whenever possible; and all in a house were to share in decision-making for their life together.

Ideas generated during the coordinators' discussions included listening sessions in each region before the quarterly meetings with the mother general and Council, social get-togethers, and suggestions for good reading. Local and regional forums, a place for airing views on significant topics and sharing good resources, were to deal with consensus-building, collegial living, issues of authority and obedience, forms of local government, prayer and liturgy, group dynamics, and ongoing forms of experimentation. There was no lack of subject matter for conversations with the sisters.

Serious questions were apparent by the first November meeting with the mother general and Council. When consensus is impossible, how does the authority of a regional coordinator extend into local autonomy? When several sisters want a more intense experience of community living and hope to move to an apartment or another convent, what can be done? The possibility of small groups within a large house had received Chapter approval; a trial period for a new form of community living was possible. But the coordinators' responsibility was only to guide discussions and facilitate decisions.

The five could report happily that house discussions on government and principles were helping to ward off polarization. Further, financial planning together was contributing to a sense of community. A tentative financial plan, to be tested for practicality, allowed for monthly stipends for individual sisters ranging from $5 to $25 and alternative methods for a local community's financing sisters' summer education. Budgeting was a totally new experience for most of the sisters, who had previously been dependent on the Community's allotment of funds to each house. Concerns of the sisters about prayer and the need for more conferences, about silence and praying apart, and about the need for courses in theology and suggestions of good spiritual books were indicative of a growing desire to deepen spiritual life. Such concerns led to the post-Christmas inter-regional institute at the Mother House.

In the summer of 1970, the regional coordinators spent six weeks at Thomas More College, Covington, Kentucky, in a program sponsored by the Canon Law Society of America. Conducted by Jesuits Tom Swift and Jim Short, it was an attempt to facilitate change in religious communities through consultation, shared resources, and common projects. The team of five Sisters of Charity of Leavenworth developed a collaborative project on communion and mission that they were to initiate after the summer. This team impressed the directors, accustomed to meeting with one community representative. Subsequently, Father Swift invited the group to participate in a collaborative renewal project with other congregations. The invitation was declined by the mother general and Council.

After spending a fruitful six weeks together, the coordinators were more confident in their assignment. They explored ways the charism inherited from Vincent de Paul might play out in the future. "We became more free," commented one of the coordinators, "as a result of wrestling with the issues." Father Swift, who had already served the Chapter as a canon law consultant, described the task of new leaders: "To stand in the midst of tension and proclaim the truth with quiet gentleness." These five were to prove its truth.

"In the beginning," remarked one of the five years later, "we were very threatening." Sisters did not know what these regional coordinators would do, asking to visit, calling house meetings, meeting with individuals. Early revelations brought home new truths: that "the unanimity we thought we had, the diversity we thought we enjoyed" as a community were not so simple. Apparently timeless structures and a Book of Customs for daily practice had prevented the sisters from realizing the range of real differences of personalities, backgrounds, views, and envisioned ministries. "We were in the middle," commented another coordinator, between the expectations of many sisters and the expectations of the General Council and many other sisters.[9]

Succeeding years brought programs on faith sharing and discernment in proximate preparation for the Chapter. Response to discernment weekends during the spring of 1973 was positive. Service opportunities during the summer were advertised with locations, dates, and descriptions of service. Coordinators encouraged cooperation with a new Social Concerns group in their promotion of peace. During 1973–1974, some sisters supported Project Equality and the United Farm Workers of America, participating in boycotts, meeting with political figures, and writing letters to Congressional representatives about appropriations for health, education, and welfare. Renewal for many meant public engagement and collaboration.

In their quarterly meetings with Mother Leo Frances and councilors, which several of the coordinators called hard work, they raised questions about more than their role and authority. They found disturbing in the lives of some sisters the time spent, not to say expense, in family visits and vacations, in certain uses of free time unrelated to community or mission, and in apparent indifference to sisters left behind in the house at holidays. Viewed in the whole, such practices revealed a growing insensitivity to the source of community in the sisters' presence to one another.

Blame for certain developments and for "not reining in abuses" was vehemently expressed at a meeting of a small group of Mother House sisters called for that purpose. These sisters voiced fears that the coordinators were dividing the Community. The coordinators in turn were hard put to explain that what they certainly had not caused were inevitable developments in the life of the Church and religious communities throughout the United States: exercise of co-responsibility through group government, individual discernment of ministry and choice of prayer forms, adaptation of rules to growing interaction with laity and public agencies.[10]

A mixed blessing, as any group must be at times to its members, the phenomenon so easily called community had been a rare achievement, regardless of how much of it depended on a common rule or individual respect and affection for one another. One who had known it in every aspect could remark on advantages in the cross section of people living together in traditional community houses. "History was saved," she said, "in the stories we told and heard." Personal growth was the pattern in daily interaction with older and younger sisters previously little known to each other—as opposed to living alone or in self-selected groups. But they were advantages overshadowed for many by growing frustration with uniform rules and limited self-determination.

COMMUNITY AT THE HEART OF RENEWAL

Reflecting on those early years of change, other sisters recalled the impact of societal values that showed itself in the 1970s, the "me-ism" typical of a self-serving culture, of a generation reared on the dubious premises, "I'm O.K. You're O.K." There developed in some the sense of a contractual arrangement that gave free reign to the attitude that "the Community owes me...." With others a strong, even innocent idealism invoked a new freedom to manifest thoughts and feelings that seemed self-centered rather than community-minded. Sometimes actions were indeed naïve, infrequently less than humane. "In the context of a nation's life," observed a sister who had given it much thought, "it was a 'coming of age' [in community] with signs of adolescence in a new freedom to choose and with the need to establish priorities, recognize limitations, and accept responsibility for the larger good of community, of the Church."[11]

Something of the pain suffered in the course of change is registered in the words of one who watched sisters move from school and hospital communities of twelve to twenty into newly formed small houses. "You suddenly realized that those you knew best in community did not have the same dreams of community, the same beliefs in community; did not pray in the same way, did not want to live community as you did, and you were devastated, broken-hearted."[12]

Thanks to the coordinators' pastoral role, they were learning what Sister Marie de Paul called the quality of "the goals, talents, and dreams of the individual sister that she had not had an opportunity to disclose before." Now such sisters were finding a new voice: "They had something to say and they said it," she continued. What was manifest was the "personal growth of many, even the transformation that was emerging from the pain of coming to grips with what the Spirit was calling us to." The desire of sisters, especially some of the young not trained in the earlier formation programs, was to work together in freedom of spirit. The outcome was,

During a term as plant manager for Saint Mary College, Sister Anthony Marie (Regina) Deitchman keeps a motor running.

for the coordinators, "the privilege of participating in the work of the Spirit in people's lives."[13]

Remembering their experience, Sister Edna said, "It was a rich time for me, getting to know sisters older, experienced, wiser, for who and what they were, but it was also a hard time." Discovering problems in their causes and realities, first hand; not remembering what she'd said when someone thanked her for it years later; bringing to birth what the coordinators had agreed on for an experiment in renewal; facing difficulties of the impact of change in persons: all this was personally transforming for the coordinators.

Sister Edna said she came to realize how the changes affected superiors and principals whose roles carried specific responsibilities. "It was impossible for many to understand another order of priorities than what had been. It was travail to accept in words and decisions what had not been conceived of before." Involuntary tears came to her eyes as she remembered the persons, the new knowledge, the self-revelations, the pain and the puzzlement.

Then she laughed. When this former grade-school teacher recalled telling a friend that she had to call the college faculty to gather for her visit and then chat with them individually, the friend replied, "They'll be glad to. It will be all right." And it was. Now she remembered how glad Sister Mary Dolorita had been that someone wanted only to listen. And how matter-of-fact Sister Mary Vincentine and Sister Mary Vincentia were, taking it all in stride. She'd been made to feel welcome. In more than a few ways it was true that "we had to re-do our lives."[14]

New meaning attached to words like *obedience* and *authority*, to *decision* and *choice*, to *spiritual development*, *collegiality*, and *subsidiarity*: they all referred in some way to what the sisters needed and to what the Community needed to do. Moreover, a new kind of leadership was appearing in people who had not sought it, many of whom had never been elected to office. Sister Edna recalled how at work with the other four coordinators energy flagged at different levels. If you stayed with it, she said of Sister Marie de Paul's persistent reasoning, the idea emerged like a "pearl of great price." But Sister Edna attributed any success to a community of women "able to move on because we were acting in obedience to the Church that asked us to renew in a life-giving way. And we set about it."[15]

In their evaluation, the coordinators did not claim success. Far from it. They had lacked the means to effect the change they were convinced was imperative. Nor can personal and communal transformation be hurried. The five had completed their charge with full report to the Council and the 1974 Chapter. A pre-Chapter evaluation survey had revealed a split between those who wanted the regional coordinator role to continue in some form and those who wanted to eliminate it. Ultimately the Chapter dropped the role.

Sister Jean Anne Panisko, principal of Annunciation School in Denver, knows firsthand the value of primary students' learning.

A major outcome of the regional coordinators' work was revision of the placement policy initiated in 1969 by the Personnel Board. A strict calendar called for consultation between the coordinators and apostolate representatives for the purpose of selecting principals and administrators who would be appointed by the mother general. Principals and the apostolate consultants then prepared assignments for the following year. Forms from individual sisters indicated their desire to remain in their present mission or to move to another institution or into another apostolate. It might or might not be possible to act on a sister's preference for a change. Employed prayerfully, discernment had prepared her for whatever assignment she received from the mother general. This was the beginning of what would become, within less than six years, a policy that approximated open placement.[16]

The coordinators' evaluation survey had garnered 461 replies, some of which recommended an earlier start to the process, job descriptions, information about community living in a given mission, and simplification of the procedure. Questions arose about whether school principals should be elected by sisters in the field, should apply for the position, and should return to teaching after five or six years of administration. According to respondents, every principal should know the quality and work record of every sister on her faculty and staff.

Responding by apostolates, sisters sought clearer role definitions for coordinators and apostolic works consultants and expressed dissatisfaction with community living. The desire for smaller groups, more closely associated with their ministries, was marked. More authority for the apostolate consultants and less power of administrators over sisters' lives was an urgent concern; an organizational chart was one suggestion. Social service and religious education sisters asked for individual contracts and freedom to make their own commitments. They asked for a voice in naming key people in apostolic appointment and for information about the Community's needs. Health care sisters asked that reasons for a move initiated by an administrator or regional coordinator be explained to the sister who was transferred.[17]

Clearly the need for professional procedures as well as training was urged as a criterion of excellence in service. When Mother Leo Frances reported on the survey, she acknowledged that the majority of changes sought for the placement policy were good for individual sisters, for community living, and for apostolic effectiveness. The ultimate outcome of these changes, she knew, would be difficult to predict.

Evaluation Necessary for Apostolates

Guided by criteria outlined in the newly written Constitutions, Part II, *Living in Charity*, the Personnel Board established policies for sisters now serving in individual ministries—their discernment, community living, and salary arrangements. Principals asked for job descriptions and placement preference forms. Faculties now annually received forms for evaluation of their performance by their professional superiors, who further had the option of self-evaluation or of requesting comments from a diocesan or Community supervisor. Guidelines for performance appraisal of teachers by their principals asked for explanations of ratings, from outstanding to unsatisfactory, on improvement of instruction, professional relationships, personal characteristics, and general school services.[18] Implementation of evaluation policies varied from one institution to another. Evidence mounted of the need for objective determination of schools' strengths, weaknesses, and needs.

Plans for objective evaluation of sisters completing the tertian program, in preparation for making perpetual vows, were progressing in the work of a subcommittee assisting the Formation Team that had begun functioning in 1970.[19] The committee revised the self-evaluation form and added to evaluations by the tertian director and Council liaison an opportunity for the tertian to select three sisters who might write open-ended evaluations to the mother general on the tertian's behalf. Tertians also benefited from a theology program, summer workshops, specially designed regional activities, and the availability of two to four personal counselors in each of the five regions.

In 1971 a seminar-retreat for all sisters under temporary vows gave them the opportunity to discuss the value of counselors, evaluations, length of the temporary vow period, and continuing formation. Fifty-five tertians enjoyed time for conferences and reflection on the vows and religious life. A booklet prepared in 1973 by Sister Kathleen Wood, newly appointed tertian director, described tertianship as a time for continued apostolic, communal, and spiritual guidance. It was an opportunity to become imbued with living traditions of the Community and to reflect on the quality of one's life and integration of all its aspects through the study of prayer, scripture, the Church, and religious community.[20] Development of mature commitment was the focus.

The sisters' prayer life was taking directions that corresponded to currents in the Church at the time. In 1971 Abbot Emmanuel Spillane, of the Trappist monastery in Huntsville, Utah, led the Community in a Summer of Prayer at the Mother House. Liturgical renewal was taking hold. In addition to adaptations of the liturgical hours for common prayer and small groups who gathered for shared prayer, charismatic prayer was a rich resource for many. Its expressive spontaneity and extended quiet time, its waiting on the Spirit were conducive to spiritual growth. As one sister wrote of it, the charismatic prayer group "nourished our spirituality for decades and opened us to sharing our spiritual lives with lay people...."[21]

Membership in the Leadership Conference of Women Religious (LCWR) brought valuable exchange of information about renewal. In 1972 the National Conference of Major Superiors collaborated with the Sacred Congregation for Religious in gathering about two hundred presidents or other delegates of some 130 national conferences from Europe, North America, Latin America, Africa, Asia, and Oceania. They heard and discussed papers on changes in community life, prayer, and positive elements of the ferment and division that were growing worldwide among religious. Cardinal Antoniutti from the Sacred Congregation urged closer collaboration with Rome and recommended mixed commissions to study mutual concerns of episcopal and religious communities. He emphasized the need for religious to participate in apostolic planning in the Church.

Tensions over change now common, though in differing ways, to religious in all parts of the world became evident. Presenters pointed to a loss of humility, simplicity, and a spirit of obedience; suggested solutions included exclaustration (departure from community) or separate jurisdiction for "dissenters." But various groups pointed to other causes in communal and ecclesial inability to accept change. Congregations were suffering from resistance to renewal indirectly encouraged by documents from the Sacred Congregation. Many voiced the need for patience with honest efforts in renewal that required personal support and evaluation by professional theologians. They cited efforts to achieve better communication, deeper spirituality, and the practice of communal discernment. They emphasized accountability with budgets and various modes of exercising authority that honored individual dignity. Apostolic teams and renewal of initial and continuing formation were surely not counter to the mind of the Church. Frustrations in these efforts, even occasional excesses and failures, these leaders insisted, were now universal and a sign of the times.

Sister Margaret Brennan, IHM, president of the LCWR, and Father Paul Boyle, CP, president of the Conference of Major Superiors of Men, made quite clear to the assembly that the National Conference of Major Superiors sought to exercise leadership, not to gain autonomy or independence. Sister Margaret also affirmed that women religious wanted justice and equality within the Church even as they continued to serve faithfully. Out of divisions within this National Conference and the LCWR grew the movement of those superiors of women who wanted to retain the original name of the organization, Conference of Major Superiors of Women (CMSW). They eventually sought recognition parallel to Rome's approval of LCWR. That dual recognition made formal a separate identity among women's congregations in the United States for those to whom renewal meant little fundamental change.[22]

Closer to home, a sister who had been a regional coordinator wrote with conviction that "no one outside a religious congregation could truly understand the wrenching and conflict of values and ideals nor the depth of personal and interpersonal struggle and searching that Vatican II caused. For us the Council was not just an historical and ecclesial event."[23]

A Benedictine monk who had been chaplain to the Mother House and Ross Hall sisters for more than thirty years and instructor of religion in the Academy until it closed died at the beginning of 1973. Born in Germany, Father Justin Sion, OSB, was torn by the conflict during World War I between two countries he loved. His ministry to German prisoners of war at Wadsworth, the Veterans' Hospital located near the Mother House, was a benefit to both them and their caretakers. The words he spoke on one St. Vincent's Day were something of an introduction to the work of the next Renewal Chapter: "Those who have wisdom and strength should be an eye to the blind, a foot to the lame, a support to the weak."[24]

Of inestimable value to the Sisters of Charity pursuing renewal in the 1970s were other words and facts unearthed in a brief study of the Vincentian heritage made by Sister Mary Edwin DeCoursey during the pre-Chapter Commission work of 1967. They came from archival material related to Mother Xavier Ross and from analysis of 249 letters of Vincent de Paul. "It seems to me," wrote Vincent, "that the affairs of God are accomplished little by little and almost imperceptibly, and that His Spirit is neither violent nor hasty." About the extent of the Daughters of Charity's work during wartime, he said, "They make and distribute soup every day, at the house of Mademoiselle Le Gras, to 1,300 bashful poor and to 800 refugees.... In a nearby parish they fed 5,000 poor persons, in addition to the sixty or eighty sick they had on their hands."

The Ladies of Charity, women of the aristocracy who organized themselves under Louise de Marillac, asked that the Daughters—girls from the villages and countryside—determine in every canton and parish "the number of poor persons who will need to be clothed during the whole or part of the coming winter...." They were to write their names for distribution purposes with the help of prudent persons who would see to it that the poor themselves knew nothing about it. Instructing these Daughters, Vincent told them: "Surely the great secret of the spiritual life is to abandon all that we love to Him by abandoning ourselves to all that He wishes, in perfect confidence that all will be for the best; and hence it has been said that all things turn to good for those who serve God."[25]

Asked early in the new century what particular strengths she saw in the past half-century of change, a sister on the missions thoughtfully replied, "Diversity of response reveals what is typical of our Community—individuality."[26] She spoke for many who would say the same in different words.

St. Vincent de Paul

Individuality comes hidden and touted, in office and without any authority whatsoever, with and without noticed talent: it is the way of grace. From the astonishing leadership of Louise de Marillac, marshalling her noblewomen and country maids, to Mother Xavier and a small band of pioneer sisters willing to brave an unknown frontier, and a century later to some eight hundred of her followers taking on challenges with unpredictable consequences, the Sisters of Charity have indeed been individuals, each of whom has contributed to the shape of things to come. The bonds that crossed those centuries were not to be easily undone.

CHAPTER 7

Drama of Renewal, Continued

Chapter sessions convened between 1968 and 1974 were on a continuum of renewal. The time between them encompassed hopes for changes to come, fears of their consequences, and the dual phenomenon of mounting departures and internal reconciliation. Addressing the Twelfth General Chapter at its opening session in July 1973, Mother Leo Frances reminded the delegates of what the Community had told them in surveys, conversations, and position papers throughout the previous year. Their primary concern, she said, is "that we search together for an expression of our common vision as Sisters of Charity of Leavenworth." She quoted Mother Xavier: "Those who are called, are sent," and added that their foundress had "sent herself and her companions into service...by teaching, by witnessing, by caring for the poor, the sick, youth, adults, the uneducated, the handicapped, the rejects of society, the minority groups: American Indians and the black." Then Mother said, "We must look forward as we are looking back, and it is in this forward look that our greatest force for good will be."

Her questions echoed implications of a search for common vision: "What do we see as the best plan—the right direction?...What is holding us back?...What does God ask of us?...What is the nature of our witness? What are our commitments to the Church? How do we live?" Her conclusion about the hard work facing the Chapter implied more than anyone at that time could fully realize: "Our goal is the greater good of the Community as a viable force in the Church."

Mother's perception of the Community's strengths could bring no quarrel: a sincere desire to know God's will and a willingness to pay any price to accomplish it; fidelity to the spiritual and apostolic heritage of its founders; and the expressed desire of the sisters for a deepened prayer life and "for a credible religious life where honesty, love, trust and respect for each other

Drama of Renewal, Continued

will prevail despite differences." Her account of the Community's weaknesses, on the other hand, must have given pause:

- unwillingness to accept change or desire of change for its own sake,
- individual interpretations of local authority,
- reluctance or refusal to assume co-responsibility,
- selective observance of the Renewal Chapter's enactments,
- lack of loyalty to one another, and
- a "prophet-of-doom role that generates fear, apprehension, confusion."

Conscientiously heard or read, Mother's assessment left no one unscathed. It was the willingness to pay any price that was about to be tested. But that depended, in turn, on the individual sister's conviction of how God's will was manifesting itself. About the proposals of the Chapter she spoke with authority:

> What this assembly accepts...this assembly must support both individually and collectively...in our lives in the community as well as in our agreement here. To do otherwise is to betray the trust the Sisters have placed in us....We must strive to reach a unity of hearts, a unity which witnesses the presence of the Spirit among us. It is our obligation to be a reconciling force when and where we meet division.

Then she appealed to the communal obligation to place itself in time: "It was never easier in any period of history for Christians, for religious, to attain mediocrity. Yet the signs of our times are clamoring for heroism.... Heroism is a hard road to travel, and it is often a lonely one." Pointing to social affluence in the face of the world's hunger, Mother cautioned against the selfishness that change and adaptation can bring and appealed to the love that had brought each sister to pledge herself to God in this Community. She quoted from some novices' prayer for their first-vow liturgy: "We begin our religious life by the voluntary and complete surrender of our individual lives, in the interest of that deeper and wider life which we are to have in common." She concluded with the exhortation, "What a serious obligation is ours—to be that faith community they willingly embrace."[1]

Citing a traditional Chapter ritual to this extent needs justification. Mother Leo Frances spoke in responsibility as the head of the Community but, more to the point, out of a profound conviction that the Community stood on the brink either of fruitful change directed by the Spirit or of lasting and destructive alienation. She knew it was divided at the core. Her words reflected, throughout, the grief division had brought to many and the hope that a stronger unity might come of suffering itself if the sisters were true to the spirit of charity that had originally bound them together.

There was apprehension and a prudent caution in her suggestion that selfishness, mirroring the social milieu, might bring the Community to the point where "our renewal will burst into a demand for reform." Finally, she framed a realistic picture of the Community as it was: in need of a healthy self-appraisal, in need of healing, in need of discernment, and in need of vision. Allowing for the decades that followed this crucial Chapter—decades of growth to a mature and unifying commitment to the poor—it may yet be admitted that Mother's call for unity of purpose and heroism in action prefigured questions to be raised thirty years later before the first Chapter of a new millennium.

The newsletter published during the weeks from June 28 to July 13 summarized Chapter proceedings. Two days of pre-Chapter meetings included a forum on common vision before a day of prayer on July 1. Reflection on the past uncovered an image of Sisters of Charity as "Christian women entrusted with a mission...all gifts to each other...more Martha than Mary...more practical than visionary in meeting new frontiers: where there was a need we filled it." The following questions brought the discussants up short: Should the lived expression of that heritage be uniformly expressed? Why are we no longer at home with each other? How can we best work through the issues causing discomfort? Is vision cloudy because of cultural changes, different views of authority, a matter of semantics, individualism in our witness, or the "insidious poison of fear?"[2] Quite a range of impediments to vision—and material for a year's worth of forums.

A pervasive concern expressed in questions about religious authority prompted an invitation to Bernard Häring, CSCR, who was teaching a course in moral theology in the college, to address the Chapter. Insights gleaned from his remarks were guidelines for the coming weeks. Common convictions must precede common laws. It is necessary to acknowledge at least two views on all critical issues. Authority originates in living the Gospel. Authority, further, is at the service of conscience. Right conscience acts in shared experience, looks to the common good, is conscious of a burden put on others by law, and is Christian only if it takes account of the conscience of others. We cannot even speak of conscience unless we are conscious of God and of the effects of our actions on others. To build community, we must act with compassion and sensitivity.

Father Häring spoke to the nature of vows and norms. While obedience is not selective, it must be discerning about the observance of norms, with clear reason for non-observance. Reasons must come from conviction. A "chaos of values" can follow from attaching equal importance to all norms. On the other hand, individual interpretation of Chapter directives must be honest as to motives. We learn to discern these by learning together how to pray, by obeying the Holy Spirit, and by acknowledging that self-righteousness hides the will of God. The vow of celibacy, he said, means an undivided heart, a non-possessive love.

Chapter directives are justified, he said, as response to the needs of the times. They are necessary for building community, for mission, and for reform. External signs of religious identity are not single but diverse. Abstention from material goods should be a redemptive action, not a battle cry for *Perfectae Caritatis* (the Vatican II document on religious life). Father Häring emphasized that the juridical source of authority for a pontifical institute—like the Sisters of Charity of Leavenworth—is from God through the whole Church and, insofar as the Holy Spirit is working in her, through the individual sister. Rather than impose legislation, a Chapter might write a letter to the sisters in community to be read together in God's presence.

To renew the life of prayer, the priority should be to make decisions "confronting the Lord together." Father Häring declared unequivocally that charity is the first goal and norm: only that is infallible, not steps taken to achieve it. True community spirit is ready for open-ended compromise and for a covenant never to criticize; when a decision follows shared reflection, he asserted, "stick to it."[3] Three or four days followed for delegates' final work in commissions on proposals for Chapter. Elected by the members when they first met in December 1972, the chairperson of each group presented its proposals to the assembly.

For the Commission on Life in Community, Sister Mary Janet McGilley began by saying that theirs was the "story of an experience, with its own rhythms—rather than a report." From their diverse experiences in community the group had undertaken at the beginning of their task to rediscover and reaffirm their common call in Jesus to be together as Sisters of Charity of Leavenworth. Trying to be honest about the questions that divided them, they asked, "Do we really want to be reconciled? Is it best for the Community, for the Church? Is it what Christ wants?"[4]

Confronting specific and concrete issues, like the veil and religious attire, they knew from the start that the range of responses in this group reflected the spectrum of views in the Community. To find genuine reconciliation meant movement from the individual and the particular toward a common vision and the possibility of mutual trust and acceptance. The pain of the process for delegates, they realized, mirrored the larger Community's suffering. Months of study intervened before they could move from suffering to hope. To begin that journey this commission had looked at their predicament in a context. The most telling witness for people convinced of their values is the reconciling power of the Gospel. But how to sort out opposing views in order to plumb that power together?

Seeking a common ground of principles and facts, they read and studied

- the documents of Vatican II and of Pope Paul VI,
- the Community documents, or new Constitutions,
- the recommendations and concerns of the sisters,
- the laity's responses to questions on religious life posed in diocesan Call to Share sessions,
- the survey of former Community members,
- the evaluations of house governments, and
- twenty-two norms on community life in the original Constitutions.

The commission's objective in this intensive work, carried on parallel to duties of ministry, was to seek renewal through the deepening of life in community, admitting many levels of meaning in the term. The deepest level was that of communion. Their conclusion was that, in view of membership in Christ and union through Jesus with the Father and with one another, community indeed may be the all-encompassing reality and a unique call to be together as Sisters of Charity. Emphatically voicing the truth was a first step. Finding how to re-achieve a lost sense of community was the problem.

The days of commission sessions at the beginning of Chapter awakened the tensions foreseen in mid-winter meetings. The years of experimentation had deepened contrary views of what the common vision of the Community must be. Disregard by many sisters of the revised norm on attire and on certain retained norms convinced many others that fidelity to the vows and to community was in question. Opposing views both identified obedience as essential to religious life. This meant for many that obedience to all community norms is likewise essential, and to many others that obedience to particular norms is not of the essence of religious obedience. The divide was reflected in responses to the pre-Chapter opinionnaire: while 73 percent of the sisters concurred on basic concepts of religious life, only 55 percent agreed on a basic cause for the polarization. Almost half had different opinions about what is essential to living that life. The need to better understand what could deeply divide a community of committed religious women was clear.

Dealing with the Issues

In the first general session for consideration of issues, the delegates were in agreement on essentials of vocation, community, the vows, grace and response to the Spirit, mission, and charity. But the deep sense of alienation within this Community found a strong voice. Paradoxically, most found local community life more or less satisfactory. The tension existed between local houses and within individuals in relation to the whole—the reversal of situations prevailing before the last Chapter. The discomfort experienced by house groups of high tolerance or like lifestyle interacting with groups living by traditional observances was symbolized usually in differing response to particular norms. But when customs and observances that had provided a sense of identity with the large community disappeared, and there were no replacements, all felt a loss of *esprit de corps*. All agreed too that the Mother House was no longer the center of community, for many no longer felt welcome coming home.[5]

In the emphasis on particular norms and individual response as failure of obedience, the Chapter recognized that questions of authority—its own and implicitly that of canon law—were at issue. If questions of particular norms were symbolic, that meant they were real. But on another level, deep down, the question was one of value, the nature of what one was committed to for life. That was what lay on the table. For some, it took the form of fear of loss of a great good, the community as they had known it and might not know it again. For others, it took the form of need for the freedom to act and to live as conscience or the call of charity directed.

A Chapter, moreover, as the highest authority in the Community, represented the fears and the needs, the insights and the ideals, and the ordinary, everyday assumptions of the women who had elected them to this task. That human limitations beset every delegate and every sister who had voted for her only sharpened the edges. With full confidence in the Community's strength, Mother Leo Frances had named weaknesses of selfishness, lack of loyalty, and "the poison of fear" in order to inspire their correction. Father Häring had warned against self-righteousness, lack of sensitivity, and rules without common conviction as dangers to the renewal going forward. Recourse to principles was a search for common ground.

Accepting the Gospel of Jesus Christ as the first source of authority in the service of conscience placed every issue in a personal dimension of mutual respect. Looking to diverse convictions forced consideration of honest motives and the risks of freedom. Keeping essentials in view curtailed the leveling of norms and assigning touchstones of allegiance. The challenge to the Commission on Community remained: How to find a way to live companionably in one community with two opposing bedrock convictions about obedience? Alternatives appeared but did not satisfy: to separate along ideological lines? to devise a structure to support lifelong efforts at reconciliation? Other communities were resorting to these or other strategies; scholars were identifying such moves by sociological patterns.[6] This group of sisters thrown together by their own choice of a commission and its topic decided to seek immediate help at the source.

In four days they had reached virtual consensus on two norms concerning the sisters' vacations and retirement. They were at a standstill with a previously revised norm on religious attire requiring the veil with a modified habit and a norm prohibiting all use of alcoholic beverages except for medicinal purposes. Earlier discernment had uncovered strong convictions against allowing contemporary dress: losing the habit meant loss of corporate visible witness in the secular world; the habit speaks publicly for "what I am." Strong reasons against allowing moderate use of any alcoholic beverage were fear of addiction and loss of a corporate stance as a weakening of values.[7] Only a few days remained for commissions to complete the proposals they were to bring to the general assembly. Without setting reconciliation as their goal, the group agreed to spend a day in prayer and discernment, putting to themselves the question, "What can we propose in two norms on these questions, as if a total decision for the Community rested with each one?"

Telling this part of the commission's story, the chairperson said, "We had instinctively set ourselves on that course. Perhaps it was not instinct, but grace: the old Sister of Charity reaction toward a job to be done and in the doing it, to find something more."[8] The something more was the basis within differences for agreement:

- that religious life is witness to the transcendent, to God's loving care, and as such is of great value;
- that there is need to seek the spirit of the law and provide for legitimate diversity of response, never compelling anyone to act against her conviction;
- that the veil is an authentic external sign of religious consecration, but not the only sign;
- that drinking is not morally wrong, but potentially dangerous, addictive, open to giving scandal or to a spirit of worldliness; and
- that a spirit of balanced moderation, characteristic of the Community's traditional attitude toward mortification or total abstention, may have high witness value.

The foundation of agreement was solid, with space for the contrary views that had inspired the search for it.

In revising the norms, commission members emphasized essential principles, avoiding absolutes of expression and providing for a pluralism of conviction with respect for differences. The revised norm on attire emphasized the dress of a religious as witness to a consecrated life. In addition to the modified habit, it included a fourth option allowing for the possibility of witness to a contemporary society in which traditional signs have become less meaningful for many. The individual was responsible to choose what she judged most effective for her circumstances.

Trust that each sister would reflect on her choice with maturity and sensitivity to companions at home and at work ran parallel to faith in reconciliation and an end of judgment. Simple and modest contemporary attire, as well as a habit with veil, "should signal who we are, and we are Sisters of Charity. To the degree, then, that our lives are lives of charity will the sign of dress be an authentic witness."[9] This revision brought consensus among 80 percent of the commission members and, in the assembly, a consensus of two-thirds of the delegates.

The move toward consensus before the necessary adoption of a proposal by formal vote was a modification of the discernment process that was now a common practice in the Community. It involved the presentation of reasons for and against a proposal, personal weighting of these reasons, then prayer and reflection before a straw vote. Not only did consensus facilitate the work of revision, but also, in the difficulty of achievement, it affirmed openness to the Spirit and a firm desire for reconciliation.

The second norm worked out by the commission was written in a spirit of joy and thanksgiving to the Creator of all things, pledging the use of these as a blessing insofar as it helps in attaining the Kingdom, refraining from use as it hinders that progress. Responsibility to others, to the Community, and to the Church for the witness value of one's acts was the emphasis. Freely abstaining from the use of such things in sacrifice for a greater good was a personal choice. Corporate witness must spring from common conviction with care for individual conscience. This norm brought consensus from 90 percent of the commission and, with a brief addition, from more than two-thirds of the Chapter delegates.

Transcending Divisions

A proposal that preceded these two in the commission's presentation to the Chapter was an appeal from experience. "Somehow," Sister Mary Janet said, "a reconciliation had taken place: Not total understanding. Not acceptance of one another's views. But acceptance of one another. Respect for different views. Trust that behind these lay mutual and deeper values held in common. And a lot of charity." Here was yet more that had come from doing, in faith, what needed doing. The commission members then asked the delegates to undertake a like journey and to invite the entire Community to do so. It had not been an exercise in piety seeking an unopposable and unrealizable ideal. It had been the hard work of prayer, discernment, and dissent without any certainty of the goal in sight. The chairperson continued:

> If we could humbly own [the task], acknowledge individually and collectively our separateness from one another, our divisions, our alienation, our continual need of redemption. If we could admit our need to help each other, heal each other—so that we may know to what we are called individually and corporately, and may respond to that call with clarity and enthusiasm....

Posited on that *if*, the members of the commission placed before the Chapter a formal proposal that they "exhort the total Community to accept with us...the task of Active Reconciliation." Its implementation in each local community was to be a program for personal and communal actions that symbolized reconciliation. Concrete suggestions for faith-sharing, discernment, liturgy, and hospitality would follow. The Chapter accepted the proposal at the end of its last session.[10] Mother Leo Frances urged the sisters to receive it as their goal in community for the coming year.

Sister Mary Liguori Horvat reported to the Chapter that the Commission on Spirituality had worked from the question, "How can our renewal strike deeper and deeper roots?" To answer it, they had spent months of study with materials from the pre-planning committee: opinionnaire results, recorded suggestions from the Community, summaries of house discussions on essentials of religious life, reports from the Renewal Committee, the study of withdrawals from the Community, position papers, and the Constitutional norms on vows, prayer, and formation. Questions the commission brought to their pre-Chapter sessions asked how the Community and individual sisters might better witness to the Gospel, consistent with the spirit of Vincent, Mother Xavier, and Community traditions.

Specific questions about the vows, they reported, called all to change their hearts. A genuine spirit of poverty asked the sisters to let go of their judgments of people and their behavior. It meant concern for the poor and oppressed, sharing the lot of Jesus in his poorest members. Accountability would appear in budgeting a monthly allowance and in sharing common goods with simplicity. If local community was to challenge the values of each member, its guidelines should be the needs of ministry and the income level of those served. Concrete expressions of the vow of poverty were many. The vow of chastity or celibacy, the commission's spokesperson said, must be a daily priority and a deepening of personal relationship with Jesus Christ. It required commitment in friendship to members of the Community and mutual support. The celibate life, moreover, should give evidence of joy and unrestrictive affection rooted in prayer and asceticism. Practice of the vow as the commission described it was altogether positive.

While obedience was to become the fulcrum of both division and reconciliation, the commission's remarks on the vow were simple, direct, and few. Obedience manifests itself, they said, in seeking the will of God in daily life, being accountable to the sisters in community, and being loyal to community agreements. Noticeably absent was emphasis on obedience to persons in authority as representing the will of God. For the commission, the chairperson asked for action on the sisters' need for theological background on the vows and for clarity about their practice. The group proposed a ministry of prayer and study of the possibility of a Community house of prayer with a report to the Chapter in 1974.[11]

"Mission encompasses our total life and demands communion with all." So declared the Commission on the Call to Mission through its chairperson, Sister Marie de Paul Combo. "It includes our very presence" in its quality and manner. The commission considered questions the Council had posed to them:

- How do our corporate works witness the authentic values of our common vision?
- Where is our witness particularly needed in the American Church?
- What priorities should determine new ministries?

Ranking high on the list of priorities in the pre-Chapter opinionnaire was the need for a means of corporately discerning the Community's direction in mission. In response, the commission proposed a survey, to be completed by the 1974 session, of present apostolic works, principles regarding service of the poor, the impact of institutional resources on issues of social justice, and a personnel assessment of future needs.

Asking, "How will the cry of the poor find an echo in our lives?" the commission spoke to individual and corporate lifestyles as the daily expression of a priority for the poor, especially the poor of the earth who go to bed hungry each night. Closer to home, they addressed needs of the Church in locales where sisters served.[12] Concern for social justice did not rank among the top ten priorities listed in the opinionnaire. Need for information about issues and education in the social teachings of the Church, especially the 1971 statement of the American bishops on economic justice, were crucial if the Community were to fulfill the Church's mandate. Conversion necessary for Christian witness was the challenge of global needs and of the pervasive perversion of the American creed evident in contempt for human life, disregard for the rights of others, and a determined pursuit of pleasure.

The commission proposed a Community-wide assembly for the following summer to deepen communal solidarity in union with the Church and to formally renew the traditional experience of "being sent forth" from the Community's home into its now diverse missions. Personnel policies were the current means of implementing such goals by enabling sisters to discern their ministry as consonant with commitment to the poor, witness to the Gospel, and education to social justice. The commission called for a revision of those policies after a Chapter-mandated study of apostolic works.[13]

Passion of conviction was evident in the questions the group put before the Chapter and the Community. Eventually their urgent call for education led to an office of peace and justice. The numbers who already desired to commit themselves to direct action for the poor spoke to a unity that would come to flower in later Chapters. But the very freedom of discernment and diversity of ministries that were to develop in the next three decades contributed to repeated calls for a unity of purpose and direction of mission that would identify the Sisters of Charity of Leavenworth.

Commitment to the poor was rooted in the history of the Community and a firm tradition in its institutions. Nevertheless, many new and individual forms of it, though true to the Vincentian heritage, tended to diffuse the common vision that was sought. The very means of serving the poor, whether in institutional ministries or in support of individual ministries, was the Community's income and investment. Mutual support in an aging community and stewardship for the future precluded dramatic renunciation of goods or property. Simplicity of life was to remain a challenge, if not a conundrum, for many in professional apostolates and for a religious community's common identifiable image as well. Once members discerned a call to ministry with God's people wherever they lived and worked and often suffered, a visible unity of communal mission became a goal rather than an assumption.

Sister Mary Edwin DeCoursey reported to the Chapter for the Commission on Governance. Its members had studied the Community's total governing structure, reviewed experiences of similar congregations, clarified the functions of various offices in the Community renewing itself, and explored concepts of authority, leadership, accountability, collegiality, and subsidiarity. Now they formally reaffirmed the authority of the mother general, the regional and local coordinators, while emphasizing the significance of building solid community at the local level as co-responsibility and accountability gained credence. Their practice was especially binding, the chairperson commented, in those houses that chose to share together the roles of the local coordinator—the option of group government.

Before reporting progress toward proposals, the chairperson expressed concerns that had surfaced in each commission's work but that took a distinct direction in each case: the need for reconciliation within the community, the need for spiritual conversion and education on religious vows, the need for unity in addressing the prior claim of the poor. The words of the commission best distinguish its direction. As commission members consulted various resources, it became increasingly clear "... that our lives in charity still lack the sense of Gospel vision and witness. As a community... our response has been an imperfect one in many respects. The pain and sorrow of the past few years is still very real. It is the feeling of this Commission that we are near a new level of maturity in our lives together, and that we will best display this if we build solid community at the local level with an awareness and acceptance of true accountability."[14]

They exhorted the Community "to make an intense effort during the coming year to think and pray about our local houses where we live and struggle together." They recommended careful reflection and discernment about the type of government to be adopted and choice of a structure that would facilitate subsidiarity. The principle implied handling of decisions at the local level with recourse to a regional coordinator if this proved an insurmountable problem.

The commission's concern for this had serious implications:

> We maintain that failure to take the needed action violates individual and corporate responsibility. We urge each member of the community to make a careful study of her own acceptance of accountability. We further urge each local group to address itself prayerfully and with concern to its living out of co-responsibility at the local level.... Our plea to you is to live freely and responsibly as the daughters of our loving and peaceful Father, who have accepted His authority as it is manifested to us by those we have chosen to govern our community.[15]

A forthcoming proposal would recommend further study of the Community's government structure, the possibility of facilitating the work of the general officers, and the need to clarify roles and expectations. The above statement, however, depends on an assumption that religious authority resides in elected officers. Implicit were principles of conscience, collegiality, and mutual respect. Absent is reference to the significance of common conviction in living by common norms, to diverse understandings of authority and obedience, and to the absolute rule of charity. Not that these would be denied—only that much room remained for division and distance. A transcendent value must make the Community one.

CALL TO SOMETHING MORE

In her letter to the Community of July 19, 1973, Mother Leo Frances cited the call to communion and mission declared by the central committee of the Eleventh General Chapter at the close of its first session. "It became more and more evident," she wrote, "that to find communion we had first to find each other. We had grown apart." Her words were perhaps as true and as understated as might be found to describe the condition in which the Community found itself that crucial summer. Acknowledging the alienation many felt, whatever their convictions, she exhorted the sisters to accept, individually and corporately, the proposal of active reconciliation presented by the Commission on Community to the Chapter. It was clear that here was no simple report on a proposal accepted by a majority of votes. Here rather was a call of the Spirit to *metanoia* and to a change of heart that, given free response, would change the course of the lives of all Sisters of Charity of Leavenworth.

The Commission on the Call to Mission, Mother recalled, sought a deeper understanding of ministry as much more than the works we do. She emphasized that mission encompasses one's total life and requires communion with all who share it. Life will be fruitful in proportion to the validity of our witness, and that depends on intimate communion with God. Before we dare speak to others of the ills of society, she said, healing must take place within ourselves. Only then can we heed "the cry of the poor" and go to meet the needs of a global community. While the Commission on Government reaffirmed the authority of the mother general and General Council, it emphasized the need for personal accountability to the local community and to the Community as a whole. Failure to take necessary action at the local level, it asserted, violates responsibility to one another; taking action requires courage and a sense of justice.[16]

The Chapter session had been a traumatic encounter. Its seriousness and impact could not have been predicted. In the fall of 1973, seven apostolic work consultants visited Community missions to gain information as background for discussion of a future apostolic direction. In addition to the traditional ministries of education and health care, social services that included child care, foreign missions, and religious education were now formal apostolates. Apostolic studies conducted by the schools and college since 1968 and long-range planning from 1972 to 1975 provided data and developments at all levels of education. Religious education showed a shift from catechetical work to pastoral roles.

Health services reported from retreats, regional work sessions, and a questionnaire regarding the recommendations of Cresap, McCormick, and Paget. Withdrawal from ownership of five hospitals followed appraisals of primary need and effectiveness. Social services recorded ministries to those least able to help themselves, to minority groups and migrant workers, work with other agencies and advocacy. Homes for children registered change from custodial care to residential treatment services and structured recreational, educational, and follow-up services. The Latin American missions reported on administrative changes and preparation of sisters for mission work. Independent ministries included public health nursing, special education in public schools, higher education posts, diocesan housing, and a migrant project.[17]

Mother Leo Frances's formal report to the Chapter opened the second session in July 1974. It provided a factual overview of her second term of office, the six years since 1968. The Community's membership had declined from 964 to 724, by reason of seventy-one deaths and 194 withdrawals in that period. The latter averaged more than thirty-two annually, reaching a peak in 1969–1970. The number of those professing first vows—the initial confirmation of an applicant's commitment—had moved from 170, the six-year total in 1968, to 25 in 1974, an average of about four newly professed each year.

Sisters serving in elementary education in 1968 had numbered 354; in 1974 they were 196, a 44.6 percent decline. The number of elementary schools had dropped from fifty-seven to thirty-five, in patterns of adjustment in the Catholic school system developing throughout the country.[18] Other

As one of her novitiate ministries, Sister Mary Margaret (Peg) Johnson accompanies school children on her banjo.

apostolates registered fewer but serious losses: more than a quarter of the 138 sisters in secondary education in 1968; something under a quarter of the 64 sister nurses. In contrast, the number of sisters in religious education and pastoral ministry had tripled, to 33, the apostolate showing the greatest gain. Swiftly moving trends, even more than raw numbers, fed concerns for future directions.

Postulant Dorothy (Sister Jean Marian) Redlinger gets the feel of catechetics for young believers.

Changes in the formation program reflected the work of the team. Of nineteen applicants over the six years, twelve had been college graduates or RNs; thirteen of the group persevered to the novitiate; seven were accepted for first vows. Criteria and screening necessarily affected both numbers applying for entrance and numbers accepted. The initial period of formation had been made flexible depending on the individual's readiness to move into the next phase. Ordinarily six to eleven months, the postulancy could extend up to two years.

Novices began their canonical year with reception of the white veil and their names in religion—usually the baptismal name. After this first year of prayer, reflection, and individual direction, they spent a year in full-time apostolic work and preparation for profession of vows. A few professed sisters besides their director were invited to live in community with the young women in formation. Simplicity continued to mark ceremonies of reception and vows, as well as community participation. In 1970, the sisters for the first time made their vows with their parents at their side in the sanctuary of the chapel. The time of temporary vows was a period of spiritual growth and renewal during early years in ministry. Its term was ordinarily seven years but the sister could extend it.

The Professional Education Board screened more than five hundred requests for study, mostly in the summer, and centralized information-gathering for individual sisters. The Council recognized the need throughout the Community for comprehensive planning for professional education, career development, and retirement. The initiative was to come in proposals prepared for the second session. The committee, making a concentrated investigation of retirement, had studied programs of other communities with on-site visits and sponsored a workshop, "Focus on the Future," offered in the college's summer session. Application for Social Security eligibility and establishment of the Community's retirement fund were necessary moves toward support of retired and semi-retired sisters. Budgeted by local communities, assessments from each sister during her years of active service contributed to the reserve fund.[19]

Proposals for Action

The model of government structure proposed to the Chapter for approval aimed at eliminating fragmentation, strengthening local government, and simplifying the roles of central authority. The Community director was to lead the Community; five general councilors were to be responsible, with executive authority, for the sisters in health care and four geographical areas, facilitating their spiritual and communal development and apostolic placement. For the first time, nominations from the Community of a limited number for each office would produce a list of names with the specified highest number of nominations. Sisters could withdraw their names from the list; at the time of voting, names could be added from the Community at large. A General Forum of twenty-five elected members was to deal with major concerns such as retirement, community life, and social issues and be advisory to the Community director and Council.[20]

Another proposal allowed for appointment of a director of missions from nominees submitted by the sisters to be assigned to Latin America. The Personnel Board was to consist of representatives of apostolic works appointed from those nominated by sisters in their apostolates. Insuring representation by the nomination process was an attempt to democratize the centralized government structure, trusting that advisory roles of the Sisters' Forum and the Personnel Board would suffice to communicate concerns and issues from the missions to the governing Council. The liaison and authoritative roles now assigned to the five councilors increased dependence for these desired effects on the persons elected to the central offices.[21]

A proposal from the Commission on Community provided a plan for aging sisters; it was characterized by flexibility and a variety of options for service and community living. Trained personnel were to design and implement the program. Their goals were to increase awareness of older sisters' needs for psychological and spiritual support and for development of new skills appropriate to volunteer work. Guiding principles of a second proposal emphasized the value of older sisters' presence in local communities and the honor due them accompanied by the same care they may have found in their families. Freedom to live in a local community, to return to the Mother House, or to join the Ross Hall community for care of infirmity was paramount. Education of the Community in general measures of healthy living was a prescient rider on the proposal.

A further proposal asked the Community to find ways of sharing prayer, work, and leisure with friends and others in a spirit of hospitality. Such a spirit would include due respect for the rights of individuals in a house to privacy and quiet. A study of communications in the Community was delegated to the General Forum, with emphasis on the need to reinforce a common vision, to personalize ties between community members, and to share both common and differing views of community life.[22]

Proposals accepted by the Chapter from the Commission on Mission provided for the study of apostolates to evaluate resources and make recommendations to the Community Council on the future direction of ministry in response to needs of the Church. Emphasis on the public value of a simple way of life prefaced a statement of principles. Witness as a counter to social ills that impoverish the human spirit now enlarged the meaning of mission. As a visible influence on America's action in the global community, the role of women religious was responsible leadership and service. Visible moves toward such witness included cooperative planning with appropriate agencies, continued presence within existing structures, expansion in new directions as the Spirit calls, and continuing assessment of apostolic efforts. The Commission on Spirituality proposed statements on the vows that incorporated active concern for the poor and moderate consumption of goods, simplicity of life and responsibility to the general community fund, deepening and widening of bonds in community, and practice of reciprocal accountability at all levels.[23]

In the final session of the Chapter, the delegates elected Sister Mary Kevin Hollow as Community director; Sister Mary Serena Sheehy as her vicar and first assistant; Sisters Mary Liguori Horvat, Agnes Virginia Hamm, and Rose Dolores Hoffelmeyer as councilors; Sister Mildred Irwin as health care representative to the Council; Sister Mary Julie Casey as Community treasurer; and Sister Marie Kelly as Community secretary. Four were new to the Council; Sister Mary Julie was treasurer for the first time.[24]

Sister Mary Kevin Hollow, Community Director, 1974–1986

Drama of Renewal, Continued 137

Community Officers, 1974–1980: *(top row)* Sisters Mary Kevin, Mary Serena Sheehy, Mary Liguori Horvat, and Agnes Virginia Hamm; *(bottom row)* Sisters Rose Dolores Hoffelmeyer, Mildred Irwin, Mary Julie Casey, Community Treasurer, and Marie Kelly, Community Secretary

Whatever had happened in the minds and hearts of the delegates during the two summers of this second Renewal Chapter, they chose a director and council firmly committed to preserving the heritage handed down from Mother Xavier, a heritage of service to one's neighbor, especially the poor, in every need the Community's resources could meet. That service remained largely in institutional ministries. The traditional structure of central authority remained, with new channels of advisory consultation and recommendation.

Urgent calls for expanded ministry to victims of structural injustice depended essentially on Community-wide education to such needs. As things stood in the first decade of renewal, the repeated plea for mission and witness in simplicity of life and commitment to the poor echoed in communal exhortations. But none were so eloquent as Sister Mary Seraphine's impassioned appeal to the Chapter before it closed:

> We are American religious women, and as such we belong to one of the most influential groups in the world today—certainly in the Church. We are the largest group of religious women in any one

country. We live in a country where we have freedoms unknown to most countries, especially to religious women in those countries. We are the best educated... but we have been affected in our lives by the affluent society in which we live. We have come to a somewhat placid acceptance of the standard of living... related to that affluence.

But the time has come. Is it [not time] now for us to examine our responsibility and our ethics? To examine the quality of life in our houses and to determine what we can do about this quality? We will never come to an understanding of our world and its needs unless we give ourselves time for reflection and prayer.... From such an atmosphere we can move out to touch in a thousand ways the wounds of the world.

Do we [not] as American religious women, in this last part of the twentieth century, have the greatest obligation, the strongest mandate ever given to anyone, to willingly undertake to witness by the quality of our lives the responsibility we have to the global village?[25]

Behind Sister's words were experiences of that part of the global community where Sisters of Charity ministered in Peru. The diary she kept of her days there bear stark witness to the contrast between the everyday affluence Americans take for granted and the touching beauty she had seen in the ways of children, women, and men living in dire poverty. What was to come of the challenge of Sister Mary Seraphine's plea lay hidden in the continuing renewal of the next thirty years.

CHAPTER 8

Getting from Here to There

Asked in person what were the strengths of the Community, a sister who had lived long enough to escape easy sentiment answered, "Our strength is love. Much in our Constitutions says that: 'The beginning and end of our coming together is our Lord Jesus Christ.' Our spiritual life and our community life: if we keep true to those we have great strength." If this was the transcendent quality, the "more than we sought" from doing the work of the Chapter of 1973–1974, it was implicit in the move toward reconciliation and explicit in many proposals. Responses to a Community-wide survey affirmed the strength discovered in daily life. "In my early years," wrote one, "a sense of belonging and on-going education" were bonds of community. A second spoke of the influence of Vatican II documents in "re-thinking...who we were"; of their invitation "to become a part of the fray, to take part more fully in the messiness of life." Another identified the Community's strength as "faith. The Spirit gives insight to each from [her] unique experience and work."[1]

One could scarcely find a more powerful combination of traits to hold a community together than these: a sense of belonging to a communal effort, union with the people of God in their experience of life, and faith in the Spirit speaking in each one. The chief motivating force of the Apostolate Survey, mandated by the Chapter, was to find further the direction or the mission to which the Community was called by the Church in these times. Ideally that would contribute to if not determine the common vision the Community sought. To involve all the sisters in each apostolic field in as many ways as possible, to judge from a sound and thorough base of information, and to be guided by recommendations of the apostolate groups were the purposes of the Council as it initiated the study.

The Apostolate Study mandated by the Chapter was conducted by the Personnel Board appointed in 1975. Ad hoc committees studied the statistical results of a Community survey, evaluated personal and material resources of given apostolates, and researched ways to revitalize the Community's witness in the world. Only then did the Board member for each apostolic area carry recommendations to the Community Council to help set future apostolic directions. Results from the general opinionnaire professionally tabulated and utilized by each group were not as unambiguous, except in a few clear instances, as one would hope. Reports after three to four months of concentrated study in apostolate groups pointed to a strong focus on ministry to the underserved wherever they were found, ministry either by Community institutions or by individual sisters working with others.

The dilemma lay in applying broad criteria to determine whether to continue in a particular school, home, or hospital or—given the shrinking number of sisters—to turn it over to the diocese. In some cases the turnover involved another congregation or the civic community. The decision in many cases depended on how the Community, withdrawing from a school or hospital, could serve a given parish or city in new roles planned with the Catholic community. Gone were the days when a call for help from a bishop, pastor, or community could be answered in terms of the number of sisters available or not available. That was the case when an area or a growing parish had no Catholic educational or health care institution and the sisters were missionaries in every sense of the word. Now, as the Community document *Living in Charity* stipulated, cooperative planning with responsible agencies produced comprehensive decisions "to insure better use of personnel and resources." In a spirit of faith, those decisions were to be the fruit of communal discernment based on clearly stated common criteria for apostolic service.

DECREASE IN NUMBERS	FROM 1968	THROUGH 1974	% OF CHANGE
Membership	964	724	-24.9%
deaths	71		
withdrawals	194		
newly professed	25		
under temporary vows	147	33	-77.6%
median age	c. 42	50	
elementary school sisters	354	182	-48.6%

The decrease in membership between 1968 and 1975 coupled with few applications and a rising median age reduced the number available for apostolic works. Excluding those in general administration and Mother House staffing and those fully retired or released for study, the total number of sisters in the field was 550. Staffing of elementary schools presented the most serious challenge.[2] All but three of the schools staffed by the Sisters of Charity registered declining enrollments. Nevertheless, criteria for judging whether to stay in or withdraw from a school or hospital included much more than attention to numbers. According to the Community document, continued presence required evidence

- that the sisters' presence penetrates structures and gives voice to Christian conscience;
- that their work advances community in the area;
- that it fulfills its professional purpose, that is, gives excellent service;
- that it contributes to meeting needs of the time, especially those of the poor; and
- that it is the best possible utilization of the sisters' talents and experience.

Further, each apostolate should consider what alternative services, if the sisters withdrew, would meet the pupils' or patients' needs, especially those of the poor and neglected.[3]

The general opinionnaire revealed that a substantial majority of the sisters were satisfied that their life as a Sister of Charity contributed to their service of others and that they were responsible for promoting unity and energy in their apostolate. An even larger number thought that both community needs and individual choices were important in choice of ministry. Considerably more than two-thirds of the respondents wanted leaders in the apostolates to be identified by a combination of Council authority, apostolate membership, and self-initiation. Fewer than two-thirds saw lay and religious, qualified and competent, equally eligible for staffing and leadership.

Although most concurred that implementation of Vatican II documents had influenced apostolates, opinion was divided on effects of change. One sign of uncertainty was the range of views about the number of sisters needed for Catholic identity of an institution. More than 40 percent wanted a quarter to half of a staff to be formally religious personnel; more than 30 percent favored half to total staffing by sisters. A full-blown lay and religious partnership was only in the making.

SIGNIFICANT FOR COMMUNITY APOSTOLATES	CHOICE OF
living as Sister of Charity greatly enriches service	73%
present lifestyle contributes to service	70%
individual responsibility for strength of apostolate	74%
vitality of Community evident in taking risks	74%
increasing governmental effects on institutions	71%
Community needs + individual discernment important in choice of ministry	77%
leaders to be identified by broad consultation	71%
lay and religious staffing and leadership	60%

Estimation of their apostolates' value, however, by the sisters engaged in them was not ambiguous. Combining the *very good* and *satisfactory* responses, one could say that 80 percent was a high rating for the apostolic effectiveness of the institution in which they served. On the other hand, one could say that a 44 percent rating of *very good* was not satisfactory. Evaluation of schools staffed by Sisters of Charity for their apostolic and professional effectiveness fell somewhat below the norm. Numbers declined on development of social consciousness. Continuance of apostolates, however, with two exceptions was viewed as *very necessary* by more than half to two-thirds of the respondents. Judging them *somewhat necessary* boosted the rating to more or less than 80 percent.[4] The difference between *very* and *somewhat* again qualified the ratings. High standards of performance in all apostolates was the source of these careful, critical evaluations.

Self-evaluations suggested more than standards of excellence and personal modesty. Only a quarter of the respondents saw themselves as agents of change; somewhat less than a third, as early followers. Respondents registered general agreement that women religious were to lead the way in meeting contemporary needs. Few more than half, however, saw themselves as very important to their apostolate; considerably fewer than half

ESTIMATION OF APOSTOLATES' VALUE		
attitudes toward change	*to be tolerated* 25%	*element of growth* 33.3%
institutions' apostolic effectiveness	*very good* 44%	*satisfactory* 36%
institutions' professional effectiveness	52%	33%
elementary schools' quality of education	48%	28%
development of social consciousness	20%	34%
continuance of apostolate	*very necessary*	*somewhat necessary*
hospitals	67%	rises to 80%
elementary schools	60%	rises to 83%
Saint Mary College	55%	rises to 78%
secondary schools	52%	rises to 79%
homes for children	39%	rises to 66%
Latin American missions	39%	rises to 59%

felt very important to their local community or individually effective in their apostolate. While approximately 60 percent of the respondents approved of the Community's provision for their personal and professional development, only half thought they were taking adequate advantage of opportunities. Nevertheless, more than 90 percent of the respondents reported themselves happy in their present apostolate.[5]

What appears as paradox at best is consistently honest reporting and self-evaluation for those who lived through the twelve years of the

SIGNIFICANCE OF PERSONAL ROLE IN APOSTOLATE	
self-evaluations	
agent of change*	26%
early follower**	31%
cautious follower	41%
happy in present apostolate	91%
very important to present apostolate**	55%
very important to local community	41%
individually effective in present apostolate	44%
women religious: to lead healing ills of time	94%
semi-retired sisters staying in local convents	92%

*slightly less than
**slightly more than

Community's early renewal. These were women who had just weathered the conflicts and tensions of the second Chapter of Renewal. They were determined together to bring the Community and its ministries to the maturity sought by the documents of Vatican II. They were certainly not complacent about the institutions they staffed nor about their personal performance in apostolic assignments. Nor were they dispirited about what they saw as imperfect progress toward difficult-to-reach goals. Yet they did not see themselves as directly influential in decision-making about that progress in renewal. What the survey revealed about the sisters was as significant as what it told the Council about the health of its apostolates.

    Considering priorities for the future of the Community's apostolic life, almost half the respondents saw the needs of contemporary society as the determining factors. They were equally divided on whether present Community commitments should take priority over new apostolates. Reasons for choosing either priority reflected a sense of obligation to the people of God with varying experience and understanding of how that obligation

PRIORITY FOR COMMUNITY APOSTOLATE			
needs of contemporary society		48%	
present Community commitments	Yes 51%		No 49%
best way to alleviate needs of poor:			
phase out some present commitments		42%	
willing to work with economically poor		43%	
with preparation		46%	

could be realized. When 65 percent of respondents marked themselves as somewhat but not too much aware of the resources required for the operation of community projects, a serious information gap complicated the picture. As for the best way to alleviate needs of the poor, appreciably fewer than half the respondents thought phasing out some present commitments would address the problem, while almost 90 percent were personally willing to work with the economically poor, especially with preparation.[6]

These and other responses suggested something more significant than ambiguity or uncertainty. They reflected differing development of thought about the Church and its mission and about roles of the non-ordained in ministries of the Church. Collaboration on a large scale and at every level was to be the keynote of change to come in all aspects of religious life. That was an evolution that sisters themselves were to effect. The Apostolate Survey of 1975 mirrors something of the depth of division in religious communities working hard at renewal. More important, it reveals the depth of responsibility that women religious assumed for renewal of their personal and communal lives and their particular calling in the life of the Church.

Replies to the opinionnaire were either too close to the center or too much in need of relevant information to guide the Council clearly. Based on data and a clear rationale, recommendations of those in the field were to be more telling. The elementary education group looked at performance assessments and goals and talents of each sister; at the attrition in the elementary field and prevalent low morale; at results of opinionnaires given to pastors, parents, and school boards. They combined the general Community criteria for the schools with their own, which included:

- opportunities for significant Christian impact on public and social life,
- attitudes of parishioners,
- mutually acceptable goals of pastor and sisters,
- availability of comparable opportunities for Catholic education in the area,
- postconciliar spirit in the parish supporting catechetical instruction,
- diocesan leadership in renewal,
- opportunities to use innovative methods to attain academic excellence, and
- services to the poor as a priority.

Immediate application of the criteria to particular schools to determine continuance or withdrawal clearly could have combustive, perhaps irremediable, effects. Implicit in the criteria was the necessity of consultation and collaboration in key decisions between clerical or lay authorities and the sisters who administered and staffed the schools. These priorities, the decreasing number of sisters in the apostolate, and insistence on a high quality of education led to recommendations for fewer but better schools. This meant increasing staff for those that qualified, decreasing staff where diminished resources and enrollment justified it, and withdrawal from those schools that failed to meet a significant number of priorities. Each school was encouraged to develop strong lay leadership in faculty and on school boards, to promote the teaching of social justice issues, and to review the salary scale of the school staff.[7]

In response to the committee's recommendations, the Council could not find warrant for total withdrawal from any school because of the subjectivity of data gathered by surveys, changed circumstances in the schools or parishes, and the difficulty of objectifying factors involved in such a decision. Reduction of the number of sisters in certain schools would not solve problems, especially if some of these sisters were taking new roles in the parish. The Community would not totally withdraw from any one school; all schools had to share the impact of a probable decrease of personnel.[8]

A unique and ultimately abandoned proposal asked for collaboration on a new scale. The elementary teachers suggested that a Campus School be located on the grounds of Saint Mary College and developed into a model of quality education. It could take a leadership role as a center for educational renewal, especially for elementary personnel, and could serve as an innovative program for Leavenworth County. Such a program could become a revitalization hub for all school levels and an internship center for administrators; it could also provide an opportunity to test integration of apostolates.⁹ It is possible that a later plan for coordinating the Catholic schools of the city might have coincided at some point with this concept with unpredictable and creative consequences. The potential might have qualified as one of the "dreams" invited by the Community in the 1990s. Although the Council promised referral of the recommendation to the college, Council members suggested as an alternate means for revitalizing the elementary apostolate collaborative planning to develop leadership and growth.

Holding Steady in the Face of Loss

The secondary school apostolate group presented the Profile of a School, compiled from five opinionnaires sent to faculty and students, school boards and parents, pastors and associates for each high school and academy. Data and responses to the surveys suggested the viability of all eight secondary schools. Survey results attested to high academic quality in the schools, access to teachers and counselors, and innovative methods of teaching and learning; religious preparation for life and preparation for college or job; a spirit of community, opportunities for service through the schools, and social awareness. Faculty spoke of positive student and parent attitudes and support from the local community.[10]

Response from the Community director and councilors indicated no immediate plan to withdraw sisters from any high school staff; the losses could be sustained. They did ask, however, for a rank ordering of the schools in terms of financial need and need for a religious presence. The Council asked too that the number of sisters who could take on extracurricular activities be related to considerations of age or experience. The Council had plans for a special study of Bishop Hogan High School, enrolling 27 percent of faiths other than Catholic, 40 percent black, and growing more interracial by the year. Among the questions to be asked were: Is Hogan a place for a particular apostolic thrust? Do we have resources for continuing the work effectively? Do we have sisters skilled to teach varying ability levels and able to adjust to different cultural milieus?

The Council pointed to Sister Mary Jo Coyle's plan for personnel distribution and for amending imbalances of student/staff ratio. They mentioned an ongoing study of resources for continuing the ministry of education and the relationship between this apostolate and others. Identifying and developing leadership potential was to include release-time, when possible, for study and internships. The bicentennial gathering would be a good opportunity for general sessions and workshops for the secondary apostolate and for collaborative meetings with elementary and college apostolates.[11]

Conclusions from a self-study and a summary of a consultative view from the college sisters stood at the center of Saint Mary College's report. Its apostolic effectiveness and witness to the Gospel pointed to the educational potential for developing Christian community and to need for the sisters' growth in theology, especially that of Vatican II. A strong campus ministry program, students' self-direction in the Goals curriculum, opportunities for career exploration, and experiences of community on campus were clear benefits of the program. Marketing the mission and vision more effectively and finding means to diminish a perceived isolation from other apostolates and from the civic community were ongoing needs.

In the long view, recognition of expanding possibilities for women in society and finding new roles for college personnel in Church and society were contemporary means of racheting up the value of a woman's college in the Middle West. The Council concurred with the conclusions of the report. In response to recommendations for a Pastoral Ministry–Religious Education program to meet current needs of the Church, the Council pointed to the Community's financing of pastoral work of the sisters in Peru and added that they would consider, case by case, other proposals for subsidizing sisters doing pastoral work in poorer parishes.[12]

The many and various roles assumed by sisters living in the Mother House go far to explain the need for the apostolate of special services. It was inaugurated in 1974 to signal the contribution to ministries of the Community of sisters living in the Mother House who were working full time. Their offices and tasks were essential for maintaining health insurance records, accounting, purchasing, and housekeeping. These sisters provided ongoing service in health care, the campus post-office, the library, sacristies, the switchboard, and social work with the poor. There was a sharply felt need by some in the Mother House community for acceptance as a cohesive group and for counseling and re-training. As community living became more flexible and functional groups were formed, organizing a special apostolate was seen as no longer necessary.[13]

In 1975, sisters in social services numbered twenty-five. Seven held master's degrees in social work; six more in other disciplines. These sisters found consensus in a philosophy that guided their commitments. All ministered on a non-sectarian basis to minority persons or groups, to the economically poor, and in a variety of social service ministries. They served in the Community's homes for children; in Catholic social services and public agencies; in the Rural Life Conference in Washington, DC; in adult education and home visitation programs; in corrections, prison work, and juvenile court; in casework with families and children; and in housing for low-income families and the retired. Their vision embraced quality of life for those living in poverty, with particular concern for African American, Mexican American, and American Indian people. Sisters in this apostolate set such goals conscious of their own need to be healed of fears, prejudices, and complacency. Their questions about placement policies and the status of the Community's homes for children met with specific response from the Council.

The recently published *Mission Assignment Policy and Procedures* spoke to Community-wide concerns. Decisions about continuing operation of Mount St. Vincent's Home in Denver and St. Vincent's in Topeka depended on the relationship of these homes to the Sisters of Charity Corporation. Ownership of the Home in Denver allowed the Community to decide its future; separate incorporation was under consideration with legal counsel. As owner of the Home in Topeka, the Archdiocesan Office of Catholic Charities had secured its incorporation in the fall of 1975. The Council asked administrators to develop a statement of philosophy that would reflect the basic beliefs and values that governed the homes' operation. Programs of treatment and personnel policies were to correspond to those beliefs, whatever the source of monetary support. Recommendations for follow-up studies of the homes' residents and evaluation of services were approved.[14]

Pastoral ministry claimed thirty-eight sisters with a median age of forty-three. All but two held a bachelor's degree in theology or religious education; twenty-one held graduate degrees in these disciplines or in counseling and guidance. They predicted remaining in the ministry for three to five years, with probable role changes. The number of roles within the ministry suggests the reason for changes: pastoral minister, parish worker, pastoral team member, and co-pastor; religious education director, campus minister, director of prayer groups and retreats, and nursing home visitor; and diocesan directors of vocations and modern media. The group asked for early implementation of a permanent Spirituality Commission to enhance the sisters' prayer ministry and envisioned a reflection and renewal center for the sisters. They sought commitment of one or more sisters to the task of education to justice and asked that the Community pay one or more salaries for sisters in pastoral work in economically poor parishes.[15]

The health care apostolate used three questionnaires to capitalize on evaluations by individual sisters, local communities, and the total apostolate. In all hospitals of the Community, 164 sisters had ministered in 1968; now 136 did so, a drop of just 17 percent. The 26, however, who were not in a Community hospital almost doubled the number who had died or withdrawn from the Community. The median age of sisters in health care was fifty. Each facility had at least 5 sisters, including sister administrators. A profile of the nine hospitals showed across-the-board accreditation and, except for one hospital, occupancy rates in keeping with state and national trends. Each institution had short- and long-range goals; eight of the nine had conducted financial feasibility studies.[16]

Mount St. Joseph, the Home for aging women and men included in the health care report, was characterized in its methods of care as a living witness to dignity of life for employees, volunteers, families of residents, business acquaintances, and professional providers. The residents made as many decisions as possible and formed meaningful relationships. Though licensed for intermediate nursing care, the Home was identified by Social Rehabilitation Services as the nearest to skilled nursing and total care of any home in the northeast section of Kansas. Its resident load was 42 percent dependent on Medicaid; all were on fixed income. The state's reimbursement left 22 percent of the cost of daily care to be absorbed by the Home. Lack of space and personnel hindered development of enrichment programs and outreach to the area.[17]

The report from the total health care apostolate recommended a professional study to test attitudes among all constituents—patients, personnel, medical staffs, civic and religious communities.[18] This would open all to the risks of broad evaluation; the recommendation came from sisters who desired such an assessment. Alternatives to a particular hospital's continuing in service were transfer of ownership to the diocese or another medical facility and transfer of sisters to other Community institutions for work in home health and clinics. Continuing to own and operate all facilities without increasing the number of sisters assigned rested on the premise that effectiveness depends not on the number of sisters but on the quality of service and sense of religious dedication.[19] Indicating that ownership and operation of the health care facilities would continue, the Council encouraged opportunities for personal, professional, and religious education for the sisters.

If data from the Community opinionnaire represented complex conditions for decisions about apostolic commitments, certain responses reflected more subtle problems. Significant variations in self-estimation among sisters in given apostolates had particular causes the survey could not uncover. Patterns suggested, however, the need for attention to factors of morale. Confidence that life as a Sister of Charity greatly enriched their apostolate fell below the Community percentage for sisters in health care and religious education. Hospital sisters rated their lifestyle considerably lower for its contribution to their service.

As many as 10 to 20 percent fewer of respondents in these two apostolates and the college rated the apostolic effectiveness of their work as very good. In rating their effectiveness as satisfactory, the college sisters leveled with the Community number. But a sense of personal importance to their apostolates and of individual effectiveness was considerably less common among hospital and college sisters. Demands of institutional accreditation and professional standards may have affected these self-evaluations. An alarming number of hospital sisters, however, felt less than very important to their local community. Almost 40 percent of these respondents viewed service to the disadvantaged as a greater priority than phasing out commitments in determining the Community's apostolic future.[20] In contrast, a majority view from the general survey of some commitments as dispensable in terms of their service to the poor suggested lack of knowledge about wide-ranging effects of institutional ministries.

SIGNIFICANTLY VARYING RESPONSES IN SPECIFIC APOSTOLATES

	COMMUNITY	HEALTH CARE	RELIGIOUS EDUCATION	COLLEGE
living as Sister of Charity greatly enriches apostolate	73%	65%	64%	
lifestyle contributes to service	70%	55%		
apostolic effectiveness of present apostolate				
very good	44%	36%	29%	25%
satisfactory	52%	36%	45%	53%
personally very important to present apostolate	55%	48%		39%
personally very important to local community	41%	29%		
individually effective in present apostolate	44%	28%		27%
priority for Community apostolate:				
phase out some commitments to meet contemporary needs	42%	31%		
emphasize service to disadvantaged	31%	39%		

Self-Concepts a Hidden Concern

The final recommendation from the health care apostolate was a signal relayed across ministries. The need for programs to upgrade sisters' self-concepts of personal worth and professional effectiveness echoed from apparent contradictions in particular responses in the general opinionnaire. A 94 percent conviction that women religious should play a leadership role in healing societal ills contrasted with the quarter who saw themselves as initiators of change. While nearly three-quarters called themselves early or cautious followers, considerably fewer than half saw themselves as effective in their present apostolate. A lesser but significant gap prevailed in estimations of the local community's attitude toward change.[21]

It might well be concluded that the patterns of community life and service had required maximum responsibility, individual and corporate, for meeting needs and demands for sisters' services. On the other hand, no parallel acknowledgment was required of the value of the sisters' presence, experience, knowledge, and ministry from hierarchical, civic, and sometimes Community authorities. Women religious were not inclined, nor did they have time, to seek public or even communal recognition or advancement or the honor of consultation from those who might have profited from such reciprocal action. The inequities did not diminish their motivation, which was anchored solidly in "the beginning and end of our coming together... our Lord Jesus Christ" and in his poor of every kind. Further, the sisters clearly enjoyed their work. They admired sound leadership; few found its potential a talent in themselves.

One powerful side effect of renewal was the gradual unfolding of what decades of willing labor with minimum resource and honest regard for authority had produced in the psyche of perhaps most women religious. They had come to equate humility and simplicity with being taken for granted and underestimated for their potential.

In its response of December 1975 to the recommendations brought to it by the Personnel Board, the Community Council addressed the major concerns that drew consensus from the apostolate groups. It first endorsed a community-wide, ongoing program directed toward updating the sisters' education in theology according to the principles of Vatican II. The principal planner was to be the Commission on Spirituality already announced in October. Second, it endorsed the concept of a broadly-based, consensus-forming process to be designed for corporate reflection within and across apostolates to discern future apostolic direction. A well-thought-out plan for consensus-building should boost community morale, a concern voiced by the Personnel Board.[22]

But the Board's expressed goal of a corporate response to social ills, though it anticipated a national conference of the United States bishops on liberty and justice, had no broad base in the Community. At this time, views on the Community's apostolic direction had little in common. The participatory process could be a step toward Community morale but could also fall short. Honest dealing with issues and differences in the Community, required for consensus-building, could fail to target concern for the individual self-image projected in the opinionnaire. That had deeper roots than either a corporate stance or a consensus on apostolic direction could uncover.

A third response of the Council endorsed the concept that women religious should play a leadership role in healing the ills of the time with action that included encouragement of young religious to consider administrative positions. This would entail a study of the ministry of administration to stimulate motivation for leadership and courses in management for present and potential administrators. Consultation would uncover roles of leadership at national, diocesan, and professional levels. Services of career exploration and development opportunities were to be the responsibility of a full-time director of the Personnel Office to be nominated by the Community and selected in the spring of 1976.

The leadership role for women religious is a concept, however, that involves more than just study of administration and management. Motivation for leadership and administrative potential do not spring from the same sources; one possessing the second might lack significant potential for the first. Leadership in women shows itself in more ways than study and administrative experience allow.[23]

In their introduction to the Apostolate Study, the Personnel Board had stated its purpose: to provide for the future direction of SCL ministries in light of the mission of the Church in the contemporary world and the goals and traditions of the Community. Given the exchange of reports and responses, given the largeness of hope or the realism of expectations, and given the responsibilities assigned to the apostolate representatives on the Personnel Board, at its conclusion participants in the study experienced a variety of reactions, ranging from feeling let down to feeling reassured. Some were simply perplexed. A perspective of thirty years allows for re-assessment of results.

Only six years had elapsed since the first Renewal Chapter, and the Apostolate Study had been mandated only months earlier by the second. Conditions created urgency: withdrawals continued, candidates were fewer, the median age of the sisters was rising, and morale in one of the Community's three original ministries was low. Pastors and parishes were waiting on news of a recommitment of sisters to staff their schools. Ideas for change and renewal in education were pouring in from too many sources too fast to adequately test their worth. Sisters themselves, in fulltime ministry, projected possibilities with no time to collaborate in their planning or to seek financial support. A study conducted in two months with another month for response allowed neither for sufficient sounding of constituents' satisfaction nor for the kind of continuing conversation in which questions and ideas can grow.

The sisters had just made their way through a discovery of how far apart they stood on matters of utmost importance and a determination to reconcile differences in order to remain who they were, all Sisters of Charity in one Community. The search for a common vision, they knew now, was to be a long one; to revitalize traditional ministries born of their charism and to find support for new ministries in a renewed way of living was beyond the reach of a study. But they tried. How they tried. More than 550 strong, they surveyed, conversed, brain-stormed, compared data, and condensed their conclusions in a rational form. And their representatives on the Personnel Board wrote, and wrote, and wrote again. All this is an achievement of the same order as that of their forebears who tackled impossible problems with the panache of pioneers who did not consider themselves or their situations extraordinary.

Beyond that fundamental accomplishment, the study yielded clear directions of the way they must continue the search: in closer company and conversation with one another on a continuing basis and in collaboration with colleagues and authorities who might not desire it or see its necessity. That was a built-in task of leadership for those who had to bring it off. They had then to probe the areas and parishes where they worked for the real needs and clearest suggestions of the people to whom they ministered or hoped to minister. They had to read, to imagine, and to re-imagine the alternatives to standard ways of organizing a curriculum, of handling oversized classes, of attending to the individual needs of the highest and the lowest and the middling achievers with challenges for each one. Student-centered learning and learning-centered schools and patient-directed health care with mounting costs and divided resources were challenges multiplying by the year, by the day.

Listening: A Priority for Leadership

Perhaps the greatest challenge lay hidden in the power of one: one idea, one voice, one group, one overwhelming problem. To release that power through structures of authority that remained largely the same even while modifications at the local level enlarged freedom of action was no obvious or simple task. Listening was the newly recognized art of the ministries of administration and governance. Trusting that one would be heard was the paradoxical attitude of genuine humility and self-respect. During their orientation to the roles assigned them during Vatican II, the people of God had gotten intimations of new responsibilities in the Church and for the Gospel that sisters, perhaps uniquely, might model in all simplicity.

Habits of mind are more difficult to change, however, than habits of action. A prudent and tried practice of waiting on others to experiment had to be tested against taking the initiative. Stewardship that had carried the Community so far could not, with any sort of reasoning or fact, be called self-interested, as some interpretations of simpler living suggested. Theories and practices of successful business did not take into acount the potential of individual women, proven leaders and effective followers. And full regard for the poor, boundless in number and a relentless presence, was the special heritage of daughters of Vincent, Louise, and Xavier. Commitment to their care and their partnership in action was the most powerful force of all.

The nation's Bicentennial was the perfect occasion for the Community's celebration of this passage in the search for a unifying vision. Little more than a century apart in their founding, the young country and a vigorous midwestern religious community had much in common: a heritage of pioneers who had re-created the frontier and horizons that stretched in new directions and across the globe. The Community had as many reasons to celebrate as it had members to claim.[24] The keynote for three days' gatherings was struck by Sister Nadine Foley, OP, in her paper, "Ministry and Leadership of Women Religious in the Church Today." Fragments of thoughts offered in original papers prepared for Heritage sessions, read thirty years later, are prophetic of what was to come in the lives of women religious.

Sister Nadine asked her audience to consider what had happened to the American dream that had been for many "so integral to our religious faith as to seem almost inseparable from it." Recent wars, global famine, unbridled exploitation of resources, the moral implications of developing technology, and the country's contributions to all of these had obscured that dream. Now, she told her listeners, "the Christian faith community is a people in mission.... If leadership is a need today it seems to me that women religious are uniquely qualified to exercise it for this kind of purpose."[25]

Sister Kathleen Wood brought life to that statement with her image of Mother Xavier: a woman "deeply and enthusiastically in love with God and His people. She lived her life as a simple daughter of the land." Her sense of humor seasoned a "marvelous balance of practicality and trust in Divine Providence."[26]

Pointing to the social sin hidden in structures that violate human dignity, stifle freedom, and impose gross inequality, Sister Marie de Paul Combo introduced the theme of freedom and justice. Because it facilitates individual acts of selfishness and thrives on the complicity of those who do not take responsibility for its effects, social sin, she said, is an evil that prophets must address. "In the Eucharist Jesus Himself calls His new people, His Body, to faithfulness.... We must respond in community...."[27]

Continuing the emphasis on justice, Sister Frances Russell cited corporate profits, military spending, and trade policies that have power, she said, to create or destroy life for millions "who are undernourished, ill housed, under-educated.... It is not enough to *have* a vision. The vision must come alive. If there is validity to a Church, a religious community, it must be because people therein can stand together, act together in regard to human life *and* the life beyond...."[28]

"The most exciting aspect of American Catholicism," declared Sister Mary Lenore Martin, "is the growth of religious communities.... I think it is important that our community came from the seed of American foundations, not from the transplanted European tradition.... The egalitarian tradition is too strong in American life to allow, for very long, a monarchial community structure to survive." She closed with a challenge: "If the community is to grow, to attract new members, it will be because each of us plays a heroic role in her own life style, and because we choose to be a community."[29]

Sister Mary Janet McGilley recalled the hour she stood on a rocky hillside above the Cuidad de Dios, the City of God, "marked off into dusty streets, strewn with shanties—the homes of 300,000 people" living outside a city in Peru. Told by city officials that the land could not be leveled as a site for more such homes, the farmers who had left their barren farms to seek a livelihood for their families "borrowed an earthmover and moved a mountain in one night." So, she said,

> If we are to be part of the future, we must identify, be one in the Spirit...with the have-nots, the young, the disenfranchised, the alienated, the seekers, the poor. Only in that root way will we, I think, be part of the future that will be delivered full-grown into other hands than ours and in another time. For us: a time of waiting, watching, preparing. An Advent time.... If only we believe more in what we already know, who we are and who we are together...in who He is in us. Then we could go about the humane business of moving mountains, just as surely as He said we could, just as surely as those Peruvian workers did....[30]

When Sister Mary Kevin, the Community director, closed the three days of reflection and celebration, she asked, "Will this gathering mark a watershed—a crucial turn in our history?" She pointed to the Community's strengths: the Word of God and the Bread of the Eucharist, a deepening spiritual life and hunger for prayer and solitude, the Sisters of Charity who preceded us, our saving sense of humor. "We...are more closely bonded, I believe, in our laughter than we would think." And the weaknesses:

- the loss of "former friends with whom we shared so much...";
- "the throes of governing ourselves in a new way...," uneven success with group government and unclear authority at the local level;
- the need to accept in faith "decisions made by those in leadership positions from a perspective that is uniquely theirs";
- the need to examine attitudes and practices of poverty "to see whether or not we continue to be credible"—the critique of a consumer society that we once were;
- the loss felt by many of "our sense of community"—a need to honor "our pledge to fidelity in community relationships."

"On balance," she concluded, "our strengths outweigh our weaknesses. So we look toward our ministry to a 'society gone random' as religious women, members of a Pilgrim Church."[31]

These were a few of the telling words of the summer of 1976. Four months later, on November 8, three days before the annual observance of Founders Day, Mother Mary Ancilla died. If any Sister of Charity of Leavenworth was to be identified by a singular quality, it was this handmaid of the poor. Asked to characterize leaders of the Community as they knew them, more than half the sisters who responded emphasized her compassion and deep love of the poor. Some perceived in her concern a personal affinity for those in need, an identification that went beyond commitment and devotion. After her death, the Community memorialized her dedication in the Mother Mary Ancilla Fund, a source for meeting unexpected needs of families or the housebound known to the sisters. The more immediate memorial lay in a personal memory recorded in the survey: "The poor wept at her funeral."

An intuitive kindness marked Mother's relationships with her sisters. Approachability, loving concern, and understanding were terms that described it; her listening, her fairness, and her unfailing respect characterized her actions. Many remembered the sisters' confidence in her stewardship and business acumen. A professional businesswoman before she entered the

Community, Mother Mary Ancilla was attentive to legal and financial requirements for stable growth. Years of volunteer social service produced what one sister called "groundedness" in the realities of life. Repeatedly, her sisters remarked on the wisdom and awareness that shaped her vision. In the spirit of Vincent, Mother expanded traditional services with carefully calculated risk. A natural leader, she evidenced what the Community sought in renewal—a "clear congruence between life and mission."[32]

In work like that of the Apostolate Study, women who led and formed community in the decade following Vatican II were of the sort that the Church and a significant portion of the world depended on. If at times perplexing or stubbornly determined, they were dedicated to the task at hand and bent on whatever the times and renewal required of them. One thing these particular women had decided for sure: they were in it together. The passions that moved them, at times into conflict, were for a past that in its essentials had to endure and for a future that needed to bring the power of community to the aid of the most vulnerable. The convictions they held would require distinguishing the relative value of externals from the one absolute: the call of the Spirit to women and men of faith to transform their world or that small part of it they could reach.

Theirs was a power they themselves did not think much about—nor had many women who had helped to civilize a frontier. To discover the new frontiers of their charity, these sisters recalled the words of Paul, writing to his Philippians: "that your love may increase ever more and more in knowledge and every kind of perception, to discern what is of value... confident of this, that the one who began a good work among you will bring it to completion by the day of Jesus Christ" (Phil 1:6).

CHAPTER 9

A Heritage of Care: Children and the Aging

The years between Renewal Chapters were not primarily a time of surveys and experiments and preparation. They were years of growth and expansion in traditional apostolates and of fruitful initiatives in both old and new ministries. That these initiatives occurred in long-established institutions was as much a sign of progress and renewal as any fresh undertaking.

It is important to realize that the changes in religious life that began in the 1960s did not constitute an abandonment of Catholic institutions, schools in particular, for the sake of individual ideals and motives. Rather, women religious continued traditions of ministering to the young, to the ill and aging, and to those uncared for by public agencies. The latter have always included a vast number of economically poor; physically, mentally, or culturally deprived; and those segregated by race, religion, criminal record, or other social stigma. In the story of the next few chapters, traditions continue and evolve in ways required by uncertain conditions; pioneers emerge where needs demand them; and the Spirit brings people together for purposes that erase lines of religious denomination, color, rank, or social acceptability.

Care for children in need has been a ministry of the Community since its founding. True to the heritage of Vincent and Louise's extraordinary mission in seventeenth-century Paris, Sisters of Charity of Leavenworth continued to care for youngsters in need of consistent parenting and special assistance. Mother Xavier's devotion to children gave impetus to her work first in Tennessee, then in Leavenworth, where an orphanage grew from her lodging homeless children. The first few lived in the cottage on Kickapoo Street. When they became too numerous for the space, room was made for them in the academy and later in St. John Hospital. A fair sponsored by Catholic and Protestant women of Leavenworth in the early 1860s raised $7,000, enough to build a two-story brick home, "with a good basement," on lots at 6th and Kickapoo opposite the academy. Blessed by Bishop Miege in 1866 as St. Vincent's Orphan Asylum, it served until 1885 with an average annual occupancy of about forty-five children. Not all facts about St. Vincent's were available to earlier Community historians; this account reaches into the century before 1955 to include them.[1]

To support the orphans and the Sisters of Charity who lived with them, the bishop began an association of lay people whose monthly allotment of twenty-five sous (roughly a quarter) was a principal source of income. Hundreds of members contributed. To add to the orphans' coffer, the two sisters assigned to care for the children took up dressmaking for women of the city, using *Godey's Lady's Book* as a guide to fashions.[2] Space for growing numbers of children prompted the move to the country in either 1885 or 1887 to a site "on a beautiful elevation, commanding a view of Leavenworth City and vast fertile farm lands." Provided by Bishop Thomas F. Lillis, the diocesan orphanage, still staffed by Sisters of Charity, stood on eighty acres of land once inhabited by the Muncie Indians. A farm, garden, and orchard extended from playgrounds that surrounded the four-story brick structure. With its three classrooms, chapel, infirmary, dining rooms, and dormitories it was home for approximately ninety children.[3]

In 1866, a portion of Leavenworth's citizens had not yet been assimilated into the population. As they got the schools, hospital, and orphanage under way, the sisters taught African American youngsters in Sunday school and housed children of both races. Though limited by segregation laws for the schooling of children, by 1872 the sisters were able to teach African American children in a small house opposite the convent on Kickapoo. Thirty-five girls and twenty-five boys made a substantial enrollment.

In 1877, when Father Martin Huhn established Holy Epiphany, the first Catholic church for Negroes west of St. Louis, the school was transferred from Kickapoo to the church basement. Sisters of Charity taught both Catholic and Protestant children there for ten or eleven years until Father Huhn obtained Oblate Sisters of Providence from Baltimore to tend to his orphans and pupils. Fourteen boys aged four to sixteen were their charges in the first Guardian Angel Orphanage for African American children at 22nd and Dakota. Sister Baptista Roberts, OSP, who was to spend the next fifty years in Leavenworth, took over the school; by the turn of the century its enrollment had topped one hundred.[4]

When the Oblate sisters and forty orphans moved to the country in 1899, their new home was an old farmhouse on forty acres of what had been the Whittier property. Without stove or electricity, they welcomed the cow given them by their neighbors, the Sisters of Charity, to provide milk for the boys. Later a calf and a hog provided much more. In 1905, a

Holy Epiphany Home for Girls opened. Over the next quarter century, additions and improvements made room for ninety orphaned girls and boys. Twenty Oblate sisters cared for them and also taught several hundred children. In 1947, when the Sisters of Charity moved their charges to St. Vincent's Home in Topeka, the Oblates moved Guardian Angel Orphanage into their former quarters. There they stayed until 1960. In seventy-two years, the Oblate Sisters of Providence had ministered to a growing parish and to some two thousand children.[5]

Between 1896 and 1945, twelve Oblate Sisters of Providence died and were buried in Mount Olivet Cemetery. Mother Xavier Ross was buried in April of 1895 directly opposite the grave of Sister Mary Gabriel who had died in February; the other eleven were buried in the row that the Oblate sisters came to call "our small green dormitory."[6]

For the Juneteenth Celebration in 1999, co-sponsored by the University of Saint Mary and the Richard Allen Cultural Center of Leavenworth, four Oblate Sisters of Providence were guests of the Sisters of Charity of Leavenworth and were publicly welcomed at the dedication of the city's first historical marker, commemorating the Community's seventy-two years of service there. In her remarks, Sister Sue Miller, Community director, alluded to the parchment copy of the 13th Amendment housed in De Paul Library on the campus and to the graves of the Oblate Sisters buried in Mount Olivet. All of these sisters, she said, "lived and worked and prayed and suffered and died in this community, serving the God and the children they loved. Surely, their lives can speak to us as powerfully as the 13th Amendment."[7]

The ceremony and events of the week that followed brought to life what mere records do not show. In the first city of "bloody Kansas," common sympathies and convictions between women religious and committed clergy, between these and believers of various denominations had done much to heal wounds and bridge divisions of race and religion, a goal that only many more years of care, education, neighborliness, and faith would achieve.

The population of St. Vincent's Home that necessitated the move to the Muncie land included thirty-three boys and thirty-six girls. Their schooling emphasized religious instruction and moral training, especially with respect for others' rights and practices of self-restraint. Responsibility came with assigned daily chores. Play was as important as work: each child had a sled for Kansas snow. The children's training in hygiene, physical and mental health, and social conduct was exemplary. Cleanliness and the daily bath were primary rules. As resources and information advanced, the children's health care included an annual physical examination and vaccinations.[8]

St. Vincent's Orphanage on Muncie land south of Leavenworth, 1885, successor to the first St. Vincent's Orphan Asylum on Kickapoo Street, 1866

The curriculum as well as the environment were organized according to state requirements and the Community's standards. They were such that St. Vincent's Home became a student-teaching laboratory in 1932 when Saint Mary College opened a four-year baccalaureate degree program. In return, residents of the Home had library privileges and use of recreational facilities in the college. In eighty-one years of service, between 1866 and 1947, when the diocese removed it to Topeka, the Home had sheltered and educated upwards of three thousand children. Until 1960, St. Vincent's Home provided residential care and schooling for nearly five hundred dependent children. Sister Rose Vincent Staten administered the Home from 1953.[9]

The late fifties and early sixties, however, marked radical changes in institutional care of the young. Parentless children were commonly placed by the court in foster families or relatives took them into their homes. Single-parent families frequently had special needs. Children emotionally or physically deprived by neglect required professional care. Coordination of services from public and private agencies became a necessity. As reported in a booklet published during the Year of the Child, 1979, St. Vincent's Home was affiliated with the National Conference of Catholic Charities, the Northeast Kansas Coalition of Children's Services, the Kansas Association of Licensed Private Child Care Agencies, and the University of Kansas School of Social Welfare. Licensed by the Maternal and Child Health Office, the Home was partially funded by a purchase-of-service agreement with the Kansas Department of Social and Rehabilitative Services. Financial support from the Archdiocese of Kansas City in Kansas came from the annual collection for orphans taken up in the parishes on Christmas Day.[10]

In 1967, Sister Frances Russell, MSW, became administrator of St. Vincent's Home in Topeka and worked to shape its program of services according to changing needs of troubled families. Referrals for service continued to come through the local Catholic Charities Office and both county and state Child Welfare Departments. The population at St. Vincent's Home included single children and sibling groups, as well as children from differing racial and religious backgrounds. To meet the needs of the children referred, additional program consultation was sought through the Child Psychiatry Program at the Menninger Foundation, the Social Work Program at Washburn University in Topeka, and the Special Education Department at the University of Kansas.

In 1970 thirty children, eighteen of them Catholic, received the equivalent of 8,800 days of care. Eight children were being prepared for foster home placement; ten were receiving individual psychiatric care; both individual and family counseling were provided by the social worker at the Home. Because of varying educational needs, children in residence attended twelve elementary or secondary schools in Topeka. Some resident children had emotional problems related to past parental neglect and abuse. Others lived with the insecurity associated with lack of family stability. Providing an emotional and social safety net to enable these children to heal and grow, then preparing them to leave the Home was the mission and the challenge of the staff at St. Vincent's.

St. Vincent's Home in Topeka, 1957

To best replicate and carry out models of child and adolescent group care, children were placed in appropriate age groups that normally included six to eight children. Two of the three child care groupings were designed for teen-age boys and girls and were located in separate wings of the building. These "departments" were usually filled to capacity, which the staff set at eight children. A major goal of each department was to help the child heal and grow through individual and group care. The main child care worker and assistants were responsible for the twenty-four-hour, day-to-day care of the children. To assist the staff and to accommodate the children, other resource persons, both volunteer and paid, were called on. Opportunities included participation in fine arts and in cultural and sports events, and education in life skills such as shopping, cooking, and driving. With increasing independence after the age of sixteen, youngsters graduated into group home facilities located in the city.[11]

According to a report to the general officers in 1971, the Sisters of Charity of Leavenworth contributed 20 percent of the total budget for St. Vincent's Home. This amounted to more than $100,000. Six Sisters of Charity and eight lay persons were employed full time. The sister staff included a full time administrator and social worker, four child care workers, and a special education teacher. The lay employees served in child care, education, and recreational services. A pediatrician and psychiatrist were staff consultants but were not on the payroll. The first lay board of directors, chosen from the Topeka area, was in place by 1973. Members served in an advisory capacity and assisted in planning.[12]

Change Imperative

Within the space of little more than a decade, the model of the diocesan orphanage had undergone a transformation. The women religious staffing homes now had acquired the education and certification necessary for a vastly different resident population. Admissions were determined by need and assignment, not by religious affiliation. Patterns of common care for large numbers had yielded to requirements of case management. Qualified lay staffing was essential. As with all such change, costs had mounted exponentially.

By the end of her term at St. Vincent's, Sister Frances Russell, with master's degrees in education and social work, had appeared before the state legislature to appeal for increased funding for the needs of residents. Her influence made itself felt on the boards of the Community Resource Council, Catholic Social Services, Inc., and the Topeka Chapter of Social Workers. She was chair of the Chapter's Committee on the Division of Professional Standards and of Shawnee County's Housing for Youth

Program. In 1973 she was elected president of the Kansas Association of Licensed Private Child Care Agencies. Other staff members exerted leadership on wide-ranging issues. In expanding social concerns, Sister Sheila Karpan supported the Native American community in its petitions for land rights. Sister Marie de Paul Combo participated in the Ecumenical Peace Seminar active in the Capital City.[13]

As announced in the diocesan newspaper in 1974, Sally Northcutt, MSW, succeeded Sister Frances as administrator of St. Vincent's Home. At that time, the staff included thirteen full-time and seven part-time workers. Six Sisters of Charity remained at St. Vincent's: Sisters Marie Noel Bruch, Marilyn Page, Susan Yerkich, and Antonella Gonzales in child care; Sister Mary Arthel Cline, social worker; and Sister Therese Bangert, teacher. Sister Rita Marie Anderson spent mornings in a special education classroom for children with specific learning disabilities.

In the early eighties, Sister Mary William Sullivan, Daughter of Charity, became administrator of St. Vincent's Home. She hoped to continue the services needed by the children and their families and to generate long-term financial support. Within a short time, however, archdiocesan authorities decided to discontinue the residential program; the Home was closed in the fall of 1983. Among the factors that led to this decision were a growing ambivalence regarding assumption of responsibility for the treatment of children who were public wards and the difficulty of obtaining committed qualified personnel.[14] A largely lay salaried staff, a smaller number of sisters with specialized training, and a population of children and adolescents assigned by civil agencies and in need of highly individualized treatment were components of child care no longer encompassed by a traditional concept of the Catholic orphanage. The vision and commitment needed for professional group care of children was to take new forms in the decades that followed.

Those who ministered at St. Vincent's Home in its final decades continued in leadership roles in social work and teaching. Sister Marie Noel Bruch received recognition in Montana for beginning the state's Open Adoption Program for Children and continuing its work for a quarter-century. Sister Rita Marie Anderson was named Outstanding Teacher of the Year in Kansas for her work with children with learning disabilities. Sister Susan Yerkich developed innovative mathematics programs for junior high students in Lawrence, Kansas. Sister Sheila Karpan designed a model social service program for Latino families at Annunciation School and for other Denver schools. Sister Mary Arthel Cline pioneered the Mother-to-Mother Program in Kansas. Marilyn Page earned a doctorate in social work before being named director of Marian Clinic in Topeka, where Sister Therese Bangert was a tireless advocate in the state legislature for families in poverty.[15]

Homeless children in Helena, Montana, were the stimulus for equally collaborative efforts once the sisters began to house them. In 1881, a father from Butte brought his small children, whose mother had died, to the sisters at St. John's Hospital. Without facilities for their care, two sisters stayed with the children in a small building in the hospital yard. The makeshift orphan's home acquired forty homeless infants before Mother Mary Josephine, then superior and administrator at St. John's, made moves to build St. Joseph's Orphanage in the Prickly Pear Valley on land part gift and part purchase from the Jesuits in Helena. Contributions from the town's businessmen made groundbreaking possible in 1892.

Expanding the Family

Ready the next year, St. Joseph's provided for orphans and children from broken homes with no criterion except need. It was the first facility of its kind in the territory of Montana. Standing on 220 acres—most of them under cultivation—and equipped with play and study rooms, the Home housed infants, toddlers, and school-age children who were enrolled at St. Mary's parochial school in town. More than two hundred residents left no room for another hundred in need of shelter and care. With necessary contributions and loans, the sisters expanded St. Joseph's in 1903 to include a three-story schoolhouse, laundry, bakery, dairy barn, garages, swimming pool, and larger living space. Twelve years later, in 1915, twelve infants were transferred to a former bishop's residence that became

Original St. Joseph's Orphans Home, Helena, Montana

the St. Ann Infant Home. Before the earthquake of 1935, the Home had offered care to 460 infants.[16]

Historical documents record that at the time of the continuing earthquakes in October of that year, twelve sisters, thirty-three boys, and fifty girls lived in St. Joseph's Home. That no life was lost in the original disaster witnessed to the providential care of God and to the swift and courageous action of sisters and children alike. Older boys carried toddlers to safety; the sisters bore infants and directed the children's steps in darkness down the stairs that remained, past exposed wires and fallen brick. The barn was a refuge that night, while three patrolmen who came to the rescue sent out word of the children's need.

Families opened their homes; thirty infants were carried to the rectory and moved into St. John's Hospital the next day. Empty Northern Pacific coaches on sidings in the railroad yards served as temporary lodgings. Within days, two heated buses provided by Intermountain Bus Lines transported sisters and children to Boulder Hot Springs to live as guests in a hotel owned by Senator Joseph E. Murray. By March, the standing portion of the Home was made safe for occupancy with room for eighty-five children. Quite a few youngsters were adopted before the move took place.[17]

Orphaned infants and the children of single mothers previously admitted to St. Ann Infant Home were now transferred to a special department of the Community's St. Joseph's Hospital in Deer Lodge. The people of Deer Lodge welcomed their new charges and the hospital kept for them the name of St. Ann Infant Home. Ten years later, in 1946, Holy Child Nursery opened for daytime services at St. John's Hospital in Helena. Children from two to six years of age received care and prekindergarten training from eight to five daily.[18]

On its sixtieth anniversary in 1941, St. Joseph's Home had ninety-four children enrolled, with more than four thousand in its history of care.[19] Its school for the orphans had been accredited by the State Board of Education and received a Superior rating in 1938. Its teachers held elementary life certificates. In the 1940s, however, as Social Security was providing aid for parentless children in homes and foster parents were multiplying, occupancy declined. The school closed and its students were transported daily to Helena's schools. Only an accident of the Cold War prevented the Home's closing earlier. At the beginning of Fidel Castro's regime in Cuba, parents sought placement for their school-age children in North American homes and academies. Sister Mary Claude Templeman obtained permission from Mother Leo Frances and Bishop Raymond Hunthausen to admit fourteen Cuban children, along with five North American girls, into the diocesan Home.

By 1963, the number enrolled reached forty-six, the majority Cuban refugees. As Cuban children in the States were reunited with their families, however, the number of residents at St. Joseph's Home rose and fell between seventeen and twenty-seven; by the end of 1964 it was twenty-two. In April of 1965, Mother Leo Frances and Bishop Hunthausen, in consultation, decided to close the Home; Sister Mary Claude was asked to delay announcement of the close until July. She also faced the formidable task of placing the children then living at the Home with adoptive or foster families. With this closing, the Sisters of Charity ended eighty-four years of institutional child care in Helena.[20]

A Home for Boys

Mount St. Vincent's Home in Denver has a long and dramatic history as the only home for children owned and operated by the Sisters of Charity of Leavenworth. The twofold dream of Bishop Joseph Machebeuf was fulfilled when both a hospital and a home for children opened early in the 1880s. A fire in 1902 that destroyed much of the structure and all records of 247 children housed in St. Vincent's Orphanage had major consequences. Because existent homes could welcome the girls, only boys returned to the rebuilt but reduced quarters. In thirty years of operation from 1902, Mount St. Vincent's was home to almost four thousand boys.[21]

A home for infants, named in succession St. Ann's, the Baby Annex, and Holy Child Nursery, provided for the youngest orphaned children with resources from St. Joseph's Hospital. By 1957 in its new location, admissions to Holy Child had topped 2,000 with more than 1,200 adopted. Accepted from all hospitals and maternity homes in Denver, ten to twelve infants were cared for at a time; from seventy to seventy-five were adopted each year. Catholic Charities conducted the study of prospective parents; a social worker interviewed each couple and investigated home conditions. A six-month trial period preceded the final adoption process. "No effort is too painstaking," wrote one of the sister staff, "no work too exhausting" to insure a safe and suitable placement for each child. In 1960 alone, 235 unmarried mothers applied to Catholic Charities for assistance in placing their child.[22]

St. Joseph's building program, begun in 1961, brought the nursery to a close, with plans to provide in the new hospital treatment for infants in need of specialized care. The youngest infants went to the diocesan Infant of Prague nursery; older babies went to St. Vincent's Home, the only Catholic facility that continued to offer residential care for boys. In Phase I of the Home's post-fire history, the children, who ranged from infants

Suited up for a game, St. Vincent boys get extra coaching from a visiting football veteran.

to fourteen-year-olds, had been orphaned by death or abandonment, had single parents unable to manage their care, or came from a farm family wanting a Catholic education for their boy. In the late 1940s, the population reached a peak of 125 children. To accommodate growth, two wings were added in 1958. In 1968 the cost was still but three dollars a day.[23]

The sisters' discipline of the boys was kin to a mother's care. Testimony comes from many who experienced it. One of the sisters described the time Sister Frances Floersch, superior at the Home from 1944 to 1950 and for three years in the 1960s, washed the feet of a runaway before sending him to bed. She knew they must be "worn from walking all those miles." A twenty-seven-year-old man, sorry to have caused her such trouble, told the story. Sister Jean Patrice (Jacquelyn) Kreuger described the delicate balance required for the care of children bearing "battle scars of beatings and broken hopes.... Somehow we must try to be the cure for all the heartaches which they bring. Yet, from the moment they come, we are preparing them to leave."[24]

But the Sisters also knew that boys need a father or at least a father-figure. With the cooperation of the Jesuit staff of nearby Regis College, they initiated a College Boy Program whereby students earned their board by relieving the sisters part-time in the junior and senior departments of eleven-to-fourteen-year-olds. They took over the athletic program and planned entertainment for all ages. A Big Brother program brought Regis sophomores who chose little brothers and worked with them individually on homework and with any problem the child confided to them. A social worker at Catholic Charities, under whose auspices the Home functioned, called the sisters at St. Vincent's "one of the most professional groups of individuals with whom I have ever worked."[25]

From 1961 to 1965, Sister Daniel Stefani was administrator of the Home and principal of its school. Then after securing a master's degree in social work from the University of Denver, she spent two years at the Kennedy Center for developmentally disadvantaged children at Saint John's Hospital and Health Center in Santa Monica before returning to St. Vincent's. Having studied carefully the complex needs of children, especially in the Denver area, Sister Daniel asked in 1969 that St. Vincent's become an institution with professional staff for the care of emotionally disturbed children, both boys and girls. The General Council studied the evidence she brought, inquired into conditions and costs, staffing, resources, and legal implications, and approved the conversion. It was at once a vote of confidence in Sister Daniel's vision and an investment in children's care fraught with risk and unpredictability.

Sister Daniel Stefani and residents greet a newcomer to the family of Mount St. Vincent's Home in Denver.

Transformation of a Home

Phase II of the Home's history began in 1970 when Sister Daniel began to secure and administer grants that transferred the Home into a residence designed to assist disturbed youngsters, boys and girls, to function in a unit. Three cottages were built and licensed to house thirty-six children, aged six to fourteen; they lived in units of twelve each, two for boys and one for girls. The program involved parents and other family members. Richard Saucier, MD, child psychiatrist, established a beneficial relationship for the Home with the Northwest Mental Health Clinic. Charles Dallas of Catholic Charities worked full time with the program. St. Anne's Lodge, opened in 1976, was a mountain getaway for children and staff built on land given by the Mary Dower Foundation, with funds provided by Anne Straub.[26]

Under a contract with the County Social Services for funded care and education, children were referred by the county department, by psychiatric departments of local hospitals, and by family physicians. Special education was funded by contract with the State Department of Education in classrooms made available by the Denver public school system. As principal of the Home's school, Sister Mary Rachel Flynn administered the program. Residents and day students attended grades one through eight. A daytime therapeutic pre-school accommodated children from three to five. In the early 1980s, renovations provided a spacious dining room, a recreation room and gymnasium, and tile flooring laid by a man who had been reared at the Home.[27]

Sister Daniel's staff credited her with a spirit and style of administration that endeared her to residents and employees alike. The children knew her in every facet of their lives. She comforted them in grief or illness, played their games with evident enjoyment, ran the dishwasher and cleaned a floor with the best of them. Sister herself attributed the climate of the Home to her staffs over the years. Five in particular, from 1954 into the 1990s and beyond, ministered at the Home: Sisters Mary Gerald (Roberta) Furey, Mary Anselma (Josephine) Bustos, Michael Joseph (Ann) Moylan, Jean Marion Rilinger, and Antonella Gonzales.

In 1979, Sister Daniel and Sister Roberta with four residents of the Home participated in an exchange program sponsored by Sheseido Foundation of Tokyo. Commemorating the International Year of the Child, twenty-one Denver children from three homes traveled to Japan for a two-week tour to promote cultural and professional understanding. A documentary, "Every Child Has a Beautiful Name," was telecast on Channel 9 in Denver.[28]

Under the Community's sponsorship, in 1983 the corporate board of the Home named Sister Daniel its administrator, soon to be executive director. Another decade of service to the Denver area established St. Vincent's as a primary child care institution in the state of Colorado. Every resource that could assist the staff to enable the children to live naturally in a family environment was available. Weekly consultation with the staff psychiatrist was complemented by native common sense and habitual prayer.

One sister recalled an incident in her primary classroom of several six-, seven-, and eight-year-olds. A new boy came in late because—as she learned later—he had caused such a row in the unit when told it was time for school. On arrival, he yelled, "I ain't going to learn. You can't teach me!" and plopped himself on the floor. Sister simply said, "Okay." Then she took all the things out of his desk. The children were playing a knowledge-game, clearly enjoying themselves. Shortly, the boy crawled up to the teacher and asked to play.

One of three cottages, home to twelve residents of Mount St. Vincent's Home

At another time, the testing of authority was crucial. An aide was trying to calm down C.B., who was causing a problem in the hall. In reaction, the boy jumped up on the stairwell banister which overlooked a three-story drop. Another aide rushed for help from a sister in a nearby classroom. With a prayer for the right words, she went out and announced to the child, "C.B., you have not finished your work. Get in there and finish it!" Climbing down, he did.[29]

On the 110th anniversary of St. Vincent's in 1993, Sister Daniel received the Service Award at Regis High School's first annual Ignatian Dinner. The diocesan newspaper recognized St. Vincent's continuum of services that provided as far as possible for children in special need a natural family situation. It reported forty-five resident students and twenty day students at the Home, all referred by court order, state agencies, hospitals, and public, private, and parochial schools. By this time the Ryan Home in Lakewood, a Denver suburb, had extended St. Vincent's services to boys, eleven to fifteen, in a supervised community-based program.[30]

The Holy Father, John Paul II, blessed St. Vincent's with his visit to the Home on August 15, 1993. In its coverage of the event, *The Rocky Mountain News* acknowledged Sister Daniel's leadership of a staff of seventy-five in a non-denominational treatment center. Two years later, as Sister Daniel retired after thirty-four years of service to Mount St. Vincent's, the Community honored her with an endowment for the Home.[31]

Sister Daniel's untimely death in September of 2003 followed on a period of service in Billings, Montana, as outreach director at St. Vincent's Hospital. That fall she was to return to St. Vincent's Home in Denver to begin writing its history. The account of her work in Billings published at her death ran under the headline, "Advocate of Poor Dies in Denver."

At her retirement party, Sister Daniel receives greetings from Michael Durkin and his young son.

Sister Daniel's advocacy at state offices and the legislature, her name on state and regional boards, and her periodic visits to city hall in Denver during three decades were legendary—and effective. The most valuable testimonials were notes from the children at St. Vincent's thanking her for serving them breakfast, assuring her of their love, and chiding her for leaving them.[32]

SPECIAL CARE FOR THE AGING

Mount St. Joseph's Home, Kansas City, Kansas, 1946

In 1945, when the Community accepted from Archbishop Paul Schulte the challenge of transforming the old Grandview Sanitarium into a home for the aged, Sister Hypatia Coughlin asked Sister Mary Adolph Scheule to help her begin the job. Sister Mary Jane Wilson, artist and craftswoman, and nine others helped prepare common spaces and individual rooms to accommodate varying levels of care. A year later, over the early months of operation, Sisters of Charity welcomed forty-eight women and men to Mount St. Joseph's on a landscaped twenty-six-acre campus. It was the first home of its kind in Kansas to be served by Red Cross volunteers. The chapel and a resident chaplain were available to all, whatever their religious affiliation.[33]

Late in the 1960s, one of the Home's guests asked Sister Mary Adolph to accompany her on a trip to Europe; it was to be a gift for Sister's golden jubilee. Her need of a passport initiated a fruitless search for birth or baptismal record. Although she had voted regularly, Sister discovered—with the help of the immigration office—that she was not a United States citizen. Sister remembered only that as a girl of eight she had come with her family from Germany on the "Queen Maria." Worse than the wartime blackouts at sea in 1917, she remembered the seasickness that took the life of her baby brother Gerard, who was buried at sea.

The family's sorrow and lack of knowledge of English during internment at Ellis Island were compounded by an incomplete address for Adoph Schuele's brother Karl, their sponsor. A place called Kansas City was all they knew. Contacting German-speaking citizens there, immigration officials found a man who had gone to school with Karl, Father Herman J. Koch. The Schueles soon found themselves on a forty-acre farm outside Atchison, Kansas. It was to be their family home; reunion and welcome hard work blotted out all thought of citizenship papers. Fifty-two years later, Sister Mary Adolph passed the test and took the oath that formally made her the good citizen she had been all her life.[34]

Sisters Mary Adolph Schuelle and Agnes Ann Kneib pause to chat with a resident of Mount St. Joseph's.

According to testimony in the Community's apostolate survey of 1975, the Home gave witness to the dignity of life in the staff's methods of care for its residents, leaving as many decisions as possible to them. In their evaluation of the Home's facilities, Social Rehabilitation Services (SRS) rated St. Joseph's as nearest to the level of skilled nursing and total care of all such homes in northeastern Kansas, though it was licensed only for intermediate nursing care. SRS cited the Home's coordinated plan of care, occupational and physical therapy facilities, psychological and social services, lab and X-ray facilities, nursing and physicians' services, dietary and pharmaceutical services, spiritual opportunities, and program of daily activities.[35]

By the late 1970s, handicaps were limited space and income, costs of consultants and services, and necessary training of personnel. Of the residents, 42 percent were on Medicaid; all were on a fixed income. Receiving no archdiocesan funds, the Home was dependent on the state for reimbursement. That source left 22 percent of daily costs to be made up by donations. As director, Sister Mary Adolph conducted fund-raisers that involved residents and the Friends of St. Joseph's Auxiliary. With its over-65 population reported at 11 percent, the Church in Wyandotte County faced a challenge in care for the aging that every diocese shared.[36]

In 1978 the Archdiocese of Kansas City in Kansas assumed ownership of Mount St. Joseph's, renaming it St. Joseph's Nursing Care Center with Sister Mary Adolph its director; Sister Mary Brost, pastoral care minister; and Sister Mary Kenneth Messina, activities coordinator. In 1983 the facility was relocated to the renovated building that had housed St. Margaret's Hospital. There, not only the elderly of the archdiocese but also homeless and runaways with no other recourse found a welcome, food and shelter, care, and new personal dignity. Soon after her sixtieth jubilee, Sister Mary Adolph received the Community Leadership Award made annually by the Community Development and Housing Department of Kansas City, Kansas. In the presentation, she was acknowledged as "the last, best hope for the city's destitute."[37]

As residents multiplied, Sister Mary Adolph urged the need for new quarters and additional staff. In 1999, after a study of demographic statistics and projected needs, Archbishop James P. Keleher approved the facility's move to a vacated nursing home in nearby Olathe. Villa St. Francis opened as a long-term care and skilled nursing facility. Sister Mary Kenneth Messina remains on the staff; Sisters Mary and Mary Adolph retired to the Mother House in 2004. At the age of ninety, Sister Mary Adolph had served the senior citizens of Wyandotte County for more than sixty years.[38]

The ministry of caring for and educating children transformed itself in many ways when the Community established its South American missions, the first in 1963. In Talara at Santa Rosa parish, Sister nurses opened a clinic for expectant mothers and immunization of children in addition to home health visiting and social work. Others taught in the schools and trained lay catechists for religious instruction. Sister Agnes Klein, principal, continued to build a native faculty. By 1970, faced with a pressing need to teach in fiscal or government schools where religion was a required subject, the sisters relinquished the school to lay administrators. In 1971 three Sisters of Charity joined the pastor of San Fernando parish in Chalaco. Sisters Florence (Catherine) Nichol and Blanche Marie Remington came up to the mountain village from Talara to teach the children and conduct pastoral ministry in a *communidad de base*, the base community formed by villages attached to Chalaco. Sister Marie James Simms, RN, traveled from the States to open a parish clinic and administer health care. In this new mission they were to receive help from unexpected and distant benefactors.[39]

Mission in the Midlands

When a parish in the Midlands of England wished to adopt a parish in the Third World, their pastor, Monsignor H. F. Davis, told parishioners what he had learned about Chalaco and the Sisters of Charity of Leavenworth from Bishop John McNabb, primate of the Diocese of Chulucanas in northern Peru. It was a village of two hundred families with fifty more villages of thirty to sixty families each reached by mule, the farthest of them

Hermana Clorinda Timana rides past San Fernando Church in the town of Chalaco on her way to a mission down the mountain.

six or seven travel hours from Chalaco. The region had recently been devastated by an earthquake.[40] Beginning in 1971, the parishioners of St. Gregory in Birmingham raised enough funds from morning coffees, white elephant jumbles, concerts, and garden fetes to send an annual check amounting to $1,000 for the mission. Some years they sent more. Agnes Robin led the initial projects, which generated thousands of dollars by 1986 when the project continued for a short time in an adjoining parish.

Sister Mary Liguori Horvat, area councilor for the Latin American missions from 1974 to 1980, carried on a lively correspondence with her English friends for more than a quarter of a century. Agnes Robin, her son Ernest and his wife Polly, Angela and John Maguire, Anna Browning and her daughters, the Shaws, the Plummers, and others gathered as much as $3,600 in a given year for Chalaco. Besides personal contributions, biannual sales of hand-woven apparel and costume jewelry, children's clothing, recycled cards and gifts, and homemade cakes, jams, marmalades, and chutneys drew increasing numbers.[41] Sisters in the missions sent grateful letters about their people and their work. The rare intercontinental friendship has grown stronger by the year, as the triangular "Midlands Connection" brings substantial benefits to a Peruvian village, benefits that the benefactors can only imagine.

Today, the Chalaco parish mission is staffed by Sister Ruth Reischman and Hermanas Esther Vilela Gutierrez, Julia Huiman Ipanique, and Deidy Abad Pulache. The mission is one of the Chulucanas diocese's sixteen parishes, each of which includes from 35 to 110 villages along the coast and in the mountains. This was the first diocese to adopt the Better World Movement for the religious and social education of its nine thousand native people. Chalaco is also one of six parish centers where sisters and laity teach in a monthly School for Women or School for Families. Emphasis on women's roles in the home and family structure gradually affects the traditionally machoistic culture. Husbands now attend school sessions

A Heritage of Care: Children and the Aging

with their wives and prepare the main meal each day. Trained native teams plan the liturgy or prayer service and conduct social ministry for youth. This is the mission that a parish in the Midlands of England joined as a partner almost thirty-five years ago.[42]

Homes for deeply distressed youth, ministry to families in both Americas, and residences for aging women and men without independent resource bear eloquent witness to faith in Providence and persistence in preserving the dignity of the powerless. The ministry is subject to social change and responsive to the most demanding professional standards. It yields a story of commitment to life: welcoming the unwelcome from birth and those declining into death; crossing borders of culture and condition; bridging the gap between those without means and those wanting to share whatever means they have. Mother Xavier's coming to Kansas, along with fifteen other women and four orphan girls, was a journey into mission territory that grew to a heritage of undiscriminating and unstinting care.

CHAPTER 10

The Care of Teaching

In the Community's heritage of education, the ministry of teaching has been the personal care of more than 1,100 sisters, or approximately 56 percent of all, up to the present, who have taken vows in the congregation.¹ From their founding in 1858, the Sisters of Charity of Leavenworth opened or staffed eighty-nine elementary schools, all but twelve of them undertaken in the first century of the Community's history. For various reasons, including diocesan finances and a fluctuating frontier, the Community had withdrawn from twenty-five of these schools between 1873 and 1960.² During the next thirty years, the disposition of Catholic elementary schools took different directions depending on variant winds of change: shifting populations within cities, moves to suburbs and out of rural communities resulting in shifting enrollments; a temperamental national economy; new priorities in religious education; and differing views on the efficacy of Catholic schools. A significant factor was the diminishing number of sisters to staff them; hiring lay replacements put an unprecedented strain on parish budgets. Pastors and parishioners had to think about their schools in new ways.

The story, however, is more complex than simple facts can make it. No single interpretation can do justice to that complexity, but one thing is clear: the evolution of Catholic education over the last fifty years represents deep change that has only begun. The mission of Catholic schools for the century preceding the Second Vatican Council was to nurture the growth of faith in generations of children whose ancestors were for the most part European immigrant parents. The means were familiar: training in the basic subjects necessary for human welfare and responsible citizenship and careful catechizing in the beliefs that prepare one for the sacramental life of a Catholic. It was a mission for pioneers in a country just growing out of missionary status in the Church. The women who staffed these schools turned pioneering into a profession both respected and adapted to conditions of American parochial life. Their frontiers advanced as schools opened by the hundreds and as educational theory and methods developed by the decade.

Thousands of young Catholic women were attracted to this way of life, and growing religious communities were able to staff the schools almost as soon as pastors and bishops appealed to them. The blessings of volume meeting the pace of demand, however, were not unmixed. The Sisters of Charity of Leavenworth shared in burgeoning numbers both of applicants and of staffing requests. The Community's procedures for mission assignments were comparable to those of most religious congregations: observation by superiors during initial formation of a young woman's talents and temperament, and consultation with the supervisor of schools about personnel needs of each school. Completion of course work for a degree, when the sister had not graduated from college, was relegated to summer study.

Into the 1960s, elementary school principals usually taught an upper grade and were responsible for the effectiveness of five to twenty teachers. Students in classes might number forty to fifty; sixty in a primary grade with a veteran teacher was not considered outrageous. Until the practice changed in 1968, the make-up of a given faculty was uncertain before August 15 when each sister received her mission assignment from the mother general. From that year forward, decisions about changes were communicated to principals and pastors in the spring; gradually a measure of stability was assured with three-year assignments. This did not eliminate for some the prospect of a new teacher coming from the novitiate equipped with college courses but with little if any classroom experience.

Mentoring provided by practiced teachers, like Sisters Mary Philippa Rock and Charlotte Marie Howell, in reading, phonics, and classroom environment virtually saved many young sisters from despair. Little other recourse was at hand for a teacher unsuited to the classroom. If a problem persisted, complaint from a principal might bring a change of assignment. These were the hazards of growth and response to need out of a working structure that changed from within, though not without cost, in two brief decades.

First steps in the process began with the Community's adoption in 1968 of the Sister Formation Program for degree-completion before teaching assignments. Although Sister Rose Dominic Gabisch, dean of the college's Graduate Division, was executive secretary of the organization, that did not guarantee full participation in a program that would withdraw sisters from the schools for full-time study. Repeated appeals from the Community's leading educators reached an urgency in the first Renewal Chapter of 1968–1969 that finally overcame opposition and doubts. Between 1969 and 1973, 119 elementary teachers had earned their baccalaureate degree with majors in professional education.[3]

Meanwhile Vatican II had wrought long-term effects on the teaching of religion in the schools. Addressing the people of God, the council had called the laity to full participation in the mission of the Church. However others saw them, sisters were fully aware that they were of that laity. The Gospel that inspired their way of life was proclaimed by the council as a mandate for Catholic teachers to strive for justice for the poor and oppressed of the world. Educated insight into scripture and doctrine was to guide the writers of religious texts. Along with deeper understanding of the human person and the ranges of intelligence, the principles of developing post–Vatican II theology were to transform the teaching of religion. The same forces were influencing sisters to look beyond the classroom to pervasive needs for adult religious education and to parents as the primary religious educators of their children.

Seven years after the council in 1972, the bishops of the United States issued a pastoral letter, "To Teach as Jesus Did," that mandated specific programs in education to justice for all Catholic schools. The Community's response was thoroughgoing. Principals with their faculties adapted suggested curricula to their local situations, teachers developed imaginative methods and materials, and students were engaged in projects that took them into their communities. Assessment of the program after early implementation revealed that a sense of community and respect for human dignity inspired a strong emphasis on service.

Comprehension of other cultures, however, as well as motivation for leadership and understanding of racial and ethnic prejudice were slower to come.[4] The realization of justice in the salary schedule of lay Catholic teachers and staff was a goal just as vital but even more difficult to achieve. Parallel to this intrinsic change in Catholic religious education was the depletion of personnel by a gradual but steady withdrawal of sisters into other ministries or out of religious life. Raises in tuition, due to budgeting for increased lay staffing, contributed to falling enrollments that in the 1970s afflicted the nation's schools.[5] Other factors included parents' and educators' questions about how best to nurture faith in the young. As renewal affected assignments, discernment reinforced continuity in some missions, depleted staffing in others.

The tensile thread that connects all the evolutions within the Catholic school system is a philosophy exemplified in the mission of education expressed in the Constitutions of the Sisters of Charity of Leavenworth. In the chapter on Mission, the Community proclaims:

> *In all our ministries we see Christian education as one of the great acts of charity: serving others at the fullest points of their needs and ministering*

> to their need to know and come to truth, to be opened to the good and the
> beautiful, to understand the past, to confront and help shape the future, to
> be called to justice, to be more fully and completely human and Christian.[6]

This is the ideal. The struggle to fully realize it underlies the changes recorded here. Selection of schools for specific consideration derives from (1) emerging patterns of the way dioceses and parishes negotiated change, (2) priorities of the Community's educational mission as it developed in the schools, and (3) examples of particular strength in transitions to lay leadership.

In 2003, a former lay administrator of the coordinated system of Catholic schools in a city served by the Community since its foundation defined the Catholic educational mission as central to the mission of the Church in the world. In a new era, he said, the administrator must motivate the strengthening of relationships between the school's lay staff and the diocesan owner and among pastors, parishioners, parents, and the sisters who first opened or staffed the schools.[7] Such relationships nurture strong leadership and collaboration. From these, this layman said, comes the vision that conceives of new forms for religious education within school and family, realizes necessary roles of the laity, and consistently re-creates the original mission.

Almost thirty-five years earlier, Father Harold P. Arbanas, superintendent of schools for the diocese of Great Falls, Montana, had insisted on the strength of just such relationships for the quality of a school system. The first question to ask, he said, is whether what we have to offer "is altogether unique, completely special, that nobody else has." Behind that lies the question of who the decision-makers are in the parish, the school board, and the diocese and among the parents and the women religious who staff the school. Then he made a significant point that prefaces the story of schools staffed by the Sisters of Charity of Leavenworth. In a decision-making process often frustrated by duplications and inaccuracies, he speculated that "perhaps the one group that is really free...is the sisters." Not that they could move independently of the diocese, the parish, or the people, but that they were best qualified "to step out and say, 'This is what it has to be.'" He believed that people would pay and volunteer for "undertakings that are truly vibrant, and creative, and new, and touch life as it is right now."[8]

Stories of the schools suggest that Sisters of Charity initiated change in curricular programs and educational environments as priorities of ministry and professional developments required. A clear priority was always service to those most in need. If mergers were an economic necessity, they also required the highest degree of collaboration with parents and pastors. Changes in religious life opened the way to cooperation with public agencies; a natural partnership with the lay women and men on school staffs took new forms. In most cases that partnership grew from its beginnings in the 1940s and 1950s to a strength that became a transfer of leadership at various times in the last quarter of the century. Hidden within that transfer was the quality of education that developed in the sixty-five parochial schools staffed in 1960 by approximately 360 Sisters of Charity of Leavenworth in nine states and twelve dioceses and archdioceses.[9]

Forty years before assessment became the watchword of educators from pre-school through university, alert superintendents in diocesan offices and school supervisors in religious communities were devising strategies for evaluating the work of teachers and learners. A manual created in the mid-sixties by a team of educators including Sister Mary Sarah Fasenmeyer assisted the process. *The Criteria for Evaluation of Catholic Elementary Schools* guided principals in reviewing with their teachers everything from curriculum to faculty meetings, with special emphasis on pedagogical methods. Sister Joseph Cecila (Mary Ann) Gausz, superintendent in Kansas City–St. Joseph, then in Helena, Montana, introduced the ungraded primary coupled with individualized instruction. Ungraded skills courses at all levels preceded the open classroom common in the 1970s and 1980s. Methods of teaching reading and spelling affected texts and ultimately educational theory. What was natural to the ways of the mind survived difficulties and influenced other fields. The "new math" and "new science" and the inquiry method introduced in the social sciences exemplified the process.

What waited on long-term outcomes, like the renewed teaching of religion, depended on what could be assessed only a decade and more later in maturing students' and adults' understanding and practice of their faith. A religion program that showed great promise was the primary series called "Come to the Father." Involving parents through workshops on the way their children were learning the story of salvation was a key to the program's effectiveness.[10] Insistence that every child have the chance to realize potential was the teacher's and the school's responsibility. That was the motive for fund-raising and for collaborating with the public system.

Title I allowed St. Joseph School in Grand Junction, Colorado, to hire faculty and expand technology for small-group work with Hispanic children whose learning had been impeded by disabilities, the difficulties of a second language, or interrupted schooling. A curriculum coordinator praised the interaction between public and parochial schools under the Title I program. Inner cities were prime territory for the individualized instruction that dramatically facilitated learning and followed from teachers' in-service, principals' leadership, and available grants. St. Louis School in Kansas City, Missouri, was overflowing its classroom space in 1954 with an enrollment of 450. Ten years later, parish families were less than half what they had been and the school's racial integration was at risk. A nongraded program with enrichment courses and peer tutoring were structures that allowed students to learn from and with one another and teachers to tailor instruction to individual needs. The goal was the same, whether in an inner city school of 260 or in a school with more than 1,000 at St. Daniel the Prophet in Chicago.[11]

DEMANDS OF JUSTICE

If principals and faculties were enterprising, that did not reduce the dilemmas that faced supervisors and superintendents. Sister Gregory (Eileen) Sheehy, supervisor of elementary education in the Kansas City–St. Joseph diocese, and Sister Marie de Paul Combo in the Kansas City, Kansas, diocese had to design programs that fit both the two-room school and the suburban plant, provide resources for the culturally deprived child and the spiritually hungry one, and aim at equity between under-funded and affluent parochial systems.[12] Justice was a complex affair. If teachers had a penchant both for apt pupils and for those deprived of basic conditions for learning, they also had to awaken the indifferent or bored and to motivate the underachiever or the unchallenged. There was no question of leaving any one of them behind.

Those motivations and innovations inspired Sisters Virginia Flanick and Anna Mary Lawrence, each of whom had spent about half a century teaching first grade. Sister Anna Mary taught for twenty years at Sacred Heart and in the Xavier Elementary School System in Leavenworth before returning to her home parish, Blessed Sacrament in Kansas City, Kansas. In 1977, out of eight hundred nominees, she was named Teacher of the Year in the archdiocese. Thanks to her genuine affection and a rollicking sense of humor, accounts of exchanges with her six-year-olds became legendary.

Dramatizing scenes from the Bible was a favorite method of teaching religion and Sister encouraged her young charges to bring the stories to life. Their retelling of the story of creation was especially imaginative. Dressed as trees, animals, flowers, and fish, the small creatures danced their delight and sang, "Thank you, God, for making us!" and God replied, "You're welcome!" The performance on the first night went fine but the next day the lead actor, facing a second performance, was home in bed with an unnamed indisposition. A classmate offered his services to a much-relieved director, saying he knew all God's lines. As the curtain rose, the lad stepped forward, climbed the ladder to his throne, and announced, "I'm not the real God. The real God threw up and went home." Astonished applause welcomed the opening scene.

On principles of individual dignity and personalized learning, Sister introduced pupil-teacher conferences to her first-graders. They were free to choose the topic of consultation. Seats too hard for a day's work, a troublesome neighbor, impatience for recess, and fear of failure were among the complaints and confidences she received. Some she could act on; others were food for young thought about the business of growing up in the only world we know.[13]

Sister Virginia Flanick spent most of her teaching years in Kansas and Missouri, with intervals in Billings, Montana, and Los Angeles. No child left her classroom who had not completed the course of reading in readiness for the next grade. "If you set ideals high," she said of young pupils, "they're going to aim for them." That proved true for all her students in largely Caucasian parishes and in predominantly African American parishes like Our Lady–St. Rose in Kansas City, Kansas. But it was literally dramatized with her group of eighty first-graders in Billings, Montana.

Choral reading was a favorite way of teaching them speaking skills and they responded with pride. Their articulation in exchanging stanzas of poems and their portrayal of characters in Christmas plays attracted notice beyond the school. A local station televised an all-school mime show narrated by two first-graders. A popular classroom project was the Eskimo igloo, "built" of newspapers with openings for light. The reward for a day's hard work was time inside the igloo for reading. The all-time favorite, marked by rules for order and cleanliness, was Pet Day, when dogs, cats, birds, turtles, and rabbits shared classroom space and recess—all but lunchtime.[14]

Just as necessities of financing brought mergers of parishes, so schools merged, especially in areas limited by socioeconomic conditions. Since their origins in the nineteenth and early twentieth centuries, parishes in Wyandotte County drew Sisters of Charity of Leavenworth as pastors sought help. In 1927 sisters taught African American children for Franciscan pastors of Our Lady of Perpetual Help. Forty-one years later in 1968, when the friars were forced by their shrinking numbers to withdraw from Our Lady's and other city parishes, it was necessary to merge St. Rose's and Our Lady's. After a century of segregated worship and schooling, pastors met resistance from both Caucasian and African American parishioners.[15] Principals and their school staffs worked with the pastors to effect reconciliation.

Hope fed by enormous energy brought substantial support to Our Lady–St. Rose School when its area became part of a federal model cities program. Applications replete with facts about the school's program and its clientele made it the first in District 500 to get a hot-lunch program. Visits from Senators George McGovern and Robert Dole led to further assistance, including breakfast for the students of this private interracial school. Two years and many application forms later, funding for an Educational

Students at Our Lady–St. Rose learn from Sister Mary Timothy Hoban how airwaves and earphones serve their education.

Development Laboratory (EDL) provided salaries for a study skills specialist and assistant and in-service training for the school's staff. Title I funds paid for a full-time math and reading teacher and part-time counselor. With these, three Sisters of Charity, and a bi-weekly music instructor from the University of Missouri in Kansas City, Sister Mary Timothy Hoban administered a traditional curriculum in innovative ways.[16]

A mainstreaming program of the Economic Opportunity Foundation subsidized adults who got their job training at the school serving the students' hot-lunch program. Hired to supervise them, Georgia Dwight, a member of the parish, baked fresh bread daily and saved to put her own children through Catholic schools. A two-week workshop on theory and practice of working in the inner city surfaced problems, myths, and prejudices encountered daily by African American children and their parents. Panelists and presenters were educators, pastors, police personnel, social workers in every level of government, members of the Human Relations Commission of Kansas City, and program directors from the Office of Economic Opportunity. By 1976, pride in their inner-city parish was evident in the people's calling themselves a "community of brotherhood" and in their tithing from parish revenue to help a diocese in Nigeria and Catholic Charities in Kansas.[17] Because of uncertain financial resources, it was necessary to close the school in 1985.

Blessed Sacrament School in Kansas City, Kansas, still had six sisters as principal and teachers as late as 1984 and four in 1990. In 1980, the upper grades were organized as a junior high and a kindergarten served the parish. A pre-school program with variable sessions was open to families in the northeast section of the city and suburban West Wyandotte County. The next year Sisters Barbara Aldrich and Ellen Dore, co-principals, emphasized shared responsibility through weekly review and planning fed by their own part-time classroom teaching. By the end of the decade, having grown into a "rainbow bridge school" that crossed borders of socioeconomic inequalities, of race and religion, Blessed Sacrament lacked adequate financial support.

A Case Statement for the school year 1989–1990 made clear the achievements of a student population 90 percent African American and 30 percent Catholic and the budgetary limits of tuition and parish support. An archdiocesan subsidy was not forthcoming; a community campaign failed. According to the staff counselor, students felt their school "was not important enough...." On a large scale, its termination was part of a pattern of inner-city school closings in Wyandotte County. Sister Nancy Bauman was the last principal to serve before the archbishop closed the school in 1991.[18]

On the Missouri side, as African American families moved south from the center of the city, Blessed Sacrament and St. Louis schools merged in 1974 to become St. Martin de Porres, named for the seventeenth-century Dominican friar who died serving poor natives of Peru. Sisters of Charity had taught the children of the three dozen or so Catholic families who made up Blessed Sacrament parish in 1916. A principal and faculty of eight staffed the school through the parish's integration in the 1950s and assisted the growth of the African American culture that characterized the area by the 1960s and 1970s. Open education, patterned on a British model, freed students at Blessed Sacrament and St. Louis to develop, with a teacher, a curriculum and schedule to maximize their individual development.[19]

The Community had staffed St. Louis, which was conducted as a free school since 1925. St. Louis's parochial school orchestra of more than seventy youngsters made a name for itself in the city during the 1950s. Enrollments in both schools peaked during the 1960s. Then mixed forces of family economics and changing parish populations pushed numbers downward at an alarming rate. Pastors worked with principals within the two parishes to effect the school merger.[20] In 1974 St. Martin de Porres enrolled 250 children. A third of the students were Catholic and 99 percent of them were African American. Parents wanted the moral and religious training as well as the individual attention and strong academic program that the school offered. Goals for students' reaching their potential—reading well, thinking and articulating clearly; knowing fundamentals of math, science, and history; and behaving responsibly—brought approval of people and pastors for the next seventeen years.

Eight Sisters of Charity of Leavenworth, including Sister Mary Helen McInerney, principal, five lay teachers, three paraprofessionals, and six office personnel first staffed the school with assistance from a school board formed from both parishes. Two other Sisters of Charity served as school counselor and reading consultant. Within a few years, St. Martin de Porres stood as a symbol of stability and security in the neighborhood in its commitment to students' learning mutual respect, discipline, and honesty and as adults assuming leadership in their communities.[21]

A result of a study of mission effectiveness, the Covenant of Sharing was an inter-parish enterprise in 1985. Father James Lyons, pastor of St. Charles Borromeo in North Kansas City, initiated a working agreement among four parishes in the central city north and south of the Missouri River to reinforce their budgets with a common pool of material and personnel resources. Student exchanges among the Covenant schools were one of its unique advantages. The schools were St. Martin de Porres and St. Augustine on the east side of the city and St. Patrick and St. Charles in North Kansas City. St. Augustine's was staffed by Sisters of Charity from 1929 for more than fifty years.[22]

A prime example of elementary principals' coping with expanding budgets and declining numbers of sister faculty was Sister Kathleen (John Bosco) Coman's initiative as principal at St. Charles School in North Kansas City. Two classes for every grade required a double number of faculty, a challenge that neither the Community's number of elementary teachers nor the budget's limits for lay teachers' salaries could meet. With the pastor and school board members, several sisters participated in a TWA conference in the early 1970s that offered a business model called Reach Out. It proved adaptable to a school's organization. Two classrooms for one grade were converted into a presentation classroom with an attached laboratory managed by teaching assistants. Parent volunteers experienced the program first hand.[23]

Under the leadership of the principal, George Cascone, St. Patrick's School in Kansas City North introduced a child-centered curriculum in 1973. Grouped by educational needs and abilities, students progressed at their own pace to mastery determined for given levels.[24]

Maintaining Priorities

The Community's commitment to St. Monica's Unified School in central Kansas City, Missouri, grew out of a continuing determination to minister to underserved children. Early in the century Bishop John Hogan proposed a Catholic school for African American children on Kansas City's east side. Francisans came to teach and Mother Katherine Drexel contributed what was then a large amount to the opening of St. Monica's in 1910. A community organization tended its growth until the consolidation of central city schools decades later. In 1989, when a new St. Monica's opened with an enrollment of nearly five hundred, the Sisters of Charity of Leavenworth provided a chief administrator for the two sites that accommodated elementary and intermediate grades and a Montessori Early Childhood program. Students from families of four parishes attend the school. Two-thirds of these families are at or below the poverty level.[25]

A long tradition of service to the Topeka, Kansas, Catholic community kept Sisters of Charity in its schools for 138 years. Ethnic origins governed certain national parishes and school populations for a considerable time. St. Joseph's German families opened their school in 1867. On the other hand, Assumption School, situated across from the state capitol building, had from its opening in 1874 drawn students of varied backgrounds. Our Lady of Guadalupe School opened in the church building in 1920 for children of the Mexican families brought north by jobs on the Santa Fe railroad. Sacred Heart School served its parish of Russo-German families from 1921. Though economic conditions varied across parish lines, parents' strong belief in Catholic education supported their schools.

The city's growth during the first half of the twentieth century saw two new parish schools appear almost within a decade of each other, Holy Name in 1941 and Most Pure Heart of Mary in 1952. Each opened with an enrollment of more than five hundred. Even as development moved westward, Holy Name, now more of a downtown parish, drew good numbers to three daily Masses. Needs broadened as the church in Topeka flourished.[26] Nor did a tornado that ripped across the center of the city in 1966 deter its growth. A new parish on the east side, St. Matthew's, called on Benedictine sisters to staff its school.

But as Interstate 70 cut across the north end of the city in the 1960s and surrounding residential populations declined, St. Joseph's

Sister Mary Corita Conlan, on retirement from her office as Assumption School's principal, drew thousands of Topekans to a Mass of Thanksgiving and reception in her honor.

School lost two-thirds of its normal enrollment of three hundred and merged with Assumption in 1970. During the seventies, the movement of sisters into houses for more intentional communal living and losses in the number of teaching sisters left convents open for parish uses. Pre-schools housed in each of them helped to boost diminishing enrollments caused by population shifts as the city grew toward the west and south. In the eighties, Assumption School faced a different sort of problem. Located in the heart of the city, it was drawing students from twenty zip codes; parents welcomed a pre-school and a kindergarten. Sister Mary Corita Conlan, principal at Assumption since 1967, needed additional classrooms. Vacated by the sisters' moving into houses for small group living, a convent above the school provided space.[27]

From 1920 to 1990, Our Lady of Guadalupe was fully staffed by 109 Sisters of Charity of Leavenworth. Sister Mary Jo McDonald was principal from 1967 to 1980. Overseen and executed by Sister Mary Joan Eble and Abel Valdivia, a mural depicting the history of the Mexican American community in Topeka was painted on the Branner Bridge in 1984. It commemorated the parish established early in the century to serve Mexican families. The bridge, which dated from that time, divided the immigrant community from the rest of Topeka's population; Mexican residents were not to cross it for shopping or other needs.

When Sister Mary Ephrem Shanahan was principal in the 1940s, she knew that the graduating eighth-graders would not be able to interview for jobs unless they were appropriately dressed. Each year before commencement, she went downtown to the shops to ask for white shirts for her boys. Decades later, Mexican men remembered her as a saint. The mural recalled the new school, built after the 1951 flood, that became a center of unity in the Oakland area. A sister briefly home from the Peruvian missions in the late 1960s worked with elementary teachers and lay catechists, translated for families in need of assistance, visited elderly and ill parishioners, and led discussion groups.[28] But dual-language teachers and pastoral ministers were not commonly available to immigrant parishes.

The next fifteen years gave ample evidence of the social and intellectual potential of Mexican American children. After its first annual Fiesta in 1984, the parish financed a trip to Washington, DC, for five students who competed in a national History Day contest with their dramatization of the story of Hispanic women of their neighborhood. Four years later, IBM brought its Adopt-a-Student program to Topeka; Gus Torrez, a senior administrative specialist for IBM and a graduate of Our Lady of Guadalupe, was assigned to make the program work at his alma mater. On the seventy-fifth anniversary of the school, Juan Sepulveda spoke to a large audience. A 1977 alumnus of Guadalupe, he received his undergraduate degree from Harvard University and attended Oxford as a Rhodes Scholar. When Sister Mary Julitta Doerhoff retired in 1998 after eighteen years as principal, she knew well what a former student said of the school as she came back to teach there: "You have something special at Guadalupe."[29] Sisters still volunteer at the school.

Urban sprawl created new churches and schools in some locations but swallowed up existing parishes in others. For example, in an area variously called Hornif or Bethel in western Wyandotte County in Kansas, St. Patrick's parishioners worshiped in a white frame church; their children went to school in two classrooms. The sisters assigned in 1949 to teach there lived in the same building. As the parish made the transition from serving largely rural communities to operating on the outskirts of a city, the people financed a convent and an addition to the school, then a new modern church. By 1966, the plant was a landmark on Highway 24-40 out of Kansas City, Kansas. After the turn of the century, St. Patrick's church was neighbor to the new Kansas Speedway and commercial development called Village West.[30]

Developing Partnerships

Approximately twenty-year intervals marked the development of St. Peter's Cathedral School in Kansas City, Kansas. Opened in 1908 with elementary and secondary classes in the same building as the church, the school moved into its own building in 1927 with eight sisters assigned to eight grades and eight to the high school. By 1960 and throughout the decade, St. Peter's Elementary School had generally eight or nine Sisters of Charity on its faculty. The number diminished throughout the 1980s until 1993. The last sisters to teach and administer at St. Peter's were Sisters Lorraine Leist, Sharon Marie Parr, and Ann Lucia Apodaca. After almost a century of the sisters' commitment, the next fall St. Peter's welcomed a lay principal and faculty.[31]

In contrast, Sisters of Charity began only in 1955 to staff St. Ann's School in Prairie Village, Kansas, with Sister Agnes Mary Brickley assigned as principal. The last principal to serve St. Ann's was Sister Regina Erbacher from 1980 to 1986. Sisters remained on the staff until 1993.[32] In other urban settings school programs grew strong, maintaining high numbers of sisters on faculty and staff until the early seventies or eighties. Opened in 1948, Visitation School in Los Angeles enrolled almost eight hundred students by 1964, with a faculty of thirteen Sisters of Charity of Leavenworth. Sixth through eighth graders were learning from discipline-based faculty in junior-high fashion. A funded Program for Intergroup Enrichment (PIE) capitalized on mixed ethnic and socio-economic backgrounds. But a three-year plan for staffing in the seventies with improved use of personnel could not forestall the sisters' withdrawal at the end of the school year in 1972.[33]

First staffed in 1949, St. Daniel the Prophet School in Chicago had more than one thousand students enrolled by 1958. A faculty of sixteen included twelve Sisters of Charity of Leavenworth. Besides the benefits of a traditional curriculum adapted to contemporary demands, the school boasted a music program that placed it among the outstanding schools in the city. Annually students carried off trophies, medals, and music scholarships. Despite strong support from a school board, Boosters and Parents' clubs, and a public relations committee, the Community found it necessary to withdraw from St. Daniel's in 1985 after thirty-six years of service.[34]

The story of schools in the West reveals similar patterns of commitment, growth, cultural change, and collaboration. For a half-century after opening in 1890, Annunciation School was maintained by its Northeast Denver parish and staffed by Sisters of Charity. The original faculty of four had grown, decade by decade, to an average of sixteen sisters in the 1940s offering a strong curriculum that served students advancing either to college or the workplace. Already by the 1950s, that number had been reduced to eight, with Sister Mary Loretta Beier as principal. When the original building at 37th and Humboldt was condemned by the city engineer in 1968, the principal, Sister LaVonne Guidoni, was given a week to relocate Annunciation's three hundred students. The next year grades 4–8 moved into the recently vacated Annunciation High School. During seventeen years in her office, Sister marked 80 percent minority students enrolled, 65 percent of them Hispanic. She saw 85 percent of those students graduate.[35]

Because not all Annunciation parents could afford the negotiated tuition implemented in the early 1980s, Sister LaVonne began to canvass Denver's business community on behalf of a vital portion of the city's school-age population. She literally "walked 17th Street" and organized the Fund for Support of Denver's Inner City Elementary Catholic Schools. In a drive to raise a million-dollar endowment, the campaign leaders' guiding principle combated stereotypes. "The real poor," they said, "will not come [to the schools] if they can't pay for it."

Sister Ann Lucia Apadoca shows one of her young pupils at Annunciation School how to complete an assigned project.

Within a few years, alumni of the ten Catholic

high schools contributed through fundraisers, nicknamed by a local sportswriter Paroke for their young parochial school beneficiaries. Total support from the parish and community mounted to 56 percent of the budget; tuition supplied 24 percent. Through grants secured by the next principal, Sister Jean Anne Panisko, to complement the archdiocesan subsidy and through continuing collaboration with parents, Annunciation kept education within reach of the parish's families into the twenty-first century.[36]

With a few exceptions, smaller communities in the West supported their parochial schools in similar ways. Parish subsidies and tuition revenue varied depending on economic conditions in given areas. In the mining town of Leadville, Colorado, families' support was consistently generous. Mining, however, was not a stable financial resource. Nor were sisters available in sufficient number by 1973 to supply a faculty. In contrast, the parish of St. Bernadette's School in Lakewood supported a lay faculty and administration after the sisters withdrew in the mid-eighties. Three sisters remained at St. Therese in Aurora through the nineties, two—Sisters Marjorie Feuerborn and Marguerite Grogman—until 2005. A year later, the school celebrated the fiftieth anniversary of its staffing by the Sisters of Charity.[37]

The only Catholic elementary school in Wyoming for some time after its opening in 1914 was Holy Name School in Sheridan. An unusual financial commitment to Catholic education allowed Holy Name to remain tuition-free until 1979. Into the 1990s, annual income from the Holy Name School Foundation and the Thornerider Foundation plus a parish subsidy kept tuition affordable.[38] Sisters of Charity administered the school from its beginnings. The faculty numbered seven in the 1960s and 1970s, five in the 1980s, and three—including a principal—as late as 1992. Five hundred alumni returned for the first all-school reunion in 1994.[39]

Though unique in many respects, Wyoming parochial schools represent patterns repeated elsewhere. In 1951 six Sisters of Charity of Leavenworth went to Laramie to staff St. Laurence O'Toole School in its new building. Sister Mary Carlotta Flynn was the first principal, Sister Mary Sarah Fasenmeyer, the second, with a faculty of seven and an enrollment growing to 370. By 1975, three Sisters of Charity and seven lay teachers made up a strong faculty for grades 1–6. The proportion of lay teachers at St. Laurence O'Toole grew until 1993, when a lay principal succeeded Sister Elizabeth Skalicky, the last Sister of Charity to head the faculty. Sisters remained on staff until 1998. When St. Laurence's parish celebrated its forty-fifth year in 1997–1998, the school's six grades and kindergarten were open to any child in the city and its student-teacher ratio was a healthy 17/1. In May, as the sisters ended the Community's near half-century in Laramie, they left the school in the hands of an eight-member lay administration, faculty, and staff.[40]

Merging Accelerates

In the same half-century, two schools in Rock Springs, Wyoming, merged after two parishes had sustained them for twelve years. In 1951 the opening of Sts. Cyril and Methodius School fulfilled a sixty-six-year-old dream of parishioners. When it opened in 1952, Our Lady of Sorrows enrolled 150, almost equal to Sts. Cyril and Methodius at its peak in 1966.[41] Planning for coordination of the two schools began in 1968 with four lay teachers and twelve sisters on the two-parish committee. The incorporated Rock Springs Catholic School, with grades reduced from eight to six, opened in 1970 with three sisters at Sts. Cyril and Methodius and three at Our Lady of Sorrows; a music teacher served all grades. By 1984, Sister Mary Kenneth Messina was the last Sister of Charity to teach in the school.[42]

At the time of the merger, an editorial in the daily paper expressed regret at the loss of the junior high and extolled the benefits of Catholic elementary schooling, whose purpose, he said, is to integrate religion in the total education of the child. The cost of such education was considerable; 60 percent of the total parish income went to the schools. The writer then pointed to the benefit these schools brought to the taxpayer. By his calculation, the 450 students graduated from the Catholic junior high over the previous eleven years represented a savings to School District No. 4 of four million dollars. Such savings would now convert to expenditure. Should the elementary school ever close, he concluded, a much greater cost would accrue to the public school system.[43]

A classic account of merging and closing schools took place in the Helena, Montana, diocese over the three years between 1966 and 1969. Butte's elementary schools numbered nine for ten parishes. Sisters of Charity of the Blessed Virgin Mary staffed four; the Sisters of Charity of Leavenworth, five. In September of 1966, it was announced that Sacred Heart School would close in May of 1967 and that St. Mary's and St. Lawrence schools would merge the next fall. When parents learned that no first grades were to be available in 1968, they began to plan for the merger and negotiated a new eight-grade dual school, Saint Raymond's, named for Bishop Hunthausen. St. Lawrence was to house the primary grades and St. Mary's, grades five through eight. A consolidation model new to most Catholics at the time was conceived of by Butte parents for the education of their children.

In the fall of 1967, Bishop Hunthausen learned from both religious communities serving the schools of his diocese that cutbacks in the numbers of sisters to be assigned were inevitable. The limited reach of parish budgets made alternatives to Catholic schooling as it had been a viable issue. Early in 1969, the bishop announced the decision of an ad hoc committee that Helena's Catholic High School and all elementary schools of the diocese were to close in May. Funds were not available to meet the debt on the new high school whose enrollment had not grown as predicted.[44]

Faced with the closing of their remaining grade schools, Butte parents formed an all-parish council to discuss in open meetings the future of the city's Catholic schools. In prolonged discussions they considered a necessary choice between Catholic schooling for the very young or for pre-adolescents and teen-agers. Consequently, in the fall of 1969, all seventh and eighth graders formed two feeder schools for the newly consolidated Butte Central High School. Thirteen years later, the two schools evolved into Central Junior High School with Sister Roberta O'Leary as principal. In 1989 Sister Mary Patricia Lenahan concluded twelve years as principal of Butte Central High; the last six years she served too as superintendent of the Butte Catholic School System.[45]

On the Community's 125th birthday, at Butte's Central Elementary School, Sister Paula Marie Tweet welcomes a very young Mother Xavier, Vincent de Paul, and Louise de Marillac.

By the late 1980s, the people of Butte were ready to re-open a Catholic elementary school for their children. Representatives from every parish and from the coordinated school system met every Saturday for almost a year with the school principals to consolidate the primary, middle, and junior high grades. In 1986 Butte Central Elementary opened with a lay faculty, Sister Roberta continuing as principal, and Sister Elizabeth Skalicky named as coordinator of grades one through five. Sisters of Charity remained in Butte schools into the new century. For seven years from 1996, Sister Mary Jane Schmitz was principal of the elementary school system.[46]

The junior-high model was a guide to other mergers. In Grand Junction, Colorado, the new Immaculate Heart of Mary and the old St. Joseph's combined as Holy Family Junior High School. In some cases, like St. John's in Lawrence, Kansas, diminished resources and availability of the public junior high brought reduction of the eight-grade program, common in Catholic schools, to six grades.[47] Diminution, however, was not a universal pattern.

On the whole, parents were partners with the sisters in the schools they staffed. Traditionally the partnership flourished through parent-teacher organizations, fund-raising events, and attendance at students' public performances. Volunteers assisted with transportation, in offices, and with study groups. In the 1960s and 1970s, advisory councils became school boards. More than a few times confusion rose from unclarified roles in decision-making about curriculum, student conduct, faculty appointments, and budgets. Parents educated to the professions and practiced in critical judgment were more apt to question than to assume the qualifications of teachers and administrators assigned to or hired for a parish school. Already in the 1970s, Sisters of Charity were engaged in individual self-assessments as well as institutional evaluations by the supervisor of schools according to national and Community criteria.

In her 1980 report to the General Council, Sister Bernadette Helfert commented that parents were frank about incompetency and found it intolerable in programs supported by their sacrifices. Nor did they appreciate any perceived sense of superiority in a teacher or principal. On the other hand, they expected the sisters to exercise the leadership necessary for their jobs.[48] Common expectations on the part of educators and their constituents and commitment to results were the only firm path to change in the final decades of the century.

In the face of adaptations, maintaining standards of teaching and administration was of paramount importance. Supervision of the schools had been crucial throughout the Community's history. The Irish-born Sister Mary Baptista Ward, assisted by a compatriot, Sister Mary Afra White, was the school supervisor for the Community from 1940 to 1966. During that quarter-century the dominant goal was to staff the schools for which bishops and pastors sought Sisters of Charity and a multitude of other women religious. Periodic bulletins from Sister Mary Baptista brought instructions and suggestions for teaching all subjects, for assisting backward students in hours after class time, and for matters of discipline and school administration. Above all, in times of stress and change, Sister Mary Baptista wrote, "let our teaching be solid, thorough and enduring...."[49] Stories of the supervisors' regularly scheduled visits to the schools are Community lore.

Perhaps Sister's most memorable trait was a combination of high demands and humane consideration. It was such humanity that moved Sister Patricia Canty when she heard the story of Sister Mary Baptista—then retired and tutoring students with difficulties at St. Daniel's—standing at a window of the convent on a snow-bound morning in Chicago, tears running down her face. One of the teachers who passed through the room asked her what was wrong and she replied, "I had so much to teach them today."[50] Accord with pastors in their parochial schools was a priority for sisters assigned to them. Deep reverence for the priesthood mixed well, nevertheless, with a practical sense of what human relationships required. One principal named to a school where others had found real difficulty functioning with the pastor recalled Sister's quiet direction for the job: "See what you can do with the man."[51]

Sister Agnes Mary Brickley succeeded Sisters Mary Baptista and Mary Afra in 1966 as Community school supervisor. Two years later during the first Renewal Chapter, her title became "director of education," with all that this implied for a period of significant change. In the first year of her job, she learned from the *Eastern Kansas Register* of the closing of St. Joseph's School in Topeka, one of the Community's oldest parish schools founded in 1867. The sisters teaching there as well as the pastor learned of the closing in the same way. Closings by the diocese or withdrawal of sisters by the Community came about without everyone's grasp of a full range of reasons. A further challenge to a supervisor during the 1960s and into the 1970s was meeting sisters' requests for education—a semester at the college, a theology course available where they were missioned, workshops whenever they appeared. Not all long-term requests were granted, though Sister Agnes Mary was not always able to say why. A sister's choice of a local community sometimes complicated the business of apostolic assignment.[52]

Over these decades, sisters' leadership in the schools took varied and quiet forms. Sisters of Charity of Leavenworth served as supervisors of diocesan and archdiocesan elementary schools: Sister Joseph Cecilia (Mary Ann) Gausz in Kansas City, Missouri, and Helena, Montana; Sisters Agnes Mary and Perpetua McGrath in Kansas City, Kansas. Others worked on archdiocesan committees for teaching methods in disciplines, training to teach in central city schools, and student assessment. As Community supervisor of the elementary schools after the Chapter of 1974, Sister Bernadette Helfert directed the Apostolate Study designed to assess the strength of the Community's traditional ministries.

Between 1974 and 1980, the apostolate of elementary education suffered a 24 percent decline in the number of sisters involved in it. By 1980 the elementary teachers' median age was fifty; the number of those between twenty and forty-three years of age had declined by 73.3 percent within a decade. In an aptitude/preference survey, 44.3 percent or 66 of the sisters in elementary education listed that apostolate as their top priority; the total number interested in elementary education, however, was 113 or 58.4 percent. Many of those were veteran teachers who had no wish to change ministries but were nearing retirement; others had grown into teaching as integral to their community life. As reported in 1980, individual school enrollments had declined anywhere from 2 to 34 percent. More than half the schools with Sisters of Charity on their staffs had lost more than 10 percent of their students.[53]

NEW INITIATIVES EMERGE

A uniquely American spirit that had brought the parochial school system to birth fostered its growth for more than a century. In the next two decades, it produced a model of collaboration that depended on existing strengths and called for courageous risk and imagination. In Leavenworth, where the Sisters of Charity had opened their first elementary schools, planning continued for fifteen months before the Leavenworth Regional Catholic School System was announced in 1979. Xavier Elementary Schools, with a projected enrollment of 500, were to be housed by grades at three locations: first and second grades at Sacred Heart; third through fifth grades and the pre-school at St. Joseph's, sixth through eighth grades at Immaculate Conception. Immaculata High School's estimated 280 were to remain at Sixth and Shawnee. Sister Katherine Franchett was administrator of the Xavier school system from 1979 to 1986; Sister Ann McGuire succeeded her. Margaret O'Sullivan served as chief administrator from 1991 to 2003.[54]

As the system grew, 10 percent of the students represented faith traditions other than Catholic; 8 percent were from diverse ethnic groups. Students came from the Leavenworth/Lansing/Fort Leavenworth community and from four nearby smaller towns. The summary study of 1982–1984, however, revealed that enrollment from nine parishes in Xavier schools ranged only between 30 and 63 percent of their school-age children; 80 percent was the goal. Support from the parishes in the form of student enrollments was desirable both because education in a Catholic setting was still a bulwark of parish life and because income from tuition was the principal way to reduce parish subsidies.[55] By the 1990s, the goal remained far down the field.

In 1997 a fourteen-member board of trustees inaugurated a long-range plan for sharing resources with the public school districts, long-term financing mechanisms, and marketing strategies. A chief executive officer for the system was to relieve principals of all but educational responsibilities. During the tenure of CEO Rolland Dessert, enrollment in the total system reached 740, near the number needed for stability. Badly needed capital improvements included upgrade of electrical systems and Internet access, air-conditioning, and parking lots. Computers for faculty and students were donated and purchased. An Early Childhood Center opened in the former St. Casimir School. The priority of justice led to adjustment of salaries. The parish subsidy, which kept the system in operation, had risen over time to 65 percent of the schools' revenue. By 2001, with increased momentum in development, a 50 percent level lowered to a 30 percent annual average over four years.[56]

Assigned to Billings, Montana, Sister Katherine met similar conditions. Three Catholic elementary schools had served the parishes of St. Patrick's, Holy Rosary, and Little Flower for almost forty years since they had reached their peak enrollments at mid-century—seven hundred at Kate Fratt Memorial School and five hundred at Holy Rosary. After Little Flower, staffed by Dominican sisters, closed in the late 1950s, the new west-side parish, St. Pius X, opened its school in 1959. The schools fed enrollment at Billings Central. But numbers were dropping seriously at all four schools by 1980. During the three decades after 1953, seventy-four Sisters of Charity staffed Holy Rosary; from its beginnings as St. Patrick's up until 1986, almost 200 staffed Fratt Memorial. In that year, two sisters were missioned to each of the three elementary schools and the high school.[57] Parish budgets reflected the declining income and increasing salary outlays.

In 1987 Bishop Thomas Murphy and the pastors in Billings accepted a plan for the consolidation of these schools from the Billings Catholic School Board. The bishop was particularly anxious to hear the people's response to the unification plan. Two hundred parishioners attended three hearings held at the high school. The kindergarten and primary grades were housed at Holy Rosary, grades 3–5 at St. Pius, and grades 6–8 at Fratt Memorial. Sisters Dolores Erman and Mary Ann Petrich were teachers at the upper school. In her announcement of the opening of the newly coordinated St. Francis School System, Sister Katherine said the reorganization meant that "Catholic education is here to stay."[58]

Her leadership and that of her successors gave the promise substance into the next century. Chief administrator of Billings Catholic Schools from 1986 to 1995, Sister Katherine was appointed superintendent of schools in the Great Falls–Billings Diocese in 1990. Five years later, she oversaw full-time the twenty-one Catholic schools of Eastern Montana.

Sister Elizabeth Youngs succeeded her in 1995 to direct the Billings Catholic Schools for the next six years. Continuity in leadership came with the appointment of Sister Jean Martin Dawson to the office of school superintendent of the Great Falls–Billings Diocese in 1997.[59]

Forms of Catholic education were evolving in the closing decades of the twentieth century. New pioneers were yet to be born. Overriding concerns that had accompanied the intense growth of schools remained as dioceses coped with mergers, systems, and budgets unsupplemented by sisters' contributed services. Concerns for the unique quality of religious education and for material means to support it united parents and pastors in new ways. Sisters were no longer the reassuring resource they once had been, but numbers were never a guarantee of quality nor did sisters' stipends constitute a sound economy. As educators by their Vincentian charism and with firm priorities, Sisters of Charity were able to raise hard questions with fellow laity and search for alternatives in a time that called for untried collaborative ventures in Catholic education.

CHAPTER 11

Teaching an Investment

An educator who worked with the Sisters of Charity for twenty-seven years developed a philosophy of education that guided him as classroom teacher and coach, as high school principal, and then as superintendent of archdiocesan schools. His philosophy echoes the commitment of the sisters and their lay colleagues to the mission of education. The common vision that "Christ is the reason" for each school is the source of his conviction that all can learn and can touch success once in a while. Self-respect and respect for one another are reflected in students' language and behavior. Such students refuse to give up and expect no free rides; their schools become neighborhoods. He believes that teachers are true heroes who care passionately about what really matters. At great personal cost they have invested in young lives as promise for the future.[1]

Convictions like these inspired the small beginnings and continuing life of secondary schools staffed by Sisters of Charity of Leavenworth. Evidence of the strength of these convictions informs the accounts of the evolution of these schools from the Community's full staffing to lay administration. Reasons for the evolution are many and complex. Catholic secondary schools in the United States were products of an educational heritage developed during the century that followed the Civil War. During the half-century that followed the Second World War, deep changes in society, culture, and the Church reflected aspects of revolution that affected schooling as well as college and university life. That a significant number of Catholic schools remained stable in their educational ideals and operations is an accomplishment that begs for accounting. The women religious who staffed them from their beginnings skillfully managed the transition of these schools' mission, their administration, and their faculties to lay women and men.

Between 1859, when St. Mary's Academy opened in Leavenworth, and 1956, when the Community opened St. Pius X High School in North

Kansas City, the sisters staffed twelve high schools and six academies. The academy enrolled students from five to eighteen or nineteen, both boarders and day students. Unlike many religious communities, the Leavenworth Sisters of Charity had no rule prohibiting the sisters' teaching adolescent boys nor did the schools limit their enrollments to Catholics. These policies were a matter of both principle and practical advantage in frontier towns and growing cities.

Saint Vincent's Academy in Helena, Montana, opened in 1869 before the territory claimed a diocese. In 1900 Immaculate Conception High School in St. Mary's, Kansas, was the first parochial secondary school in the Leavenworth diocese. Butte Central consolidated in 1969 to serve seven parishes. Integration was natural. In Laramie, the only African American students in town were enrolled in the academy; in Topeka, they attended Catholic elementary schools and Capitol Catholic High. The sisters raised the money to buy or build a structure for the academies. They initiated high schools by adding a ninth grade to an elementary program and then building enrollment and grade levels until the space could no longer contain the students. Tuition was commonly $1 or $2 a year; a resident student in an academy paid $20 a month.[2]

The quality of education in both academies and parish or central high schools proved itself in student performance. Early coursework in algebra, science, Latin, English, history, and moral philosophy was standard, reflecting the classical learning of the teachers educated in Ireland and in American academies. From regional and state competitions for public and private schools, students brought home first-place ribbons and numerous awards in speech and debate, essays, mathematics and science, and music. Teachers reinforced their own knowledge and methods of instruction in summer institutes featuring scholars brought from universities as distant as New York. The Community sponsored these institutes in both Leavenworth and Helena as early as 1899. Diocesan school boards, the first initiated and organized by Mother Josepha Sullivan, issued examinations and certification for teachers that anticipated government accreditation.

By 1913, the Community had withdrawn from four of the six academies to concentrate personnel elsewhere or, in the case of Central City, Montana, because of total lack of material support. By 1960, only one of the high schools had closed.[3] The remaining eleven led colorful and persistent lives. An earthquake had closed Saint Vincent's Academy in Helena in 1935; like a phoenix it rose from the rubble the following year with a new name, Cathedral High School, and a co-ed population. Faculty accustomed to teaching boys in the elementary schools accepted their presence as a matter of course. By 1954, Cathedral High was housed in a wing of the elementary school and in 1966 in a handsome new building. Its faculty annually included ten to eleven Sisters of Charity. But expansion required more lay teachers than the diocese could support. The school closed in 1969 when financial dilemmas troubled the Helena diocese and a program of total parochial Christian education replaced the schools.[4]

HALF A CENTURY'S FOUNDATION

In Butte, Sisters of Charity of Leavenworth and the Irish Christian Brothers had staffed Girls Central and Boys Central in separate buildings in 1927 and 1924 respectively. In 1951 Bishop J. M. Gilmore dedicated a new Girls Central at Park and Idaho. In the fiftieth year of Catholic secondary education in Butte, 1958, Girls Central enrolled 440 students. By then, however, financial support of nine parochial schools and two high schools in Butte was becoming a serious burden.[5] While students' accomplishments multiplied, their faculty advanced professionally through workshops, conferences, and summer study. The *Prix d'honneur* went to a Girls Central 1962 senior for performance in a French National Merit contest. Awards in Latin, journalism and business, history, science and math, and the performing arts were recorded repeatedly throughout the 1960s. A 1967 graduate became Girls Central's first Papal Volunteer when Sheila McGlynn, RN, went to Guatemala. During her term as principal, Sister Mary Seraphine Sheehan was named state chair of the National Catholic Education Association and vice president of the Helena Diocesan Association for Secondary Schools.

Administration of Butte's schools was growing complex, however, as resources diminished. Under Bishop Raymond Hunthausen, each diocesan high school was administered by a priest director with a principal.[6] When the crisis of Butte's schools in the late 1960s brought even tougher problems, diocesan and pastoral consultations led to an announcement that the high schools must close. Parents' committees quickly formed and in parish-wide meetings reversed the decision. Debating the significance of a school environment at different stages of a child's development, the parishioners decided that the Catholic high school was essential. The need of Boys Central for a new building, however, posed an impossible financial challenge. Intense discussions of alternative plans led to a difficult decision, that a co-ed Butte Central and junior highs for seventh and eighth graders would meet immediate needs.

Under co-principals—a Christian Brother and Sister Mary Kathleen—the Boys Central student body moved to the Girls Central building for the fall term of 1967. It took a year for the students, especially the boys, to accept their integration. A decision by the bishop in 1968 that a priest should be the single principal of every high school brought the exodus of the

Christian Brothers and new responsibilities to clergy inexperienced in a principal's duties. Sister Mary Kathleen served as curriculum director before she was assigned to a new mission in 1972; Sister Mary Julianne O'Flannigan succeeded her.[7] The faculty at that time included twelve Sisters of Charity, seven lay women and men, and ten pastors who taught religion.

The significance of the sisters' contributed services is clear from the expenditures reported for 1967–1968 to the pastors of the city. In a $55,700 budget, lay faculty salaries collectively amounted to $23,215. Provided with housing and utilities, the sisters received a collective stipend of $8,000.[8] Until the 1980s, this pattern was not uncommon in diocesan high schools. Equitable salaries for lay teachers and contracted salaries for teaching religion became growing concerns over the last quarter of the century. In diminishing numbers, Sisters of Charity continued on the staff of Butte Central until 1990, when Sister Mary Regis McEnroe retired from a quarter-century of teaching Centralites.

A Quiet Revolution

From its beginnings as Catholic High in 1908 with twenty-three enrolled, Bishop Ward High School's population exploded by the decade. A new structure was necessary in 1912 for 250 students. The building housed more than 450 in 1931, when the school adopted a new name honoring Bishop Johannes Ward. A decade later Ward claimed 960 students. In the mid-1940s, Bishop Paul C. Schulte, rejecting racial discrimination, made a decision that would seriously affect that enrollment. Through a letter to the pastors read at every Mass and published in the

Bishop Ward High School, Kansas City, Kansas, 1931

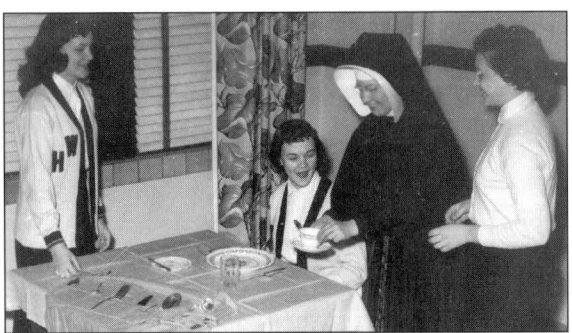

Sister Elizabeth Ann West shows Ward's home economics students how to set a table and serve their guests.

diocesan newspaper, Catholics of Kansas City, Kansas, learned that Bishop Ward High School was open to all, regardless of creed or color.

Backed by the school's president, Msgr. Joseph P. McKenna, and its administrators, the decision met its first test in 1945. A number of parents withdrew their children from the school or refused to enroll them. Some of the students who remained found it difficult to accept as classmates and teammates those they had never seen as equal to themselves or known as neighbors. Nevertheless, thanks to the example set by faculty, staff, and many classmates, within a few years integration was a natural condition of life at Ward.[9] Margaret Fay, the second lay person in 1938 to join Ward's faculty, recalled that a spirit of cooperation characterized the school. A teacher could expect that any serious problem with a student would be resolved in a conference with the principal. Recourse to parents was rare. Sisters of Charity continued to manage the school throughout the 1950s. In 1959, Father Francis Maher was named principal by Bishop Edward J. Hunkeler.

Academic rigor matched popular and widely supported athletics; an honors program and membership in the National Honor Society encouraged achievements of learning. During the 1960s, a strong faculty and a curriculum that included both classics and pre-professional courses bore fruit in student awards, regionally and in the state, in dramatics, art, and music; science and math; speech and journalism; business and Latin. Awards for service took top billing at commencement. Faculty attended conferences in their disciplines as far afield as Ohio and New Jersey. With NSF and NDEA awards they studied in the summer at Boston College, UCLA, and other universities. In 1966 during National Catholic Youth Week, students and faculty—1,350 strong—marched fifteen miles from 18th and Central through downtown Kansas City, Kansas, with banners identifying their faith and their school. By 1967, graduates numbered 263; twenty-five Sisters of Charity served on the faculty and staff. The late 1960s also brought flexible scheduling and team-teaching to Ward. Students' self-paced study and lab investigations were the daily round.[10]

The 1970s brought radical change. In 1971, Ward's school board, representing sixteen parishes, hired Blake Mulvaney as principal to succeed Father Raymond Davern who had been named a pastor in the archdiocese. Thanks to external factors having to do with public school integration and population shifts, Ward's enrollment had declined almost a third by 1973 from its mid-1960s peak. Yet a full-time faculty of thirty-eight included twenty Sisters of Charity of Leavenworth.

Overseeing a budget of $560,000 that carried a $700 expenditure per pupil and a $10,000 outlay for scholarships and grants, the new principal faced tasks far beyond that of an instructional leader. He called on long-time colleagues as his mentors. These included Sisters Mary Clarence (Madelon) Burns, Joseph Mary (Jomary) Schwieder, Susan Rieke, Judith Jackson, and Virginia Bartolac. Nevertheless, tasks of public relations, budgeting, planning, and fund-raising suggested reorganization. As in post-secondary institutions, the latter duties fell properly to the office of a president. Blake Mulvaney first filled the position in 1978. Sister Maureen Craig was development officer; Sister Therese Steiner directed a program for communication with parents.[11]

A monthly letter written in 1979 reveals the spirit that had characterized Ward for more than fifty years. The president wrote of a school built by faith and sacrifice and pointed to national recognition given Christian social action classes and to more than $94,000 raised by Ward constituents in fund-raising events. Sister Mary Constantia Towle, who taught at Ward for twenty-seven years, spent a month calling graduates for contributions to the drive for capital improvements on the building. She raised enough to fund scholarships as well. Ward's multi-generational family made the drive a success.

By 1981–1982, financial aid to students neared $44,000; tuition of about $1,500 was negotiated for students in need; costs and benefits were the same for students not of the Catholic faith. Students enrolled for 1982–1983 numbered 674, served by a full-time faculty of thirty-seven, including nine Sisters of Charity of Leavenworth. The student-teacher ratio was a healthy 18/1. Dual enrollment for college courses was available at Rockhurst College; 78 percent of the students elected the college prep curriculum. A community-based career program was open to all and special classes served both learning-impaired and gifted students.[12]

A smaller Ward, firm in its traditions and adapting to contemporary demands, stood on the threshold of a new era. Sister Rita McGinnis, associate administrator for a year, took the reins in 1984 and over the next seven years led Ward to further national recognition. A Parent Network created to combat the growing threat of drugs and alcohol to teenagers got strong support from a new Parent Club dedicated to social and educational activities for all students. Two National Merit semi-finalists in 1985 exemplified the academic standards maintained at Ward High School for decades.[13]

Continuing Tradition in New Ways

Founded in 1909, Immaculate Conception High School in Leavenworth became Immaculata in 1923, affectionately dubbed I-Mac by students and faculty alike for years to come. Eight Sisters of Charity made up its faculty at the time; by 1960 more than seventy had taught at I-Mac.[14] This small, private secondary school drew students from the Catholic elementary schools, from parents who sought a college prep education for their teenage children, and from military families at Fort Leavenworth who had heard of the school's quality from predecessors scattered around the globe. In 1964 students still made an annual retreat when Sister Mary Dolorine Eakes became principal. Awareness of social issues was growing. Immaculata students excelled in dramatics, debate, geopolitical history, and government in action. Officers from the Command and General Staff College at Fort Leavenworth were guest speakers. Visits to city and state government offices were annual field trips.

During Sister Mary Elizabeth (Marie Aquina) Kelly's term as principal, modular scheduling allowed for advanced courses in film and nuclear science and the advantages of independent study and seminars. Dual credit from Saint Mary College courses were factors in producing a National Merit scholar and a National Science Foundation student grant-winner. Athletic programs included the usual high school sports and cross-country track, golf, tennis, soccer, and wrestling.[15] Enrollment held steady at around three hundred into the 1970s.

In 1972 when individual discernment was part of the mission assignment process, no other Sister of Charity was available for the post of principal although sister teachers remained. Convinced that the Community's presence at Immaculata was a tradition not to be lost, Sister Mary Jo Coyle offered to take on the job and recruited four sisters to teach full- or half-time as they were free to do so, replacing several lay and religious on the school's faculty. A golden jubilee celebration in 1974 honored founders and named twenty-nine women and men who had responded to religious vocations since 1924. They included twenty-five Sisters of Charity of Leavenworth. I-Mac's building had seriously deteriorated, no funding was in sight, and responsibilities of the school board were not clearly defined. Sister Mary Jo made successful grant applications, oversaw restoration of physical facilities, and laid foundations for the future. Consultation with the school's lay council led to initiation of the annual Greenway Auction in 1978–1979.[16]

Immaculata High School, Leavenworth, in the 1950s

Immaculata had turned a corner in terms of administrative organization, public image, and financial resources. But broader support was needed. It came in the way of the Leavenworth Regional Catholic School system that coordinated the Catholic elementary schools and included Immaculata in a plan for sharing resources, reducing expenses, and developing new sources of revenue. An Education Foundation, under archdiocesan auspices, formalized a system of investment in the schools, and earned interest on loans that would finance improvements in programs and facilities. In 1979 Sister Ann Barton, principal, established a development program with offices in one of the schools, with Marietta Gregor, graduate of 1952, in charge. In addition to the tuition and parish subsidies that supported less than 70 percent of the budget, fund-raising depended for the most part on parents and alumni. Despite all efforts, development provided only about 4 percent of the total revenue.[17] That had to change.

When Sister Rita Smith became principal in 1995, she capitalized on the mission statement: "IHS offers a program of academic excellence and builds a foundation for a lifetime." New teachers of mathematics, science, and English strengthened the faculty. Dr. William Krusemark, of Saint Mary College's music faculty, directed chorus and taught individual students one day a week. At the state music festival, I-Mac students received highest ratings in all categories. Stories issuing from the development office informed the public of students' achievements, the numbers of graduates who went on to college, and the satisfaction registered among the three thousand individuals educated at Immaculata over more than fifty years. A memorial program for deferred giving and the 2024 Century Club aimed at tuition assistance that would guarantee graduates for the next twenty-five years and more.[18] Under lay administration, Immaculata High School was ready for a new century.

Unique Collaboration

St. Mary's High School in St. Mary's, Kansas, was born of initiatives peculiar to a rural community grounded in a religious tradition. At the turn of the century the townspeople asked the Sisters of Charity in their elementary school to offer secondary school courses. By 1944, Immaculate Conception High School graduated seventeen. Two years later, when enrollment stood at seventy and the public high school had only forty students, school officials proposed that the two schools consolidate to swell the student population and thus increase the annual state tax revenue from $5,000 to a possible $14,000. Combined with local resources, this income secured threatened curricular programs in music, vocational agriculture, and domestic science. The state Board of Education welcomed the plan, considering it acceptable for Episcopalian, Lutheran, and Catholic parochial high schools throughout Kansas. The integrated school's name was St. Mary's High School; John M. Browne was principal. In the old Catholic high school building, three sisters taught English, Latin, and history and oversaw the library. Their salaries in excess of $50 each went to Immaculate Conception parish.[19]

Sister Rose Dominic Gabish's study of the schools in the late 1950s clarified the school's unusual history. The year 1953 marked the fiftieth anniversary of the first graduation excercises of the first Catholic high school in the Archdiocese of Kansas City, Kansas. In its collaborative form, however, the sisters had no voice on policy decisions or curriculum design in the school. St. Mary's Jesuit pastor in 1959 was reported to have said, nevertheless, that "the Sisters have caused the breakdown of prejudice and have a strong influence for good on all the students." Mother Mary Ancilla's decision in 1961 to withdraw the two remaining sisters from St. Mary's rested on several considerations: great need for sisters elsewhere, little formal opportunity for sisters at the high school to exert influence on programs, and considerable financial loss in the mission.[20]

A People's School

With an early start in 1914, Annunciation High School in Denver began its proper history housed in the grade school in 1925. Because the Depression forestalled building, that structure was reinforced in 1938–1939; in 1951 the school moved to its present location at 36th and Lafayette. By 1953, 47 Annunciation students were among the 486 Catholic high school graduates who received their diplomas from Archbishop Urban J. Vehr in a joint commencement ceremony. Annunciation was already making a name for itself with a band, essay contests, stage productions, art exhibits, and achievements in business, science, and math.[21] Only in 1958, however, could the campaign to build a new high school begin. Sister Mary Thomas O'Flannigan was named vice president with a priest principal.

In 1960 fund-raisers provided $160,000 for the addition of two classrooms and a gymnasium to the already crowded building. That year Annunciation enrolled 376 with a faculty of twenty that included thirteen Sisters of Charity of Leavenworth.[22] In 1964 Annunciation received national recognition from the United States Department of Agriculture for its low-cost lunch program. Ten Sisters of Charity were teaching religion as well as other subjects on a faculty of thirty. The school's doors were always open, that year to the Poor People Marchers on their way to Washington, DC. Faculty and students welcomed them to a hot meal. Sister Ann de Sales (Agnes) Lobeck was principal when in 1966 modular scheduling was introduced to meet needs of the individual student. Annunciation students' accomplishments in public speaking gained national recognition. Sister Mary Georgette Groh guided the school's chapter of the National Forensic League to an award for excellence and acclaim as one of twenty-five groups selected from a thousand chapters in the nation.[23]

By 1968, with Sister Mary Ernest Marsh as principal, Annunciation's population was two-thirds Hispanic and about a third African American with small percentages of other races. In its third year of modular scheduling it was the only co-educational school in metropolitan Denver with a developmental program. Devised from individually designed schedules, the master timetable provided released time for special subjects at the public school and dual credit for English classes at Regis College. That spring, however, the parish met an insurmountable problem. After the city condemned the grade school building, its students moved to the high school, where half-day schedules were followed during the final month of the school year. But there was no money to build. According to sisters writing for the Community's magazine, *Relay*, that summer marked the end of a school and its singular era. For more than four decades, the sisters had patterned growth and change to the needs of their students. At Annunciation they not only taught but also learned from a warm and grateful people.[24]

Necessary Decisions

Erected in 1939 in Topeka, Kansas, Hayden High School was designed by Maurice Carroll, architect for major buildings of the Community and

College in Leavenworth. The school had undergone three transformations since its opening by Father Francis Hayden as Assumption High School in 1911. Successively renamed Topeka Catholic and Capitol Catholic, in 1946 it was re-named Hayden High to honor the school's founder. Sixteen years later, West Hayden High accommodated juniors and seniors in a new building at the west end of town. Like other central high schools, it served all the parishes in town. Principals from mid-century included Sisters Mary Patrice McInerney and Mary Columba Connaughton, and Father Henry Beier.[25] By 1960, when Father Raymond Davern took charge of almost 800 students, new quarters were necessary. The price tag for a building to house junior and seniors was $1,300,000.[26] But challenges more than economic were day-to-day fare for the Irish-born principal. He presided over a school bristling with talent, diversity, competition, and parochial ethnic loyalties. Father Davern's congenial and cordial manner concealed a firm control that he exercised as occasion required. Students who failed to perceive this quickly learned the power of quiet authority.

Hayden buzzed with life. A Future Nurse's Club reflected career interests of students and civic interests of many who supported the school's growth. St. Francis Hospital provided hospital experience for the students. Father John Stitz told students about PAVLA, Papal Volunteers for Latin America, and Father John Vianney Brinkman, OFM, introduced them to the Franciscan missions in the Philippines. Staffs of student publications won national Catholic press awards with new conceptions of the yearbook and literary magazine.[27]

Hayden High School, Topeka, built in 1939

In 1967 when a North Central evaluating team visited the school, Hayden boasted more than 950 students and a faculty of sixteen Sisters of Charity and twenty-one lay teachers. Sister Charles McGowan was curriculum director. Comparable staffing continued for another fifteen years under a new principal, Father Thomas Santa. During the 1970s Hayden High School joined PACE, the national organization for support of Catholic schools called Parent Action for Christian Education. Students grew more community-minded with projects inspired by Let's Help, Inc., and contributions to the Emergency Center. Nevertheless, problems with a divided student body were begging for change. Freshmen and sophomores downtown needed the influence of older students who were proud of their school.

When Sister Mary Jo Coyle was asked to take over duties as principal in 1979, the need to combine all classes was imperative. Archbishop Ignatius Strecker, commending the commitment of Topeka's Catholics that had built Hayden East and West, asked them now to support a move to one site.[28] Faced with falling enrollment, a cost per pupil of almost $1,700 in a budget of more than $900,000, and a North Central accrediting visit, Sister employed Marilyn Krueger, Saint Mary alumna and former Sister of Charity, to direct the study and set about informing the public and feeder schools of the city about Hayden's strengths. Graduates were satisfied with their educational preparation in percentages that ranged between 84 and 96 percent. Support and cooperation from colleagues was felt by 86 percent of faculty and staff; attitudes of students toward teachers were favorable up to 94 percent.

In the early 1980s, the faculty and staff numbered thirty-one lay women and men and five Sisters of Charity of Leavenworth.[29] When Dan Elsener, Hayden's first lay principal, took over in 1983, he said that on coming to Topeka "when you mentioned Hayden everyone listened and responded with respect and admiration." About two-thirds of the staff were graduates or had served four years or longer. A *Pacemaker* writer observed that these tenures reflected Hayden's "resolve, stability and strength." The last Sister of Charity to serve on its faculty was Sister Mary Bridget Mullen, who left in 1986.[30]

Spirit Personified

In 1920 a ninth grade opened in Fratt Memorial School in Billings for a brief three-year term and reopened as St. Patrick's in 1943. An annex functioned as the high school of that parish until the new Billings Central Catholic High School opened in 1947 on the site of the old Children's

Hospital of St. Vincent's. Its first graduating class numbered thirteen. By 1957 the faculty, under Sister Genevieve Tebedo, principal, included eleven other Sisters of Charity of Leavenworth and five lay women and priests. Father Patrick Donovan was superintendent.[31] By then, the rousing spirit of its students and the public relations talents of principals like Sisters Ann Patrice Harrington, Francetta O'Donnell, and Mary Pauline Degan did much to allay suspicion of Catholics in this eastern Montana city that had never known frontier missionaries.

When the students numbered more than a hundred in 1959, Ed Piess, a sportscaster who had covered Billings Central games for thirteen years, wrote, "Central is the best behaved group I have seen in attitude toward one another, toward visiting teams, and toward officials. I have never seen such school spirit as Central students have." That same spirit had shown itself when Kerry Feldman was named one of four Teen Guest Editors for an issue of *Extension Magazine* in 1958. So many Centralites contributed interviews, articles, art, and photography that he won the national award for the most entries worthy of publication. Their activity, wrote one student, "swept Central like a summer thunderstorm."[32]

In the early 1960s, the school was acquiring its reputation for academic excellence, sending graduates with scholarships to colleges and universities especially on the West Coast. A Centralite was state winner in the "Voice of Democracy" contest. The school participated in a national science talent search. A different type of national search brought senior Dave McNally a contract with the Baltimore Orioles. Students excelled in the arts, moving their teachers to undertake ambitious productions like a stage version of "Pride and Prejudice."[33]

Sister Mary Lenore Martin was principal during the school's ascendancy. The largest Catholic high school in eastern Montana, Billings Central was

Billings Central Catholic High School, erected in 1947

second largest in the state. By 1968 its roster of alumni numbered 1,744. A faculty of thirty-five included fifteen Sisters of Charity, two Irish Mercy sisters, and twelve lay women and men.[34] In 1971, Sister Mary Rau, principal, introduced modular scheduling described at length in the school newspaper. According to students and faculty and the principal, its distinct advantages were flexibility in student-teacher contacts, independence of students with responsibility for their own learning, new initiatives and collaboration among teachers, and more effective preparation of students for college.

A historical review published in the *Billings Gazette* in 1975 evaluated four decades of service by Sisters of Charity of Leavenworth. Two Sisters of Charity, Maureen Kehoe and Linda Lohman, remained on the staff in 1977 under Sister Mary Blaise Power, RSM, principal. In 1979–1980, about 150 students elected to make retreats and parents attended two evenings of recollection. Billings Central's original philosophy still prevailed in commitment to spiritual values, to the individuality of students in their learning, to the importance of self-worth, and to the preparation of graduates for active life in the Church and civic community.[35]

Distinctive Hogan

The only high school built by the Community, Bishop Hogan High School stood on Kansas City's "Holy Hill" half a block from the Benedictine Convent of Perpetual Adoration. Co-educational from its opening in 1940, it was urged upon Mother Mary Francesca by Bishop Edwin O'Hara who knew from his work in Montana that co-ed, multicultural central schools were soon to succeed academies in the Midwest. Rivalry in academics and athletics with Rockhurst High School led to frequent communication between the Jesuit and SCL principals. Mutual respect and cooperation resulted, especially in questions of necessary discipline. As principals in the 1950s and early 1960s, Sisters Francetta O'Donnell and Mary Pauline Degan enjoyed the confidence of a vigorous parent-teacher association. In the mid-1950s, Hoganites were distinctive both in academics and personal choices. Between 1944 and 1960, eighty-one Hogan graduates responded to calls to religious life and the priesthood; fifty-five of these entered the Sisters of Charity of Leavenworth.[36]

When Sister Agnes Virginia Hamm became principal in 1963, she had taught dramatics and English at Hogan for seventeen years. The school newspaper dubbed her director of a cast of seven hundred. Interest in issues of social justice intensified during the decade, as did participation in musicals, the band, and the visual arts. Saturday science classes given by a professor on the faculty of the University of Missouri in Kansas City qualified students for the Junior Academy of Science. Foreign exchange students came to Hogan from France, Peru, Germany, and Panama. Catechetics based on scripture and the liturgy enlivened the teaching of religion. The Youth Corps drew student volunteers for projects to better the community, especially to work with poverty-stricken families or individuals. By 1965, enrollment reached a peak of 630.[37]

The school's population was becoming interracial. In 1969 sixty African American students were enrolled at Bishop Hogan; by 1978 they numbered 260, half of the student body, whose numbers were declining. In 1975 a professional study recommended moves to find new sources of revenue, to counter uninformed negative images of the school, to form a board for policy-making, and to communicate to all those involved the decisions of the Sisters of Charity about staffing the school. Financed by tuition, diocesan subsidy, and contributed services of the sisters and lay faculty, the school operated with a deficit of $12,000. With the help of parents' fund-raising, Hogan made up the deficit. Enrollment, however, had dropped by 100 in a year's time. About 70 percent of Hogan's graduates were accepted by colleges and universities, many with scholarships or grants.[38] To maintain that record and the philosophy that governed the school would require major commitments.

Hogan took pride in its role as a stabilizer in a changing society. Assisting the student to develop values of a Christian committed to a better life for all in a more viable democracy was a demanding goal. Religion classes were required with the serious condition of no proselytizing. No objections had been registered from a student body only 60 percent Catholic. Yet the transition to an integrated school was not uncomplicated. The spirit of ownership by students and their parents who had committed much to the school's maintenance and reputation was deeply rooted. Many students resisted the leadership of African Americans on the student council and playing fields. Strongly principled parents resolved to stay but "couldn't stick it out."

Bishop Hogan High School flourished with the support of students, faculty, staff, and parents.

In the early 1960s, Sisters Mary Bridget Mullen, Mary Leo McNamara, and Agnes Virginia Hamm gathered around a fire engine on the grounds of an annual outing sponsored by the Parents' Club. In 1970 the same adventure delighted Sisters Mary Helen Bristow, Edna Hunthausen, and Rosella Mary Hehn.

The tenor of the faculty in adapting to needs of new students was misinterpreted as misplaced favoritism.

Recalling the time, Sister Ann Barton, principal in 1973 with a faculty of thirty including thirteen Sisters of Charity, said the "teachers were the backbone of integration." They met with parents, students, and facilitators for three intensive days of exercises in welcoming strangers and learning from cultural differences. Faculty members Louis Read and Mike Day as well as Al Brooks, president of the Parents' Club, and other parents were of special help throughout the first year. Much of the principal's time was spent breaking up fights. But students grew up to the challenge and took charge the second year. Joe Alpo, student council president, Cleon Brown, and Lester Blare typified those who were bigger than the contentious issues. Whatever we do, they told her, "we're going to have fun."[39]

Confronting Change

Mandated in 1975, the special study of Hogan went on for two years. In 1977, Sister Victoria Perkins became principal, with eleven Sisters of Charity on a faculty of thirty and two sisters on a staff of seven. One result of the study was consultation with David L. Brecht, OSA, of Villanova College, on elements of success in the predominantly African American schools staffed by Augustinians. Hogan's faculty focused on quality in the students' critical thinking, writing, and study skills and on practicality in preparation for parenting and managing personal finances. The student population of 475 was diverse not only in race—African American, Caucasian, Hispanic, and a small number of Asian students—but also in cultural, economic, and religious backgrounds. Recognition of Hogan's achievement came with the Black Catholic Caucus Award and materially with a capital improvement campaign that raised a million dollars.[40]

A survey of sisters who knew the school brought a 75 percent return and revealed positive attitudes with serious uncertainties about the sisters' future at Hogan. Out of sixty-four replies, 55 percent answered *yes* to the question of whether the Community should continue staffing Hogan if the non-Catholic population continued to grow. Only five answered *no*; about 40 percent were uncertain. With the interracial ratio as it then stood, 65.6 percent were willing to teach at Hogan, slightly fewer if the number of African Americans increased. A desire for education in their culture was registered by 53 percent of the respondents. Suggestions were many: alternate plans for meeting needs of exceptional students, visits to the Augustinian schools, stronger PR in feeder schools, Hogan as a magnet school and as a mission serving students of other faiths.[41]

In 1985 the school celebrated its fortieth anniversary. The next year Sister Barbara Aldrich succeeded Sister Vickie, who was appointed superintendent of schools in the Kansas City–St. Joseph, Missouri, diocese. Like her predecessor, Sister Barbara considered ethnic diversity one of the greatest strengths of the school. During her five-year term, she fostered alliances of mutual benefit with the diocese, the neighboring St. Peter's parish, and Rockhurst College. Hogan housed the licensed Bishop Helmsing Early Childhood Center that served the students' graduation requirement of a class in parenting. A covenant agreement with St. Peter's formalized the exchange of facilities and services on school board and parish catechumenate. A partnership with Rockhurst engaged college students as tutors and offered college credit to Hogan seniors in language and history taught at their school and physics at the college. Professors observed the high school classes; Hogan gained an unbudgeted physics teacher.[42]

Despite the number of sisters who hoped for a continued role in developing a new Hogan, the Community found resources inadequate and handed over administration of the school to the Archdiocese of Kansas City–St. Joseph in 1989. With Sister Katherine Franchett on its board, Hogan became a charter school in 1999. Donna Miller was principal of Hogan Preparatory Academy when the Community released the building in 2003. Of almost sixty years of service at Bishop Hogan High School, about a third of that time constituted a gradual transition to its governance by the people who continue to support it.[43]

Small But Mighty

During their forty-five years at Sacred Heart High School in Falls City, the Sisters of Charity formed many friendships with young Nebraskans and their parents. Re-opening the school in 1941 during World War II, the sisters succeeded the Ursuline sisters who had staffed Sacred Heart Academy from 1896 to 1941.[44] By 1954, the parish had financed at a cost of $185,000 a one-story building of modern design to house both parochial elementary and secondary students. In 1963, as principals of Sts. Peter and Paul and Sacred Heart respectively, Sisters Georgeanne Desch and Ann Teresa Conroy initiated IMPAC (Instructional Media Production Advancement Center), a program of independent study. Individual student record-keeping called on a rich store of films, records, and models of learning in every field.

A three-year program integrated science and advanced math courses. Drama took young Nebraskans into classics such as Aristophanes's *The Birds* and Moliere's *Imaginary Invalid*. A sixty-two-piece band won first place ratings at festival time. Graduation from Sacred Heart, frequently with honors, was the first goal of Sts. Peter and Paul students; completing college or university was the second. Master's degrees were not uncommon among alumni.[45]

Sisters Marie Carmel Dunning, Mary Hilaria Phipps, and Mary Denise Sternitzke succeeded as principals of Sacred Heart into the 1980s. In 1983 the school graduated eleven. Declining enrollments, rising costs, and a limited number of sisters brought the decision to withdraw from Falls City in 1991. Sisters Virginia Flanick and Mary Eugenia Floersch were the last to teach there, and Sister Mary Paulette Fitzgerald was the last to serve in the office, ending a century of the presence of women religious, fifty years that of Sisters of Charity of Leavenworth.[46]

Growth in North Kansas City

St. Pius X High School opened in North Kansas City in 1956,[47] thanks to the initiative of Bishop Charles LeBlond and the Community's response to his invitation to staff the school. Sister John Berchmans (Alice) Leist was principal and Sister Mary Adelaide (Mary Alice) Grellner assisted her, with a faculty of five for forty-one students lodged for a year in Saint Michael's Grade School. The new St. Pius X attracted students from the many families who had resided north of the Missouri River for decades and from families moving into housing developments mushrooming near Kansas City International Airport a few miles to the north. Within a year, enrollment had more than tripled; the faculty of thirteen included five more Sisters of

St. Pius X High School, opened in 1956

Charity. A strong curriculum with many opportunities for student leadership generated applications; by 1960 enrollment had reached 520, with a prediction of 1,150 by 1968.[48]

Sister Rose Carmel McKenna was principal in the mid-sixties when the school's guidebook placed education on a continuum with life. Its aims were the deepening of Christian life in the student, development of intellectual habits, and development of physical, social, and emotional maturity. One reason for the phenomenal growth was the annual tuition of $100 kept within the reach of area families. Mrs. Ethel Leist, mother of Sisters John Berchmans and Lorraine, made financial arrangements with discretion. With expenditure per student at $370 and receipts at about $290, the gap of $80 had to be met with fund-raising. Pius X was a new school on its own.[49]

A board of directors established in 1970 became the immediate governing body for policy-making and strategic planning for financial support. An associate board for scholarships and funding took responsibility for assisting qualified students short of funds for tuition. A development committee included representatives of various faiths from the North Kansas City community. This governance and support structure modeled changes to come gradually and partially elsewhere. Under a priest appointed president, Sister Mary Thomas O'Flannigan was principal from 1969 until 1978; Sister Rita Smith succeeded her. The number of sisters on faculty and staff rose from nine to twenty-two during the 1970s. Students progressed in academics, in public performance, and in athletics under Coach Joseph Monachino, Sr. Modular scheduling allowed for faculty mentoring, self-initiated learning, and expanded resources. A testing and guidance program facilitated transition to college and to employment.[50] Despite the school's strong reputation and the decade's touted strong economy, enrollment did not continue to climb.

In 1979, the board of directors opened the position of principal to applications. After making sure she was not competing with lay persons who wanted and needed the job, Sister Rita Smith applied for the position. Hired by the board, Sister sought the assistance of an administrative team: Sister Renee Washut as vice principal; Sister Rose Marie Catudal, coordinator of scheduling; and Joseph Monachino, coordinator of student welfare. Enrollment, which had declined with an increase in tuition, began to rise again. Active recruitment efforts to draw students from feeder schools included a video of St. Pius X created by Shirley Koritnik, visits to parents' homes, bussing students, communication with pastors, and a scholarship program. Stan Grabowski, chair of the associate board for funding, led major drives. The closing of De LaSalle Academy by the Christian Brothers and of Lillis and Glennon High Schools sent students to Northland in the 1970s and 1980s.

As many as twelve Sisters of Charity were on the faculty and staff of St. Pius X High School in 1986 when Sister Rita retired from her position. By the 1990s, the number had declined to five: Sisters Ann Victoria Garcia, faculty; Regina Mary Link, librarian; Rose Marie Catudal and Catherine Laboure Conway, office staff; and Sister Mary Sharon Verbeck, registrar.[51] The latter spent thirty-three years at Pius, teaching math and serving as counselor, registrar, and sacristan before retiring in 2002. Hundreds of students and alumni were proud that Sister Mary Sharon knew each of them by name. Sister Mary Lenore Martin served on the board of trustees from 1995 to 2002.[52]

From the heyday of these high schools a former teacher recalled pep rallies, Friday night games and Saturday paper drives, the fund-raisers to pay for supplies and field trips, the endless rounds of meetings on aims and objectives that left one glassy-eyed, cafeteria duty, stacks of papers...and survival. "You remember the Honor assemblies that everyone had to attend," she said, "and gave you special pain because you taught the less proficient students, and the idiotic joy you felt when you saw eyes light up as one of your slow-starters 'just got it!' You remember the parents and their loyalty, digging into what were never deep pockets for yet another drive. These schools had to go it alone. Their only modus vivendi was 'pay as you go' to keep the doors open and the lights on."[53]

The energy that fired administration and teaching in the secondary schools staffed by the Community did not disappear. Nor was it simply channeled elsewhere as numbers of sisters declined. Transition to lay leadership required continuing attention to each school's original mission, quality of service, and current problems. The responsibilities of ownership and support of schools, both elementary and secondary, fell to the diocese and parish. But as personal discernment of ministry became an essential factor in mission assignments, the traditions of staffing a given school weighed heavily on individual sisters and the Community. Students, graduates, and parents were personally known to sisters who had taught and served there for crucial years of many young lives. The influence of these women's teaching and service and personalities was embedded in the school's history and in countless memories.

The love of teaching itself was always something of a mystery, instinctively detected by students in a teacher's unbridled enthusiasm for the subject, an ability to raise questions and find some value in every answer, a stubborn insistence that there was a fact or a truth worth looking for. One veteran English teacher pleaded with her students—in a poem: "...Enjoy a class or hate it, / but please, I beg you, learn. Take one word said.... / let it touch the core of your bones,...May you / be unsettled, unhinged, unhappy, may you / be one word more yourself when you leave this class...."[54]

But teachers varied. There were those who couldn't let a student fail whatever the demand on both of them; others who believed that failure by able students was their own responsibility. Now, with the turnovers of time, a sister's contribution to the staff as principal, teacher, librarian, alumni director, counselor, development officer, liturgist, social action coordinator, or board member meant the continuing presence of the Sisters of Charity of Leavenworth.

Reflecting on causes of teachers' leaving the schools, Sister Susan Rieke, who was on Ward High School's English faculty for eleven years, surmised that a long time in the same ministry and the need of a break contributed to changes in ministry. The aging factor or a sense of diminishing effectiveness provoked honest self-appraisals. In the 1960s and 1970s, broadening roles for women in parish life offered new opportunities; a few desired direct pastoral ministry to adults. Advanced degree work carried for some an assumed move to another level of education. But working toward a master's degree was an accreditation requirement for secondary school faculty; it did not motivate many to seek more. The simple force of change and freedom to make it was felt, Sister Susan said, by a relatively small number of secondary teachers.[55]

Strength Underlying Change

Given the numbers required to staff the schools as they had multiplied during the first two-thirds of the century, joy in teaching with readiness for the job was not a universal experience. Increased confidence and professionalism came with the degree completion mandated by the Renewal Chapter of 1968–1969.[56] Significant patterns of strength in curriculum, teaching, and programs emerge from even an incomplete account of the schools. Development in the faith with solid learning in classic subjects was the end; personal attention to individual need, resource, and capacity the essential means. A firm place for the arts characterized the curriculum at every level and led to performance directed by trained musicians, directors, and artists. Service to those without means or privilege became a way of life for some students moving into adulthood. Graduates won scholarships, obtained good jobs, and achieved civic recognition. Outcomes of their learning fill alumni records.[57]

Teachers generally renewed their own learning in professional organizations; many won respect in their fields. Lay and religious faculty worked as equals and partners. Administrators adapted to the demands of team teaching and flexible scheduling, the need for counseling services, and long-range planning. Perhaps an indefinable aspect of sisters' leadership in many instances was the ability to function effectively under the authority of a priest administrator. The number of Sisters of Charity not ready to retire who by 1980 had elected ministries other than formal education approached only eighty.

The number of teachers who had left the Community by then, however, was more than 200.[58] Besides diminishment by deaths and retirement, the loss to the educational system that had been supported by the Sisters of Charity of Leavenworth over the previous century and a quarter was dramatic. Further, as events were to prove, these teachers would not be replaced by newcomers to religious life. The Catholic family culture that had nourished religious vocations was changing radically. Though still valued by innumerable parents, choice of the priesthood or religious life was not so clear-cut as it once had been.[59]

Causes more profound, however, than personal preference and cultural influences were at work in the lives of women religious. Staying the course *or* changing direction within the Community often took courage and required prayerful discernment. Reasons for leaving religious community altogether were too complex to explain with generalities. What remains a unique mystery is how, in individual ways and communal experiences, Sisters of Charity shared new problems with unprecedented energy and faced inexplicable dilemmas. Renewing an original commitment was a challenge peculiar to their way of life in a troubled time when each one's vocation, reverberating daily, was calling her to continue or to change the shape of her ministry to the people of God.

CHAPTER 12

The Maturing of a College

A perusal of mission statements of Saint Mary College from its first commencement as a four-year institution to the present decade reflects an evolution in the post-secondary education ministry of women religious. It represents a centrifugal movement from a powerful center, the Christian tradition of liberal learning, to expanding circles of engagement with the world. Acknowledging the value of "vocational power" that enables the graduate to achieve economic independence, Saint Mary aimed in 1933 "to inculcate in her students the power of self-knowledge, self-reverence, and self-control through response to ideals... deeply rooted in religious convictions."

From 1939 into the 1950s, the goal for its students was living "a full rich life, guided by the light of faith and reason" through development of character, preparation for material demands of life, and cultivation of relationships. For some dozen years from 1955, the college's principal objective was "to lead her students to the perfection for which they were created" through intellectual and spiritual growth in qualities needed to "fit them for marriage and motherhood, for occupations and professions suited to women, and for civic, social and apostolic responsibilities." The center was expanding within accepted parameters.

In 1969 the stated purpose of Saint Mary College was to graduate "a woman of her times, yet not swept along with the tide and tastes of her

The Maturing of a College

times.... Her concerns are the world's. She is an articulate Christian with a drive to serve in a democratic, pluralistic society." Twenty years later the college, now co-educational, sought "to prepare graduates to live value-centered lives of learning, service, and character rich according to the best resources within each person." In 2004, the mission statement read: "The University of Saint Mary educates students of diverse backgrounds to realize their God-given potential and prepares them for value-centered lives and careers that contribute to the well being of our global society." Its values, deriving from belief in each person's dignity, continued to be "community, respect, justice, and excellence." Further, the last mission statement was the product of collaborative efforts by 120 members of faculty, staff, and administrators of the newly named University.[1]

Faculty and administrators educated during the twenties, thirties, and early forties established that firm center of learning and faith and provided a core of leadership in the college that extended into the 1960s and 1970s and beyond. The influence of these sisters who established the strength and initial reputation of Saint Mary continued throughout the century in the teaching and administrative roles of former students who entered the Community and received the education needed to staff a growing academic institution. In 1980 these sisters numbered almost 30 in a faculty and staff of 128.[2]

Both personal growth and cultural change in Church and society brought major developments to the college as well as significant leadership of lay faculty and staff. The institution moved from the status of a four-year liberal arts college for women to that of a co-ed university offering the baccalaureate and master's degree in day and evening/weekend programs on three sites in Leavenworth, Wyandotte, and Johnson Counties. The story of this evolution falls into three periods over the last half-century: the years from 1950 to 1964 when Sister Mary Paul Fitzgerald served as vice president and sisters who had helped to found the college in the 1930s remained in strength on the faculty; the twenty-five years of Sister Mary Janet McGilley's presidency; and the decade and a half that ushered in brief terms of recruited presidents and the early presidency of Sister Diane Steele, a time of separate incorporation and sponsorship by the Sisters of Charity of Leavenworth.

The closing of St. Mary's Academy in 1950 made room in two historic buildings, St. Mary and Xavier Halls, for an expanding college program. The Graduate Division, established during Sister Mary Paul's vice presidency, enabled school personnel to become more effective in their professional roles and to enrich their general and special knowledge in the field of education. The dean of this summer program, Sister Rose Dominic Gabisch, enrolled fifty-one in the first class and guided thirteen of them through to their master's degree in the first commencement in 1955. Forty-three principals of the Community and 19 teachers had graduated by 1966, when 159 sisters from thirty-one communities were enrolled. By 1970, when the division closed, 228 students had completed the master's program. They included 17 lay teachers, a priest, 112 sisters of other communities, and 98 Sisters of Charity of Leavenworth. By 1977, 427 Sisters of Charity had earned the bachelor's degree from Saint Mary College.[3] Because of its quality, the education department, chaired then by Sister Mary Kevin Hollow, gained strength in student enrollment, reputation in the educational community, and grant support during the years that followed.

Departments were growing in the 1950s and early 1960s, during the presidency of Dr. Arthur M. Murphy and under the guidance of teachers with advanced degrees bringing new strength to their departments. Science students benefited from Sister Agnes Marie Horner's participation in the NSF-sponsored Nuclear Isotope Studies program at Oak Ridge, Tennessee, and her licensed ham radio operation. Her faculty included Sister Mary Aquinas Haas and Sister Marie Pierre Leonard. Sister Ann Elizabeth Shea taught mathematics until her untimely death brought to Sister Andrea Johnston the responsibility for shaping the growing program. Sister Mary Florentia Schouten taught the business courses that later developed into a dual major department under the leadership of Sister Mary Corine Pohle. Modern languages flourished under the guidance of Sister Mary Vincentine Gripkey, who designed the language laboratory in the new Miege Hall. Sister Rose Paul Tetyak directed the nursing education program.

At the death in 1966 of Father Edward Lillie, OP, who had guided the theology program since 1957, Sister Mary Jude Redle succeeded him as chair of the department. Father Edward McGinnis, college chaplain, taught in the program. Sister Mary Edwin DeCoursey chaired the budding philosophy department. The art department matured as Sister Theresa Fagan drew on experiences of study abroad and Donald Tefft joined the faculty. Developing music and drama departments were the charge of Sisters Rose Vincentia Tomlin and Mary Camilla Montgomery. Sister Mary Catherine Floersch began the china and crystal collections that enhanced coursework in home economics. Her faculty included Sisters Mary Hugh Dearborn and Mary Edwina (Dorothy) Harvat. Sister Mary Ernestine Whitmore led an English faculty that included Dr. Catherine Jarrott and Sister Leo Gonzaga Erbacher, who modeled writing for publication for students of the Writing Lab. Sister Margaret Clare Herron, classics professor and dean of the college, was the first to be named professor emerita on retirement.[4] The history department grew under Sister Mary Paul, who brought Dr. Agnes Sirridge and Sister Thomas Aquinas to the faculty.

The Maturing of a College

St. Mary's Hall, once Mother House of the Community and site of St. Mary's Academy, now Administration Building for the University of Saint Mary

Year after year, the 1960s were to see building of every kind. At the north end of the campus, the new Miege Hall housed business and home economics departments and science and language laboratories. To free construction space for the new dining complex, the first forty feet of the old Miege was removed in the fall of 1962; the foreshortened building was renamed Aquinas Hall, home for the humanities and arts. Blessed in the spring of 1963, St. Joseph Dining Hall and kitchen was erected between the Georgian Berchmans and Victorian Mead and St. Mary's, a tribute to the architectural ingenuity of Maurice Carroll. By the end of the academic year, resident students looked forward to new rooms in Maria Hall, to open in the fall of 1964 with suites for four occupants and spacious lounges.[5]

Saint Mary's growth was evident to a broad community. The performing arts sought audiences that the Academy's Xavier Auditorium could not hold. In the fall of 1962, Sister Mary Dolorita Flynn, new chair of the drama department, took her cast and crew of *The Miracle Worker* to the Music Hall in Kansas City, where the music department's spring festivals had drawn crowds for ten years. With a faculty of accomplished musicians, Sister Rose Vincentia brought the community/college orchestra, founded in the 1960s, to forty members. The beauty of halls and lounges on campus was enhanced by art treasures given the college by Sir John Craig, of Tulsa, Oklahoma—oil paintings, small sculptures and stained glass.[6]

Academic achievement was at the heart of the operation. Individual performance according to ability with attentive advising was the priority. Requirements in philosophy and theology were at the core of the student's program. Science majors prepared for advanced study and careers

Berchmans Hall, erected in 1930 for student residence and student affairs offices

in research or medical technology; assignments in social science took students from classroom to urban housing and ghettoes under the guidance of Sister Frances Therese Shea. An Honors Colloquium, directed first by Sister Mary Janet McGilley of the English faculty, then by Sister Mary Rebecca Conner, chair of the art department, brought qualifying students into dialog with faculty and guest presenters.

The year of Latin America drew speakers from the Command and General Staff College at Fort Leavenworth and concluded with a study tour to Mexico. Later topics were Russian culture, Eastern Orthodox icons, the Orient, and American Colonial history. History major Maureen Burke, the first recipient of a scholarship honoring Sister Mary Paul, and English major Kathy Dlabal spent their junior year studying at the Extension of Loyola University in Rome with students from the United States, Europe, Africa, and the Communist bloc. In subsequent years, juniors studied in Bolivia, Colombia, and France.[7]

The decade saw a resurgence of volunteer social work and the lay apostolic activity that had marked Catholic college campuses of the 1940s. Students developed leadership skills through participation in the National Federation of Catholic College Students, the civil rights movement, and a new Resident Assistant program in Student Services. Camps and day care for special children, tutoring high school drop-outs, visiting nursing homes, and teaching religion in the diocesan CCD program were steady drawing cards. Missions at home and abroad attracted Saint Mary graduates to the Extension Lay Volunteers and the Papal Volunteers in Latin America. Rosemary Hughes, '60, first lay missionary, served in Belize, British Hondura; Pat Olive, '61, and Rose Schopper, '62, in Lima, Peru. A dozen graduates of 1964 and 1965 were missioned to Brazil, Venezuela, and poor parishes in southern states. A graduate of the clinical nursing program served with the Red Cross in Vietnam. In 1963 fourteen Saint Marians from four classes entered the novitiates of five religious congregations.[8]

When she first addressed the college as president in the fall convocation of 1964, Sister Mary Janet McGilley invited the students to an examined life. Quoting John Henry Newman, whose *Idea of a University* she and Sister Mary Kevin had brought to Saint Mary's curriculum from their study at Boston College, she said, "What I'd like to lobby for here is...that you give yourselves root room...time enough, space enough, patience enough, talk enough, quiet enough to let the roots go deeper that the fruit may be better...." She was to spend the next twenty-five years, an unprecedented

St. Joseph Dining Hall, topped with a skylight that centers mealtimes, university gatherings, and public events

term for a college president at the time, trying to make room for students to plunge their roots into good ground.⁹

During those years, Sister Mary Janet expanded the legacy inherited from the college's founders. New visibility in the Leavenworth/Lansing community derived from cultural offerings of high quality. Through programs in the 1970s and 1980s, Sister extended the reach of the college to the underserved: working adults in need of a degree; residents of Wyandotte County, especially women, otherwise unable to manage a college education; and inmates of federal and state prisons who qualified for college courses aimed at associate and baccalaureate degrees. Doing so, she committed the college in a new era to the Vincentian ideal of ministry to those most in need.

In procession with the graduating class of 1965, Sister Mary Janet accompanies the Honorable Mike Mansfield, commencement speaker.

Expanding the Base

Supported by faculty and staff, Sister Mary Janet laid the groundwork for that future with repeated moves toward separate incorporation, with campus-wide conversations about issues related to male residency, and with the beginnings of a substantial endowment. New professional programs and master's level courses in education responded to needs of a growing urban population. Successful capital campaigns and grant applications along with generous scholarship gifts supported the principle of good stewardship but did not lessen its burdens. A curriculum grounded in liberal arts, sciences, and humanities was the lodestar of Sister Mary Janet's endeavors.

Two months after the 1964 convocation, on November 10, Dr. Arthur M. Murphy, former president of the college, died. He had retired the previous spring after more than thirty years' presiding over Saint Mary and serving the civic community. Innumerable students had taken his courses in sociology, anthropology, and the papal encyclicals. A member of the board of directors of the Kansas Foundation for Private Colleges and of the executive committee of the National Catholic Education Association, he had been a Leavenworth city commissioner for eight years. Most valuable for him, however, had been his personal contact with students and volunteer teaching at the United States Penitentiary.¹⁰

During the first three years of her presidency, Sister Mary Janet sought friends and leaders in the civic communities surrounding Saint Mary to bolster support, to build a public image, and to assist in planning. She welcomed students' parents into their own association, invited women and men to Leavenworth/Lansing and Kansas city councils, and created a President's Council for advice on finance, recruiting, and student life. When she announced the Women's Associates as an appropriate way of broadening the base of friends of the college, she had the ideal sponsor in Sister Agnes Eugenia Finn who hosted the group at annual luncheons and informative tours of the Mother House and college.[11]

Though small and relatively isolated thirty miles from Kansas City, Saint Mary and its towered buildings stood on a hill marked by frontier and Civil War history. Its founders had lived in Leavenworth when Lincoln visited, forty miles from Lawrence, raided by Quantrell a few years later. Originally, children of officers stationed at Fort Leavenworth were schooled at the academy; later daughters and mothers took degrees at the college. At times, retired officers found their managing and administrative skills or their teaching experience welcome in college offices and classrooms. Situated between Leavenworth and Lansing, the college served the incarcerated in federal, military, and state prisons in the 1950s and 1960s with informal classes in literature, sociology, and religion. An Interfaith Choir drew sisters from the campus. Both lay and religious faculty continued the spiritual ministry and choirs that Sisters of Charity had begun in the prisons during the previous century.

Sister Mary Janet McGilley, President of Saint Mary College, 1964–1989

Vigorous and visible leadership was necessary for a Catholic institution in such an environment. As the college grew, educational networks were taking shape across the nation and in each state. Saint Mary faculty and students participated in a consortium, the Kansas City Regional Council for Higher Education, and profited from membership in the Association of Independent Colleges of Kansas (AICK). In 1971, Sister Mary Janet was elected to the executive committee of AICK, which met with Governor Docking's new Planning Commission for Education in Kansas. The following year she became president of the Kansas Foundation for Private

Colleges and chair of the board of directors of the Kansas Independent College Fund. Early in the 1980s, she was invited to the Commission on the Status of Women in Higher Education of the American Council on Education. In that decade too, she was elected vice-president of North Central Association's Commission on Institutes of Higher Education.[12]

Recognizing the need early for a development office, she asked Sister Mary Vincentia Maronick to direct it. Eight years on the faculty of the mathematics department and ten years in the office of the freshman dean had familiarized Sister with the curriculum, the faculty and staff, the quality of incoming freshmen, and the idiosyncrasies of college students in general. It had not acquainted her with the perils of cultivating prospective donors and soliciting major gifts—the twentieth-century art of begging—or with the techniques of office management, budgeting, public relations, and deferred giving. Mary V, as she'd been nicknamed by students, had more in common with Sister Mary Janet than undergraduate memories. Born teachers both, they took on the responsibilities of administration with little preparation, with firm determination to do the job, and with profound faith.[13]

Faculty brought the same kind of energy and initiative to their responsibilities in the late 1960s. Sister Edward Mary Brown, chair of the physical education department, introduced archery and recruited professional teachers for a dance program that extended students' choices in fulfilling their physical education requirement. She organized the Women's Athletic Association, the annual Wyandotte picnic, and intramurals in volleyball and basketball. Education students mentored by Sister Gregory Sheehy participated in CUTE (Council for Urban Teacher Education), a student-teacher semester in inner-city Kansas City schools funded by the United States Office of Education. The program became a demonstration center and model for other cities and received an award from the American Association of Colleges for Teacher Education.

Lay women and men who spent much or all of their teaching careers at Saint Mary were recruited in the 1960s. Hadley Crawford came to the music faculty; Anthony Molina developed and directed the college/community orchestra. Michael Paul Novak joined the English faculty, contributing to the department's growth for the next thirty-seven years. Terry Brungardt taught sociology and anthropology for thirty-five years, chairing the department for twenty of them. A native of Puerto Rico, Virginia Monserrate began her long stint in the modern language department, with Carmen Lederer teaching French. After emigrating from Cuba, Ada Herrara had joined the science faculty, teaching at Saint Mary for the next thirty-one years.[14]

Bible Week at Saint Mary, celebrated annually since 1943, reached a peak in the 1960s when Sir John Craig, donor of the college's extensive Bible col-

Entrance to De Paul Library, with a window view from one of three study areas

lection, and Sister Mary Mark Orr hosted Rabbi Herman E. Schaalman of Temple Emmanuel, Chicago; Carroll Stuhlmueller, CP, and Roland de Vaux, OP, director of l'Ecole Biblique, Jerusalem. Crossing centuries of scriptural texts, the collection includes illuminated manuscripts on vellum of the Gospels, Acts, and Epistles; the sixteenth-century Antwerp Polyglot Bible in Hebrew, Greek, Aramaic, and Syrian translations; and a first edition of the Douay-Rheims, first Roman Catholic translation of the Bible into English.

Another lasting resource for students' learning was the Lincoln Collection, a gift to the college in 1969 of Dr. Bernard Hall of the Community Mental Health Service, Roosevelt Hospital, New York City. Dr. Hall was serving as a senior clinical consultant and Distinguished Visiting Scholar in Psychology at the Menninger School of Psychiatry when he became a member of Saint Mary's President's Council. Judged to be the finest assemblage of documents and memorabilia of Abraham Lincoln west of Illinois, the collection of ten thousand items includes newspapers, portraits, a letter of sympathy signed by President and Mrs. Lincoln, and one of thirteen original souvenir copies of the Thirteenth Amendment bearing Lincoln's signature.[15]

Student movements usually reached the Midwest a year or two after they originated on the coasts. Except for the Universities of Wisconsin and Michigan, this held for the civil rights and anti-war demonstrations. In the late 1960s, two faculty members, Michael Novak and Bela Keryafalvi, organized a group of students in protest against the Vietnam War. In November of 1969, with students from nearby campuses, they marched more than a hundred strong from the college campus to Wolman Park, where they rallied with brief but impassioned addresses, songs, and readings from Ghandi and Martin Luther King Jr. Immediate reaction to the Kent State tragedy came from students who invited faculty to participate in a memorial service.[16]

Divisions of sentiment on campus about the war grew so tense that Sister Mary Janet felt obliged to make a statement in the student dining room—a rare and reluctant action for her. She spoke to the values of liberal education in the Christian tradition that protected every individual's right to speak in dissent from or in support of public actions and political positions. The principles of human dignity and freedom that education safeguards require respect for such rights and at the same time invite critical judgment, the foundation of a viable democracy. Her words brought a sense of calm to all who heard her.

From 1970 to 1972, Saint Mary College was represented on every continent except Australia: Father Imre Kekessy in Latin America; Father Lee at his home village in China; Sister Mary Edwin DeCoursey and Sister Mary Lenore Martin with groups of teachers in India; and Sister Mary James Harrington studying in Europe. On the summer faculty of the Catholic University of America, Sister Mary Corine Pohle taught business education. As a member of NEA's Teaching Corps, Sister Dorothy Harvat traveled to Ethiopia to instruct secondary-school teachers in food and nutrition. In England, Sister Marie Paula Hardy studied with Dorothy Heathcote, pioneer in dramatic improvisation as a method of teaching. Sister Mary Liguori Horvat participated in an Asian Seminar that took her to Tokyo, Hong Kong, and Honolulu.[17]

Growth in Many Directions

The 1970s brought creative expansion in the curriculum, student associations, and public relations. Fall 1970 enrollment was the highest since 1966, when the pre-clinic program for nurses had opened. Sister Francetta O'Donnell, director of admissions, worked with Ellen McCarthy, in charge of recruiting. Many faculty initiated recruiting efforts that continued over the next two decades. Retention stood at 77 percent and a total of almost six hundred students showed an increase of one hundred, in contrast to the national trend. A federal degree-completion program for veterans of the Vietnam War brought military personnel from Fort Leavenworth to the campus until government support for these "bootstrappers" was terminated later in the decade. Both students and faculty benefited from an exchange program that operated between 1966 and 2000 between Saint Mary and the Jesuit Sophia University in Tokyo. As the program developed, two Saint Marians enrolled for Sophia's summer term and a Japanese student came to the college for the regular school term.[18]

During a sudden Kansas thunderstorm that interrupted the commencement ceremony in 1971, the Saint Mary Center at the University of Kansas was born. On their way to Xavier Auditorium, Sister Mary Janet and Chancellor W. Clarke Wescoe, the commencement speaker, exchanged thoughts about how the university and the college might pursue mutually beneficial arrangements. Ideas that bore fruit included reciprocal graduate credit for summer workshops, class audits and mutual library privileges, collaboration in teaching internships, and faculty exchange. The house of study for Saint Mary students opened on the university campus in the fall of 1971.[19] Nevertheless, visibility of this small women's college, for many years outside the reporting radius of the *Kansas City Star*, was a perennial problem.

A degree of fame came to Saint Mary unexpectedly in 1972 with the Remnants, a stage band that began its life in the 1940s as "Dot and Her Dashes" when Dorothy Ditmars, Betty Martin, and Eleanor Long were fellow musicians at Saint Mary. Some twenty years later, Sisters Madeleva Ditmars, Mary Lenore Martin, and Dominic Long recruited several other Sisters of Charity of Leavenworth, assigned to the college and to high schools in the Kansas City area, to form a contemporary stage band. Their reputation grew as they played at college functions and at the Community's hospitals and schools in the area and performed with the Saint Mary Madrigals for the Kansas City Plaza Christmas lighting ceremony. During Christmas vacations they went on the road to Montana and California.

After a performance at Saint John's Hospital in Santa Monica, the Remnants attracted the attention of *The Lucy Show*'s producer. Numberless telephone calls, permissions, and contracts later, they returned to Hollywood for the taping session of "Lucy and Her All-Nun Band." An audience of three hundred stage hands, sound and prop, make-up, wardrobe, and transportation crews were all guests at a reception for the sisters at the Universal Studios commissary after the taping session. Interviews with AP and UP International, syndicated radio interviews, a front page story in *Variety*, and features in the *Los Angeles Times* and *Photoplay Magazine* provided ample publicity for the airing of the show November 1, 1972. Sister Mary Lenore, in charge of the recording of Remnant favorites, reported sales of about five thousand tapes. Materially, the Remnants' contribution to the Community—to missions where they performed and to the central fund for support of its works—amounted to about $100,000. Their contribution to the spirits of those who enjoyed their music was immeasurable.[20]

Keeping firm the foundation of a liberal arts education in the Christian tradition was the continuing priority of Saint Mary College. President's Grants encouraged professional development of faculty and staff through funding of personally designed projects of research, course preparation, and travel. Academic leadership created a challenging co-curriculum. The annual agenda of Delta Epsilon Sigma, national honor society with a chapter on campus since the 1940s, united the campus community in discussion of faculty lectures and readings and of students' honors papers. Sister Barbara Sellers, chapter sponsor, served a term on the national board.

For six years, the annual Classics Day brought student competitors from surrounding colleges and universities to test their knowledge of mythology and the Greek epics. Continuing innovative traditions of the Science Club, Jean Emerson and Sister Susan Chase added an annual canoe trip for seaworthy students and mentored majors for graduate study and research laboratories. Sister Mary Erwin Baker perfected self-paced study packets for math students that heralded student-centered learning in its early phases. Returning from doctoral research in medical sociology in urban and rural areas of Ghana, Sister Constance Phelps intensified the intercultural thrust of the behavioral science curriculum. In an outreach of the business department that he chaired for twenty-four years, Robert Russell organized a campus chapter of Phi Beta Lambda to cultivate students' leadership skills and professional standards. Sister Thomas Aquinas established a Phi Alpha Theta chapter for history majors.[21]

The Jubilee Scholarship, established by Mother Leo Frances Ryan in 1973 in the name of the Community, did much to raise the bar of academic achievement. More than a decade later, the Ross Fellowship emphasized service and leadership as well. Presidential and Honor scholarships attracted other promising students. The perpetual scholarship honoring Agnes T. Sirridge, Ph.D., was established by Drs. William T. and Marjorie S. Sirridge to honor the history professor's nineteen years of teaching in the college.[22]

The arts flourished. Over two decades, Xavier Theatre offered to college and civic communities performances ranging from *The Trojan Women* to *The Children's Hour*. Sister Bonnie Bachle formed a concert dance group that performed with the college/community orchestra. In later years the drama and music departments, led by Van Ibsen and William Krusemark, collaborated in a performing arts major, presenting Gilbert and Sullivan musicals, opera workshops, and children's theater. Graduates left Saint Mary prepared for every job in theater including set design, costuming, direction, house management, and the daily demands of a touring company. Thousands of school students came to campus annually for the Christmas children's play.

On request from a state organization, Sister Anne Callahan organized the annual Delaware League Music Festival that continued for five years with the help of Sister Dominic Long. The festivals brought some one thousand grade school and eight hundred high school students, teachers, and families to campus. In the early 1970s, the Concert Choir went on tour to St. Louis via Jefferson City, visiting six high schools and academies. The Sounds of Praise, a liturgical choir organized by Sister Rose Tomlin, traveled to parishes in Kansas City and Denver. Later in the decade, the Saint Mary Singers journeyed to Romania in an international performance program.

On campus the International Club, sponsored by the foreign language department, drew students from the Middle East, Europe, Latin America, Africa, India, Japan, Micronesia, and the Philippines to share their cultures with North American students. Virginia Monserrate, Emilie Gordon, and Yvonne Mauton prepared students for hosting duties and performance.[23] A living source of intercultural learning and one of the most beloved figures on the campus, Father Stephen Lee drew both Catholics and students of other faiths to his course in world religions. He took classes to the collection of Oriental art and sculpture at the Nelson-Atkins Gallery and to the local Jewish synagogue for evening worship. A student of Sanskrit, Father sought speakers on Islam and Hinduism. Chaplaincy at the federal prison during his years at Saint Mary and assistance at area churches brought Father Lee a host of friends. At his death in 1995, a crowd of students, faculty, townspeople, and representatives of the prisoners he had instructed filled Annunciation Chapel.[24]

That spiritual and cultural development was an essential element of Catholic higher education was a first principle of the college's mission. Student retreats took on various forms under the sponsorship of Campus Ministry, Student Services, and anyone with particular resources. Recalling classes, campus events, and hours of conversation, alumnae witnessed to the personal influence of faculty and staff, many of whom became lifelong friends. In the informal manner of the generation that had preceded them, faculty taught, advised, and provided a spiritual resource that challenged students' thinking and, by their own testimony, changed them for life.[25]

With initiative and encouragement, faculty managed to produce articles for professional journals in education, the sciences, literary criticism, and the arts. Michael Novak edited the letters of Rolfe Humphries, a classical poet, and three small volumes of his own poems, one of short fiction. Sister Susan Rieke published a book of her poems and later joined forces with Sister Mary Janet and Michael Novak in an anniversary volume of poetry. Dr. Terry Brungardt saw the publication of his basic text on juvenile delinquency.

Faculty regularly lectured on special topics, reviewed books, and served as consultants for civic organizations in Leavenworth and Lansing.

Enlarging the Vision

A major channel of collaboration between the college and civic community was joint grant application for Kansas Humanities programs in public adult education. From 1972 to 1974, the college co-sponsored with the Leavenworth community a series of town forums on public issues. History and English faculty continued to serve as book-discussion leaders and speakers for the next decades. Perhaps the most dramatic collaboration was the College Community Cultural Council that offered an annual program of drama, musical events, and lectures to the Leavenworth/Lansing/Fort Leavenworth community. Sparked by the leadership of Sister Mary Dolorita Flynn, the Council of some thirty townspeople and several college faculty and students met in working groups to plan and host each year a half-dozen programs presented by nationally recognized artists and scholars and offered to the public free of charge. Post-performance receptions were cross-cultural experiences for artists, students, and local residents alike.[26]

Guests who visited campus over the years for lecture series, for program development, for commencement, or in collaboration with neighboring colleges stimulated conversation across disciplines and professional experience. Hosted by students working with faculty committees, they included Senators Nancy Landon Kassebaum, Mike Mansfield, and Julian Bond; authors Rosemary Haughton, Eugene McCarthy, Stephen Ambrose, and Richard Rhodes; educators Jonathan Kozol and Frances Marian Berry; poets Richard Wilbur and William Stafford; and performers Hal Holbrook, Irene Dunne Griffin, and the Alvin Ailey Dancers. Guest speakers on an anniversary theme, "The American Journey," were Gary Wills, political philosopher, and John Altman, Kansas City filmmaker.[27]

The winter interim four-week term was an opportunity to concentrate on a unique area of learning. It ran for eight years until increasing off-campus enrollment lessened its feasibility. Courses in bioethics, criminal justice, Old Testament figures, Shakespeare, opera, and the world of Thomas More competed for numbers while other students traveled with teachers—to Florence and New York City, to sites of Colonial America, to Mexico and Guatemala, to Santa Fe and the Southwest, to London and Dublin, and to France. Faculty who came to the college during the 1980s and taught through the 1990s included Robert McAllister, Nancy King, and David Greene, behavioral sciences; Van Ibsen and Danielle Trebus, theater; Freda Proctor, music; Sister Susan Rieke, English; George Steger, history and international problems; Jean Emerson, biology; Robert Schimoler, philosophy; Les Rubenstein, business; Sisters Helen Forge, Mary Patricia Lenahan, and Frances Juliano, education; and Sister Kathleen Wood, theology.[28] Sister Madonna Fink came to stay in De Paul Library.

What Student Services called the "hidden curriculum" was a range of programs that included vocational and personal counseling, campus employment, health and recreational programs, and social and religious activities. Dean of students Sister Marie Therese Bride led a staff of developing professionals: Sister Margaret Petty, who re-organized the campus ministry program; Sister Bernadette Marie Teasdale, counseling and guidance; and Sister Mary Carol Conroy, RN, director of nursing service. To strengthen a traditional liaison between the college's students and administration, young alumnae—Mary Ann Slattery, Jeannie Harrington, Mary Morgan, and Penny Lonergan—were invited to the staff.

A major resource to both students and staff for more than twenty years, Dr. C. Kermit Phelps, clinical psychologist, traveled weekly to the college for individual counseling and group sessions. As chief of Psychology Services at the Veterans Administration Hospital in Kansas City, Missouri, and member of the faculties of the University of Kansas and KU Medical Center, Dr. Phelps complemented clinical practice with public and professional services. His work with students at Saint Mary and other Catholic educational institutions was an outlet for what he most enjoyed, teaching and counseling on interpersonal relations. Training at the Menninger foundation in Topeka enriched his background.[29]

Appointed dean of students in 1973, Sister Mary Elizabeth Kelly responded to students' requests for educational programs on drugs, for changes in curfew, and for an experiment in the dress code. In the 1980s as departments were arranging pre-professional internships for their majors, counselor Paula Timmons organized internships in corporate businesses in Kansas City and with alumnae throughout the country. Joanne Bangert established the annual Health Fair that provides testing and consultation with health professionals for students, staff, and faculty.[30]

In unusual ways, the college's traditional outreach brought contacts that students would not otherwise have enjoyed. Summer Stock, a two-week music theater camp for high school students, fostered talent in a non-competitive environment. The lecture committee addressed ecumenism through dialogue with Leavenworth clergy. A panel on prison reform included officials from Kansas State Penitentiary, the Disciplinary Barracks, and the Legal Aid and Defender Society. Students traveled with their instructor to Pine Ridge, South Dakota, for a site study of Plains Indians history. As chair of the history department, Sister Mary Lenore Martin was a member of the Leavenworth County Historical Society for years. The Leavenworth County Museum, a three-story mansion willed by the Carroll family to the county, offered first-hand experience of a home built in the Victorian style popular in the early decades of the First City of Kansas.[31]

Early-childhood education became a special program in the preparation of teachers when Sister France Juiliano completed doctoral studies. The Ancilla Center, opened in 1980 to serve both the college and civic communities, provided field experience for early-childhood majors. In a specially designed area, dozens of children enjoyed either pre-school learning or supervised day care under a certified director and staff. Especially valuable for health care providers in the area, the bachelor of science degree program in nursing came under the direction of Susan Hildebrand in 1984.[32]

Deeply Vincentian

A gradual and genuine expansion of students' world vision and moral sensibility developed over the years during the chaplaincy of Father John Stitz, who joined the college community in 1972. A native of Baileyville, Kansas, Father Stitz came to Saint Mary as college chaplain and pastor of Corpus Christi parish in Mooney Creek northwest of Leavenworth. Inviting students to minister there, he called his parish their west campus. Father's homilies were calls to live by the Gospel as champions of the poor and the oppressed and to oppose vigorously all forms of injustice. As director of the archdiocesan office for rural life, he brought a group of German farmers to campus on their tour of midwestern farms, and twice took Kansas farmers to China to discover how Asian people keep their vast land productive.[33]

The Vincentian spirit that flourished in both hidden and visible ways informed student programs and college undertakings. Under many influences—of teachers, counselors, and one another—students committed themselves to others in need. A program called CO-SWAP integrated college training with practical experience in providing services to central city families. Collaboration with fifty agencies in Kansas City made it possible for students to assist social workers and to prepare for work with the poor in rural areas. The Lighthouse program at Plaza Park in Bain City, a low-income area of Leavenworth, engaged thirty students in tutoring and organizing recreational programs for fourth to sixth graders from three schools. It was one of seven projects of Community Action chaired by Joann Sistrunk, class of 1974.[34] After the tragic church bombing of 1980 in Atlanta, Saint Mary joined the nation in ministering to children with a summer camp for African American youngsters. The most valuable recognition at commencement was the Ancilla Award, honoring Mother Mary

Ancilla and her devotion to the poor. Chosen by vote of students, staff, and faculty, the student judged to be most mindful of others' needs and active on their behalf receives the annual award.

Within the decade before its fiftieth anniversary, the college celebrated five of its longtime faculty and administrators as they retired. A master teacher of German, Sister Rose Dominic Gabisch became academic dean of the college in 1953. Invited to membership on state and national councils of education throughout the fifties and sixties, she was elected in 1964 for a three-year term as executive secretary of the Sister Formation Conference headquartered in Washington, DC. After serving Saint Mary as institutional research officer for six years, Sister Rose Dominic retired in 1973. An educator in the broadest sense, Sister consistently appealed to her representatives in Congress about the political situations in Central America, about hunger in Africa, about funding for Women, Infants, and Children (WIC), and in opposition to the death penalty. In retirement Sister served on the new archdiocesan Board of Total Education formed in 1974 and lived another active decade before she died.[35]

During her twenty-two-year tenure as academic dean of the college, Sister Mary Louise Sullivan had an open-door policy that Father Stitz mentioned in his homily at her funeral Mass in 1997. "Whoever came through those doors," he said, "found a friend, a professional educator, and a committed religious woman with incredible faith." Qualities of integrity, directness, and fairness distinguished Sister during six years of teaching chemistry and physics before being named academic dean in 1952. While in that office she was elected by the Chapter of 1956 to the Community Council for a six-year term. Her foresight, sense of stewardship, and habits of prudential judgment held the college on a steady course. The Sullivan Award for Teaching Excellence funded by Brother Peter Clifford, FSC, then president of the college, honors her each year as well as a faculty member selected by students and colleagues.[36]

Sister Mary Mark Orr directed the college's library for thirty-six years until she retired to become the Special Collections librarian. Before entering the Community she taught in a one-room schoolhouse at a distance from her farm home near Beattie, Kansas. Sister bought herself a Model T for the commute. In the summer of 1944, Sister Mary Mark attended the Inter-American Institute Seminar for Religious Teachers at the National University of Mexico. Because of anti-clerical policies of the Mexican government at the time, she and her companion, Sister Theresa Fagan, had permission to wear secular clothes. One of the paradoxes wrought by the Mexican people's faith was the pilgrimage, witnessed by the sisters that summer, of 3,400 men and boys, walking as many as nine miles in the sun, to pay homage to Our Lady of Guadalupe in the cathedral of Mexico City. During her tenure, images of Our Lady of Guadalupe identified the entrance to De Paul Library's special collections.

Over the years, Sister acquired for the library a valuable assortment of WPA dolls—fully costumed in ethnic traditions—made by unemployed men and women during the Great Depression, as well as a large number of German beer steins and valuable editions and memorabilia of Shakespeare. Sister Mary Mark enlarged holdings to approximately 110,700 volumes by 1972 when she relinquished direction of the library to Sister Anna Rose Hanne.[37]

Dean of students for twenty-one years, Sister Marie Therese Bride came to the college in 1952 after serving as teacher of Latin, assistant dean of women, and principal of St. Mary's Academy. With a master's degree in guidance and counseling from Saint Louis University, Sister developed the staff who established standards for campus life and social behavior that fed alumna conversations for decades. She retired in 1973 to work on the development staff as executive director of the Alumnae Association until 1979. With meticulous oversight and alumna support, Sister administered phonathons, Christmas luncheons, and annual reunions. In 1990, the college and alumnae honored Sister Marie Therese with three perpetual scholarships.[38]

In fragments of an essay, Sister Mary Ernestine Whitmore wrote, "In my own mind I was a child of the prairie, although I actually lived in a small town...." An affection for her past surfaced in rare comments Sister made about teaching Nebraska youngsters, first to eighth grade, in a one-room country schoolhouse near Indianola where she grew up. From childhood, she learned to love words and the books they filled. While she chaired the English department of the college for thirty-six years, Sister initiated *The Leaven*, a student literary magazine; advised *The Taper*, the college newspaper; and sponsored regional journalism conferences. The first alumna newsletter, *The Mary-Go-Round*, was her creation. The "E" Award for Excellence in English that Sister initiated with jubilee gifts recognizes a beginning English major at commencement. Sister's dissertation was published by the Catholic

Sister Mary Ernestine Whitmore, chair of the English department, 1936–1972

University of America in 1937 and reprinted in 1972 by Cooper Square Publishers in New York as *Medieval English Manners and Customs in Chaucer's Works*.

A line from Sister Mary Janet's address at the college's memorial convocation for Sister Francis Therese could commemorate these women and others who staffed the Community's schools for decades of their lives. "Sometimes if you're lucky, part of what is true is made flesh for you, incarnate in a teacher."[39] In 1973 the college community celebrated its golden jubilee with a birthday party that addressed the question Ann Ross's father had put to her when she told him she would become a Catholic sister: "What can a woman do?" Dorothy Day's visit to campus introduced the birthday year; students heard her speak and received her as a saint rather than as a celebrity.[40]

Sister Joan Sue Miller became academic dean in 1974 and, with the support of the faculty, facilitated extension of the college's resources to those in particular need of completing their education. Saint Mary enlarged its mission to include a degree-completion program offered in evening courses on the Donnelly College campus in Kansas City, Kansas. Called 2 Plus Two, the program enabled working adults to complete a junior college education or to return from a necessary break for their baccalaureate degree. Manifest but difficult to market was the personal impact of teachers on adults often doubtful of their capacity for advanced college work. Sister Mary Patricia Lenahan, education professor and frequent observer of student teachers, exemplified the kind of teaching that older hard-pressed students needed to help them persevere.

James Murphy and Karin Gagne were two who administered the program in its early years. Monica Horvat took responsibility for the two sites in Wyandotte and Johnson Counties in the 1990s. Patricia Howard succeeded her as site director of Saint Mary College in Kansas City, offering the baccalaureate degree and, in time, five master's programs to professionals who wished to extend their education, specialize in their fields, or simply challenge their minds.

Meanwhile in Leavenworth and Lansing, Kansas, courses leading to the associate of arts degree were offered at three state and federal penal institutions. Saint Mary had first offered college courses at Kansas State Penitentiary in the fall of 1966. When federal legislation authorized tuition grants for prisoners who qualified, Saint Mary won contracts with the state and federal governments for both associate and baccalaureate degree programs. Academic advising and coursework began in 1974 at the state's largest prison, now called Lansing Correctional Facilities (LCF), with at the time three sites: Maximum, Medium, and Women's.

Within the twenty years before the Pell grants were terminated by Congress, 111 men and 12 women at LCF earned the AA degree. Twenty-three men earned the BA or BS degree; fifteen more were pursuing the baccalaureate at the program's end in 1994. Under the degree program maintained at the United States Disciplinary Barracks at Fort Leavenworth from 1983 to 1989, fourteen military prisoners earned the associate of arts degree. Between its inception in the spring of 1987 and December 1994, Saint Mary had awarded the baccalaureate degree to sixty-two inmates of the United States Penitentiary north of Leavenworth. Three men had earned a second degree; ten were pursuing the baccalaureate at the program's close. The associate of arts degree was earned by eighty-three inmates. Commencement ceremonies included a valedictory address by the graduate with the highest academic standing.

The educational director of the college program was John Estes, succeeded in 1990 by academic dean Sandra Van Hoose. Sister Edward Mary Brown was admitting registrar during its final four years.[41] In the mid-eighties, the college contracted with the Kansas Bureau of Corrections for educational training services (ETS) designed to enhance the employability of disadvantaged adults. Prisoners benefited from basic and advanced computer training.

A combination of these services, courses in English as a Second Language (ESL), and instruction for the General Education Diploma (GED) were offered on campus in 1984 and then relocated as the OutFront program in downtown Leavenworth. In 1989, under the direction of Kitty Goeters Bronec—alumna of academy and college, class of 1967—OutFront enrolled approximately 300 in the three programs. At that time those completing their programs came to campus with their families for their own graduation ceremony. A special program for single parents was inaugurated in cooperation with Kansas Social and Rehabilitation Services.[42]

Engaging the Whole

At its operational level, governance was the quiet dynamo fueling the daily life of the college. As programs grew, students wanted more self-determination in their studies and resident life. A matrix model extended the base of participation by faculty and staff in decision-making from 1976 to 1984. The college's commitment to students of all socioeconomic backgrounds was steadily expanding the need for financial aid. Traditionally tuition had been held at a level that made the degree program accessible; faculty were responsible to see that its quality was not diminished. The Kansas tuition grant, passed with the help of two years' hard work by private college presidents, brought substantial assistance to students who were residents of the state. Application for federal and foundation grants grew at a smart pace.

With increasing responsibility as programs multiplied, Sister Xavier Andre became treasurer of the college in 1973, serving for the next thirteen years as the first business manager. In 1973 and again in 1981, Sister Mary Janet re-submitted her previous request for separate incorporation of the college; at neither time did the board of trustees find sufficient reason for such action. In 1974 the board approved Sister's formation of an administrative council to assist in decisions of governance.[43]

Accountability became the keynote of students' assuming roles in academic planning and campus life during the seventies and eighties. Representatives from the Student Government Association were welcomed to faculty meetings and committees. A model for student self-governance in residence hall communities and a Goals curriculum with individualized academic advising made students more responsible for their educational progress and for living accountably with their peers. In later years Sister Barbara Sellers, as associate dean, created a program for peer academic counseling that created strong ties between the peer academic counselors and freshman counselees.[44]

Faculty and students together took a hard look at curriculum in a campus-wide "Think Day." A task force on general education addressed assumptions about teaching and learning and effective ways to organize the learning process that would make students consciously responsible for their own progress.[45] Emphasis on writing and on the critical thinking that guides it was a hallmark of the curriculum from the start. The ability to see the whole of an issue, to integrate knowledge and adapt it to a wide range of problems, was the desired outcome of this goal-directed learning. Primary texts introduced entering students to origins of their own and other cultures and to the disciplines of knowledge. Immediate experience of the arts in their development and in studio production was a significant graduation requirement.

At the initiative of the academic dean with the support of grants from the National Endowment for the Humanities, the core curriculum extended into the evening/weekend programs. For more than twenty years after implementation, full-time working adults and prisoners in degree-completion programs were viewing classical drama and contemporary films, reading Newman on liberal knowledge, and producing papers acceptable for their writing portfolios. Grants from the Fund for Improvement of Post-Secondary Education and the National Science Foundation provided special training for faculty in teaching adults and in initiating the faculty's educational use of computers. Sisters Barbara Kushan and Mary Erwin Baker had introduced the computer science program in 1978 with up-to-date equipment necessary for coursework. Faculty were engaged with Benedictine teachers in summer institutes for teachers of chemistry and physics.[46]

On the 125th anniversary of the Community's founding, 1983, the college dedicated for new academic uses the renovated St. Mary's, Mead, and Xavier Halls, historic buildings of the Community's foundation in Leavenworth. The new De Paul Library, housing the education department on its ground floor, and the Student Center in the renovated Berchmans Hall had been in full operation since 1981.[47] Capital campaigns financed the building projects in its two phases. Gifts from alumnae, faculty and staff, and friends of the college testified to the faith in its mission that inspired the leadership of the campaigns. Exceeding the goals set by the President's Council, two drives funded the college endowment, scholarships and student financial aid packages, and faculty/staff and program development. Leavenworth and Kansas city councils of professional, business, and civic leaders as well as the Alumnae Association contributed initiatives, solicitations, and material resources to the campaigns.[48]

In the anniversary year, for the first time, the college's enrollment exceeded one thousand. Successive directors of admissions, with support from consultants, maintained total numbers, but enrollment of residential students did not rise. In the Midwest, a small liberal arts college for women located within forty miles of universities and several private co-ed institutions had difficulty selling itself. More than a means of increasing numbers, offering the full experience of Saint Mary's home campus program to men became a serious option.

After Sister Sue Miller, who had served as academic dean for thirteen years, was elected to the General Council in 1986, Carol Hinds was named to that office and Sister Constance Phelps became dean of students. Planning for the possible transition of Saint Mary as a college for women to that of a co-ed institution was in large part theirs. With most of the faculty and staff in agreement in 1987, the board of trustees voted unanimously to extend the college's full service to women and men. At a beginning ratio of 60:40, the first class of residential women and men was admitted in the fall of 1988. In the long-range plan, a three-year campaign included funding for a sports facility to serve both student populations. Membership in the National Association of Intercollegiate Athletics was part of the proposal formulated by a task force on sports and recreation, led by Sherry Mouille Kipp, chair of the physical education department. She was assisted by Dr. Nancy King, professor of behavioral science, who

Traditionally, students process to Annunciation Chapel for the convocations that begin and conclude the academic year.

researched requirements under Title IX for equity in athletic programs for women and men.[49]

Nearing completion of her twenty-fifth year as president of the college, Sister Mary Janet announced her retirement in the spring of 1989. A stable administration was in place; academic divisions now unified faculty across their departments. Retention was rising and male students of good quality were proving their worth. A surplus budget was on record after much of the loss from the national market crisis of 1987 had been recouped.[50] Recommendations were taking shape for a multi-purpose sports facility and playing fields; Saint Mary was accepted as a new member of the National Association for Intercollegiate Athletics.

Commending her quarter-century of service to the Community and college, the board of trustees accepted Sister Mary Janet's relinquishment of office, naming her president emeritus and distinguished professor.[51] The period of Saint Mary's history that ended with Sister Mary Janet's retirement might best be summed up in words about ends and means taken

Students stroll down the red brick lane laid in 1870 through the wooded expanse that Bishop Miege and Mother Xavier chose for the home of the Sisters of Charity of Leavenworth and Saint Mary.

from her final budget message to the board of trustees: "The end, for us, is something human and humane, something indeed with a touch of the divine. For we are about education in the fullest sense. One of our human tasks, as I see it, is to transmute money into full and valuable lives. And the agent for this change is Christian education."

Sister's campaign message nine years earlier had paid tribute to the founders of that tradition of education in schools, academy, and college: "Saint Mary is a legacy from those pioneer American Sisters of Charity who braved the frontier over one hundred and twenty years ago to plant their lives in this singular and particular place."[52]

CHAPTER 13

A Heritage of Healing

Without equipment, facilities, or staff, Vincent de Paul set about the business of healing children, soldiers, refugees, galley slaves, and many that could not be healed, only comforted as they died. Volunteer professionals and aides, lay women and men, wealthy and powerful patrons came to his assistance as he set up emergency stations and shelters, eventually the hospital at St. Germaine in Paris. What was counted impossible became ordinary as crises multiplied. That kind of transformation attended the opening of the Community's hospitals on the Great Plains, in the mountains, and on the west coast between 1864 and 1952. What the next fifty years brought followed a familiar pattern: respond to a need, gather resources, keep an eye on the horizon. In pioneer parlance, it's called circling the wagons.

A master of the art was Sister Joanna Bruner, a registered nurse who led the small band of sisters assigned in 1888 to St. Stephen's Mission on Wyoming's Wind River reservation. During a visit in 1990 to the mission's Heritage Room, Sister Dorothy Henscheid noticed a portrait of a sister who looked familiar. The young Arapahoe woman who tended the room identified the sister as Chief Big Squaw. "She spoke," Sister Dorothy wrote later, "with feeling and vibrancy as if the Sister had just left the reservation two weeks before." That was the effect this Sister of Charity—bountiful of body, mind, and heart—had on the people she served in Kansas, Wyoming, or wherever she was. She died in 1903, yet "the young Indian woman spoke of her warmly and proudly in 1990—a hundred years later."[1]

Sister Joanna was a prototype of the women who administered the hospitals that were opened or staffed by the Sisters of Charity of Leavenworth between 1864 and 1942. Six years after they came to Leavenworth, the fledgling Community built St. John, the first private hospital in the state. Within a century they had taken on seventeen more hospitals in Montana, Colorado, Wyoming, New Mexico, Nebraska, Kansas, and California. In every case, after an initial commitment by the local community, the sisters assumed major responsibility for raising the funds to build, staff, and then expand the facility they had been asked to establish or take over. People were generous, but for the most part their means were scarce. Begging, under the euphemism of "collecting," was the practice from city to city and coast to coast. What marks the story of these hospitals is the quality of the women who administered and staffed them. They possessed a keen eye for the needs of people in expanding areas and deepening distress, and they had distinct capacities for bringing to bear on those needs the resources of those with ample means.

Of the fifteen hospitals staffed by the Community at the midpoint of the twentieth century, six were closed or acquired by local providers by 1973. Extensive study and evaluation of local resources and changing needs prompted withdrawals from Our Lady of Perpetual Help in Falls City, Nebraska, in 1955 and St. Joseph's in Deer Lodge, Montana, in 1962. In 1964 St. Vincent's Hospital in Leadville, the highest city in North America, opened the High Altitude Cardiac Research laboratory staffed by cardiologists from the University of Colorado medical center under federal funding.

The laboratory culminated decades of research at St. Vincent's conducted on newborn infants, athletes, and different age groups to determine effects of high altitudes on heart, blood cells, and lungs. More than 500 adults and children participated in research that attracted doctors from England and Peru as well as the United States Army and scattered universities. By 1972, however, the hospital's future in Leadville was uncertain; the mining families of the community had supported it throughout to the full extent of their means. Sisters on the staff under Sister Michael Marie O'Leary left Leadville laden with the affection of its people when the Community handed over St. Vincent's to the citizens' board.[2]

At St. Ann's in Anaconda, staffed by the Sisters of Charity since 1889, concern for growing problems of medical practice, for a shortage of doctors to staff emergency and other services, and for qualified support staffs led the Community, after outside review and consultation, to transfer ownership to the local community in 1973. During 103 years of service to Helena, St. John's had survived poverty, earthquake, and the Great Depression before its rebuilding in 1939 and expansion by 1965. At its centennial in 1970 it had earned a rating of Excellent from the Joint Commission for Accreditation of Health Care Organizations. A detailed study of the remodeling and construction necessary, however, to maintain its high standards of safety and care of patients brought an estimate of $8 million, a cost beyond the resources of a community with a second general hospital. St. John's closed in 1973.

Six years before the Community's withdrawal from St. Anthony's in Las Vegas, New Mexico, Lay Extension Volunteers had complemented its nursing and laboratory technician staffs. Additions in 1959 to the hospital's surgery, radiology lab, therapy department, medical library, and admitting offices had strengthened its services. Nevertheless, the impact of government regulations, multiplication of the area's medical needs, and duplication of facilities and services in Las Vegas's two small hospitals made the 1973 merger advisable.[3]

The unique histories of hospitals now sponsored by the Sisters of Charity of Leavenworth are the shared story of hundreds of sisters and thousands of lay people collaborating in the mission of healing. However sophisticated the technology and administration, the story of this mission is one of self-gift and heroic determination. Names from the past mark the record; they symbolize a heritage that stands as challenge for a future of collaboration and consolidation in forms emerging by the decade. Mother Josephine Cantwell, third major superior of the Community from 1877 to 1886, governed at a time of enormous debt, when hospitals in Leadville, Colorado, and Butte and Anaconda, Montana, were needed. Nevertheless, as Sister Mary Carol Conroy observed in a historical account, her administration brought "a tradition of stability to the community not previously experienced." Her name marks Cantwell Hall, first location of the Sisters of Charity of Leavenworth/Health Services Corporation.[4]

Mother Irene McGrath is credited with investigations and reports that became the basis of a code of hospital ethics endorsed by the hierarchy for Catholic hospitals at the turn of the century. Both Mother Josephine and Mother Irene were nurses. In 1938 the General Council delegated the responsibility of overseeing the Community's hospitals to a councilor qualified for the task. Sister Rose Victor Felsheim, a nurse, filled the role for twelve years.[5]

Sister Cornelia Donnelly was the General Council's hospital consultant from 1950 to 1969, years of concentrated health care expansion. With a bachelor of science degree in nursing from the Catholic University of America—an uncommon academic accomplishment in the 1930s—she was responsible for nursing education for the sisters under Mother Mary Francesca Shea. Under Sister Cornelia's leadership, nine hospitals operated accredited schools of nursing. St. Vincent's was the first in Montana and one of the first three in the Northwest recognized by the American College of Surgeons. She was the first woman religious elected to the board of directors of the Colorado State Nurses Association.

As general councilor, Sister Cornelia initiated combined meetings for medical staffs and administrators in Sisters of Charity hospitals. Memories of this woman are keen among hospital sisters for many reasons. Familiar with blueprints, she "was quite at home walking along the scaffolding several stories up, while overseeing the work.... She was greatly respected by architects, contractors, and the laborers as she had a keen mind and an understanding of the field."[6]

Sister Hypatia Coughlin gained much the same reputation as she supervised the construction of the Mother House in the 1930s. No error in the placing of steel, pipe, or brick escaped her notice. Before its opening in 1942, Sister Hypatia supervised the building of Saint John's Hospital in Santa Monica, California. When the contractor, Luigi Pozzo, heard that his crew's construction boss was a nun, he was virtually speechless. Later, his astonishment was eloquent: "Good grief, she could build, she could boss, and she straightened out my life and my language."[7]

Sister Hypatia's comment that raising monies in California was "quite different" proved something of an understatement. This may have been a reference to the luncheon hosted in the spring of 1946 by Sister Ann Raymond Downey, administrator, for Hernando Courtright, president of the Beverly Hills Hotel. Her aim was to gather names of potential donors.[8] It was the beginning of Saint John's association with generous friends of the Los Angeles and Santa Monica communities. Sister Ann Raymond personified the spirit of Vincent, who was a master at bringing together those of great power with those who had none. Without apparent effort, her charm conquered business executives, socially sophisticated women, hospital workers from ground floor to nursing stations, physicians, bishops, and children. More than charm, she radiated the Spirit. That accounts for the acclaim Sister received after eleven years of ministry in the Archdiocese of Santa Fe, chiefly as administrator of St. Anthony's hospital in Las Vegas, New Mexico.

The Archbishop John Baptist Lamy Award, the highest award given by the Church in the Santa Fe archdiocese, was conferred on Sister Ann Raymond in a public ceremony in 1970. Her service was characterized by Archbishop James Davis as a "continued concern to make all of those who were sheltered in any way under the roof of the hospital, a real community—a family."[9] Sister had a talent for building medical staffs and strong support guilds in every hospital she managed—Providence in the 1930s, Saint John's in Santa Monica in the 1940s, St. Vincent's in Billings in the 1950s, and DePaul in Cheyenne, Wyoming, a hospital she opened in 1952. When she died in 1995, Sister Ann Raymond had been a volunteer receptionist at Providence Health Center.[10]

Reared on an Indian Reservation near Deer Lodge, Montana, where her father maintained a business to serve the Native American population, Sister Kathleen Keenan learned early to recognize the face of human suffering. As administrator of Providence–St. Margaret Health Center, her care for patients and staff was legendary. During a fire at the apartments near the hospital in Kansas City, a photographer caught a memorable shot of Sister Kathleen with one arm around a blanketed woman and the other extended to hold an elderly man's hand. The cutline read, "Sister Kathleen Keenan, as always, where she's needed most."[11]

Before her extensive term with the Health Center, Sister Kathleen had administered St. Francis in Topeka and been named the first president of the Kansas Catholic Hospital Association. Notice of her appointment to the Kansas State Board of Health by Governor George Docking reached the national wire services and the *New York Times*. She participated in collaborative planning in Cheyenne for DePaul's million-dollar five-year expansion program announced in 1964. Appointed executive director of Providence–St. Margaret's in 1973, Sister Kathleen later became vice president for development and public relations. Before retirement she took on direction of the pastoral care department.[12]

Sister Mary Asella Delaney, born in County Tipperary in 1891, entered the Community at age sixteen and became a nurse. When she received *in absentia* the Distinguished Service Award from the Medical Care and Research Foundation of Denver in 1970, she sent four simple facts for the introduction. During twenty-four years at St. Joseph's, she had been a medical and surgical nurse, served in the operating room, directed the nursing program, and been superintendent of the hospital. The Foundation's director found much more to say. From its original goal of financial assistance to patients with overwhelming illnesses, the Foundation developed the broadly based Denver Clinic. Sister Mary Asella's original vision of St. Joseph's as a teaching hospital had evolved, "despite unbelievable opposition," into a residency training program that ultimately supplied the clinic with many of its doctors.[13]

Sister Mary Asella Delaney observes closely while Sister Mary Andrew Talle breaks ground for St. Joseph's mid-1960s expansion.

Sister was adept at uniting doctors, nurses, and sisters in support of St. Joseph's growth. In the first two years of her administration of St. Joseph's, she initiated a doctors' house staff program that became a model in the region and beyond.[14] In an interview in 1960, a reporter was impressed with what he called a "combination of simplicity and shrewdness." Sister herself said at the time, "Faith is our cornerstone, yes. But one needs prudence too...."[15] As director of development in the early 1960s, Sister led a fund drive to support the building of the new St. Joseph's at a cost of $9,000,000.[16] When Sister Mary Andrew Talle was assigned as administrator of St. Joseph's in 1964, Sister Asella agreed to stay on at the hospital for a year to mentor her in the job. She did so, relinquishing all authority and offering no decision-making advice.[17]

Initiatives of Leadership

Even as women like these brought the Community's hospitals to high standards and exercised leadership they had not aspired to, the nation was looking to growing needs in health care. Under the Hill-Burton act of Congress in the 1940s, federal grants had funded the building of hospitals to guarantee equal access to urgent medical care for all citizens.[18] Mother Mary Ancilla Spoor supported the growth of the Community's health care ministry of the 1950s. Thanks to the continuous counsel of Sister Cornelia, she saw the problems brewing: expanding budgets with increased hiring; continuing education of medical staff and employees and the public in preventive health care; demands for research departments; increasing outpatient care; and voluntary health insurance.

The Council approved in 1964 a landmark gathering of all the hospital administrators for a three-day "Management Manifesto" at St. Mary's Hospital in Grand Junction. Professionals in specialized areas of health care and its developing challenges provided a "short course" in management for two days before the sisters themselves spoke to immediate concerns. Hospital by-laws, assignment of sisters, the spiritual atmosphere of a hospital, and communication among hospitals were the topics of Sisters Mary Walter Swann, Mary Andrew Talle, and Ann Raymond Downey, all hospital administrators.[19]

From his correspondence with Sister Cornelia in the early 1960s, it is clear that Thomas E. Havel, MD, chief of staff at Saint John's in Santa Monica, foresaw the need for standardization of procedures and staff regulation in view of increasing "governmental interference." Both saw in collaboration between physicians and sister administrators implicit benefits for all ministries of the Community. The Medical Staff Assembly of 1967 focused on roles and responsibilities for patient care resting respectively in hospital boards, the Community governing board, the medical staff, chiefs of service, and the civic community.[20]

Before the Renewal Chapter of 1969, Sisters of Charity in health care met at the Mother House for a retreat and seminar on managerial styles and conflict resolution, development and trends in health services, and the future of the apostolate. Change did not come suddenly to the health care apostolate. Nor did it come without the professional competence, readiness to consult specialists, and willingness to risk that mark top-flight executives.

Looking to the future, Sister Cornelia planned with the General Council under Mother Leo Frances Ryan a major review of the Community's health care facilities, needs, and potential. They engaged the management consultancy firm of Cresap, McCormick and Paget, Inc., to conduct an in-depth study that would clarify the future of the Community's apostolic mission in health services. The consultants interviewed more than one hundred officers of the SCL Corporation, directors of apostolates, the personnel consultant, and in the hospitals, sisters, physicians, administrative lay personnel, and community residents. From records they found a 13 percent decrease since 1950 in the number of sisters active in health service. No formal method existed for planning future commitment to the health care apostolate. Concluding the study, the firm recommended that the Community move in five directions:

1. to broaden goals and objectives to reflect needs of the community being served, involving lay representatives in governance, participation and leadership in area-wide planning, lay personnel in management, high levels of education and research, and care for mentally ill, aged, and addicted as resources permit;
2. to strengthen top organization for managing the apostolate with administrative support: a Director of Health Services with a consulting staff in administration, finance, and personnel management;
3. to establish a governing board for each hospital of members chosen by the board of trustees, a chair from its own members, standing committees, and local incorporation;
4. to establish management capability to exploit advantages of system; and
5. to establish personnel policies for sisters, including a long-term planning mechanism with annual review, personnel records system, management orientation to assigned roles, performance evaluation; and for lay employees, job descriptions, skills inventories, benefits, and continuity of tenure in transfers.[21]

After studying the report thoroughly, the Council took a larger action than the recommendations explicitly suggested. On December 19, 1972, they filed Articles of Incorporation for the Sisters of Charity of

Leavenworth/Health Services Corporation (SCL/HSC). Those on the General Council were corporate members and the board of directors of the corporation; they were also corporate members of each hospital corporation. The comprehensive plan meant, the sisters knew, more involvement of lay persons on hospital boards and in hospital management through shared leadership. The parallel incorporation of each hospital signaled delegation of responsibility and authority.

An ad hoc commission drew up the philosophy of the central corporation, and a committee worked out personnel policies. Objectives included promotion of comprehensive health care to individuals, families, and communities through preventive measures and acute care, rehabilitation and health education, and support in the final stages of life. All decisions were to be guided by needs of the local civic community; care was to be characterized by compassion for human infirmity and respect for the human person. Development of operating budget systems and strategic plans and encouragement of partnerships and collaboration with local hospitals were long-range objectives.[22]

Elected to the General Council in 1968, Sister Mary Dennis (Mary Margaret) Shea was the first president of the Health Services Corporation from its beginning in 1972; Sister Mary David (Mildred Marie) Irwin was vice president. Sister Mary Dennis summarized the expected benefits of the corporation:

- to bring the hospitals into a more unified system bound together by a common philosophy;
- to secure the assets of the Community, especially funds for the education and retirement of the sisters,
- to provide financial advantage to individual hospitals, especially in corporate borrowing capability, and
- to provide services that included consulting, group purchasing, and educational seminars.[23]

Sister Mary Dennis's graduate study in theology deepened her vision for needs of the Community as it prepared for the Chapter of 1973–1974. In her pre-Chapter report she emphasized the apostolic principles that must guide the ownership and management of hospitals and the managerial principles that apply to motivation and development of personnel. Adequate assessment of individual potential and environments conducive to professional, social, and spiritual growth were concepts that were to guide planning and mission assignment in years to come. Mutual responsibility of the sister and the Community for development and decision-making were to be key ele-

Sisters Mary Aloys Powell, Mary David Irwin, and Marie Madeleine Shonka wield the shovels that signaled the beginning of construction on Saint John's new entrance in 1983.

ments of renewal. Sister died on Christmas Eve, 1979.[24]

In 1974 Sister Mildred Marie was elected to the General Council and returned from her mission to Saint John's in Santa Monica to serve as health services consultant and the second president of the Health Services Corporation. She was particularly sensitive to concerns of the hospital CEOs. The Health Services Commission, part of the central structure, arranged bi-monthly meetings of the corporate officers and affiliate administrators or their representatives.[25] The present head of SCL/Health System, William Murray, said of Sister Mildred Marie's leadership of the corporation: "She is really the one who carved out its role, balancing the need for some central office functions with the needs [for autonomy] of the hospitals."[26]

Sister Mary David, as everyone knew her then, initiated coordinated strategic planning and engaged General Electric to teach its planning methodologies to the administrators and board members. She saw that hospital administrators needed formal preparation in graduate programs with an emphasis on business principles and that business managers of hospitals needed extensive financial background. Looking to the future, she knew that lay people would assume top-level management positions as the Community's hospitals became medical centers. Sister conceived of an umbrella of Catholic health care services from religious communities working together.[27]

By 1978, with her assistant, Sister Ann Marita Loosen, and treasurer, Sister Mary Julie Casey, Sister Mary David knew that the developing organization needed to expand managerial assistance and clearly define its central office. Mark Dundon was hired as the corporation's first lay executive director, Margaret Anne Kearns as assistant to the Community/Corporation treasurer, and Dean Laefflebein as director of materiel management. From his early experience with it, Dundon said the Health Services Corporation was ahead of its time in offering to its affiliate hospitals opportunities for team building, conflict resolution, and organizational change. Corporate and affiliate boards learned the methodology of strategic planning. With her election to the Community Council in 1980, Sister Macrina Ryan became president of the SCL/Health Services Corporation. During the next twelve years, she expanded corporate services and staff while responding to the growing needs of the affiliate hospitals.[28]

As compensation for hospital services began to diminish due to Medicare regulations and managed care restrictions, subsidiary corporations at local levels became a means of reimbursing costs and providing sources of revenue free of external controls. SCL/HSC provided a framework, Caritas Inc., with criteria for establishing such subsidiaries. Examples were commercial laboratories to serve physicians' offices, medical office buildings, pharmacies, and independent surgeries. Incorporated subsidiaries were established in six locations of hospital affiliates in 1982. Technological expansion, staffing, and meeting space required new quarters for the Health Services Corporation, which moved its central offices in 1987 to Cantwell Hall, a renovated former college building.

During her tenure, Sister Macrina oversaw development of the SCL/HSC Creed. Emphasizing its long-held values, she called it "a definitive statement to emphasize the mission and spirit of our system." The full statement included demanding goals:

- to establish standards for corporate and institutional performance and quality of care,
- to encourage development of innovative and alternative delivery systems, and
- to influence national health care legislation.

Under her leadership, corporate offices for mission integration, strategic planning, human resources, legal counsel, and financial planning centralized operations of the tenth largest Catholic health care system in the country.[29]

Providing for Nursing Care

Parallel to the Community's far-flung provision of medical services in the hospitals was development of nurses' training and educational programs. The first training school for nurses opened at St. Joseph's Hospital in 1900; eight more started up in Community hospitals in Kansas, Montana, and Colorado during the first quarter of the century. Student nurses learned from their work in wards and with special cases, in operating rooms and from physicians' lecturing on their specialties, from dietitians' instructing them in nutrition and diet therapy, and from nursing supervisors who were their role models. Sister Rose Orchard remembered the cumulative effect of moving from one department to another during training and later the deep sense of responsibility for supervision of nurses in a department where she had learned on the job.[30]

From 1932, Saint Mary College provided the diploma program of pre- and post-clinical coursework for nursing schools at Providence, St. John, and St. Francis Hospitals. In 1939 the college supplemented the diploma with a program that led to the bachelor's degree in nursing or nursing education. The Kansas hospitals became clinical sites for both the diploma and the supplemental degree programs. St. Joseph's and St. Mary's Hospital schools of nursing were affiliated with the college's program as the Colorado unit.[31] Schools of Nursing at St. Vincent's, St. James, and St. John's in Montana consolidated as the Sisters of Charity School of Nursing at Carroll College, Helena, in 1946. At the program's termination in 1964, the bachelor's degree in nursing education had been awarded to one hundred registered nurses; through the college's diploma program more than nine hundred nurses had been registered since 1943.[32]

The quality of the Community's nursing schools manifested itself in the education of their directors, in leadership roles assumed by their faculties, in collaboration between directors and college administrators, and in close attention paid to currents of change. In the 1950s, nurses qualified by education and experience were assuming the duties of clinical instructors, releasing nurse supervisors to oversee the needs and performance of student nurses.[33] In Kansas hospitals, the sister directors of schools of nursing moved naturally into hospital administration, positions on the General Council, and health care ministry in the Community's Latin American missions.

At the close in 1969 of Saint Mary College's thirty-seven-year-old nursing program, 337 nurses had earned the degree supplementary to the three-year nursing program. From 1969 forward, the Community's nursing schools closed,

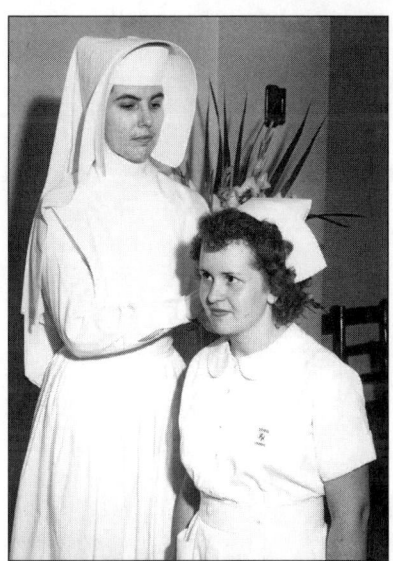

Sister Alice Marie Schwieder caps a new nurse at Providence Hospital's School of Nursing in Kansas City, Kansas.

having graduated more than 6,100 women and men. By 1973, a seventy-three-year-old tradition of nursing education gave way to four-year degree programs. Advancing knowledge of nursing was submerged in programs of medical science. Major changes in state board exams reflected the compartmentalization of medical knowledge and duplication of content in coursework. Consistent with the philosophy of the original nursing schools, the patient stayed the center of care in church-related nursing degree programs, including those of Saint Mary and Carroll Colleges.[34]

In 1979 the bachelor of science degree in nursing was offered by Saint Mary College for those graduated from diploma and associate degree programs. It was an opportunity for nurses to renew professional competencies, broaden their intellectual base, and qualify for supervisory and administrative roles. The program continued until 1981 when the nation's need for nurses declined.[35] The story of nursing education within the Community reveals a ministry that evolved according to manifest need with characteristic leadership raising the bar of professional standards and remaining focused on comprehensive care of the individual patient.

A Hospital and Its People

Like its academies, the Community's hospitals had their beginnings in Leavenworth. As with all Catholic institutions, the hospital depended on close cooperation between the sisters and the area's citizens. For its 140th birthday celebration in 2004, St. John Hospital recorded dramatic data for its many constituents. The hospital's first patients in 1864 were a poor white family from Alabama who had fled General Sherman's army. The first civilian hospital in the state, St. John was administered by the first trained nurse in Kansas, Sister Joanna Bruner. Two years after its opening, the average annual patient population was 185; in 1954 the registration record showed 1,670, an increase of about 89 percent over ninety years. St. John's home, the first city of Kansas, had grown proportionately.

But the building, almost a century old, could not contain the growth. In 1959 St. John Hospital closed for three months

St. John Hospital, 1864–1963

St. John Hospital built new in 1963 at the insistence and with the support of the community of Leavenworth

that allowed for necessary but temporary improvements. A succession of meetings and initiatives made clear that the people of Leavenworth wanted a permanent Catholic hospital. Led by Erwin Baker, two groups of citizens formed to work for a new St. John, one group for fund-raising, another for planning. Former mayor Jack Miller chaired the campaign that raised the two million dollars needed. Consultation with administrator Sister Mary Owen Horner and with Community officers facilitated progress over the next five years. Reflecting on the collaborative effort, Baker said publicly, "The people built the hospital. The community supported us 100 percent."[36]

The new St. John was accredited under Sister Aurelia Henry as a sixty-five-bed Class A hospital. At the centennial mark of the original St. John, 1964, Sister Robert Marie (Bernice) Himmelberg administered a medical staff of more than 90, a nursing and support staff of 250, and more than 200 volunteers. Sister Jeanne Marie (Margaret Gertrude) Zeugen succeeded her.[37] Early in the 1970s under Sister Mary Francine Stubbs, the hospital developed specialized centers and its outreach to area residents. Leavenworth's first CT scanner supported a twenty-four-hour emergency room. The Life Line helicopter lift served six counties in two states. Outpatient services in downtown Leavenworth and a home health program developed over the decade as St. John admitted patients from northeast Kansas and northwestern Missouri.

With Sister Ann Marita Loosen's leadership, new pediatrics and infant care facilities and a physiotherapy department expanded the hospital's services. In 1974 St. John's lay advisory board was succeeded by a board of directors as the hospital was affiliated with the new Health Services Corporation of the Sisters of Charity of Leavenworth.[38] To help maintain quality in the nursing field, St. John Guild set up an annual scholarship for study toward the baccalaureate degree. Established early in the 1980s under Ross Marine, St. John's first lay administrator, a Woman's Center was staffed by board-certified physicians in obstetrics and gynecology. Services of the Outpatient Centre by that time included cardiopulmonary testing and treatment, rehabilitative nursing care, and dietary counseling. St. John was one of forty hospitals in the United States and Canada to offer infant hearing assessment.[39]

Under administrator Sister Mary Aloys Powell, coordination with St. Francis Hospital in Topeka enabled St. John Hospital to offer treatment for adolescent chemical dependency. The Family Centre staff now included medical and psychological specialists, social workers, and counselors. Pastoral care directed by Sister Jeanne Marie Zeugin went forward in coordination with the Leavenworth County Clergy Association. Services to the community and to employees included health checks, fitness evaluation, pain management, and classes in weight control, stress management, back care, and diabetes. Children from kindergarten to fourth grade enjoyed Discovery Days.[40] In 1988 the Joint Commission for Accreditation of Health Care Organizations accredited the hospital for three years. By the next year, the twenty-five-year-old new St. John had recorded upwards of 60,000 admissions, more than 100,000 emergency room visits, and 6,000 births. Surgeries numbered more than 1,000 annually. Employee salaries amounted to $49 million.[41] Leavenworth and its hospital were growing together well into St. John's second century.

Meanwhile, reimbursements for Medicare and Medicaid patients and HMOs were decreasing and health-management regulation of patients' treatment was rising. Partnerships were evolving throughout the world of health care. In 1992 St. John allied with Providence Health Center for advantageous sharing of resources and services. Sister Mary Andrew Talle became the hospital's executive vice president and chief operating officer in coordination with the president of Providence, Sister Ann Marita Loosen.[42] It was an alliance made possible by the combined assets and administration of the Sisters of Charity of Leavenworth/Health Services Corporation.

Extending the Charism

When Sister Rosalie Mahoney was elected to the General Council in 1980 and given responsibility for Latin American missions, she was already convinced that clinics were a needed and viable health care ministry for the Community. After serving as director of nursing in six Community hospitals for fourteen years, she had volunteered for the Peruvian missions where over a decade she organized community nursing in Talara and opened midwifery training cooperatives on the coast and in the mountains.

Returning to the States in 1973, she served as director of Home Health among the Blackfoot Indians in Browning, Montana, and as director of the Silver Bow County Home Health Agency in Butte.[43] In 1984 her proposal to the Council and the Community's Health Services Corporation was a plan for providing access with continuity of health care for people unable to afford it. The plan included a city-wide network of community resources in Leavenworth, coordination of referrals with the local health department, and services for housing, jobs, and disability compensation. According to the 1980 census, more than half the households in Leavenworth County lived on less than $1,125 a month and one in thirty-five persons depended on assistance.[44]

Within two years, St. Vincent Clinic opened in Leavenworth under the direction of Sister Anna Totta. Two phenomena suggested the proposal was well founded: the number of uninsured families and individuals who came for services and the number of physicians, dentists, nurses, and technicians who volunteered time for those services in a generous and welcoming medical community. Six months after its opening, 500 clients had come to the clinic for help. A majority of the patients were women under thirty without health insurance. In 1986 Sister Mary Jo Downey, full-time Physician's Assistant, joined the staff. The volunteer medical director, Dr. Robert Parker, oversaw doctors who provided services to patients. Dr. Mary Rardin, OSB, soon joined the staff and became the clinic's medical director.

The clinic grew quickly into a community project with volunteer services from physicians, nurses, and laboratory technologists averaging about nine hundred hours a month. Donated items came from doctors and area hospitals. Cushing Memorial and St. John cooperated with laboratory and X-ray services. Drs. William Allen Sr. and William Allen Jr. did radiology readings. Sister Joy Duff was the full-time RN and Elizabeth Johnson, the volunteer coordinator. VISTA volunteers completed the

St. Vincent Clinic, Leavenworth

Duchesne Clinic, Wyandotte County

staff. Local pharmacies gave drug discounts. The charge per visit ranged from one to ten dollars; if the patient could afford them, prescriptions and lab work cost two dollars. Outreach sites within a radius of twenty-four miles soon opened in Easton and Linwood.[45]

In 1989 St. Vincent Clinic Inc., the parent corporation for the Leavenworth clinic, opened Duchesne Clinic on the ground floor of the former St. Anthony School in Kansas City, Kansas. According to statistics, that city's inner core had the highest concentration of poor in the state. Wyandotte County residents who carried no health insurance needed what the clinic offered: primary medical care for minor injuries, basic cancer screening, medical examinations, and treatment of common physical and mental conditions, with referrals and health counseling available. In its first year, the "Best of Wyandotte County" award went to Duchesne Clinic along with the Kaw Valley Habitat for Humanity and Associated Youth Services.

Outreach to St. Mary's Food Kitchen, Shalom House, and the Salvation Army Family Center publicized the clinic. Four area hospitals—Bethany, Providence, Shawnee Mission Medical Center, and St. Joseph Health Care Center—offered services and supplies. Sixty-two professional volunteers and twelve clerical volunteers worked on site; seventy-four volunteers took referrals from the staff under the leadership of Sister Anna Totta. In its first year, Duchesne served approximately 350 clients monthly. Donations funded 88 percent of a $350,000 budget that drew the comment: "We operate close to the edge." The facts were reminiscent of the clinic's patroness, Rose Philippine Duchesne, a Religious of the Sacred Heart who spent thirty-four years in missionary work in the nineteenth-century Midwest. Three or four of those years were with the Potowattomi Indians in Linn County, Kansas.[46]

Caritas Clinics Inc. united the two clinics of Leavenworth and Kansas City, Kansas, in 1993 with the mission "to provide quality health care in a spirit of justice and charity to the medically underserved in Wyandotte and

Leavenworth Counties." Approximately thirty thousand people qualified for such service in Wyandotte County; and an estimated eight thousand in Leavenworth County qualified because they lived on a limited income and did not qualify for Medicaid or government benefits or did not have health insurance. Sister Amy Willcott, the combined facilities' first executive director, could report that, after three years of operation, annual expenditures were more than matched by individual and public contributions, a grant from the Sisters of Charity, and in-kind and donated services. Caritas Clinic's report for 1995 recorded 2,122 patients, almost 48 percent of them unemployed, almost 55 percent people of color, and approximately 20 percent homeless. All but 5 percent lived in Wyandotte County.[47]

A COMMUNITY'S CLINICS

Meanwhile, in Shawnee County, Marian Clinic had opened in 1988 in response to the Topeka community's documented need. Seed money from St. Francis Hospital under Sister Ann Marita Loosen's administration provided for three full-time staff, Pat Hurley, RN, executive director; Sister Concepta Mock, RN, patient care coordinator; and Sister Sue Cush, CSC, office manager. Seventeen physicians, nine nurses, and six office personnel formed the first volunteer staff. In its second year, Marian Clinic offered dental services, psychiatric counseling, and eye examinations thanks to the Kansas Eye Institute's provision of space and equipment.

Community support grew with the help of a Resource Council's special projects and the Good Samaritan Stewardship program that provided for monthly contributions, especially from Topeka's churchgoers. Within two years, two-thirds of Marian Clinic's funding came from the Topeka community— individual and corporate contributions, foundation funds, area churches, and civic organizations. The remainder came from the Sisters of Charity of Leavenworth, the SCL/Health Services Corporation, and St. Francis Hospital and Medical Center through

Marian Clinic, Topeka, Kansas

in-kind services for hospitalization and laboratory work. Additional donated space in the Medical Plaza building allowed for physical expansion.[48]

Within five years, 154 physicians served patients, volunteering hours in the clinic's examination rooms or by referral in their offices. Twenty volunteer nurses complemented the staff of four RNs. With three part-time contracted dentists and three dental assistants, twenty-two volunteers served more than 300 patients a month. A limited Home Nursing program served low-income patients. In its new outreach program, the Menninger Institute sent resident doctors to work at the clinic. An obstetric program was the first of special services for women: a well baby clinic, a new-mother empowerment program, extension family and nutrition education, a pediatric clinic, and participation in the Kansas Breast and Cervical Cancer Initiatives. Partnership between patient, clinical staff, and physicians was the trademark of Marian Clinic from the beginning, made concrete in the initial confidential interview about family resources and contribution. Collaboration with civic agencies and the regional medical community was essential to a philosophy that encouraged patients' self-support and responsibility for their health.

In 1997 when Marilyn Page, college class of 1972, became director, patients numbered more than 650 a month. For the 10 to 13 percent of Shawnee County residents with no health insurance in 1998—14 percent of them children and 11 percent women—Marian Clinic recorded more than 12,000 medical and dental visits. Service from the medical community continued and financial support remained strong. By the summer of 1998, the anniversary campaign goal of $100,000 was on target: the equivalent of seven $10,000 gifts was pledged or in the bank. Carolyn Saenz Zimmerman, class of 1963, directed the development office.[49]

By that time, too, Martin de Porres Dental Clinic was up and running in East Topeka. Sister Margaret Finch, outreach director for St. Francis, had recognized the need for such a service in 1992. According to records, half of the households in Shawnee County's medically underserved areas had incomes below or near the federal poverty level. In 1995 St. Francis Hospital and Medical Center shared in a centennial project grant of $25,000 awarded by Piper Jaffray Companies

Marian Dental Clinic

Foundation to the Community Health Clinic co-sponsored by Stormont Vail and St. Francis. That share included seed money for dental services offered at Marian Clinic in 1996. These services included preventive dental education, cleaning, and all standard treatments to people suffering from years of neglect. Local dentists donated equipment to the mini-clinic staffed by the director, a full-time dentist, and two dental assistants in addition to Sister Margaret.

After its move to a renovated commercial building on East Sixth, the clinic served an average of forty patients a day, or four to five hundred a month, who made approximately ten thousand visits annually. According to their resources, clients were charged at three levels of payment, providing a third of the clinic's funding. Contributions from St. Francis Hospital and Medical Center, grants, and gifts provided the rest.[50]

When the Board of St. Mary's Hospital and Medical Center in Grand Junction, Colorado, decided to open a clinic to serve the uninsured of Mesa County, it appointed a twenty-one-member task force to study the project. With its own annual operating cost estimated at $150,000, the hospital committed $80,000 seed money to the clinic's foundation. The experience of one task force member provided something of a model working plan. Mary Freund, class of 1985, had for a time directed the original St. Vincent Clinic in Leavenworth; she opened Marillac Clinic as its director in the spring of 1988. With the help of VISTA volunteers, an optical program started up in the clinic's second year and an adult dental program two years later. A pharmacy gave patients access to low-cost prescriptions.

In 1992 Marillac Clinic received the El Pomar Foundation's Award for Excellence as the best non-profit small health care facility in Colorado. The dental program won the state's American Health Education System Facility Award for its training services. By 1994, a Saturday schedule was necessary to meet needs.[51] The clinic was committed to a philosophy of sharing resources through cooperative efforts of local hospitals, physicians, optometrists, and other providers working with the support of local businesses, clubs, and civic organizations.

That principle proved its worth when the Robert Wood Johnson Foundation awarded a four-year grant of $471,000 to the Mesa County Health Consortium. Marillac's participation in this Local Initiative project brought amounts to be matched dollar-for-dollar by local funding partners. Together they were to expand on an interagency model of collaborative health care. Marillac Clinic was to administer the funds, which were awarded to Colorado West Mental Health, the Center for Enriched Communication, St. Mary's Psychiatric Center, and Marillac Clinic. By the time the clinic completed its first decade, a case management staff and collaborative care counselor complemented medical care. Annual patient visits were in excess of 6,500; dental visits, more than 4,200; and optical visits, more than 700.[52]

Transcending awards, the mural that reaches across a wall of Marillac Clinic's waiting room attracts the attention of adults and children alike. The artist, Ruth Fields, a resident of Grand Junction, studied the history of the Sisters of Charity and of St. Mary's before she began her work of painting, ceramics, photography, and quilting. The Missouri River unifies figures of Vincent de Paul, Louise de Marillac, and children; traces the Community's history from France to Leavenworth; and marks modes of transportation on the frontier. School children contributed to the mural with thousands of buttons they collected and arranged by colors to reflect the river's flow.[53]

Proximity to the facilities and staffs of the Communiy's hospitals was significant for the clinics' operations. All of them were extensions of the immediately accessible health care that the hospitals had offered in clinics and outpatient services for the past four decades. In a questionnaire distributed during the Apostolate Study of 1975, the hospital sisters recognized in their health care institutions strong witness to the Gospel as the heart and soul of their mission. Without exception, their hospitals served all who came in need, without regard for ability to pay and with close attention to the poor and uninsured of their communities. Provision of social services to patients and employees, directly and by referral, was common. In their local areas they stood for justice in management, ethical principles of patient care, and respect for life in all its manifestations. Educational programs and free services in response to area needs were characteristic of each hospital. Moving westward from Leavenworth into the Rockies and to the West Coast, Sisters of Charity developed centers of health care that exemplified the ministry of healing brought by thousands of women religious to the American frontier.

CHAPTER 14

Expanding Frontiers of Healing

St. Joseph's Hospital cherishes the memory of having been founded, in effect, by Mother Xavier, who visited the frontier city of Denver in the summer of 1873. In 1900 a new St. Joseph's raised its octagonal twin towers seven stories high; they stood for more than half a century over a complex that covered about half a city block. From 1958 to 1960, the percentage of occupancy increased from 87 to 96 percent, exceeding the other three Denver hospitals. Returning for her third term as administrator in 1957, Sister Mary Asella, with the good counsel of Denver financiers and her medical staff, undertook in carefully graduated steps an expansion program that culminated seven years later in the dedication of the new Twin Towers. As St. Joseph's Hospital approached its centenary, the towers dramatically signified a second century of health care offered to an area that stretched from Boulder to Pueblo and from Colorado Springs to the Western Slope.[1]

Initiated a century earlier in 1893, a program of residency and postgraduate education unique in the Rocky Mountain area had developed under Sister Mary Linus Harrington after its approval by the American Medical Association in 1914. Annual clinics in a post-graduate program recognized by the American Academy of General Practitioners were held in late summer. In 1957, 311 doctors from nineteen states gathered to hear papers written by their colleagues.

Exempla St. Joseph Health Center, Denver, Colorado, 1997

The hospital's strong medical staff and volume of patients allowed for gradual expansion of the residency program to four fields: internal medicine, surgery, family practice, and obstetrics and gynecology. On its centennial in 1993, the teaching program numbered more than a hundred residents, a fraction of the annual applicants from the nation's foremost medical schools.[2]

Dr. William Rainer, a thoracic and cardiovascular surgeon, joined the staff in 1954 and over four decades developed the Continuing Medical Education program. Its reputation attracted to the annual lecture series physicians from Zurich, Munich, and Vienna as well as major centers for thoracic surgery in the United States. His own research in heart and lung technologies contributed much to clinical residency studies. Dedication of the Rainer Learning Center testified to Dr. Rainer's lifelong commitment to residents' and staff physicians' breadth and depth of knowledge.[3]

Before the Twin Towers were quite completed, Sister Mary Andrew Talle took the helm of St. Joseph's in 1964. In view of duplicated services and rising competitive costs, she invited the five private midtown hospitals to consider an unprecedented alliance. Although the nascent partnership did not last long, Sister pursued the concept as president of the Midtown Hospital Association.[4] Recognizing the far reach of St. Joseph's, geographically and on the medical frontier, the Colorado Hospital Association appointed Sister Mary Andrew to its board of trustees. In 1965 a new outpatient facility, Caritas Clinic, opened in the Midtown building. With twenty family practitioners on its medical staff and nine residents in an autonomous unit, the Family Practice Center, dedicated in 1969, aimed at ambulatory primary care and included the intensive care nursery in its services.

A special Senior Care program at the Center offered diagnosis, transition to treatment, and family and health counseling to patients fifty-five years of age and older.[5] As the Denver region's population passed the million mark in 1970, annual births in St. Joseph's exceeded 3,000 and more than 22,000 patients sought its medical services. In 1973 a surgical outpatient pavilion was added and a dental clinic was added soon after. Medical service to rural areas was possible with individual physicians' travel. Dr. John Holyoke, an avid mountain climber, drove long miles to outlying towns and isolated dwellings to perform procedures in makeshift quarters.[6]

Volume at St. Joseph's was increasing steadily. In 1972 more than a million clinical lab tests threatened capacity, while almost 60,000 radiology treatments begged for more staff.[7] When increasing government regulation and competitive markets made alliance with a professional health care management system imperative, Sister Mary Andrew entered into agreement with Kaiser Foundation Health Plan of Colorado to receive Kaiser Permanente physicians as the majority of the medical staff under a Kaiser medical director. With four area hospitals taking Kaiser Permanente patients, Dr. William Reimers chose to come to St. Joseph's in 1974. Two decades later, members of Kaiser Permanente made up 60 to 65 percent of the patient population.[8]

St. Joseph's was known for its ecumenical impact and consistent moral principles honoring the sacredness of life and dignity of the individual. It was the first private hospital in the city to offer psychiatric care. The Women's Pavilion, opened in the early 1980s, soon made a name for itself with its public education program in obstetrics and gynecology.[9] By the late 1980s, a statistic of great advantage to the Denver populace came from the Colorado Health Data Commission: St. Joseph's Hospital recorded the highest number of patients at the lowest average daily charge. At its centennial, the Health Center listed a medical staff of 1,300 physicians and employed 3,000. It claimed 12.5 percent of Denver's market share, serving twenty-one cities and towns in Colorado, Nebraska, Kansas, and Wyoming with specialty care. It was the largest private teaching hospital in Colorado and surrounding states, ranked by leading national health care firms as one of the 100 best hospitals in the United States.[10]

Atwill Gilman, first president of St. Joseph Hospital Foundation, worked with Sister Mary Andrew for almost a decade of her quarter-century as administrator, president, and CEO. He came to admire her knowledge of the hospital's people; a monthly visit to some 300 patients brought understanding of their condition and family situation.[11] Sister's business acumen was keen. With productivity markers for every department, the actual outlay of a given year's budget came within two-tenths of one percent of its projection.

Widely recognized for running a good business, Sister was chair of the State Health Planning Agency for several years, treasurer of the Mountain States Employers Council, and a board member of Denver's Chamber of Commerce and United Banks of Colorado, Inc.[12] Before she retired in 1989, Sister Mary Andrew received the National Samaritan Award for significant contribution to human health and growth and for religious sensibility in her work.[13]

West Side of the Rockies

By 1881 Butte, Montana, had grown in three years from a small town of four thousand to a small city of fourteen thousand. A boom in the purchase of its three hundred mines brought jobs to five thousand men and occasioned

St. James Community Hospital, Butte, Montana, 1960

the transformation of St. James Home into St. James Hospital staffed by Sisters of Charity of Leavenworth. Early patients were immigrants from Continental Europe and the British Isles, the Scandinavian countries, Canada, and China. They came to the hospital injured in fires, explosions, and accidents and afflicted with consumption, pneumonia, and erysipelas, an acute inflammation of the skin. When times were hard, families in need could count on food from St. James. Merchants carried the hospital when the cash flow was low; they knew the sisters would pay when they could.[14] An essay written by Sister Mary Seraphine Sheehan in 1980 about the hospital completing its first century in her hometown throws light on this kind of relationship:

> *Sisters* is a faceless kind of term which embraces all those heroic women religious who braved the rigors and trials of the opening territories in the West. None asked for any recognition, nor did they expect any personal commendation.... When tragedy struck the city [of Butte], the victims were taken care of by the Sisters; when disease assumed epidemic proportions, the Sisters dealt with their share of it. If they contracted the illness, then they were cared for as were the other victims. In 1918 when the city was ravaged by the flu, the schools were closed and the Sister-teachers came to spell the Sisters at the crowded hospital.[15]

This was the bond that sustained St. James from its opening. When the Anaconda Minerals Company that had built and equipped Community Memorial Hospital for the people of Butte at mid-century found a decade later that it was not a viable operation, they offered the hospital with its outstanding debt to St. James. The company contributed a third of the total cost of remodeling the hospital over the next decade as the new St. James. For the remainder, the Sisters of Charity matched citizens' donations dollar for dollar. A cobalt cancer treatment center, a respiratory therapy department, a neo-natal intensive care unit, a diagnostic ultrasound facility, and a nuclear medicine department were serving patients by the end of the 1960s.[16]

During the administration of Sister Mary (Leo Catherine) Canjar, the Alpha Center opened, the first of its kind in a Montana hospital. Thanks to recognition by the American Medical Association in the late 1950s that alcoholism is a disease and to AMA's recommendation that hospitals admit alcoholics desiring medical treatment, special centers were being established in various parts of the country. Visits to facilities in Michigan and consultations with medical professionals and members of the Southwestern Montana Council on Alcoholism preceded a feasibility study for Silver Bow County. The Sisters of Charity in Butte provided a former nurses' aide training center as a residence; the Community Council provided a medical director; and a psychological counselor was available part-time on the staff that had Alpha Center ready to open in April 1968. Its objectives emphasized education, rehabilitation, and productive sobriety as well as prevention of incipient alcoholism, especially in the young.[17]

By the end of the 1970s, St. James offered to residents of Silver Bow County and southwestern Montana the most modern acute care in the region. A $3.4 million addition, itself a boost to Butte's economy, was financed by eight years of accumulated savings in the depreciation fund. An airlift brought patients to the hospital from a dozen towns in southwest Montana and Wyoming for emergency or long-term care. The *Montana Standard* acknowledged St. James as the third largest employer in Butte and as the largest business run by a woman.[18]

At its centennial in 1981, St. James physicians and nurses had ministered to 350,000 patients and brought 21,000 infants into the world. Many of the physicians, surgeons, dentists, and ophthalmologists on staff, employees, and volunteers contributed time to coaching and coordinating summer camps for asthmatic children, to Scout troups, and to Junior Achievement projects.[19] The purchase of Silver Bow Community General hospital in 1982 gave St. James a second site in East Butte for outpatient surgery. Acquisition of the county's chemical dependency and stress centers unified Butte's medical services to addicted and severely pressured residents. A $2 million cancer treatment center, dedicated in 1986, eliminated patients' travel to Billings or Missoula. A primary care clinic extended the hospital's services to the uninsured and underserved.

Sister Mary Serena Sheehy, administrator, confirmed St. James's commitment to become a first-rate regional medical center.[20] With a budget dependent on the collaboration of citizens and sisters, St. James Community Hospital entered its second century of service maintaining the second largest payroll of the most hospitable mining town in the world.

Community Hospital for a Wide Region

A year after St. Mary's Hospital in Grand Junction, Colorado, celebrated its sixtieth anniversary, 1896–1956, Sister Vincent de Paul Paul [sic] visited the city. One of the last living sisters who had known Mother Xavier, she recalled the early career of this pioneer health care venture on the western slope of the Rockies. The hospital grew over time between the Colorado silver rush of the 1890s, the next century's uranium boom of the 1950s, and the oil shale boom of the 1970s. From the time the new St. Mary's opened in 1951 on Grand Junction's famed Rose Hill, it was a collaborative venture. By decision of the mayor and Town Company president, three lots came from the city for a dollar and Mesa Junior College sold First Fruit Ridge for $100. The hospital's price-tag of $2.5 million was shared by the people to the extent of their resources and the Sisters of Charity of Leavenworth. Sister Mary Alexine Hollenbeck was administrator during its final planning and construction.[21]

By 1958, admissions, surgery, and birth statistics justified a new fund drive. Well over 60 percent of the budget fed Mesa County's economy and 60 percent of the patients came from towns beyond Grand Junction into Utah. Almost 80 percent of the patients were not Catholic. With occupancy at 100 percent, no one questioned need for expansion. A major feature of the three-story addition was provision of progressive care, the first to be designed for a Rocky Mountain area hospital. Sisters Mary Sylvester McGowan and Zita Marie Cotter administered St. Mary's during this decade of growth.[22]

During the 1950s as well, in a small laboratory maintained by two technicians, Dr. Geno Saccomanno, pathologist at St. Mary's since 1948, began his research on lung cancer detected among uranium miners. Assisted by federal grants from Public Health Services, the Department of Energy, and the National Institute of Environmental Health, he directed a team of technicians and specialists in pathology who tested 17,700 miners over a thirty-year period. In 250,000 procedures annually, they employed Dr. Saccomanno's original method of extracting cells from sputum for diagnosis and combining results with patient demographics. Refinements of extraction and isolation of tissue and a tumor registry extended the impact of the study. The research revealed that habitual smokers among uranium miners very nearly tripled their chances of developing lung cancer. By 1980, early detection had increased the five-year survival rate of cancer victims by 48 percent and of lung cancer victims by 12 percent.

Unilateral research conducted with Hiroshima and Nagasaki cancer victims compared effects of nuclear blasts and those of direct contacts with ura-

St. Mary's Hospital and Medical Center, Grand Junction, Colorado

nium. Dr. Saccomanno's medical text, *Diagnosing Pulmonary Cytology*, came into use by the American College of Pathology and teaching institutions worldwide. The uranium mining industry was able to significantly reduce the radiation suffered by miners. More significant for Dr. Saccomanno than the National Service Award he received from the American Cancer Society was the country's first Cytotechnology School and the Cancer Research Institute he established at St. Mary's before he retired in 1984. Because of their faith in the hospital, Geno and his wife, Virginia, located the Saccomanno Education Center on the medical center campus.[23]

Typical of Colorado's spirit, Veronica Sabina Lally O'Malley was the legendary volunteer who worked at St. Mary's for fifty-two years after her husband's death in 1906. In 1969, Sabina died at St. Mary's, where her body lay in state as hundreds of friends, volunteers, politicians, migrant workers, sisters, clergy, and families came to acknowledge her and her work. One of the Community's earliest partnerships with the poor was the bond between St. Mary's Hospital and Sabina O'Malley and her friends.[24]

Countless residents of the region made progress possible during the early 1960s under Sister Mary Aloys Powell's administration. In 1967, Sister Michel Pantenburg saw need for expansion of departments and purchase of property for a hospital that served residents within a 250-mile radius. On the hospital's seventy-fifth anniversary in 1971, Project Responsibility got under way with a four-phase $44 million development plan, aimed at growth over the next twenty to twenty-five years. Ground was broken in 1973 for the Ambulatory Care and Surgery Center, needed for a hospital growing into the Regional Medical Center for western Colorado and eastern Utah.[25]

When a community-based internship and residency program started up in 1977, the new A. H. Gould Family Practice Center, a twenty-four-hour emergency center, and the ambulatory surgery center offered residencies to a limited number. Rotations in seventeen disciplines taught by half the hospital's medical staff preceded an "externship" in underserved rural areas in western Colorado and eastern Utah. A burn unit served emergency and outpatient departments as well as the inpatient population. Home Health Care nurses relieved physicians in follow-up care.[26]

By the mid-eighties, under the leadership of Sister Marianna Bauder and then Sister Mary Aloys Powell, St. Mary's was the only medical center between Denver and Salt Lake City offering primary and critical care in four states on the Western Slope. Air Life made the outreach possible. Attended by constant risk in mountainous territory, the helicopter service brought care into inaccessible and underserved areas. A certified family nurse practitioner was the medical staffer on an occasional flight. As in all hospitals, nurses were often unsung, or un-headlined, heroines. A veteran called the scrub nurse of the operating room "boss of the sterile technique," crucial for the integrity of the surgery. Commemorating Ute Chief Ouray and his daughter Chipeta who had successful cataract surgery at St. Mary's, the Ouray/Ridgway Family Medical Center of the Western Slope opened in 1985.[27]

At the close of its oil shale industry in 1982, Grand Junction lost thirteen thousand residents, and jobs were scarce. Over three years, the Health Center suffered a drop in admissions and a necessary cutback in employees. With strong efficiency measures, St. Mary's held its own and was designated sole community provider for Medicare reimbursements with regulated referral status. Nevertheless, when Sister Marianna Bauder became president of St. Mary's in 1986, morale in the hospital and city needed a boost.

A series of small construction projects and team building throughout the hospital contributed to recovery. The expanded Shriners' Burn Center, a well-staffed open-heart surgery and heart center, and the Senior Life Center served local and regional needs in a mountain area of 34,000 square miles. A perinatal center and psychiatric unit boosted the hospital's census. St. Mary's became one of the largest employers in western Colorado. After a year-long study of needs and resources by a community task force, Marillac Clinic was incorporated in May 1988. In its first year, the clinic registered more than 3,000 medical visits.[28]

By 1989, as Sister Lynn Casey took over administration, the hospital and its home community were gaining new financial stability. Though debt remained on the two-decade expansion, St. Mary's charges were 15 percent lower on average than those in Colorado hospitals of equal size and 25 percent lower than those in urban hospitals. Medicare reimbursements fell short of costs by more than 50 percent, but the Medical Center maintained its service to the indigent and the underserved without diminishment of access or quality. St. Mary's was selected by the national Centers for Disease Control for a five-year pilot project to develop a model program for prevention and early detection of breast and cervical cancer. At the hospital's centennial in 1996, the hospital's Foundation established a Memorial Aid Fund honoring the physicians and civic leaders who had created the lasting ties between Grand Junction and St. Mary's Hospital and Regional Medical Center.[29]

Outreach Unlimited

Martha Jane Canary and a Canadian doctor had much to do with the coming of Sisters of Charity to Billings, Montana. The first was a competent and compassionate nurse who ministered to the sick in this new railroad town that functioned without other medical resource. The second was Dr. Henry Chapple who, with his brother James, came in answer to Canadian families' pleas and set up a pharmacy. When Dr. Chapple, an Episcopalian, and the new pastor of St. Joachim's, Father Francis Van Clarenbeck, traveled to Leavenworth to request the sisters' aid, they were confident of success. The $40,000 hospital, built on land given by the Billings Realty Company, opened officially in 1899. Broad collaboration was the keynote of the city's health care from its beginnings.

Physical expansion during the 1950s was imperative for a hospital growing at a tempo set by the medical advances wrought by World War II. In 1954 Sister Ann Raymond, working with advisory board president Arthur Lamey, initiated the fund drive for an addition to be completed at a final cost of $1,200,000. The new five-floor wing, dedicated in 1959, housed extensive rehabilitation facilities, the first such unit for inpatient and outpatient care in Montana. Sister Concepta Mock oversaw renovation that enlarged the maternity department and new construction that included an intensive care unit equipped for coronary patients.[30]

In Montana's centennial year, 1964, St. Vincent's outreach to five states—eastern Montana, Wyoming, Idaho, and North and South Dakota—included diagnosis and treatment for cancer, diabetes, and ostomy. Looking to community outreach as well, administrator Sister Alice Marie Schwieder lent support to city and county home health programs and initiated patient education, in-service classes, and social services for employees. Her attention to just benefits produced a new pension plan and percentage raises for all employees. An Employees' Council in turn maintained an emergency relief fund for unpredictable crises, contributions to those in need, and purchase of hospital equipment. Sister Alice Marie personally informed patients of reasons for the increasing cost of medical care.

A long look ahead ushered in the 1970s. Prompted by a report from the Hospital Area Planning Committee of Billings, St. Vincent's and Deaconess hospitals announced a plan to locate all obstetric services and birthing facilities at Deaconess. It failed in the face of renovation costs. A new neonatal intensive care unit at St. Vincent's expanded throughout the decade to full-service maternity service with prenatal care, birthing suites, support groups, and education for new parents.[31] Her characteristic leadership brought Sister Alice Marie appointment as a Fellow in the American College of Hospital Administrators; she was the first in the state to receive the title. Sister was also the first woman to be elected president of the Montana Hospital Association and to hold that office in the Wyoming Hospital Association. Acknowledging St.Vincent's comprehensive health plan for a large area of Montana and neighboring states, the Mountain States Regional Medical group named the hospital the Learning Center for Southeast Montana.[32]

Sister Michel Pantenberg, administering the hospital at 95 percent capacity, oversaw the planned construction of a five-story tower of single-occupancy rooms served by nursing teams and an ancillary surgical suite. Completed in 1977, intensive care and cardiac care units were supported by new communications technology; a giant bus designed by NASA was the terminal first used for satellite medical consultation. On a national computer network installed in the hospital, radiologists stored data from electrocardiograms; doctors throughout the country phoned in EKG results for use in any place open to the network.

Most dramatic in its outreach was HelpFlight, the Clinical Care Air Transportation system staffed by an emergency medical response team that operated in Montana, Wyoming, and the Dakotas. A helicopter ambulance later gave the team access to stranded or critically ill patients within a 150-mile radius.[33] In 1979 Sister Michel was named chairperson-elect of the Montana Hospital Association, which counted more than sixty hospitals and nursing homes on its rolls.

That year saw the opening of the region's first burn unit and the New Hope Regional Rehabilitation Center, created for long-term recovery from traumatic injury or disease. A dramatic hospital-wide

St. Vincent Healthcare, Billings, Montana

vote gave evidence of employees' satisfaction as well as loyalty to St. Vincent's. Unions had been making bids for membership; by large majorities the appeals were rejected. The long-range strategic plan drawn up by Sister Michel and the hospital board in 1984 projected a four-year development at a total cost of approximately $21,700,000. At its completion, a second nursing tower, a Women's Pavilion, enlarged intensive and critical care units, dedicated orthopedic and cancer surgeries, and comprehensive cardiac care served a multi-state region.

Sister Michel's formal service to St. Vincent's closed in 1985 with a year as director of the Saint Vincent Hospital Foundation that funded development, promoted employee and community health and care for the elderly, and worked to prevent child abuse. Two hospital programs strengthened special bonds with the community. Since its inauguration, pastoral care had been an ecumenical service. On its tenth anniversary, the Foster Grandparents senior and junior volunteers honored Sister Jane Ellen Furey, the program's first coordinator.[34] William M. Murray, executive vice president and chief operations officer, succeeded Sister Michel as president and chief executive officer of St. Vincent's as it prepared for the final decade of its first century in Billings.[35]

Tending the Roots

While the Community's hospitals in Montana and Colorado were expanding facilities and services, two close to home in Shawnee and Wyandotte Counties—St. Francis and Providence—were growing at a slower but steady pace throughout the first three decades of the twentieth century.

When St. Francis Hospital opened in 1909 on West Sixth, three hospitals of long standing served Topeka: Christ's Hospital, founded in 1884 to serve "not only the sick in Topeka, but also strangers and travelers from around the state and, above all, those unable to pay"; the Jane C. Stormont Hospital and Nurses Training School, opened in 1894 "for treatment of women patients" and "the less affluent sick"; and Santa Fe Memorial Hospital, established originally for railroad employees and their families. Though its doors were open to all who came, St. Francis was a welcome recourse for the growing Catholic population of the capital city. Within half a century it grew from a small private hospital to an institutional leader in the state's health care program.[36]

With the addition of an east wing in 1959, St. Francis benefited from an enlarged bed capacity and clinical laboratories, a new surgical suite, and a pharmacy. At the beginning of the next decade, Sister Mary Andrew Talle developed an intensive care unit through professional partnering with physicians. To meet patients' special needs, she initiated the first collaboration with the Menninger Institute. Two neurologists who served St. Francis's patients purchased houses to secure property needed for the patients' follow-up care.

During the early 1960s, Sister Mary Walter Swann, who moved St. Francis through almost twenty years of growth, strengthened administration of the personnel department and management staff with in-service education and a retirement plan for employees under a comprehensive hospital budget. With the help of a lay advisory board, she developed plans for a 100-bed nursing home with a self-help unit to complete the home's programmed-care cycle. By 1964, expansion of the original hospital building brought cardiac and cancer treatment, surgeries, delivery rooms and nurseries, to advancing levels of care and rehabilitation.[37]

In response to the Topeka community's need for developing health services, Sister Mary Walter and the administrator of Stormont-Vail Memorial Hospital consulted with coordinators of Health Planning in Kansas. One outcome was an arrangement with Topeka State Hospital that eventually brought St. Francis the Bell Award from the Mental Health Association. The Menninger Foundation's Division of Psychiatry and Mental Health asked the hospital to participate in a case study to examine interaction between the individual and the institution. St. Francis also provided clinical facilities for the State Practical Nurse training program. Collaboration of a different sort with the Jesuit community at St. Mary's, Kansas, provided regular sacramental ministry and spiritual counsel for patients. Problems attending racial integration of patients were the subject of discussion with NAACP representatives.[38]

Every resource of the hospital was tested in 1966 when a tornado ripped through the center of Topeka. Complex treatment of about 150 injuries brought immediate assistance from nurses, priests and ministers, medical staffs of Menninger's and the State Hospital, and the Sisters of St. Joseph and Sisters of Charity communities. Staff members who lost everything came to the hospital to help others; elderly victims of the destruction received care along with the injured.[39]

Toward the end of the decade, St. Francis Hospital was transformed by a $6 million expansion of its facilities. In a campaign chaired by Alf M. Landon, the people of Topeka contributed one million of the funds. The Sisters of Charity of Leavenworth matched Halliburton federal funds of $2.5 million. Community-wide planning aimed at meeting needs and avoiding duplication.[40] A full-page spread in the 1970 health care issue of the *Topeka Daily Capital* informed the public that after sixty years of service to the community, Saint Francis Hospital was to open a new facility with expanded bed capacity.

St. Francis Medical Center, Topeka, Kansas, 1977

In 1974 a cancer research and treatment center stood at the center of the enlarged hospital. By the end of the decade Sister Mary Roselle Kroetch, RN, was working as Cancer Resources coordinator with Dr. John Travis, chair of the medical staff and director of the radiotherapy center. Dr. William Roy, director of medical education and professional services, developed programs to implement legislative changes in the state's health care systems.[41]

Meanwhile, Stormont-Vail had purchased the Cross Ambulance Service. Questions of possible joint ownership, a multi-hospital corporation, or a joint board of directors for a city-wide service had no easy answers. But they were only symptoms of a deeper problem. St. Francis and Stormont-Vail had not collaborated effectively for a long time. When a civic and business leader familiar with both hospitals and with the Sisters of Charity of Leavenworth congregation suggested that the administrators and boards of directors come together over lunch for a far-ranging conversation, the interested parties readily agreed. After the event, mutual good will and significant concessions resolved immediate issues.[42]

In 1977 St. Francis opened a Capital Region Radiotherapy Center supported by a $2.5 million investment by the Sisters of Charity of Leavenworth/ Health Services Corporation. The Center served from fifty-five to sixty patients a day with a team approach to spiritual, psychological, and social as well as physical needs. A nursing outreach team provided support groups and an educational program. Research carried on in conjunction with the Menninger Foundation was funded by the National Cancer Institute. In 1980 St. Francis Health and Medical Center was incorporated in Kansas with Sister Ann Marita Loosen as its administrator. By 1981, a community-wide oncology program emphasizing education and preventive care was under way.[43]

Named president and chair of the board of directors in 1985, Sister Ann Marita was elected chair of the Governmental Affairs Committee of the Kansas Catholic Health Association for 1987–1988. The post required precise knowledge of legislation affecting health services. By 1988, St. Francis served as a tertiary referral hospital for twenty-five counties of northeastern Kansas. It maintained units in chronic renal dialysis, comprehensive care for cardiac and oncology patients, a chemical dependency treatment program and rehabilitation unit, a StayWellness program, and a Golden Care Plus hospice. In Topeka, 24 percent of its services were for outpatients.[44]

Positioned for the future in 1991, St. Francis admitted approximately 120,000 patients a year. In-service programs assisted employees with incentive plans. The pastoral care department under Sister Mary Francine Stubbs ministered to patients, families, and staff. Rehabilitation for stroke and accident victims, a sleep disorder center, and the Kansas Eye Institute offered new services. Behind strong patient satisfaction reports, competitive staff retention rates, and a steady increase in the market share stood a single priority: "The patient is Number One." The staff turnover of 6 percent, contrasting dramatically with the national average of 26 percent, was attributed to the hospital's commitment to primary nursing care. Assignment of a specific nurse to a patient from admission through dismissal with a reference card for follow-up calls created a bond of trust that frequently brought requests for the same nurse from returning patients.[45]

In more than eighty years of service, the hospital had weathered vicissitudes of nature, concentrated growth, rising costs of medical advances, and conflicts that could have grown to crisis dimension. Instead, persistence in a mission of first-rate holistic health care and spiritual well-being had brought St. Francis into varying degrees of partnership with four other hospitals, government agencies at all levels, and a community of citizens who wanted its services. This was a result of a great deal of committed leadership and an invincible spirit of professional collaboration.

Hospital with Staying Power

From the opening of Providence Hospital in 1920, its story dramatized its name. St. Margaret's Hospital at 6th and Vermont had opened in 1887 with one hundred beds, staffed by the Franciscan Sisters of the Poor. At the urging of Bishop John Ward, who was concerned about St. Margaret's staffing difficulties, the Sisters of Charity reluctantly and without sufficient resources agreed to build Providence. The bishop offered $2,000 and a loan at 3 percent. The sisters obtained a loan from Massachusetts Life at 5 percent and from their hospital in Deer Lodge, Montana, at 8 percent. These were the funds in 1920 that provided the sixty-five-bed facility at 18th and Tauromee. A three-story annex built on the west side of the hospital in 1946 brought beds to 150.[46]

In 1955 Marian Hall, a three-story residence hall, opened for nurses and one hundred nursing students. A four-story addition to the west unit provided space for a nursery, X-ray laboratory, physical therapy unit, emergency room, intensive care unit, and cancer clinic. In 1963 a Providence doctor performed a cardiopulmonary bypass, one of the first open-heart surgeries in area private hospitals.[47] As the administrator of Providence from 1966, Sister Kathleen Keenan oversaw a study in 1968 with administrators of St. Margaret, Bethany, and Douglass hospitals to determine possible advantages for Wyandotte County of merging their facilities.

Archbishop Ignatius Strecker opposed such a move. He proposed instead three years later the merging of St. Margaret's and Providence in a new non-profit corporation operating from the two sites near downtown Kansas City, Kansas. Both administrators and medical staffs continued to function. The archdiocese, sponsor of the new corporation, was expanding westward along with the city; the population of the western three-quarters of Wyandotte County was expected to double in a foreseeable time. By a decision made in 1973, the two health care facilities were to relocate within three years in a new medical complex on thirty acres between Parallel and State near the forthcoming I-435 freeway. The site was to provide access to the new hospital for residents of both eastern and western Wyandotte County. As executive director of Providence, Sister Kathleen directed the move. With a $24.5 million bond issue, ground was broken in 1975.[48]

Providence–St. Margaret Health Center opened the following year. Its first board of directors included Vincent W. DeCoursey, chairman, Bernard J. Ruysser, James J. Owens, Joseph Butler Jr., Thomas Daly, Michael Sambol, Stanley Szczygiel, and Sister Mary David (Mildred Marie) Irwin, president of the Sisters of Charity of Leavenworth/Health Services Corporation. In its first year, the Health Center recorded 11,600 admissions and approximately 16,500 and 16,700 emergency and outpatients respectively. Within two years, occupancy stood at 80.8 percent. Enterprises to bolster revenue, incorporated as Health Care Facilities, included a medical office building and the Midwest Magnetic Imaging Center. In 1980 the Keenan Education Center opened to offer programs of preventive and follow-up care to health center staff and the residents of Wyandotte County.[49]

During the 1980s, state-of-the-art instrumentation facilitated open-heart surgeries, cancer detection, radiology procedures, and pulmonary functions. Outreach provided home health services and, in affiliation with Children's Mercy Hospital, neonatal care. In 1991 the archdiocese returned sponsorship of Providence–St. Margaret Health Center to the Sisters of Charity of Leavenworth. The Community called Sister Ann

Providence Medical Center, Kansas City, Kansas, 1992

Marita Loosen to the health center as president and chief executive officer. The next year, St. John Hospital in Leavenworth came under her administration with Sister Mary Andrew Talle as executive vice president and chief operating officer of St. John. The alliance allowed for sharing of resources and integration of some services, each institution retaining its own medical staff and board of directors.[50]

At its diamond jubilee in 1995, collaboration with resources of Greater Kansas City and neighboring counties strengthened Providence's primary care services. Behavioral health service was offered in collaboration with the Menninger Institute. Programs of the Women's Centre were geared to the needs of outpatients. A spirituality and healing seminar enriched the social services of a Family Care Center. Free health education programs served approximately 4,000 residents of Wyandotte County each year; 5,500 came for screenings. The Medical Center cared for uninsured and low-income patients at a cost of more than $3 million.[51] It was poised for the last quarter of a century of healing ministry to the people of Leavenworth and Wyandotte Counties.

Called to the Coast

Winding rivers, mile-high mountains, and a nearby desert had been settings of Sisters of Charity hospitals for eighty years. In 1942, the sisters missioned to the Santa Monica Bay area of Southern California found quite another environment. The sisters came because a group of doctors, along with the archbishop of Los Angeles, had kept alive for twenty years the dream of a hospital west of the city in Santa Monica. On their second trip to Leavenworth in 1939, Mother Mary Francesca O'Shea was able to commit the Community to the project. With the site on 22nd Street purchased and $20,000 raised in pledges, the civic community had reached its limits; an $800,000 loan secured by the Sisters of Charity was an act of faith in God and in the people who were to support Saint John's for decades to come. Articles of incorporation were filed with the state in 1940; the hospital opened its doors in 1942 to eighty-nine patients.[52]

In its first decade, Saint John's offered the first mental health services from a non-profit facility on the West Coast; enlarged the coronary care, maternity, and pediatrics departments; provided facilities for cancer research; and expanded orthopedic and pulmonary care. A strong resource was a lay advisory board of professionals from the Santa Monica and Los Angeles communities.[53] Clinics that Saint John's conducted in the 1940s and 1950s in specific areas of Santa Monica were obliged to close in the wake of Medicare and Medicaid, but their services continued through outreach programs.[54]

The hospital continued to attract physicians experienced in medical practices initiated during World War II. Small beginnings were a specialty with Sister Mary David Irwin, administrator of Saint John's for fourteen years. At the initiative of Tony Sturdivant, MD, the hospital opened in 1951 a twelve-bed unit for the mentally ill that developed into the Ross Center for Behavioral Sciences. Under George Corbett, MS, a team of volunteer psychiatrists offered outpatient services from Xavier Clinic in 1959. Both facilities commemorated Mother Xavier Ross. By the end of the next decade, Saint John's Hospital Community Mental Health Center accommodated almost ninety patients with all the services of a total psychiatric facility.[55]

The Michael Burke Foundation was established in 1953 by a family grateful for the care given their three-year-old son before his death. With advanced technology and research funded by the Burke and Harold McAllister Foundations, Saint John's cardiac specialists were among the first to perform open-heart surgeries and to provide alternative treatments of heart disease.[56] Looking to the future of nuclear medicine, Sister Mary David encouraged John Richards, MD, to set up a department in a patient room to test procedures for "tracking" the heart."[57] George Hummer, MD, established a School of Medical Technology to help staff the pathology department he directed into the 1970s. With Dr. Daniel Levinthal in 1955, Sister Mary David welcomed a group of women, eventually called the Hope Guild, who wanted to work with children afflicted with cerebral palsy.[58]

When Cardinal James MacIntyre asked Saint John's to establish a child guidance center for children with special educational needs, support came from many sources: the Lt. Joseph P. Kennedy Jr. Foundation, the

Los Angeles Archdiocese, the Hope Guild of the hospital, the Catholic Study Clinic, and the Sisters of Charity of Leavenworth. Opened in 1962, the Child Study Center served developmentally disabled and emotionally disturbed youth between infancy and eighteen years of age. Evis Coda, MD, was medical director; Sister Mary Serena Sheehy led the professional staff. In 1974 the state of California declared the facility a regional center for developmentally disabled children.[59]

The South Wing, a twenty-year development funded at $11,000,000, was completed as Sister Mary Aloys Powell succeeded Sister Rita Louise Cunningham in 1967. She responded to a request from Phillip Rossman, MD, for medical services for families in the clinic he founded in Venice, a low-income area of Santa Monica. Another outlet for service to families was St. Joseph's Center, which maintained day care, a food pantry, a thrift store, and family advocacy at five locations in Venice. With volunteer help from Saint John's professionals, the center offered mental health assistance as well.[60] When the Native Sons of the Golden West, founded to honor their pioneer forebears in California, came to Saint John's in 1969 offering their assistance, Leslie Holve, MD, proposed a fledgling cleft-palate program. Within months he organized a team of plastic surgeons, pediatricians, nurses, speech language pathologists, audiologists, and a social worker who collaborated with the parents of each young patient.[61]

Saint John's Health Center, Santa Monica, California, 1994

From its beginnings, Saint John's entered the nation's battle against cancer. In 1967 Sister Mary Aloys made radiologist Thomas E. Havel, MD, responsible for tracking developments in the technology and treatment of the two hundred diseases that are commonly called cancer. Supported by grants from the W. B. Keck Foundation totaling more than $2,000,000, research and purchase of technology new to the field focused all services in a cancer unit opened in 1976. Directed by Donald Wagner, MD, a team of oncologists, radiologists, and nuclear medicine specialists included therapists, pastoral care and social workers, and dieticians.[62]

Pioneer orthopedic surgeons performed innumerable joint replacements during the first three decades of Saint John's history. By 1972, Leonard Marmor, MD, had developed the knee replacement that came to be known as the "Marmor knee."[63] Responding to the rapidly increasing number caught in the net of drug abuse, Saint John's created a chemical dependency center that offered a program of education, interaction with peers, and counseling in a setting designed to attract the patients to a self-respecting way of life.[64]

When Sister Marie Madeleine Shonka became administrator of Saint John's in 1973, she brought her experience as associate administrator since 1969. Long-range planning and financing of major capital improvements became the tasks of the Saint John's Hospital and Health Foundation, incorporated in 1975 with seventy-five trustees in three-year terms. In 1978, with Saint John's designation as Hospital and Health Center, Sister became its president and chief executive officer.[65] Addressing a seminar, "Health: Whose Responsibility?" in 1979, Sister Marie Madeleine explained the marketplace model that she foresaw must govern strategic planning in health care. Incentives to hospitals for mergers and consolidation must be matched by their husbanding resources; physicians must be informed consultants about alternative treatments and just charges.[66]

The Foundation's first major undertaking was to raise the funds necessary for the ambulatory care center that Sister had envisioned when she first read the signs of major change in health care traditions. Opened in 1980, the center demonstrated that follow-up care at home rather than admission to inpatient status compensated for increasing government regulation of hospital stays; the volume of outpatient treatment and surgery supported the extended availability of high-tech procedures. Within a three-year period, ambulatory laboratory visits doubled and cardiac procedures more than tripled. Within two decades, more than 50 percent of the Health Center's surgeries and 140 types of surgical procedures were performed in the ambulatory surgery unit.[67]

A board member of regional and state health care organizations, Sister was the first person to be named Humanitarian of the Year in 1988 by the

Anti-Defamation League of B'nai B'rith International.[68] A Walker Foundation Fellowship allowed Sister Marie Madeliene's travel in 1989 to Canada, England, France, and the Netherlands for first-hand study of the health systems in those countries. Questions of universal health care that enveloped and transcended concerns about HMOs and government programs were the focus of her report.[69] In 1992 Saint John's efforts to address such questions were manifest in its Circles of Excellence: Coronary Care, the Cancer Center, Orthopedics, and Women's Services; and in its 14,500 inpatient admissions and 165,000 outpatient visits. One among its many support organizations, the Jimmy Stewart Relay Marathon in its thirteenth year, 1992, numbered 5,000 runners and 30,000 spectators; it brought the Health Center $3 million.[70]

The strategic planning process and cost management systems at Saint John's moved forward with a debt-free budget and a substantial investment portfolio. At the heart of the Health Center's operation, however, was its annual allowance for uncompensated care of uninsured, underserved, and homeless citizens and for free services to children and families with special needs. This contribution to the Bay Area community was a priority in Saint John's expenditures and an effective source of partnership with its many benefactors.

Four Decades of Health Care

When it opened in 1952 in Cheyenne, Wyoming, DePaul Hospital admitted five patients, the first of them the infant son of a migrant couple. He was suffering from dehydration and malnutrition. Sister Ann Raymond Downey was the first administrator of the only Catholic hospital in Wyoming. She led the formation of its medical staff and of the DePaul Hospital Guild necessary for major support. The Sisters of Charity had agreed to staff DePaul after the community raised $200,000 toward its building.[71] Sister Alice Marie Schwieder, administrator from 1954 to 1960, was able to purchase equipment for deep therapy radiation with funds from the King Merritt Memorial Foundation and a Ford Foundation grant. The Hope Guild contributed a heart-monitoring cardioscope and equipment for pathological diagnosis of premature infants.[72]

During the decade of the sixties and into the seventies, plans for a second addition at a cost of $3 million projected expansion of surgery suites, the coronary care unit, and outpatient facilities to serve an area beyond Cheyenne that included southern Wyoming, northeast Colorado, and western Nebraska.[73] Under Sister Michael Marie O'Leary, the new wing opened in 1976 with a 24-hour emergency unit and ambulatory care center. An education center offered programs of in-service for staff and preventive health care for the community. Home Health Care registered eighty patients. Collaboration with Laramie County Memorial Hospital and the physicians' Pathology Group provided centralized laboratory services and divided specializations in pediatrics and obstetrics.[74]

Sister Mary Francine Stubbs was named administrator of DePaul in time to organize the hospital's celebration of twenty-five years of service to the people of Cheyenne. The year 1977 also marked incorporation of the hospital with a lay board of directors. When Sister Mary Clarice Lousberg succeeded to administration, needs of the area were expanding. In 1981 the chemical dependency unit's 28-day program of treatment recorded 66 percent of its patients rehabilitated. Radiology and nuclear medicine departments operated with state-of-the-art technology and sophisticated rehabilitation followed neurosurgery.[75]

1985 was the year when consideration of Cheyenne as a one-hospital city first surfaced. A letter addressed to the physicians of Laramie County from James A. Helzer, president of DePaul's board of directors, laid out the benefits of enlightened cooperation between DePaul and Memorial Hospital. Coordination of services and collaboration with the Laramie County Health Planning Committee, together with benefits accruing from DePaul's affiliation with the SCL/Health Services Corporation, gave promise of increasing vitality to the community as a health center and of reducing out-migration. The prospectus was coolly received.[76] In 1990 the first lay Foundation was planning for a new addition to the hospital. The move for a merger remained strong, however, and in 1992 the Sisters of Charity withdrew after the consolidation of DePaul with Memorial Hospital in Cheyenne was complete.[77]

DePaul Hospital, Cheyenne, Wyoming

Extraordinary Women

Not one of the women who administered the hospitals of the Community would claim major credit for the progress of their institutions. When they spoke to their employees, doctors and nurses, volunteers, and support groups with gratitude for their fidelity to the mission of healing, they meant every word. In turn, it needs to be observed that administrators served the people of God without regard to religious affiliation and in close collaboration with the civic community in which they served.

Particular qualities gleaned from the evidence in these stories attended their ministry. The concern of these women for every individual, employee or patient, manifest in a word, a personal visit, or a quiet provision for aid that leaves dignity intact was simple humanity exercised with particular grace. Their spirit of stewardship, responsible while magnanimous, saw to the maintenance and management of buildings and systems that needed to wear well even as they grew redundant. The sisters did not flaunt their ability to grasp operational detail while keeping up with government regulations and medical research; it was part of the job.

Theirs was a gift for bringing those of means to the willing service of those in sometimes desperate need; they were natural and graced collaborators. But what lies perhaps most hidden is the vision that put them on the firing line and would not let them rest. It was the vision of what could come of generous resources, advanced technology, and human ingenuity put to work for those suffering, vulnerable, and needy.

This humanity, stewardship, integrative grasp of detail, collaborative genius, and vision are qualities that both embrace and transcend the principles of efficient management, public relations, the market, and strategic planning that courses in business administration aim to instill. They are qualities of dedicated women at work, relating to colleagues, taking the lead where it is needed, and ministering to God's *anawim*, the poor and unknown ones. They are the fruits of a freely accepted gift of love.

Chapter 15

Ministry in a Post–Vatican II World

Viewed as communal ministry in the mission that is God's life in the Church, certain institutions staffed by Sisters of Charity of Leavenworth for the first century of their history continued to grow in strength and effectiveness during the following half-century even as the number of sisters available for staffing diminished. But distinctions in institutional ministry are significant. Change within the health care ministry carried its own challenge and recognition year by year. In contrast, outcomes of education and religious development were by their nature delayed and immeasurable.

A second distinction in institutional ministry lay in ownership and governance. Early incorporation of the Community's hospitals affected operation and long-range planning by the Health Services System and its individual affiliates. Boards were accountable to the Community Council for decisions regarding corporate offices and assets and for fidelity to mission. On one hand, as corporate sponsor, the Community was responsible to its own members for the corporate institution's implementation of mission and ministry. On the other hand, one home for children and all of the schools but one were owned by dioceses. Operational decisions were largely left to administrators; budgeting and planning were functions of pastor, parish, and bishop. Owned by the Community, the college depended on two-tiered governance by administrators responsible to the Community Council.[1]

This chapter chronicles the evolution of individual ministries from decades of service in educational and health care institutions. Along with causes related to community life and personal development, some sisters left institutional ministries because they wished to carry the experience and competence acquired in the institutions into forms of ministry they could more directly help to shape. These were developing from conditions and needs with which they were already familiar in pastoral ministry, religious education, growth in the spiritual life, and alternative modes of health care delivery. If the Community's reduced membership—caused by deaths, departures, and falling entrance rates—were the sole cause of institutional withdrawals and staff turnovers, this story would be simpler to tell. Recorded facts do not account for the work of the Spirit in the renewal of the Community's mission through its ultimate source in renewal of individual members' lives.

A few comparisons clarify changes that puzzled more than a few observers in the 1970s and 1980s. In 1968 hospitals staffed by the Community numbered thirteen; Sisters of Charity administered and staffed ten secondary schools and fifty-seven elementary schools. By 1986, the Community still administered nine hospitals; administered and taught in nine high schools; but staffed only twenty-five elementary schools. In 1968 there were 22 sisters ministering individually in health care, public education, the foreign missions, social work, and pastoral ministry. By 1986, the last two ministries—social services and pastoral ministry/religious education—claimed 109 sisters working with church and public agencies and in parish and diocesan offices. The range of their services was virtually unlimited.[2] Reasons for such change, focused as it was in particular areas of ministry, were more complex than the numbers reveal.

Vincent de Paul's genius for attracting collaborators and employing gifts is a lens for viewing the charism that inspired his foundations and hundreds of congregations that descended from them. He recognized in Louise de Marillac a partner whose talents for organization and leadership complemented his own. His spirit deeply touched men and women of means and influence who were moved to support both the Daughters of Charity and his Congregation of the Mission. His vision knew no limits as he risked opposition and failure in opening the Hotel Dieu for victims of war, disease, and poverty. Bridging the gap between the powerful and the powerless, he encompassed the works of mercy and the more elusive work of justice.

Three centuries later, the call to renewal brought the Sisters of Charity of Leavenworth to commit themselves to a mission in Latin America; to catechetical and sacramental ministry beyond the classroom; to ministries of healing in clinics for the uninsured; to care for the homebound and the homeless, for prisoners, and for Native Americans. Advocacy and collaboration for change in systems that perpetuate poverty were twentieth-century equivalents of Vincent's challenges to wealth and power. Sisters' competencies and experience recommended them to pastors, bishops, and public administrators for posts that often called for leadership. Many of these ministries were not new but developed from institutions the Community sponsored or owned. Individual initiatives and personal discernment, as well as community living in support of diverse ministries, were the catalysts for deep and expansive change.

The costs were considerable. In 1972 the Leadership Conference of Women Religious reported on the meeting of 130 National Conferences of Major Superiors—both women and men from nine countries—with representatives from the Sacred Congregation for Religious. Papers dealt with consequences of change in community life: no little ferment and division, but also desire for the riches of prayer life, a deeper sense of relationship with a personal God, and inner discipline. Cardinal Antoniutti, of the Roman Congregation, urged collaboration among communities, mixed commissions to study mutual concerns of bishops and professed religious, and participation of religious in diocesan apostolic planning. For their part, religious superiors called for patience and personal support, evaluation of changes, accountability with budgets and varying modes of exercising communal authority, and attention to both initial and continuing formation. They insisted that the complexity of laudable efforts, excesses, and frustrations of religious was universal and a sign of the times. A further sign was their desire for justice within the Church and for leadership within their national conferences.[3]

The previous spring, major superiors of women religious in Kansas and Missouri had met with their bishops to discuss the progress of renewal in women's religious communities. The sisters' emphasis on individuals' interior renewal as more significant than external changes prefaced pleas for cooperative diocesan planning in education and attention to pastoral work and team ministry in hospitals and parishes. Proposals met with approval—not an uncommon outcome of such meetings. But the historic nature of the gathering was undeniable for more reasons than its uniqueness.[4] Judging by statements from women religious at home and in national conferences, they were ready for renewal and striving to realize it in a deepening life of the spirit. Within their communities they were experiencing energy for new ministries along with caution about directions of change. What is generally not understood is the degree to which change came about within and outside of the institutions themselves.

Tutoring a Natural Evolution

One of the earliest ministries that grew directly from the schools staffed by Sisters of Charity of Leavenworth was tutoring adults who lacked schooling and youth who needed help getting through school. School sisters acted in collaboration with public school systems and community programs. As early as 1968, the Leavenworth Community Action Program used facilities at Sacred Heart School. The principal, Sister Lorraine Leist, coordinated the tutoring program; her faculty and hospital sisters spent evening hours with a special education teacher from Nettie Hartnett Public School. Results were tangible: a father was happy to sign his son's report card for the first time; a young man learned to count to ninety in order to write his own checks; a woman in her mid-fifties could at last read the morning paper.

Similar programs went on at the Mother House and at Immaculata High School. At Blessed Sacrament School in Kansas City, Kansas, some 300 attended classes in an ecumenical Volunteer Adult tutoring program. In Kansas City, Missouri, sisters supervised high school students from Bishop Hogan and Pius X in the Kansas City Inner-City Tutors Inc. and the Methodist Inner City tutoring programs. In Topeka, Kansas, at Assumption School and Hayden High School, sisters tutored students in the Youth Basic Education and Neighborhood Youth Corps programs. Home visiting was part of the work with students.[5]

A stranger approached a sister walking down the lane on the campus in Leavenworth one summer evening and asked who might teach him to read. She took him up to the Mother House and found Sister Mary Laurentia Sullivan, who tutored adults in the evening. The man worked as a civilian at Fort Leavenworth and his daughter was now in school there. His own education as an African American in Alabama had been limited to a few years in a one-room schoolhouse where he and his classmates had shared one reader a public school teacher had given their instructor. He had never learned to read but told his pre-school daughter stories from the picture book he bought her. Sister Laurentia taught him three nights a week; Sister Maureen Craig, the other two nights for an hour. She said she wept the night he read a full story the first time.

Catechetics, or religious education, in the Catholic school classroom and beyond was a major mission of the Sisters of Charity of Leavenworth, from their founding. After the beginning of the Confraternity of Christian Doctrine in the 1940s, Saturday CCD classes and correspondence courses were extra assignments for full-time teachers and, where they were available, semi-retired sisters. With renewal after Vatican II, catechetics became a parish ministry as the Catholic population outgrew the parochial school system and Catholic children in public schools needed education in their faith. Both theologians and professional educators contributed to the theory and practice of religious instruction in the weekday Catholic classroom and evening and Sunday morning groups taught by volunteers. In the 1970s, the ministry took on formally what had been integral to catechetics from the start: the education of lay teachers of religion.

Sister Mary Pauline Degan was appointed director of Adult Religious Education for the Archdiocese of Kansas City in Kansas in 1969, with Sister Charlotte (Maureen Therese) Smith her assistant. From August to December of that year, they worked throughout eastern Kansas, meeting with full-time religious education teachers, religious and lay, and with

CCD and adult education boards and committees. The two sisters spoke to CCD groups of Helpers, Parents, and Educators about their assigned responsibilities and to discussion club leaders and executive boards.[6]

Through summer institutes, in-service workshops during the academic year, and second degrees, sisters were deepening their own religious knowledge. Theology had been developing under the influence of biblical studies; major theologians were contemplating the doctrines of grace, sin, and salvation. In a secular age, a renewed realization of individual personal value permeated philosophical reflection and the social and behavioral sciences. Effects on the formal teaching of religion were not all equally happy; new religion textbooks and new writers on the spiritual life were at best creative and exploratory, at worst prematurely authoritative. But genuine developments in doctrinal, moral, and sacramental theology reached hundreds of sisters home from the schools for the summer in courses scheduled by Saint Mary College and taught by recognized scholars. Principles of sound pedagogy and growth in the life of prayer were mainstays that transcended change.

Transitions were a fair challenge to good teachers. Students adapted with some aplomb. More than one became a master of the art of collage. But outcomes reached far beyond creative assignments. That their faith meant they were in the care of a loving God day by day and forever was fundamental for children, adolescents, and adults. That Jesus Christ in the Eucharist was their bond with every other human being was Revelation made new. And that the Spirit lived within them rather than above them was a lifetime's lesson. Critical judgment and imagination were necessary for educators faced with the need to express the tradition of faith in new ways.

These were also times of growing awareness of issues of social justice. Civil rights became more than an abstract term. Students were often enamored of their new knowledge and enthralled by charismatic political leaders. When teenagers came home with impassioned statements about the evils of war and condemned the nation's action in Vietnam, fathers who had served in World War II or Korea remembered why they had fought. The dinnertable could turn into a battleground. Assent to racial integration of a Catholic high school required a bishop's public statement. Religious faculty committed to clarifying the social teachings of the Church had to be sensitive to family conflicts. Sisters of Charity in schools next to Fort Leavenworth with officers' children in their classrooms taught principles of peace along with patriotism and personal respect.

In 1969 in Butte, a team of seventeen religion teachers, priests, and parents implemented a plan for coordinating teachers of religion in each of nine parishes. Sister Helen McDevitt with Father Robert Shea facilitated the parish coordinators' work and established the Religious Education Center for training teachers and assisting city-wide liturgy groups. In a given year, approximately 175 catechists learned about teaching religion from ten Sisters of Charity and a priest, the center's staff. Their students, grades 1–12, numbered roughly two thousand. Each sister worked with thirty to forty catechists and more than two hundred families. Their own revitalized faith life moved some of these adults to seek formal classes in scripture, Church history, and liturgy; in-service workshops served them all.[7]

Catechetics Transformed

Mature believers' desire to know their faith in greater depth fed such growth. In Billings, Montana, the St. Pius X parish council and board of education voted to release one sister from the parochial school to work full time in the parish religious education program. With the pastor, that sister acquainted volunteer teachers with the texts and materials for classes designed for school children, adolescents, parents, and other adults. The Eucharist and liturgical celebrations were integral to instruction. A six-week program, "Christian Living in Modern Billings," initiated by Sister Rose Delores Hoffelmeyer, reached across denominational lines. So did the city-wide "Through-the-Week Religious Education" for elementary and secondary youth who missed a basic religious understanding not achieved in weekly religion classes for public school students. Eastern Montana and Rocky Mountain college students congregated for religious discussions at one of the convents that was home to St. Vincent's Hospital nurses.[8]

Vision, courage, and know-how were the qualities attributed by a *Relay* correspondent in 1964 to a small team of sisters and priests who initiated a program in the principles and experience of catechesis of the adolescent. Teachers of religion in high schools and elementary schools throughout the

With a team of practiced religion teachers, Sister Maurita Postlewait plans catechesis for teenagers.

dioceses of Kansas City, Kansas and Missouri, enrolled in summer workshops and a year-long course taught at Ward High School and credited by Saint Mary College. Sister Maurita Postlewait and priests of the group, who had studied under Father Gerard Sloyan at the Catholic University of America, taught and exemplified the witness that is the catechist's charge issuing from full participation in the liturgy.[9]

Children and parents were students in the Sunday-morning classes directed by Sister Mary Helen McInerney for the three-parish program of catechetical instruction and sacramental preparation shared by Blessed Sacrament, Annunciation, and St. Vincent's in Kansas City, Missouri. The five sisters who lived in one of the first experimental local communities spearheaded the program, soon joined by sisters from other parishes and lay parishioners. Residents of this first "Olive Branch," located in a neighborhood of low-income African American families, soon became familiar neighbors and their home a parish center with its Friday afternoon eucharistic celebration followed by a light supper.

Certified in special education, Sister Rita Marie Anderson taught in the public schools in Topeka for twenty-five years. Experiencing it "as a public witness to the Church and religious life," she felt no need to wear religious garb, for her identity was well known. "In a conservative 'Bible Belt' city," she wrote, "striving for professional excellence and treating children and parents with respect and compassion, my 'missionary work' was clear. In return, I was given a widened circle of friendship and ecumenical experiences of spirituality." Sister Phyllis Stowell pursued a different sort of missionary work as principal of St. Francis of Assisi School, first- and second-time winner of the Quality New Mexico Pinon Award. In 2006 she led a staff of sixty-four serving 530 students in Santo Niño Regional Catholic School, Archdiocese of Santa Fe.[10]

As a special education teacher, Sister Rita Marie Anderson is a resource for Topeka's public school system.

Founded on professional preparation, years of in-service, and advanced degrees, teaching experience was an entrée into the life of the Church in city, suburb, and country. The demands of that life depended on distances and terrain of parishes in the Middle West or in the mountains. It depended too on the welcome of sisters into the total life of the parish. Many had spent extra-classroom hours directing choirs, training altar boys, and managing sacristies; wide-ranging skills and leadership were now in demand. Teachers of special subjects sometimes moved into pastoral ministry in half-time roles, maintaining a presence after the Community's withdrawal from a school. Wherever they ministered, sisters realized the need for sound theological preparation and a maturing life of prayer.[11]

These were hidden resources for the Holy Name School sisters in Topeka, Kansas, who found themselves one day in 1968 suddenly confronted with violent death in their convent neighborhood. Accustomed to dealing with classroom crises, the suicide of an elderly man living alone nearby brought home the realization of what aging and loneliness can bring. Assisted by a priest counselor from the Menninger Foundation, the sisters formed a Senior Citizens Group with advice from three elderly persons they knew. Meetings turned into regular Sunday afternoon social hours with some two dozen people. Contributions paid for games, prizes, and refreshments. The convent, said the organizers, "became more truly a part of our parish and neighborhood."[12]

Moonlighting was a common practice among school sisters in these years. Ward High School faculty continued to visit patients at Providence Hospital next door, tutored Spanish-speaking students in English, directed an adult ESL program, backed up Search retreats for college and high school students, and volunteered for a program to assist elementary science teachers. This was a pattern repeated in varying degrees in all cities where Sisters of Charity staffed schools. When the Community had to withdraw from the elementary school in Deer Lodge, Montana, in the early 1970s, the people asked that the Tiny Tot Nursery, opened by Sister Alice Clare Hill in 1969, be maintained. So a presence of Sisters of Charity for ninety-eight years remained.[13]

After thirty-two years of secondary school teaching in drama, speech, and English literature, Sister Margaret Marie Mitchell applied for parish work in ministry to the elderly and homebound. Ultimately it led her to a position on the staff of Truman Medical Center where she daily visits clinic patients and comforts young mothers who have borne a stillborn child or given a newborn up for adoption. The county facility welcomed her presence.

Sister Jeanne Marie Jette had taught successfully for twenty-two years before she became director of the Argentine Catholic Center in Kansas City, Kansas. Her responsibilities included programs in adult education, religious instruction, and remedial training. In pastoral ministry to the elderly, direct work with the poor deepened her commitment to social change and political advocacy. On the staff of Congressman Jim Slattery in his Kansas City, Kansas office, Sister Jeanne Marie dealt with issues of children, the poor, the elderly, and the underserved. She recruited tutors

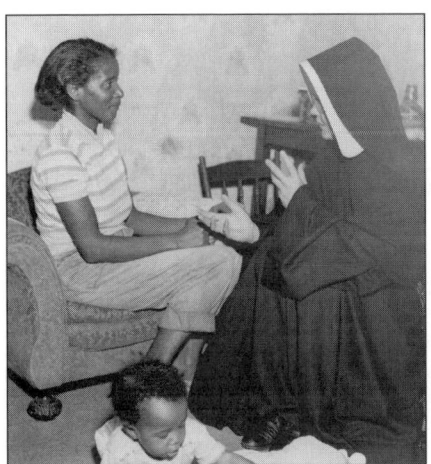

A mother's visit with Sister Mary Edwin DeCoursey doesn't interrupt her child's play.

for the diocesan REACH program of religious education for the handicapped and volunteers for ministry in the central city Bethany Medical Center.[14]

Wolcott was a rural town between Leavenworth and Kansas City where Mexican families lived in buses while all able-bodied members harvested the annual sugar beet crop for Valley Growers Packing Co. Inc. Sisters Mary Ernestine Whitmore and Mary Liguori Horvat, of the Saint Mary College faculty, were the first to visit in 1963. They observed the care with which mothers kept their families' clothing clean and received assurance that sisters would be welcome to teach their children and prepare them for the sacraments. Teamwork followed. Medicines and unobtainable food and clothing were basic provisions; instruction from volunteer school teachers continued throughout the summer and drew increasing numbers. When members of the Kansas Council of Churches attending the families' needs learned of the families' Catholic background, they accepted the sisters' teaching them. During the summer, Archbishop Edward J. Hunkeler established the Apostolate of Migrant Workers for the Church in Kansas City, Kansas.[15]

An unexpected fruit of those summers was the long memory of a young woman who glanced at the check given her by Sister Francis Marie Grady for groceries at a check-out register in a Texas town on the Mexican border. She looked up and asked if the customer were a Sister of Charity. Assured that she was, the woman thanked Sister on behalf of all her family "for the many kindnesses and the concern" the sisters had shown them when they lived in Wolcott, Kansas, working as migrants. Although she had been only seven at the time, the woman was still grateful for the groceries, cleaning, and teaching that her family would never forget.[16]

The RCIA Journey

One of the most influential factors in renewal was the Rite of Christian Initiation for Adults (RCIA) restored from the apostolic age and first centuries in the life of the Church. It was the journey of preparation for full membership in the Christian community through the sacraments of baptism, confirmation, reconciliation, and Eucharist. In 1976 four pastors of inner city parishes in Kansas City were looking for sisters to implement the rite and its adaptation for children, RCIC. Sister Rosalie Curtin, representative to the Community's Personnel Board for some thirty-five to forty sisters in pastoral ministry and religious education, had become familiar with RCIA as pastoral associate for Risen Christ parish. She and Sister Lillian McGuire, with Sister Jeanne Stewart, ASC, and Brother Terry McGlennon, FSC, made up a team to work with about fifteen catechumens and their sponsors in each parish. Weekly inquiry and discussion from the scripture readings for Sunday's liturgy led naturally to doctrinal instruction. From their experience the team produced the manual, *A Practical Approach to RCIA*.[17]

In a small town parish in the Ozarks, a team of sisters discovered the personal impact of teaching religion to pre-schoolers, adolescents, and adults. Leading catechumens through the RCIA, they found that responses to questions about Catholic belief deepened their own life of faith. A professional educator, Sister Eileen Sheehy learned that young people and parents trained to proclaim the word often read so prayerfully that people closed their Mass books to simply listen. Sisters Bonnie Bachle and Susan Newland found that every aspect of the liturgy enacted reverently appealed to the young.[18]

In the Far West, the need for sisters' pastoral presence evolved from limits of the environment and availability of priests. After teaching for twenty years, Sister Letitia Lenherr spent a decade ministering to the elderly but missed her earlier work with Catholic families in school and parish. In a pastoral ministry role in Gilette, Wyoming, she directed religious education for children in public schools, worked with adults in RCIA, prepared for eucharistic liturgy and funerals, counseled the young, visited the housebound, and coordinated parish outreach programs. Her ministry became a genuine partnership with the pastor.

Help on a practical project is welcome from veteran teacher Sister Ann Louise Eble, volunteer in Sister Mary Laura Huddleston's Hispanic ministry.

Study for a master's degree in theology and ministry brought Sister Therese Steiner into contact with a pastor looking for a director of family-centered religious education in his parish, located near the University of Wyoming in Laramie. In a two-pronged campus and parish ministry, for a decade she taught children, students, and adults. Further study took her into retreats, adult classes, and spiritual direction for the diocese of Cheyenne. In the Big Sky and West Yellowstone parishes of Montana, Sister Patricia Toeckes still serves as parish administrator for the sacramental minister to both communities.[19]

Roles for sisters multiplied as parish renewal progressed. In Butte Sister Mary Jo McDonald brought more than twenty years' experience as teacher and principal and two master's degrees in counseling and administration and in pastoral ministry to St. Ann's parish. Welcoming her as a partner, the pastor turned over to her tasks of business management, planning, and parish ministries. Sister oversaw allocation of funds and expenditures, upkeep of buildings, and projection of needs; she shared decisions of parish council and pastor on the best use of parish property. Her ministry included counseling walk-ins and planning inter-parish trips to Mexico for youth and adults to work on housing projects for those in need. Social justice issues taken up by parishioners resulted in a food bank board and legislative advocacy. Pastoral ministry in the 1980s and 1990s was only another face of the services of Sisters of Charity to the people of Butte since 1881.[20]

In Helena, Montana, Saint Mary's parish welcomed three Sisters of Charity in 1982. Sisters Patricia Sullivan, Mary Jo Quinn, and Mary Agnes Hogan came as directors respectively of religious education, liturgy and music ministry, and pastoral care and social concerns. When the parish completed renovation of its worship space and service complex in 1998, the people dedicated the new tabernacle in the Blessed Sacrament chapel to the Sisters of Charity of Leavenworth for their services to the Saint Mary's community.

Sister Mary Jo Quinn, music minister, participates with the choir in the Easter Vigil service at St. Mary's Parish Community, Helena, Montana.

As race riots ravaged inner cities from Detroit to Los Angeles and National Guard units were restraining attacks on African American students in the deep South, large numbers of parishioners in Kansas City, Missouri, were learning first-hand one another's cultural roots and values. In 1990 Sister Irene Skeehan became pastoral associate at St. Thomas More church with a staff in the Social Justice and Peace office who were proactive in educating themselves. They organized a consortium of six parishes that met regularly for celebration of the Eucharist and an intercultural program. Each parish took its turn planning the liturgy and supper menu and securing speakers and performers. Exchange after the Rodney King incident in California led to mutual understanding.

A parish group traveled to their sister parish in Guatemala early in the decade. Working with the poor was a call heard repeatedly by Sister Maureen Hall during her early years as a teacher and later as director of novices. Three months in 1988 with Hispanic families living in the Rio Grande Valley helped prepare her for pastoral ministry in central Kansas City parishes, at St. Joseph the Worker and Good Shepherd during the 1990s and as pastoral associate at Holy Cross for the first four years of the new century.[21]

Bishops found that practiced teachers had highly developed skills of arbitration and mediation. Nine lay people and Sister Mary Rachel Flynn made up a Due Process Council for mediating disputes among church members in the diocese of Cheyenne, Wyoming. Sister Rose Dolores Hoffelmeyer was a diocesan consultant on social studies in the Great Falls diocese where she made presentations on the inquiry method of teaching. After thirty years as a teacher and principal in parochial schools, Sister Perpetua McGrath served in both Kansas City, Kansas, and Kansas City–St. Joseph, Missouri, diocesan offices. She was director of religious personnel for Catholic Charities in the 1990s.[22]

As the Community withdrew from elementary school staffing, sisters equipped with a master's degree in education or another field looked to levels of teaching not commonly open to them so long as they were needed in the schools. Donnelly, an inner city diocesan community college in Kansas City, Kansas, welcomed qualified teachers from the Community. Among the Sisters of Charity who joined its faculty was Sister Marie Kathleen Daugherty, who proved her worth teaching philosophy and chairing the Humanities division.

In 1990 Sister Peter Parry applied for an opening in the mathematics department of Penn Valley Community College in central Kansas City, Missouri. Almost thirty years in the elementary schools and fifteen years teaching GED students for Donnelly College had prepared her for a diverse population. Her work with students, attentive to individual needs and capacities, kept her on the Penn Valley faculty for more than a decade. Sister Mary O'Rourke, who had taught chemistry and physical science at Saint Mary College for thirty years, joined the science faculties of Rockhurst College and Penn Valley Community College as an adjunct professor.

In the 1980s, Sisters Mary Jo Coyle and Mary Ellen Beyhan accepted positions in physics and chemistry respectively on the faculty of Iowa Western Community College. Sister Mary Jo later taught at Donnelly

College and at community colleges in Kansas City. With years of experience at Saint Mary and area colleges in training faculty and developing computer curricula, Sister Barbara Kushan came well equipped in 2004 to the position of graduate coordinator of Management Information Systems at Park College in Parkville, Missouri.[23]

Gifted as a writer, Sister Mary Catherine Daugherty was a teacher and administrator in the schools for twenty-eight years before she found a niche in the world of journalism. After her service in religious education for the Helena, Montana, diocese, the bishop invited her to edit *The Western Montana Register*, changed to *Westmont Word* in 1971. Three years later she was named to the United States Bishops Conference Bicentennial Committee to assist with publications. In 1979 the Council asked her to set up an office of communications for the Community. From that office for the next twenty-two years, Sister Mary Catherine published *Connecting* and videotaped conferences, workshops, and Chapter sessions that constitute a file for use and research. Her recommendations led to a Community study that produced a computerized communication system and website.[24]

INVITED TO LEAD

A Jesuit provincial who conducted a retreat at Regis College in the late 1970s asked a question of Sister Margaret Hogan that eventually led her to pastoral ministry. She was a teacher of twenty-five years and loved her work. When she expressed her hope to the retreat master that Jesuits would continue their work of spiritual direction, he replied, "Why don't you do that?" The question persisted. Study in spiritual theology, a thirty-day retreat, much discernment, and finally pastors' invitations drew Sister Margaret to work in a Butte parish, then in Hamilton, Montana.

In this small town in the Bitterroot Valley of western Montana, Sister Margaret found parishioners wanting to develop a more vigorous spiritual life. The pastor encouraged her shaping a program for days of prayer, especially in Advent and Lent, for weekly group and individual spiritual formation, and for ongoing direction in the Spiritual Exercises of Ignatius of Loyola. The Jesuit parish in Missoula invited Sister Margaret to share with a team of lay ministers her experience of the Spiritual Exercises throughout much of her religious life.[25]

Father Ed Hays had a long relationship with the Sisters of Charity of Leavenworth, not simply because his sister Jane entered the Community in 1946. From seminary days through his subsequent years as a priest, Father Ed ministered with them in the high schools, conversed with them in renewal workshops, celebrated their liturgies of jubilee and profession days, and welcomed them as parish associates when he was pastor at St. Dominic's church in Holton, Kansas. After his sabbatical year of prayer in monasteries of Europe and the Middle East, Father Ed directed Sisters of Charity in the spiritual life at Shantivanam, the retreat center Bishop Ignatius Strecker assigned him to build west of Leavenworth. When she had charge of the Mother House grounds, Sister Jane Hays extended an image of her brother's Forest of Peace to the campus with a grove of pine and red maple trees behind the original Marillac, a small house of prayer.[26]

Experience of need for a deepened prayer life was a fruit of the intense ministry pursued by sisters during the decades of renewal, whether they remained in institutions owned or staffed by the Community or were employed individually in professional fields. After fourteen years of teaching, counseling, and development work at Saint Mary College, Sister Bernadette Marie Teasdale sought a new ministry. A degree in pastoral ministry from the Jesuit School of Theology in Weston, Massachusetts, requiring lay teamwork in the field, prepared her for the parish Renew program of the Denver diocese. There Dom Thomas Keating, a Cistercian abbot, invited her to train lay facilitators in a pilot program for a spiritual journey of renewal. Seventy parishioners of Spirit of Christ church agreed to the training, which included workshops, classes in the Spiritual Journey lecture series, and mini-retreats with the abbot four times a year. In the 1980s, Sister worked with an ecumenical team in the international Contemplative Outreach program developed by Abbot Keating and operative in twenty-two countries and almost every state of the union.[27]

Dubbed "Mother Earth" by her sisters, Sister Jane Hays tends a plant that will go to one of many gardens on the campus.

New Ministries of Prayer

Teaching for thirty-three years in elementary and secondary schools and in the art department of Saint Mary College, Sister Carmen Echevareria increasingly recognized the intimate exchange between her creative life and growth in prayer. With formal preparation beginning in 1980, she undertook a ministry of spirituality through the Focus program at the University of Seattle and at the Stillpoint Spirituality Center in Oregon. Enriched by the retreats of Dom Thomas Keating, OCSO, in the 1990s, she took her experience in centering prayer and the Ignatian Exercises to the Spiritual Life Center of the Diocese of Wichita, Kansas, where she offered retreats and spiritual direction. The serenity and restraint of Oriental art deeply influenced her creative work.[28]

Their prayer life and creative gifts moved many sisters to express themselves in poetry, music, and the visual and plastic arts. The wood sculpture of Sister Bernardine Hon brought serenely simple figures of Jesus and Mary from her Chop Shop in Berchmans to many rooms and chapels on the campus. Discerning a call to retreat work, Sister Francis Marie Grady made of her convent home in Texas a spiritual center and studio. At the Mother House, Sister Maurita Postlewait photographed Kansas skies and vibrant seasonal life for gift packets of greeting cards. In three unbound volumes, Sister Mary Janet McGilley gathered a thousand poems, only a hundred or so publishable—by her standards. Musicians wrote, cantored, and directed choirs for liturgies; performed tirelessly; and entertained students, staffs, boards, benefactors, and countless children. Dozens of contemporaries and successors to such artists enriched community life and ministry.

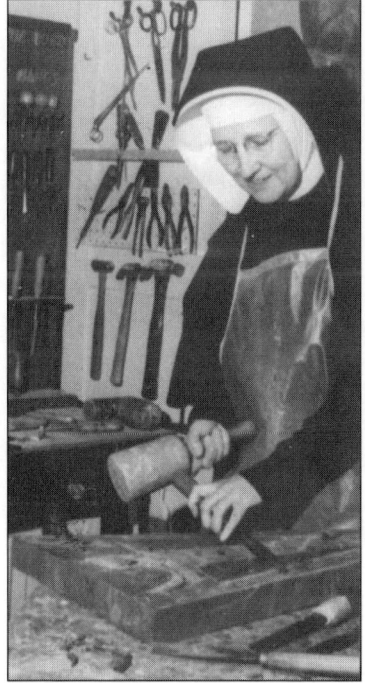

Creating a human image from one of her salvaged wooden beams, Sister Bernadine Hon works in her Chop Shop on ground floor, Mead Hall.

The post–Vatican II decades witnessed a spiritual hunger that manifested itself within and beyond the Church. In the midst of change wrought by renewal, Sisters of Charity experienced a need for deepening spiritual life that manifested itself in requests for theological and spiritual studies, directed and thirty-day retreats, and sabbaticals of renewal. One of the most urgent requests as the Community approached the Chapter of 1980 was a plea for a Community house of prayer. Speaking for others, Sister Gloria Solomon wrote of the very real and very deep need of prayer as the heart of conversion. Such a need is the beginning of the *metanoia* Paul speaks of. This turning around, this maturing in a person's spiritual life, can come in the course of daily living; or it can come in response to suffering or to an immediate experience of God. From this maturing the knowledge of what is needed to pursue a deeper life of prayer is sure and clear. Citing words of Mother Leo Frances Ryan, the Community Constitutions, and lines from Thomas Aquinas and Thomas Merton, she pointed to a principle of the Gospel, that "a call to a contemplative way of life...feeds both the individual's active life, when she returns to it, and the apostolic life of the community."[29]

The house of prayer Sister hoped for did not immediately follow, but the sisters' need for a maturing life of prayer appeared in diverse ways. Charismatic prayer groups formed in many places, sometimes including college students, more often lay associates. Benefits attested to by many from prolonged periods of both personal and shared meditation carried over years and influenced personal and community prayer. Shared prayer in small groups became habitual in some convents or took the form of common petitions in morning and evening prayers. Mindfulness of others' needs and attention drawn to human suffering in all parts of the world extended the reach of those petitions.

A Ministry's Self-scrutiny

As early as 1968 the Sisters of Charity of Leavenworth were asking themselves questions about their ministry of health care, questions prompted by mounting medical costs, financial and ethical problems posed by growing governmental control, and decreasing availability of religious for supervisory or administrative positions. Besides these conditions, the apparent paradox of women religious committed to increasingly big business transactions and the reality of new needs in health care outside hospitals prompted further questions. Criteria formulated by the committee assigned to study the situation were immediately practical:

- Are the needs of the Church as witness to the Gospel being met?
- What are the sisters' commitments to the civic communities of the hospitals?
- Are present facilities adequately utilized?
- What is the potential for development in the ministry of health care?

New prospects for ministry as well as problems soon followed. Owning and operating hospitals might offer unique opportunities for witness to Christian principles through increasing participation in civic roles of leadership and decision-making. Community-centered health services were expanding already in public health education, social programs, outpatient and mental health clinics, rehabilitation centers for recovering addicts, and mobile units to serve low-income areas. But the concept of a non-profit institution was also changing: justice to employees in a living wage, absorption of costs for uncompensated services, and the commitment to care for each one in need regardless of means made the individual institution in a given community particularly vulnerable. Add to that the desire of some sisters to minister directly to the poor and expansion to new ministries of health care looked promising.[30]

Outreach to those with arrested or troubled mental and emotional development began where Community hospitals had appropriate staff and facilities. Beginning in the 1960s, treatment programs for children and youth affected by the drug culture and rescue operations for homeless persons who were mentally afflicted became part of the hospitals' outreach. Sister Nancy Svetlecic had taught for ten years and begun study for a master's degree before she entered the Community.

Work as an associate in a Montana parish led her to a second master's degree in pastoral counseling. Proving her ability as an intern, then as a diagnostic and assessment counselor at the Community Research Foundation in San Diego, Sister Nancy became full-time coordinator of a treatment unit for clients with addictive and emotional disorders. With authority in her unit over all phases of care from admission to stabilization and dismissal, she was welcome as a religious on a professional team of counselors, clinical psychologist and medical psychiatrist, and program directors.[31]

HEALTH CARE AT HOME

With twenty-five years of nursing, supervision, and administration in Community hospitals behind her, Sister Kathryn O'Neill applied for a position opened in 1970 by the Butte/Silver Bow City/County Public Health System. In need of an administrator for an independent Home Health program to be sponsored by the Butte/Silver Bow office, Cy Delaney, the system's administrator, hired Sister Kathryn to develop policies and procedures compliant with the strict standards necessary to maintain federal funding. Subsequent practice revealed that the responsibilities of a home health nurse required application of all she had learned in training, from specialized coursework, and from long experience. Assessment of a patient's need for hospital care and for the physical and psychological preparation for it was her sole and immediate responsibility. The role demanded all the confidence she had gained in bedside nursing and as a clinician and supervisor.

Sister's competence quickly gained the full trust both of the doctors and the patients she served. Five years with Home Health in Butte and Silver

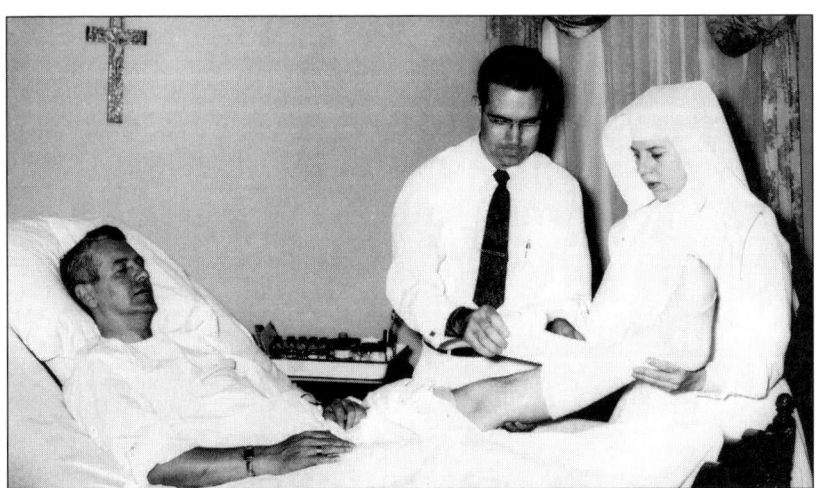

Before she was called to establish home health programs in Montana, Sister Kathryn O'Neill served as a registered nurse in the Community's hospitals.

Bow County in collaboration with St. James Community hospital brought Sister Kathryn an assignment in 1976 to establish the program for DePaul Hospital in Cheyenne, in conjunction with the Public Health office. In 1982 she was missioned to Livingston, Montana, to assist in care of her mother. There she set up a Home Health program for the Westmont Health System serving Helena and its region. It was a short step to the State Department of Health to help develop a Home Health program for all of Montana. Back at St. James Community Hospital at the end of the decade, she directed a federal program for home visiting with the services of twenty volunteers.[32]

While working as director of patient care at Catholic Family and Community Services (CFCS) in Kansas City, Missouri, Sister Elizabeth Henry, who had assisted Sister Kathryn in Livingston, welcomed summer volunteers. One of them was Sister Bernard Ann (Pam) Hinkle, who soon joined the staff as a geriatric social worker and advocate for the elderly. Both sisters influenced systems.

Sister Elizabeth was elected secretary of the newly formed Missouri Association of Home Health Agencies in Jefferson City. As secretary of Aging Inc. she was instrumental in opening a multi-purpose center in Kansas City's urban core for senior citizens in need of referral services. After five years, Sister Elizabeth left Kansas City to administer Westmont Home Health Agency in Helena, Montana. In her role at CFCS, Sister Bernard Ann helped the aged find their place at a nursing home, secure Meals on Wheels service, or apply for Medicare and other financial assistance. She became acutely aware of the many unmet needs of elderly persons who had no knowledge of or access to sources of assistance.[33]

When she left St. Mary's in Grand Junction in 1977, Sister Jean William (Jean) Lockett brought with her to Ross Hall, the sisters' infirmary, valuable experience as director of the Health Center's physical and occupational therapy department. For fourteen years, she served the sisters of Ross Hall and the Mother House as a licensed physical therapist. In 1991 she became one of six members of a private Home Health group in Topeka, Kansas, offering special services to people in twenty-seven counties. The team included licensed specialized social workers, a registered nurse, a clinical psychiatrist, a family therapist, and Sister Jean. After earning a master's degree in social work, she served in Catholic Charities. She continues her ministry with Woodrich Counseling, a team of therapists and psychiatrists based in Topeka and serving a broad outreach of clients.[34]

Frequently sisters' own parents were in need of care that only a daughter in religious life could offer. The Community commonly missioned such a sister to her home town or freed her to live with her parents when that was necessary for a time. From such an assignment Sister Mary Georgette Groh accompanied her mother, then her father to the end of their journey on earth. The experience took her into pastoral care as an intern in Clinical Pastoral Education (CPE) at St. Francis Hospital in Topeka. After an eight-year stint at St. Mary's Hospital and Medical Center in Grand Junction, she returned to her home state as chaplain for Midland Hospice Care in Topeka.

With a small staff, Sister Patricia Field, missioned to Butte where her ailing mother lived, directed St. Patrick's parish program of sacramental preparation and visiting at hospitals and nursing homes. She made funeral arrangements for pastors of four parishes. While she cared for her mother in her final years, Sister Mary Depner taught band in the city's four Catholic grade schools and served as librarian before becoming director of music at St. Patrick's co-cathedral. During her eighteen years at this post, she was honored by the American Guild of Organists.

A respiratory therapist at St. John Hospital in Leavenworth, Sister Patricia Connolly traveled to Council Bluffs, Iowa, every weekend in 1976 to assist her mother, increasingly incapacitated during recovery from surgery. Need for her assistance only grew with her mother's death, the subsequent death of a single-parent brother, and illness of her father. A parentless school-age niece made discernment necessary; the Community readily confirmed Sister's new ministry. During these years, she volunteered as respiration therapist at Edmundson Hospital.[35]

After five years in the Latin American missions, during work in the States with Hispanic students and parents in school and parish, Sister Mary

Joan Eble undertook the hospice ministry. For six years from 1994, she served as chaplain at the Veterans Administration and St. Mary's hospitals in Grand Junction, Colorado, through Hospice of Grand Valley. Since 2005, she brings her experience to In-home Services for the elderly, maintained by CSJ Care, a ministry of the Congregation of St. Joseph sisters.[36]

Pastoral care in the hospitals was an evolution of the practice of visiting patients and of the personal attention consistently given by nurses and supervisors. Needs of patients approaching death and of their families led to formal programs for assistance to the dying at hospitals staffed by the Community. The new liturgy for the anointing of the sick was a particular learning challenge for the pastoral care team. Traditionally the department of pastoral care included the services of ministers of all Christian faiths and Jewish rabbis; the ecumenical thrust of Vatican II confirmed and intensified its inclusive policy. Care for the spiritual needs of all patients, whether or not members of a religious body, became a growing concern for health care workers.

New Call to Pastoral Care

At the same time, in the 1970s and 1980s, licensing of pastoral ministers and accreditation of their training programs became important, somewhat as academic preparation of nurses had dominated the previous two decades. The Clinical Pastoral Education (CPE) program, established in the late nineteenth century by Protestant health care workers, came to the fore in Catholic institutions as administrators and pastoral ministers foresaw the demands. Sister Bernice Himmelberg, a pastoral associate, was one of the first Sisters of Charity of Leavenworth to receive such training through the Pastoral Care program directed by Sister Rose Carmel McKenna at St. Joseph's Hospital in Denver.[37]

After thirty-six years of teaching physics and chemistry and with a second master's degree, Sister Rose Carmel turned to rehabilitative and vocational counseling. In 1974 she was licensed in CPE by the Institute of Religion and Human Development at the Texas Medical Center in Houston. Her residency was at M. D. Anderson Medical Center in Houston and Presbyterian Hospital in Philadelphia. She directed the CPE program at Mercy Hospital, Sacramento, California, and pastoral care programs at St. Joseph's Hospital, Denver; Providence Medical Center, Kansas City, Kansas; St. Joseph Medical Center, Wichita, Kansas; and St. John's Hospital, Oxnard, California. Sister was accredited as a pastoral associate supervisor by the National Association of Catholic Chaplains when the organization numbered only priests on its rolls. In 1980 she received the Diplomate Award as "one of the grandparents of the Association."[38]

In retrospect, what the Community's institutional ministries had both hidden and revealed during its first century of mission to the people of God was the strength and power of relationship. Responsibility of administrators to boards, pastors, parents, and patients was both public and moral. The power of the individual sister's relationship to patient or student or child was altogether personal and frequently unperceived but indelibly remembered. But the source of that power and the effect of that responsibility were put to the test during the decades of renewal. In the first place, sisters increasingly felt responsible for their professional effectiveness. In their self-examination and individual evaluations, they looked to what contributed to or detracted from their competence and to what leadership rightly expected of them. With emphasis on discernment of ministry, assignment was no longer sufficient reason to remain in a work for which they did not feel fully qualified.

Moreover, the effectiveness of Catholic school education was under intense scrutiny even as the development of post–Vatican II theology was affecting religious instruction with mixed results. Curriculum, pedagogy, and growth in faith were complex issues rather than an accepted status quo. The conditions of child care were changing from surrogate parenthood in a close-knit community to specialized and limited treatment preparatory to foster care and adoption. Hospitals were faced with growing regulation and costs paired with decreasing compensation from managed care corporations and government. The foundations of ministry were shifting with unprecedented impact on personnel both lay and religious. Education and updating of sisters for ever more demanding roles in administration and staffing was a *sine qua non* for religious communities already coping with diminished numbers.

What lay hidden, however, was the most significant relationship of all, that of the individual sister with the Spirit, source of her initial call to religious life and source of her Community's vitality. Whatever strength might come of renewal lodged in the interior life of each sister. Only from her growth in prayer, in union with God, and in communion with her sisters in community—only from such relationship would the real power of ministry, new or continued, manifest itself. Out of that relationship had to come the discernment of whether to change or to remain in one's ministry. Clearly, the factors of effectiveness, preparation for change or updating, and the Community's needs and resources required communal as well as personal discernment. That in turn called on maturity and openness to the Spirit. However forthrightly acknowledged, these were not guaranteed by a way of life. The source of both lay in the deeply personal relationship ordinarily called the mystery of grace.

CHAPTER 16

Mission Unlimited

A sister's words reported in the media sum up one of the motives of those engaged in social service ministries throughout the decades following Vatican II: "People of faith have the responsibility to speak for those who can't and to empower the voiceless to speak for themselves." The first responsibility is that of advocacy; empowering people implies more. One who spent twenty-two years of her professed life working with Native Americans said, "I wanted to be in a place where I would have to...experience being a minority in a dominant culture." That meant, on the face of it, living apart from the Community and learning with those she hoped to teach and lead forward in a society that was not their home.

Yet another, ministering to her native Mexican people for more than twenty years, realized that "here in the [Rio Grande] Valley...I've learned what having faith really means. Here I discovered my own poverty as I share in the struggles of others.... It is here that I've discovered 'the richness of the poor': rich in their spirit of hospitality, rich in their trust in God, and rich in their ability to celebrate life."[1]

Their words reveal much of what sisters in direct ministry were learning from experience, that the call of the Gospel reached into the world's far corners and crossed all lines of congregation, faith, culture, and commitment. No government or institution could meet needs that beggared imagination and now called to women religious in unique and specific ways. These women and most of the others who entered the social services ministry had been teachers in parochial schools for anywhere from fifteen to thirty years of their religious life; a few of them early on were assigned to the Community's homes for children. They valued and built on those institutional experiences. This chapter records stories of leadership not sought but of natural growth from personal gifts and experience in this and other ministries and from initiatives taken for people in hidden and mortal need.

In preparation for the General Chapter of 1986, members of the social services apostolate reached consensus on priorities: the responsibility of each sister to lodge her ministry on a strong spiritual base, respect for life, and Community solidarity; the need for multi-disciplinary centers to be administered by teams for advocacy, education, counseling, and health care in poverty areas; ministry to the severely disadvantaged—physically, spiritually, and educationally; and signs of the times to be found in the talents, dreams, and visions of individual sisters.

Except for the first, such broad goals quietly called for measures undertaken largely through existing communal and ecclesial structures. In 1985 the thirty-five Sisters of Charity of Leavenworth in social services were still ministering in Community institutions, in parish and diocesan roles, and under public auspices. Three were in prison ministry or criminal justice work; seven were ministering in diocesan housing for the elderly and low-income families; others were in Catholic social services, hospice care, child care, counseling and education of minority youth and adults.[2] But these and sisters like them were implementing strategies that bridged gulfs of income and power and that brought research and resources to bear on political and corporate decisions.

Between 1970 and 1983, the United States Conference of Catholic Bishops issued pastoral letters on justice in the world, racism, world peace, and Catholic social teaching and the U.S. economy, all more revolutionary in their principles than many realized. Further, radical principles wanted sound formats for implementation. Women religious were generally ingenious in finding or inventing such formats where need was apparent. Many in social service grew adept at the business almost in proportion to the obstacles that stood in their way. As demonstrated in Denver's archdiocesan project on housing, sisters could manage on proverbial shoestrings, could organize families and elderly dependents in complex structures, and knew how to provide for the spirit as well as the body.

In 1970 Sister Mary Lucy Downey was asked by Bishop George Evans, vicar of rural and urban affairs for the Archdiocese of Denver, to move from the faculty of Annunciation School to be social coordinator for the new housing commission responsible for low-income families and the elderly. Incorporated in the early 1970s, Archdiocesan Housing was governed by a board of professionals that included lawyers, doctors, gerontologists, architects, and engineers. With their support and advice, Sister Mary Lucy successfully applied for HUD funds and searched for land on which to build two-story structures of family units. The first complex rose at 37th and Humboldt, site of the first Annunciation School.

Sister recruited managers from her own and other religious communities. With their help and with the resources of Denver's St. Vincent de Paul

Society, she found baby cribs, living room furniture, beds, kitchen appliances, and anything else that goes into the making of a home. They furnished 160 apartments in four family complexes. Abiding by HUD requirements, Sister opened facilities to persons of all religious persuasions. To serve elderly and disabled persons without family resources, she oversaw the building and management of six high rises in Denver and manors in Cheyenne and Caster, Wyoming. Denver's Cathedral Plaza produced models for interviewing applicants, writing reports, and mentoring new teams. Applicants more than tripled the number of spaces available in a given facility.[3]

Early on, Sisters Owen Marie and Marie de Lourdes Falk and Sister Mary Lyons began twenty-five-year stints in management and purchasing. Once Sister Lucille Degenhart obtained the first van for transportation, social activity coordinators escorted residents to Denver's numerous parks, museums, and galleries and on day trips into the mountains. For some, the most memorable entertainment was line dancing. The Falks learned it at the Mother House and brought the music on tapes back to Denver where a dozen lay staff and sisters made a name for themselves doing western boot-stompin' boogie and matched-rhythm dances for Plaza residents and other senior groups in the city. At an annual Christmas party for some 150 Board members, HUD officials, and contractors, the Plazette line dancers were in top form.[4]

In the 1990s, townhouses of four or six units each, totaling sixty-four apartments, were erected for families of workers in four mountain resorts between Aspen and Glenwood Springs. Before she died in 1992, Sister Mary Lucy served three years as chief executive officer of the Archdiocesan Housing Commission Inc.[5] Sister Mary Loretto Lyons succeeded her as director of archdiocesan housing. Similar responsibilities fell to Sister Ruth Ann Hehn as director of the Cheyenne, Wyoming Diocesan Housing Management Services.

A century-old tradition of ministry to prisoners that Sisters of Charity began when they first settled in Leavenworth became a formal mission in the early 1960s when, at the chaplain's request, Mother Leo Frances assigned Sisters Magdalen Ford and Anthony Marie (Regina) Deitchman to teach religion at the Kansas State Penitentiary. By 1966, Saint Mary College was offering courses there and faculty were in dialogue with prisoners during informal seminars at the federal prison. Inter-faith choirs attracted sisters at both facilities. Between 1977 and 1998, the college held contracts with the state and federal governments for granting associate and baccalaureate degrees to incarcerated men and women. At the turn of the century, sisters continue a ministry of Communion service and prayer with inmates of a holding facility in Lansing. As members of the Bethany group of lay women and men who have ministered at Kansas State Penitentiary for twelve years, half a dozen sisters share with prisoners reflection on scriptural readings for the Sunday Eucharist.[6]

A veteran of ministry in all four local, state, and federal prisons, Sister Darlyne Kern originally taught a course in scripture, with never fewer than twenty in her classes. Her theology course was one that met the requirement for the associate of arts degree from the college. When the degree program was terminated in the 1990s, Sister got certified in library and information studies and taught prisoners skills needed to run a library: cataloging, a check-out system, reviewing books for recommended purchase, and generating reports. For nine years, Sister Darlyne was a staff member of Outside Connection, an organization for helping families of prisoners. In 2000 she was recognized as Kansas State Volunteer of the Year for the Department of Corrections.[7]

A different kind of learning went on at the Kansas State Penitentiary during the 1970s while Sister Dolores Brinkel was director of the criminal justice ministry, an office she organized for Catholic Charities of the Archdiocese of Kansas City in Kansas. In pastoral ministry at Kansas State Penitentiary, Sister motivated members of the Lifers Club to apply for grants from the Kansas Humanities Council to fund symposia for informing the public on conditions and issues of incarcerated men and women. Educators, pastors, legislators, and civic leaders participated in panels and heard prisoners' presentations in programs designed for mutual benefit. The Lifers Club sponsored the "Seventy Times Seven" program aimed at biblical understanding of criminal offense, restitution, and forgiveness. At the same time, Sister Dolores served as president and board member of the Kansas Council on Crime and Delinquency. Advocacy for penal reform became a central focus as she continued to teach social studies at Ward. Each ministry fed the other.

Alternative punishment for nonviolent and first offenders, training programs for prison personnel, and professional help for inmates highlighted the Community Corrections act passed by the Kansas legislature in 1977. On the board of Catholic Charities USA during the 1980s, Sister Dolores facilitated a policy statement by the Committee on Corrections that passed at the 1984 national conference. Through her parish work and in coalitions of labor leaders, the mental health association, the League of Women Voters, and the Kansas Council of Churches, Sister led successful efforts to persuade Kansas legislators to restore welfare funds cut from the state budget.[8]

With a view to preventing juvenile offenders' further crimes, Sister Margaret Mary Driscoll began her work with them in the 1970s. During formal study for the ministry, she spent an internship as a "street worker" in Spanish Harlem at the northeast end of Central Park in New York City, where she learned what succeeded and what didn't with kids adrift. The degree certified her as a deputy juvenile officer in the Protective Services branch of the Jackson County Juvenile Court of Kansas City, Missouri. She quickly became assistant administrator of Hilltop School for girls, established in collaboration with the Metropolitan Community Colleges.

Five years later, Sister was in charge of the McCune Home for boys in Independence, funded and staffed by the courts with teachers drawn from the Kansas City school district. With twenty-five professionals serving the forty-five to fifty residents, Sister set up three cottage programs for age groups between eleven and seventeen, operating with a firm but non-oppressive discipline marked by goal-setting, self-assessment, and involvement of parents who were willing to cooperate. She summed up the ruling philosophy of the Home: "We don't write off any student."[9] The Archdiocese of Kansas City in Kansas claimed Sister's services in the 1980s for the criminal justice ministry and as associate director of Catholic Social Services.

Sister Margaret Mary Driscoll with two youngsters in the foster care of sisters at Ancilla Place.

Of lasting impact was the Victim/Offender Restitution Service (VORS), which Sister Margaret Mary instituted to aid victims and their families as well as to bring offenders, especially young potential criminals, face-to-face with those they had harmed. A major effect of the program, which included sixty to eighty cases a year, was frequent reconciliation after the personal encounter mediated by a trained professional and concluded with appropriate restitution. A team of volunteers assisted in the program, eventually turned over to a lay director.[10]

Because graduate programs in psychiatric social work were new, Sister Margaret Groh, after being assigned to study, found the best at the University of Michigan. A year in the religion and psychiatry division of the Menninger Foundation in Topeka, Kansas, complemented her degree. In her first ministry after internship, Sister was on the staff of a New York counseling center for African American children living in poverty; she later served at the Tidewater Psychiatric Institute in Virginia. More than two decades followed of clinical ministry and direction of the diocesan counseling center in Tucson, Arizona. Her work recommended her to the bishop of Tucson for counseling of priests.[11]

Diocesan Doors Opening Wide

During the early decades of renewal, collaboration with pastors and parishioners evolved naturally into leadership roles for women religious. A small number of bishops and priests came to realize in the 1970s that women religious may be prepared by experience in parishes for ministry to Catholics in troubled marriages. Bishop George Fitzsimmons of the diocese of Kansas City–St. Joseph, Missouri, shared this conviction with the judicial vicar for the diocesan marriage tribunal, Father Richard Carney, who invited a Sister of Charity of Leavenworth to study at the Catholic University of America. Late in the decade, Sister Mary Helen McInerney was certified for tribunal work in a class of 130, twenty-five of them lay men.

Initial experience as a procurator preparing cases for couples seeking annulments qualified her for responsibility as the first woman in the diocese and one of the first in the country to be named defender of the bond. By prescript from Rome, renewed annually, Sister Mary Helen spent twenty-three years on the tribunal, transforming the role that made of annulment a healing process. Personal interviews pertinent to a given case and a simpler procedure at the formal hearing deepened fairness and fostered peace. No fee for expenses was required when that was a question; the social status of parties was of no moment.[12]

In 1987 Sister Virginia Bartolac was asked by the Community to exchange her secondary teaching schedule for the study of canon law. After earning her doctorate, she became canonical consultant to the Sisters of Charity of Leavenworth. At the same time, she served as judge and defender of the bond for the marriage tribunal in the Diocese of Venice, Florida, then as appellate judge for the five-diocese province of Atlanta, Georgia. Nearer home in 1995, Sister Virginia became the first woman to be named chancellor of the Diocese of Jefferson City, Missouri. Four years later, as director of the Metropolitan Tribunal for the Diocese of Kansas City–St. Joseph, Missouri, she said of her work, "We act like a bridge in the facilitation and investigation of marriage cases.... We are there to listen." That attitude made her a valuable member of the diocesan pastoral council in developing and implementing diocesan policies.[13]

In 1980 Bishop John J. Sullivan formed pastoral ministry teams in Kansas City, Missouri, with priests and Sisters of Charity missioned to parishes there; lay members soon followed. These were the beginnings of the Center for Education of Laity for pastoral ministry. With a master's degree in theology, Sister Mary Cele Breen was invited to help direct the Office of Worship, implementing the RCIA program for the diocese. Training lay ministers led to her full-time coordination of the New Wine renewal program. Sister's weekly column in the *Key* reflected mutual learning among laity, sisters, and priests in scripture, theology, worship, and the daily plight of the poor and the marginalized. By 1992, the diocese numbered 370 non-ordained ministers on parish staffs, up by 56 percent from 1982. Of these, 85 percent were women, almost 60 percent of them lay women and two-thirds of these married. National figures represented a "virtual revolution in pastoral ministry" in the Church.[14]

As pastoral associate in a new parish, Sister Eileen Hurley, holding a master's degree in education with emphasis on religious studies and liturgy, designed a program to educate laity in sacramental theology and train them for ministry in the diocese. By the end of the 1980s, she was directing an intergenerational religious education course for use in the home. Teachers met with the children enrolled in public schools; they took material on their subjects of study home to their parents. Teaching moments that resulted, especially for young parents, were reinforced by teachers' visits to walk the children through their approach to the Eucharist. Before the new church was built, small faith communities bringing families together made the Church personally real for children and parents together.

In Montana, as pastoral administrator for four priests who traveled among rural parishes for sacramental ministry, Sister Eileen oversaw all other ministrations for the parishioners, from cradle to grave. A lay administrator succeeded her when she was called to Holy Rosary in Billings as the city's first parish administrator with lay associates for two ordained sacramental ministers. In the Great Falls–Billings diocese many parishes without resident priests had as many as seven or eight mission churches. It was a natural evolution of Sister's ministry to move to the diocesan office for preparation of lay ministers. Teaching, facilitating, and coordinating components of a two-year foundational faith-formation program in theology, scripture, sacred liturgy, world religions, ministry, and social justice took her repeatedly across the diocese for sixteen weekend sessions in several towns. At the turn of the century, eighty graduates from the program were certified as lay preachers and committed to continuing education and serious peer critique in biannual workshops.[15]

The first woman to lead St. Mary's Bundschu Memorial High School of Independence, Missouri, Sister Rita McGinnis administered a student population from six areas of suburban Kansas City. The environment, standards, and spirit of the school drew high praise from North Central accrediting teams on annual visits; Sister Rita attributed St. Mary's edge to the ultimate partnership of parents, students, and faculty. After twenty-six years in secondary education, she found a "continuum between education and pastoral responsibilities" as she participated in institutes of theology and pastoral ministry and in the Focus on Leadership renewal program at Gonzaga University.

Early in the 1990s, Sister Rita joined the parish community of St. Mary's in Helena, Montana, as director of religious education. The experience and her extensive preparation qualified her for responsibilities as director of the pastoral office of the Helena diocese, leading the Pastoral and Renewal Division. There she facilitated a support program for school principals and coordinated the three-year diocesan celebration, "Crossing the Threshold to the Third Millennium." In 1997 an ecumenical reconciliation service in the Helena cathedral opened the observance. A few years into the new century, Sister Rita was invited back to the diocese as director of the Office of Pastoral Planning and to serve as the bishop's delegate for men and women religious.[16]

In 2005 Sister Lynn Casey was appointed chancellor of the Great Falls–Billings diocese with responsibilities as executive coordinator of the diocesan pastoral council and as the bishop's liaison in diocesan planning. On the diocesan outreach team, she provides workshops for lay ecclesial ministers and support for parish teams in their spiritual development. In the same year, the diocese appointed Sister Lillian McGuire as coordinator of Native American ministries. During the 1990s, Sister Lillian was in charge of the RCIA program for four Billings parishes, including St. Patrick's Pro-Cathedral.[17]

Sister Jean Martin Dawson, who had originally wanted to be a nurse, found teaching and administration challenges she enjoyed for twenty-two years. Serving as principal in Montana and Colorado led her to the office of educational consultant for the Diocese of Kansas City, Kansas, in 1988. As associate administrator in the mid-nineties of Saint Mary College's new degree-completion programs for working adults, she learned to value adult education. A doctorate prepared her for the post of superintendent of the thirteen schools in the Great Falls–Billings archdiocese. During her administration, the mission statement adopted by the schools emphasized partnership with the family and the Church.[18]

While she was principal of Bishop Hogan High School in Kansas City, Missouri, during the 1980s, Sister Vickie Perkins earned a reputation for keeping a culturally diverse institution up to the mark academically and in good financial shape. The achievement brought an invitation to the Kansas City–St. Joseph diocesan office of education, where she oversaw thirty-nine schools with approximately eight hundred teachers and twelve thousand students. A Central City School Foundation Board was organized to benefit eight schools of the diocese with insufficient means to support themselves. Leaders of these multicultural schools' associations committed themselves with Sister Vickie to bring some two thousand children up to high educational achievement. The Kansas City Partnership for

Children worked with her to secure endowment support from four major family foundations in Kansas City. Three million dollars in the first three years of the campaign set the pace.[19]

Invitations came from universities as well. Medical research in these decades discovered or confirmed phenomena of the interaction of body, mind, and emotions, a truth that health care professionals knew from long experience. Many centers of spiritual renewal inserted principles and practices of holistic health into their programs. Sister Michel Pantenberg, RN, hospital administrator for more than three decades, took a sabbatical in the mid-eighties at the Holistic Institute, Berkeley, California, and at the FOCUS in Leadership program of Gonzaga University in Spokane, Washington. Her qualifications and experience in administration brought an invitation to direct the program, with Sister Dominique Long coordinating its specifically spiritual components. Between forty and fifty women and men from Sri Lanka, Holland, Ireland, and the British Isles commonly made up the global community gathered for physical and spiritual renewal and theological enrichment.

After a stint at Spokane's Deaconess Hospital in clinical pastoral education, Sister Michel was invited to direct workshops in the States and a thirty-day retreat for Ursuline sisters in Java. She spent several more weeks visiting FOCUS programs in Indonesia, Australia, and New Zealand and came home with a vision of health care that integrated body and spirit and embraced the peoples of the globe.[20]

Sister Mary Sarah Fasenmeyer's call to university administration followed on eighteen years of teaching and administration in the elementary and secondary schools staffed by the Community. Assigned to pursue a doctoral degree in higher education administration, she earned the University Founder's Day Distinguished Scholarship Award at New York University and accepted an invitation in 1968 to direct the Curriculum Development Center at the Catholic University of America. Within two years, she was appointed dean of the School of Education and subsequently named a consultant to the National Catholic Educational Association in Washington, DC. In 1974 St. John's University in Jamaica, New York, chose Sister Mary Sarah as dean of its School of Education and Human Services, where 2,600 students in the educational division included graduates and undergraduates.

Seven years later, a call from Carroll College to serve as academic vice president and dean of faculties took her to Helena, Montana, where she co-chaired a task force that prepared a document for the United States Bishops' Conference pastoral on women. Sister's research on the recruitment and retention of minorities, on multicultural challenges in education, and on the psychological and spiritual praxis of aging produced

Giving Form to the Vision. This work on moral and religious education and the formation of teachers led to workshops and seminars in western states, New York, and England. In 1980 the NCEA (National Catholic Educational Association) selected Sister Mary Sarah for the Presidential Award for outstanding service to Catholic education.[21]

A deep ordinary conviction that she wanted to do theology stayed with Sister Susan Wood throughout the 1970s as she taught English and religion at Hayden High School, then English and French at Saint Mary College. Degree work in theology and doctoral research on the works of Henri de Lubac sharpened her desire to write as well as teach. A faculty position at St. John's University in Collegeville, Minnesota, led to mentoring graduate students and teaching seminarians, as well as to publications in systematic theology. Membership on an interim commission in the Lutheran–Roman Catholic dialogue brought subsequent ecumenical responsibilities in the dialogues with Orthodox and Anglican religious bodies. Sister Susan's conference presentations and published work on the sacraments of initiation and orders brought an invitation to the theology faculty of Marquette University in 2004.[22]

CALLS TO THE BORDER

Encouragement to work directly with the poor led a number of sisters to communities of native people living without sufficient resources to develop their lives with dignity. Their rights to physical well-being, education, and spiritual development were in effect denied. Renewal of religious life opened ministries once reserved to missionary communities.

After she had taught for eighteen years, the last five at Our Lady of Guadalupe School in Topeka, Sister Margarita Padilla requested an assignment to St. Joan of Arc parish in Weslaco, Texas, as religious education coordinator. There for the next eighteen years she trained catechists for five parishes in the Rio Grande Valley, organized delegations to the Texas legislature, and served as vicar of religious appointed for the Diocese of Brownsville by Bishop John Fitzpatrick.

Sister Margarita Padilla, named vicar of religious by Bishop John Fitzpatrick, makes her home in the colonia, *or village, of La Paloma on the Mexican border.*

Sister's advocacy and leadership affected the lives of 1,400 campesino families and migratory laborers who lived in *colonias*. These small plots of land with their shanties, built from cast-off boards, and gardens of vegetables and flowers are clustered across some six hundred miles along the Mexican border. Within two years of her coming to the Valley, Sister had almost seventy volunteers to teach 1,000 children, teenagers, and adults in RCIA and to prepare 175 First Communicants in a population of something over 3,000. Five weekend Masses and sixty *communidades de base*, or small groups gathered for discussion of their faith, were the responsibility of a Belgian pastor of St. Martin's in Alton, Texas, and Sister Margarita, his associate.[23]

Of 650,000 residents of the Valley, 85 percent were Catholic; they included Mexican Americans, Mexican immigrants, and Latin American refugees. The Valley, rich in fruits and vegetables, cotton and sugarcane, also stood, in Sister Margarita's words, for "poverty and poor housing, in many cases without good drinking water, drainage, sewer systems, or paved roads." The greatest need was for economic development and good jobs in a population predicted to double within twelve years. In the diocese, the number of priests would shrink from 115 to 50 over the same period while candidates for lay ministry in 1988 already numbered 1,400.

Collaboration for the good of her people prompted Sister's participation in Valley Interfaith, a coalition of churches in the Judeo-Christian tradition that organized advocacy programs, citizenship classes, voter registration drives, and delegations to the capitol in Austin. Its purpose was to seek justice for the thousands who lived in 150 *colonias*—more equal educational systems, job-training skills, and improvement of infrastructures. Sisters who ministered for shorter periods in the Valley worked with Catholic Charities and parish chapters of the St. Vincent de Paul Society to set up a store for clothing at low prices. County Extension employees taught nutrition and English as a Second Language; Vista Volunteers worked where needed. But immigrant women initiated classes in sewing, personal care, cake decorating, and other homemaking skills. From these, women developed their own home industries for extra funds. Prayer groups brought sisters, volunteers, immigrants, and parishioners together in ways that made permanent impressions.[24]

At the northern end of North America, Sister Mary Ermin Lambrecht lived in Anchorage, Alaska, with seven other sisters who ministered to Native American families and parishes. Together they represented five religious congregations. A registered nurse, sister had served thirteen years in Community hospitals before assignment to study for the degree in nursing education. Two years at Neighborhood Health Center in Denver preceded more study for a master's degree in public health nursing, with certification in midwifery from Johns Hopkins University. Sister Mary Ermin and the Community saw needs in the West similar to those of native peoples served by the sisters in Peru and Bolivia. Missions in Arizona and New Mexico were preparation for her assignment as nurse and midwife in the Alaska Native Medical Center in Anchorage.

When Sister Mary Ermin died in 1981, Archbishop Francis Hurley in an editorial for *The Anchorage Times* recalled her as "unassuming and gentle, humorous and refreshing, perceptive and spiritual," touching all "with the presence of God...." Doctors who had worked with her for five years at the medical center had named her an "honorary pediatrician" because "she delivered babies as well as any doctor."[25]

Native Americans a Magnet

Sister Kevin Marie Flynn had come to Anchorage the year before, to collaborate with Archbishop Hurley in establishing a Native Alaskan ministry. For seven years, she directed the office, reaching out to the various tribes of Eskimo Indians dwelling in rural areas as well as in the city. The mission followed six years of pastoral ministry to Blackfoot Indians in Browning, Montana, where she had learned how to incorporate Native American culture into teaching the Catholic faith, how to cultivate community leaders as spiritual models, and how to live in poverty and cold that reached 50 and 60 degrees below zero.

After a lapse of eight years, full-time ministry to the Blackfeet had resumed in 1974 when Sisters Linda Dean and Agnes Therese Weir began their work in religious education at Little Flower parish on the reservation. During summer breaks from school, sisters had worked with the pastor and lay ministers to prepare hundreds of children for First Communion besides instructing youth and adults in their faith and visiting the elderly in their homes. From that time, continuity marked the mission to the Blackfeet.

In 1975 after her term as a regional coordinator, Sister Edna Hunthausen went to the parish and its three missions as associate to a Native American pastor. The reservation covered eighty by fifty miles next to Glacier National Park and was home to about half of the Blackfoot tribe of sixteen thousand. In RCIA and in planning eucharistic celebrations and prayer services, Sister combined native ritual and liturgical elements. Twelve Step programs met the needs of many young men afflicted with alcoholism. Northeastern Montana was home for Sister Edna for the next thirty years.

A pastoral worker on the Browning team for four years until 1980, Sister Therese Klepac was called to the Crow Agency in Montana as director of religious education. She served seven years before need for a pastoral associate at Our Lady of the Snows in Mayetta, Kansas, brought ministry to Pottowatomie Indians, the first to welcome Bishop Miege in 1854.[26]

Gertie Heavy Runner, of the Blackfoot Indian Nation, and Sister Edna Hunthausen prepare for a traditional Mass at Little Flower parish church in Browning, Montana.

In 1981 Sister Mary Hilaria Phipps, with thirty-five years of teaching and school administration behind her, was hired as a teacher by the Oglala Sioux principal of Red Cloud Indian School in Pine Ridge. Recognized statewide for its programs, the school enrolled five hundred children of the families who lived on a reservation of five thousand square miles, one hundred miles long and fifty miles wide. Sister lived and taught with a number of sisters from other congregations on a staff that included Jesuit priests, brothers, and scholastics, who ministered as well to the sixteen Catholic chapels on the reservation. During her fourteen years at Pine Ridge, Sister Mary Hilaria taught journalism to students who published the Red Cloud newspaper and yearbook, oversaw science fair entries, and mentored students into medical school at Headlands University.[27]

The Crow Indian Reservation of four thousand drew Sister Mary Frances Kirkpatrick to St. Xavier Mission in 2000. A counselor at Bishop Hogan High School, she made a summer visit to the reservation in her native Montana. The people's urging her to come and teach them led Sister Mary Frances within a few years to the Pretty Eagle Catholic School of 140 pupils, largest of seven such schools in Montana. She found her home in a volunteer ministry with its own challenges. "They do not hand out their trust free," she said of her young charges and their parents. Sister's assignment in 2000 to administration of mission churches in Columbus and Absarokee assisted the pastor's sacramental ministry.

Sister Dolores Erman learned some of the same respect for traditional culture in her post-retirement mission as pastoral associate for a Capuchin pastor to Crow Indians on the North Cheyenne Reservation in Wyoming. The sovereign nation of some five thousand reveres its prophets, or holy elders, and its relics. The pastor of the church at Lame Deer, in the southeastern Montana corner of the reservation, knows that special prayers chanted after Mass are perhaps three centuries old and of much value to his parishioners. With unemployment at 85 percent, "the poverty level," said Sister Dolores, "is unimaginable." A deep spirituality transcends it.[28]

Ministry to Native Americans in New Mexico began with Sister Ruth Barron, mission worker and director of religious education for Navajo Indians at Tohatchi from 1981 to 1985. A registered nurse, Sister Clara Scherr entered pastoral ministry after retreat discernment in 1989 and found herself not at home in an affluent parish. Six years of teaching nursing to the Oglala Sioux followed. Then, at the suggestion of the Community director, she answered the plea of a Franciscan pastor of St. Anthony's Indian Mission in Zuni, New Mexico. There on a reservation of close to eleven thousand Zuni Indians, she ministers to approximately two hundred families by assisting with the liturgy, directing religious education, visiting the elderly, and serving at Our Lady of Guadalupe School as needed. The Zuni people, descended from prehistoric tribes, settled on the land around AD 700, having migrated from Mexico and southwestern Arizona. Their rituals of the winter solstice and the new year are sacred and attended by fasting and continuous prayer.[29]

From her post on the faculty of the Cheyenne River Sioux Nursing Program, Sister Marie Bernard Martin, physician assistant, moved to public health nursing in Washakee County, Wyoming. At this certified Home Health agency, she teaches prenatal care, serves women and children in the WIC program, and visits homebound elderly clients. Adult Health Maintenance Clinics reach a wide Native American and Caucasian population.[30] Her mission work knows no borders.

In the early 1980s, Sister Kevin Marie Flynn had spent fourteen years in ministry to Native Ameican tribes in Montana and Alaska. While assisting in the formation program at the Mother House, she learned of work with AIDS victims in Kansas City, Missouri. After much prayer and discernment, she entered the volunteer training program of the Good Samaritan Project. She had no intention, she said later, of bringing spirituality to others. "They already have it. It's just my job to find it, and it doesn't take long."

Thursday night dinners for residents of the SAVE Home, reserved for terminal patients, became a routine, favorite dishes an anticipated treat. With encouragement from the staff, Sister coordinated a buddy program to complement case management. Sitting with mothers of patients nearing death was one of the most beneficial things a buddy could do. One of the staff said, "She taught me how to listen with my heart." Within a decade of her ministry, Sister Kevin Marie accompanied five hundred AIDS clients in their dying and supported their families. In 2002 she received the Marion Kreamer Ribbon of Hope Award from the Kansas City chapter of the AIDS Service Foundation.[31]

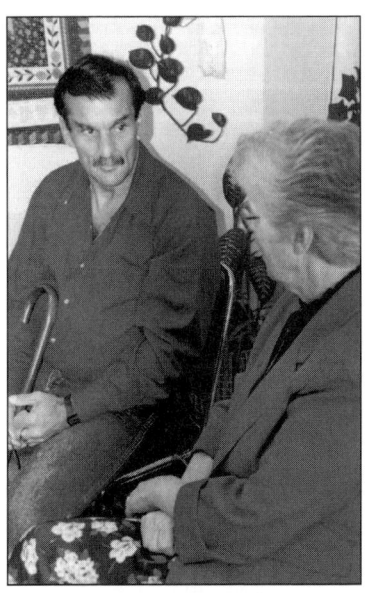

Sister Kevin Marie Flynn chats with one of her friends at SAVE Home, a residence for terminally ill AIDS patients in Kansas City, Missouri.

When L'Arche Heartland, home for adult men and women with mental handicaps, opened in Overland Park, Kansas, Sister Lucy Walter was ready to apply for the position of associate director with Sister Christelle Buser, CSJ. Since having met Jean Vanier, founder of an international federation of such homes, she had felt a call to his work, extended since 1964 from Canada to the United States, Mexico, Central America, Australia, Africa, the Middle East, the United Kingdom, and Europe. Sister Lucy assisted in the opening of a second home for four residents in Kansas City and became assistant director in 1989.

Driving residents in their bus to programs at the University of Saint Mary opened new horizons. Half a dozen of them flew with Sister Lucy

Residents of L'Arche Heartland gather with Director Sister Lucy Walter (middle row) and Sister Mary Joan Eble, assistant (top row), at their home in Overland Park, Kansas.

to Notre Dame for a weekend retreat with Henri Nouwen, CSC, whom they then assisted in a talk at a local parish. After seven years at L'Arche, Sister Lucy ministered in Lawrence at Community Living Opportunities for severely handicapped adults.[32]

Throughout twenty-five years of teaching, pastoral work at Our Lady–St. Rose parish, adult education, and family crisis counseling, Sister Mary Jo Downey hoped one day to go to Africa to minister in a clinic in Kenya. Founded by her cousin and his wife, Lalmba, "Place of Hope" sponsored clinics in Kenya and the Sudan that offered life-saving health care for African refugees. At her request, Sister Mary Jo was assigned in 1983 to study in a physician's assistant program at St. Francis College in Pennsylvania.

Three years of clinical experience followed in the family practice clinic at Fort Leavenworth and the Community's St. Vincent Clinic in the city. In 1989 Sister joined the staff of Matora Clinic on the shores of Lake Victoria, ten hours from Nairobi. Transportation to patients was by foot or bicycle; housing was a grass-thatched hut; the diet was sturdy and unvaried. The simple life of her African staff, patients, and friends appealed to her. On her return to the States, Sister joined the medical staff of Duchesne Clinic in Kansas City, Kansas, as physician's assistant. To be fully effective with a broad Hispanic clientele, she learned Spanish.[33]

No sister would claim to represent the Community's ministry to the poor. Three who would shun the title served in the Leavenworth Emergency Assistance center and ministered from the Mother House during the decades of change. Their actions recalled years of attention to immediate urgent needs: providing food before the next paycheck arrived, turning over a providential gift just in time to pay the rent or an electrical bill, finding articles to furnish an apartment, referring a single mother to a hospital or clinic that would give service regardless of material means, scrubbing floors and washing windows of an elderly woman's bungalow, finding a car to rush a child to the doctor. Emergencies were brought to sisters at any hour of the day or night without application form or explanation.

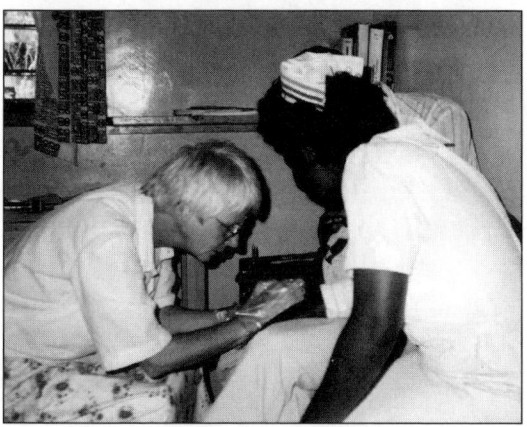

With a native nurse, P.A. Sister Mary Jo Downey examines a patient at Matora Clinic in Kenya.

Strengthening a Tradition

For twenty-six years, Sister Ann Margaret Noonan, having retired from teaching at Bishop Hogan in 1973, administered from the Mother House Mother Mary Ancilla's special poverty program funded at about the same time. Collaboration with lay volunteers, the Emergency Assistance Center, and other agencies in Leavenworth was Mother's *modus operandi*; Sister Ann Margaret picked it up. Callers in need were greeted at the front door of the Mother House and brought into the parlor. The operations room, however, was on the ground floor where supplies were kept and boxes filled. Bookkeeping was simple: "Keep a little tab," Mother said. Shopping was selective at local stores where long-term shelf items and end-of-day foodstuffs were offered to Sister Ann Margaret for her far-flung needs at cost or less. She recalled generosity: "I don't know how they gave us so much."

The veteran of Emergency Assistance service was Sister Valeria Monnig who, according to Sister Ann Margaret, died working. Sister Valeria's assistant and successor, Sister Leo Marie Cooper, endeared herself to hundreds of people living in and passing through Leavenworth. Her service continued from the Mother House after she retired. Perhaps the most significant assessment of her ministry came from one who knew her well: "She never stopped doing the lowest thing. People loved her."

Equally persistent and invisible in their direct work for those in dire and daily need were some that Sister Ann Margaret knew from living with them or remembering their assistance. Sister Andrea Johnston ran a "Give-Away, Take-Away" benefit and "Charity Corner" in the college for years; others weekly picked up baked goods from regular outlets, repaired equipment and houses, and helped fill hundreds of Thanksgiving and Christmas boxes. Three apostles of poverty named by Sister Ann Margaret and affirmed by many who knew their hidden work were Sisters Mary Vincentine Gripkey, Mary Borromeo Brose, and Mary Florentia Schouten.[34]

In the footsteps of Mother Mary Ancilla, Sister Ann Margaret Noonan arranges a box for personal delivery to an elderly shut-in.

In the vanguard of the Community's concerted efforts for peace and justice, Sister Marie de Paul Combo learned principles of action and advocacy from her parents. Her father organized fellow miners in defense of their rights within an international corporation that controlled state politics. As a teacher and then supervisor of archdiocesan schools in Kansas during the 1960s, she acted from the premise that education is the necessary path to social justice and to world peace. She worked for racial integration in the schools and advocated for fair housing and civil rights legislation.

On the faculty of three colleges—Saint Mary, Donnelly in Kansas City, Kansas, and St. Thomas Seminary in Denver—Sister Marie de Paul influenced students and peers by her actions as much as by instruction. While associate dean in charge of field work in pastoral and social services for seminarians, she stood with groups opposed to the development of nuclear weapons, in support of women's rights, and on behalf of the oppressed people of Central America. In 1984 Sisters Sheila Karpan and Marie de Paul joined thousands gathered in Washington on the anniversary of Bishop Oscar Romero's assassination for a week of advocacy against military aid to Nicaragua. The only midwesterner among thirteen delegates to that country selected by the non-denominational Witness for Peace, Sister spent two weeks in 1986 helping to harvest coffee beans for a man whose three sons had been taken by the Contras. Such contacts led to acquaintance with the people who formed Peru Peace Network/USA.[35]

At home, Sister was a charter member of Bread for the World and of Network, the organization of women religious who practice advocacy in government offices and across the globe. Her continuous witness with those of every culture and faith, her self-education in the systemic causes of poverty and oppression, and the depth of her commitment led to Sister Marie de Paul's appointment in 1987 as director of the Community's new Social Justice office. A network of volunteers made the ministry of peace and justice a Community undertaking.

In 1992 Sister Marie de Paul received the Bishop John Sullivan Award presented by Catholic Charities of the Kansas City–St. Joseph diocese for her long-term commitment as a member of the Latin American Task Force of Catholics for Justice. Four years later, on its twenty-fifth anniversary, Network chose Sister Marie de Paul as one of twenty-five Women of Justice they wished to acknowledge for creative commitment to the Gospel-inspired change necessary for a just society.[36]

What moved thousands of religious and lay women and men from the 1960s onward was the vicarious experience—gained through study and mutual support but mostly by personal encounter—of suffering. No document, not even a well-planned immersion experience in an unfamiliar cultural setting, guaranteed the effect of seeing what another had suffered from violence or deprivation. A youth facing death from self-inflicted damage, a mother watching her infant die for lack of medicine or food, someone of another color numbed into acceptance of neglect or rejection—these and unimaginably more were living motives for those who ministered in new ways during the 1970s and 1980s.

Hospitals continued to minister to such as these in incalculable numbers. Schools continued to educate to the insights and obligations of an awakened conscience. But the decades of renewal brought many women religious to ministries that put them in personal touch with those who suffered from systemic and remediable causes. They were meeting people up against impossible odds, coping with intractable conditions due in part to political and economic decisions made miles and countries and continents away. They also met those who brought upon themselves most of what they endured. The sisters were committed to whatever care might promise a manageable future for anyone who had little apparent cause for hope.

CHAPTER 17

"The beginning and the end of our coming together..."

When a people unite to identify and govern themselves, they write a constitution. So too do the members of a religious community. That document states as well as words can do the purposes of the founders, the charism or spirit by which the members intend to live, and the parameters within which they will conduct their daily lives. In the second half of the twentieth century, it was necessary to revise the constitutions of all religious

Mother House of the Sisters of Charity of Leavenworth where more than 650 sisters celebrated the nation's Bicentennial and the Chapter of 1980 received the Community's new Constitutions.

communities that were heeding the Vatican Council's call to renewal. The Sisters of Charity of Leavenworth began that task with the first Renewal Chapter of 1968–1969. A group of sisters were asked to write a document that would retain the substance of the original Constitutions in a way true to the spirit and direction of renewal.[1] The twofold document, *A Life of Charity* and *A Living in Charity*, opened with the words:

> *The beginning and end of our coming together*
>   *as Sisters of Charity of Leavenworth*
> *is our Lord Jesus Christ,*
>   *who in His church*
>   *has called us now, in these days,*
> *to worship the Father with our whole lives.*
>
> *In the strength of this calling*
>   *and in this Spirit,*
> *we vow our lives in Charity*
>   *to love and serve one another*
>   *and our neighbor,*
>   *whoever he may be*
>   *and whatever his need.*
>   (A Life of Charity, *Book I, 3*)

The second part of the document contained the directives produced by the Chapter concerning life in community, the vows, prayer, service, formation, and government. Together the two small books expressed the nature and mission of the communal life a Sister of Charity of Leavenworth professes by her vows. Given to each member of the Community on Easter Sunday of 1970, this two-fold document had to prove itself through the crucial Renewal Chapter of 1973–1974, the inevitable struggles of evolving change, and the impact of ministries that took a number of sisters to new convents and places of work during the decades to follow. Revised after subsequent General Chapters, the Constitutions were submitted to the Sacred Congregation for Religious in Rome. Approval there represented the full circle begun with the exhortation to renewal of religious life that came from Pope Paul VI and the Second Vatican Council.

In December 1978, Sister Mary Kevin Hollow, Community director, invited a second group of sisters to make whatever additions and revisions were necessary to adapt the new Constitutions to requirements of canon law and to incorporate changes required by the enactments of the Chapter of 1973–1974.[2] The accomplishment of their predecessors was such that they determined to preserve its style and substance. Completed within a year, the revised Constitutions were presented to the General Chapter of 1980.

Preparation for the Chapter was vigorous. In common, the sisters engaged in a year of prayer. In local communities and the General Forum, emphasis fell on the Community's charism, qualities of leadership, and the vows. The Personnel Board coordinated Mission and Evangelization workshops for area meetings and apostolate groups.

In her report to the Chapter, Sister Mary Kevin emphasized the themes of the Council's work over the previous six years:

- emphasis on strong communal government and daily life in local houses,
- priority given to common prayer and practices of the Community's characteristic virtue of simplicity, and
- reflection on poverty and justice as encompassed in each apostolate.

Sister observed that group government, the form most commonly chosen, was effective when evaluated periodically and implemented with accountability. Failures followed lack of leadership for decisive action and lack of experience and maturity in self-governance. Potential for the necessary leadership was in large part undeveloped. A tendency to request a community living assignment with sisters of a compatible lifestyle made for peaceful interaction, she said, but the long-range effect on the Community could be devastating.

On the other hand, Sister Mary Kevin reported that community life at the local level was growing stronger, especially in the practice of common prayer and evening meals together. Indicative of the struggles of renewal was her simple assurance that "after some very difficult transitional times, [the sisters] seem more accepting of and are enjoying each other more.... On the whole," Sister concluded, "...we are a deeply spiritual community." A portent of what lay ahead, daily Eucharist was becoming increasingly difficult for many. The sisters' growing consciousness of poverty and simplicity of life was evident in their annual participation in the development of house budgets. These frequently manifested solicitude for the poor in the moderation of consumption of goods.

Some estimations, however, of what the Community's poverty should be were uninformed about total costs of providing for the sisters' daily life and ministry. "Whatever we do," Sister pleaded, "...let's be real. Let's not talk to each other in broad theoretical terms that belie what we have by way of...personnel and resources. General Utopian terms may be heartening but they make us uneasy because [of] unreal goals."

Questions before the Chapter concerned dimensions of poverty and justice in apostolic ministries, criteria for Community investments, and collaboration with agencies committed to systemic change—Network, Center of Concern, Pax Christi, and the Liberty and Justice campaign of the U.S. Conference of Bishops. New ministries that lay in the Community's tradition of direct service to the poor Sister Mary Kevin identified as pastoral ministry in hospitals; care for battered children and unwed mothers; assistance to the jobless; and sacramental preparation of youth and adults in parishes.[3]

The report set the tone for the Chapter's deliberations with clear priorities, honest cautions, and hopeful signs of a Community's gradually renewing itself. Like the election of a broader range of delegates and the Community-wide nomination of officers, the publication of daily *Chapter News Notes* revealed a growing need for members' participation in Community governance. In the tradition of the first newsletter of 1968–1969, the *News Notes* were a significant unifying force. Another was the financial report of Sister Julie Casey, who detailed the Community's assets, restricted funds, operating and general fund expenditures, health insurance and retirement funds, income and expense of the Latin American missions, Community charities, salary income where applicable, and Community indebtedness.[4] Her thoroughness and clarity with appropriate charts were reassuring even to those without comprehension of financial operations.

Testament to Community

Reports from three commissions focused the Chapter's agenda. Speaking for the study group on Government and Community, Sister Constance Phelps invited attention to fundamental social laws. Documents, she said, provide for structural change but do not alter attitudes, perceptions, or behavior. "Commitment to community," she continued, "is essential to religious life as a way of intensifying obedience to the Gospel.... Community is our primary apostolate. Loving one another, living for the same ideal, sharing in the same gifts, bearing the burden of life together—this is the unity of religious family."[5]

Areas of necessary change according to the Mission and Ministry Commission included justice as "integral to all that we are and do as Sisters of Charity," presence to the poor "by preference and priority," and experience of life situations of the poor to allow for mutual evangelization. Defining the poor as "those most in need and those who have no economic or social power" was essential to the commission's proposal. If the 1970s, they said, were a time of spiritual renewal, the 1980s must bring an outreach of this spiritual deepening.

The Commission on Spirituality and Formation reported that eighteen of the thirty-five young women who had entered the Community since 1970 were now vowed members. They recalled Sister Francis Therese's challenge of 1968 "to renew the spirit of St. Vincent in our lives" and to provide opportunities for sisters to live and work among the economically poor and oppressed. Delegates asked if the Community was going far enough in this direction or if a middle-class way of life had taken hold. Others insisted that, given a poverty of time for direct service, most were doing all they could working for the poor through Community and public structures.[6]

The hard work of Chapter emerged from draft proposals prepared from consensus of commission members. Suggestions for change in the operation of the Community's central government focused on the director's term of office, the councilors' responsibilities, and participatory or advisory roles of the sisters. None reached proposal form. A voiced need for long-range planning required clear priorities for determining commitments to new and traditional ministries. A draft proposal for a Community-wide, in-depth study of assignment policy and procedure was to proceed from a theology of mission that might well test the depth of the Community's commitment.[7] Provision for a theology of mission was not put to a vote.

A proposal for close collaboration with the laity in the life and ministry of the sisters recognized the crucial need for lay colleagues' participation in decision-making in the apostolates. Commitment to the rights of women, especially those who were poor, elderly, or victims of injustice, was unanimously affirmed, as were proposals for lifelong formation in the life of each sister through the aging process. Long-range planning for ministry to the aging was to show special concern for women, the poor, and the sisters. The Chapter affirmed the personal moral responsibility of each sister for cultivating habits conducive to health and for seeking help when needed. In discussing these proposals, the delegates applauded Dr. C. Kermit Phelps for his work with the Community on issues of aging and provision for a productive life in retirement.[8]

The common ground of obedience for all Chapter delegates was a lively relationship to God discerned in personal conscience, the needs of others, legitimate authority, and communal responsibility. A proposal for obedience that focused on corporate decisions guided by fidelity to the Spirit made known through needs of the times, leaders of the Church, and resources of the Institute passed by only a narrow margin. Some delegates found the proposal ambiguous. It could reinforce central authority or it could allow a corporate stance on given social issues. Read either way, the proposal met objections to its lack of clarity about the role of individual participation in corporate decision-making.[9]

Paradoxically, while the prior claims of conscience and discernment in religious obedience could diminish traditional emphasis on authority lodged in individual persons, it could also limit the power of a community to speak for all its members. The individuality characteristic of the Sisters of Charity of Leavenworth was both a rich resource for spiritual development and ministry and a check on the Community's pace of change.

Approved proposals, or Chapter enactments, on government reflected the tension between individual freedom and communal response to need. Local communities were to determine annually the form of shared responsibility by which they would order their life: group government, a team, or a local coordinator elected or appointed at their request by the Community director. Emphasis was on making a home that witnessed to Christian charity, on unity and mutual support among its members, and on open communication with the Community councilor who represented the direct religious authority that canon law required.

All were to participate in planning, budgeting, making decisions affecting the house, and evaluating progress toward goals. The councilor was responsible to consult with each sister in her area about her apostolic experience and discernment for her next term of ministry. The director in turn was responsible to lead the Community toward the accomplishment of its mission in the Church, strong community life, fidelity of all to the call of the Spirit, and the preservation of values implicit in a common ideal.[10]

The Chapter passed unanimously the proposal that committed the Community "to participate in the continuous development of the Church's understanding of its social mission" and "to recognize justice as fundamental to our mission of charity." A companion enactment called the sisters "to be present to the poor by preference and priority either directly or by ministering ... with a consciousness of the poor and growing in solidarity with them."[11] Clearly, sisters of the second half of the century were searching for immediate knowledge of others' suffering the lack of what life in community afforded them.

Sister Ruth Reischman visits with (left to right) novice Deidy Abad, postulant Isabel Sandoval, and Hermanas Laura Rumiche and Susana Córdova, director of formation.

The Latin Americfan missions were a concrete commitment to justice for people with extraordinary material and spiritual needs, a commitment both for the Community and for individuals who volunteered to serve in Peru, Bolivia, and Guatemala. Historical changes came to fruition in the Chapter of 1980. For the first time, a director for the missions was to be appointed from nominees to be submitted by the sisters in the area. She was to have direct personal authority in facilitating, with the Community director, the sisters' communal and apostolic life. As early as 1974, in their second regional meeting, the sisters in Latin America came to consensus on a proposal to open a native novitiate. Now, unanimously approved, a formation program for native South American sisters was to include the postulancy, novitiate, and tertianship before perpetual vows.[12]

Other enactments provided for a vocation committee to assist in the formation personnel and mandated an Associate program to establish a formal connection with the Community for lay persons who desired it—women and men, married or single.[13] A major step toward achieving grassroots participation in implementing Community goals was the Chapter mandate for Local Forums. These were to meet biannually in each geographical area to voice concerns, initiate projects, and make proposals to the General Forum that met annually. A second channel of communication regarding mission assignments was the Personnel Board, to be enlarged by representatives from each apostolate.[14] Without decision-making authority, however, neither Forums nor the Personnel Board proved effective in the long run for effective participation in the Community's governance. So far as majority decisions by Chapter delegates revealed it, support for centralized authority in the Community remained firm.

The Chapter's election of the Community director and her Council demonstrated faith in that authority and reliance on its traditional forms. Sister Mary Kevin Hollow was elected to a second six-year term of office. Her first assistant was Sister Mary Kathleen Stefani; the other councilors were Sisters Bernadette Helfert, Gabriella Connell, and Rosalie Mahoney. Sister Macrina Ryan was elected to the Council as representative of the SCL Health Services. Sister Mary Julie Casey was re-elected Community treasurer and Sister Marie Kelly, Community secretary. The Constitutions approved by the delegates in November were to be amended, section by section, as Chapter enactments and editorial suggestions required. Sister Mary Kevin, accepting the responsibilities of office, referred to the document's completion as a "historic moment for the Community." It revealed, she said, as it must the Community's essential character.[15]

Participation in the analysis of Chapter decrees conducted as part of the LCWR-sponsored Sisters' Surveys indicated how closely the Sisters

Community Council, 1980–1986: (seated) Community Director Sister Mary Kevin Hollow and First Assistant Sister Mary Kathleen Stefani; (standing) Sisters Gabriella Connell, Rosalie Mahoney, Macrina Ryan, Bernadette Helfert, Julie Casey, Community Treasurer, and Marie Kelly, Community Secretary

of Charity of Leavenworth paralleled, fell behind, or outstripped other women religious of the United States in their progress toward renewal. Revised constitutions and directories were the ultimate gauge of such adaptation. The evaluation of documents from 273 religious communities derived from principles of renewal applied for consistency and taken from the documents of Vatican II; the encyclical of Pope Paul VI called *Development of Peoples*; the papal letter, *Call to Action*; and the Bishops' Synod document, *Justice in the World*.[16]

Constitutions in Context

The document submitted by the Sisters of Charity of Leavenworth for evaluation was the original two-part Constitutions, *A Life of Charity* and *A Living in Charity*, accepted by the Renewal Chapter of 1973–1974. The revised Constitutions and Directory approved by the General Chapter of 1980 were submitted later. (These documents will be identified subsequently as *LLC* in reference to evaluation of the submitted documents.) As revealed in the national analysis, the Sisters of Charity held in common clearly renewed principles of religious community. Statements in their documents revealed a concern for the world community that makes women religious a very part of it, the recognition of and provision for privacy and solitude, and a conviction that life together and prayer are the bedrock of community. With broad consensus on the second and third concerns, about a quarter of the other documents emphasized the first.[17]

In the section on the apostolate, *LLC* statements emphasized service—in terms of the evaluation instrument—as that of a pilgrim people responding to human needs with priority given to eliminating causes of poverty and injustice. Although a quarter of other documents defined ministry as a pilgrim's response to Christian mission, only 11 percent indicated the same priority. Just 14 percent of all documents manifested clear planning for members' understanding of the political, social, and economic conditions of the world's peoples. *LLC* statements revealed a conscious effort to move forward from within institutional works. A tolerance of individual choice was coupled with a preference for mission as *being sent* by the Community. Approximately 25 to 30 percent of other documents affirmed the same principles.[18]

Of all the documents, 42 percent made no provision for members' real power to initiate or implement transforming action. *LLC*'s norms told evaluators that consultation of membership was valued, though without participation in major decisions; a quarter of the other documents manifested the same views. Half of the documents, including *LLC*, afforded much local autonomy. Just under 30 percent directly involved members in decisions, with the central government responsible to the whole assembly.[19] Decentralization was not a common direction among religious communities of the 1970s and 1980s.

It must be remembered that the evaluated documents issued from congregational Chapters of Renewal that generally occurred in the early 1970s. Emphases from Sister Marie Augusta Neal's report in 1980 on a second survey of a smaller representative group revealed women religious as well on the way toward aligning themselves firmly with the mission of the Church. By then they recognized that proclaiming the Gospel of Jesus required collective action to bring justice to the oppressed, freedom to captives of poverty, and peace to all peoples. At the same time, the report revealed women religious as not yet comprehending the practical reaches of their role in the action.

That the Church should focus primarily on social justice as God's will for humanity was the conviction of more than 60 percent of the respondents in 1979–1980. Only 7 percent, however—given the question in these terms—recognized God speaking to them in cries of the poor or dispossessed.[20] As many as 80 percent of the respondents affirmed that "this generation of religious is being asked to rediscover evangelical poverty" while they sought realistic ways to be meaningfully poor and with the poor here and now. Only 46 percent, however, were in favor of specific actions by the Church to eliminate causes of poverty.[21] Discrepancies in survey responses revealed the transitional nature of renewal at this juncture.

An Evolving Image

In the choice of an image of their congregation as an ideal of women religious, responses to the 1979–1980 survey revealed either that few had contemplated the question or that few were ready to shift the ground of their thinking. Slightly more than a fifth saw their congregation as "women sent to manifest God's love through availability, hospitality, acceptance and concern for all." From twenty-three choices, this statement drew the largest consensus. Fewer than half that number saw their community as "women furthering the mission of the Church" or as "radical responders to the Christian gospel of universal love." A minimal number of responses suggested that few considered commitment to the poor as a corporate identity. Only 1 percent of respondents affirmed as an image of their congregation "women sent to effect change in social and political structures" and only 2 percent saw themselves as "women sent to be in solidarity with the poor not as an option but as a sign of the Kingdom."[22]

Responses to other questions revealed, however, a deepening realization of God's call in Jesus to radical systemic change in the name of justice for every person created and redeemed. Concluding her report, Sister Marie Augusta foresaw further and deeper renewal: "That God dwells with the poor in this transforming action is only on the very edge of our consciousness.... A conversion [is] in process, but only just begun. The wonder is that women religious are in the forefront of its realization."[23]

If parallels and contrasts in the Sisters of Charity's new Constitutions with those of a national group were the only point of this summary, they would hardly justify the detail. Analyzed for a larger purpose, they reveal much about where the Community found itself on the eve of the 125th anniversary of its founding. Combined with the evaluation of documents, the 1979–1980 survey results suggest how renewal in both the Community and its sister congregations took an uneven pace and produced perplexing ambiguities along the way.

Clearly, the Sisters of Charity of Leavenworth grew more and more keenly aware of their Vincentian heritage and its implications for their mission in the

WOMEN RELIGIOUS AND MISSION OF THE CHURCH (C. 1980)	
Changing concept of mission	
Social justice as God's will	62%
God speaking in cries of poor	7%
Church to act	
for social change	70%
on problems of women	70%
against racism**	66.6%
Community to act	
in commitment to poor women*	50%
for alleviation of effects of poverty	60%
for elimination of causes of poverty	40%
Influence on choice of ministry	
freedom to follow conscience*	60%
needs of corporate mission**	40%
Images dominant of women religious	
sent to manifest God's love*	20%
furthering mission of the Church**	10%
sent to effect structural change	1%
with poor as sign of the Kingdom	2%

*slightly more than
**slightly less than

decade of the 1980s. Identification with the poor was the ground of that mission; envisioning it as one with that of the post–Vatican II Church was the foundation. Understanding how the Church's social teachings, developed in the century that embraced the Council, implied radical changes in the very concep-

Sister Mary Joan Eble reads the newspaper with young Peruvian friends.

tion of the Church—her liturgy and sacraments, her structures, and her relationships—was a challenge overwhelmed by the business of renewal.

Given pre-renewal constraints on women's formal study of theology, providing communal means for internalizing the ramifications of Vatican II documents was a serious undertaking for women's religious congregations. Reading and discussing selected documents in preparation for the Renewal Chapters was a first substantial step taken by the Community toward common understanding. Annual institutes and consultation with theologians during years of experimentation were follow-up resources. Courses offered by Saint Mary College in summer months taught by well-known theologians provided systematic instruction and topical studies for approximately two decades. Many educated themselves through reading and reflection and by taking advantage of lectures and workshops in areas where they lived. Perhaps the greater wonder of it was that so many learned so much so deeply in the brief span of a decade and a half filled with full-time ministry, continuous planning and meeting, and discernment of both personal and communal direction.

This was true of a large number of Sisters of Charity of Leavenworth. Nevertheless, a systematic program of education in the theology of Church, sacraments, and mission was a virtual impossibility for a community of far-flung and increasingly diverse active ministry. Summer courses in theology during years of renewal were a beginning. Later, under the aegis of the Ongoing Formation Committee, a three-year series of workshops in post–Vatican II teaching conducted by sisters holding degrees in theology from some of the strongest programs available drew active participation and high praise. Readings were preparatory; authors were recommended. But as an apostolic order founded in frontier territory, the Community had no tradition of common study and dialogue. The very words *justice* and even *poverty* brought tension to some conversations because for many the new and urgent emphases implied that these concerns had not been the focus of all previous decades of service.

An even greater source of potential tension evident in daily life was the duality of convictions about religious obedience taken in its broadest sense. Ultimate authority regarding essentials of Catholic belief and of vowed life was for many vested in *persons* of authority, while other manifestations of truth, morality, and mission in community and human needs were subject to interpretation. Though belief in the Gospel as God's revelation of the mission of Jesus in the Church united the sisters, the development of that mission, as expressed in Church documents and now to be discerned personally and communally, was a complex exercise of conscience and obedience to the Spirit. Furthermore, mature exercise of growing personal freedom with full regard for the demands of community was the clear and present challenge for all members in local houses and in governance of the whole.

Two remarkable documents that came from the Long Range Planning Committee mandated by the Chapter and from the Personnel Board reveal directions these groups envisioned for the Community in 1983 and 1984. They reveal as well the sharp awareness of their members of the kind of world in which they aimed to further their Community's mission. The first document was a set of social and political assumptions that underlie the Planning Committee's goals and objectives.[24] Societal changes that conditioned all planning included

- a growing realization of the finiteness of world resources, the interdependence of peoples and impact of Third World countries on the world's economy, and the persistence of poverty in the wealthiest country on earth;
- rising expectations of people who want better living conditions and increased control over their lives as a challenge to the economic and political status quo; and
- the continued closing of service institutions.

Effects of these changes included growing polarization between rich and poor countries with the victimized ever more ready to take violent means to destroy oppressive systems and the powerful inclined to rationalize the kind of violence available to the national security state. Instruments of international cooperation were to become inevitably more fragile. Christians would have to face tests of faith and imagination. Read now, the assumptions are acutely prophetic.

Other changes offered hope in a return to spiritual and humanistic values and renewed interest in religion, recognition of the interdependence of humankind, a commitment to systemic thinking and planning, and a new acceptance of limits with reassessment of needs. Aware that meaningful systemic change requires interior transformation and willingness to risk failure, the Planning Committee raised what it trusted to be implicitly strategic questions:

- How to define the Community's area of competence to effect significant consequences for the lives of the needy?
- How to move toward a future of renewed traditional ministries, simplicity of lifestyle, and openness to new ways to meet the needs of the human community?

A silent tension between the questions may have been the crux of the strategies to follow. The key to their success lay in the assertion that "the SCL community as a unified force can effect change and growth."[25] How to unify that force was the unvoiced strategic question.

The second document issued from the Personnel Board and accompanied the outline of a program of study and reflection on ways of collaborating with the laity, especially women, in the sisters' ministries. The document was "A Chicago Declaration of Christian Concern" that the vision of Vatican II for dynamic lay leadership in the Church had been sidetracked. According to the signers, internal issues like the ordination of women and a married clergy were consuming time and drawing attention from questions of peace and justice—the special arena of the laity. There the Church "is present to the world in the striving of the laity to transform the world of political, economic and social institutions."

The document was signed by lay women and men, sisters, and priests who invited members of the Church throughout the nation to associate themselves with the declaration asking for "a new sense of direction, a new agenda" for developing lay responsibility for the world. "It would be one of the great ironies of history," the declaration concluded, "if the era of Vatican II which opened the windows of the Church to the world were to close with a Church turned in upon itself."[26]

In *A People Adrift: The Catholic Church in America*, published twenty years after this declaration, Peter Steinfels analyzes the potential tragedy of a Church divided within by questions the educated laity of the 1980s could have helped it address had they been more seriously consulted. How one religious community called lay women and men into partnership for its mission is part of the story of those same twenty years. In a larger sense, it is a story of how the Sisters of Charity of Leavenworth struggled to give concrete shape to a mission that had matured but wanted still the common vision that would embrace both overt and deeply hidden diversity.

CHAPTER 18

Seeking a Common Voice

Achievements of the six years following the Twelfth General Chapter might be called up as evidence of the contrast between political and communal processes. Given nominations, voting, proposals, parliamentary procedure, and offices of authority, a Chapter in community has the trappings of secular government. A constitution is its normative document and enactments are mandates. But the effectiveness of all this issues in much more than an ordered common life within community. A Chapter serves the mission of the Community and its outcomes depend on a deep sense of personal responsibility in community members, on dialogue and persuasive argument, and on discernment of the Spirit rather than on legal structures and compromise, executive enforcement, and judicial review. Though the constitutional structures of a congregation do conform to canon law regarding religious life, sisters work within those structures by their own cognizance and determinations. This was strikingly apparent in the persistence of Sisters of Charity of Leavenworth in pursuing their goals throughout the 1980s.

To understand the difficulties of implementing a mission as firm as founders had made it and at once as fragile as any living organism, it is necessary to recall the years that followed the second Chapter of Renewal. In the mid-1970s, nations lived in the tension of potential nuclear holocaust; Latin Americans shed blood in rebellion and intensified oppression; and the economies of free peoples widened distances between rich and poor. Sisters of Charity were struggling to identify what united them in the face of continuing change and to discern effective forms of self-governance and ministry. Those struggles and certain ineluctable events reveal the sisters' genuine progress in renewal and ambivalence among them about its directions. The events were a birthday celebration of the Community's foundation in Leavenworth and the death of Sister Charlotte Swain, a midwife in Bolivia where the Community had only recently come to birth.

A Forum of twenty-five elected representatives from five geographical and professional areas had operated from 1974 to surface Community concerns. In 1979 a survey revealed that seventy-five sisters were willing to work with a group charged to assess how sisters in each locale were moving forward on the U.S. bishops' Call to Action. The episcopal document's six areas of action were education for justice, family life, the Church's people and parishes, economic justice, human rights, and world hunger. From packets returned in the survey, the Peace and Justice Committee learned that many sisters viewed action for social justice as a responsibility of the individual sister, that justice must begin at home, and that many needed education on the issues. Nevertheless, communication about what individual sisters and Community institutions were doing on behalf of social justice was a priority. The Council encouraged the committee to search out the information.

In further response, the committee urged local houses to promote

- understanding of social problems and cultural conditions,
- methods of social analysis and theological reflection,
- formation of a social conscience,
- knowledge and skills necessary for leadership on boards,
- education of lay leaders and of sisters for social and pastoral ministry,
- consumption patterns sensitive to national economic inequities,
- just dealing with employees, and
- a communal program of corporate responsibility.[1]

The survey confirmed that sisters in the field wanted to be heard and to be more closely involved in directing the future of the Community. Attention focused on leadership roles and relationships and delegation of responsibility throughout the Community. Questions were asked about diminishing numbers in the face of change and conflicting interpretations of past Chapter enactments. In a formal Focus on the Future initiated by the Forum, sisters asked for statement of a philosophy for life-long growth and service and implementation of a long-range planning process.[2]

A significant question raised by the Forum of 1980 concerned participation in governance. Tension between those who desired a more active role in decisions and those who favored centralized decision-making was clear and did not disappear. Following the 1980 Chapter, fifteen Local Forums across the Community began to meet twice yearly with two stated objectives: to carry out tasks conveyed by the Community Council and to prepare recommendations for the next General Forum. Because proposals for a corporate stance on given issues had been debated at length and rejected during Chapter, the question of public witness now became a matter for Local Forums' discussion and decision.³

Task forces and surveys began to uncover local problems; discussion of community service centers or hunger projects produced concentrated action. Hopeful for some form of corporate stance, sisters learned more about nuclear disarmament, Central America, the death penalty, and conditions of women in Third World countries. Needs for a social justice coordinator and improved placement policies were uppermost, though felt in different degrees throughout the Community. Language describing Forum procedures and qualifications of nominees became appropriate to a faith community moving in discernment to consensus.

Forums a Vital Force

In 1982 the General Forum distributed to Local Forums a tentative agenda for its annual meeting to get suggestions and further a sense of ownership. Continuing their concern for communal action on issues of peace and justice, members clarified the pros and cons of a corporate stance. Responsibility for giving tangible evidence of the Community's response to the Gospel and its mission, unifying and educative effects of preparing such witness, and its value for systemic social change were strong recommendations of a public stance. Risks of dissension and of separation from benefactors and friends, the complexity of issues and difficulty of education on necessary facts, and the Community's tradition of respect for individual concerns and of conservative action were objections to public corporate statements.⁴ Looking ahead to the summer's celebration of the Community's 125th birthday, Local Forums urged progress toward a corporate stance on disarmament, including research, education, discussion, and reflection.

The General Forum's response to these concerns took shape in three major proposals to the Community Council:

- for a social justice task force to form a network and to study models for a permanent Justice and Peace Commission,
- for collective response to major justice issues deriving from critical analysis and theological reflection, and
- for a task force to produce a model for corporate response to issues of social justice.

Forum members expressed additional concerns for solidarity and trust in the Community, for a spirituality of the Beatitudes, and for response to the bishops' letters on peace and justice with special focus on Central

America. To encourage renewed commitment to a simple way of life, the Forum disseminated a report on the cost of living in community. It revealed that for 508 sisters the average individual monthly cost was $383, an annual cost of $4,594.[5] Though the average covered a wide range of individual expenditures, it suggested that sisters personally considered their manner of living as contributing to or countering a consumer culture that supported a national economy of abundance. All of the issues of the 1983 Forum coalesced in the desire for a communal commitment to stand against causes of endemic poverty and a culture of domestic and global violence. How to achieve that commitment in personal and communal living was the fault line of continuing discussion.

A report from the personnel director, Sister Kathleen Coman, signaled both concern for communal stability and regard for individual qualifications and choice. She presented a Mission Assignment Policy and Procedure that emphasized individual discernment, consultation with apostolic representatives for recommendation to the Community director, and three-year commitments. Periodic evaluation and programs for summer and sabbatical study were to advance professional competence. That the procedure was evolving in 1983 was a sign of the radical change from an established practice of annual apostolic appointments to a consultative and reflective process.[6]

Action by Local Forums in subsequent months drew attention. At the end of the following year, 1984, a Social Justice Network representative reported statistics from Leavenworth County to stimulate discussion and action by Local Forums in Kansas. Approximately one-third of the county's households earning less than $13,000 and an average of only thirty-five individuals per thousand were receiving assistance. Of these, 90 percent lived in the city of Leavenworth. In the county for the month of September, average assistance payment from all programs was $253.89 per household and $104.89 per individual. From 1978 to 1983, grants for families on welfare increased by less than 15 percent; the cost of living went up 50 percent.[7]

Proposals issuing from the Forum for the Council put a priority on implementation of the Chapter's enactment on women. Every apostolate was to give tangible evidence of commitment to women's needs. Education toward sound judgments about roles of women in Church and society was a Community-wide focus. Solidarity between women religious and lay women in professional and civic groups fostered respect for freedom of conscience. Action on behalf of suffering women, especially in Nicaragua and other Central American countries, was reported from Local Forums.[8]

By 1985, these priorities that echoed the scriptural call to justice and urged action for the good of women suffering impoverishment and indignity were taking shape in alliances, advocacy, and formal ministries. Sister Constance Phelps was named facilitator of the Social Justice Network. Saint Mary College offered a summer schedule of courses and workshops that placed issues directly within the context of Catholic tradition. Subjects for study included the liturgy and sacraments of initiation, arms control and disarmament, Central America, and the bishops' pastoral letter on the economy. Public policy-making and legislative processes were areas to be pursued for informed advocacy. In support of long-range planning, review of the Community's financial situation and re-evaluation of individual lifestyle and stipends was beginning. Spiritual growth throughout the life cycle was the emphasis in the formation program. Nevertheless, unity of purpose in the General Forum and intensified action across geographical regions did not yet reflect a unified community.

Reporting sheets gathered from Local Forums to identify key issues for the approaching Chapter of 1986 showed that none of the attempts to implement collegiality and give voice to the sisters in determining ministry, community life, and communal direction had fully succeeded. Contributions to broader initiative and interaction came in turn from Regional Coordinators, the Personnel Board, a full-time communications director, the Forums, a Social Justice Network and task force.

Taken together, they did not yet provide the sense of ownership that was patently desired. Investing general councilors with authority for geographical areas was a move toward mutual accountability between individual members and the governing body, but depended largely on each councilor's skills of interpersonal relations and time management. Local house government, while subject to problems of incompatibility and conflicting views of community, was perhaps the strongest source of personal development and maturing exercise of freedom and responsibility. On that level, sisters came to know the depths and demands of their life of charity. Regardless of differences in views, the very concerns voiced in the reporting sheets indicated the depth of desire for unity.

The overarching issue for the coming Chapter was participation in determining the future direction of the Community. A major task was to find structures and processes for determining community leadership, with emphasis on evaluation of ministry in the light of the Community charism. A second task was to find ways to engage the total Community in Chapter proceedings. Concrete suggestions included discussion and nomination of candidates for election to the Chapter and Local Forums' review of a tentative agenda. It was recommended that there be intensive study of the previous Chapter's enactments on women and the laity and the bishops' pastorals on the economy and on war and peace.[9]

Meanwhile, actions of the General Council in response to Chapter mandates kept large issues in view. Assignment of Sister Rosalie Curtin to study religious formation resulted in a far-reaching program born of her pastoral experience. She co-authored an adaptation of the Rite of Christian Initiation of Adults to candidates' journey into religious life that led to significant change in the Community's initial formation program and influenced formation programs in the United States and Canada. Its foundation in scripture, sacramental theology, the spirituality of the Beatitudes, and the Church's call to justice made for a basic understanding of vowed life as response to the Gospel. While the primary companion for each novice was the formation director, partners on the journey were professed sisters, a group selected as a novitiate community. In time, first-year candidates lived in community with their own director; experiences in ministry contributed to this formative year. Sister Kathleen Wood, who was an experienced formation director, and individual professed sisters were companions for young sisters on their journey to perpetual vows.[10]

Responding to a proposal from the Social Justice Network, the Council introduced the Community to the sources and purpose of social analysis and theological reflection through workshops conducted in 1982 and 1983 in Leavenworth, Denver, and Billings.[11] Construction of a new wing for Ross Hall and appointment of a health insurance committee were steps in a long-range program for care of Community members. Issues of retirement and the needs of an aging community concerned a growing number. The committee recommended a medical insurance plan for the Community.

In Annunciation Chapel the Community began to celebrate its 125th anniversary.

Renovation of Annunciation Chapel was a response to the Constitution on the Sacred Liturgy issued by the Second Vatican Council. Structural changes transformed the classical sanctuary of the chapel—a faithful replica of the Renaissance church of St. Alphonso in Rome—into a sacred space surrounding the table altar for celebration of the Eucharist by a presider united with the assembly of the faithful.[12]

A Liturgy Committee for the Mother House was to promote the sisters' education to full participation in the prayer of the Church. A full-time director of prayer programs was appointed in 1983 to provide for a wider range of annual retreats and seasonal days of recollection. The first Marillac, a cottage on the Mother House grounds, became the Community's first house of prayer.[13] In that same year in response to Forum proposals, the Council approved community-living stipends for unfunded work among the poor. The revised Constitutions were forwarded to the Sacred Congregation for Religious; Sister Mary Kevin informed the Community of the formal approval of the document on August 15, 1983.[14]

Growing to a Birthday

Significant for understanding common objectives and real divisions in the Community were carefully tabulated responses to a question posed by the Personnel Board on Apostolate Day during the 125th celebration of July 1983: "Given the mission of the Sisters of Charity of Leavenworth and our limited personnel, identify visions of SCL ministry in the next ten years for addressing needs of the Church." Sisters numbering 438, or approximately 70 percent of the Community, responded individually to a list of options prepared with professional consultation; then they met in thirty-five randomly selected groups and later in apostolate groups to choose top priorities for their vision of ministry.

Approximately one-third of the sisters participating in Apostolate Day affirmed the concept of "conversion to a life of faith and prayer in community as the source of ministry." The top priority for 16.6 percent of the respondents was "serving the poor and disadvantaged and promoting justice and peace." Close behind, "renewing and adapting ministry to needs of the times" was the top priority chosen by 11.7 percent of the respondents. Contrary to public images of sisters changing to satisfy personal inclinations, "provision for individual needs and development of talent to enrich service of the Church and the world" was a top priority for just 7.5 percent of the respondents. Leadership attracted still less attention. While only two groups made training sisters for leadership with influence on policy their top priority, two more listed it as second. Initiating leadership by laity was the top priority for only one group, and second for two other groups. Ministry to women remained the first priority of only one group, the second choice of another.

More significant perhaps is the last place taken by certain items in the total listing of priorities. Though indirectly, these items pointed to a future direction for the Community not yet commonly envisioned: "educating for leadership in justice"; "working for systemic change, reconciliation, and bridge-building"; "education of sisters in theology, law, and education"; "developing individual talents in response to needs"; and "exercising leadership in the Church." Why they were not more prominent in group and individual priorities is a complex question involving community climate, personal motives, group dynamics, and the absence of encouragement.

Before the group discernment of priorities on Apostolate Day, the Personnel Board had inquired into the sisters' preference of ministry. Results combined with priorities may have raised serious questions. More than a third of 438 respondents expressed preference for ministry in the spiritual life and community. A combination of two categories, serving the poor and working for justice, produced the preference of less than a fifth. Education in its broad reach was the preference of approximately 16 percent. Leadership attracted only 6.8 percent of the respondents. That 21 percent of the sisters responding had miscellaneous preferences suggested increasing diversity of ministries and little motivation to direct changes that many desired. Again, the inquiry raised more questions than it answered.[15]

Having produced the Placement Policy and Procedures Manual and reported evaluations of its work, the Personnel Board prepared two recommendations in anticipation of the 1986 Chapter:

1. for an advisory group to be nominated from the Community at large to assist in the study of initiatives for new responses to needs, to evaluate individual sisters' commitments, and to help develop a sense of Community direction; and
2. for an Office of Ministry to coordinate placement procedures, maintain sisters' professional files, and communicate openings in all ministries as well as resources for life and career planning.

Strategies that accompanied the Long Range Plan depended largely on individual need, motivation, and local communities' initiatives.[16] Whether the Personnel office, the Ongoing Formation Committee, the social justice facilitator, the vocation director, or the area councilor designed and encouraged their use, plans for personal growth and forms for reflection and self-evaluation did not generate wide acceptance.

One example, however, of the energy and high motivation that infused sisters' thinking about their ministries was the goal expressed by the thirty-five sisters in social services. Development of multiple-discipline centers for integrated service, especially to families, would call on a wide range of the sisters' competence and experience. A center would include schooling adapted to needs of individual children at different stages of readiness, counseling for students and for family members, health care as needed, and teams for advocacy. If directions were not yet firm, ideas were not in short supply. From the Communications office came a report on newsletters that preceded *Connecting*, new since 1979, and on the publicity and resources provided by the full-time director.[17]

On the Community's 125th anniversary, six hundred sisters came from twenty-eight elementary and three high schools; from nine hospitals and the college; from numberless parishes; from social work with children, the aging, the needy and dispossessed, prisoners, and the homebound; and from the Mother House. The century and a quarter of history, recorded in media stories and photographs, told of first foundations in the four-year-old frontier town of Leavenworth and of subsequent missions in eight

Sisters re-enact the Founders' arrival in Leavenworth on the Missouri River in 1858. Sisters Mary Gertrude Glotzbach, novice Mary Mikijanis, Sisters Margaret Dolores Green, Ann Louise Eble, Katherine Franchett, and Nancy Bauman; postulant Loretta Ann Frick, orphan Angela Rose Barbieri, and postulant Ann Lucia Apodaca move toward their new home, led by Sister Ann Barton standing in for Bishop Miege.

states, Latin America, and Alaska. The stories told of continuing commitments to health care, to care for the young and the aging, and to education that changed lives of students of all ages from half the states and abroad, of working adults in inner city and suburbs, and of prisoners aiming at a college degree.

A special gift of monies contributed by each house of the Community for distribution to the poor was presented to the Community director by the oldest professed sister and the youngest. Holistic Health Day featured guest speakers on wholesome adult living and concurrent sessions conducted by Sisters of Charity with special interests and training. At the Leavenworth County Historical Society Museum, a sister portrayed Mother Xavier in a living history. Heritage Days in July and September began with celebration of the Eucharist and welcomed visitors to both Mother House and college. Heralded by the bells of St. Mary Hall, second home of the Community in Leavenworth, the fall festivities began with a tree planting on campus and continued with a family fair for the people of Leavenworth and Lansing. Perhaps the most memorable feature of the year-long birthday party was its spirit of joy, gratitude, and universal welcome.[18]

Sister Marie Kathleen Daugherty portrays Mother Xavier during the Community's anniversary celebration in 1983.

Death at Home in a Foreign Land

Within a year of the celebration, on the feast of St. Vincent de Paul, Sister Charlotte (Mary Cabrini) Swain died in Coripata, Bolivia. As a licensed midwife, she had served the Aymara Indians and Mestizos since 1966 in the mountainous area of Coripata and the thirty-eight villages surrounding it. At about 6,000 feet, the mission included the *marquirivi*, a tropical river area 2,000 feet below, and wound up the road toward La Paz, the capital, at 14,000 feet above sea level. For twenty-three years with Sister Lucille Harrington, catechist, and Sister Mary Patricia Kielty, RN, Sister Charlotte learned the complex culture of the people and gradually gained their confidence. Sister Joan Kilker, RN, was with them for twelve of those years.

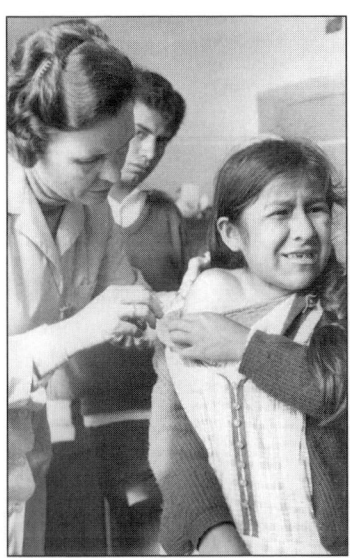

Sister Charlotte Swain ministers to a child at the clinic opened by the Sisters of Charity of Leavenworth in Coripata, Bolivia.

Under their instruction in nutrition, homemaking, and pre-natal and child care, they saw children grow from half the size of North Americans the same age to normal height and weight. When the priests left the mission in their hands under a pastor, Monsignor Robert Walton from Kansas City, Missouri, the sisters taught the women reading and writing and made them aware of their role in the Church. Understanding of their faith and of responsibilities of home and family gave the women a sense of equality and partnership with their husband catechists. Continuous health education stemmed some of the effects of communicable diseases, intestinal disorders, malnutrition, and the tubercular condition of 80 percent of the population. Sister Charlotte had said in an interview during a home visit that during complications in childbirth, a missioner with no recourse except her own skill learns the power of faith and prayer.[19]

Suffering advanced effects of psoriatic arthritis for several years before she died, Sister Charlotte wrote in an intermittent journal in 1982 of the discouragement she felt in prayer.

> I wonder am I asking wrongly... am I knocking at a locked door....
> I am tired of asking. I am ashamed to continue to ask others to intercede... and with this I receive an answer. It is so humiliating to admit my need. It's humiliating to admit my poverty. Lord, I realize you are teaching me to be humble.... Lord, I need conversion— conversion into you.[20]

Little more than two years later, after a day's work, feeling not up to evening prayer in the church, Sister spoke with her sisters throughout most of eight uneasy hours before she died in the early morning of September 27. She had asked to be buried with her people in Bolivia. The women with whom she had worked prepared Sister Charlotte's body for burial. With their husbands, they made everything ready for the Mass of Resurrection celebrated by Bishop Adehmar Esquivel and priests of the diocese.

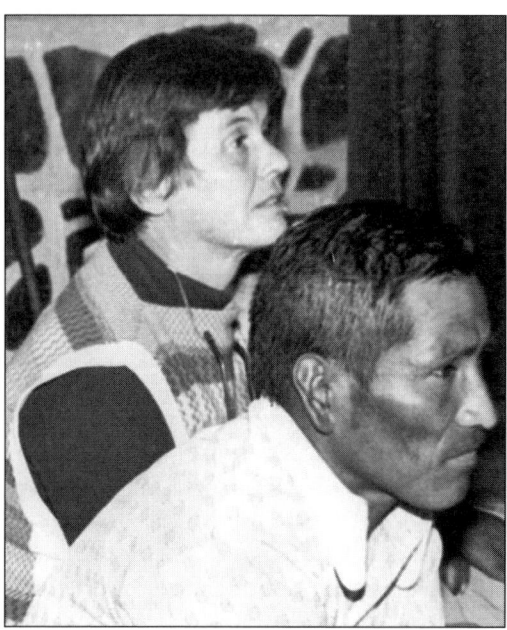

A parishioner and Sister Charlotte pray together at Mass in Coripata's church of Santiago.

The bishop had insisted that a picture of Mother Xavier Ross be on the card commemorating Sister Charlotte. When the sisters did not have one at hand, he brought forward his own. "Your charism is hers and it has to continue," he said. He wanted the Community's coat of arms placed below Sister Charlotte's name on the headstone of her grave. "Your charism has no face," he said. "All of you are the charism...." Beneath the symbol were engraved the words, "All she did was love." Charity just began to flower in Coripata, said the bishop in his homily, on the day of Sister Charlotte's death. Later, at the Mother House, the sisters gathered for a memorial service to celebrate the life of Charlotte Swain, SCL, the first North American missionary to be buried in Bolivia.[21]

Without their full awareness in the mid-1980s, the Sisters of Charity of Leavenworth were experiencing events that promised to lead them forward. The anniversary celebration of 1983 threw light backward on a past that awakened new pride. Sister Charlotte's death the next year pointed to years of growth into a North-South Community of Charity. If the data from Apostolate Day revealed more differences than many wanted to recognize and divisions that blurred a vision of unity, the same data suggested qualities crucial for further renewal.

In April 1983, a letter from Pope John Paul II to the bishops of the United States directed their attention to sections of the document, "Essential Elements in the Church's Teaching on Religious Life." These emphasized the evangelical and ecclesial witness of religious in their corporate apostolate. Loyalty to the mission of Christ and the Gospel in communal identity was the touchstone of the authenticity of new works. Loyalty to humanity in these times was one with loyalty to a community's charism. In the character of their mission, women religious were distinct from the laity in their proper apostolate. Temptations of professed religious include trying to do everything, leaving aside stable works for others related to social needs, and scattering resources.

The letter came from the bishops to religious communities during the following months.[22] Given the cautions implicit and explicit in the papal letter and the recently mandated study of women religious in the United States, few would likely have taken comfort from the essential elements carefully underscored. Papal documents, like scripture, must be read for principles to be honestly and prudently applied to conditions and issues that develop in time and place.

In their discernment of priorities, the sisters made loyalty to the mission of Christ and his Gospel the first criterion of their ministries. In their commitment to the poor, however diverse its forms, they were loyal to their charism and heritage. The sisters' firm intention to support the laity—whether in the light of their own declining numbers or in a desire for genuine partnership and lay leadership—recognized the distinctions between celibate and family life, community and individual apostolates. Selected priorities manifested the clear conviction that stable works, social needs, and stewardship of resources were interrelated. What stood more threateningly in the way of a unified vision were sources of disunity that lay hidden.

Faithful insistence on a deepening prayer life and a generous Providence did not necessarily translate into the contemplative living that transforms apostolic action and unites disciples. Even stubborn fidelity to the poor can take individuals as well as a community into directions that fail to speak the Gospel in a unified voice to those who control resources and power. Yet further diversification of ministry was to develop from the very policies designed to give it clear direction. Sources of tension, however, did not lie in policies and procedures nor were they discoverable in studies and surveys. The sisters had grown so proficient in conducting and responding to these, implementing enactments, and evaluating performance that the volume of their paperwork threatened the trees they loved.

What appeared to divide the Community was more than differences about lifestyle and commitment to justice. It had to do with the developing life of the Church itself. Like the diocese, parish, and family, a religious community is the living image and contributing organ of the Body of Christ. Shortly after the close of Vatican II, Yves Congar, a Swiss theologian, wrote of "the Church which looks to the future and to the past." It is a church that ever looks back to her historical reality while she always looks ahead, seeking what God calls her to be, a "Church between the times."[23]

Twenty years later, the Sisters of Charity of Leavenworth found themselves to be a "Community between the times." Only hindsight can recognize that strong forces in the Community and its leadership were looking forward with a firm grip on the past and that other forces were equally faithful to the past with insistent moves toward a new future. Tensions of the struggle made communal self-knowledge and recognition of prophetic voices next to impossible. The determination ten years earlier to remain one community bore fruit in continuous efforts toward reconciliation and equally serious efforts to deepen renewal. This indeed may have been the most prophetic decision of all. It did not eliminate friction and delay. Only stubborn fidelity to God and to a call heard with conscientious though diverse convictions bound the sisters in charity for the enterprise ahead.

CHAPTER 19

Seeking a Common Vision

Drawn from records of the previous six years and from analyses of their progress by every apostolic group and working committee, the Community director's report to a General Chapter is as objective an account of the Community's situation as anyone can give. In 1986, at the beginning of the Thirteenth General Chapter, Sister Mary Kevin Hollow reported a decrease of 9.3 percent in total Community membership and an 11 percent decline of active sisters. This reflected a rise in the median age from fifty-five to fifty-nine across the total of 559 sisters. Withdrawals from the Community had decreased from the fifty of the previous six years to twenty-seven between 1980 and 1986, while newly professed in the same periods were fewer—eleven in contrast to seventeen.

Declining numbers in apostolates varied substantially. Between 1980 and 1986, the number of sisters in elementary and secondary education declined by 36 percent. The total number in health care declined by 12.6 percent except for hospital nurses, almost two-thirds of whom changed to another area in the field of health care. Numbers in higher education, the Latin American missions, and general community services stayed steady. In contrast, the number of sisters in pastoral ministry and religious education increased by 53.5 percent and the number in social services by 34.6 percent. Sisters had assumed twenty-four new positions in pastoral ministry since 1980.[1]

Similar statistics characterized dozens of religious communities during the decade. More significant were trends and challenges reported by apostolate representatives from their groups' evaluations and planning. In-service topics for elementary educators were education for justice, financial aid for students, identity of the Catholic school, and increasing roles for laity. Challenges to be faced were serious:

- incentives to draw and keep good teachers,
- the changing role of the family in education,

- the need for basic changes in school structure and educational delivery, and
- a reformed global curriculum in collaboration with civic leaders.

Principles of justice required examination of salaries, consideration of individual students' special problems, and consensus in decision-making. Teaching justice as integral to religion and moral values assumed respect for one another and for people of all cultures.

For secondary educators, collaboration with laity in leadership and mission was coupled with the need to deepen students' and parents' commitment to the Christ-centered and counter-cultural education that the Catholic school represents. The group addressed strategic questions:

- How to develop more literate, faithful Catholic youth?
- How to strengthen family and home life?
- How to awaken social awareness of the poor and the elderly?
- How to provide leadership while letting go of roles?

In 1986 a changing population of Saint Mary College students included 67 percent commuters over twenty-two years of age; the resident number had declined 21 percent since 1980. Sixty percent were of faiths other than Catholic or of no religious preference. Financial aid, always a major portion of the budget, now went to 93 percent of registered students. Sisters of Charity made up 54 percent of the full-time faculty at a median age of forty-nine. The budget was balanced and debt-free; an endowment had grown by more than 90 percent over a decade of capital campaigns aimed at offsetting the anticipated decline in the sisters' contributed services. The Saint Mary Center offered hospitality service and space to ecumenical and educational groups seeking spiritual and professional renewal. Increasing lay leadership and a population of more working women, more minorities, and more part-time students were predicted developments.

The six-year interval included experience of other groups that clarified planning. Recommendations from Latin America emphasized exploration by native sisters of mission possibilities, residence for a short time in the country before mission commitments by North American sisters, and exploration of future funding. The social service group emphasized need for specialized training and internships for sisters entering the apostolate. Effective ministry to the severely disadvantaged—physically, spiritually, educationally—depended on discernment of individual talent and vision.

The pastoral ministry apostolate included seventy-four, some of whom were double-listed in overlapping ministries. Spiritual direction and retreat work were developing as parishioners sought them. Ecumenical ministry grew naturally out of a wide range of duties. A less-recognized character of pastoral ministry was its immersion in varied ethnic and geographical populations—African American, Native American, Hispanic, rural, central city, and suburban. The group recommended education of sisters in canon law, gerontology, communication, management, theology, and spirituality. Evangelization of both churched and un-churched young and old was the model proposed for preparation and study.[2]

Unmistakable in all the reports was concern and planning for the future of Community institutions increasingly different but evolving from their past. Growing dependence on the laity was uppermost. This paralleled the expanding outreach of sisters responding to women hungry for deeper faith and prayer; youth caught in the cycle of poverty, petty crime, and parole violation; and children in need of pre-school and after-school care and training. Education to the sources and abuses of justice was the crying need of all—the sisters themselves, those they taught, and their parents, leaders, and legislators.

New structures or channels for ministry called for integrated resources and disciplines that bridged traditional apostolates and sectarian identities.[3] Ecumenical advocacy programs, collaborative ventures in child and elderly care, government- and foundation-sponsored initiatives, and board memberships brought sisters into every sphere of public and private enterprise. Titles and roles many times lost significance as horizontal arrangements virtually displaced vertical and hierarchical structures.

Proposals that helped shape the Chapter's agenda came from 111 sisters. Individual and group position papers spelled out specific needs with ideas for addressing them. Enactments provided for a standing commission to emphasize the spirituality of Vincent and Louise de Marillac, the spirituality of women, and education in the Eucharist as central to religious life in ongoing formation. An enactment on integrating the demands of justice in education and practice through Community Forums, the Social Justice Network, and inter-congregational collaboration passed without difficulty.

Speaking for the Latin American mission, sisters emphasized its demands: openness to another language and culture, willingness to let a native culture dominate, and the ability to live in a small religious community in an isolated area. The delegates did not enact proposals for new models of Christian education to serve the poor in collaboration with laity, for learning uses of media in ministry, or for education of the sisters to roles of the laity in the Church and to leadership in shared responsibility.[4]

Nevertheless, the practice of soliciting individual proposals and both individual and group position papers was a channel of participatory governance in its impact on Chapter agenda and long-range change, a channel not sufficiently recognized for its value in Community until it virtually disappeared. In the 1990s and later, formal participation was designed to engage as many sisters as possible through regional gatherings, circle conversations, and organized table conference during the Chapter. Contributions were funneled through note-taking and summaries that produced concentrated agenda reflecting priorities and scheduling discussion. In the event, breadth of participatory exchange was taking precedence over depth of study and time for dialogue. The Community had sufficiently experienced both by 2004 to evaluate benefits and losses.

Results of the new process for the election of Chapter delegates were revealing. Taking together all categories of age, location, and ministry, representation was varied and widespread. The practice of depending on long-recognized authority and experience was still evident but diminishing. Two delegates had been in every Chapter for the last twenty-four years; four more had been elected to Chapters since 1962; twelve, or 29 percent, had not been in Chapter before.[5] From the total Chapter membership of forty-one, nine sisters were nominated for Community director.

Sister Mary Kathleen Stefani won the necessary majority. Councilors were elected by similar margins. They included Sister Bernadette Helfert,

Community Council, 1986–1992: (seated) Sister Mary Kathleen and Sister Rosalie Curtin; (standing) Sisters Bernadette Helfert, Joan Sue Miller, Mary Serena Sheehy, Community Treasurer, Rosalie Mahoney, and Macrina Ryan

first councilor; Sister Rosalie Mahoney, re-elected; and Sisters Rosalie Curtin and Sue Miller, first-time councilors. Sister Macrina Ryan was re-elected Health Services representative on the Council; Sister Mary Serena Sheehy, was the newly elected Community treasurer; and Sister Marie Kelly was re-elected Community secretary.

Common to all remarks from delegates at the close of Chapter was an abiding sense of challenge, a call to deeper renewal and even sacrifice, and of growth in openness and mutual concern. The term most often repeated was "simplicity of life," with its parameters of solidarity with the poor and personal discernment of need.[6]

Sister Mary Kathleen Stefani, Community Director, 1986–1998

It is possible to draw alternate conclusions from outcomes of this Thirteenth General Chapter, the first after formal approval of the Community's Constitutions re-created from almost twenty years of renewal. With basically the same central governing structures firmly in place, broad participation in decision-making was limited to communication of urgent concerns through Forums and recommendations from working committees and networks. The desired unity of direction for the future was subject to expansion of ministries and lasting divisions of thought and conviction about community life dependent on differing experiences of almost every kind.

Further change was the business of individuals and groups or local communities; its approval and implementation was the task of the Council insofar as broad Chapter enactments provided for it. A united Community in its manifest daily living depended on mutual charity, tolerance of differences, and cheerful compliance with numerous plans and exhortations.

An alternative reading of Chapter outcomes might begin with words taken from the revised Constitutions:

> *As Sisters of Charity of Leavenworth*
> *our essential mission*
> > *is to witness and share the mission of Jesus....*

We are called
  ever to renew and recreate
  our works and our witness
uniting justice and charity in our lives
  as servants of the poor....
We foster community by
  a presence to one another
  a sense of being part of each sister's endeavors...
  a concern for the programs of the whole Community...
  a simple hospitality which welcomes others into our homes
  a sense of oneness with the human family: its care, hopes, and dreams....[7]

To reinforce the bond of community enjoined by this and other norms, each local house found ways to ensure that the Constitutions were read together throughout each year. Personal fidelity to the document was a way of life undertaken by religious vows. Sisters elected to governing offices were bound by it no less than those who never held an elective or appointed office. The effectiveness of their leadership was dependent upon that universal personal fidelity. This fact, moreover, was coupled with the authority they held from the Chapter, an authority defined by the ideal expansiveness and practical limits of a Chapter's enactments. Though instruments of the Spirit, the words of both Constitutions and Chapter were left in the hands of individual human beings acting together as best they could.

Volunteer assistants to the chef, Sisters Mary Edmund Pratt and Mary Gregory Dusselier, residents of Ross Hall, prepare vegetables for the evening meal.

Furthermore, fidelity to the document they had endorsed came down to what a Community's real convictions and sentiments allowed. Recognition of a need for education to justice did not erase ambiguities of personal experience. Very few knew the deprivations and degradation of radical poverty; many had known the sting of injustice in community or professional life. All had committed themselves to life in community; no reflection journals or evaluation sessions or celebrations would diminish its challenges, which had been experienced by most for more than half or even just a fifth of a lifetime. The most deeply held values of fidelity, solidarity with the poor, justice, and commitment were not to produce a common vision and unified Community by any imposed formalistic means.

The overriding fact of religious life was a growing emphasis in and out of Chapter on diversity of ministry and on the communal structures and expenditures it entailed. Because of their tendency to group like-minded sisters together, smaller diverse communities diffused, if they did not weaken, the energy of healing and reconciliation enjoined by Chapter delegates with such hope and significance. Add to this the repeated echo of the word "simplicity" in enactments and evaluations of the Chapter, and what was emerging as the key to interior renewal was difficult to define for sisters living what they themselves called a middle-class life. Such ambiguities were to prolong the search for a communal identity and unity of vision that it was hoped would confirm and mature the fruits of renewal.

Models of Fidelity

Sisters willing to express in a confidential survey their impressions of the Community director who had led them during the twelve difficult years after the 1974 Chapter identified qualities that marked Sister Mary Kevin's time in office. Unquestionable integrity and fidelity to her convictions underlay the fairness and justness of her leadership. Its foundation was loyalty and humility "without guile." Habitually unassuming and straightforward, she did not lack courage. One who knew said that Sister was fearless with bishops. Her action, further, was always for the good of the whole; she worked for unity in the face of opposition to the point of self-sacrifice. Devotion to the Community, its works and traditions, and its organizational needs made Sister a sign of stability in time of change.

"A sister among sisters," she was willing to listen and to work out situations, though she herself, according to some, was difficult to know and kept much within. Her interest in each one was thoughtful, down-to-earth, and decisive. Her sense of principle some would call unyielding. Very many found her kind and approachable, intelligent and astute, with a ready sense of humor.

Her taste for politics and commitment to education reflected a cautious vision and ability to stay the course, to exercise calm leadership in a difficult time. Perhaps the most insightful assessments of one easily called conservative came from those who saw in Sister Mary Kevin simplicity "in all its implications," clarity of vision open to the future, and a "woman of quiet prayer."[8]

Near a turning-point in the life of the Community, the extended illness and subsequent death of Mother Leo Frances Ryan on August 11, 1988, was a poignant reminder of what change and renewal had cost. Having served on the Community Council with Mother Mary Francesca and Mother Mary Ancilla, she was elected mother general in the Ninth General Chapter of 1962 and re-elected in the Renewal Chapter of 1968–1969. During those twelve years, she had seen 235 sisters leave the Community, 82 of them in two years at the turn of the decade. It was her responsibility to interview each one, seeking reasons for her departure before signing the requisite form.

With the burden of such knowledge and a natural reserve, Mother Leo Frances was subject to interpretations that varied sharply. Nevertheless, both those who knew her well and many who did not consistently acknowledged her spirituality and profound faith. Habitual serenity and patience under trial signaled a prayer life and intimacy with God that mystified the postulants she directed after her two terms in office. Long-suffering and steadfast courage were the marks of her leadership that respondents mentioned most often.

For many reasons, Mother Leo Frances was not easy to know. She could read people deeply, her first councilor Sister Mary Seraphine said of her, and this discernment brought her firm friendships. But election to office cut her off from many. A playful lightness of wit endeared her to many but not all. She loved to cheat at cards and laughed easily—too easily for some, Sister added. She could make people feel that an interest of theirs didn't matter, that something of a wall stood between them.

This friend observed too that Mother may have been more fragile than was apparent, affected by rheumatic fever contracted early in her religious life. Many attested to her kindness and gentleness, to her generosity with her time. A lay friend commented that to have survived such turbulent times signaled a healthy personality, but to live those times in such a spirit of joy was the sign of a saintly woman. A retreat master confided that of all women religious he had known, she had had the deepest faith.[9]

Again, the cycle of death and new birth drew the Community together in certain initiatives. During the late 1980s in response to Chapter mandates, the Ongoing Formation team proposed a pilot year for a program to test affiliation of lay women and men with the Sisters of Charity of Leavenworth. Designed by a subcommittee of the team, the program had as objectives:

- to enhance the mission of the Community and to enrich the lives of both sisters and lay persons committed to its spirit;
- to acknowledge the common call to holiness of laity and religious and to draw on the resources of both for mutual benefit; and
- to join with lay persons in the search for fundamental values of Christian life as a counter-culture in contemporary society.

An agreement stating expectations and a commitment to share specific resources was formalized in a symbolic ceremony. All persons eighteen and older, financially independent, and able to relate effectively with others were candidates for the association. By 1993, Associates numbered 116, of whom 93 were women and 23 were men.[10]

In 1987 the Council invited Sister Marie de Paul Combo to serve full time as facilitator of the Social Justice Network. Sister's immediate experience and extensive knowledge of Nicaragua and El Salvador and of the effects of the U.S. government's policies in Central America gave credibility to her reporting. Annual themes came from the bishops' pastoral, *Economic Justice for All*; from a widely recognized need to preserve planet earth's resources; and from the North American continent's Columbian quincentenary observed in the light of Catholic social teaching.[11]

From 1982 to 1986, only three candidates entered and moved to first vows. To gain a broader experience, they learned the meaning of religious life in company with formation groups of neighboring Benedictines and of the sixteen congregations of the Sisters of Charity Federation. Working directly with the poor introduced them to the mission of the Church in realistic ways. To learn how professed sisters of all ages had been attracted to the Leavenworth congregation and to encounter firsthand the spirit of the Community, the candidates met with them individually and in their local houses.

In Latin America, growth took almost the same pace. Cultural differences and desire for independence from North American influences were problems for some candidates. Young professed sisters stood in need of education at either a university or a normal school. Promotion of vocations loomed as a primary need. The formation program included a year of education in central doctrines, prayer, health and sexuality, the history and current situation of Peru, and the lives of Vincent, Louise, and Xavier. Work with the people complemented the study.[12]

From an office of Vocation Ministry, set up in 1989, Sisters Noreen Walter and Linda Roth initiated summer volunteer programs, retreats, weekend convent live-ins for young women interested in religious life, vocation nights on a state university campus, and presentations to diocesan and congregational groups. Approximately twenty-five women participated as volunteers in poverty programs during four summers in Denver, Colorado; Brownsville, Texas; and Billings, Montana. They experienced prayer and community with Sisters of Charity missioned in these places. Sisters in sixteen states contributed to vocation brochures on "Being a Sister of Charity" and "Community Charism and a Legacy of Service."

Sister Victoria Lichtenauer organized an annual Vocation Voyage that took young college women interested in religious life to the Mother Houses of religious communities in Kansas and western Missouri. Most evident for the ministry was the need to make spiritual growth and community accessible to many who might or might not seek vowed membership.[13]

Since 1979, the job description of the director of communications had focused on publishing a community newsletter, managing publicity, setting up a resource media center, and serving as staff support for the Council and Personnel Board, the General Forum, the Spirituality Commission, and the director of vocations. Sister Mary Catherine Dougherty completed these assignments and assisted with major community projects as well. The monthly *Connecting* was mailed to all houses and Associates and to former Sisters of Charity. An issue was translated into Spanish to observe the twenty-fifth anniversary of the first Peruvian mission. Photographic, video and audio, and computer services meant purchase and updating of equipment and development of skills Sister had acquired as editor of the Eastern Montana and Denver *Catholic Registers*. Her recommendations initiated the Communications Committee formed in 1992.[14]

In the summer of 1989, as many sisters as could came home for the first midterm gathering, known as Rainbow Reflection Days, designed to strengthen community bonds and a sense of shared mission. In her welcome to the sisters, Sister Mary Kathleen cited concern for crucial issues as the centripetal force that unites community members toward their common end:

- How to adapt our traditional religious apostolates with a decrease in personnel?
- How to maintain a distinct presence in all our apostolates with the pressure of secular values at work within?
- How to minister to the poor and bring about systemic change?
- How to meet the needs of this age: the refugees, the victims of AIDS, the single parent?

In the opening event, several hundred sisters and Associates celebrated in paraliturgy the fourfold cosmic theme of earth, water, fire, and air. In pilgrimage to Mount Olivet Cemetery they called on all Sisters of Charity of Leavenworth buried there and in the West to bless their gatherings.[15]

In 1990 the Ongoing Formation team distributed to the Community the Book of Life, a daily record for remembrance in prayer and congratulations of sisters' and Associates' birthdays, their entrance into life, and anniversaries of their entering eternal life.

CALL TO THINK BEYOND

Most telling for the Community's self-appraisal at the beginning of the century's final decade were accounts by the general councilors of dialogue they had initiated with ordained and lay Catholics and persons of other faiths who knew Sisters of Charity of Leavenworth as colleagues, pastors, or administrators. Councilors' questions touched on priorities of need and concern, roles of women religious for future service to the Church, and diocesan plans of which the Community should be aware. They visited ten bishops and forty-six priests in fifteen dioceses, lay employers, administrators, and directors of centers for pastoral life and lay ministry. Several dominant themes emerged.

The desire of laity to develop their own spirituality, their deep hunger for prayer and spiritual development, and need for formation in the discipline of faith and leadership roles all suggested collaborative planning. Ample evidence of understanding of their sacramental call to mission and of their potential contribution to the good of the whole ecclesial family came from lay participants. Many were open to the role of parish administrator. Laity in general expressed deep concerns for youth and apparent neglect of them by the Church as well as concern for interaction with ethnic groups. Ecumenism got almost no mention. On the whole, lay people were positive about the Church, its renewal, and its challenges.

Although some notions of the ways in which religious and lay life intermingle were at best ambiguous, other statements by clergy and laity alike suggested firm conclusions:

- Sisters have great credibility that makes it possible and imperative for them to invite laity to ministry.
- Sisters are critical to the future of the faith community in its family-centered sacramental life.
- Sisters by their presence awaken inquiries among the young about celibacy as a way of life, about commitment and prayer as life values.
- Sisters of Charity are at the heart of mission and ministry.

Comments clarified the last claim. Their gift is in "combining a vision of the whole with direct service—the work of their hands." Focusing on the macro-vision of the Church, they manifest an "uncanny ability to implement that vision in the here and now, at the local level." Diocesan planning with dialogue and needs of the poor were priorities for ordained and lay alike.[16]

Whether or not Sisters of Charity stopped to compare, they had fundamental qualities in common with other congregations. In the introduction to her early work, *New Wineskins*, Sister Sandra Schneiders, IHM, raised the question of why women religious who had responded most energetically to the Church's call to renewal had not produced any new theologies of religious life. Her twofold conclusion from long observation was that experience took priority over theory in their reflection, which produced only occasional writing about it; and that collaboration governed both reflection and action. Neither left much time for theorizing.[17]

This image of Christ at the entrance to Mount Olivet Cemetery was created by Sister Bernadine Hon, her only bronze sculpture, to replace the corpus that had been vandalized.

A Vincentian charism newly examined taught the Sisters of Charity to apply new energy to the needs of neighbors now recognized within and beyond parochial borders and institutional ministry. The Community and its members sought to collaborate actively with laity, clergy, and whoever shared a vision not yet clear even to themselves. Like their founders, they looked both past and forward to discern the call of the Gospel in times and places ready for the reign of God. Questions about the viability of religious life for the future were surfacing in secular as well as religious publications.[18] For their own part, the sisters did not consider themselves lost or invisible to the faithful or to the general population. They had more immediate concerns on their minds.

III

AS WE ARE BECOMING...

CHAPTER 20

Re-envisioning the Charism

At the end of the second millennium the threat of nuclear proliferation and the randomness of both senseless and purposeful killing deepened the shadows darkening the world, even while inability to control such forces distanced the danger. In the Western Hemisphere, the United States under four successive presidencies nurtured multinational investments and a flow of capital that multiplied markets, took jobs abroad, and justified corporate subsidies. By the middle of the decade, 5 percent of the population controlled 20 percent of the national income, while 40 percent of the country's people lived on a little more than 14 percent of its wealth.

A global economy flourished under some two hundred free trade agreements that with unbalanced benefits widened the gap between wealthy and poor nations.[1] The earth's resources were being ravaged in the search for minerals, waterpower, and soil that fed massive multinational production and transport. Gains of trade and employment from foreign investment in the Third World were overshadowed by losses of native industry, agriculture, and control of resources. Ironically, the first years of a new millennium darkened horizons across the globe.

Then at the dawn of the twenty-first century for the first time in its brief history, the United States suffered an assault on its own land that within minutes took more than three thousand lives in terrorist attacks using passenger-laden airplanes as weapons. The directed fury of 9/11 and the suicidal resistance to coalition forces who rescued Iraqis from tyranny had causes deeply embedded in East-West relations. Early attempts at reconstruction did much to exacerbate them. A pre-emptive retaliatory war and assurances of military withdrawal could not substitute for what was lacking: the force of a united world community. That unity needed the strongest kind of moral leadership and political will. Neither was at hand.

Nor could the integrity and good will of Pope John Paul II, acknowledged by much of the world, be brought to bear with any pervasive effect.

The bridges he was building across religious and cultural gulfs were not yet strong enough to bear such violent pressures. Only in the final decades of the twentieth century were the leaders of the world's religions making substantial headway in sustained ecumenical dialogue. Since 1981, a joint commission of Orthodox and Catholic bishops had met annually to discuss common traditions and historical differences in their creeds that came to major resolutions by 2004.

In that same year, the Midwest Regional Dialogue of Catholics and Muslims met at the headquarters of the Islamic Society of North America to consider values and virtues common to living both faiths in a changing society. Bishops in thirty-four state conferences, including Kansas, gathered annually to prioritize issues of Catholic social teaching—health care, welfare, abortion, education, capital punishment—that they then brought to the attention of state legislators and executives for serious consideration.[2]

Meanwhile, within the Roman Catholic Church internal failures reported in the media were shattering an inexplicable silence. The scandal of sexual abuse by clergy preoccupied the public and justly enraged a multitude of faithful who felt betrayed. A deeper concern grew swiftly among laity and clergy alike for the invisible structures of authority that had enabled bishops to prolong what became irreparable damage. Attempts since 1985 to remedy both causes and effects had been hampered by the very nature of the hierarchical organization that virtually isolated bishops in the exercise of their office.[3]

A serious study of that organization, going forward at the time though unknown to most Catholics, planted seeds of hope for radical change. In the middle of the 1990s, Pope John Paul II asked in his encyclical letter, *Ut Unum Sint*, the Catholic bishops of the world to study the office and primacy of Peter. In 1983 the pope had asked Archbishop John R. Quinn of San Francisco to examine the issue and to report directly to him. Thinking in collaborative terms, John Paul II posed the question of how forms of papal ministry might be open to "a new situation"—of a thirst for unity among Christians, the displacement of more than fifty million refugees, rising consciousness of the dignity of women, the growing gap between wealthy and poor nations, and deep divisions within the Church. Concluding the study, Archbishop Quinn called on original principles that could restore the college of bishops to their full responsibility to the Body of Christ. In regular communication with their people, they would be the true conduit of the mind of the faithful to their brother and head, the bishop of Rome. Such a renewal would imply a re-conception of the Curia as a necessary functional body in service to the whole people of God through their First Pastor and the bishops.[4]

The hope engendered by such actions is of slow growth. Relatively unrecognized for its impact was the work of religious congregations in the closing years of the twentieth century. Though its spirit was necessarily practical and present-minded, it was no less the work of a Church in travail. It might be argued that in their deepening renewal and determined preparation for a vigorous though decidedly different future, women religious mirrored and projected the developing life of the Church. What marked the work of the Sisters of Charity of Leavenworth in the last decade of the century was resolute attention to the need for prayer and Eucharist, a persistent search for unity within increasing diversity, and a characteristic cheerful energy. Their year-long preparation for the Fourteenth General Chapter of 1992 reflected all this and a growing consciousness of responsibility to the people of God wherever they found them at home, in their nation, and across international borders.

As the country took satisfaction in the swift progress of the Persian Gulf War, a prayer service provided in 1991 by the Social Justice Network used words of Pope John Paul II, U.S. bishops, and a United Nations report to decry war's devastating consequences for all who wage or suffer it. Invited by the Community Council to prepare throughout the year for the approaching Chapter, individual sisters and local houses engaged in reflection on transformative elements for religious life of the future.[5]

Reports on reflections bore witness to values of the Gospel, contemplation as a way of life for the whole Church, and the poor and marginalized as focus for ministry. Implications of these perennial elements for their realization in contemporary society and community life were the new challenges. Allowing for changes in terms, the transformative elements were the traditional challenges of religious life shaped by prophetic charisms, dependent on conscious union with God, and dedicated to meeting immediate human needs. During the year preceding Chapter, the Sisters of Charity translated the principles offered for their reflection into terms of their own experiences of ministry and their Community's heritage.

Educating sisters to issues of justice, developing skills to deal with opposition, and encouraging communal decisions about corporate stewardship —actions sought by the members—required leadership. Significantly, that quality did not rank high in surveys of community priorities. The very meaning of a contemplative attitude and the demands of simplicity of life were repeated topics for discussion but basically dependent on personal discernment and spiritual experience. Solidarity with and direct ministry to the poor were developing largely through individual choices of ministry and the Council's actions of witness and corporate support.

Trends recorded by the councilors for pre-Chapter reflection included expanding diversity in ministry and sisters' working in direct service more often than in leadership roles. This did not exclude leadership exercised by sisters in diocesan offices; on parish and community boards; and in administrative roles in social services, education, health care, and pastoral ministry. One councilor concluded her report with the observation that "religious life is at a crossroads and the SCL Community is right in the middle of it. We are at that moment when the status quo is becoming uncomfortable but the desired future is still unknown."[6]

Patterns of community living gleaned from the reports revealed sisters' greater selectivity about living companions and a tendency toward groupings of two to five; increasing enculturation into middle-class living; and more energy expended on ministry than on enriching life with one another. A reluctance to call one another to accountability weakened growth in community while the tendency to stay a long time in one place occasionally made life difficult for newcomers. While faithfulness to retreats was marked, personal modes of prayer and ministerial demand were taking precedence over communal prayer. Openness to ancient religious practices and contemporary spiritual trends paralleled lessening commitment to traditional spirituality. Increased awareness of and response to social justice issues reflected leadership from the Justice Network and its director even as increased consumerism conflicted with expressed desires for simplicity of life. Trends in ministry were diminishing contact with young women who might be potential candidates for the Community. The councilors found a sense of common life eroding.

A realistic appraisal by one councilor concluded that sisters were tired but stable and attentive to one another, especially in times of crisis or pain. Taking its toll, change was revealing fissures in what had been and risks in what was developing. With good cooperation in central financing, a growing independence was apparent in monetary matters. The cost of rental properties for community living and of cars for travel to ministries necessitated a larger general fund to which local houses contributed yearly. A given group had little common identity except a faithful community life, the fabric of which was fraying. Nevertheless, community was of the essence to vowed life and its well-being a general and individual concern.[7] Personal and communal discernment were clearly in order.

Persistent Search for Unity

In June 1992, 366 sisters gathered in Leavenworth for the Fourteenth General Chapter, preceded by three days of theological reflection.[8] Given the personal and communal reflection of the previous several months, this was the broadest and most direct participation in a General Chapter the sisters had experienced. The insistent patterns of the three days revealed a community calling itself to a new depth of renewal, a community aware of its problems and determined to move inward to its center and outward to unfamiliar territory. Evaluating lifestyles, ministries, and institutions from the perspective of the poor and building community with responsibility were recurrent themes. In various ways, each group called on the Chapter to reassess governance structures with attention to roles of Community councilors, collaborative processes, effective communication, and maximum use of individual talent and corporate resources. Fostering leadership, taking necessary risks, living with limits, sacrificing self for the common good, and deepening an intimate, direct relationship with God were singular phrases that forcefully supported the major themes.[9]

Motions unanimously approved—the equivalent of the traditional Chapter enactments—derived from the three days of theological reflection and three subsequent days of concentrated discussion:

- that the Social Justice Office continue with a full-time director to address issues of justice,
- that a vehicle of collaboration and communication be created between the sisters and Community leadership,
- that the Community director and Council provide for study of procedures for nominations and elections of delegates and Community officers to be effective in the General Chapter of 1998, and
- that the Associate Program continue to evolve.[10]

Given the thorough reports of activities and recommendations, the first and last motions were predictable in their outcome. The second motion for a "vehicle of collaboration and communication" between membership and leadership was an echo of concerns voiced in General Forums and at every Chapter since 1980.

Membership in the highest governing body, the General Chapter, had been enlarged with better representation of age groups, regions, and apostolates. Many hoped that improved communication and collaboration would follow on further expansion in numbers of delegates and processes of nomination and selection that moved toward consensus. In the exuberance of commitments gathered from a year of reflection and seven communal days of focused prayer, conversation, and discernment, the sisters generally did not perceive a motion for a vehicle of collaboration and communication to imply more responsible participation in governance of the Community. A Chapter of Affairs was its ordinary vehicle. This Chapter, however, concentrated on the palpable need for deeper unity and renewal of original purpose. Further, the mode of its action from theological reflection to re-commitment of life and mission did not ask for specific mandates or re-alignment of structures. Direction rather than decision was the order of the day.

In the mission statement fashioned by a trio of delegates from the recorded work of the reflection tables, the sisters found a sense of renewed conviction:

> *As Sisters of Charity, we commit ourselves, here and now,*
> *to embrace anew the charism given us by Vincent, Louise, Mother Xavier:*
> *to love the poor, to love one another, to live simply,*
> *and to unite the whole of our lives in the poor and loving Christ.*[11]

During the eucharistic liturgy preceding elections, the common direction of the Chapter was identified as "the face of Jesus in the faces of His poor" and in each sister. The condition of "complete simplicity" was to cost "not less than everything." Elected Community director for a second term during the session that followed, Sister Mary Kathleen Stefani spoke of "the energy and spirit generated during these seven days together." Sister Sue Miller, elected first councilor, referred to the waters of baptism and the commitment to charity "made unfalteringly together."

Community Officers, 1992–1998: (top row) Sister Maureen Hall, Sister Mary Kathleen Stefani, Community Director, Sister Barbara Aldrich, and Sister Helen Forge, Community Secretary; (bottom row) Sisters Marie Damian Glatt, Joan Sue Miller, Mary Julie Casey, Community Treasurer, and Helen Therese (Marie Elena) Mack

Re-envisioning the Charism

The other three regional councilors, Sisters Barbara Aldrich, Maureen Hall, and Helen Therese Mack, pointed to a sense of ownership generated by the theological reflection process and the risk entailed in a common vision. Sister Marie Damian Glatt, elected as councilor for Health Services, anticipated above all growth in access to health care for the poor. Having served as treasurer from 1974 to 1986, Sister Mary Julie Casey was re-elected to that office both for the Community and for the Health Services Corporation. Sister Helen Forge, elected to succeed Sister Marie Kelly as Community secretary, affirmed that the Chapter called each "to journey in a deeper way with the poor."[12]

CHALLENGES OF SPONSORSHIP

Developments in sponsored works of the Community during the first half of the 1990s more than satisfied the Chapter's challenge to renew and re-create traditional ministries to meet changing needs, especially those of the poor. The depth and breadth of change in human conditions, material resources, and modes of care defied prediction. It inspired the leadership, collaboration, and adaptation that had marked the sisters' administration of schools and college, child care, and health care for the past two turbulent decades. Maintaining a mission of service that derived from a clear religious identity was the balance wheel for Catholic institutions in a society constantly being redefined by pluralistic principles and a profit-driven market economy.

Separate incorporation of Mount St. Vincent Home brought a board of directors that included lay persons who had long supported its mission and knew Denver's resources. No one, however, could have conceived of the headlines that marked the Home's 110 years of service to children and families celebrated in 1993. At the end of his sojourn in Denver for World Youth Day, Pope John Paul II visited Mount St. Vincent to meet and bless the children.[13]

On his visit in 1998, Pope John Paul II greets Sisters Jean Marian Redlinger, Roberta Furey, and Mary Donalda Orleans, staff members at Mount St. Vincent Home, Denver.

On his walk from the helicopter with Sister Daniel Stefani, the Home's director for thirty-two years, and her sister, the Community director, Sister Mary Kathleen, the Holy Father learned how forty-five youngsters lived with resident supervisors in cottages equipped for a family-like environment. He learned of the twenty who were in day treatment for emotional and behavioral problems. He met a few of the staff of seventy-five who helped the young people adapt to full participation in home and school life. But the children's unique achievement on August 15 was to win the full attention of the pope as he chuckled at their questions, surprised them with his answers, and blessed the crowd of 260 gathered in the small chapel. Before leaving he embraced each child who approached him. According to comments after his visit, the children liked best his hugs and his laughter; one boy wished the pope could be their teacher.[14]

An extensive study undertaken by the Sisters of Charity of Leavenworth/Health Services Corporation led to the formation of a strategic direction plan that focused on integrating lay leadership into governance of the system. Vice president of planning since 1987 and president of the SCL/Health Services Corporation (SCL/HSC) since 1992, Sister Marie Damian Glatt worked with the first combined lay and religious board, chaired by Sister Mary Corita Heid, RSM. The long-range plan focused on leadership development, mergers and partnering opportunities, and mission integration. Goals and objectives emphasized a social accountability process to ensure visible commitment to the poor and to report on and assess the quality of community services. Partnering with physicians and other providers, collaborating to control costs and conserve resources, ensuring just and equitable dealings with employees, and maintaining an adequate margin to further the ministry were major pillars of the plan. Major bond financing and a centrally managed investment program were actions guided by anticipated needs.[15]

A significant initiative in the centralization was the office of vice president for mission integration, filled for ten years by Sister Charlotte White, a veteran science teacher in high schools staffed by the Community. Introducing to affiliates a specific role for what had been both essential and peculiar to each hospital's history and culture for decades was a task more daunting than facing reluctant teenage learners. That the mission of an institution become integral to every aspect of its ministry and individually owned by the physicians, nurses, and staffs who exercised it was the challenge.[16]

A report by the Catholic Health Association in 1993 revealed a growing decline in the number of Catholic hospitals in the United States. According to the director of research, the chief cause was Medicaid's reimbursement policy requiring hospitals to accept less than costs for health service to the poor.[17] The government had no balance wheel for non-profit

A very young patient comforted by a nurse, here in Obstetrics/Gynecology, is a familiar image at any of the Sisters of Charity hospitals.

hospitals' mission to the underserved. HMOs, Medicare, and insurance companies set limits to hospital stays and reimbursement for services. Independent medical centers and clinics contributed to the competitive market inherent in a technology-driven profession. Implacable forces were sending hospitals into mergers and systems that meant survival as well as growth.

Facts from the early 1990s are a testament to the Sisters of Charity hospitals that maintained excellence, sought partnerships and collaboration, and expanded compassionate ministry in the face of insurmountable obstacles. In their Midwest and Far West locales, specific hospitals extended services as regional medical centers and contracted with research and independent physicians' programs. Administrators looked to a future beyond foreseeable control and dependent on stewardship responsible for the health care of those least able to meet its cost.

St. James Community Hospital recorded a million dollars in care for poor, elderly, and indigent patients in 1992 after negotiating a new contract the previous year with nurses seeking salary and overtime increases. President of the hospital since 1986 when she succeeded Sister Mary Serena Sheehy, Sister Loretto Marie Colwell led the negotiations. As inheritor of a generous pledge by the Butte District Community Relations Team of Mountain Bell, she saw to development

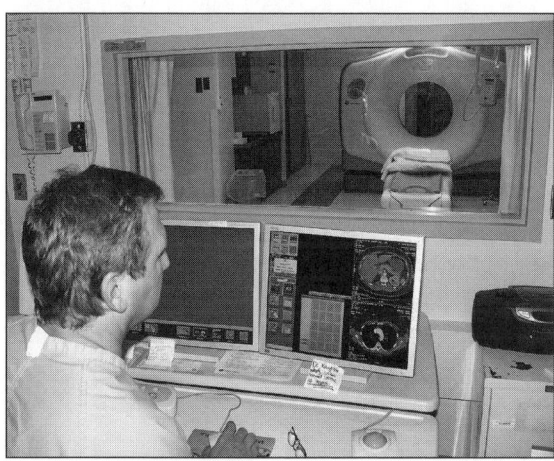

As at every system affiliate, the C-Scan at St. James Community Hospital, Butte, facilitates diagnosis and treatment.

of the Regional Cancer Treatment Center. Approximately 80 percent of its service went to outpatients who came from the Butte/Silver Bow County area of southwestern Montana.[18]

Mission Goes Abroad

In years that followed, St. James with thirteen other Montana hospitals undertook a medical mission at long range to Santa Clara in Guatemala. Dan and Rose Casazza of the Helena diocese carried incubators to the village for a small hospital the people were building. Thousands of dollars in equipment and supplies were sent from Montana to help two St. James physicians with a Spanish-Indian native doctor treat five hundred people in the first three days after the hospital opened. Back in Butte, an ecumenical team of eight local ministers volunteered time on-call twenty-four hours daily for crisis situations at St. James Community Hospital in a program coordinated by the pastoral care department. In 1993 a Regional Psychiatric Family Center opened and both physical and occupational therapy were offered in cooperation with the Occupation Therapy Association of Butte.[19]

When he succeeded Sister Michel Pantenberg as president and CEO of St. Vincent's in Billings, William M. Murray had served seven years as her executive vice president and chief operations officer. For three years he continued to work with Deaconess Medical Center and physicians' groups to forge a public perception of Billings as a collaborative regional medical resource, keeping services on the leading edge of national developments. James Paquette inherited that legacy and in 1990 opened the Elizabeth Seton Prenatal Clinic for women who could not afford needed services. Fees operated on a sliding scale according to family size and income. A certified nurse midwife, Pat Loge, attended the newborns and their mothers, backed up by physicians from OB/GYN Associates.

Community education programs were offered at five locations in Billings. Specialized clinics drew hundreds of aging clients yearly. Six family practice clinics in the city offered services to all clients regardless of ability to pay; clinics multiplied in half a dozen towns between northern Wyoming and the middle of eastern Montana. At the initiative of Sallie Arellano, head instrument technician, St. Vincent's undertook in 1990 a mission to Honduras.[20] Later in the decade, an allocation of interest from SCL/HSC investments allowed the hospital to purchase a twenty-acre plot for housing homeless youth, jobless families, and released prisoners. A second amount went to Billings Housing for condos built for small families unable to build or rent. With St. Vincent's leadership, a coalition of

Billings health care providers collaborated in a medication assistance program, a dental program, a campaign to support family health insurance for the working poor, and a Habitat for Humanity house.[21]

Early in her term as president and CEO of St. Mary's Regional Health Center in Grand Junction, Colorado, Sister Lynn Casey, with the hospital's Development Foundation, initiated a Natural Resource Campaign to develop facilities that served the Grand Valley region of some five hundred thousand people in western Colorado and eastern Utah. The Prenatal Center grew to include a twenty-four-hour newborn and maternal transport reaching women in far-flung areas. Doctors in small communities provided externships for residents and participated in rural training advisory meetings. Averaging twenty thousand visits a year, the Family Practice Center served the medically indigent and provided health care workers for migrants.

St. Mary's Cancer Center was approved by the American College of Surgeons as a comprehensive cancer program unusual for its outreach to a vast rural area. Hospice and Home Care services augmented the hospital's aid to families in more than a thousand visits a month. To strengthen ownership of their common mission, Sister Lynn initiated a dialogue project, engaging physicians, nurses, and staff in exchange and mutual learning.[22]

Originally the Catherine Mullen School of Nursing, now home of St. Joseph Hospital's Foundation, the "clustered-brick" facade and art deco interior designed by Temple Buell is a monument to the generous donors who support the health care ministry of each affiliate of the SCL/Health Services Corporation.

Prompted by observations of patients' diagnoses and treatments, Janet Cameron, executive director of Marillac Clinic, implemented in 1994 a study of five hundred patients to determine connections between biomedical and mental health problems. The collaborative care program, an interagency undertaking of the Mesa County Consortium on Health, produced long-term evidence that 51 percent of the clinic's low-income patients suffered one or more mental disorders, in contrast to the national norm for medical patients of 28 percent.[23]

For years, St. Joseph's Hospital in Denver had maintained Ave Maria Clinic on site and sent surplus supplies to needy clinics abroad.[24] In the early 1990s, Sister Marianna Bauder, president and CEO, led a steering committee of fifteen doctors, nurses, friends, and other sisters to plan further ways of alleviating poverty at home and abroad. A Mission Office, directed by Sister Mary Walter Swann, organized shipments of supplies and equipment to villages and cities in forty countries in North and South America, Africa, India, and Eastern Europe. During the first three years of operation, teams spent time in thirteen countries. Local missions served migrant workers and homeless women and children; Denver hospitals and private donors contributed equipment and monies. Tepeyac Clinic was the work of Our Lady of Guadalupe parishioners assisted by Sister Paula Rose Jauernig.[25]

Celebrating 120 years of service to metropolitan Denver and the Rocky Mountain region, St. Joseph's Hospital and Health Center in 1993 recorded for the previous year more than 25,500 admissions. Families chose St. Joseph's for 20 percent of Colorado's births and 17 percent of those in Denver. Dedication of the three-story Russell Pavilion in 1995 enhanced educational resources and mentoring partnerships for a record one hundred resident doctors with swift access to all departments for outpatient services. A Women's Pavilion offered specialized programs for wellness in all of life's stages and to provide women with services they could not afford.[26]

When St. Francis Hospital and Medical Center carried more than seventy programs and services to communities of northeast Kansas beyond Topeka, no one including Sister Ann Marita Loosen, president and CEO for eleven years, could have predicted the results. A team approach in psychosocial treatment to assist cancer recovery included spiritual resources of the pastoral ministry staff. Two radiation oncology vans traveled 155,000 miles each to deliver treatment to outlying communities. The Children's Miracle Network Telethon brought the Topeka community and St. Francis together in new ways in 1991 to contribute a record amount for treatment of area children in financial need.[27]

In the summer of 1993, approximately one thousand volunteers from the community and one hundred St. Francis employees made a collective effort in a names project that produced the AIDS Memorial Quilt. A special care team had studied the physical, emotional, and spiritual needs of AIDS patients and educated hospital staff for the past seven years. Sister Loretto Marie Colwell, president and CEO from 1992, spoke to a principle not yet operative in all health care institutions: "Our responsibility is no different to people with AIDS than it is to those who suffer from any other disease.... We have never questioned our role in caring for them."[28]

Planning for the 125th anniversary of St. John Hospital's founding in Leavenworth, Sister Mary Aloys Powell, president since 1986, realized it was a hospital that belonged to the people as well as to the Sisters of Charity of Leavenworth. The Family Centre offered treatment and education in chemical dependency as well as support from social services. A Lifeline provided personal emergency response. Speech and hearing tests and treatment complemented physical and occupational therapy. Few health care records could equal the work of the five Zeugin sisters, three of whom had volunteered for the twenty-five years since the new St. John's opening and two of whom, Sisters Jeanne Marie and Mary Ellenita, were assigned by the Community to pastoral care in the hospital.

Recalling the thirty-two sister administrators of St. John in its 125 years, *The Leavenworth Times* reported the new hospital's quarter century of admissions, emergency visits, and births. In 1989 the teamwork of physicians, nurses, technologists, and support staff was the achievement of a medical staff led by Doctors Derrick DeSauza, William Allen Jr., Robert Parker, and Debra Hudgen, and a nursing staff led by registered nurses Pat Hegarty and Ann Hess. Officers of the board of directors Royal Brown, Jerry Reilly, and Clyde Graeber worked as partners with the sisters. Employee salaries during the period contributed $49 million to Leavenworth's economy.[29]

The beginning of the decade for the new president and CEO of Providence–St. Margaret Medical Center, Sister Ann Marita Loosen, was marked by the death of the health center's strong support and collaborator, Vincent W. DeCoursey Sr. President of the board of directors and brother of Sister Regina, he had been a member since 1980 and was instrumental in establishing the Founders' Fund to help finance Providence's care for those without health insurance or financial means. A tribute recalled his role as executive director of the Kansas Catholic Conference and his steady involvement in the task of "establishing justice on earth."[30] Dedication of the Vincent M. DeCoursey Diagnostic and Treatment Center followed a memorial Mass in November 1991.

At the end of 1992, Providence–St. Margaret Medical Center and St. John Hospital integrated their services to Wyandotte, Leavenworth, and surrounding counties for increased efficiency, resource, and outreach. The boards of both hospitals initiated plans to assess community needs and implement services. Alliance with Physicians' Resources of Kansas Inc. made possible later the opening of West Glen Primary Care medical offices in Shawnee County. By the middle of the decade, Providence–St. Margaret was ready to celebrate its diamond jubilee.[31]

Jubilee and Acts of God

When Saint John's Hospital and Health Center in Santa Monica celebrated its golden jubilee in 1992, major developments were in planning, negotiating, and implementing stages. The joint venture with Harbor-UCLA Medical Center brought Saint John's Heart Institute and cardiovascular research program significant medical and fiscal advantages. The John Wayne Cancer Center had sought residence at Saint John's for its research facilities and reputation. Community services of educational programs, free testing and inoculations, Venice and Xavier Clinics, the Child Study Center, and mental health outreach to the homeless continued Saint John's mission to the Bay area.

Cost accounting in all departments, programs, and planning was governed by a procedural standards tool from the department of budget and reimbursement, the first of its kind to be used in the country's health care systems. A debt-free investment portfolio provided high interest to be sent home to the SCL/Health Services Corporation. Saint John's Foundation of seventy-three members led fund-raising committed to the Health Center's programs and to its service of the indigent and uninsured.[32] Continuation of such service was to face a daunting test of courage and determination.

At 4:31 AM on January 17, 1994, a 6.5 earthquake struck Los Angeles and damaged eighteen hospitals in the Northridge area. Twelve miles from the epicenter, Saint John's took crippling blows throughout its main wing and adjacent towers. Though it suffered a violent shock, the hospital remained structurally habitable the first day as personnel carried patients in the severely damaged north wing down stairways to safety. Thanks to swift action, no lives were lost; only one employee suffered minor injury. Labor and delivery continued as necessary in the recovery unit; surgery was limited to one room. Significant aftershocks within the next three days brought evacuation orders from state officials after site visits to all hospitals disabled by the quake. By the afternoon of January 20, Saint John's had been totally evacuated by nurses, physicians, administrators, and personnel and their families.[33]

Operational less than a month after the quake in ambulatory services, Saint John's physicians and patients had access by late February to all major departments and minor surgery. The south and main wings were available for inpatients early in October. At the ribbon-cutting event, Gov. Pete Wilson praised the reconstruction that brought continued services in a reduced but secure setting.

After the quake, Sister Marie Madeleine, president and CEO, described the most grievous loss: necessary termination of seventeen hundred employees, "many of whom were the heroes and heroines" identified from the beginning. A local Employee Relief Fund received contributions

Sisters Marcianna Trujillo and Mary Owen Horner offer a Christmas box of food and gifts to a grateful father at Saint John's Hospital, Santa Monica.

from individual Sisters of Charity, SCL/HSC, employees from affiliate hospitals, board members, physicians, and trustees.[34] During the month after the quake in a previously scheduled event, Leland Kaiser, Ph.D., authority on the country's health care system, told Saint John's people that their hospital would "be rebuilt on the spirit of its past," calling the quake "an acceleration of God's grace to show you where you should be going."[35]

Within nine months, plans for a new Saint John's were on drawing boards and a public campaign was being planned to help support construction of a health center designed for the twenty-first century. A grant of ten million dollars from the W. M. Keck Foundation supported the redesign and helped preserve research and technological development under way at the hospital. The new Health Center was to be the first to meet requirements against earthquake damage under a Seismic Hazard Mitigation program.

A *Los Angeles Times* editorial commended plans for a streamlined Saint John's that would continue its "history of charity." The example cited was the health center's half-century provision of free surgery, obstetric care, and laboratory work for the poor and homeless clients of the Venice Family Clinic.[36] The selflessness and resilience of staff, sisters, and residents and the generosity of people—friends or strangers—were memorable. The story of Saint John's recovery added an extraordinary chapter to the beginning of its second half-century.

New College Leadership

Less visibly but in long-lasting ways, the Community's sponsored educational institution, Saint Mary College, contributed consistently to the mission articulated by the 1992 Chapter. In their offices as academic dean and dean of students, undertaken in 1986, Dr. Carol Hinds and Sister Constance Phelps had assisted the transition to the college's first lay president in twenty-five years. On Sister Xavier Andre's sudden death in the summer of 1986, Sister Dorothy Harvat was appointed treasurer of the college until she became registrar. Jo Adams was business manager into the 1990s. In 1988, William Kiel followed Annabel Willcott as director of development. In 1989 this administrative team welcomed Brother Peter Clifford, FSC, who came to the college as president from Washington, DC, where he had served as director of the Secondary Division of the National Catholic Education Association.[37]

Not until 1993 did the Community Council approve the college's separate incorporation. With additional compelling reasons, Brother Peter repeated the case that Sister Mary Janet had presented during the previous decade. A new and enlarged board of trustees was charged with direction and management of the college still owned and sponsored by the Sisters of Charity of Leavenworth. From his first year, Brother Peter encouraged faculty and staff in initiatives that would sharpen the image of Saint Mary as a source of leadership in Church and community. The Ryan Sports Center was dedicated at the completion of a capital campaign begun in 1989. Saint Mary Center hosted ecumenical groups and spiritual programs monthly. Campus Ministry sponsored spring break trips to Appalachia and inner-city Chicago.

Under renewed contracts, faculty teaching at the United States Federal Penitentiary garnered a feature story in the *New York Times*. Brother Peter expanded the degree-completion program for working adults with a second site in Johnson County that grew tenfold in its first three years. As coordinator of the program, Sister Mary Sarah Fasenmeyer recruited and advised students through commencement. A master's degree in education served graduates in a five-county area. Total computerization of the college and its Kansas City sites, as well as administration of all programs on the campus and in the prisons, became an urgent necessity.

With a year's collaboration in the application process led by John Estes, a Title III grant made possible what had begun in 1981 with a second National Science Foundation grant secured by Sister Barbara Kushan. The early grant had provided for computerization of academic departments, extended training for faculty and staff, and computer education programs for area secondary teachers. Now Title III funded hardware for the college's infrastructure, upgrading the Enterprise Resources Planning (ERP) system that facilitated central administrative procedures.

With no little foresight, Sister Mary Mercita Jackson, cataloger of De Paul for almost a quarter of a century, had begun the conversion of 100,000 volumes of De Paul from the Dewey Decimal System to the Library of Congress System appropriate to a growing academic library. Before she retired in 1991, Sister Mercita had completed 90 percent of the conversion, her only staff a few work-study students. Computerization of the holdings, which had grown to 120,000 volumes, began with the Title III grant.[38]

Father John Stitz was an early recipient of the Caritas Award, inaugurated in 1993 for recognition of exceptional service to marginalized and underserved people. Though he spoke of the prison programs, Brother Peter included the entire college when he said, "What distinguishes the programs of Saint Mary College is our total and absolute commitment ... that the Lord will be served even among the poorest by our academic efforts."[39]

That the Community's sponsored works were channels of the commitment to the poor mandated by the General Chapter of 1992 was in many ways clearer to the beneficiaries of the institutions than to many sisters no longer directly involved in their ministries. Communication of the effects of these ministries as well as of those undertaken by individuals and groups of sisters was to become more than a need of the decade to follow. It figured in the very image of women religious and their communities before the public and in the Church. Were they still a viable, even vigorous part of the life of the Church, or were they in danger of becoming irrelevant as well as largely invisible?

Page after page, file after file, the record of more than one community attests to the determination of sisters in the last decade of the century to pursue their commitment to the people of God, especially the poor and vulnerable, in the spirit of their founders but with new energy and in new modes of ministry. Further, that commitment was now a growing partnership with the laity and across lines of faith and tradition. Numbers notwithstanding, they were women sent to do the work of God wherever it called them and with whatever means lay at hand. They were not simply moving to new frontiers; they were re-envisioning them.

CHAPTER 21

Crossing Borders

The hundredth anniversary of Mother Xavier's death, April 2, 1995, reminded the Sisters of Charity of Leavenworth not only whence they had come but, more urgently, how they had to travel if they were to emulate her courage. Diversity was their heritage, division a hazard they had skirted more than once. The renewed unity and direction they sought in recommitting themselves to their founders' charism lay now on distant frontiers and close to home. Deepening their alliances with laity, strengthening bonds across the Americas, joining the Charity Federation, and collaborating in ministries, sponsored and new, forged the dynamic of the 1990s. Strengthening foundations of community in security for retirement and in integration of new members generated confidence in the future. Nothing in the past encouraged anything but practical realism and absolute trust in Providence. The midterm report of the Community director, Sister Mary Kathleen Stefani, suggested the need for both.

Through task force recommendations, the Council tried to give shape to the inchoate desire expressed in Chapter for greater participation in community decisions. Regional meetings in fall and spring replaced the local and general Forums with an agenda that continued theological reflection on Vincentian spirituality. Issues of aging and retirement generated a survey of living preferences and a study of living spaces on campus and in mission areas. The retirement fund was to grow from gifts and annual assessment of local houses. A comprehensive study of medicines in use, charges by suppliers, and methods of purchase was completed for implementation.[1]

A Community-wide inventory of self-reported talents, experience, and preferences for service on community projects led to numerous appointments to the Social Justice and Vocation Networks, to standing committees, and to specially charged task forces. A Ministry Development officer, Sister Margaret Mary Driscoll, was named to facilitate change and identify openings for new mission assignments. On invitation to form

"Dream Teams," five groups took initiatives in education, community living devoted to witness and welcome, and specialized ministry to women and children in deprived circumstances.[2] One group began planning for what would become Duchesne Clinic serving the uninsured of Wyandotte County. Several sisters spent the summer of 1995 with families on the border of Texas and Mexico in order to experience the economic realities of their daily living and the riches of their social and spiritual culture.

Collaborative ministry with other congregations in Kansas was the subject of conversations among community officers of Benedictines, Ursulines, Dominicans, Sisters of St. Joseph, and Sisters of Charity. Crossing barriers of age, race, religion, socioeconomic strata, and way of life characterized specific ventures. Xavier Community in Denver became the first house to invite young women to residence for a temporary experience of the common life of women religious; they contributed to the house budget from their individual salaries. In Kansas City, Missouri, Menuha House became a place of reflection and quiet on a given day or weekend for women whose lives were otherwise filled with family, professional schedules, and volunteering.

In Leavenworth, a Mother-to-Mother ministry assisted families of men incarcerated in the area's state and federal prisons. Sisters partnered with single mothers in need of housing, clothing, and medicines for their children. Leavenworth's Alliance Against Family Violence attracted volunteer hours, contributions, and advocacy of sisters respected in the statehouse. El Centro, founded in 1986, was an archdiocesan center of education, job training, and social gatherings for the Hispanic community of Kansas City, Kansas. It continued to draw the services of Sisters of Charity for teaching, translation, and program management.[3]

Perhaps most laden with blessings for the future was the Community's decision in 1995 to join the Elizabeth Seton Federation of Charity. This association of Sisters and Daughters of Charity holding in common the Vincentian legacy of ministry to the poor and vulnerable numbered thirteen congregations located on the east coast of Canada and the United States in cities westward from Baltimore to Leavenworth.[4] The immediate benefit of Federation membership was participation in the collaborative Formation program. *The Seton Legacy*, the history of the Sisters of Charity of Leavenworth, and the life of Mother Xavier were texts for candidates' study. Intercommunity dialogue confirmed what directors perceived in candidates: need for theological education, acquaintance with local communities and sisters in ministry, continuity between initial and pre-profession formation, and experience of new models of living in community.[5]

To reinforce its commitment to the Latin American missions and to strengthen personal ties between North and South American sisters, the

Community sponsored immersion experiences for groups of sisters who wished to learn about mission life firsthand. Nine spent twenty days of prayer, conversation, and ministry with the sisters of Santa Rosa in Talara, Peru, in the first of such journeys. Elected to the Community Council in 1992, Sister Elena Mack resigned that position and returned to Peru in 1994 to resume her direct work with the poor. Over the next few years, the Council approved new missions in exceptionally poor areas of Ecuador, the city of Quito and the rural area of El Chaco.[6]

Meanwhile, twelve North American mission sisters and eight native Hermanas de la Caridad prepared for an event that was to sharpen common understanding of the Community's mission in Latin America. In 1995 Sisters of Charity in Kansas, Missouri, Colorado, Wyoming, and Montana formed eleven cluster houses to plan the welcome of native Peruvian sisters into their convent homes for the days preceding the June gathering called Converging Paths. Learning Spanish, exchanging letters with those assigned to each house, preparing an agenda of visits, meetings, and ministry experiences was task enough. Raising the money for the travelers' airfare personalized all efforts and made the civic community aware of the value of the Community's Latin American mission. Pray-ers remembered the Come North project daily; Associates participated in every effort.

Hermanas who came north from Peru in the summer of 1996: (left to right, back row) Lourdes Abad Pulache, Laura Rumiche Morales, Liduvina Dominguez Córdova, Susana Córdova Castillo, and Maria de los M. Orozco Olaya; (front row) Julia Huiman Ipanaque and Trinidad (Trini) Orozco Olaya.

Reflection questions informed prayer and conversation during weeks before the event anticipating the next General Chapter:

- What kind of a people do we want to be?
- What will be our role in the world?
- What are the responsibilities of one generation to another?
- What are the obligations of the "haves" to the "have-nots?"
- What limits will we put on individual freedom for the sake of the common good?

By the summer of 1996, approximately 450 North American Sisters, 60 Associates, and 20 South American *hermanas* were ready for the Community gathering in Leavenworth.[7]

Experience of community bonds reached a zenith that summer. The Heritage Room, designed and constructed by Sister Mary Rebecca Conner, chronicled the Community's history with carefully identified artifacts, photographs, and century-old gifts from friends in Nashville, Tennessee, and clergy in Kansas and Montana. Showcases focused attention on its origins and earliest foundations. Central panels detailing the Latin American missions and missionaries with pictures of Peruvian and Bolivian parishioners, children, and *hermanas* brought the history up to date.[8]

Ties with laity in mission and ministry took new forms during the decade. The Rosalie Mahoney Award, commemorating the sister who had inspired clinics for the uninsured, recognized Therese Horvat, a veteran of twenty-one years' service at Providence Medical Center. An Associate of the Community, Therese served the Archdiocese of Kansas City, Kansas, as news editor of *The Leaven*.[9] In sponsored institutions, parishes, diocesan offices, and far-flung missions, religious and lay women and men were to deepen the wells of life and faith for the people of God across all borders of resource and culture.

In her call to prepare for the Fifteenth General Chapter of 1998, Sister Mary Kathleen Stefani, the Community director, reminded the sisters that congregational Chapters are meetings of the Church. "The whole ecclesial community," she wrote, "benefits from the fruits of the Chapter." For a community of 438 members with a median age of sixty-nine, slightly less than half in active ministry and more than a third active in retirement, it was important to engage all the sisters in prayer, discernment, and leadership as their condition and gifts allowed. Those choosing active participation committed themselves to three days of theological reflection discerning the challenges and signs of the times. Among reflection materials were 188 individual challenges gathered from sixty-three discussion tables at six regional meetings.

Readings from contemporary theologians emphasized global realities of a Church reaching beyond all borders and nourished by the blood of martyrs in El Salvador.

This preparation led to the process of personally inviting sisters to leadership positions, electing delegates, and nominating sisters for the offices of director and Community councilors. Out of 102 invited, 39 sisters agreed to be listed for nomination. A considerable pool of potential leadership evolved from the process. In evaluation, 82.4 percent of 296 sisters responding rated it effective or highly effective.[10] Under the theme, "Igniting the New Fire of Charity," the Chapter convened in June for a week of deliberation, discernment, and celebration.

Closing the first "Day of Water," sisters and Associates traveled in buses to the town's Riverfront Park to bless a plaque commemorating the first sisters' arriving in Leavenworth. From every river that marked their missions in California and Washington; Montana, Wyoming, and Colorado; Minnesota, Illinois, and Kansas; Washington, DC; Texas, Arizona, Peru, and Ecuador, they brought vials of water to be poured into the Missouri River where the founders had landed. On the "Day of Light and Fire," Sister Mary John Mananzan, OSB, president of St. Scholastica's College in Manila, issued a challenge to women religious for the third millennium. She called them to stand against forces of injustice and oppression, to take seriously the earth's ecological crisis, and to accept responsibility for women's role in opposing violence, discrimination, and exploitation. Facts and experience generated Sister Mary John's account of suffering and protest in the Philippines. The action she sought clearly issued from a contemplative and compassionate spirituality.[11]

In her report to the Chapter, Sister Mary Kathleen put serious questions to the sisters about the prior claims of their communal prayer and the centrality of the Eucharist to their daily life. Sister clarified the two-tiered governance structure of the Community's sponsored institutions. Predominantly lay boards are accountable to the members, the Community director and Council, who assume responsibility for the corporate entity's mission and Catholic identity. As part of the patrimony of the Church, sponsored institutions carry the sacred obligation to use their resources to further the mission of Jesus.

Costs of a Chapter

Meeting the needs of the times, Sister said, posed "simple but dangerous questions..., dangerous because the answers will cost us. They will cost us our preconceived notions; they will cost us our ways of doing things; they will cost us our carefully constructed comfort; they will cost us everything."[12] Community councilors' reports emphasized implementation of the 1992 Chapter enactments and revealed at close range common currents of community life. According to these reports, the sisters evinced a strong desire for a deepened prayer life and grasp of Vincentian spirituality with its call to live simply and to love the poor. For many, prayer was the unifying factor in the local community. Determined to live faithful to their founders' spirit, they frequently asked themselves in theological reflection: "How is this [decision, action] going to affect the poor?"

The reports indicated that for many participants a major goal of the Chapter was to share in directing the future of the Community. Evident in attendance at regional meetings and in initiatives for Community projects, the effort extended to Associates and interaction with the Latin American sisters. Sisters looked for shared purposes between members and elected leaders of the Community. The spirit of sisters approaching retirement, surrendering control, and risking the unknown inspired the councilors. Finally, the potential of women centered in relationship to God, to the earth, and to one another was a source of both energy and concern among many of the sisters. While they saw roles of women opening in the Church and parish structures, sisters found mixed attitudes among the clergy. Hiring practices in some dioceses diminished prospects and threatened sisters' financial security.

The councilors' overview of six years' interaction with the sisters raised significant questions:

- How to nurture the common life so as to build community in all circles of influence?
- How to develop accountability while fostering leadership?
- How to translate the founding charism into demands of necessary employment and good stewardship of limited community resources?
- How to challenge society rather than mirror it?

In the report from Latin America, increasing diversity in response to needs, especially those of women, marked ministry in Peru and Ecuador. Of the nine native sisters, six had made perpetual vows. *Hermanas* were working with Jesuit fathers in educating the poor and with women in programs of personal growth. One of the sisters was to direct the archdiocesan office for health promotion. Projection of needs took into account a growing market economy that left the poor behind and a potential for family breakdown in a secularized society. Conditions magnified the importance of women's collaboration with pastors and work on parish teams, not to say their diocesan leadership. Growth in self-esteem and access to education were mounting priorities in the initial formation of Latin American sisters.[13]

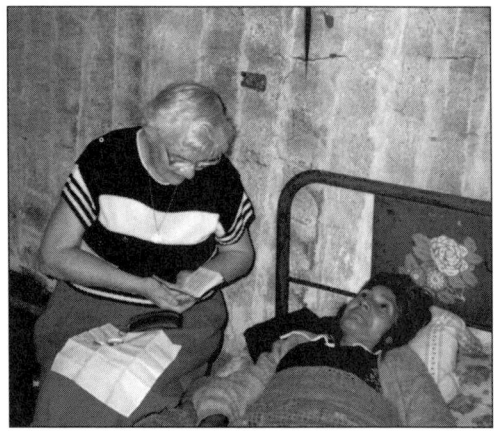

Sister Rose Dolores brings Communion to a woman of Cristo Resucitado parish in Trujillo, Peru.

Sponsored institutions' reports revealed significant growth during the previous six years in outreach to the underserved, development of programs, and public collaboration. Mirroring its 115-year history to more than fifteen thousand children and families, Mount St. Vincent's Home in Denver marked growth in service to families with no place else to turn for mental health needs and support to stabilize their lives. Accredited programs included a therapeutic pre-school to assist early intervention, residential and day treatment for children five to twelve, and a school for children unable to handle the regular classroom.[14] Sister Vickie Perkins served as executive director of the Home from 1995 until called to another ministry in 1999. She was succeeded by Dallas Rychener.

Saint Mary College reported on its new board of trustees with a majority of lay members, new majors, and new master's degree programs in management and applied psychology initiated by the Johnson County site director. The joint venture with St. Thomas Aquinas High School for a new building to house the Johnson County program had been forwarded by Dr. James Reid in a brief presidential term. Sister Constance Phelps succeeded him in the spring of 1997. Scholarship Friends of Saint Mary made major investments in students eligible for college study but unable to bear its cost.[15] The first WomanSpirit event co-sponsored by the college and Providence Health Center was hosted on campus in the fall of 1997.

In the spring, Saint Mary College celebrated its diamond jubilee with a gala hosting the Leavenworth/Lansing community and the inauguration of Father Richard Mucowski, OFM, as president. During the next few years, he advanced the visibility of the college with expansion of athletic programs that were to make their mark in intercollegiate play. With careful planning and development, the playing fields enhanced rather than diminished the beauty of the front campus. As a Division II member of the National Association of Intercollegiate Athletics, the college put eight sports teams on field, diamond, and court.

It was a new millennium when the Spires baseball team, coached by Rob Miller, won the Kansas College Athletic Conference Tournament Championship, first in the history of the program. The head football coach, Lance Hinson, led the Spires to a record-breaking season and was named KCAC Coach of the Year. More significant, perhaps, was the wide range of students engaged in athletic programs and intramural sports while maintaining the requisite academic standing. A major event of 2005 was the dedication of the Ryan Sports Center basketball/volleyball court to Sister Madonna Fink, faithful patron of all Saint Mary athletic teams. For years, students sought her out for academic assistance in De Paul Library, for prayer to open each game, and for sustenance in away-games. Students to come will find her name just above the playing floor.

By the 1990s, the Catholic health care ministry was re-ordering its mode of operation. Systemic collaboration to maintain its mission and to find a common voice for political advocacy were fundamental to both survival and mission. Strengthening alliances, the Sisters of Charity of Leavenworth Health Services joined the National Coalition on Catholic Health Care Ministry and Consolidated Catholic Health Care. To centralize services and to influence legislation to meet needs of the poor, SCL/HSC partnered with the Daughters of Charity and Carondolet National Health Systems. Socially responsible investment and a centralized mission integration office aimed at deepening the commitment of all administrators and employees to the healing ministry that identified each health care institution of the Sisters of Charity of Leavenworth.

When the Health Services Corporation observed its twenty-fifth year in 1997, living sisters who were serving or had served in the health care ministry numbered 193. They included medical personnel, staff, and a dozen volunteers. Sister Marie Damian announced the institution of a Mission Fund and the annual Mother Xavier Ross Award to support projects exemplifying the founders' charism and legacy. Statistics from the clinics showed that their service to the uninsured had grown in budgetary terms by approximately 20 percent over three years.[16]

To continue the legacy of Catholic health care for the people of Miles City, Montana, whom they had served since 1909, the Presentation Sisters transferred sponsorship of Holy Rosary Hospital to the Sisters of Charity of Leavenworth in 1997. The history of both congregations ran parallel. Called to Kansas, then Montana, by a missionary bishop to serve in rural areas and the first to enter into managed care contracts with the Anaconda

Holy Rosary Healthcare, acquired by the SCL/Health Services Corporation in 1997

Company, these frontier sisters, first neighbors, were now partners in a potential statewide system of Catholic hospitals.[17]

Reports to the Chapter from standing committees filled out the six-year picture. The Ongoing Formation team focused on transformation as the goal of the sisters' spiritual life. Recommendations emphasized the need for theological understanding and sabbaticals for spiritual renewal.[18] Part of a national phenomenon, the Associate Program reported growth to 125, with 14 in the application process. Sharing in all-Community projects during the previous few years had added to Associates' sense of belonging. A newsletter, *SCLA Connection*, kept sisters and Associates informed.[19]

Since 1995, the Social Justice Executive Committee had promoted the use of social analysis and theological reflection on issues of justice integral to Vincentian spirituality: reverence for the earth and prophetic challenge to socioeconomic and political structures. A workshop on welfare reform was followed up by information on health care for women and children. Materials from the Seamless Garment Network inspired by Cardinal Bernadin's consistent ethic of life informed opposition to war, abortion, poverty, racism, the death penalty, and euthanasia. Education of the sisters to U.S. policies in Peru, to political responsibility in national elections, and to the impact of globalization had contributed to preparation for the 1998 General Chapter. On the horizon was the potential for systematically engaging Associates in the Community's work for justice and peace.[20]

Intercommunity Ties

Thanks to collaboration developed since the 1970s and resources of the Charity Federation, the Initial Formation and Vocation Teams worked hand in hand. The trend in North American communities toward one-by-one entry instead of in groups required inter-community association, a benefit not known to earlier women religious. The Federation's Collaborative Novitiate in eastern cities engaged the Community's youngest members in ministry experiences with candidates from other Charity congregations. Recommendations for the initial formation program included a common experience with Latin American sisters before final vows, and language learning in English and Spanish across the North-South border.[21]

It is significant that the vocation director called hers a ministry of accompaniment, not of recruitment, of young women on their journey into religious community. Four years on the board of the National Religious Vocation Conference had deepened her thinking. Conversations with young adults, women's retreats that emphasized the role of the home in nurturing vocations, and listening sessions with parents revealed complex currents in the spiritual development of the millennium generation.[22]

Charged to create vehicles of collaboration and communication with the Community and to deepen the call and commitments of the 1992 General Chapter, the Communications Steering Committee had moved as practically as possible given the breadth of its assignment. Guiding principles emphasized collaboration at all levels and participative processes to foster ownership of Community ministries and projects.[23] A canvass of the Community generated plans for electronic communication of information and news. These required house budgeting for computers and consultations for their purchase.

For a year prior to these reports, in house discussions and regional meetings sisters had been thinking about the direction they wished the Community to take in its immediate future. From the dozens of challenges produced by this communal reflection, key areas of concern emerged for the Chapter's consideration. During two days, 230 delegates and active participants met in full assembly for free exchange, then in self-selected groups on the topic of first significance for them. Their task was to formulate a succinct proposal for enactment or recommendation by the Chapter delegates. The broad participative process and the difficulty of casting a group's thinking into clear, convincing language put limitations to some groups' work.

Despite deep frustrations, the assembly perceived the action of the Spirit in the Vision statement adopted by the Fifteenth General Chapter:

> to partner—locally, nationally, globally—with the poor for
> mutual transformation with special focus on women and
> children, and
>
> to actualize our preferential option for the poor
> in living and deepening the charism
> given us by Vincent, Louise, and Xavier.

Proposals for implementation asked for a deeper realization of the transforming power of the Eucharist in prayer and ministry; witness through living simply according to Gospel values; development of a ministry for the aging; exploration of new membership options; and furtherance of mission in the use of computer technology.[24]

Enthusiasm for the work was nourished on the evening of the second day by celebration of the eighteen years Sister Mary Kathleen Stefani had given to Community leadership, twelve of them as director. For eighteen years as well, the Community treasurer, Sister Mary Julie Casey, had advised and overseen leadership with regard to the Community's material resources in sponsored works. Admiration of her acuity and professional knowledge was common among sisters and colleagues. With the skill of a master teacher, she communicated at home and on the missions the Community's accountability to its employees, members, and the people served by their ministries.

In response to a Community questionnaire regarding renewal, sisters indicated qualities that gave them confidence in Sister Mary Kathleen's leadership. With all the marks of a creative, intelligent, and clear-thinking teacher, she carried these as well as the precision and method of the sciences she had taught into the responsibilities of her office. Decisive, focused, and astute, she exemplified the talents of an administrator and more. According to respondents, Sister quietly led the Community in the right direction. Sensing the deep need for unity, she endorsed all-community gatherings, made improvements in Ross Hall, and initiated practices to enhance community spirit in the Mother House. On the other hand, Sister supported sisters in various ministries and was open to uncharted courses and collaborative endeavors. One called her term a "breakthrough to truly contemporary community life."

Sensitive to the sisters' needs, Sister Mary Kathleen made herself available to them. Many, young and older, knew her devotion to aging sisters. While some perceived her as aloof and impersonal, others found her approachable, a good listener, and kind. All recognized her integrity, a firmness of principle that called for courage and willingness to confront issues. She was conscientious, trustworthy, steadfast, and direct. All who knew her saw her prayerfulness and deep-seated faith.[25]

Confirming a Direction

Sister Joan Sue Miller, Community Director, 1998–2010

Community Officers, 1998–2004: (from bottom left to right) Sister Joan Sue Miller, Community Director, Sisters Constance Phelps, Barbara Aldrich, Katherine Franchett, Community Treasurer, Helen Forge, Community Secretary, Marianna Bauder, and Rita McGinnis

A day of reflection and discernment and a prayer service preceded election of the general officers on the Day of Wind and Spirit. With the Chapter delegates' election of Sister Joan Sue Miller as Community director, the assembly paused for a communal rite of acceptance. Sister Barbara Aldrich was named first councilor and Sisters Rita McGinnis, Marianna Bauder, and Constance Phelps were elected councilors to complete the leadership team. Sister Helen Forge was re-appointed as Community secretary. New to her post, Sister Katherine Franchett was named Community treasurer. No one doubted that a clear direction now unified the Community. That demands of transformation were not altogether clear and that roles of women in the transformation of the Church were yet to be realized did not deter these women from action to come. The depth of transformation and the extent of its range were neither evident now nor subject to future control. "A sense of oneness with the human family" and "an active concern for... projects of the world community"[26] were, by their rule of life, serious if unplumbed guidelines for following Jesus sent by God to the world they knew.

At issue for that world were implications of rampant poverty in both developed and developing nations. By the 1990s, more than one theologian and not a few sociologists[27] were exploring the intrinsic relationship between sisters' solidarity and ministry with the poor and the absolute need of oppressed peoples to reclaim governance of their lives. Sisters had to learn, such thinkers were saying, from their ministry what they lacked in the structures and processes by which they lived and ministered. The issue was much larger than that of communication; collaboration was much more than a way of strengthening resources and sharing good works. The overriding question was one of vision and leadership. These qualities were hard won and not always recognized in a community like the Sisters of Charity of Leavenworth. They were so important as to require unlimited extension of five fruitful Days of Light and Fire, Water, and Breath of the Spirit.

CHAPTER 22

Jubilee:
"Year of Favor from the Lord"

Called to prepare for the millennium by a Church declaring 2000 a year of Jubilee, the Community summoned all the energy reinvigorated by Chapter and initiated plans in 1998 to "keep the sabbath," first phase in the Jewish tradition of observing Jubilee. Doing so, the sisters cast their lot with all who desired peace for the world and justice for those oppressed by poverty, tyranny, and alienation. Under the umbrella of this theme of the Fall Regionals, sisters were invited to remember the sabbath Sundays of their journey in faith. The rich significance of sabbath produced all other themes of preparation for Jubilee: forgiveness, liberty, justice, and celebration.[1] Their realization in the first century of the third millennium would give new meaning to the biblical "year of favor from the Lord" (Isa 61:2).

Before the year of preparation began, a longtime friend of the Community closed thirty-two years of service with the Sisters of Charity of Leavenworth. Father Daniel Shea, OSB, born in County Kerry, Ireland, in 1909, came to the Mother House as chaplain in 1966 to succeed Father Justin Sion. Priests from St. Benedict's Abbey in Atchison, Kansas, had been missioned to Saint Mary uninterruptedly from 1926. Father Justin was chaplain to the sisters at the Mother House from 1933 to 1955 when he grew ill. Until 1960, Fathers George Spiegelhalter and Joseph Staudinger, OSB, successively served as their chaplain. From 1952, Father Alcuin Hemmen, OSB, was chaplain to the sisters in Ross Hall until Father Justin returned, the first to be officially appointed as chaplain to the sisters in both the Mother House and Ross Hall. He ministered to them for six years until injury from an accident brought his retirement in 1966. Father Francis Broderick, OSB, shared Father Justin's duties during the last two years of his chaplaincy.

Father Daniel came to minister to the Mother House sisters and to teach classes in the vows to novices and postulants. Assisting him, Father Imre Kekessy ministered to the Ross Hall sisters for eight years; Father Joseph Haller, SJ, for six years; and Father Stephen Lee from 1984 until his final illness in 1995. Occasional visits to Father Dan's family in Ireland were gifts of friends. On his retirement in 1998, he was declared an honorary member of the Community; soon after he celebrated his seventieth year as a Benedictine. Communication with the sisters continued until he died in 2002. To assist Father Michael Zoellner, OSB, who succeeded Father Dan as chaplain, Sister Anne Callahan was appointed director of liturgy with a reformulated liturgical committee.[2]

In January 1999, Sisters of Charity and Associates gathered at the Mother House to begin Community-wide implementation of Chapter commitments. In self-selected committees and task forces, they provided for partnerships with the poor in the spirit of their founders, immersion experiences in unfamiliar cultures, and global mission study. One group focused on preparation for Jubilee 2000. In response to an initiative from Pope John Paul II and the U.S. bishops, Leavenworth Charities, as members of the Federation of Sisters of Charity, petitioned for cancellation of the debts of heavily burdened poor nations.[3]

The Partnership Task Force began its work with three Sisters of Charity and three members of the Vincentian Center for Spirituality and Work in Denver. Funding and clear criteria for projects and teamwork with associates were initial strengths of the operation. Projects for coordination of crime awareness and victims' assistance efforts and for a day center's micro-credit system got early funding. In the summer of 1999, funding went to projects for medicines and equipment sent to hospitals in Latin America, promotion of dental health for senior women, ministry to AIDS patients, adult job training, and ministry to wives of prisoners.

By the spring of 2000, the Partnership Committee was supporting projects proposed by seventy SCLs, HCLs, and SCLAs with partners in Montana, Colorado, Kansas, and Peru. Awards ranged from $300 to $10,000. Among the partners were medical residents who worked with families and health care workers in Peru and women of all faiths who sought quiet and prayer with sisters in their convent home. Abused women and their children and handicapped individuals were partners with sisters and Associates for support in their needs. Individuals initiated projects with agencies, parishes, clinics, and schools.[4]

Teenagers partnering with Hispanic families in Montana contributed to Esperanza International, a home-building program for poor families in Mexico. Twenty SCLs and SCLAs contributed $10,000 and at least five hundred hours to help a low-income couple build their Habitat home in Butte. In a program designed to improve prenatal care among clients of Caritas and Family Practice Clinics at Exempla St. Joseph's in Denver, staff and volunteers partnered with pregnant women to provide for prenatal visits, childbirth education, and home care. Holy Rosary parish in Billings, Montana, partnered with AIDSpirit to furnish a home-cooked meal six days a week for women and men with AIDS. Community Partners in Teaching united parents and parishioners in training to become substitute teachers in seven inner-city Catholic elementary schools in Kansas City, Missouri.[5]

Immersion Experiences took North American sisters and Associates to distant places for immediate knowledge of living as the minority in a given culture or without means for living in humane conditions. For some, the experience of immersion came from ministry of the previous five years. Besides ongoing ministry at nursing homes, emergency centers, and food kitchens, sisters in their areas described work with the homeless, prison inmates, and poor families. A two-week stay at Catholic Worker House and ten weeks of job training at El Centro provided diverse experiences of minority people without work or family life. The Christian Appalachian Project and Caritas Missions in the East engaged several sisters. Living with the poor in foreign cultures took thirty sisters and Associates to Mexico, Haiti, Jamaica, Ecuador and Peru, Guatemala and El Salvador, China, Africa, Armenia, and the Ukraine. In all places, they served with native people and shared their professional resources.[6]

Over three years, the Theology Update task force engaged sisters in reading, reflection, and dialogue about fundamental theological developments in Christology and ecclesiology. Workshops on "The Church: Called to Communion" focused on its global nature, communal structure, and evolving roles of laity. Resources for study of the Vincentian spirit came from the Ongoing Formation Committee.[7]

By the summer of 2000, the Communications Committee was implementing workshops on conflict resolution, large-scale communication by e-mail, development of a Community web site, and professional standards for all communications. With a lay director for the Communications office, technologically proficient sisters assisted in audiovisual production and website maintenance. Called *SCL Spirit*, a newsletter provided stories about ministries, millennium projects, and sisters celebrating their jubilees.[8] A cohesive statement of purpose for communications with a long-range strategic plan waited on a Chapter to come.

In the spring of 2001 in Chicago, the U.S. Bishops Committee on Women in Society and in the Church consulted with approximately 150 women in diocesan leadership on subjects significant for women and for the Church at large. Sister Eileen Hurley took an active part in the conference. Lay women and sisters described the journey of women in the Church since Vatican II. That journey had brought them to diocesan offices of chancellor and vice chancellor; to direction of communications, development, human resources, community services, family life, religious education, and evangelization; and to responsibility for AIDS ministry, Respect Life programs, and projects for racial justice.

Concluding recommendations focused on recruitment of women in under-represented groups such as African Americans, Hispanics, Asian Americans, and Native Americans; and on priestly formation in areas of spiritual development, administrative skills, and teamwork with women. Participants urged education of parishioners about realities of the priest shortage to cultivate acceptance of lay ministers.[9]

In May 2001, a life-size bronze sculpture of Mother Xavier Ross, sitting with hand outstretched in welcome, was installed on the fountain circle in front of the Mother House. On her lap lay a book inscribed with her words: "Look forward to the good that is yet to be." The sculptor, Sister Margaret Beaudette, Sister of Charity from Mount St. Vincent College in New York, attended the installation. Its cost and the cost of the new fountain were gifts to the Community from anonymous donors. On a sunny day, Ross Hall sisters assisted by wheelchairs, canes, and nurses' aides made the long trek from their infirmary to the fountain for their own personal visit. The figure of Mother Xavier and its setting attracted young people in particular—University of Saint Mary students from across the campus and groups of visiting youth in summer months.

Later in May, the sisters welcomed approximately ninety members of the Sisters of Charity Federation to the Mother House for the annual leadership meeting. The gathering signified their unity in the worldwide Vincentian tradition and that of Elizabeth Ann Seton, founder of the first congregation of Sisters of Charity in the United States. The presider at the weekend's eucharistic liturgies was the Vincentian Father Tom Nelson of Denver. Sister Susan Wood's paper on Sisters of Charity as Daughters of the Church placed their history in an ecclesial context.[10] Guests returned to the East with new images of Church and religious community in a Midwest many of them had never before visited.

The enormous energy and genius of organization that fueled the work of the three years since the 1998 Chapter poured into the mid-point gathering, "In the Spirit of Charity," that began on the Fourth of July in 2001. After a rousing celebration of the nation's birthday by sisters of both Americas and Associates, reports from the committees and task forces brought participants up to date. The third day opened with an impassioned address by Ada Maria Isasi-Diaz, author and professor of theology and ethics at the Theological School of Drew University. She asked for a deeper understanding of justice as the struggle for liberation of all oppressed peoples.

She spoke of priority for the poor as growth of understanding between those who have means to live with dignity and those who do not. Their recognition of mutual interest and worth, she said, is essential to growth in relationship with Jesus and all who are neighbors to one another.[11]

One piece of information provided by the Social Justice Network came from the Charity Federation's office of its NGO representative to the United Nations. The report put flesh and bone on the morning's injunctions. In their interventions before the Economic and Social Council, non-governmental organizations including the Federation asked for full cancellation of the poorest nations' debts and linked the debt burdens to education, the struggle against AIDS, and deprivation of services essential to life.[12]

A Royal Welcome

A "red carpet" rolled out at the entrance to the Mother House on the fourth day of celebration to welcome 157 women who had been part of the Community during the past fifty years. Uninterrupted visiting filled the afternoon and dinner hour. Evening brought a performance in Ryan Center that recalled events, customs, and charges familiar to everyone who had experienced novitiate and convent life in the decades before the seventies and eighties. That evening, native wit and common memories evoked laughter that carried a sense of gratitude for what some 300 women gathered in the hall had experienced together twenty or thirty or forty years earlier. Before the Sunday morning liturgy in Annunciation Chapel, the guests returned to Ryan Center for reflection on a Celtic belief in a "thin place" where past, present, and future all meet for a brief moment in time.[13]

Evident in everything was the Jubilee Committee's intention that the welcome home would acknowledge the contribution of former sisters to the mission and ministry of the Church, the sacramental dimension of all the baptized who partake of the Eucharist, and the developing international dimension of the Community. The event was to ask how all might move together as women in the Church, recognizing a common history with years "in between" that had been a time of grace for all. Subsequent comments from those who attended bore out impressions of the weekend. Realization of the original Jubilee theme of "coming home" was a historic event of reconciliation and reunion with implications for the future of religious life and the people of God.[14]

A survey distributed to the Sisters of Charity of Leavenworth early in 2002 asked for insights into their experience of renewal. Designed to elicit the sisters' views of the Community's evolution over the past forty years, the survey brought a generous response of 81 percent, or 293 of 361 surveys distributed. Guidance from an academic researcher in the behavioral sciences ensured validity of format and content; thirty readers reviewed a first draft with suggestions that were incorporated into the final form. Its comprehensive reach asked for considerable time and reflection from respondents.

Analysis of data produced more information than can be used for a significant overview; it is available for another kind of possible research. Decisions for present use of the data clarify the interpretative statements: (1) For highest ranking items of the number requested, percentages of first and second choices are combined to indicate relative significance. (2) Percentages of third and fourth choices are added for further significance of totals. (3) Responses entered as "Other" are identified when ranked as first, second, or third choice.[15]

As Sisters Saw Themselves

THE COMMUNITY'S CHIEF STRENGTH AS PERCEIVED BY THE SISTERS	PERCENT OF CHOICES
the sisters themselves, in their union with God	48.81
all our ministries, in their quality and diversity	14.33
the heritage of those who have gone before us	11.26
union of the community in charity	8.19
the charism of Vincent, Louise, and Xavier	7.85
our service to the Church	4.78

The central question asking for one response revealed a deep conviction about the value of each sister. According to almost half the respondents, the greatest strength of the Community was "the sisters themselves in their union with God." Three respondents chose an "other" form of the item, omitting the final phrase or rewording it. A fourth "other" item indicated "willingness to serve wherever there is a need," certainly a reference to the sisters themselves. Of the remaining eight items, none came closer in percentage of choice than "all our ministries, in their quality and diversity." Next in line were the "heritage of the Community," its union, and its charism. Relatively few as were these latter choices, "service to the

Church" was marked by less than five percent, suggesting that in the sisters' thinking their ministry and the heritage of the Community were not yet consciously identified with the mission of the Church.[16] As the Community's greatest strength, local community, validation of one's ministry, and stewardship of resources were each the choice of approximately 1.33 percent of the respondents.

The first question that required ranking of selected items asked what events or developments in the life of the Church in the past half-century had most deeply affected the life of the Community. Firm choice of the Vatican II

EVENTS IN THE LIFE OF THE CHURCH MOST DEEPLY AFFECTING COMMUNITY	1&2	3&4	TOTAL
Vatican II document on religious life and its renewal	83.94%	10.04%	93.98%
Vatican II document on the Church in the modern world	67.59	16.48	84.07
diminished number entering religious life	27.03	40.99	68.02
sisters' withdrawal from many Catholic schools	23.03	38.79	61.82
Vatican II document on liturgy and its renewal	20.54	44.64	65.18
Holy Father's call to serve in Latin America	15.04	36.85	51.89
women exemplifying role of religion in 21st century	14.96	25.98	40.94
role of women religious in institutional Church	14.03	33.92	47.95
role of laity in Church's institutional life	13.29	39.30	52.59
poverty, especially of single mothers, and welfare reform	6.06	18.18	24.24
justice of national and international policies	2.24	24.72	26.96

document on religious life and its renewal reflected solid conviction born of remembered experience. Upwards of two-thirds marked the document as their first choice. More than two-thirds in their first and second choices indicated the influence of the document on the Church in the modern world. Another consistency appeared in the percentages of those who chose items immediately related to community life: diminished numbers of women entering religious life, sisters' withdrawal from many Catholic schools, and the Vatican II document on the liturgy and its renewal.

For most respondents, global conditions in the life of the Church had considerably less impact on the Community than common internal experiences. In primary choices by 15 percent or less, the Holy Father's call to religious to serve in Latin America was matched by women exemplifying in their initiatives the role of religion in the twenty-first century; the role of women religious and of laity in the institutional life of the Church came next. All of these appeared as third and fourth choices made by more than a quarter to almost 40 percent of the respondents. Poverty, especially of single mothers, and effects of welfare reform was not seen as a primary influence on community life, though it was marked as fifth or sixth in significance by more than half the respondents; justice of national and international policies was marked at the same level by more than 40 percent.[17]

The last two data points suggest that intensified efforts on behalf of social justice had made an impact but without widely perceived deep effect on the life of the Community. What does not appear in the responses is the fact that many sisters had known and served mothers in every kind of need throughout their religious life. They knew the effects of poverty in personal relationships. Causes of that poverty were not yet for many in the realm of concerted action. Realization of the need for action was to grow sharper, however, within the next few years.

Although women and children living in poverty had been traditional beneficiaries of the Community's health care and social work ministries in both North and South America, it had been only three years since the Chapter of 1998 had committed the Community to active and effective solidarity with them.[18] The effects of Chapter statements of 1992 and 1998 were to deepen with years of theological reflection and dialogue within and beyond the Community.

A second qualification colors the data. Given results of a later question about issues exerting the strongest impact on sisters' thinking, responses to this question may allow alternative readings. One implies respondents' simple *experience* of effects in Community from listed developments; another implies *evaluation* of the extent of such effects. Allowing for this measure of ambiguity, perhaps the most significant conclusion to be drawn from the data is that the social teaching of the Church had not, for most of the respondents, led to a realization of connections between poverty in its causes and public policy on national and international levels. That women collectively, lay and religious, might take leading roles in seeking justice through such policy was not yet a first principle of mission held in common.

When it came to selecting secular events or developments since the end of World War II for the most significant effects on religious life and on the Community, choices yielded emphatic patterns. Changes in the status of women, whatever the cause, were the most significant factor in community life, although the phrase had no single value or reference for the number who chose it. The next most important factors were increasing opportunity for service to those in need and the civil rights movement and all forms of racism. New consciousness of individual responsibility was highly significant for its effect on community living. Similarly, more than

SECULAR DEVELOPMENTS SINCE 1950 AFFECTING LIFE OF COMMUNITY	1&2	3&4	TOTAL
changes in status of women	59.26%	25.00%	84.26%
increasing opportunity to serve most needy	43.75	29.68	73.43
civil rights movement and all forms of racism	41.59	31.85	73.44
new consciousness of individual responsibility	36.00	33.33	69.33
decline of two-parent family and growth of single-parent households	34.17	30.84	65.01
global issues: economic, political, environmental, social	30.63	32.95	63.58
new consciousness of individual freedom	28.15	37.04	65.19
expansion of gap between very rich and very poor	26.98	38.09	65.07
climate of the times	19.20	41.60	60.80
suffering and needs of Third World people	14.77	39.78	54.55

a third saw effects on religious life in the decline of the two-parent family and growth of single-parent households.

Global issues—economic, political, environmental, cultural, and social—were perceived by somewhat fewer as having had a major impact on religious life and on the Community. Related but secondary to individual responsibility, new consciousness of individual freedom was ranked as most significant by more than a quarter of the respondents, as was expansion of the gap between the very rich and the very poor. The economic gap and the suffering of Third World people gained considerable weight as third and fourth choices. Finally, the raised consciousness of individual responsibility and freedom and the climate of the times ranked in that order of significance for a third to more than 40 percent of the respondents. A perceptive addition to the listed items given top ranking as an influence on community life was TV.[19]

Given the persistence of certain percentages, concentrations of choice emerge. They reveal clear convictions among the sisters about effects on religious life of the changing status of women and the family, of racism and poverty, and of responsibility for personal freedom. Nevertheless, connections between universal suffering, the sacramental life of the Church, and communal responsibility were in need of contemplation and theological reflection.

Responses to a question about the influence on the Community's ministries of the increasing role of the laity revealed that a clear majority were convinced that collaboration strengthened lay leadership and brought mutual benefit. Roles of laity on institutional boards were acknowledged as influential. More significant, however, was the near 80 percent of those who, in first through fourth choices, saw partnership with laity as widening Community horizons and opening new roles for religious in parish ministry.

The perception by 40 percent of the respondents, recorded in first and second choices, that lay positions diminish or eclipse sisters' roles in institutions and parish life may be read either as a simple fact of experience or as a qualifier of the perception of widened horizons. The number of respondents who perceived the contrary is decidedly significant. Further, the number who reported in first through fourth choices a deepened respect for the laity, their gifts and commitment, indicates strong relationships. These led to realization by more than two-thirds of the respondents that many lay persons desire a deepening spiritual life.

Clear patterns in the overview may suggest different depths of experience in working with lay persons in their developing roles. An "other" item for this question written in by a respondent defined the number one influence of laity in ministry as clarifying the need of sisters to redefine themselves—"who we are [over against] what we do." Addition of two items to the eight that ranked highest reveals a significant benefit claimed by more than 60 percent of the respondents in first through fourth choices—that partnerships with laity clarify the value of vowed community life in the Church. That they encourage growth in numbers and initiatives of Associates was for many a desirable consequence. That the laity enable Community ministries to continue was acknowledged as significant.[20]

INFLUENCE OF GROWING ROLE OF LAITY ON COMUNITY MINISTRIES	1&2	3&4	TOTAL
lay boards influence institutional ministries and sponsorship	41.00%	25.46%	66.46%
collaboration and growing freedom strengthens lay leadership	40.89	28.13	69.02
partnership with laity widens horizons and vision	40.08	39.67	79.75
role of laity tends to diminish or eclipse sisters' roles	40.00	22.22	62.22
their role deepens respect for gifts and commitment of laity	37.66	31.17	68.83
opens new roles for religious in parish ministry	36.97	41.18	78.15
threatens life of Catholic institutions for the future	28.58	28.58	57.16
emphasizes growing desire for deepening spiritual life	27.96	39.34	67.30
clarifies value of vowed community life in the Church	20.23	41.57	61.80
influences growth in numbers and initiatives of Associates	11.76	37.82	49.58

The growing influence of laity and awareness of the value of partnering with them were factors to be realized by the time of the next Chapter and its preparatory Circle sessions. Further education to sponsored institutions and participation of Associates in regional meetings were to provide new opportunities for understanding both distinct and collaborative roles of laity and religious in the mission of Church and community.

Asked what issues confronting the Church were the most determining factors in respondents' thinking over the past several decades, the sisters were certain about what had influenced them. Half marked in this order as

ISSUES CHURCH FACES AS DETERMINING FACTORS IN SISTERS' THOUGHT	1&2	3&4	TOTAL
dire poverty of more than half the world's people	50.00%	23.09%	73.09%
roles of women in the Church	49.49	28.06	77.55
sacredness of life, especially mercy killing and legalized abortion	45.14	24.57	69.71
leadership of laity and religious in the life of the Church	31.49	29.95	61.44
control of institutional Church by male hierarchy	29.45	28.77	58.22
strengthening sacramental life of the Church	22.73	16.67	39.40
waste and ruin of the earth's resources	17.10	27.46	44.56
divisions within the Catholic Church	16.00	19.00	35.00
violence in American culture and national policy	14.95	31.96	46.91
the death penalty	14.91	28.07	42.98
the Church in relation to other world religions	14.45	21.11	35.56
other issues added by respondents	38.46		

decisive: the dire poverty of more than half the world's people, roles of women in the church, and the sacredness of life, especially [violated] by mercy killing and legalized abortion. Participation and leadership of laity and religious in the life of the Church weighed most heavily with almost a third. Control of the institutional Church by a male hierarchy was most influential with almost 30 percent.

More than a fifth of the respondents were most deeply concerned for the sacramental life of the church. Waste and ruin of the earth's resources and divisions within the Catholic Church were primary influences on somewhat fewer. Because of the total percentages of first through fourth choices, three items merit mention for their impact: violence in American culture and national policy, the death penalty, and the Church's relations to other world religions.[21]

None of the seventeen items listed was omitted in the total ranking. All but two were at least someone's first choice. Moreover, the number, amounting to very nearly 40 percent, of those who added "other" items indicated further the scope of sisters' thinking and concern about the Church. Three of these added items converged as a first choice variously worded: concern for authenticity as religious in a culture of opposing values, fidelity to the Gospel of Jesus, and the role of the religious as prophet. While the lesser emphasis on theological issues was notable, the weight of concern for the sacredness of life, for the world's poverty, and for leadership in the life of the Church by the non-ordained, especially women, signaled expansive growth in individual concern and commitment within the Community.

Finally, respondents were asked to choose and rank eight changes in the Community over the previous fifty years that most significantly affected their life together as Sisters of Charity and their service to the people of God. Of the eight requested for ranking, two were selected by more than half the respondents; two drew the same percentages in the first four choices. In order of ranking, the eight were greater responsibility for personal decisions; changes in local community—structure, prayer, co-responsibility; growing emphasis on deepening the life of prayer; the "exodus" of many sisters in decades following Vatican II; the departure of many sisters from primary ministries of education and health care; the relationship with the director and councilors, especially in making decisions; the emphasis on the charism of the Community in the lives of Vincent, Louise, and Xavier; and direct involvement of sisters in Chapters, committees, and new ministries.

Combined third and fourth choices added to the significance of seven more items: collaborative and developing Chapter statements; options in attire; parish ministries and diocesan leadership; regional councilors and Forums; changes in liturgical worship; expansion of ministries; and the call

CHANGES MOST SIGNIFICANT FOR LIFE IN COMMUNITY AND SERVICE	1&2	3&4	TOTAL
greater responsibility for personal decisions	58.82%	23.98%	82.80%
changes in local community—structure, prayer, co-responsibility	50.48	24.52	75.00
growing emphasis on deepening life of prayer	37.37	24.21	61.58
"exodus" of many sisters in decades following Vatican II	31.40	30.58	61.98
departure of many from ministries of education and health care	22.22	29.86	52.08
emphasis on charism in lives of Vincent, Louise, and Xavier	21.28	25.54	46.82
relationship with director and councilors, especially in decisions	21.28	25.54	46.82
direct involvement in Chapters, committees, new ministries	15.91	30.68	46.59
call to missions in Latin American and growth of Community there	15.65	19.13	34.78
options in attire	15.55	33.33	48.88
expansion of ministries and Community sponsorship	11.85	25.18	37.03
regional councilors and Forums, for development and community	11.83	25.80	37.63
changes in liturgical worship and sacramental celebration	9.46	25.68	35.14
ministries in parish life, including leadership in parish and diocese	9.20	29.88	39.08
more collaborative and developing Chapter statements	7.02	35.09	42.11

to missions in Latin America. A full third of the respondents added their own "other" items. Added as first choices were Vatican II, changes in the Community's Constitutions, diversion from following the Christ of the Gospels, and authenticity of lay people in the day-to-day struggle to live unselfishly by Christian values. Human rights under totalitarian regimes and the living example of women religious were major concerns. Second and third choices ranged even further.

The evident care with which sisters responded especially to this question justifies the extended breakdown of their choices. Further analysis would prove worthwhile. For example, on the last three questions about lay involvement, issues confronting the Church, and changes affecting community life, arranging items in order of total percentages, rather than first and second choices, has significant and several startling effects. As it stands, particular patterns—convergence in the highest ranking choices, emphasis on personal responsibility and deepening prayer life, and value placed on involvement in community structures and decision-making—characterized the responses of a community in developing renewal. They suggest also the individuality that had characterized this Community from its beginnings.[22]

A line quoted during discussion of Jubilee themes defined a prophet as one who "knows what time it is." At the beginning of a new century, the Sisters of Charity of Leavenworth knew they were called to new horizons but on the whole did not think of themselves as prophets. True to the character of their forebears, they found Jubilee an urgent time to confirm in action the deepening knowledge of who they were. A simple question at the beginning of the survey, as well as subsequent questions asking respondents to mention three characteristic qualities of the directors of the Community over the past fifty years, revealed what they valued in their identity as Sisters of Charity of Leavenworth.

In Sister Sue Miller, elected as Community director in 1998, a decided majority—more than 87 percent—of those who responded to the question and more than 70 percent of those who responded to the survey—found in her prominent qualities of leadership. These included high intelligence, vision, willingness to risk, foresight in planning, decisiveness, courage, capacity to listen, and administrative skills. Emphasis on her strength in living out the mission of the Church, of Mother Xavier, and the Community came to focus in particular comments, that Sister is "willing to dare new possibility for the future" and is able "to discern and articulate the spiritual dimension" of Community. The ability to meet new organizational needs while keeping Community structures viable was of special note. Respect for individual differences and openness to suggested alternatives particularly characterized what for many was a collaborative manner.

Qualifications in a few responses acknowledged strong qualities while observing a certain distance from common concerns, less contact with the sisters, inclination to control, and failure to seek broad Community participation in decisions. As personal experience must influence any general survey, so it is the ultimate source of a community's continuity and measured pace of change. A desire for both of these appeared in respondents' perception of Sister Sue's deep love and concern for the individual sister's welfare and her "unflinching pursuit of task" in fulfilling the duties of office.

The compassion and empathy many experienced reflected a deeply prayerful life of faith in Providence, integrity, and commitment to justice. Frequent mention of her approachable, down-to-earth simplicity paralleled observations of her creative talent and warm hospitality. Perhaps the most significant mark of a magnanimous and gentle spirit lay in the comment that Sister Sue "communicates peace."[23]

As Others Saw Them

Two effects of renewal observed by appreciable numbers of the sisters—a deepening of their prayer life and the growing influence of their Vincentian charism—appeared indirectly in responses to a survey sent to colleagues, friends, and Associates in 2002. Of 237 surveys sent, 115 or 48.5 percent were returned, approximately a third of them from friends, slightly fewer than a quarter from colleagues, almost 12 percent from Community Associates, and just under 9 percent from institutional board members. Students and alumni, employees, and parishioners responded in lesser numbers. Others identified themselves as chaplains, retreat directors, college faculty, volunteers, clergy, family, and legal counsel. Several categories overlapped in respondents' identification of themselves. Association with the sisters ranged from four to eighty years, with small concentrations at twenty and thirty years. Slightly more than 60 percent were lay persons.[24]

Because the mailing list derived from sisters' suggestions, the respondents do not constitute a random sample. No question in the survey required rank ordering of choices. Nevertheless, the listing of response percentages in tables below uncovers clear patterns that suggest reliability of outcomes. Asked to choose qualities that signified the Community's strength, well over 80 percent marked professional competence. Slightly fewer chose evidence of spirituality. In equal numbers, close behind were commitment to the poor, especially women and children; service to those in need; and evident happiness or peace in religious life. Joyfulness in min-

QUALITIES SEEN AS COMMUNITY'S STRENGTHS	PERCENT OF CHOICES
professional competence	83.48
evidence of spirituality	79.13
service to those in need	78.26
commitment to the poor, women, and children	78.26
evident happiness or peace in religious life	78.26
joyfulness in ministry and relationships	77.39
kindness and sensitivity to another's situation	73.43
intellectual acumen or leadership	68.70
creative energy and initiative	68.70
willingness to share spiritual experience with others	66.95
prudent use of resources, personal and material	66.09
unity as Sisters of Charity, with tolerance of diversity	65.22
freedom of spirit and flexibility in service	62.61
fairness and directness in dealing with others	60.00
contributions to civic community where located	60.60

istry and relationships and kindness and sensitivity to another's situation followed. A second pattern included intellectual acumen and leadership matched by creative energy and initiative. Willingness to share spiritual experience and prudent use of resources were another pair. Approximately two-thirds of the respondents observed unity with tolerance for diversity among Sisters of Charity. Sixty percent or better saw a freedom of spirit and flexibility in service, fairness and directness in dealing with others, and contributions to the civic community where sisters were located.[25]

Numbers who identified weaknesses fell considerably. The quality marked by somewhat fewer than a fifth of the respondents was failure to collaborate in roles of leadership. Approximately 15 percent of the respondents marked overextension of resources in ministry, apparent lessening of a spirit of community, and a lifestyle at variance with professed poverty. In another pattern, stress in work relationships with lack of a joyful spirit, reluctance to delegate responsibility, high priority assigned to work, and failure to assume leadership in religious or civic undertakings drew attention. Fewer still marked inadequate knowledge of social issues. Work-related issues, like delegation of responsibility and priority placed on work, suggest links with weakness in collaboration; the data, however, cannot confirm a connection.[26]

QUALITIES CONSIDERED WEAKNESSES	PERCENT OF CHOICES
missing opportunities to collaborate in leadership	19.13
over-extension of resources in ministry	15.65
apparent lessening of spirit of community	15.65
lifestyle at variance with professed poverty	14.83
stress in work relationships, lack of joyful spirit	12.17
reluctance to delegate responsibility	11.30
high priority given to work	10.43
failure to assume leadership in religious or civic undertakings	10.43
inadequate knowledge of social issues	9.57
lacking initiative in cultural, intellectual, or creative activity	6.95
little acquaintance with contemporary movements or ideas	5.22
behaviors inappropriate for religious	5.22
reluctance to share resources and benefits of prayer	3.48

OBSERVED CHANGE IN MISSION AND SPIRIT OF SISTERS OF CHARITY	PERCENT OF CHOICES
continued growth in service to those in need	80.87
relinquishment or inadequate service to those in need	35.65
continuing growth in spirit of charity	68.70
diminishing evidence of spirit of charity	15.65
continuing witness of sisters in their community living	60.00
diminishing evidence of such witness	12.17
continuing growth in simplicity—unencumbered living consistency in relationships	51.30
diminishing evidence of spirit of simplicity	24.35

Asked about change observed in the mission and spirit of the sisters, a majority of the respondents saw continuity or growth rather than diminishment in service to those in need. More than two-thirds saw the same in the spirit of charity. Encouragingly by this time, 60 percent found continuing witness of the sisters in their community living. Only half, however, perceived simplicity as characteristic of the sisters in an unencumbered way of living and consistency in relationships.[27]

Significant but limited influence of association with the Sisters of Charity appeared in responses. Chief among benefits was increased understanding of the life and ministry of women religious and, to a lesser degree, of contributions of women to religious and civic life. Influence on respondents' spiritual life and sense of purpose was considerable for slightly fewer than two thirds of the respondents. For half or fewer, affirmation of the value of collaboration and of their roles in service to the Church was a benefit. Just 30 to 40 percent deepened their understanding of the Church, of the Mass, and sacramental life. The spiritual maturity of respondents may well account for the patterns; limitations of the question in listed choices may also have affected its results.[28]

INFLUENCES FROM ASSOCIATION WITH SISTERS OF CHARITY	PERCENT OF CHOICES
in understanding of life and ministry of women religious	80.86
your view of roles, contributions of women to religious and civic life	73.04
your spiritual life, sense of purpose	63.48
affirmation of importance of collaboration	51.30
in understanding your role in direct service to the Church	50.43
in understanding of charism and mission	48.70
in understanding of the Church	41.74
in appreciation of the Mass and sacramental life	31.00

As for preferred service to God's people by Sisters of Charity in the next half century, 75 to 85 percent of the respondents marked ministry to the poor and disadvantaged, health care, and social services. With no limit on choices, approximately two-thirds marked ministry to women and children and parish ministry, including pastoral and administrative roles. More than 60 percent included collaborative work in ministry, leadership roles in the Church, parochial schools, work for peace and justice with influence on political and economic decisions, and spiritual ministry. Clearly, these respondents placed much confidence in the sisters' experience in ministries developed during renewal. Consistency and certitude were characteristic of their expectations. Continuing ministry for sisters in Community-owned institutions, marked by slightly more than 40 percent, reflects not only understanding of reduced numbers available but also confidence in lay leadership of sponsored ministries.[29]

Individual comments themselves produced instructive patterns. A simple remark set the tone: "The community was about its mission and service to the poor before I worked with [them]." Respondents had decided views about the sisters' ministry in areas of great need. Two observations that the sisters "have a tremendous impact in the inner city" and show concern for staffing and fund-raising for inner-city schools were reinforced by a state-

Jubilee: "Year of Favor from the Lord"

ment that traced earlier changes on a national scale. "Confusion, fragmentation, relinquishment of inner-city education [and] hospitals" followed "a venture into individual apostolates" that led to losses. "Some communities completely dissolved," the respondent continued. "The SCLs held on.... They weathered the storm. Gradually, they again returned to these apostolates, only in forms necessary for the modern world."

MINISTRIES IMPORTANT FOR COMMUNITY IN SERVING GOD'S PEOPLE	PERCENT OF CHOICES
ministry to poor and disadvantaged	85.22
health care: hospitals, clinics, home care	75.65
social services: children, aging, youth, families, counseling	73.91
ministry to women and children	68.70
parish ministry: RCIA, scriptural study, music, youth, pastoral and administrative roles	64.35
collaborative work in ministry with God's people	62.61
leadership roles in the Church	61.74
parochial schools	61.74
work for peace and justice, influence on political and economic policy	61.74
spiritual ministry: retreats, spiritual direction	59.13
in developing countries	48.70
collaborative roles in civic community	43.48
Community-owned institutions	40.87
public education	26.96
public agencies	24.30

Another respondent was specific about "education of the young in elementary and high schools in the inner-city, care of the sick, especially the elderly, care of abused children" and leadership in these fields. Houses like a Spanish-speaking community in the inner city drew mention from one who saw in Martha and Mary's Way in Lawrence "a prime example of ecumenical community sharing." One who had heard sisters express their desire to work with those too poor to afford the assistance saw the Community subsidizing their work.

The Mission Fund of the SCL/Health Services Corporation demonstrated to others a commitment to projects for those without medical resources. New medical outreach to low-income persons in Leavenworth and Topeka was a sign of mission for the future. Decades of association lent perspective. Two respondents found the sisters much more intentional in their desire to help the poor and vulnerable than twenty years previously and viewed them as consistently spiritual in those endeavors. Another remarked how well they worked with those "really in need, the ones looking for someone of faith." Approval of the sisters' decision to reaffirm the charism of Vincent de Paul summed up such observations.

Reservations and questions about increased lay leadership of schools and sponsored institutions reflected regret that sisters were no longer much in evidence. One respondent expressed the "need for a concrete presence of religious life within a lay community." Another said the issue is not their "continuing witness" but the diminishing number with few to succeed them and the growing consolidation of hospitals. Dismay at changed administration for some stood parallel to another's admiration of growing charity in the same institution, making it one of the "most generous hospitals in the region." Perceptive observations of sisters coping with the tension of "living in the world" provoked a comment that women religious, "struggling with how to sustain their charism and mission," are "one of the strongest units in the Catholic Church." Formation and training of lay leaders was commended. One remarked that "as demand for our services grows our best champions are the sisters...."

A number of respondents recorded effects on their lives and service. Long association contributed to observations of constancy of purpose, unwillingness to be overcome by adversity or challenge, exceptional leadership, and a practice of continuously evaluating their goals. One expressed awe at the sisters' "steadfastness in providing for the poor and needy." Others recalled a motivation to re-examine life and ministry and significant opportunities to show their own faith and expand their roles. A long-time partner in leadership said that "the sisters are a beacon of values, spirit and service. They are the one constant in our lives that humbles me," and a reason for continuing to serve.

The witness of individual sisters in their community life as religious was especially powerful for many respondents. Some named sisters they knew well as examples of giving, loving, and "a true spirit of justice." Others saw a consistent attitude of simplicity or even its increase in sisters holding leadership positions. Contrast came in comments on loss of a common life in moves to small groups or apartments and adoption of up-to-date attire. Individual observations of sisters "acting like corporate executives" or of apparently more importance attached to job or apostolate than to community witness were reminders of how readily behaviors and words impress others.

One who had lived in religious community said that sisters who live apart miss "an important component of what it means to be an SCL." Another admired the commitment within the congregation to live in community rather than singly and occasions of all the sisters coming together for special meetings and decision-making.

But above all, reference to deep communal affection and loving service characterized responses. A respondent recorded words of a store clerk who pointed to sisters she had just waited on: "I can always tell [sisters] because of the kindness they show to each other." Others remarked the "joyful and open expression of love toward one another," great fondness and a care for each other, a sharing of life.

One respondent found the sisters "pure in spirit, meaning ready to serve; ready to drop whatever they may be engaged in to be with someone in need, to provide comfort...." The symbol offered for such comfort was a "covered dish being brought to a home or person in need." That simplicity echoed in another observation: "I never doubt the commitment to God and service to others. Yet they do it with such joy and zest for the simple pleasures of life." The same respondent said, "They are serious about their vows."[30]

Though it comes from only a fraction of the hundreds of co-workers, friends, and clergy associated with the Sisters of Charity of Leavenworth over the past fifty years, such affirmation of their developing mission in the life of the Church witnessed to the unity they sought in the last decade of renewal. Their clear identity as daughters of Vincent de Paul and Louise de Marillac and as pioneers in ministry on American frontiers was a credit to their founders. What lay largely hidden from the general public and from many in the Church was continuity between the visible and much loved religious community as it had been and the smaller, less visible, and widely dispersed community of women who still claimed their name with pride, continuing loyalty, and love. What they unconsciously cherished, without realizing its full impact, was the witness they gave to what traditionally identified the first Christians: "See how they love one another."[31]

CHAPTER 23

Motto for Community: "Choose Life"

It was as if the heart of the world, filled with compassion, reached out to the victims, their families, and heroic rescue workers of September 11, 2001. Images of the World Trade Center's twin towers crumbling, of firemen and police plunging into smoking rubble, and of human beings flinging themselves out of flame's reach repeated themselves on screen and in dreams for the days and weeks that followed. The united resolve that met the tragedy spoke a kind of invincible hope that would not be humbled. But the strength of humility, distinct from humiliation, lay hidden in individual hearts and minds.

The Community Council invited the Community at large to prayer for victims and perpetrators. They pledged recommitment to nonviolence, to the sacredness of human life everywhere, and to respect for the common home of the earth. Approaching the anniversary of September 11 the next year, the Community took heart from the mission statement of an advocacy organization, "September Eleventh Families for Peaceful Tomorrows." It declared "a commonality with all people similarly affected by violence throughout the world" to break the cycle of "violence and retaliation engendered by war."[1] Along with religious congregations throughout the country, the Sisters of Charity invited residents of the Leavenworth-Lansing community to join them in vigil each Friday evening in Annunciation Chapel. Sister Constance Phelps, Community councilor, engaged sisters in creating the hour's Taize prayer for peace throughout the world.

Sister Constance's work on the Community Council found parallels in regional and national assemblies of the Leadership Conference of Women Religious. Evidence of her practiced leadership, profound spirituality, and capacity for vision brought election the following year as vice president of the Conference. The office entailed a three-year commitment to serve as president in the second year and past president in the third. In its thirty-year history as LCWR, the organization had promoted the spiritual welfare of women religious of the United States, ensured increasing efficacy in their ministries, and fostered cooperation among religious congregations and with the hierarchy, clergy, and lay associations. Issues of social justice and peace entered their agenda as Pope Paul VI closed Vatican Council II declaring the Church to be for the world. During the decades that followed, LCWR united the voices of its members who, by 2002, numbered one thousand congregational leaders representing some seventy-six thousand women religious in support of Gospel principles and protest against their abuse.

Sister Constance Phelps, President of LCWR, 2003

With other members of Region 13, Sister Sue Miller and councilors met in El Paso, Texas, in the summer of 2002 and crossed into Mexico for a first-hand look at programs assisting families, especially women and children, in need. Social and religious agencies in Mexico and Texas sponsored a women's center, housing projects, counseling services, and assistance for immigrant communities. For ten to fifteen years, women religious had trained women on the border in leadership skills and in methods of building covenant communities of faith.

The dignity and direction of LCWR's statement in 2003 concerning the crisis of allegations of clerical abuse typified the organization's clear purposes and fearless action:

> We are saddened, by the suffering and violation of the victims and their families, the actions of the perpetrators, the allegations against the falsely accused, the way in which the actions of some have implicated the whole clergy, the institutional Church's pattern of silence, the erosion of trust in church leadership among the faithful, and the deep hurt experienced in all parts of the Body of Christ.... In spite of the dark place in which we find ourselves at this time, we are filled with hope. We know that we are all part of a broken world; and, in our faith, we trust that the brokenness can be healed.

In the national assembly of 2003, the members welcomed Sister Constance to the office of president.[2]

A religious community is as strong as its individual members acting for the good of the whole, an ideal that persistently exceeds their grasp. The pioneer founders of the Sisters of Charity of Leavenworth had encountered that truth in the physical frontier that beckoned them and required resources they did not know they had. A century and a half later, their religious leaders and innumerable new neighbors depended again on the willingness of women to trust together a Providence leading them to horizons beyond clear vision and apparent resources. The strength of the Community depended not upon numbers, but upon their fidelity. This chapter recounts individual and communal actions that demonstrate fidelity to an original compelling purpose and hope in a future no one could see with any certainty or reassurance. The persistent mark of that hope was a habitual cheerfulness in the face of discouragement and an abiding, if sometimes unperceived, joy in a common endeavor.

These qualities in their sisters were invaluable for those who were aging, infirm, or approaching the unfamiliar territory of retirement. Visiting sisters in Ross Hall was a faithful practice of many community members. These included not only longtime friends but also the youngest sisters who acquired the habit from postulancy days. A particular comfort in years of illness was the company of blood sisters. Their number was a sign of what had contributed to the early growth of the Community. Since its foundation, ninety-seven pairs of sisters, seventeen sets of three, and three sets of five had entered.[3] Early recruitment of young women from Ireland explained some of the numbers.

No simple fact, however, could explain the longevity of many sisters who lived their final years in Ross Hall. Still a phenomenon at the turn of the century, one hundred years of living drew attention from the media and brought family and friends to the campus for celebration. Sister Ann Dolores Muckenthaler, who had been growing more and more forgetful for a year before her hundredth birthday, found herself on the day of celebration surrounded by nieces and nephews and her youngest brother, "Sam m' lamb," whom she had helped to rear. Enlivened by her company, she chatted for two hours with a *Kansas City Star* reporter, answering every question with energy and no little wit.[4]

A Harvest Committee's project, designed to discover common threads and practical attitudes in the thoughts of those aging and nearing retirement, included 111 conversations with sisters and 24 with Associates working full- or part-time or retired. Common themes ranged from anxiety about physical loss to amazement and gratitude for life as it broadens and deepens. Thankfulness for each new day and the need to grow in awareness of God marked conversations in all groups. Responsibility for one's well-being within limits imposed by aging was another. A sister's voicing "great faith in our young sisters" found its echo in an Associate's desire "to be present to the young."⁵

Spanning the Decades

A committee in the long range study drew up a Philosophy of Aging developed in consultation with Mother House and Ross Hall sisters as well as many on the missions. Among beliefs flowing from the commitment of Sisters of Charity to live Gospel values were convictions that each sister, whatever her age or ability, is a contributing member of the Community; that the stewardship of physical, mental, and spiritual health is a lifelong responsibility; and that the gift of life is a call to return this gift in full freedom to God.⁶

Attention to and growth of young members, urged in more than one of the conversations on aging, constituted the developing program of initial formation in the new century. Ten years' work in vocation ministry proved the mettle of Sister Noreen Walter, who in 2000 was one of only three vocation directors to be honored nationally for contribution in that ministry to the Church in the United States. The award for her service and leadership came from the National Religious Vocation Conference. Early in 2001, Sister saw renewed interest in religious life among young women responding to programs like Vocation Awareness Days, discernment retreats, and Come-and-See Weekends. At the Third Continental Congress of Vocations in Montreal in 2002, she spoke of these signs to eleven hundred delegates all involved in vocation work and youth ministry: young adults, parents, priests, bishops, and members of secular institutes.⁷

In the Rite of Acceptance into the novitiate celebrated at

As assistant coordinator of the Mother House, Sister Irene Hanley wears many hats, not least important playing hostess at a Fourth of July party.

the Mother House in August of 2000, Elizabeth Adams and Melissa Camardo were formally welcomed as candidates by the Community. The commitment made before family, friends, sisters, and Associates who responded together to their words quietly dramatized the spiritual force of religious symbolism and ritual. In her work with prospective candidates, the vocation director, Sister Sharon Smith, called on young sisters and applicants for accounts of their recognizing a call to religious life and identifying a community by its charism.[8]

Narratives like these from some of the youngest members of the Community witnessed to the initial formation program they had experienced under Sisters Nancy Bauman and Kathleen Wood from 1996 through 2002. After assisting in the program and studying at the international Institute of Religious Formation in Chicago, Sister Mary Beth Minges became director of initial formation in 2002. With three other professed, she led the creation of a community environment for two candidates in the fall of that year. Volunteer work with sisters in the Mother House and conversation with sisters in area houses were priorities of their schedule.

In a letter of March 2002 to Sister Sue Miller, Community director, Sister Susana Córdova Castillo, formation director in Peru, wrote: "Cordial greetings from La Arena, our hot little city of beautiful countryside and simple people who in their daily lives live with confidence in the God of life. This time of Lent our loving God leads us to look at our lives and the lives of the poor and to make personal changes in order to follow him, recognizing and accepting his merciful love."[9]

With a view to forging strong connections among the sisters who entered the Community after 1970, the Council hosted a gathering at the Mother House after Christmas of 2002. These young sisters had grown up in community without the ties of large novitiate groups; many had not lived in houses with sisters of wide age-range bound by common ministry experience. About a third Peruvian, the group of thirty-eight represented almost as many ministries. In the invitation to the gathering, the planners wrote: "We look forward to a future at which we can only guess.... It is important that we know with whom we face the days to come.... We stand between a past that has immense import and significance and a future of unimaginable challenge." The group called themselves "Between Alpha and Omega: *el fuego del amor nos urge*."[10] The paraphrase of St. Paul's words, "...the love of God urges us on" (2 Cor 5:14), suggested that unknowable ends were to be the fruit of their beginning in charity.

Recognizing bonds of even longer duration, the Community began to celebrate forty years in Latin America in August of 2003 and continued

On the fortieth anniversary of their first mission in Peru, Sisters Irene Skeehan, Patricia Kielty, and Susana Córdova greet Archbishop Oscar Cantuarias P. after Mass.

through the following June. Forty-six Sisters of Charity and Hermanas de la Caridad who had lived in community and ministered to the people of Peru, Bolivia, and Guatemala over the four decades were honored in the liturgy of Founders Day, November 11. A Christmas gift, a statue of the Virgin of Evangelization, designed by the late Max Inga of the Chuculucanas Diocese of Peru, came from his family, with small models for every house of the Community in the United States.

The climactic event, however, for the Peruvians was the homecoming of one of the first missionaries, Sister Irene Skeehan, in November 2003. Sister Helen Forge, Community secretary, made the journey with her. Monty Mace, from the staff of the archdiocesan paper, *The Leaven*, traveled to Peru to photograph and narrate the event.

The two-week festivities began with Mass celebrated on November 8 by Archbishop Oscar Cantuarias, prelate of Piura/Tumbes. Parishioners from Talara down the coast and Chalaco and Ayabaca up in the mountains came during days that followed to welcome the Hermanas de la Caridad. Endless stories of first encounters with the sisters from the North and of the people's own work now in pueblo, town, and countryside filled the time. A daughter of a Talara family told of her prison ministry; a husband boasted of his wife's taking Communion to the sick—works that women could not think of doing when the sisters first came. Training the people in catechetics, health care, and pastoral ministry was the initial work and primary achievement of the missionaries.

Delayed in her missionary calling for thirty-six years, Sister Rose Dolores Hoffelmeyer spent ten years in Peru before she was asked to write the history of the Community's Latin American missions. She completed the work in 2004. Although she enjoyed her teaching in elementary and secondary schools staffed by the Community, beginning in 1987 Peru became her home. Her narrative included special ministries of the young *hermanas* who envisioned during their three-year formation period what needs of their people they hoped to meet.[11]

Hermana Julia Huiman Ipanaque undertook civic activity in Chalaco, where poverty is deep. Making materials and helping to build adobe houses and organizing health programs and small pharmacies only suggested the range of her competence. She counseled women in the home on child-bearing, child-rearing, and schooling and organized *trebago* (worker) communities. Hermana Esther Filela Gutierrez taught religion at the high school level in four districts including Talara and conducted weekend retreats for public school youngsters. She was one of four teachers chosen by students to work for protection of children and elders against sexual abuse and violence.

Trained as a professional reflexologist, Hermana Maria de los M. Orozco Olaya practiced in four locations and taught methods of reflexology to approximately fifteen women each week. Her work in Promotores Sociales, community organizations dedicated to improving systems, gave her much influence with civic officials and other male leaders.[12] Between 1995 and 2003, Hermanas Maria and Laura Rumiche in succession coordinated the archdiocesan office of health ministry, Pastor de Salud, in Piura/Tumbes.

Realizable dreams for the future of the Peruvian community included a St. Vincent Center in the Santa Rosa parish that would offer health and social services, counseling, reflex therapy, and ultimately ministry to a

Cheerful schoolboys at Ignacio Merino in Talara listen to Hermana Esther Vilela's instructions.

growing AIDS population. An alternative school in Chalaco was drawing for its organization upon the *hermanas* trained in teaching. The Jesuit schools of Fe y Alegria, Faith and Joy, were sites for their observation. Five Peruvian sisters were engaged in pastoral ministry. Offered by the Conference of Religious, a course in leadership for religious life proved beneficial for three *hermanas*, with others to follow. In 2005, the community numbered nine Peruvians who had been Hermanas de la Caridad for five to twenty years and six North American Sisters of Charity.[13]

Hermanas All

Despite physical distance, unity between sisters across continents seemed more realizable at times than unity within diverse ministries. More than a decade of determined efforts by the Community to find communion in mission was bearing fruit by the turn of the century in support of sponsored ministries and in rallying points for individual initiatives. More than six thousand neighborhood volunteers started early and worked through rain into the evening of a Christmas-in-October Saturday, 2003, in Wyandotte County, Kansas. Approximately seventy Sisters of Charity were among the number that made 412 houses safer and more habitable in addition to repairing a few community centers and schools.

In her thank-you note of the previous year, Sister Mary Jo Coyle, organizer for Habitat for Humanity projects since 1988, acknowledged the help of relatives, friends, co-workers, and young people recruited by the sisters for their Quindaro Street project. She admired the fact that, "as the work gets harder, your numbers grow." In Leavenworth, the Community contributed substantially to the Kaw Valley Habitat for Humanity; sisters served on the Kaw Valley Habitat Board and Selection Committee and worked in on-site projects.[14]

Concerned for the decline of neighborhoods in Kansas City, Kansas, Sister Mary Geraldine Yelich became a "drive-by inspector" who informed appropriate city officials about the location and dangerous condition of unoccupied houses. Her persistence week after week, month after month, brought action on many houses; she continued to badger officials about others that were visible contradictions to the city's public pride. Sister Mary Lex Smith, retired from ten years of teaching and fifteen years of parish ministry, joined the staff of Safehome Inc., a shelter for battered women in Johnson County. The work qualified her as domestic court advocate for victims of domestic crimes. In that role, she assessed victims' situations for the court, supported them in hearings, and followed up severe cases. Her work prepared her for broader responsibility in 2000 as coordinator of the Victims' Assistance Program in the district attorney's office in Wyandotte County.

At El Centro in Kansas City, Kansas, Sister Linda Roth instructs adults in life skills and clerical competencies.

A different but related undertaking affected lives of Wyandotte County residents. Early in her twelve years of service at El Centro Inc., Sister Linda Suzanne Roth designed Keyboards to Success, a computer-based clerical job development program. Within the next decade, the program moved approximately six hundred adults from little or no employment to skilled clerical positions. Beginning in 1993 with five borrowed computers, Keyboards trained students in computer applications, life skills, and office competencies. The women and men grew not only in skill but also in self-esteem and confidence. On the program's tenth anniversary, Sister Linda was recognized for her work by the Kansas Department of Human Resources and by Mayor Carol Marinovich and the Unified Government of Wyandotte County and Kansas City, Kansas.[15]

An unusual kind of assistance to veterans came with Sister Jane Albert Mehrens's persistent efforts to find a place of transition for men recovering from treatment but uneasy about living on their own. Administrators of Dwight D. Eisenhower Medical Center in Leavenworth sought the help of Catholic Community Services in providing for the veterans. In collaboration with officials of the Medical Center and the City of Leavenworth, Sister Jane Albert studied possibilities and saw the potential of a former administrator's home on the grounds of the Center. All work on the house was done by Robin Frank, interior decorator, and volunteers from Pilgrim Church and the community of Leavenworth.

Reveille House opened in 1996 and welcomed twenty-three residents in four- to six-month stints during its first year. Its success proved contagious. A second home, Reveille Annex, was prepared by Frank with new volunteers from military families of Fort Leavenworth. Recommended by the director of planning and community development, Sister Jane Albert received the Audrey Nelson Community Development Achievement Award in a ceremony hosted by the Veterans Administration in Washington, DC, in 1996. Serving as director of Catholic Social Services for eleven years prepared her for her next ministry as outreach coordinator for Leavenworth's Alliance Against Family Violence.[16]

Consistently supporting individual and group initiatives, the Community continued its commitment to systemic reform and collaborative relief efforts on behalf of the most helpless victims of poverty. With firsthand knowledge of conditions in Haiti, the Council responded to the request of a veteran missionary, Sister Janet Cashman, to work for two years in a mission of the Daughters of Charity. She helped care daily for some forty malnourished children aged six months to five years before she moved to a food distribution program organized by the Vincent de Paul Society. Young adult professionals and students, not too far removed from poverty themselves, served the center and gathered weekly to reflect on scripture and works of the Vincentian family. Before returning from Haiti, Sister Janet trained ten eucharistic ministers for the parish to bring Communion to more than sixty elderly and chronically ill in their homes.[17]

During a two-week break from her job as nurses' aide at a diocesan housing facility in Denver, Sister Rosella Mary Hehn traveled to Cochibamba, Bolivia, and to Peru with a group from Water for People (WFP) to learn how the organization operates. Working with native citizens, WFP builds holding tanks, filtering systems, reservoirs, and pipes that bring fresh water to a central pump. Training a local management team was crucial to long-term maintenance in approximately ten communities of the region that provide some five thousand people with safe water, sanitation services, and health education.[18]

Sister Paula Rose Jauernig, nurse practitioner, returned to Jamaica for the third time in the summer of 2004 to work with health care volunteers of all faiths in a mountain village clinic built by Johnson County Disciples of Christ. "We gave them time and supplies," Sister said of the young and old who came for assistance. "They gave of themselves.... It is humbling to see how they get along so well with so little."[19]

Networks within the Community and with national organizations of women religious were uniting the sisters in a grasp of their broad significance for the mission of the Church and for fidelity to their Vincentian charism. In 1989 the Community took a corporate stand against capital punishment. With the Charity Federation, LCWR, and countless other groups, it joined the Jubilee 2000 campaign for debt forgiveness for heavily indebted poor countries. Associates' earliest formal participation in an ongoing Community structure was membership on the Social Justice Executive Committee. Approximately fifty SCLs and Associates were among forty-five hundred persons who endorsed the public statement of December 2001, "A Catholic Community Responds to the War: Living with Faith and Hope."[20]

In 2002 the Community Council named Sister Therese Bangert, longtime advocate in the Kansas Legislature, to succeed Sister Marie de Paul Combo as Social Justice coordinator. While at St. Vincent's Home, Sister Therese had been chaplain for the Topeka State Hospital for thirteen years and ministered to prisoners. With her appointment to the Kansas Sentencing Commission and the Mental Health and Corrections Committee in 1991, she worked as special advocate in the juvenile system and later became assistant coordinator of the Kansas Coalition Against the Death Penalty. The Archdiocese of Kansas City in Kansas called on her as a consultant on rural life and ministry and as an advocate for welfare reform. As chaplain to police officers of Wyandotte County, she learned conditions and effects of crime firsthand. In her role in the Peace and Justice office, she joined the Community director in signing with other religious leaders a 2003 published statement of support for the United Nations.[21]

Nourishing the Spirit

Deepened attention to bonds of spirituality had been growing in deliberations of the Community Council during the last decade of the century. The first Marillac, adapted in 1977 for use as a small place of prayer, was razed in 1998 and a number of sisters asked for its replacement. At the close of their term that summer, Sister Mary Kathleen Stefani and the Council recommended construction. In view of developing needs of the sisters for assisted living, Sister Sue Miller and the new Council undertook plans for a new Marillac that would provide a fully equipped spirituality center adaptable if necessary to residence for aging sisters. Renovation of the Mother House for gradations of retirement and health care was part of the planning.[22] Initial work of the Renovation Committee was presented to Community members at home in 1999; consultation with representative groups from the

Marillac Center welcomes individuals and groups seeking quiet accommodation for conference, recollection, or retreat.

Mother House, Ross Hall, and the novitiate brought suggestions and concerns to light.

As its mission statement indicated, Marillac Center provided "an environment of prayer, peace, hope, and transformation" for those seeking "to grow spiritually and deepen their quest for God." Connected to both the Mother House and Ross Hall, the Center's spaces accommodate retreats of every kind for individuals and groups up to fifty. More than 250 sisters, Associates, and guests assembled for the dedication of Marillac Center on the feast of St. Louise de Marillac, March 15, 2003. After blessing of the cornerstone, Sister Sue Miller, Community director, recognized Sister Mary Loretta Beier, director of the original Marillac Place of Prayer, and introduced Sister Noreen Walter, director of the new Marillac.

From that time forward, the Center calendar was filled weekly with guests of many faiths, professions, volunteer organizations, and Community ministries from Leavenworth and Lansing, nearby areas of Missouri and Kansas, and distant states. Almost 50 percent of them came for retreats throughout the year and days of recollection during Advent and Lent.

The Center proved true to its mission of sharing the holy ground, the story, and the charism of the Community. Diverse groups found the quiet and beauty of the place conducive to prayer, discernment, and planning. Witnessing to the spirit of hospitality, over the first two years of its life the Center hosted retreats directed by thirty-eight Sisters of Charity of Leavenworth, seventeen sisters of other communities, a Christian Brother, and priests from eighteen different congregations and dioceses. Collaboration with other spirituality centers in the area led to an exchange of schedules, program information, and referrals for specific needs. An advisory committee to work with Marillac Center staff included Sisters of Charity, friends, and Associates.[23]

Honoring the late Mother Mary Francesca O'Shea, the O'Shea Conference Center was dedicated in February 2004. At the dedication, Sister Sue Miller acknowledged the contributions of and extended the Community's thanks to Pete and Pat Zink, who had served both Mother House and University for more than twenty-five years. Retired from his position as manager of physical facilities at Fort Leavenworth, Pete became plant manager for the campus and supervised all major building projects of the Mother House and the University. Gratitude took the form of a new organ for Ross Chapel, commemorating the Zinks for their generosity.[24]

The Mother House sisters concluded the renovation of their home by affirming the mission statement written by several of their number and posted for all to read:

As the Mother House of the Sisters of Charity of Leavenworth, our mission is to be a welcoming, heart-centered home where we witness and proclaim God's love for all. We commit ourselves:
  – to love and care for each other and for all those who enter our doors,
  – to respect the dignity of all creation, and
  – to create an atmosphere of prayerfulness and joy.

Evidencing the deepening desire among many for spiritual growth and experience of community, sisters took other initiatives in sharing their resources. Xavier Community in Denver was a model for a similar Xavier House in Kansas City, Kansas. Four young women joined the sisters to share in their daily community life and prayer. A doctoral candidate, a student teacher, a chemist, and a social worker pooled their monies, helped pay bills, and shared homemaking tasks with the sisters. Within a few years from the opening of the House of Menuha in Kansas City, Missouri, a group of clients formed a board to manage long-range planning and development. They wanted the project, initiated by Sister Ann Loendorf, to continue with its quiet time and place for women to rest in purposeful, if brief, retreat.

Mutual enrichment was the experience of a number of women who came to know Catholic sisters as partners as well as a resource for spiritual growth. Martha and Mary's Way, an inter-faith ministry, took on permanence with the acquisition of a forty-two-acre wooded plot southeast of Lawrence, Kansas, a place for prayer, reflection, and respite. Sister Irene McGrath, with twenty-five years' experience in pastoral ministry, and a collaborative board had started up a small project while at Corpus Christi parish. In 2000 she was invited back to direct the facility.[25]

Deep in the Smoky Mountains surrounding Maggie Valley, North Carolina, Sister Francis Marie Grady pursues prayer ministry at Living Waters Reflection Center, an Augustinian retreat house. A professional painter and former college teacher trained for spiritual direction, she serves on the staff as sabbatical advisor and resident artist. Teamed with a member of the Cherokee Nation, a professional storyteller and instructor in Cherokee spirituality, she leads retreats set in the solitude of forests and mountain streams.[26] Artists in the Community in retirement from teaching, Sisters Mary Rebecca Conner and Carmen Echevarria, nourish and share their gifts with sisters at home in studio, gallery, and the quiet places of Mother House and campus.

In a mountain setting on the Yellowstone River high in the Rockies, Sister Dominique Long has ministered for seven years in St. Mary's parish and school and to the sick and the dying in the community of Livingston, Montana. After twenty years on the staff of Jesuit programs—Ministry Training Services in Denver and Focus on Leadership in Spokane—Sister sought direct ministry to her own Community. Discernment with her councilor led to residence in Livingston where she composes music for religious and public markets. Her scores for the poetry of John of the Cross and in the mystical traditions of East and West give wide range to her talent as pianist and composer. Grateful for the Community's blessing on her time in the West, Sister funds her work with grants from the Wasmer Foundation of Spokane and similarly assists other musicians in the Community. Sister Dominique believes that the contemplative spirit flowing from the arts is a need in community life.[27]

CONTINUITY WITH THE PAST

Renewal had taken root among the Sisters of Charity at the level of their radical commitment to live in response to the call of Jesus expressed in the counsels of the Gospel. Maturing in the spiritual life produced not complacency or routine, but the desire for deeper union with God. Ministry remained at bottom Vincentian in character and direction. It required a rigorous and demanding life of prayer and a unity more dependent on desire than on organization. The demands and the desire were bearing fruit in the quality of community life and in commitments that brought the sisters together in collaborative approaches to ministry and in acknowledged needs. Perhaps the most concrete instance of that unity appeared in continuing care for and attention to the needs of children and the aging in a new century.

During thirteen years in Archdiocesan Housing in Denver, Sisters Mary Clarita Sternitzke and John Vianney Martinez, accredited residence managers, inaugurated a Celebration of Cultures with displays and a musical program recognizing the clients they served whose origins lay in twenty different countries. A lay woman, Mary Boland, and the board of directors were committed to the primary focus of Archdiocesan Housing: subsidized and affordable housing for low-income seniors and families of all faiths. Sisters Mary Siefkin and Karen Guth were responsible for HUD properties.[28] Under the combined leadership of bishops, pastors, religious, and laity, the faith community of the Denver archdiocese embraced its elderly and its children with equal affection.

At Mount St. Vincent's Home in the fall of 2002 at the groundbreaking for a new school, Dallas Rychener, first lay executive director, called on the community of Denver and the state of Colorado to elevate the children to the priority level that they deserve. The $3.5 million structure, to be named in honor of Sister Daniel Stefani, was to serve special needs of the Home's residents and day-time population.[29] This common ground of the Community's legacy and Denver's generosity had been harrowed and planted over the past decade.

What began as a fund to support seven inner-city Catholic elementary schools became by 1996 the Seeds of Hope, a charitable trust maintained by major benefactors of both schools and Mount St. Vincent's Home. High school basketball teams, parish volunteers, the Denver Broncos, Amoco employees, U.S. West Airlines, telephone company volunteers, and the school children themselves were partners in the enterprise. At Mount St. Vincent's 120th anniversary celebration, alumni in their eighties returned to recount stories of growing up there in boyhood. Four Sisters of Charity on a staff of ninety-two, Sisters Jean Marian Rilinger, Roberta Furey, Josephine Bustos, and Michael Delores Allegri, welcomed them even as younger sisters came in a new century to fill new posts at the Home.[30]

Sister LaVonne Guidoni enjoys supper with residents of Mount St. Vincent's Home, Denver.

Three Sisters long experienced with children and licensed for foster care took youngsters into their convent homes during the 1990s when many were suffering from extraordinary problems and social agencies' overload. Sister Michael Dolores, who entered the Community hoping to teach first graders or care for orphans, learned instead the ways of adolescents, teaching them for twenty-three years. Missioned to Mount St. Vincent's as an intermediate unit manager responsible for eight- to eleven-year-olds day and night, she was ready to oversee a group home when it opened on the campus. When the Community Council in 1999 saw the foster-parent role bearing good fruit and realized there was available space in the original building at Mount St. Vincent's, they assented to Sister Michael Dolores's request to provide a home with personal care for five children. Year by year, Sister received referrals from social agencies and Catholic Charities through the courts.[31]

Broad effects of the sisters' evolving experience at Mount St. Vincent's, however, were systemic as well as profoundly personal. Their leadership throughout the last decade of the century in collaborative efforts to raise standards of foster care was crucial. Strict requirements for placement, licensed care-givers, trained foster parents, and oversight of care in foster homes were not yet common after 2000 in judicial and social service systems. Adequate education and compensation of caseworkers were basic but not the rule. Advocacy with the governor and legislature of Colorado was a priority on the agenda of Mount St. Vincent's administrator. Sister Amy Willcott became executive director of the Home in 2004.

Awards acknowledged the initiatives of individual advocates but could not measure the effects of their ministry. Over twelve years in the eighties and nineties, Sisters Margaret Mary Driscoll and Anna Mary Lawrence

A young resident registers with Sister Amy Willcott, director, for a cottage at Mount St. Vincent.

Sister Marie Noel Bruch evokes a smile from Fuli, brought from China through International Adoptions.

had served as foster parents to sixteen girls and boys between the ages of five and twelve. Before they retired from the ministry, Temporary Lodging for Children, the agency responsible for referrals, found adoptive parents for Brian, aged twelve. The sisters did not recommend the adoption but had no authority to prevent it. Abusive discipline, applied to the boy and his adopted siblings over the course of more than two years, caused Brian's death. Public mourning and belated investigation prompted local change that signaled need for broader reform and a study of inflated impersonal systems. The experience of twelve years convinced the sisters of the need for a continuum of care for each child, with strict criteria, review, and oversight at each stage of foster parenting, adoption, and aftercare.

While administering the Community's office of Ministry Development, Sister Margaret Mary collaborated with the Sisters of St. Joseph in Adoption Ministry, a licensed child placement agency in the state of Kansas. With broad networking and sound knowledge of client families, they remain in support throughout the adoption process. Eleven years at St. Vincent's Home in Topeka prepared Sister Marie Noel Bruch for her work for Catholic Social Services of Montana. From the end of 1981 through 2002, she counseled birthparents and their families, conducted home studies of adoptive parents, and arranged for placements of infants through open adoption. The work took her across endless miles of western Montana.[32]

Three new residential cottages were completed by 2000, each of them accommodating twelve youngsters, with a resident staff member, in a homelike environment. Schooling of both resident and day treatment children at Mount St. Vincent's Home in Denver was certified both by North Central and by the Council on Accreditation of Services for Families and Children. An evolution of the personal attention given children at the Home, the Individualized Education Plan (IEP), adopted at the turn of the century, required participation of a parent. Convincing the mother, particularly of an abused child, that her contribution was valuable revealed to Sister Mary Rachel Flynn, the school's director, something of what it means to feel not simply powerless but worthless. For such a mother to learn that knowledge and love of her child were the source of good counsel for the child's future moved her toward her own healing.[33]

In many unforeseeable ways, a ministry of the Sisters of Charity of Leavenworth came full circle with these developments in child care as the first century and a half of the Community's foundation was approaching. Mother Xavier's welcome of orphaned children into the sisters' first convent home on Kickapoo Street re-echoed in the acceptance of children into convent homes in Kansas City and Denver. The story of growing strength in the smaller but vigorous Leavenworth community was a continuation of the work of Louise de Marillac, whose instincts and faith were mirrored three centuries later.

Response to Need as the Key

During the thirty-eight years of her ministry, Louise responded to needs where she found them. Education for poor women, housing and occupational training for the elderly poor, and resettlement of refugees drew her attention. Willing assistance came for food banks, homeless women and children, and indigent hospital patients. She started a system of care for infants in the Mother House of the Daughters of Charity; with the Confraternities of Charity in Paris she initiated a program of foster care in private homes and cottage care for children.[34] Subsequent generations of Sisters of Charity were moved by the same kinds of needs.

Evidence of the professional competence and deepening knowledge of what traditional and new ministries required in a new century came by way of a final survey of Sisters of Charity, both active and retired. In acknowledgement of the value of everyone's experience, the survey was sent in the fall of 2002 to 358 sisters or almost 93 percent of the Community, whose median age by then was seventy-two. A return of 55 percent reflected willingness to cooperate in an enterprise requiring faith in a less-than-clear rationale and no little concentration. Religious ministry during the previous four decades had undergone deep change, not to mention individual transitions. Admittedly, any attempt at assessment with change in swift progress was complex, if not questionable.[35]

The first question asked respondents to estimate for their primary ministry *fundamental change or continuity* (a) in religious institutions, whether or not sponsored by the Sisters of Charity of Leavenworth; (b) in Community ministries of any kind; (c) in the ministry's explicit witness to the Gospel; and (d) in their individual experience of the ministry. Items under each head specified what change or continuity they may have observed. As in earlier surveys, responses evidenced care in registering impressions and evaluating effects. In general, respondents chose to mark only those items that fell within their experience. Without close analysis for greater objectivity, the most salient results are significant.

In institutional ministries, an equal number of responses indicated impressions of change and of continuity in attention given to special needs of the individual. In spite of ambiguity in the question, broad response suggests the consistent priority of this value in the sisters' ministry. In all Community ministries, experience of work with lay administrators and colleagues left substantially equal impressions of change and continuity, with *no change* explicitly added by almost a quarter of the respondents. Between a third and 44 percent emphasized change in varying degrees in the need to educate lay leaders, in the call to new areas of ministry, and in collaboration with other institutions.

The third section of the question, a ministry's explicit witness to the Gospel, drew the highest number of responses. Attention to the poor or marginalized carried heavy emphasis on continuity, while a high number also marked continuity in attention to fairness and justice toward employees. The choice continued, though with more marks for change, in attention to justice with regard to each Sister of Charity, in attention to women and children, and in knowledge and application of Catholic social teaching. Evidence of other Gospel values varied substantially. In 2001 more than half of those responding to the item saw change rather than continuity in the power of their ministry to diminish racial discrimination. Sixty percent of a like number found change in willingness to take a corporate stance on issues of peace and justice.

Similar patterns of change prevailed in individual experience of ministry. Almost equal evidence of continuity, however, appeared in freedom to initiate or implement change, in freedom to assume responsibility for projects, and in the need for formal education in new fields of service. Such balance may well be due to varying age and experience of community among respondents. Larger gaps between change and continuity marked a growing need to consult constituents and authorities outside the Community and to educate lay women and women religious for roles of leadership.[36]

Asked to assess significant impact on witness to the Gospel of any five of the items listed, respondents both affirmed fundamental values and identified issues that either reflect or require concerted action. More than half of those who responded to the question emphasized growing attention to the poor or marginalized. Well over a third added increased attention to women and children and only slightly fewer, refashioning responsibility in mission and ministry as collaborative. Somewhat less than 30 percent listed attempts to live and work in solidarity with the laity, a corporate stance on issues of peace and justice, and attention to fairness and justice with regard to employees. A quarter of the respondents chose influence or role-modeling of women religious.[37]

Certain patterns in individual comments added both concerns and affirmations. Recognition of witness to the Gospel in the integrity of sisters' daily lives and their accountability in ministry accompanied insistence on continuing conversion and deep prayer life. Needs for education of laity in continuing spiritual leadership paralleled new awareness that lay colleagues may develop their own charism in ministry. The working premise that each sister in her ministry stands for the Community in its mission was complemented by the expressed need to inform the people of God about what sisters do and to provide visible signs of consecrated religious life.

Values of advocacy and awareness of oppressive social structures met fears of growing bureaucracy—as opposed to collaborative leadership—in Community governance and sponsored ministries. But increased involvement of laity "always and everywhere" was affirmed. Hopeful realism informed the plea to reassess the focus of community energies in the light of the laity's responsible and visible roles. Diminishing numbers require creative response to needs and collaboration with all stakeholders if the Spirit and call of the Gospel are to guide the Community's stewardship.

Change within continuity, said one, arises from overwhelming demands. To maintain its Catholic character, ministry requires theological underpinnings. It calls both members and leaders to focus on issues of peace and justice. Their role as educators asks sisters to be a prophetic voice of the Church. In the words of another respondent, justice is "the new face of charity."[38]

Response to a question about the most significant obstacles to growth of a ministry revealed certitude that lack of financial resources is the chief problem. Combining first through third choices produced the same result. With the same combination, lack of committed colleagues to carry on the work vied for second place with lack of vigorous leadership. Next in line was unawareness that lay colleagues may develop charism in their own ways as participants in the ministry of Jesus. The fifth most serious obstacle in a given ministry, according to a similar count, was basic differences in interpretation of values.

Obstacles to ministry added and assigned first rank by eight respondents may also be important to others: lack of sufficient background and help in developing a Gospel-centered spirituality that should permeate a school; influence of media, politics, and "computer trash"; [need for] understanding of who we really are and our purpose as spiritual beings; lack of structures in place to accomplish ministry; need to include anyone, regardless of race or ethnic group; official attitudes in the Church toward women; clericalism; and societal structures.[39]

Asked how the sisters are "handing over the heritage of ministry" to lay leaders, 54 percent of the respondents chose, as the chief emphasis, attention to mission as response to Gospel and to the ministry of Jesus. Slightly fewer than a third chose attention to the SCL mission and charism. Thirteen percent emphasized attention to lay members' sense of personal or corporate mission. Primary agents and means of making the transition, according to respondents' marks, are Sisters of Charity on staffs, prayer in common, and administrators. Orientation, designated Mission persons, and workshops were marked as other major channels of change.[40]

Aspects of ministry most significant for the witness of women religious in their mission and service were judged, in telling numbers, to be

- quality of relationship with student, patient, client, or parishioner,
- willingness to share fruits of prayer life and spirituality,
- willingness to be a prophetic voice when ethical or moral issues arise,
- capacity for creating community with co-workers,
- working collaboratively, and
- exercising leadership, whether directly in office or informally and morally.[41]

If repetition and statement of the obvious plagued the format of the survey, such conclusions are ample reward for respondents' hard work. These priorities, selected as concrete witness to the Gospel, source of their vowed life, and to their mission and ministry with the people of God, are substantial fruits of renewal. Individual voices, never lacking in this Community, lend urgency and eloquence to persistent themes. Whatever their age, ministry, or degree of activity or retirement, the Sisters of Charity of Leavenworth were emphatically choosing life.

CHAPTER 24

Teaching:
A Heritage Firm and at Risk

Education in the faith through a vast Catholic school system was a priority of parents, pastors, and bishops during the last half of the nineteenth century and well past the first half of the twentieth. That Catholic schools began in the 1970s and 1980s to number fewer religious on their faculties raised questions about the quality of teaching and discipline that characterized institutions of elementary and preparatory education. Doubts were frequently laid to rest by the professional performance of lay teachers and lay administrators. The partnership of religious and lay educators that had evolved over three decades and the advances these educators had negotiated together were familiar to parents, pastors, and parishioners intimately involved in their schools. Determination to maintain or build Catholic schools gathered momentum in the last two decades of the century and took various directions.

At the annual Catholic School Foundation dinner in Leavenworth in 2002, Father Charles McGlinn told the members:

> The world desperately needs men and women of Christian character, who cannot be bought; who can honor their commitments; who put character above wealth; who are willing to take risks; who will not lose their individuality in a crowd;... who will make no compromise with wrong; whose ambitions are not confined to their own selfish desire; who are not ashamed or afraid to stand for the truth....[1]

His words were a credo for Catholic schools of a new millennium. But in the same issue of the Xavier Schools newsletter, Margaret Anne Kearns, president of the Foundation, pointed to a difficulty. She said that it was unclear whether most Catholic families paying taxes to support public schools could commit themselves to Catholic education. "Maybe it's a question of will," she added, "renewed will and determination." Many had not experienced Catholic school education yet were calling in to say "they want an education with a faith component, one that has the moral values."[2]

This veteran of Catholic schooling was voicing a complex paradox facing Catholic educators at the beginning of the new century's first decade. On the one hand, parents, churched and unchurched, wanted for their children a future built on sound moral attitudes and belief. On the other hand, except for those who were financing expensive new academies of the kind they favored, parents were uncertain about who should lay the foundations for that future. Catholic schools that had evolved from the past stood at a crossroads of solvency and leadership.

Coordinated school systems initiated variously by school boards, religious and lay principals, or diocesan school offices had been flourishing for at least a decade. Sisters of Charity and their lay successors had helped to organize them in Leavenworth, Billings, and Butte. In 2003, Mike Connelly, principal of Immaculata High School in Leavenworth, was named director of the Xavier Schools. He had been at Immaculata for twenty years as teacher, athletic director, and, since 2000, principal. Susie English became the new administrator of Xavier Elementary. Individual sisters remained in the system. How to maximize their role was more than a casual question. Maintaining the charism of the Sisters of Charity was still significant for the mission of the Xavier Schools as it was conceived at the turn of the twentieth century. Experience of that mission lived in the memories of countless teachers, alumni, and parents.[3]

Appreciation of an educational heritage handed down through families, parishes, and religious communities took various forms throughout the nation. Late in the 1990s, seventeen Sisters of Charity gathered in Laramie, Wyoming, to celebrate forty-five years of Catholic education at St. Laurence O'Toole School. Two of them, Sisters Mary Cecilia Lenherr and Eileen Sheehy, were among the original nine who started the school in 1951. Five years into the new century, a crowd gathered in Oklahoma City to celebrate with Sister Mary O'Rourke as she received the Distinguished Graduate Award from the Department of Elementary Schools of the National Catholic Educational Association. The award recognized in this graduate of Rosary Catholic School distinguished service to the Catholic Church and to the nation.[4]

These were tokens of the gratitude and dedication of hundreds of thousands of Catholic parents whose faith and labor had supported a private school system for their children while they simultaneously paid their dues to the nation's public schools. If the memory of sound teaching and collaborative ventures was still significant for development drives, practically speaking it no longer informed long-range planning. When Sister Katherine Franchett returned to Leavenworth after twelve years in Billings and began to serve on the school board, she found that the base of support had indeed expanded in the region. Parishes provided a healthy 40 percent of the budget. But the challenge of enrollment remained with a reduced pool due to an aging population and smaller family size. Cultural factors inhibited perception of the value of Catholic education.

People in Partnership

The economy of scale that produced the coordinated system had saved the elementary schools. But the excellence of Immaculata High School's core curriculum and the quality of students who won Knowledge Bowls and ranked high in national standardized tests could not compete with the size and numbers of a public high school that for many meant recognition leading to university scholarships. Another factor was quietly at work. Students' formation in the faith and growth in religious understanding require both parents' and staffs' maturing in faith and participating in administrative decisions. The first means expenditure of time; the second means integrated leadership. Chaplains, campus ministers, and teachers of religion committed to students' spiritual formation were not ordinarily included on the administrative level.

A genuine renaissance or maturation of Catholic education depends on more than maintenance of familiar symbols, scheduled religion classes, and required religious exercises. It requires a depth of understanding and religious motivation that grows over years in home and school. A generation's loss in such growth led in the 1990s to what the National Catholic Educational Association identified as a "quiet crisis" of both breadth and depth.[5] What was wanted for the future was the collaboration of lay educators and parents imbued with the mission of the Church itself. Understanding of that mission was the source of renewal for both parish and religious community life entering a new century. Collaborative vision and planning were crucial.

Although conditioned by local cultures, the need was nationwide. Capital campaigns at the turn of the century in Billings and Butte, Montana, demonstrated Catholics' support of their school systems. When Sister Elizabeth Youngs retired after seven years as director of the coordinated Catholic school system, the Billings Area Catholic Educational Trust (BACET) had successfully completed a $7 million campaign. The monies boosted teachers' salaries, built the Ralph Nelles Activity Center, and raised the endowment to $1.7 million. Nelles had been Billings Central's "most valuable athlete" in his student days and was the campaign's "all-star donor." Throughout the system of three elementary schools and junior and senior secondary schools, enrollment was stabilized; day care centers and an infant-toddler program had waiting lists. The total enterprise depended on a community proud of its private schools as an alternative to the public system. One indicator of respect for the central Catholic high schools was that nearly half of their populations were enrolled from public elementary and middle schools.

From her office as associate superintendent of schools for the Denver archdiocese, Sister Elizabeth recalled an important principle she had learned from her experience in Billings—that the coordinated system worked because the schools were self-contained as successful institutions.[6] It is a principle applicable at every level: strength at the administrative center depends upon the strength of each operable part. She and the lay superintendent were applying it to thirty-eight elementary schools, five secondary schools, and seven stand-alone pre-schools in the archdiocese.

In Butte at the close of the Tradition of Excellence Campaign in 2000, special thanks to donors were expressed with sincerity by administrators of Butte Central Catholic Schools. JoEllen Estenson, principal of the high school and junior high, credited parents, students, parishes, alumni, benefactors, and staff for financial support and contribution of their time and labor. Sister Mary Jane Schmitz, administrator of Butte Central Elementary Schools, was grateful for a six-classroom addition and expansion of early childhood and day care programs. The Butte Central Foundation where campaigns originated maintained a system with scaled tuition open to all. A mission statement was crafted from drafts submitted by faculty, staff, students, and parents.

Traditions as old as Catholic schools themselves assumed new forms in fund-raisers and volunteer groups. New initiatives appeared in endowed faculty scholarships, deferred giving agreements, and a partnership between Butte's Catholic schools and more than one hundred local businesses called the BC Futures Program. Certificates for discounts on purchases benefited tuition accounts and promoted local shopping. Linking past and future, challenge grants from the Cardinal Foundation, established by the family of Thomas and Marie O'Brien MacLeod, enabled Butte Catholic Elementary School in 2004 to add a state-of-the-art classroom building that housed a sizable computer lab, the school's library, and an expanded Noah's Ark Daycare. Other Cardinal grants contributed to scholarships and faculty salaries.[7]

Such generous support, however, points to another principle voiced by a layman in the Eastern Montana Diocese when Sister Jean Martin

Dawson went to Great Falls as superintendent of schools. "The people who pay for a school," he said, "should be the ones who decide it should stay open." The question is not simply one of authority, clerical or lay. If mission implies clear Catholic identity, facts of stewardship speak to the will and determination as well as material means of the parents and parishioners who must keep the school solvent. On the other hand, decisions must take into account the needs of children locked into contingencies of local economies and family resources. The people of a diocese, the Church in small, take responsibility for one another.

The Diocese of Great Falls–Billings did not support the school system. In addition to Sister Jean Martin, only four women religious, three of them full-time, served in the diocesan school office. Financial aid to students in real need came from a budgeted amount of "real money." For the Catholic schools to remain open and accessible, it was necessary to issue to all parishes a clear statement of total costs, of cost per student, and of objective assessable conditions for individual financial assistance. Shared information included total revenue from parish assessments; the education trust, BACET; and the annual May Fair, or auction. As for the schools' Catholic identity, that was visibly dependent on common prayer, liturgy, and sacramental life. Though more difficult to discern, responsible behaviors and interaction among teachers, staff, and students were marks of the religious learning community.[8]

Meaningful integration of all this and more was the responsibility of lay administrators—not all of them Catholic—and teachers convinced of their priority. The mission of Catholic education, central to the mission of the Church, meant conversion of mind and heart if the eucharistic table was to be accessible to all who came and if its grace was to permeate both the spirit and life of the schools and those who supported them. With dramatic shifts in parish and school populations and revolutionary changes in educational methodology, diocesan school offices in the late decades of the twentieth century became more serviceable than supervisory, attentive to assessable outcomes, and open to students of diverse backgrounds. Long-range strategic planning and central funding required leadership from lay and religious educators of broad experience and deep conviction, whatever their church affiliation or spiritual values.

Constant Call of Inner City

The Central City Schools Fund, established in the 1980s by Bishop John J. Sullivan and Father Norman Roetert for the Diocese of Kansas City and St. Joseph, Missouri, is an example of new challenges for the church's educational mission. Operational allocations for schools in financial need and tuition assistance were its chief concerns. The fund's second director, Sister Barbara Schrader, spoke to sources of its major challenge: city expansion that multiplies the number of suburban parishes and enlarges the core of inner city schools; diocesan funding spread thin as costs of Catholic school education increase; growing demands on foundational support; and changing demographics in a more transient population with a larger number of families at poverty level.

The profile of a Central City school in 2004 showed 72 percent of its students from diverse racial and ethnic minorities, 63 percent living at or below the poverty level, and a third or more being raised by a grandparent or other guardian. More than two-thirds of the students received scholarship assistance, and many of the students were from families with an average annual income of less than $21,000. Nevertheless, the approximate cost per child in a Central City school was half the cost of public school education per pupil.

Strict criteria applied by review boards to applications from either a school or an individual student assured good stewardship of the funds supplied by the diocese and by foundational, corporate, and individual contributions. By the end of 2004, six Central City schools and a pre-school received support from the Central City Schools Fund. These schools were what remained from the closures, consolidations, and mergers of thirty-two Catholic schools staffed by nine congregations of women religious and one of men. Eight of the schools had been staffed by Sisters of Charity of Leavenworth who played a significant role in three of the mergers.[9]

In the Archdiocese of Kansas City in Kansas, the Gardner Institute was a legacy of Monsignor Henry F. Gardner, first superintendent of schools for the archdiocese. Its large goal was to provide programs and services for non-public schools in Wyandotte County. The Institute prevented schools in financial straits from closing and fostered standards of excellence for others in need of support. During Sister Vickie Perkins's term as director, faculty in art, language, reading, and ESL were hired and Early Childhood Centers established. A Learning Club, part of a national program, provided mentors in reading and math for participants of all ages. In 2004 the institute was subsumed under the Catholic Education Foundation of the archdiocese.[10]

That the mission of Catholic education was in good hands was evident in a *Kansas City Star* report in the spring of 2005 on building, renovation, and expansion progressing in schools of the Diocese of Kansas City–St. Joseph, Missouri, and the Archdiocese of Kansas City in Kansas. Twenty-six elementary schools and seven secondary schools evenly distributed on either side of the Missouri River served almost 13,000 students in Kansas and more than 11,600 students in Greater Kansas City, Missouri. Investment over five years of more than $40 million in Missouri and approximately $35.5 million in Kansas witnessed to the dedication of Catholic people and broad support of civic communities for schooling they respected as academically excellent and committed to students' religious and moral growth.[11] This account did not, however, reveal the difficulty of making Catholic education available to families with incomes inadequate for the schools' tuition.

Availability of education in such a tradition was not so secure for increasing numbers of Catholic youth. When she returned to St. Labre schools in southeastern Montana in the fall of 2004, Sister Bernadette Helfert realized that the mission statement, carefully drawn up by the school board she had chaired for four years, was a plaque on the wall, little more. As the new director of Mission and Ministry for three schools in a K–12 system and two elementary schools about one hundred miles away, she was responsible to the executive director who had hired her. Not a Catholic himself, he knew the mission of this school system on the Cheyenne and Crow Reservation had originated 121 years before when Bishop John Brondell had obtained Ursuline sisters to teach the young Native Americans evangelized by Jesuit missionaries. The mission of the school was integral to their culture.

Long years in education taught Sister Bernadette Helfert how vulnerable children are in their first steps of learning.

About a fifth of his faculty at St. Labre were Native Americans; at the distant Pretty Eagle and St. Charles Schools, more than half were Native Americans. Sister Bernadette set about visiting individually with each of the teachers and their Caucasian colleagues to determine whether the Mission of St. Labre was still viable. She called the enterprise "Mission Quest"; it began with stories of the schools and those who had established them. What she learned deeply impressed her. Across the board, many welcomed her explanation of the mission statement and its core values. They liked the prospect of liturgical celebrations and asked about student retreats. More than a few expressed a desire to deepen their faith. One young woman had for some time wanted religious instruction for baptism. A Mission Council for the schools was a promising prospect. The situation of St. Labre was exceptional, but it illuminated what was happening elsewhere with less immediate results.

Sister Bernadette reflected that sisters who staffed schools in Catholic communities assumed that the mission of Catholic education would continue. The schools' strength and the sisters' partnerships with lay colleagues encouraged the assumption.[12] Relatively few realized the ultimate cost of that educational mission embedded as it is in the mission of the Church. Declared in papal and episcopal documents of the decade, justice requires that the values of Catholic education deriving from the Gospel of Jesus must be open, in as many ways as necessary, to all who seek those values, regardless of a family's means or condition. Further, students' mentors must model the mission as Jesus proclaimed it. In words of Pope John Paul II:

> Catholic institutions should continue their tradition of commitment to the education of the poor in spite of the financial burdens involved.... If students in Catholic schools are to gain a genuine experience of the church, the example of teachers and others responsible for their formation is crucial: The witness of adults in the school community is a vital part of the school's identity.[13]

The U.S. bishops made an unqualified assertion in their 1998 call to action addressed to Catholic educators, lay and religious: "If Catholic education and formation fails to communicate our social tradition, it is not fully Catholic." Sharing that tradition—which insists on the essentials of human dignity for all and on rights of the most vulnerable—they declared to be an "essential part of Catholic faith...proclaimed whenever we gather to worship." This expansive mission was now to be realized in its fullness by the lay women and men who staffed schools throughout the Catholic faith community.[14] Although sisters still served the transition to lay leadership and played leading roles in developing educational ministries, they were no longer the principal voice of the church's commitment to the children and youth of a new generation.

The schools, moreover, had to be financed by a Catholic laity convinced of the mission and values of a Church not to be defined in geographical or cultural terms and not to be identified with suburban parish growth. As inner city Catholic schools with mixed ethnic and low-income populations multiplied, they required larger allocations of diocesan funds. The funds themselves grew from realization by the faithful in more favorable circumstances of responsibility to a Church that knows no stranger. Models for lay leadership and programs for strengthening Catholic sacramental life were emerging from the collaborative work of parochial and diocesan teams.

Sisters in pastoral ministry continued to draw upon their educational experience to form parish groups for catechetics, liturgy, youth ministry, ministry to the aging, retreats, and RCIA. Although they did not think of themselves as modeling an essential element of the Church's educational mission, they were doing so. One who had served with two sacramental ministers as pastoral administrator of a parish and its two missions on the Hi-Line of Montana, a few miles from the Canadian border, observed the people's vibrant faith in action. Teaching, organizing, preparing liturgy, planning with parish committees and finance councils, she sensed "that the Church here is on the cutting edge of what is eventually going to happen across the country."[15]

As pastoral associate at Blessed Sacrament and Church of the Risen Christ in Kansas City, Missouri, Sister Joanne Sistrunk drew upon people's undiscovered talents to implement programs of advocacy, direct assistance, and educational development. Through a New Horizons Assistance Corporation, she mentored staffs of residence programs for persons with mental retardation and developmental disabilities. In the parish group Kwanzaa, she organized annual celebrations of unity, collective responsibility, and creative ventures.[16]

In Our Lady of Guadalupe parish in Omaha, Nebraska, Sister Mary Marcianna Trujillo organized a staff of forty-five volunteer lay teachers for the religious instruction of children in public schools. Sacramental preparation for adults in the growing Latino community added to an enrollment that grew over fourteen years from eighty-five to six hundred. Sister was one of several women recognized by Creighton University's Jesuit community on its 125th anniversary as Women in Ministry to the Poor. In 2004 she received the Outstanding Minister Award as Parish Religious Education Administrator.[17]

Wisdom at the Source

Education of a people to the mission of their Church could not now depend on a traditional system of Catholic schooling. It had to go forward wherever and however the people of God lived. It had to call on resources deeper than professional competence, developing technology, and unlimited knowledge. In a homily to the people of Pope John XXIII Catholic Community in Missoula, Montana, in 2003, their pastor, Father Ed Hislop, told them that Wisdom is found in ordinary, faithful human living. He invited "whoever is simple, [to] turn in here, for Wisdom is the desire to eat and drink deeply of the unknown and of what is yet to be discovered." The readings were to be realized in the act of "becoming the Holy Communion" of the Body and Blood of Christ, "the Wisdom of the Eucharist."[18]

About fifteen years earlier, a parishioner in the Saint Mary Community of Helena had said things during a retreat that echoed the "Wisdom of the Eucharist." She had introduced the idea of spending money on the place for liturgy because the Sunday gathering "calls us constantly to ask the greater questions of care of one another, the poor, the oppressed, 'those who thirst for justice.' Because we worship so well, so carefully," she said, "we are able to ask such questions."

What followed were first moves of a collaborative venture in renewal. It had actually begun in 1966 with the dedication of the new church of Saint Mary by Bishop Raymond G. Hunthausen in the working-class neighborhood of Helena's east side. Three decades later, in 1995, a communal enterprise of expanding the house of worship went forward in continuous conversation, self-education, and volunteer labor of parishioners aided by professional architects and artists. A steering committee—gathered by pastor, liturgy team, and pastoral council—involved the whole parish, local artisans, and ultimately the Diocese of Helena.[19]

Sisters involved with the people in such renewal learned how profoundly the mission of the Church and of a diocese depends on the dedication of its Catholic family. Newly appointed in 2005 as director of pastoral planning for the diocese of Helena, Montana, Sister Rita McGinnis works with Bishop George L. Thomas, the vicar general and chancellor, and the Diocesan Pastoral Council to produce a five-year plan for the Helena church. The Council of twenty-four lay women and men and a liaison with the presbytery represents the pastors and parishes of the diocese.

Sister Rita emphasizes the need for lay presence around the table of Eucharist and around all the tables of planning and administering. Such presence dramatizes, she said, the historical transition from clerical to collaborative management, in full support of the sacramental ministry of the ordained and in deepening influence of the laity on every aspect of Catholic life. For such collaboration, the spiritual development of lay leaders depends on strong formation programs and a life of prayer.[20] In Portland, Oregon, Sister Mary Jo Quinn heads the educational division of Oregon Catholic Press (OCP). Calling on years of experience as director of liturgy in the St. Mary Community of Helena, she organizes and trains lay leaders for workshops on liturgy with the help of materials published by OCP.

By the end of the century, renewal of the Church was a long-term process of education not to be accomplished by attempts to restore an idealized past. Examples of such programs were the undergraduate degree in pastoral ministry offered by the University of Saint Mary, Leavenworth, and the Institute for Teachers of Religion at Benedictine College, Atchison, Kansas. Both were established in consultation with the Archdiocese of Kansas City in Kansas.

Along with a legacy of Catholic education that integrates learning, professional integrity, and faith, the Sisters of Charity who staffed Saint Mary College in the latter decades of the twentieth century inherited a history. The women who preceded them were serenely stubborn in refusing to lower intellectual standards, blur the institution's Catholic identity, or reject a student unable to pay full fare. Those who remained—fewer in number and allied with a majority of lay colleagues—proved equally ingenious and perhaps more inventive in adapting pedagogy and re-creating curricula for the needs of an increasingly diverse range of students maturing in a technological culture of continuous change. An account of programs and developments, however, tends to obscure the depth of commitment by lay faculty and staff who choose to align themselves, at no little sacrifice of material compensation, with the mission of the university.

Sister Diane Steele checks out a parade float prepared by University of Saint Mary students, assisted by mascot Spiro.

When Sister Diane Steele was asked in 2001 to move from the theology faculty to the president's office of Saint Mary, she knew what her immediate tasks were and what they portended for the future. Familiar with Saint Mary as a student and alumna since 1979 and a respected voice on the faculty since 1993, she valued the priority assigned to teaching in the college and its commitment to students capable of advanced learning but unable to bear its cost. In 2000 more than 90 percent of those enrolled received financial aid determined by parents' resources and eligibility for scholarships, grants, and loans. Part-time work on or off campus was a necessity for many. By 2004, Saint Mary continued to educate a large number of lower income students, often the first generation of their family to aim at a college degree. Naturally intelligent, they frequently lacked academic skills. Summer preparatory courses and a learning center helped take up the slack.[21]

These needs of students and competitive salaries for highly qualified faculty were primary essential costs. The core of teachers at the helm of strong departments included Sisters of Charity and lay colleagues whose professional merit and continuous contribution to curriculum and student life secured the college's academic reputation and graduates' record of achievement. Administrators of the same professional quality and tenure made up the president's Academic Council. They included Dr. Sandra Van Hoose, vice president for academic affairs and dean of the college, who had chaired the department of education for six years. To meet an immediate need, Len Bronec assumed responsibility as interim director of the Institutional Advancement Office and volunteered on the staff until his retirement in 2004 when Molly Sirridge, class of 1975, succeeded him. Dale Culver served as vice president of finance and administrative services. Staff of long-standing administered library, offices, and evening degree programs. Faculty served on visiting teams of regional and national accrediting associations. Sister Mary Lenore Martin, professor emerita of history, was college historian.

Master's degree programs in teaching, education, business, and counseling psychology brought increasing numbers of evening/weekend students to the University of Saint Mary Overland Park site, directed by Patricia Howard. Coordinators of the education programs were Hattie Gilmore, Nancy Murphy, and Sharrilyn Honacki; the coordinator of the psychology program was Mary Matzeder. Graduates of the online master's program for teachers lent considerable depth and diversity to the student community. In order to strengthen the board of trustees, Sister Diane invited new members whose knowledge and experience extended the circle of counsel for the college.[22]

Students with a Mission

During the curriculum renewal initiated in 2001, a strategic planning process began with the charge to revise the mission statement of the college. Before the process was over, the governing board and Community sponsor had reached the decision, contemplated for some time, to announce the transition of Saint Mary to university status. The change brought Ron Logan to the administrative council as dean of graduate and continuing studies. Alumni and constituents, having contributed to its name and logo, welcomed the University of Saint Mary. Surveys and interviews within the population at all sites issued in a mission statement that explicitly focused on diversity of students, their God-given potential, and lives and careers oriented to the well-being of a global society. Values encompassed by the mission are community, respect, justice, and excellence.

Renewing the curriculum for a new century proved a challenge to teachers and students alike. To identify learning outcomes true to the mission for a generation of students technologically sophisticated but underprepared for college study was the first challenge. Design of structures and interactions for maximal learning and personal development followed. Learning Communities, in line with a national trend but unique to Saint Mary in content and organization, brought underclass women and men together with professors of different disciplines in an integrated approach to contemporary questions of broad significance in a global culture. Interaction was the fundamental method of each Learning Community. Professors teamed up by choice to offer six-hour courses in literature and ethics, the Christian tradition and the fine arts, business principles and personal finance, impacts of globalization on individual lives, diverse peoples who constitute civilization, and threatened sources of the planet they inhabit.

Upper level Idea Seminars developed from perspectives of a given field, creative figures, and seminal texts. A succession of seminars enriched major study and contributed to a campus culture of inquiry and dialogue.[23] The guiding principle of the curriculum was application of the liberal arts—of language, computation, analytic thinking, and synthesis—to practical problems of daily life. In direct service to the Church and diocese, theology faculty had developed a pastoral ministry degree attractive to undergraduates and adults serving their parish communities.

Recounting Sister Mary Janet McGilley's death on September 13, 2003, the editor of the alumni magazine called it the end of an era. Sister Diane, once her student, said her legacy was the spirit of community.[24] Maintaining that spirit in a time of intensive growth was the challenge. A combined graduate and undergraduate enrollment produced commencement ceremonies that required more space than Ryan Sports Center provided. With its Olympic-size courts and flexible seating capacity, McGilley Field House, designed to serve both the campus and civic communities, was dedicated in the fall of 2004.

Indicative of the resources for learning on campus and in the Leavenworth–Kansas City area, an annual Lincoln Lecture was inaugurated late in the 1990s to celebrate the Lincoln Collection housed in De Paul Library. By 2005, seven February events included lectures by two governors of Kansas, a Lincoln scholar, the commanding general of Fort Leavenworth, the first African American mayor of Kansas City, Missouri, a film-maker, and an African American athlete. The next year, the lecturer was Michael Lind, journalist and author whose biography, *What Lincoln Believed: The Values and Convictions of America's Greatest President*, was gaining national attention. Memorabilia from the Lincoln Collection of De Paul Library were on exhibit.[25]

During the Lewis and Clark Bicentennial, the library received another gift of primary historical value, Gary Moulton's definitive edition of *The Journals of the Lewis and Clark Expedition*. The university's location in Leavenworth on the Missouri River is an unparalleled historical resource. Unique in Kansas, De Paul Library received a grant in 2005 to support the six-part documentary film series, "The World War I Years." In conjunction with Leavenworth Public Library and the university's Delta Epsilon Sigma chapter, the staff complemented the films with lectures and discussions of literary classics of World War I.[26]

In view of the expanding society Saint Mary graduates were entering, a major program in global studies started up in the fall of 2003 under the aegis of the history and political science department, chaired by George Steger. The Global Studies Institute, designed to support and foster students' research and to offer its resources to the public, sponsored a monthly seminar for students, faculty, staff, and guests on a topic of national and international significance. In the fall of 2004, Lawrence D. Starr, friend of the university and member of the board of trustees, made a bequest to the Institute, believing in its potential for the expanding educational mission of the university.

The Institute's mission of education to justice and peace was exemplified in the fall of 2005 at a lunchtime session of students and faculty with Father Michael Gilgannon, missionary and professor at the State University of La Paz, Bolivia. He brought to the discussion three decades of pastoral and academic experience and a deep knowledge of the political and economic conditions of Central and South American countries.[27]

Far-reaching in its collaborative structure and designed to meet immediate needs of the health care community, a new nursing program at Saint

Mary under the direction of Karen Fernengle, RN, PhD, received licensing approval from the Kansas State Board of Nursing. Clinical rotations for the bachelor's degree in nursing were to be in place by fall 2006. A unique feature of the program was a formal agreement with area hospitals and affiliates of the Sisters of Charity of Leavenworth Health System. The hospital's provision of full tuition for a qualified applicant's education was complemented by the student's commitment to join the nursing staff of the sponsoring hospital on graduation. Following on two years of study in the arts and sciences, the student nurse applied specialized knowledge in the practice of nursing in clinical laboratories in the department and neighboring hospitals.[28]

Continuing Saint Mary's strong tradition of performance in the arts, eight students of the Concert Chorale joined Benedictine College's chorale over winter break of 2005–2006 for a ten-day pilgrimage of music and prayer across Italy. Singing for Mass and public concerts in cathedrals, basilicas, and churches in Milan, Venice, Assisi, and Rome, they performed *a capella* religious works and American spirituals for Pope Benedict XVI. In the same vein, private vocal and instrumental instructors prepared students for professional competition. On submission of a recorded audition, a sophomore tenor was one of thirty accepted from the country for the College Light Opera Company's annual performance in Falmouth, Massachusetts.

LEARNING AS SERVICE

When Sharon and Tony Albers visited with Sister Diane Steele in San Diego in the spring of 2003, their offer of a year's service to Saint Mary was unprecedented and virtually unbelievable. Retired and mindful of Sharon's years at the college, they wanted to spend time living in Maria Hall and working at whatever furthered the mission and the day-to-day operations of the university. At ease with students, they worked in the bookstore, assisted the registrar and alumni director, tended campus gardens, contributed to classes, and undertook whatever the president requested. SpireFest, a fund-raiser that got off the ground at the historical Kansas City Union Station and moved to the new Kansas Speedway, became a major project. Their primary assignment, however, was campus-wide.

Accompanying students on a third alternative spring break trip to Appalachia in Kentucky was an eye-opener. Repairing and building houses for families in dire need was learning of a sort they hadn't realized college students desired. Campus Ministry had long encouraged the kind of learning that service brought both in Leavenworth and on journeys to El Salvador, the Mexican border, and urban and rural pockets of systemic poverty. The Albers were charged with establishing a permanent Service

Learning office at the university. Before they ended their fifteen-month visit, they had engaged almost five hundred students and more than thirty faculty and staff working with as many community partners to provide 3,200 hours of service to Leavenworth/Lansing and beyond.

Alliance with Kansas Campus Compact, one of thirty-one state partnerships across the nation, committed Saint Mary to service integrated with learning in every discipline of knowledge and campus activity. The Service Learning office and Campus Ministry offered spring break opportunities for 2005–2006 with social service agencies in St. Louis; with children in Denver; with home-building agencies in rural Kentucky; and on a rural school/community project in Guatemala.[29]

Gateway to Success, a collaborative program with Bishop Ward High School, extended the university's strategies for assisting under-prepared and financially limited students. Of the student population, 65 percent were eligible for the federal TRIO program for students in need of academic skills; 40 percent were eligible for a Pell Grant.[30] On its twentieth anniversary in 2005, the university-sponsored OutFront program had awarded approximately two thousand diplomas during the two decades of its operation in downtown Leavenworth. Ranging in age from sixteen to seventy-two, students included individuals in need of a high school diploma equivalent, women preparing to enter the workforce, and immigrants and international visitors learning English or sharpening language skills.[31]

A Mission Integration Council recognized, through monthly nomination by their colleagues, students, faculty, and staff, those who exemplified the university's mission. That mission spoke most dramatically, however, in the lives of thousands of graduates. In its decades as a women's college, students and alumnae carried Saint Mary's mission into countless roles of leadership. Margaret Martin Stuart, graduated in 1948, served for twenty-five years as head of Child Welfare Services in Montana before she was elected to the board of the Child Welfare League of America, source of national standards for all such services.[32]

A 1986 graduate in art and history, Francine Orr won the coveted Photograph of the Year Award and competitions at state, regional, and national levels. As a lead photographer for the *Los Angeles Times*, she has brought to millions of American readers vivid images of dire poverty in the Sudan, of forced exile in Uganda, of the island culture of Micronesia, and of daily life in India's teeming cities, as well as in depressed areas of Los Angeles.[33]

The first city councilwoman of Kansas City, Kansas, Carol Marinovich, an elementary education major graduated in 1972, ended her six-year term with election as the first woman mayor of the city. Her vision of renewal and

Saint Mary alums Allison Messerschmidt and Alex Robinson, '97, congratulate Mike McNally on Molly's and his newborn daughter, Maggie, at a reunion of 1990s alumni. Mike graduated in 1998, Molly in 1999.

prosperity for her hometown led the way to a unified city-county government and brought major investors, including the Kansas Speedway corporation, to realize the potential of the city and western Wyandotte County.[34]

An English major of the same class, Mary Rieke Murphy, took her junior year at Maynooth University and returned to Ireland after graduation to marry Michael Murphy and rear their daughters there. She wrote for a Dublin newspaper, edits the Spiritan Fathers' magazine, and published a first book of short fiction in 2003.[35]

At Commencement in 2005, Rose Inza Kim Surh, 1958 graduate in chemistry, received an honorary degree from her alma mater. In her native country of Korea, as an academic dean of women, author, professor, businesswoman, and mother, she won acclaim in the field of reality therapy. With an advanced degree in counseling, she opened the Korean Counseling Center, work that brought her the National Presidential Award.[36]

An unusual appointment came to alumna Judy Vogelsang, MD, class of 1974, when the Croatian ambassador to the United States traveled from Washington, DC, to welcome her as the honorary consul of the Croatian community of Kansas City, Kansas and Missouri. On the faculty of the University of Kansas Medical Center, she led relief efforts among colleagues, fellow citizens, and parishioners for the people of Kosovo during the defense of their country in the late 1990s. Consuls from California, New York, New Jersey, Pennsylvania, and New Mexico attended the ceremony.[37]

During a stint in Afghanistan and Uzbekistan early in the war with the Taliban, Captain Charles DiLeonardo, class of 1999, trained fighters in the Afghan National Army. After injury ended his military service, he returned to the States for further study and training of both military and support leaders in Senegal and Mali.[38] Named by fellow students, staff, and faculty as worthy of the Ancilla Award in 2005, Joni Aukerman spent much of her time at Saint Mary in service to students and to residents of the community. Spring breaks took her to El Progresso, El Salvador, and twice to Appalachia, Kentucky.

The stories demonstrate the power of learning with a mission inspired by the Catholic heritage of liberal education and the Vincentian commitment to the least free and most vulnerable. They demonstrate as well the equal potential of women and men for transforming the Church in its families, parishes, and communities. A living image of this power and potential was the long line of new students holding lighted tapers and circling the interior of the Chapel of the Annunciation on the day of their matriculation in August 2005. Individually named by the president of the university, they were now members of the Saint Mary community who were committed to their learning, symbolized by the light each one held. "As a Catholic university," the president, Sister Diane Steele, said, "we welcome our brothers and sisters of other Christian denominations, our Jewish and Muslim brothers and sisters, our Hindu and Buddhist brothers and sisters, and all who are still searching. All are welcome in this holy space."[39]

A month later, students native to some twenty cultures encircling the globe gathered in the convocation ceremony that officially opened the academic year. Presiding at the Mass of the Holy Spirit, Father Michael Stubbs alluded to the mighty wind and tongues of fire that had descended on the apostles and enabled everyone—all in their own languages—to understand their words. Prayers of intercession spoken by students and faculty in their native languages —Somali, Brazilian Portuguese, Urdu, Russian, Hawaiian, and English— brought the assembly together as one in an act of worship that signified their interdependence.[40]

Bagpipers lead graduates to their commencement ceremonies in McGilley Fieldhouse.

Vehicles of Catholic education had evolved during the past quarter-century in new partnerships of laity

Xavier School students cluster around the image of Mother Xavier Ross, seated at the fountain in front of the Mother House.

and religious, parish and community, professionals and parents seeking structures and resources strong enough to sustain a legacy on which the life of the Church depended. Without family nurturing and support, students lack a lifeline to learning and faith in early years; efforts of certified educators and pastors are "cut off at the knees." At the turn of the century, new forms of collaboration were developing swiftly. Sisters were servants and leaders in the enterprise because they were some of the best educated and most experienced among the people of God and because the conditions of a celibate life in community freed them to discern priorities of ministry in Church and society.

That the sisters who persisted in the ministry of formal education were still responsible by their institutional commitments for the foundation of such learning was a truth concealed by the many faces of change. That these women were now singular partners of lay teachers, administrators, board members, and clergy increased rather than diminished their effectiveness. Whether this resource now concentrated in fewer numbers was to benefit the Church with all of its potential was not to be determined simply by official decisions. The heritage of teaching in whatever guise it had taken over the last century was carved out by pioneers. These were women undaunted as well by the shifting horizons and uncertain resources of the previous fifty years. They were accustomed to shaping the frontiers that beckoned them.

CHAPTER 25

Health Care in New Hands

In the early spring of 2005, the head of the Sisters of Charity of Leavenworth Health System affirmed that the mission and vision of the sisters was "alive and present in the system" they had built up over the previous 140 years. William Murray, commissioned as president of the system in 1999, had worked for twenty-five years in hospitals staffed by the Community and had served as the first lay CEO within the incorporated system. With a close knowledge of their operations and their leaders, he said that the sisters, past and present, personified the mission and vision of Catholic health care as they ministered. Now they did so in few and diminishing numbers. How to maintain and relay their mission and vision was the challenge.[1]

Response took shape at the turn of the century on three levels of collaborative effort. The Catholic Health Association (CHA) initiated a process of defining sponsorship for religious congregations engaged in health care. The SCL/Health System—its name simplified in 2000—strengthened its office of sponsorship and mission integration with specific initiatives. Each affiliate hospital created ways of integrating the mission and responsibilities of personnel engaged in the sacred ministry of healing. Sisters of Charity of Leavenworth played central roles in all endeavors.

At the national level, CHA invited a team of theologians and health care leaders to prepare a statement and program for education to sponsorship of leaders in the affiliate institutions and health care systems of the association. Authors of the statement, "Toward a Theology of Catholic Health Care Sponsorship," were Susan Wood, SCL, professor of theology at Marquette University; Doris Gottemoeller, RSM, senior vice president, Mission/Values Integration, in Catholic Healthcare Partners, Cincinnati, and a board member of the SCL/Health System; and Charles E. Bouchard, OP, president of Aquinas Institute of Theology, St. Louis. In their reflection, they identified the purpose of Catholic sponsorship in general: "to promote and sustain

Christ's ministry to people in need." Sponsors of Catholic health care act "on behalf of the faith community... continuing the compassionate healing ministry of Jesus." Distinct from governance and management, sponsorship is *corporate* in accord with civil and canon law; *relational* or collaborative with other religious and secular institutes and with the hierarchy; and *ministerial* in its participation in the mission of Christ and his Church.[2]

Three women who strengthened the foundations of the SCL/Health System foresaw the challenge of maintaining the Community's mission in health care as they prepared for generations of lay leadership. Sisters Mildred Marie Irwin, Mary Julie Casey, and Macrina Ryan exemplified the Vincentian heritage of ministry to all who come in need of health care and of collaboration with those most able to assist the ministry. Their deaths in 2003, 2004, and 2005 threw into relief the qualities required to secure the identity of Catholic health care. In turn, these women perceived the particular needs of the communities they served, managed resources necessary for excellent care extended to the most vulnerable and neglected, and led development of the system's collaborative arrangements and strategic planning.

Having served as president of the SCL/Health Services Corporation from 1974 to 1980, Sister Mildred Marie knew its potential and the risks of its growth. After a term on the Community Council, her personal ministry took her to Sacred Heart Emergency Housing Center in Denver where she coordinated the program for homeless families. From there she returned to Saint John's Health Center in Santa Monica to serve in community relations and the outreach program for the homeless mentally ill. One of five to volunteer for the Peruvian missions in 1987, she coordinated nutrition programs for tuberculosis patients in Piura and for pre-school children in Talara. In 1990, because of health problems, she returned to Leavenworth and volunteered at St. Vincent Clinic for as many hours a week as she could manage.[3]

Between her terms as a Community councilor and treasurer touching three decades, Sister Mary Julie was vice president for finance in the SCL/Health Services Corporation from 1986 to 1992. During that time, she served on the National Committee for Federal Legislation of the Catholic Hospital Association. Faith in Providence, a habit of stewardship, and willingness to seek consultation marked her character as an administrator.[4]

As the third president of the SCL/Health Services Corporation, Sister Macrina extended the circle of the system's board, which ultimately included sisters of sixteen religious communities. Her experience in administration of affiliate hospitals gave her insight into the need for health care partnerships and state contracts. She knew that conflicting expectations between a system and its sponsoring members are a source of tension that can either diminish or build its power. William Murray characterized

Sister Macrina in a letter announcing her death: "She demonstrated trust and a fundamental belief in the honesty, professionalism, and commitment of those with whom she worked."[5]

In their inaugurating SCL/HSC in 1972, the Sisters of Charity of Leavenworth, according to Murray, were about a decade ahead in the development of Catholic health care systems. Likewise in the 1980s and 1990s, their early study of sponsorship readied them for what was becoming a national agenda. Roles and relationships of sponsoring religious congregations and the boards of their separately incorporated institutions required that a community's mission be clear and normative for governance of a system and its affiliates. The challenges of managing tensions—between stewardship and care for the poor, between system resources and local needs, between a secular culture and Gospel imperatives—such tensions Murray saw as the means of creating and preserving community. Mission becomes the way for all "to hold themselves accountable."[6]

Such thinking may come from long association with those who founded the mission of a congregation's health care ministry; most people hired to staff the hospitals, however, come without understanding the implications of that mission. Knowing this, sisters in the field learned ways and means of integrating mission into the life of a hospital and conveyed to officers and boards of the system the seriousness of the need. At the corporate level, Sister Marie Damian Glatt established a series of annual Leadership Forums designed to educate affiliate and corporate officers and board members to developing demands of impending change. Mission, stewardship, collaboration, and centralized resources were crucial issues within and across systems. During her term, Sister chaired the Board of Consolidated Catholic Health Care (CCHC).[7]

In 1998 Sister Judith Jackson was named vice president for sponsorship and mission integration. Sponsorship of a corporate health care system by a religious community required common ground for affiliates in cultivating ownership of the values and goals that constitute their Catholic identity. In her role, Sister was responsible for providing strategies, resources, and means of assessing implementation of mission integration programs.

In a new generation of lay leadership, it became increasingly clear that such commitment grew from the spiritual maturity and moral conviction, as well as the professional dedication, of board members, administrative officers, directors and supervisors, and staffs of every service to patient and family. When the mission of an institution becomes the personal commitment of every employee and governing officer and its values are apparent in their day-to-day work and interactions, mission integration is a reality and tends to generate itself. This was the discovery of those who set about to bring abstract concepts of sponsorship to life in human settings, actions, and personal relationships during the early years of the millennium.[8]

Formation of leaders in mission and ministry gained momentum as the new century began. Sister Bernadette Helfert, vice president for mission integration at St. Vincent's in Billings and later for the Montana Region, presented to regional officers the idea of educating skilled leaders in Gospel values of the health care mission. Distinct from conventional training, the experience would call directly on the personal spirituality of participants. Encouraged to give shape to the concept, Sister invited Sister Jean Casey, director of ministry formation for the Montana Region, to design a program for education in mission and ministry of all CEOs, vice presidents, directors, and managers.

Each month for eleven months, leaders in three health centers spent four hours in successive sessions reflecting on the mission of healing, the heritage of their sponsoring congregation, and essentials of the institution's Catholic identity. Experience of meditation and prayer lay at the heart of each session. Presentations on the history of the Sisters of Charity of Leavenworth, ethical and religious directives of the Catholic Health Association, and traditions of spirituality fed discussion. Participants brought diverse religious and moral convictions to bear on conversations. In its third year, the program was offered in shorter segments to accommodate schedules of frontline workers in housekeeping, food services, maintenance, offices, and staff support.[9]

More specific ministry formation of administrators and directors, then of all employees, followed. The staff led two-hour sessions four times a month in each town that had an affiliate hospital. As sessions progressed, one fruit was an observable increase of workers' mutual respect and a sense of ownership of the institution's mission. A long-range benefit was understanding of spirituality as each one's personal gift and of high value in each one's contribution to a common enterprise. Sister Jean's perception of potential leaders in ministry formation led to a new level of the program's development. Response to her invitation to department directors to prepare as teachers or leaders in ministry formation implied a serious commitment.

While openness to all traditions and beliefs characterized the process, respect for personal faith and for the Catholic identity of the hospital allowed for emphasis on the Eucharist as the source of unity and regard for the human dignity of every individual in each new community. Sister Jean's demonstration of the program as an adaptable model was welcomed by health center staffs first in Montana, then in Wyoming and elsewhere. A Mission Council focused on particular values and functions of religious diversity in a health care institution, on liturgy, stewardship, and global outreach.[10]

The Foundation: Personal Commitment

Beginning in 2000, as director of pastoral care and mission services at St. James Healthcare in Butte, Sister Mary Agnes Hogan transformed the mission integration process, as then required for affiliates of the system, into a program of individual initiative and development. Environment was a priority; the meditation room became a place apart. Equally important, the program encouraged the conviction that work turned in the direction of God is prayer. Integration of Eastern and North American traditions of prayer varied the format. An end-of-the-year retreat culminated the year's experiences of mission.[11]

Sister Joy Duff, director of pastoral care at St. James for eleven years, had made the department an ecumenical enterprise with Baptist, Methodist, and Assembly of God pastors. The spirit of collaboration grew as more of Butte's congregations contributed to formal sessions and provided spiritual support—Lutheran, Episcopal, Gospel, and Church of God, Evangelical, and Christian. The Mission Integration Council had earlier organized a mission to Honduras undertaken with eighty volunteers from the International Health Service. A surgeon, a dental assistant, and a registered nurse accompanied the group.[12]

At the 2002 biennial Health Assembly in Arizona, 240 hospital and corporate board members, physicians, and affiliate administrators heard Cindy Stergar, chair of the board of trustees of St. James Healthcare and executive director of Butte's Community Health Center, describe the impact of mission integration. She found it extraordinary that an organization should gather its members for direct experience, in prayer and personal encounter, of the vision, mission, and values of a health care organization.[13]

Almost five years of developing the spiritual programs that make up mission integration at St. Francis Health Center in Topeka culminated in the International Spirit at Work Award, presented to Sister Loretto Marie Colwell, president and CEO, at the Spirit in Business Conference in Zurich, Switzerland, October 1–2, 2004. Thirty countries were represented in the conference; ten companies received the award. In St. Francis's application, five directors worked with Lawrence G. Seidl, vice president for mission integration, to prepare an account of the program's evolution. Sister Loretto Marie described the program—the collaborative work of St. Francis staff, physicians, and administrators—at the 2005 meeting of the Catholic Hospital Association.[14]

Well known in the late 1990s as a financially stable institution, ranking repeatedly in the top one hundred hospitals in the country, St. Francis had sought at the turn of the century to become an equally recognizable, spiritually vibrant health center in the Catholic tradition. Invited by Sister Loretto Marie to a conversation about stewardship, department directors knew well that the budget's "bottom line" included commitment to the financially deprived. Now they were challenged with an extended concept of stewardship: visible presence in northeast Kansas as a culture of health care that virtually spoke of God in every service and personal relationship. The idea raised new questions:

- Would a business model based on Gospel values be strong enough in a competitive environment to maintain St. Francis's public identity?
- Would new generations of leadership and employees feel the ownership required to maintain a spiritual legacy throughout the institution?
- Could employees and patients who called God by any other name or claimed no religious allegiance feel equally welcome in such a place?[15]

Without ready answers, a working group established four general principles of what might become an enduring ministry in a contemporary business climate: a hospital-wide habit of cooperation, quality leadership, pervasive regard for human dignity, and patient/family-centered care. In weekly meetings, opened with prayer and time for silent reflection, department directors exchanged thoughts on what ministry based on faith means and requires of its members. Human Resources created questions for recruiting employees; the questions grew out of the program soon known as the Culture of Stewardship.

In a second year, an initiative that participants called Kindness Connects had dual objectives: to minimize anxiety experienced by those admitted for care and to reinforce the role each employee plays in living the mission through interaction with patients, families, vendors, and colleagues. Two-hour classes in a Caring Model, held throughout the year, focused on behaviors and provided a common language for the seventeen hundred employees who attended them. Outcomes of the program appeared in reduced turnover and increasing job-satisfaction recorded in employee surveys. Less measurable was the intentional kindness that became noticeable in departments and operations. The third initiative was a multi-step program focusing on Spirituality in the Workplace and featuring images and memories of places made sacred by experience and tradition.[16]

Mission integration at St. Mary's Hospital and Medical Center in Grand Junction, Colorado, took formal shape during Sister Lynn Casey's administration. A fourfold *Commit to Care* statement engaged administrators, staff, and physicians in priorities and goals of patient care. Emphasis on personal

Sister Michel Pantenberg

interaction, strong teamwork, and goals of excellence and courtesy permeated the statement. In 1999 Robert Ladenburger came to the office of president and CEO of St. Mary's Medical Center in Grand Junction, Colorado, with a sense of ownership in the SCL/Health System's mission. Among the first things Ladenburger did was to schedule weekly encounters with staff and to engage Sister Michel Pantenburg for development of a holistic health program for staff and patients. In 1998 Sister Michel spent five weeks studying health care in the World Health Organization headquartered in Sweden.[17]

To further ownership of the system's mission statement, LaTisha Wells Starbuck, RN, vice president for patient care services, developed with the Mission Integration Council a team of mission ambassadors who carried the statement's implications to every department in celebrations of song, prayer, and story-telling. A Friendship Fund allowed employees to apply for emergency assistance up to $1,000 and for means to volunteer services in Panama and Haiti. The Book-in-Hand project brought nine hundred books from physicians and employees for distribution to children of the Grand Valley and visitors to the community soup kitchen and clothing bank.[18]

Across the Continental Divide, Exempla St. Joseph's Hospital in Denver met challenges of the mission in a distinctive partnership. Allied in 1998 with Lutheran Medical Center Community Foundation in a corporate structure, Exempla St. Joseph welcomed Leslie Hirsch as president and CEO in 2003. In two years he made progress in forging connections and inspiring trust—the difference, he said, between management and leadership. Martin Helldorfer, at the helm of pastoral care and mission integration, affirmed that the major issue of health care leadership is the education of lay people in the spirit of the Gospel and response to God's call.[19]

For Barbara Wertz, chief nurse executive, the mission statement became a norm for interviewing applicants. Mentored by Sisters of Charity since 1957, she was drawn to St. Joseph's nursing education program. Sister Ann Schumacher, MD, the only physician in the Community, serves on the medical staff of St. Joseph's and the faculty of the residency program. Medical director of Tepeyac Clinic, she is secretary of the International Association of Sister, Brother, and Priest Physicians.

Carl Unrein, president and CEO of St. Joseph's Foundation, expressed admiration for the hospital's investment in transition to lay leadership. He saw a continuum of the mission in Exempla's commitment to human dignity, the healing presence of its staff, and responsibility for care of the indigent. Such a mission, he said, is an alter ego, a conscience for the Foundation.[20] His words reflected the original vision of E. Atwill Gilman, co-founder and first president of the Foundation; its tradition continued during the eighteen-year term of Roger Goodwin.

Saint John's mission of healing in Santa Monica brought one of the first inter-faith pastoral ministry teams to southern California. The deepest dimension of mission at Saint John's is evident in relationships and bonds—developed over decades across all ethnic and cultural lines—that constitute community. Sister Maureen Craig personifies that community bond throughout the Health Center, as do members of the pastoral ministry staff and chaplains. Integration of the mission manifests itself as well in decision-making of the Healthcare Ethics Committee, commitment of the foundation, and a Values in Action program for annual recognition of employees who exemplify the Health Center's core strengths.[21]

As vice president for mission integration at Providence Medical Center and Saint John Hospital, Sister Catrina Bones called on the traditions established by the Sisters of Charity in the ministry of health care in Leavenworth and Wyandotte Counties. Comfort for the sick and dying, long practiced at both facilities, produced a palliative care model. Respect paid to each individual has led to unexpected accommodations and consciousness of people's sacred stories. A Mong gentleman in intensive care urgently requested that, in accord with his culture, on approaching death he be fully clothed to enter eternity. Observing the heart monitor closely, his nurses managed to exchange his hospital gown for the underclothes and suit they had at hand for him. In a genuine commitment to wholeness of care, they honored his values, his traditions, and his beliefs.[22]

MISSION A MATTER OF COMMUNITY

Stewardship, the material foundation of mission in ministry to those without means, continued in many forms in the early years of the twenty-first century. *Misson Milestones*, the SCL/Health System's 2004 report, recorded care of the financially disabled in the context of community benefits. Data from each facility's and the system's services accounted for more than forty million uninsured clients receiving health care. Clinics alone reported unprecedented numbers. Approximately ten of these operate within the SCL/Health System, half of them incorporated within an affiliate hospital.

With an overflow crowd of benefactors at the blessing ceremony in December 2004, Saint Vincent Clinic in Leavenworth moved into historic renovated quarters, the original nurses' residence located half a block from the first St. John Hospital. During 2004, the clinic had logged the highest number of clients in its eighteen-year history and an increase of 14 percent in just one year.[23] The year marked a 26 percent increase in the number of Duchesne Clinic's individual patients from Wyandotte County. Between approximately 30 and 43 percent of those served by the two incorporated clinics were at 100 to 150 percent of the national poverty level.[24]

At Marian Clinic in Topeka, Kansas, under the executive direction of Marilyn Page, uninsured women who visit for care or medications are offered appointments for annual health assessments and preventive screenings for cancer. Ninety-five percent of the women accept the offer. A project designed to educate and monitor those with diabetes invites patients' active participation.[25]

In Grand Junction, Marillac Clinic and St. Mary's Hospital and Medical Center were leading sponsors of widespread community engagement in a program designed to influence health policy at local, state, and national levels. The new executive director of Marillac, Stephen Hurd, reported in 2004 rising numbers of patients benefiting from the clinic's integrated mental health care program. During harvest seasons, St. Mary's provides to migrant families help that includes housing, food and gas vouchers, second-language instruction, and referrals for immigration and employment.[26]

In 2000 Exempla St. Joseph's Family Practice Residency Program started up a collaborative effort with the Sisters of Charity missioned in Peru. Residents in family practice and internal medicine spend about a month in Peru living with local families and working with medical providers in Ministry of Health clinics run by the government. At home, collaboration with Annnunciation School provided health education for kindergartners and pupils, first through sixth grades. Sister Ann Schumacker, MD, coordinated the program.[27]

Other affiliate hospitals served the uninsured through collaboration with community agencies. St. Vincent Healthcare in Billings hosted the state's largest observance of Cover the Uninsured Week during May 2004, working closely with Deaconess Billings Clinic, the Yellowstone City/County Health Departments, and the Chamber of Commerce. The Rocky Mountain Health Network, a collaborative of St. Vincent Healthcare and approximately 430 professional providers, supports rural hospitals and doctors in maintaining local services. In 2003 the network opened a primary care clinic in Cody, Wyoming.[28] A Hospice House opened by Holy Rosary Healthcare in Miles City, Montana, reserves one of its main-floor apartments as a low- or no-cost place for out-of-town families to live while a family member is receiving hospice services. The hospice serves small towns in southeastern Montana from 40 to 120 miles away.[29]

Partnerships with area agencies complement Saint John's direct primary care to the uninsured in West Los Angeles through arrangements with community and family health centers, Saint John's-Malibu Urgent Care Center, and the Santa Monica-Malibu Unified School District. When the nurse practitioner program of the Venice Family Clinic lost its federal funding in 2000, staff members at Saint John's Health Center in Santa Monica secured new funding to keep the clinic open.[30]

To affirm affiliates' direct contribution to worldwide health needs, the SCL/Health System conducted a Global Outreach videoconference in May 2002. Personnel from five health centers reported medical mission work in Guatemala, Peru, Haiti, Swaziland and Cameroon, and Odessa, Ukraine.[31] The system's personal mission milestone was a journey of its leadership team and six family members to Peru in the summer of 2003. During visits to Piura, Talara, and Chalaco they had conversations with native *hermanas*, lay teachers and health care workers, and civic leaders.

Firsthand knowledge quickly raised questions for the North Americans about how impoverished people cope with uncertain schooling, inadequate infrastructures, and limits to employment. Inequities of free trade benefits, the imperviousness of inherited wealth and privilege, and a mounting burden of national debt preclude for 80 percent of Peruvians the dreaming that is a right for North America's middle class.[32]

Strategic planning and consultancy led to the purchase in 1998 of Bethany Medical Center in Kansas City, Kansas. The Columbia health system was relinquishing sponsorship of Bethany; with the purchase, Providence Medical Center absorbed seven to eight hundred staff members who faced unemployment. The SCL/Health System maintained the inpatient acute care inner-city hospital for three years; the outpatient urgent care clinic stayed open another year for service to residents of Wyandotte County. When the operation could no longer be sustained, reorganization as a community plaza provided a fifth year of multipurpose health care and social services. These did not sufficiently utilize the space of a complex physical facility. With federal funds, the SCL/Health System separated the mechanical systems that served the medical office building, then at its own cost demolished the hospital and prepared the land for transfer to Community Housing of Wyandotte County.[33]

Stewardship that extends resources to those most in need inspires the SCL/HS Mission Fund that covers the employer portion of benefits for employees of the clinics for the uninsured. A process for assessment of affiliates' assimilation of values, inaugurated by the system in 2004, was named MIRROR, a Mission Integration Report and Reflection on Opportunities and Recommendations. Sister Judith Jackson credited the quantitative self-assessment with valuable feed-back for affiliates' strategic and operational planning. Site visits by teams of leaders from across the system allowed for testimony from employees to the impact of spiritual programs initiated by administrators and mission integration staffs.[34]

On the West Coast, five systems addressed the question of whether institutional Catholic health ministry can survive in a culture of fiercely competitive market values and medical/legal solutions to spiritual problems of life and death. With David Blake, former vice president for mission and human resources at Saint John's in Santa Monica, Sister Judith joined system officers on the West Coast in developing a collaborative Ministry Leadership Center. Its three-year program of formation for some five hundred executives focuses on spirituality of leadership, institutional identity, integration of mission in governance and operation, and ecclesial relationships fostering social justice.[35]

Such education has been the aim of Sisters of Charity in health care and governance who saw the crisis of mission and its ramifications gaining intensity over the past fifteen years. Relatively new in the system, Providence Healthcare, now allied with Saint John Hospital in Leavenworth, renamed Providence Medical Center and Saint John Hospital, established affiliation with SCL/HS as an independent corporation whose legal acts depend on recommendation of a local board. CEO and president James Paquette realized the implications of his statement when he said, "Like it or not, we are a fairly independent lot. Our roots lie in a group of fiercely independent women. They had to be to do what they did [on the western frontier]." He had been part of the system for twenty-three years, as chief financial officer of St. Vincent's, CEO of the Montana Region, and throughout six years a board member at St. Mary's in Grand Junction.[36]

"I believe our health ministry is at a crossroads," he continued, "in a creative tension of centralization and decentralization.... We cannot stay as we are." For necessary control, he said, the system board must hold each CEO to greater accountability, requiring quality reports with uniform standards, criteria, and formats, and timely bond payments. On the other hand, consultation and conversation, minimal in the past within parameters of trust, are imperative for decisions on bigger projects and costs and in visioning for investment and expansion in each local community. What is distinct about each hospital is how its people create a culture of mission and service and how they respond to system requirements for performance. Employers in the institution must describe these in a way that affects hiring. Patient satisfaction and quality improvement are matters for assessment.

The strength of Providence and Saint John, Paquette said, is the people who work there, in their ability to forge through obstacles and take on difficult issues, riveted on resolving them. Overcoming limitations is their source of energy. Great doctors who could work in different places, he said, stay here because they believe in what these hospitals do. "At the core is everything the Sisters of Charity did when they went west."[37]

That charism was personified in Sister Ann Marita Loosen, nominated by Paquette and selected in 2005 for the Lifetime Service honor awarded annually to Heroes in Healthcare by the Greater Kansas City business community. President and CEO of the Providence/Saint John alliance from 1992 to 1995, Sister was legislative liaison for the SCL/Health Services Corporation from 1995. In 1998 she received the Charles S. Billings Award for Distinguished Service to Health Care of Kansas.[38]

EXCELLENCE THE CONDITION FOR STEWARDSHIP

The mission continues to materialize in developments throughout the SCL/Health System. After planning is complete, a replacement Saint John Hospital will be built on its twenty-four-acre site in Leavenworth. Projected for long-term growth, the facility of 150 patient beds will be linked to the new Saint John Medical Plaza. Expansion of services in Leavenworth, Wyandotte, and northern Johnson Counties will accommodate a growing population and new demands. Design of the new Saint John, begun in 2007, includes the electronic medical record system being installed throughout the Sisters of Charity Health System. Greg Madsen, administrator of Saint John since 2002, identified the hospital's strength in its maintaining the standards of quality demanded of a metropolitan health center through its alliance with Providence Healthcare.[39]

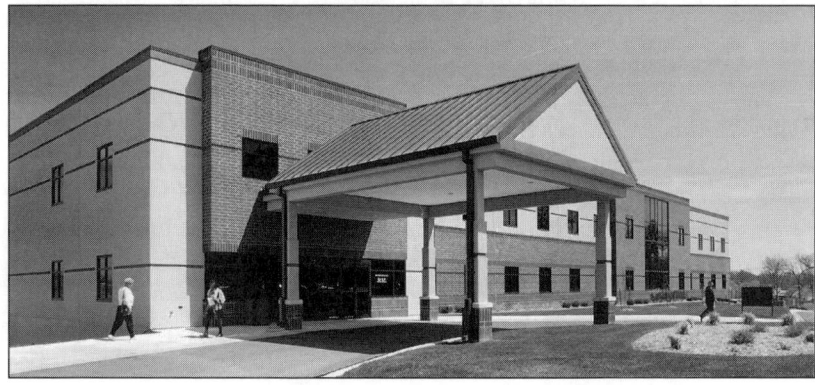

Saint John Medical Plaza, Leavenworth

Vincent DeCoursey Diagnostic and Treatment Center

By 2005, a decade of expansion at St. Francis Health Center in Topeka reflected the commitment of its physicians, the dedication of its employees, and its service to rural areas. An increasingly far-flung community consistently respects values affirmed in family life, broad employment, stewardship of resources, and a highly developed urban/rural environment. These values guided development of an intensive care unit equipped with private rooms, a neonatal center with family-centered maternity rooms, a joint replacement center, and a comprehensive cancer center that opened in 2003. Clinical visits rose by 19 percent in its first year. A freestanding cardiology center opened in 2006 to consolidate cardiovascular care and cardiac rehabilitation. Strategic planning for major renovation and construction over the next decade is under way.[40]

According to Michelle Hood, president and CEO of the Montana Region and of St. Vincent Healthcare in Billings, the strength of each institution is its people. She described the hospital as a collaboration of individuals for an end larger than themselves. Commending the SCL/Health System for the priority given local needs, she called it a corporate structure of "guided autonomies."[41] Partnerships characterize St. Vincent's response to needs of the area: with St. Alexis Medical Center in North Dakota; St. John's Lutheran Ministries in Billings; and independent physicians in the Yellowstone Medical and Surgery Centers on the Healthcare

Kansas Heart and Vascular Center at St. Francis Health Center, Topeka, Kansas

campus. Joint ventures with Deaconess Billings Clinic include the MRI Center and inter-institutional review.

Listed among the top one hundred hospitals of the country for stroke care and neurological services, orthopedic care and precision surgery, St. Vincent's won top ranking four years consecutively for its Heart Center and rehabilitation program. Through a hub at St. Vincent Healthcare, the Health Telemedicine Network provides consultation, education, and communication for rural doctors and patients throughout Montana.[42]

"St. James is an extension of this community.... It is a microcosm of Butte," asserted James Kiser in the first year of his role as chief administrative officer. When St. James Healthcare and a local union bargaining unit adopted "interest based bargaining" in contract negotiations, outcomes were not predictable, he said. At the close of negotiations, a participating labor relations specialist observed, "I have never seen management share information with such class, abundance, and factual clarity.... The desire to trust and be trusted was evident."[43]

In 2004 "Project Excellence," a four-year $45 million campaign, got off the ground to support building, renovation, and state-of-the-art medical technology. A year later, the new Foundation facility opened with Kevin Dennehy its executive director. In collaboration with the American College of Cardiology and the Montana Cardiovascular Health Program,

St. Mary's Hospital and Medical Center CareFlight on a slope of the Colorado National Monument

St. James physicians have designed standardized processes for immediate treatment of heart attacks and training sessions for staff. The program, called GAP (Guidelines Applied in Practice), is directed by Sharon Hecker, MD. An Advanced Center for Orthopedic Care distinguishes St. James and honors its origins.[44]

Under Chief Administrative Officer Greg Nielsen, Holy Rosary Healthcare in Miles City led major efforts in the area to gain a public consensus from citizens through an organized voting procedure for advocacy aimed at influencing state and national health policy. For more immediate benefits, the hospital collaborated with other organizations to obtain federal funds for a community health center that opened in December 2003. Holy Rosary has filled a gap in radiology services in rural eastern Montana with the help of a regional grant obtained by St. Vincent Healthcare. With advanced technology, Mark Irion, MD, radiologist at Holy Rosary, extends imaging and telemetric services to surrounding communities for diagnosis and treatment by their local doctors.[45]

In the first phase of a ten-year development plan, St. Mary's Hospital and Medical Center in Grand Junction, Colorado, concentrated outpatient services in a new three-story building connected with all treatment centers, expanded the intensive care unit, and increased the inpatient capacity of the Psychiatric Institute. A new Advanced Medical Education Pavilion and a five-story nursing tower will accommodate expanded emergency and critical care facilities and labor and delivery units to complete the second phase of development. A loop road will expedite access to discrete facilities of the extended campus.

With support from reserve funds, the SCL/Health System, and a public campaign to meet its cost of $200 million, the development prepares the Medical Center for a projected population growth in the Grand Valley of 66 percent by 2010.[46] In the interval, a new vice president of mission and organizational effectiveness, Terry Weinberger, SCLA, will keep St. Mary's focused on the spirit that has made the Valley's people and the Sisters of Charity partners in the ministry of health care.

On the Eastern Slope, a strategic ten-year plan that involved one hundred of Exempla St. Joseph's people laid out needs at the beginning of the new century for renovation and growth at a total cost of $400 million. Its first phase saw construction of a new outpatient building, parking facility, and patient tower to house the Cardiac and Vascular Institute. A goal to be best in the nation for patient satisfaction and clinical practice is realistic considering Exempla St. Joseph's five-time ranking among the top one hundred of United States hospitals. In a given year, fifty-eight of the hospital's physicians were named in the annual listing of Denver's top doctors. Women's and children's services care for 11 percent of Colorado's newborns.

Partnering with Metropolitan State College of Denver, the Saint Joseph Hospital Foundation established the Colorado Permanente Medical Group Healthcare Education Fund for an accelerated nursing

Exempla St. Joseph's Russell Pavilion entrance

program. The hospital's full range of diagnostic imaging, its step-down critical care program, and the busiest surgeries in the state draw applicants from across the country to medical and nursing staffs. During the second phase of the long-range plan, a third Exempla facility, Good Samaritan Medical Center, opened in Lafayette, Colorado, to extend health care services and employment to the expanding metropolitan region.[47]

In the first phase of new construction in Santa Monica, California, the Campaign for Saint John's: Creating the Future outstripped a goal of $125 million and saw dedication in September 2004 of the North Pavilion. A start-up grant of $20 million from the W. M. Keck Foundation initiated major gifts. The pavilion includes the Marion and Earle Jorgensen Patient Care Center and McAlister Women's Health Center, home of the Joyce Eisenberg Keefer Breast Center. The Leavy Foundation and Polak Charitable Foundation support research and development in the John Wayne Cancer Institute. The new Weingart Emergency Department will expand its round-the-clock relief to trauma victims of west Los Angeles. Bequests from the Flora L. Thornton Foundation support the education center that serves Santa Monica and the Bay community.[48]

The first health center in California to build on base isolator foundations, Saint John's offers the best available protection against seismic shock

The North Pavilion, inpatient facility of the new Saint John's, blessed September 23, 2004

Sister Marie Madeleine Shonka and Jerry Epstein carry major responsibilities in the fund drive for the new Saint John's.

and, in the personal investments that made the structure possible, sturdy symbols of faith. Thanks to the base isolation elements, the Health Center's infrastructure of water, power, and communications will remain operational during earthquakes or other catastrophes, a veritable "lifeboat" for the community in time of emergency. During his tenure as CEO and president, Bruce Lamoureux saw personal attention and genuine presence in every aspect of care at the Health Center as qualities essential to the Catholic identity.[49] A stakeholder of more than forty years, current chairman and originator of major Foundation events, Jerry Epstein leads the building committee for the new Saint John's.[50]

In September 2005, Lourdes Lazatin was named president and CEO of the Health Center. During an interval as chief operating officer, she learned the demands of the personalized care that makes Saint John's one of the fifty top-ranking hospitals in the state and a leader in Southern California. LaTisha Starbuck became Saint John's vice president for mission integration in 2005; Louise West continues as director of mission services. Early in 2006, ground was cleared for the Howard Keck Diagnostic and Treatment Center to be completed by 2008 on the site of the original Saint John's.[51]

Consultation with affiliates is a first principle of a far-reaching collaborative venture of the SCL/Health System that began in 2005. Called CareQuest, the first phase engaged corporate officers with consultants and a multidisciplinary team of twenty-nine health care clinicians and business personnel from all affiliates. Led by chief nurse executives and chief financial officers, the team contributed to the design of a centralized electronic system for recording and transmitting all information, from diagnosis through treatment and follow-up care, between departments, physician, and patient. The integrated system makes all services accessible online.

Richard T. Lopes, MD, is chief clinical transformation officer of CareQuest. St. Vincent Healthcare was the first affiliate to implement the technology in 2007; St. Mary's Hospital and Medical Center will do so a year later. The digitalized system will be installed throughout the system within the decade. Enterprise Resource Planning (ERP) is the business model for management of best practices in general accounting, human resources, and the supply chain at all affiliates. While improved delivery of patient care at the bedside is the goal of CareQuest, the critical importance of communication with stakeholders and consideration of local culture is a growing priority with Dr. Lopes and affiliate officers.[52]

Such priorities come to life in relationships that transform vertical lines of corporate authority into horizontal lines of collaboration in decision-making. As Bill Murray has described it, interdependence is the condition of the developing science of management. If economic issues and competition are not to enslave decisions and policies, core processes and choices must be subject to core values.[53] Interdependence must be the condition of mission as well as management.

Nothing could better dramatize the truth than the actions of the SCL/Health System in its Hurricane Katrina Relief Task Force. Five teams—Personnel, Financial Support, Aviation and Supplies, Housing, and Communications—went into action for response to immediate and long-term needs. Rapid response teams of nurses from affiliates succeeded each other in one-week commitments to relieve staff at a rural hospital located near the Gulf Coast. First funds including paid time-off donations from staff throughout the system were matched by the corporate office. The mounting total went in equal portions to Catholic Charities USA and the American Red Cross. Affiliates in their communities admitted transferred patients, met housing needs, and volunteered time to local agencies.

More illustrative, perhaps, than response to crisis was the steady climb of care throughout the system, over the first years of the new century, for those unable to pay for their care. Even as the mission of health care in the tradition of the Sisters of Charity of Leavenworth calls for technological transformations, it depends essentially on complex human factors. In an organization that by 2003 ranked in the top 10 percent of Catholic health care systems, the teamwork necessary to implement systemic change and the trust implicit in transmission to lay leadership are genuine tests of interdependence.

Less definable and more difficult to maintain is the consultation necessary to consistently identify the character and developing culture of individual affiliates. Regular conversation with sisters—not always administrators or directors—whose knowledge of local communities complements and qualifies statistical outcomes must be intentional and deliberate. Regular communication with stakeholders recognizes those who invest their daily labor as well as those who share affluent resources. The compassion and confidence manifest in personal encounter on the ground of each hospital, health center, and clinic is not measurable in margins reserved for mission.

Such relationships are the heart of a system whose boards and officers have recourse to them. They are, in the system's beginning and its continuance, the lifeline of its mission. Perhaps the hidden wisdom that lies in those relationships has to do with the dimensions of mission that transcend a given religious community's heritage. These include the sources of spirituality in lay leaders and employees who respond to a call lived and voiced by sisters for many decades and now by all who re-create an enduring and identifying mission. The call originates ultimately in the Gospel of Jesus. It sounds in the heart of each one open to the Spirit, who speaks at once in many tongues and in the profound silence of commitment and hope.

CHAPTER 26

Emerging Frontiers

A new century and millennium is a time for determinations more serious than New Year's resolutions. It is a time for self-scrutiny of a people's place in the world, of nations' and cultures' relationships to one another, and of human beings' perception of purpose in their "allotted number" of years on earth. It is a time for the Church to heed the voices of all its people, a time for religious communities to discern with renewed care their role in the mission of Jesus.

That role, in the early years of the twenty-first century, was taking visible shape for the Sisters of Charity of Leavenworth in the deliberations of their Sixteenth General Chapter, in developments of sponsored ministries, and in the new life of applicants and young sisters making vows. Invisible fruits of growth were a newly realized unity, the promise of expanding collaborations, and the aspirations of a new generation of Sisters of Charity. To see the Spirit as source of all such life was the work of faith—that of sisters, Associates, and partners in mission and ministry.

At some cost during earlier decades, the Community had resolved growing tensions of difference in religious conviction and practice through Chapters of Renewal and subsequent revision of their Constitutions. Almost twenty years later, tensions within the Church born of deep differences of conscience and theological orientation and tensions within the country born of political gambits and moral disputes fed division among believers and growing skepticism of governmental decisions. Thoughtful people longed for strong leadership informed by firmly grounded knowledge and indubitable integrity. Religious communities in continuing renewal, seeking vibrant new life, felt the same need.

Some four months before he died, in his message on the thirty-eighth World Day of Peace, Pope John Paul II mourned the violence that raged in Africa, in Iraq, and across the globe and the poverty that divides nations and peoples. He called on a Church divided within itself to find in the

Eucharist "the wellspring of all communion" with Jesus and, in him, "with every human being." Had he not in his own person reached out to many across ethnic, religious, and historical barriers, his words would have carried less weight. In an unprecedented demonstration of unity in respect and admiration, thousands of all races, ranks, and beliefs gathered in Rome on April 8, 2005, to honor John Paul's personal prophetic power and to wonder at the throng united in grief at his passing.

Yet the very model of communion, declared for the Church by the Vatican II Ecumenical Council, appeared at his death to stand at risk. Contrary forces at work within the Mystical Body of Christ, as within almost every religious body, threatened unity. In his study of the primacy of Peter, enjoined on him by Pope John Paul, Archbishop John Quinn described the fundamental concern of an ecclesial model of communion to be discernment in faith of the diversity of gifts and works of the Spirit. It must coexist in the Church with the political model and its fundamental concern for order and control. "It is always wrong," he wrote, "when the claims of discernment are all but eliminated in favor of the claims of order thereby making control...the supreme good."[1] Tensions created when the mutually necessary claims fall into imbalance—through fear of reform or impatience for change—can deteriorate into disunity. Strong leadership, capable of strengthening order while discerning frontiers, is more than ever a priority.

As for the Church, so for religious communities. At their annual joint assembly in 2004, leaders of women's and men's congregations of the United States deliberated about ways of peace building that ask for collaboration among all who seek peace, including Mennonites, Buddhists, the World Conference on Religion and Peace, Pax Christi, faith-based NGOs at the United Nations, and their own congregational offices of Peace and Justice. In a joint interactive address with the president of men's congregational leadership, Sister Constance Phelps, SCL, president of LCWR, called on the spiritual resources that "turn fear into courageous trust, agitation and confusion into stillness, isolation into a sense of belonging, alienation into love." The ability to lead, she said, "emerges from the strength and sustenance of those around us" and bears fruit in "the inner peace and bedrock confidence" that enable leaders to inspire others.[2] Those she addressed knew at first hand the challenges of renewal that required the ordering of community life with full regard for discernment of the Spirit.

By the turn of the century, the Community had achieved a balance between order and discernment that allowed for various expressions of its Vincentian charism within a common commitment to standing with and for the poor. It had done so within a central governance structure flexible enough to allow expanding participation in direction-setting Chapters. Not unpredictably, these blessings were mixed with limitations. The desire for yet deeper unity paralleled but sometimes contended with pressing needs for action in diverse ministries. The very commitment to the poor and encouragement of initiatives over the previous twelve years reinforced motivation to act on invitation or opportunity for individual ministry. While liberating sisters for service and leadership in a Church and society plagued with needs, dependence on discernment of ministry limited the Community's common resource of personnel. Diffusion of enormous talent and energy was a paradoxical effect, even as a common spirit united the sisters in their diversity.

As the Sisters of Charity of Leavenworth approached their Sixteenth[1] General Chapter, to be held in the summer of 2004, they knew that its purpose was to set direction and to choose leadership for the next six years. Questions about religious life wrestled with during the difficult transition years after Vatican II were taking new directions. Many had not experienced the demands and drama of Renewal Chapters that had dealt with such issues in common study and dialogue. Commission documents, individual position papers, and surveys responded to by large numbers in each apostolate contributed to a bank of data and reflections shared by Chapter participants. Serious study of religious community and mission, questions basic to continuing renewal, was not now a common endeavor, ironically, in part, because of fundamental change. Schedules of sisters ministering in distant places, in church offices and public agencies, and on collaborative teams prevented gatherings planned to complement and connect the workshops conducted by the Community's theologians from 1998 to 2002.

Reading and conversation issuing from the best thought of theologians and authorities on developing religious life were certainly the practice of many sisters but were not a common experience in long-range preparation for Chapter. Such study had given way by the 1990s to discussion, in local communities and regional meetings, of selected articles and questions. Excellent as some of these were, no common forum existed for raising critical questions about the future of women religious in the mission of the Church and about priorities for the Community in shaping that future. Sources of vision, the bedrock of leadership, were not plumbed together. That Sisters of Charity were seriously thinking about the questions, however, is clear from patterns of discussion in at least one regional pre-Chapter meeting.

Change had produced another phenomenon of Chapter preparation and organization. The desire for growing involvement in direction-setting and choice of priorities brought a broadened base of voting delegates, increasingly formal modes of active participation, and an agenda planned from grass roots thinking. A widespread practice among religious communities at the time was the use of facilitators to keep discussion in regional groups on track of the questions pondered in local houses and to assist the committee planning an agenda from the groups' submissions. Such a process paved the road to consensus; outcomes, however, presented problems yet to be solved. How to balance organized total participation with productive spontaneous exchange on well thought-out questions was an issue perhaps beyond facilitation and organization.

In the spring of 2003 and for a year following, Sisters of Charity of Leavenworth met in regions and in local circles to prepare for the General Chapter to be held the following summer. Delegates were to be chosen by all members for electing the Community director and Council and voting on formal proposals to the Chapter. Broad participation came by way of nominations, circle discussions throughout the year, and conversations among delegates and active participants at randomly assigned tables during the Chapter itself. Results of circle and regional gatherings were material for the elected delegates' serious consideration.

Notes from one regional meeting suggested broad areas of consensus and a hunger for further dialogue:

- Our role in the Church is more vital than ever. We need to probe the mystery of the Church together. Leadership and ministry of women now is crucial.
- Ours is a global mission, part of the mission of the Church in the world. What are our untapped and perhaps unfocused communal resources?
- Together we are Eucharist, we are Gospel. How can we better proclaim our mission in the Church?
- We desire a new sense of community—unity in ministry and voice in direction—with leadership dependent on continuing communication, planning, and implementation.[3]

Major themes rising from circle meetings that engaged self-selected members three times during summer, fall, and winter months continued the emphases with questions and concrete concerns. Themes, interpreted from reams of circle reports, were demanding:

- Unique identity and mission as an ecclesial community, visible sign of God's love for all people
- Needs of the global community, especially those of the poor
- Stewardship of the earth and its resources for ends of justice through sponsored works

- Need for increased collaboration through the Charity Federation, Associates, churches, and public agencies
- Witness of vowed community as a countercultural way of life and bridge between rich and poor

Concerns pointed to action:

- How do we exercise and train for leadership in Community and in the Church?
- What are formal channels of communication for assessment of progress, discernment of options, and exchange of ideas?
- What are concrete ways of witnessing to the poverty we profess?
- How do we diversify our communal commitment to education?
- What are ways of further commissioning lay leaders in our sponsored ministries?
- How do we become visible and hospitable to young women desiring to serve?[4]

Reports from Community councilors, sponsored institutions, standing committees, and task forces, assigned to begin the work mandated by the Chapter of 1998, completed the material given delegates to study. The groups included standing committees for Ongoing Formation, Social Justice, and the Sisters of Charity Federation; Jubilee commissions on Global Mission, Immersion Experiences, Partnerships, Theology Update, and Jubilee 2000; and continuing programs for Formation and Vocation Promotion, Associates, Ministry Development and Transition, Sisters 55 and Younger, and Marillac Retreat Center. Reports on building and renovation came from the Community director. In her address to the Chapter and all Sisters of Charity of Leavenworth, Sister Sue Miller assessed the situation of the Community in its Vincentian heritage and present responsibilities.

"AT THE HEART OF THE CHURCH..."

In our movement toward the center, she said, "God talks to us because we're so interested"—a familial way of defining hope that takes us outward to solidarity with all peoples. Alluding to Vincentian spirituality, she spoke of consciousness of the earth, of the other, and of the presence of God. In lay partnerships and through sponsored institutions, the Community can "bring to birth a culture of peace" and help to create "a Church where everyone feels at home." As "women at the heart of the Church," en-

Emerging Frontiers 489

trusted with resource of members and means, Sister said the Community can learn how better to teach what we believe, what the Gospel says to us, and what discernment of conscience requires. In the global community, we can come to be known as "women who stand against injustice and...as voice for the voiceless." Mission, she said, roots us and Chapter translates energy into focused action, transforms issues into directions. Sister Sue concluded with words of Bishop Raymond Hunthausen: "We do not go to God alone. We go as a people"—in hope and in communion within community, within the Church, and beyond.[5]

The opening of the Chapter in June 2004 involved more sisters than ever before in conversation about major concerns with successive diverse groups. A group member brought to a microphone the most salient proposal each table in turn could formulate. According to an agenda prepared by the planning committee, overarching questions focused on relationships with one another, between leadership and membership, with the Church, with the global community, and with the earth. Unfathomable as the questions appeared, proposals from the tables were the fruit of a year's prayer, thinking, informal discussion, and recorded dialogue. They asked for concrete actions, some in need of information about current initiatives and legal complications.

Written recommendations submitted with the proposals urged broader involvement with Associates, commitment to careful listening and dialogue within local communities, and investment in larger houses for communal living. Suggestions for new leadership structures sought fuller participation in decision-making through consultative collaboration, frequent area town hall meetings with a councilor, and wider use of sisters for implementation of Chapter directives. Some recommendations were conflicting. Mentoring leaders for boards of sponsored institutions while lessening councilors' membership could in fact diminish the Community's influence on corporate decisions. Other recommendations lacking consensus within given groups reflected expectations of councilors that gave priority to personal pastoral roles over responsibilities for leadership and intercommunity collaboration.[6]

But to "be the Church we want the Church to be" was a goal for all: to dialogue with honesty and to grow in credibility and integrity. A concrete recommendation for building bridges—especially with clergy and hierarchy—when in loyal dissent with particular practices found its way to the Chapter statement. Creating communities of compassion and forgiveness where people of God are not experiencing true church was an equally challenging suggestion. Standing in solidarity with Peruvian bishops and Hermanas de la Caridad in opposition to exploitation by mining companies was a recommendation that seconded action by the Peace and Justice office and the Council. Calls for further theological reflection and continuance of circle meetings echoed throughout the summaries.

The desire for collaboration with LCWR, the Charity Federation, ecumenical groups, Network, the United States Catholic Conference of Bishops, and the UN Millennium Project reflected firm resolution to strengthen relationships with the global community. Collaboration with sponsored works pointed to the University of Saint Mary's Global Studies program and to justice issues like wages, benefits, and working conditions. Seed money for small business starts by women in developing countries was a practical suggestion.

Perhaps the most essential recommendation, dependent on individual motivation and communal support, was for personal transformation in contemplative and countercultural action. Similar initiative was invoked to nurture relationships with the earth. Suggestions for water conservation, theological reflection on the interconnectedness of all life, and more responsible patterns of consumption suggested action by local communities as well as community-wide consciousness of collective buying power.[7]

The Chapter Statement—critiqued by participants and revised—opened with a recommitment to the Vincentian mission explicitly declared in the Chapter of 1992. The focus on relationships reflected a new consciousness in these women of their unity and responsibility for contemplative and compassionate presence to the people of God. The statement carried conviction.

> *We, the Sisters of Charity of Leavenworth,*
>   *who love the poor,*
>   *hear a cry and feel an urgency in these times*
>   *to unite our voices and to speak out,*
>   *to live and move as women of hope.*
> *Charged by the spirit born in us of Vincent, Louise, and Xavier,*
> *and strengthened by our life together in community,*
>   *we step into our future with a renewed sense of mission.*
> *As women called to risk for the reign of God,*
>   *we choose to nurture relationships of hope:*
>   *with one another*
>   *by creating authentic communities that welcome, support,*
>   *and challenge*
>   *by strengthening our South-North connections*
>   *by clarifying and enriching the SCLA-SCL relationship*
>   *between leadership and membership*

> *by developing community structures that lead to more participation,*
> *collaboration, and accountability*
> *by learning about our community's sponsoring role and works*
> *with the Church*
> *by sustaining dialogue with and by caring for the Church*
> *by engaging in theological reflection and study*
> *among ourselves and with our neighbors*
> *with the global community*
> *by responding to human and environmental issues*
> *through personal choices and communal actions*
> *by joining our voice with justice-centered organizations*
> *with the earth*
> *by embracing our need for full communion with all creation.*
> *As a community of believers, we open ourselves*
> *to the presence of the Sacred in each of these relationships.*
> *As Sisters of Charity, rooted in Christ and united in our convictions,*
> *we claim our responsibility as gospel-centered women*
> *and stand with all who suffer, who grieve, who hope.*[8]

The work of a General Chapter to envision and set directions for a congregation's future was complete, so far as assiduous preparation and hard work could achieve it. Outcomes reflected the ecclesial nature of congregational Chapters as "meetings of the Church," recalled by Sister Mary Kathleen in 1998. Furtherance of unity and charity, the canonical purpose of such Chapters, was a clear benefit of these deliberations. The work of choosing leadership for the next six years remained.

Prayerful discernment on the part of community members, regional meetings focusing on leadership, conversations about qualities for office, and personal invitations to individual sisters with their consent had produced nominees for Community director and four councilors. With qualifications recognized by many and eighteen previous years of leadership, Sister Sue Miller was elected by the delegates for a second term as Community director. One of the councilors was not eligible for a third term on the Council. Sisters Maureen Hall, Linda Roth, and Nancy Bauman were elected in succession and Sister Marianna Bauder was re-elected to the Council for the next six years. Their nomination and willingness to serve reflected members' acknowledgement of their qualities. Their experience in teaching, pastoral ministry, inner city job training, family shelter, initial formation, and health care gave them individual credibility. Sister Margaret Ellen Johnson was appointed Community secretary and Sister Katherine Franchett was reappointed Community treasurer.

(Top row) Sister Sue Miller, Community Director, with Sisters Maureen Hall, Linda Roth, Marianna Bauder, and (bottom row) Nancy Bauman, Councilors; and Sisters Katherine Franchett, Treasurer, and Peg Johnson, Secretary

To interpret results of any election requires more knowledge than any one person possesses; to ignore them is to close a door on understanding for the future. The method of successive table conversations among all active participants, with voting delegates at each table, had prepared the ground for consensus on large directions for the Community. It had also allowed for exchange of views about nominees in and out of office and, to a degree, for discussion of what leadership entails. Discernment of qualities necessary for leadership in religious community depends on insight—into candidates' experience and depth of knowledge—and on a prayerful spirit. Such discernment can, but does not necessarily, accompany a democratic process.

Two words, *vision* and *leadership*, had not appeared with any frequency in the voluminous accounts from the year's circle meetings. In general, the qualities were desired but understanding of what they required had not been a voiced priority. At this juncture in religious life, participation in Chapters calls for informed examination of the demands of leadership, particularly that of women, in continuing renewal of community and mission in the Church.

Election results clarified what a majority of delegates primarily sought in their choice of leadership. What may be called the pastoral role of a councilor was a dominant topic in conversations before and during Chapter. It had appeared as a concern in previous years, with suggestions of separated roles in the Council for attention to the sisters' needs and for business decisions; it reappeared in a recommendation for councilors' training in counseling. Pastoral leadership was not to be identified with participatory governance through communication with membership. But desire for the latter and perceived need for the former became the same issue and clearly affected the election.

The desire for improved communication between the general officers and members of the Community influenced discussion, found expression at the microphones, and issued in formal proposals endorsed by the Chapter delegates. Conversations during the year and in immediate preparation for the Chapter had translated the desire into a theme that dominated conceptions of leadership. By Chapter time, what was recognized as a real need for improved communication resulted unexpectedly in voting patterns that swept sisters out of and into roles of governance. Informed discernment, a communal action guided by the Spirit and invoked for the nomination and election process, required more time and perhaps more silence than full participation and planned conversations allow.

No growing movement toward participatory governance in religious communities explains how a particular community produces the forms it needs. For three decades, the Sisters of Charity of Leavenworth had struggled to achieve some measure of consultative decision-making within a basically centralized structure they had never found sufficient reason to change. An attempt to broaden the base of Chapter planning and preparation undertaken in the early 1990s had long-term and indirect effects that needed periodic discernment and evaluation. Every six years from 1991, the Sisters of Charity of Leavenworth employed facilitators to assist organization of grass roots contribution and to direct carefully honed processes of theological reflection and consensus among increasing numbers of Chapter members. By the last Chapter of the decade, however, the peace that marks consensus was for some not the result of the ordered procedures for gaining it.

Further, the rationale and programming of pre-Chapter discussions did not sufficiently allow for unexpected contributions outside planned channels of communication. Unpredictable and deeply personal concerns can reflect movements of the Spirit in a community of hundreds that careful organization, however rightly motivated, does not readily encompass. Such concerns need time for informal conversation and shared reading, opportunity for expression in papers like those of the past. By 2004, various and complex experiences of preparation, participation, and outcomes were available to guide long-range planning for the Chapter of 2010 that would follow the Community's 150th anniversary.

Time and paradoxical fruits of renewal were silent factors no one could begin to assess. From new ministries, sisters knew the needs of the poor they desired more effectively to address. Personal reports from sisters who led sponsored institutional ministries had drawn enthusiastic response from the Chapter participants. The presentations inspired a formal affirmation from the delegates; written recommendations asked for continuing education to the mission of sponsored ministries. Sisters who gladly shared a common heritage knew that community grows by fundamental laws of the spiritual life: the contemplative spirit that nurtures presence to one another depends on self-knowledge and attentive listening.

Presence of the Spirit pervades a community that knows itself and its members, one by one, in their ministries and desires to contribute to a mission that feeds the life of the Church, the Body of Christ. Without that presence to one another in the Spirit, nothing of life in religious community can flourish. For the past fifty years, the Sisters of Charity had been learning and practicing that truth. Their learning continued.

In fall regional meetings, the Community director and her Council called on such a source. Sister Sue Miller described team building by the Council and relayed the commitment to regular communication with

Charity Notes made their debut at the 150th anniversary celebration of Immaculate Conception parish, established in 1858 by Bishop John Baptist Miege, SJ. (Photograph by Therese Horvat)

members and to the sisters' influence on decision-making when possible. More personally, she invited the sisters to engage imagination "as a place of change and hope." She urged them to welcome each other in the power "that flows from the deepest, most vulnerable part of us."[9] A prayer service, opening with Matthew's account of the surprising encounter between Jesus and the Samaritan woman at the well, offered the symbol of water that brings new life. In turn, councilors explained how two initiatives flowing from the Chapter now engaged the Community.

Results of a communications audit were introduced with a brief overview and time for consideration in small groups. Wide response to a survey, conversation in focus groups, and individual comments had produced decisive ratings for every format in use for relaying information within and beyond the Community. Expressed desire for more personal knowledge of one another and a view of communication as ministry were to guide the next steps: employment of a communications director and gatherings in Wisdom Circles to exchange stories and accounts of ministry. The possibility of sponsoring a Cristo Rey school for teen-age youth unable to qualify or pay for education in a school of their choice awakened questions about staffing, material resources, and mission outreach. In thoughtful appraisals, the temper of the meetings was one of attentive listening.

In the name of the Community during the months after the Chapter the Council engaged in collaborative enterprises. These included the Charity Federation's Hunger Project, the Center of Concern's work of transforming unjust power structures, and LCWR's five-year program of contemplative action for peacemaking, stewardship of the earth, and mentorship of leaders for the future of religious life. The Council sent relief funds to Fonkoze, a microcredit bank in Haiti founded by Father Joseph Philippe, CSSP, and to Darfur and Chad through Catholic and Jesuit Relief Services. They signed on to the Religious Working Group's response to the failure of G8 finance ministers to approve 100 percent cancellation of impoverished nations' debts to the World Bank and the International Monetary Fund. At the annual Leadership Conference, they heard Dr. Mary Robinson, former president of Ireland, reflect on what women religious can bring to a globalizing world.[10]

Arriving at the Beginning

On November 12, Immaculate Conception Church hosted the sisters at a candlelight riverfront prayer service at the Landing and in the parish hall to commemorate the 150th anniversary of the parish. Few in the crowd at the soup supper realized that the lively singing by the Charity Notes, a group of thirty Sisters of Charity from area missions, represented a tradition of music that harked back to the beginnings of the Community. A few sisters remembered innumerable choir practices for perfecting the precision and flow of Gregorian chant and the difficult harmonies of polyphonic music. More recalled the colorful sounds of summer gatherings punctuated by sing-alongs and musical parodies. Made up of teaching musicians and sisters who simply loved to sing, the Charity Notes began from that first performance to develop a repertoire that brought recognition and awakened memories in every audience that invited them to perform.[11]

Sister Sue Miller spoke about Mother Xavier Ross to the crowd assembled in the parish center near the spot where Bishop John Baptist Miege had first welcomed the Sisters of Charity to Leavenworth 146 years earlier. To reduce the debt on the cathedral he built before retiring, he traveled immense distances in South America, from Ecuador to Peru and Chile and, by mule, over the cordillera of the Andes to Argentina, Uruguay, and Brazil, begging from those of substantial means for his mission in Kansas.[12]

The morning after the commemorative event, Sisters Sue and Ann Barton left for Peru to visit the fifteen sisters there engaged in discernment of mission and leadership. The prayerful process led to naming the director of Latin American Missions, Hermana Susana Córdova Castillo. It led within months to the closing of the Community's first Peruvian mission in Talara. The multi-purpose St. Vincent Center, under construction in Piura, the parish mission in Chalaco, and the new pastoral mission in the remote village of Chuschi remained. Located in Ayacucho in the southern Andes, at an elevation of seven thousand feet with a pastoral outreach to villages at altitudes as high as eleven thousand feet, Chuschi had been an initiative of the Peruvian *hermanas* in 2004. A convent for the sisters boasts a stained glass window depicting the charism of the Community and designed by one of the sister artists. Near the coast, St. Vincent Center is a resource for lay ministers in catechetics, sacramental preparation, and health education; for providing and teaching reflexology; and for parish assemblies and celebration.

The visit of the Community director and its outcomes symbolized a century and a half's development of the mission of the Sisters of Charity of Leavenworth. What began with a journey from Nashville to the Indian Territory in 1858 was still evolving by the end of 2005 for 337 sisters who now ministered in twelve states of North America, in two countries of Latin America, and through advocacy and contribution on continents across the globe.[13]

The year 2005 heralded things to come. Promise of deeper unity appeared in initiatives that drew sisters to roles they could not have imagined. In unprecedented formats, Associates joined the sisters in exploring the potential of their common mission. Avenues of communication opened in a renewed website and a newsletter requiring broad collaboration. As the number of deaths rose, young sisters brought their motivation and energy to sponsored ministries. New members applied with evident trust in the future.

Voices of Charity, edited by Therese Horvat, named by Sister Ellen Dore, and applauded by its hundreds of readers, came off the press in June 2005. Besides accounts of major events and new undertakings, jublilarians' stories, and notes about recent honors to sisters and Associates, the publication announced winners who named regular features of the magazine. One of them, "Leaven Words," highlighted Sister Ann Lucia Apodaca's photographs of Ross Hall sisters projected on a screen to music and lyrics: "My friend, you are a miracle." Another feature, "Beyond All Borders," took readers to the Northern Cheyenne Reservation in Montana, where two Sisters of Charity minister; and to Fondwa, a village of Haiti, where a Palatine priest ministers to basic Christian communities and where native religious care for orphans and offer health care to peasant farmers and their children. Sister Katherine Franchett, Community treasurer, is an active member of their Partners in Progress Board.[14]

The invisible work of grant application, pursued by sisters in education, clinics, and collaborative ventures, called on beneficent relationships between foundations and ministries, families of means and thousands in need. Grants from the Hilton Foundation for Sisters and the Seton Institute in 2005 promoted a venture begun by Sister Janet Cashman sixteen years before in Piura-Tumbes in Peru. The health care ministry, which she coordinated for six years, has prepared more than three hundred *promotores de salud* who provide training for leaders in basic health practices in thirty-five parishes of the far-flung archdiocese. Attending to the sick in their homes, resources for those who cannot afford medical care, a small pharmacy and a reflexology clinic, food kitchens, and assistance to AIDS patients are among services provided by each parish.[15]

A New Century of Promise

New life in the Community flourished in forms developed over a quarter of a century. Education in inner cities, suburbs, and rural communities; study, teaching, and scholarship in universities; health care and social services in hospitals, clinics, home health, and AIDS hospice; pastoral ministry, administration, and diocesan leadership; spiritual direction, retreat work, and houses of welcome; contemplative prayer, sometimes in musical and visual forms; mission integration in health care systems and on Native American reservations; campus ministry and ecumenical dialogue—no list encompassed the sisters' ministry to the people of God.

Perhaps the most difficult relationship affirmed in Chapter, while it appeared the easiest to strengthen, was that of the sisters with one another. On the personal level, sensitivity and openness had grown since the 1980s. Regard for individual ministries had deepened. What was apparent largely in indirect ways was comprehension of the unutterable value of each individual sister not only in her person, before God and in community, but also in her knowledge and experience. The value was more than a matter of belief and conviction; it was a resource for mission and ministry not yet fully understood. That may be because diversity of gifts with individual differences in their manifestation is a natural fact, even a scriptural principle. The fact, however, leaves people free to value the diversity and miss its implications.

Those able to articulate ideas, influence colleagues, organize projects, administer systems, and remain likeable besides get elected to offices and committees, become leaders on various levels and in different roles. Renewal had wrought major change in practices of choice by name recognition or trust in authoritative appointments and in reliance upon education or record of achievement. Attempts to broaden the base of participation through nomination and election, task force and committee work, self-selection and invitation by peers had engaged many unaccustomed to leadership. Forums, regional structures, surveys, and grass roots preparation for Chapters gave voice to all who had something to say. Yet the very talent for organization demonstrated by the Community throughout its history and developed with finesse during decades of renewal left much thinking unplumbed and wisdom unconsulted.

Freedom to seek fields of ministry that called on unexplored talent took sisters away from the center into ministries they had discerned, with or without subsequent impact on Community projects and sponsored works. When natural leaders emerged for those works and projects, the Council furthered their education and sought their continuing commitment. New responsibilities and new roles fostered dependence on principles and methods newly acquired.

On one hand, kinship of professional views and even bonds of friendship contributed to consultation, staffing, and decisions that sometimes diminished the influence or passed over the knowledge of sisters long engaged in the ministry. What had once been called patronage within a community, however much it rose from laws of human nature, now had professional parameters. It posed a potential loss of valuable personal resource in the varied experience and deep conviction of sisters unfamiliar with theory and systems but experienced in human interaction.

These forces were at work in the nomination process and in table conversations during the Chapter of 2004. They were evident in a plea for

Chapter statements free of heady language and abstract terminology. At long range, such forces pose a risk to governance of corporate structures dependent on board decisions and professional consultants but not obligated to dialogue with sisters and lay colleagues alike who may or may not be credentialed by advanced degrees but are informed by rich experience.

On the other hand, sisters who value their experience but lack self-confidence or understanding of personal characteristics do not often perceive how to make their influence felt. The Ministry Development Office of the Community offers services of self-assessment, ministry counseling, transitional planning, and discerning new ministries. In religious communities, such offices can be a vehicle for exchange between corporate officers and sisters professionally and spiritually experienced.

But mission integration is not limited to programs within institutions. Its principal resource is the power of the Spirit manifest in the competence and shared gifts of sisters whose presence is a sign of mission. On institutional staffs and in serious consultation, they are a fund of personal capital. It is a fund that diminishes year by year with unpredictable onsets of debilitating or fatal disease.

Enriched in Diminishment

In view of such loss and after extended consultation, the general officers drew conclusions about provision for the sisters' health care. In November 2005, the Health Fund, maintained by the Community since the late 1960s, was dissolved. Two insurance plans were undertaken with outside firms, one for sisters with Medicare benefits and another for sisters under sixty-five. During the previous five years, seventy-six sisters had died, an annual average of more than fifteen. Four sisters had died in one month during each of the previous two years. Because of the range of ages and causes of death, the loss was felt as keenly as the joy in their new status in the communion of saints. In the natural human cycle, nevertheless, new life replenished the community.

Sister Maureen Writt, who died in July, 2005, had just celebrated her seventy-fifth jubilee as a Sister of Charity of Leavenworth. With her, two sisters observed their seventieth year in the Community and thirteen their sixtieth year. Eleven golden jubilarians celebrated with families and friends at the Mother House. Longevity as well as lives cut short characterized this particular portion of the communion of saints on earth. So did the range of their ministry: classroom teaching and GED, administering schools, archdiocesan housing, working in clinics for the uninsured, building and maintaining low-income homes, serving on corporate boards, caring for and educating emotionally disturbed children, ministering to the life of prayer, coordinating action against family violence, accompanying youth and adults on the journey of Christian initiation.

Ministries undertaken by young sisters who first made or renewed their religious vows within the last decade reflect the life and potential leadership they bring to their Vincentian heritage. Sister Carolyn Gleoge is on the pastoral ministry team of Benefis Healthcare in Great Falls, Montana. In parish settings, Hermana Lourdes Abad Pulache ministers to youth and is a resource for teachers; her sister, Hermana Deidy, is in pastoral ministry. Sister Ann Schumacher, MD, practices in Caritas Clinic at Exempla St. Joseph's in Denver. Sister Elizabeth Adams is a child care worker at Mount St. Vincent's Home in Denver. Sister Melissa Camardo directs work force development for employees of Exempla Saint Joseph Hospital there. In 2006 Sister Victoria Ann Lichtenauer completed work for a master's degree in pastoral theology at St. Louis University.[16]

Prelude to what might become a more fruitful connection between the Sisters of Charity and their Associates, Therese Horvat's reflection during

In the soup kitchen opened by the Grand Junction SCL Associates, Donna Mae Donahue, Bob Johnson, and Terry Armstrong serve dinner to their guests. (Photograph by Therese Horvat)

Chapter witnessed to the mutual benefit of the relationship. Then she had asked how the Associates and sisters could network in more significant ways and more effectively partner in ministry. New members were named that summer to the Associate Advisory Council. A move of considerable significance took shape when the Council planned to host the morning session of Wisdom Gatherings for the fall of 2005 in Kansas, Colorado, and Montana. An overview of the history of Associates in religious communities in the United States and of the Sisters of Charity Associate Program preceded group reflections on concrete possibilities for its growth.[17] Associates and sisters received copies of the second issue of *Voices of Charity*.

At home, the traditional ministry of teaching took a direction that was to bring unpredictable unity of purpose and vision to the Community. Although schools receive generous support in dioceses where Sisters of Charity and thousands of other women religious have taught, the long-range future of Catholic education is dependent on economic contingencies and the initiatives of committed leaders. By 2005, school closings and mergings reported for metropolitan dioceses from New York and New Jersey across the Middle West to California, with concentrated numbers in Brooklyn, Chicago, and St. Louis, raised fears that inner-city cores might suffer the most grievous losses.

Based on the Jesuit model for educating children from low-income families and adopted by the De La Salle Christian Brothers, the Nativity–San Miguel Network has opened fifty-seven schools in twenty-six states over the past thirty-five years.[18] Cristo Rey high schools are a singular nine-year-old collaborative system. In Chicago, Los Angeles, Portland, Denver, and six other cities, they serve young women and men of various faiths and cultures open to the values of Catholic education and willing to work in pre-professional positions to help finance their learning. A strategic plan aimed at sixteen schools within the first decade of the new century.

In the fall of 2006, Cristo Rey Kansas City opened under the sponsorship and administration of the Sisters of Charity of Leavenworth. Seven sisters and a candidate have committed themselves to the ministry in administration, curriculum, admissions, work study training, and mission. Four friends of the Community filled out the staff of twelve. Sister Vickie Perkins is president of Cristo Rey, a college preparatory high school with a work-study program for motivated, economically disadvantaged students. Trained to the highest level of customer service, students job-share one full-time position at entry level in the corporate world. Working in teams of four, they each spend one full day at the job and rotate a fifth day every week. They abide by professional standards with regular evaluation and opportunity for summer employment. Managed by a corporate agency associated with the school, the team wage or fee meets all legal requirements and pays for 70 percent of the students' tuition.

A layman's initiative, start-up grants for a feasibility study, broad Network consultation, and arrangement with the Redemptorist Fathers for use of their converted parish school in Kansas City, Missouri, preceded a year's work by the team of sisters. They recruited one hundred students for the first year. Some sixty-five Kansas City businesses and professional firms invested in the program that serves young people and their families. Nationwide, corporate sponsors who hire the students register a 91 percent retention rate.

The integrated system of academics, work, spirituality, and extracurricular activities prepares graduates for college study and further professional employment. While many of the students come from Catholic homes and schools, others meet Catholic traditions and beliefs for the first time in a welcoming, non-proselytizing environment. A principal benefit for the Community's investment of personnel and initial support was evident from the start in enthusiasm for a new unifying educational ministry. Volunteer prayer partners signed up at the Mother House.[19]

New education vehicles at the University of Saint Mary held potential in 2005 for illuminating values implicit in public policy and uses of power. Under the direction of Randy Scott, new chair of the history, political science, and global studies department of the University of Saint Mary, the Lawrence D. Starr Global Studies Institute broadened its base of consultation and the range of topics opened to dialogue. The institute's first generous endowment invited collaboration with others who believe in the

Leading classmates, staff, Sisters of Charity of Leavenworth, and guests, Cristo Rey Kansas City freshmen move to the ribbon-cutting ceremony from Redemptorist Church after the Mass of the Holy Spirit that opened their first school year. (Photograph by Therese Horvat)

possibility of converting economic and political structures to service of those without power or privilege.

One who taught such goals during his forty years at Saint Mary died in July 2005. "A champion, who challenged us to think beyond our selfish little worlds," was the tribute of a Saint Mary alumna who knew Father John Stitz as chaplain of the college when she was there. Hundreds of fellow priests, colleagues, former students and parishioners, sisters, friends, and family came to Annunciation Chapel on the campus to honor him in a vigil service and the Mass of Resurrection. A tireless advocate for the needy, Father Stitz coordinated for the Archdiocese of Kansas City in Kansas Papal and Extension Volunteers and founded Kansas Volunteers to serve missions in the States and Latin America.

At the Eucharist, a priest he had taught described John's loyalty to a Church he often found deeply flawed; the young homilist called him a man who above all loved Jesus and lived by his Gospel as faithfully as he was able. The archbishop recalled how persistently Father John trusted dialogue even in the face of dissent or division.[20] The funeral procession, some forty cars long, wound through Leavenworth and rolling valleys of farmland to the cemetery at Mooney Creek where more parishioners waited. The graveside blessing closed with the chanted *Salve Regina* and a prayer that ended: "May this pilgrimage remind us of what we already know: that nothing dies,... is only transformed into new life."[21] Wheat that John had helped a friend plant years before rested on the box that held his body. The Community's relationship with Father Stitz was a living model of the faithful dialogue with the Church that the sisters pledged at their Chapter.

Visible confirmation of the potential for Church as communion came in an event in the life of the Sisters of Charity of Leavenworth, July 19–20, 2005, when family, friends, and fellow sisters gathered for the wake and funeral of Sister Leo Marie Cooper. Her lifelong devotion to the Blessed Sacrament governed her instructions for the wake, a Holy Hour of adoration. Parents with their children and Legionnaires of Mary formally attired knelt throughout the hour of prayer. Children and parishioners from towns where Sister ministered led decades of the Rosary. Sisters scattered throughout the chapel were recognizable only to those who knew them from the past or by acquaintance with Sister Leo Marie. At the next morning's funeral Mass, traditional Latin hymns alternated with contemporary music and an elegiac song composed by two sisters for the Mass of Resurrection. Hospitality at reception and meals was an all-community affair. Granted, all were to go their separate and diverse ways. For a space of eighteen hours, those who expressed their faith in old and new ways shared communion in genuine charity.

Sister Vicki Lichtenauer walks with her parents in the final steps of her journey to perpetual vows in the institute of the Sisters of Charity of Leavenworth.

New life was the promise of applicants to the Community and of young sisters in North and South America vowing themselves to lives of service in a mission without visible boundaries. During two weeks of August 2005, four candidates were welcomed, one in Piura, Peru, and three in Leavenworth. The three ministered during their first year of initial formation in El Centro and Donnelly College, Kansas City, Kansas, and in Cristo Rey Kansas City in Missouri. Sister Jennifer Gordon renewed her vows at her parish church in Kansas City, Kansas; she is manager of St. Vincent Clinic in Leavenworth. At her profession of final vows, Sister Victoria Lichtenauer's family, friends, fellow students from St. Louis University, and sisters filled the chapel with song. The music of stringed instruments, trumpet, flute, and marimba accompanied the liturgy that spoke Jesus' words to his frightened apostles in a storm at sea: "Take courage, it is I. Do not be afraid."[22]

With their willingness to launch out on a way of life still changing, to take up a tradition rooted in the past, and to give themselves to God in a Community unknown to them a few years ago, these young women defy perplexed descriptions of their generation. In their commitments, they joined the multitude of women religious advancing Christ's mission on earth. That the Year of the Eucharist should be marked by so many deaths was thought a blessing by the Sisters of Charity of Leavenworth. It meant that so many of their own had gone to enter the great company of "friends of God and prophets" gathered into the presence of God.[23] The Community's resources for influence on decision-making and legislation of the powerful, for ministry to the needy and powerless, were enhanced even as their numbers on earth declined. Their General Chapter had brought yet stronger unity out of reconciliation and promise of new fron-

Sister Jennifer Gordon joins Mother Xavier, imaged in bronze at the Mother House, on the day of her first vows.

tiers of ministry. Their lives, fed daily by mystery and communion, were a psalm of grateful praise.

Events at home and across the globe late that summer brought up short all rejoicing. In early September, Hurricane Katrina hit the Mississippi delta, sweeping thousands of human lives and millions of dwelling places in its wake. As images of human suffering in the southern United States crossed the world, immediate offerings of aid came from hundreds of the richest and poorest countries. The Community responded swiftly with monetary contributions, offers of shelter for families at the Mother House and local convents, the University's invitation to evacuated students for a tuition-free semester, and the SCL/Health System's assistance with volunteer teams and material contributions. Individual sisters and houses exerted themselves in assisting the southern pilgrims who came their way. Experiencing twice within four years their profound vulnerability as a nation, the American people were called to contemplate the limits of their material power, the extent of human capacity for error of judgment, and their individual and collective responsibility for one another.

In the center of France late in July, Brother Roger Schutz, leader of the Taizé ecumenical religious community, died at the hands of a crazed woman during a prayer service in the Church of Reconciliation. On a visit to the monastery in 1986, Pope John Paul II had said to Brother Roger and the community, "One passes through Taizé as one passes close to a spring of water."[24] Both men knew that new life is born from loss and reconciliation. In months that followed, floods, more hurricanes, and devastating earthquakes across the Himalayan fault line took tens of thousands of lives and wiped out villages and acres of farmland.

Death of an unimaginable scope was a stark reminder in the autumn of 2005 of the prayer before communion learned in a Vincentian retreat: "One is broken, that all may be one."[25] Words of priests gathered across the globe in Australia, at the beginning of the Year of the Eucharist, echoed their deepest convictions: "The language and the signs used in celebrating Eucharist will mean only as much as their power to speak to the hearts of broken and fragmented ordinary human beings.... Participation in the Eucharist propels us into being Christ for the poor, wounded and marginalized people of our world."[26]

The Chapter commitment to relationships of hope was sign of a Church called to bring Christ's Body to a hungering world. It was a call to deepening conversion of heart enjoined on sisters in continuing renewal. It was the Community's *Amen! Alleluia!* to the daily eucharistic doxology of praise to the Trinity, in thanksgiving for Jesus Christ through whom, with whom, and in whom all things are made, and continue gladly to be.

Epilogue

Examining their recent past, women religious are obliged to look to their future. It lies at the heart of the future of the Church. This is more than metaphor. As women are responsible, in a given time, for the life blood of a generation, so a unique woman, at a precise time past, became freely responsible for the life blood of One, the promised Messiah, to be born of her body by the Spirit. Every mother and every woman vowed to live in religious community participates in such generation insofar as she believes in and bears new life for the Body of Jesus Christ, the Church.

The renewal of religious life, as decreed by the Second Vatican Council, did not go forward for its own sake but for the sake of generations to be born into the universal community of faith. The evolutionary changes wrought by that renewal are not complete. They must relentlessly deepen life at the heart of the Church, life that depends on what women bear in their hearts, in the darkness of their faith, the inviolability of their hope, and the intransigence of their love. This continuing renewal can bear fruit only in mutual recognition by those who guide and those who serve the Church. Their full collaborative consent is needed for the Spirit's work in the world.

For two millennia, the visible Church benefited by and suffered limits of cultural and historical conditions that left decisions and structural development in the hands of men. As in the centuries before Christ's coming, so in the centuries that followed, women played crucial roles in the life of the people of God, especially at times of crisis, with faithful ministry, a profound prayer life, and courageous intellectual and spiritual leadership. Because of cultural limitations, however, they did not directly influence clerical practice and education, hierarchical authority, or curial structures. The loss that has accrued to the Church is immeasurable.

For centuries both men and women shared the consequences. Both continued to contribute to the developing life of the Church that nourished the vision and labor of John XXIII, Paul VI, and the fathers of Vatican II. Forty years later the work wants new life. Given growing divisions of conviction and practice within Church and country, given growing gaps between those of means in the world and those without, given growing hungers for spiritual nourishment, the peculiar gifts of women are an incalculable and essential resource for ministering to deepening needs of the people of God.

In the first governing Chapter of the new millennium, the Sisters of Charity of Leavenworth committed themselves to fostering relationships of hope. Pre-eminent among these was relationship with the Church in dialogue and collaboration with other laity and with clergy. Hope in such relationship relies now on the need to be heard and heeded, rather than on the long evolution of women's participation in ordained ministry. The persistence of the Canaanite woman who sought healing for her child and of those to whose stubborn faith Jesus responded is a model for this kind of hope, rooted in love.

Women, married and vowed in community, know intimately the sources of life and its nourishment. They know that issues of abortion must be addressed primarily by changes in the conditions of women, yet girls and older, who lack education and understanding of their options. That knowledge, a modicum of economic security, and psychological and spiritual support are conditions of their free choice. Women know that laws and ecclesiastical sanctions do not achieve such conditions; they know how systems work for and against women who must choose between the life and death of their unborn children. No one is closer to the origins of life than women; no one is wiser about how life in the womb and new life from baptismal waters must be nurtured. The counsel and collaboration of faithful and educated women are primary sources for sustained consultation and organized action with pastors and, especially in these times, with bishops.

As mother, physician, teacher, researcher, legislator, artist, or caregiver, a woman protects and nurtures life. Whatever her profession, the potential for guarding the life of the planet and its inhabitants lies in her intelligence. With due regard for facts and budgets, a woman knows the cost of ignoring the forces of nature and neglecting basic necessities of life for any number of human beings existing anywhere. Neither illogical nor naïve, she discerns priorities and badgers or bargains for resources. No more successful than men of like purpose and determination, she is nevertheless their strongest partner and surest counsel. That is only one reason, neither mythical nor romantic, why women—theologians, liturgists, counselors, mothers, missionaries, and women religious—need to be primary consultants in determining how the faithful are to have access to the Eucharist.

In the remotest community of faith, members of the Body of Christ need regularly the food and drink, his sacramental Body and Blood, which promises their eternal life. Increasing the number of seminary applicants, praying for and promoting vocations, merging parishes, redistributing priests for sacramental ministry, and ordaining permanent deacons are necessary measures for long-term growth. They are institutional and structural. But Christ's own compassion directs our attention to the large crowds, to the thousands in overcrowded cities and deserts, who again bring their lame, their crippled, their blind and their dumb, who wait patiently on his word and have nothing to eat. They are the poorest of the poor who might indeed collapse on the way. An urgent need for the Eucharist in any part of the world means extending the sacrament of orders for the sake of the hungering faithful.

The same urgency and hunger are familiar to many divorced and remarried Catholics, barred from the sacraments by centuries-old Church law deriving from interpretation of biblical teaching. If developing sacramental theology suggests papal and episcopal consideration of what may be discipline rather than doctrine, hope for reconciliation and renewed access to the Eucharist may change the course of many lives. The testimony of countless women—those married and remarried and those vowed in community with immediate knowledge of their suffering—is a crucial resource for such historic renewal.

Reconciliation is the sacramental grace that makes redemptive the deepest suffering. Sisters who minister to the sick and their families, attend the dying in their last moments, know firsthand how those perhaps self-exiled from the sacraments and without confidence in their infinite worth before God, can find their way home. Nowhere is the potential partnership between priest and woman religious more poignant. Especially for a prisoner awaiting death, the presence of a woman, as experience has shown, may recall the bond between mother and child that for one about to die is a promise of new life.

The death of one diminished by HIV-AIDS is more frequently than not the most lonely, a final experience of abandonment. Sisters as well as others who minister to such a one understand something of this reality. They are not called to assess the way of life that brought this or that one and millions more to their death; they only learn how to ease their passage into the Presence of God. The mystery, more than the problem, of sexual orientation becomes for such women a matter of relationship—accepted or decried, feared or exploited, surrendered to God or claimed for oneself. Its complement—not its rejection—may be celibacy, taken up into the virginity of Christ. But how can such a mystery be explored within and for the Church without fearless and welcome collaboration among women and men who have ministered to the afflicted and understand something of what ministry to all the people of God requires?

Jesus' caution about the prior place of tax collectors and prostitutes in the Kingdom is not inapplicable to questions of sexual abuse and hierarchical response. Authority creates responsibility; it does not educate to its exercise. Attempts to identify causes and remedy conditions without broad and continuing consultation with those who understand both celibacy and sexuality from experience are bound to confuse real issues and at times confound the situation. The priesthood of Jesus in all of its orders must be as broad as he conceived it. That remains a mystery not to be safeguarded by tradition but rather enlarged and enriched by the experience of time and the *consensus fidelium*. The faithful are not called such for their docility but for their fidelity to Jesus Christ, their invincible hope in his grace, their compassion and common sense.

Incomplete as it must ever be, renewal of the religious life of women religious over the past half-century has brought them to unparalleled awareness of suffering. However imperfect their response, it has deepened their spirit, their prayer, their life in community, and their need to work with others. Without claiming more for its power than is warranted by facts, the consciousness of others' pain and perplexity has humbled women who acknowledge the security of their way of life. Working hand-in-hand with lay people and priests who carry complex responsibilities and face unresolvable problems, they realize that their hard-won simplicity is a gift as much as an elusive goal. In the face of real poverty, they make no claim to live poor. The measure of their union with God is the measure of their power for good. Of these there is no measure.

Citing Mary's role in the act of Redemption, proclaimed in the Dogmatic Constitution on the Church, Pope John Paul II in encyclical letter and decree[1] exhorted all women and women religious in particular to take her as model and mentor for their lives. If the past half-century has brought sisters to lasting renewal, it means they desire honest self-knowledge in their call to the mission of the Church, seek understanding of the world they live in, and daily realize that union with God is the wellspring of their ministry. Their kinship with Mary lies there.

If the Spirit waited on her assent, and if Jesus enlisted her company and counsel for his disciples, surely his Church can follow suit in a new time. Mary knew daily needs for water, bread, and oil. She knew her own limits in rearing her Son and learned the limits of those who listened to him. She surrendered her desires for his mission to the anguish it brought. She was a realist, bred of God's own compassion. These are ways women religious find themselves emulating. These are what they hope to offer, in their time, to those who people and pastor Christ's Church.

NOTES

Introduction

1. Conversation with Sister Mary Helen McInerney, January 2003.
2. *The Official Catholic Directory, 1950,* 677–702.
3. Lora Ann Quinonez, CDP, and Mary Daniel Turner, SNDdeN, *The Transformation of American Catholic Sisters* (Philadelphia: Temple University Press, 1992), 11–12; Chronological History of Sisters of Charity of Leavenworth (hereafter referred to as CH), Archives of the Sisters of Charity of Leavenworth (hereafter referred to as ASCL).
4. Chapters of Renewal 1967–69: Former Sisters of Charity of Leavenworth Respond, 1968, ASCL.
5. Sister Mary Paul Fitzgerald, SCL, Syllabus for Study of History of Sisters of Charity of Leavenworth (1958), 1, 46, 49–50, ASCL.
6. Sister Mary Buckner, SCL, *History of the Sisters of Charity of Leavenworth, Kansas* (Kansas City, MO: Hudson-Kimberly Publishing Co., 1898), chaps. 7–8, 12, 14, 16 passim; Sister Julia Gilmore, SCL, *Come North* (New York: McMullen Books Inc., 1951), chap. 1, ASCL; Membership Record, Community Secretary.
7. Fitzgerald, Syllabus, 160–71 passim.
8. Historical Summaries of Schools, Education file; Fitzgerald, Syllabus, 27, 46, 157, 181–82, ASCL.
9. Buckner, *History*, 215–17, 220–38, and chap. 20; Gilmore, *Come North*, 121, 238; see letter from Sister Mary Clare Bergen, Victor, Colorado, Nov. 25, 1898, Sister Mary Buckner, *Chronicle of the Sisters of Charity of Leavenworth*, vol. 1, 1898–1910, ASCL.
10. Membership Record; statistics from Sister Mary Lenore Martin; *Book of Common-place Lives*, record of sisters' deaths and burial places, compiled by Sister Helen Forge, Community secretary, Heritage Room. The book's title plays on a comment by Sister Mary Buckner about the "Sisters, leading in the eyes of the world only common-place lives," *History*, 499; Annunciation Chapel, Buildings file, ASCL.
11. Archives of respective foundations.
12. Membership Record; Sisters from Ireland folder, Community file, ASCL. Sister Mary Lenore Martin has researched the origins of the Irish-born sisters and their influence on the Community's history, aided in part by a Hibernian Research Award in 1989, a program administered by the Cushwa Center of the University of Notre Dame (Personal file, ASCL).

13. Papal Approval, ASCL; James Hennesey, SJ, *American Catholics: A History of the Roman Catholic Community in the United States* (New York: Oxford University Press, 1981), 187; Jo Ann Kay McNamara, *Sisters in Arms, Catholic Nuns through Two Millennia* (Cambridge: Harvard University Press, 1996), 622.

14. Certification of Teachers, Courses of Study, Directions for Teachers, Evaluations, Education file, ASCL.

15. St. Joseph's Hospital; St. John's Hospital, Santa Monica, ASCL; Erwin H. Ackerkneckt, M.D., *A Short History of Medicine* (New York: Ronald Press Co., 1955), chap. 20 passim; Fitzgerald, Syllabus, 173, 183.

16. "The Sisters of Charity and the Care of Children," Hospitals, Baby Homes file; St. Joseph's Hospital, Baby Annex; Correspondence, St. Joseph's Home, Helena, Montana; History, St. Vincent's School, Montana, Billings file, ASCL.

17. Most Rev. Paul C. Schulte, Most Rev. Edwin V. O'Hara, Clergy, Laity file; Vacation Schools History, ASCL. The comment is from notes taken by Sister Mary Syra Kelly in 1933–34. Of the volunteers, eighteen taught in nine schools in the diocese of Leavenworth in 1929. Between 1936 and 1941, 162 sisters taught about 3,800 students in eighty-one vacation schools. This includes repeated attendance, year by year. Eulalia Erbacher, president of the diocesan chapter of the National Council of Catholic Women, planned the original vacation schools for the diocese.

18. *Centennial, Sisters of Charity of Leavenworth, 1858–1958*, 6, 18–20, 24, ASCL.

19. See an illuminating article by Michael J. Baxter, "Notes on Catholic Americanism and Catholic Radicalism: Toward a Counter-Tradition of Catholic Social Ethics," in *American Catholic Traditions*, ed. Sandra Yocum Mize and William Portier, College Theology Society (Maryknoll, NY: Orbis Books, 1997), 42:53–71.

20. Thomas A. Tweed, ed., Introduction, *Retelling U.S. Religious History* (Berkeley: University of California Press, 1997), 7.

1. Reading the Signs

1. The town of New Madrid fell twelve feet and was buried under water in the course of the quakes, each of which measured from 8.4 to 8.8 on the Richter scale. The Mississippi was reported to have flowed backward for a few hours during upheavals that created lakes and swamps, wasted forests, and caused landslides in a tract of 3,000 to 5,000 square miles. Tremors were felt coast to coast; some 1,500 aftershocks kept populations in fear for years. The New Madrid Fault, as it is called, is a rift in the earth's plates about 45 miles wide and 190 miles long, extending along parts of the Mississippi, Missouri, and Ohio Rivers in the states of Mississippi, Arkansas, Missouri, and Kentucky (*New Encyclopaedia Brittanica*, 8:639, 29:324).

2. Buckner, *History*, 34–35, 37–38; Gilmore, *Come North*, 28, 51–52; CH; Mother Xavier Ross, Minutes of Council Meetings of Nazareth Community, Notes from Nazareth, ASCL. The Chronology dates Mother Xavier's office from 1851, the year she left the Nazareth Community. *The Metropolitan Catholic Almanac and Laity's Directory* for 1852 under Diocese of Nashville included a precise listing of the insti-

tutions staffed by the Sisters of Charity, with Mother Xavier Ross, Superior (Gilmore, *Come North*, 52).

3. Walter LaFeber, Richard Polenberg, and Nancy Woloch, *The American Century: A History of the United States Since 1941*, 5th ed. (Boston: McGraw-Hill, 1998), 394–446 passim.

4. Report to the Sacred Congregation for Religious, 1951–55, pp. 36–39, Quinquinnial Reports, ASCL.

5. Tertian Program, Spiritual Life Institute, Sister Formation file, ASCL.

6. Tertians, Temporary Vow Sisters file, ASCL.

7. Report to the Sacred Congregation for Religious (hereafter cited as Report to Congregation), 1955–60, p. 40, ASCL.

8. Statistics, Surveys, ASCL.

9. Mother General's Report to General Chapter (hereafter cited as Report to Chapter), 1956, 1–2, 9–10, ASCL.

10. Ibid., 11.

11. Fitzgerald, Syllabus; *Eastern Kansas Register*, Nov. 7, 1958, Newspapers, SCL Centennial Overview file; 1956 Report to Chapter, 11–13, ASCL.

12. 1956 Report to Chapter; *Centennial* booklet, 22; Report to Congregation, 1961–65, ASCL.

13. Ann Braude, "Women's History *Is* American Religious History," in Tweed, *Retelling U.S. Religious History*, 87–107, 106. George C. Stewart Jr. records from the *Official Catholic Directory* for 1965 a total of 10,503 schools with 4.56 million students (*Marvels of Charity: History of American Sisters and Nuns* [Huntington, IN: Our Sunday Visitor Publishing Division, 1994], 428).

14. 1956 Report to Chapter, 14–15; CH; Fitzgerald, Syllabus, ASCL. Facts about nurses from Sister Mary Lillian Landauer.

15. 1956 General Chapter; CH, ASCL.

16. Survey of Former Sisters of Charity of Leavenworth, Fall 2001 (hereafter referred to as Survey 1).

17. Ibid.

18. Chronicles of the Sisters of Charity of Leavenworth (hereafter referred to as Chronicles), 13:188; CH; Historical Data, Centennial Overview, ASCL.

19. Chronicles, 14:117; *The Leaven*, Dec. 30, 1961, 9, Leavenworth Diocese, Parish Histories file, ASCL. Writer of the article was J. H. Johnston III, then a staff photographer for *The Leavenworth Times*.

20. Quinonez and Turner, *The Transformation of American Catholic Sisters*, 6–7.

21. The team included Sister Rose Dominic Gabisch, chair, and Sister Mary Liguori Horvat, both Sister Formation representatives; Sister Mary Louise Sullivan, Saint Mary College representative; Sister Mary Camilla Montgomery, juniorate director; and Sister Mary Clarence (Madelon) Burns, novice mistress. They were assisted by apostolate area consultants Sisters Mary Baptista Ward, Mary Ursula Daily, Michel Pantenburg, and Anthony Marie (Regina) Deitchman (Mother Leo Frances to Sisters, Oct. 18, 1962, Circular Letters file, ASCL). A name in parentheses is the sister's re-assumed baptismal name or her former name in religion.

22. Sister Formation file; Quinonez and Turner, *The Transformation of American Catholic Sisters*, 9–11.

23. Conversation with Sister Eileen Sheehy, January 2003.

24. The teachers were Sisters Perpetua McGrath, Anita Sullivan, and Ivan Marie (Barbara) Kushan (Personal files, ASCL, and conversations, Fall 2005).

25. The newsletter was edited by Sisters Mary Ernestine Whitmore and Mary Janet McGilley; its artist was Sister Andrea Johnston. Sister Mary Christopher D'Arcy represented the sister nurses. The semi-monthly *In Touch*, edited by the Council from 1968 to 1974, kept the sisters informed about the apostolates' work of renewal. During the same period, *Relay's* staff of high school English teachers told the stories that reflected the energy of renewal. *Perspective* was a record of the Chapter of 1973–1974. Volunteers published *Spectrum* to integrate news and views. From 1976 to 1980, *Catch-Up* was a prelude to *Connecting* and its two decades of publication (Communications file, ASCL).

26. CH, ASCL.

27. Quinonez and Turner, *The Transformation of American Catholic Sisters*, 37.

2. Responses of Head and Heart

1. Chapter of Affairs, 1962, Proceedings; Constitutions 1915–1983, 1958 reprint, ASCL. A footnote on the Chapter's decision to retain the Chapter of Faults is an entry in the Chronicles of 1964, from the Junior Sisters' house history, about an experiment initiated by their directress, Sister Mary Camilla. In order "to make this exercise more meaningful...," each sister spoke to her companions "in a conversational manner" about three things "in which she thought she had failed." Discussion and a group resolution followed, on the common failures in keeping silence (Chronicles, 16:239).

2. 1962 Chapter Proceedings; Report to Chapter, ASCL.

3. CH; St. Vincent's Home file; Book of Firsts, ASCL. The Home had stood empty since the Sisters of Providence had taken over the orphanage and built elsewhere. The cutline for an aerial photo of the campus, in *The Kansas City Star*, Apr. 22, 1963, described the new octagonal dining room, "looking like a flower from the air.... The stainless steel spire on the ruffled roof is 20 feet tall. A solar-glass 'lantern' beneath it admits sky light. Sides of the building are columns interspersed with sections of orange-colored glass. Inside, music is piped through eight chandeliers" (Chronicles, 16:14–15). The annalist reported that approximately 1,500 people attended the open house that followed the dedication ceremony.

4. This Kansas priest, a member of the St. James Missionary Society founded by Cardinal Cushing of Boston, spoke movingly of his parish, half the town's population and 8 percent of whom he saw at Mass, about 1 percent at the Sacraments. "The need is right there in those figures.... I write you with trepidation. So many have turned a deaf ear to my entreaty... that I am almost afraid to write any more. But the task lies before me...." (Newsletter from Mother House, Apr. 14, 1963,

1–2). The call to religious communities and clergy to assist the Church in Latin America came in the papal encyclical, *Princeps Pastorum*, addressing issues of mission, native clergy, and lay participation.

    5. CH; Heritage Room; Newsletter; *Leavenworth Times*, Aug. 30, 1963, and Mar. 7, 1965; *Eastern Kansas Register*, Oct. 8 and Dec. 31, 1965, Newspaper Clippings, Talara file, ASCL.

    6. Chronicles, 16:53, ASCL.

    7. CH; Book of Firsts; Chronicles, 16:9, 11, 27.

    8. SCL/HSC Health System Assemblies, 1960–69, ASCL; conversations with Sister Mary Beth Kelly and Sister Mary Pauline Degan, January 2003.

    9. Chronicles, 16:219; clipping from *Eastern Kansas Register*, Apr. 30, 1965; Chronicles, 16:228, 204, 207–9; clipping from *Leavenworth Times*, Mar. 14, 1965, ASCL.

    10. Sister Frances Therese's obituary and clippings from *Eastern Kansas Register*, Sept. 27, 1968, and Feb. 28, 1969; *Leavenworth Times*, June 29, 1969, Personal file, ASCL.

    11. Report to Congregation for Religious, 1961–65, pp. 46–47, ASCL.

    12. General Chapter, 1968, Former Sisters Respond; Report to Congregation, 48, ASCL.

    13. A practiced teacher, Sister Mary Adelaide Grellner, came to their aid, mentored them through the next ten months, clarifying the sequence of grammar assignments, lending them lesson plans and study materials, and discussing with them novels they had never formally studied.

    14. Conversation with Sisters Mary Elizabeth Strecker and Rose Orchard, November 2002.

    15. Sister Ann Marita Loosen took up a hospital administration residency at Frederick Hospital in Frederick, North Dakota, to complete her degree work at the University of Minnesota; Sister Miriam Therese Larkin went to Powell County Hospital in Deer Lodge, Montana, as a volunteer nurse (Personal files; conversation with Sister Ann Marita, Summer 2005).

    16. Hennesey, *American Catholics*, 323.

    17. In 1965 when Sister Rose Dominic took office as executive director of Sister Formation in Washington, DC, Mother Leo Frances appointed Sisters Mary Kevin Hollow and Mary Janet McGilley to the Community's Formation Committee, the former as chair. The next year the Council enlarged the group and renamed it the Formation Planning Committee. (Mother Leo Frances to sisters, Feb. 18, 1965, and Jan. 27, 1966, Circular Letters, ASCL.)

    18. General Chapter, 1968, ASCL.

    19. Former Sisters Respond, ASCL.

    20. Ibid.

    21. Conversation with Sister Maureen Craig, November 2002; Mission Assignments, Community Secretary's records.

    22. Sister Mary Emilda Gleason, Sister Hyacinth Marksman, Personal files, ASCL.

23. Conversation with Sisters Mary Andrew and Mary Josepha Talle, January 2003.
24. Story from Sister Mary Sarah Fasenmeyer.
25. Conversation with Sister Mildred Marie Irwin, Summer 2000.

3. Heeding Many Voices

1. Tweed, *Retelling U.S. Religious History*, Introduction, 10.
2. Elizabeth Kolmer, ASC, *Religious Women in the United States: A Survey of the Influential Literature from 1950 to 1983* (Wilmington, DE: Michael Glazier Inc., 1984), 19–23, 32–35.
3. Ibid., 24–25.
4. Sister Marie Augusta Neal, SNDdeN, *From Nuns to Sisters, An Expanding Vocation* (Mystic, CT: Twenty-Third Publications, 1990), 35, 40–42. It is important to observe at this point that the Sisters' Survey of 1967 has been brought into serious question by Sister Elizabeth McDonough, OP, canonist for *Review for Religious* and author of published work on renewal in religious life ("The Sisters' Survey Revisited," *Review for Religious* 63/4 [2004]: 387–401). Careful examination of her objections reveals that they do not touch the purposes and method of my use of the survey's data and their interpretation by Sister Marie Augusta Neal.

McDonough's objections derive from basic elements of Neal's research: first, the origin of her "belief scales" with regard to reliability and their use in accounting for change in religious life during the renewal decades and the designation of "pressure areas" in religious life assumed to be dysfunctional; and second, interpretation of results claimed to have influenced decisions of governing Chapters and subsequently the lives of tens of thousands of women religious in the United States.

The third area of concern is pertinent to this account of renewal by the Sisters of Charity of Leavenworth. In her conclusion as well as throughout her analysis, Sister Elizabeth at once questions, though indirectly, the legitimacy of a renewal guided by flawed research and biased premises while she apparently accepts the repeated claims by Neal and other writers of its pervasive effects. (The claims appear in Neal's *Nuns to Sisters* and in Quinonez and Turner, *The Transformation of American Catholic Sisters*.)

This chapter in particular of the present history and evidence to follow witness to the fact that this religious community and perhaps an unknown number of others made their way to renewal without dependence on the Sisters' Survey. This is not to deny the Survey's influence but only to clarify the nature of this Community's intense and extensive study in preparation for the Chapters of Renewal. Careful review of sources reveals only one reference to the Survey. For purposes of comparing change in the sisters' thinking between 1967 and 1968, the year of the Community's first Renewal Chapter, a questionnaire drew upon items in Neal's survey as well as upon the sisters' extensive study of the documents of Vatican II.

Estimating the influence of the national Sisters' Survey on the thinking of Sisters of Charity of Leavenworth—impossible in any case—would in the process identify sources used by creators of the Survey with a long tradition of the Church's social teaching, with formal decrees of a contemporary ecumenical council, and with the precepts of the Gospel. Respondents drew on backgrounds, education, and intellectual growth that both transcended and encompassed purposes and outcomes of the Survey.

To call on its data as a base of comparison between the experiences, divisions, and decisions of one community and those of the majority of women religious in the country does not require the Survey's formal validity. The parallels drawn, however, go far to demonstrate its immeasurable usefulness. Particulars of Sister Elizabeth's analysis that refer to critical identification of ultimate values and that contrast abstracted notions of fundamental beliefs suggest the need for recourse to cited sources and for clarifying dialogue with those interested in the critique.

5. *Evangelica Testificatio*, apostolic exhortation of His Holiness Pope Paul VI on the Renewal of the Religious Life According to the Teaching of the Second Vatican Council, 1971. <http://www.google.saint-mike.org/Library/Papal>, paragraph 17.

6. Neal, *From Nuns to Sisters*, Introduction, 4–5; CMSW Sisters' Survey, Part I (1966) Congregational Survey, Archives of the University of Notre Dame, Marie Augusta Neal Papers (hereafter referred to as UND: CNEA), 14; Sister Marie Augusta Neal, SNDdeN, "Implications of the Sisters' Survey for Structural Renewal," CMSW Annual Assembly Proceedings 1967, 9–10, Archives of the University of Notre Dame, Leadership Conference of Women Religious Records (hereafter referred to as UND: CLCW), 10/12. Neal, "A Report on the National Profile of the Third Sisters' Survey," Emmanuel College, Boston, July 1991. Revised February 20, 1992. UND: CNEA 40/13.

7. Congregational Survey, UND: CNEA 14; "Implications," 10.

8. UND: CLCW 66/22, #207, Sisters of Charity of Leavenworth, Xavier, Kansas, UND: CNEA 14; Former Candidates, Former Sisters, 1958–1995; Novitiates and Vow Groups, Mother Generals' Letters, ASCL; Community Secretary's records.

9. Advanced degrees in other fields aimed to fill out what a supervisor or principal needed to broaden the education of young teachers and to prepare some for administrative positions. The national picture approached what the previous generation had thought liberal with practical needs of the congregation in view: 10 percent with advanced degrees in literature, 8 percent in theology, 6 percent in history, 4 percent each in mathematics and administration, 3 percent each in nursing education and music, only 2 percent each in art, science, guidance, special education—and slightly more in all social sciences ("Implications," 13–16).

10. Report to Congregation, 1961–1965, pp. 19–22, 15; Centennial Booklet, 30–31, ASCL.

11. *SCL Relay*, Spring 1965 and 1968, ASCL.

12. "Implications,"16–17, CMSW Annual Assembly, CLCW 10/12.

13. Renewal 1966, ASCL.

14. Sister Rose Dominic Gabisch, "The Apostolate of the Elementary School Teacher," Renewal 1966, ASCL.

15. Ibid.

16. CMSW Report: Textual copies, Chicago 9/24/67, "Implications of the Sisters' Survey for Structural Renewal," 5, UND: CNEA 14.

17. Schemata, Community Study, 1967–68, ASCL. The schema does not identify a specific source for these words of Paul VI. In language and tone, however, this quotation strongly resembles a passage from *Evangelica Testificatio*. Selected lines from the Vatican website translation of the apostolic exhortation read: "How then will the cry of the poor find an echo in your lives? That cry must, first of all, bar you from whatever would be a compromise with any form of social injustice. It obliges you also to awaken consciences to the drama of misery and to the demands of social justice made by the Gospel and the Church. It leads some of you to join the poor in their situation and to share their bitter cares.... You are aware... that the needs of today's world...make your poverty more urgent and more deep." See *Evangelica Testificatio*, 18, 22.

18. Unfortunately, the source of the passage was not indicated.

19. Community Study, 1967–68, Schemata, passim, ASCL.

20. "Implications,"18–19, CMSW Annual Assembly, CLCW 10/12.

21. "Implications," 6–7, CMSW Report, Textual copies, CNEA 14.

22. The Research Committee of CMSW, Cover Letter, Sisters' Survey, Apr. 1, 1967, UND: CNEA 14.

23. Only professed sisters responded to the survey. No age group under twenty was recorded. Other demographic facts fill out the picture. Almost 87 percent of community members were white, and very nearly a third of them second-generation American citizens. Close to 40 percent of the sisters perceived theirs as working-class families, nearly half as middle-class. About a quarter came from families of six to eight children; another near-quarter, from four to five siblings. Only about 22 percent grew up in a city or suburbs, 15 percent on a farm, more than 40 percent in towns large or small. More than 75 percent were not studying full time for a degree at the time of the survey (Individual Order Analysis on Program A, Order No. 307, UND: CNEA 14).

24. Present and former superiors ranked significantly higher in their estimate of service to the poor and awareness of local needs. Between 30 and 40 percent of all respondents saw renewal in local houses going forward, whether rapidly or slowly. The survey's national statistics revealed that 83 percent of the responding sisters were not working with the poor ("Implications," 17, CLCW 10/12).

25. Individual Order Analysis, UND: CNEA 14.

26. Ibid.

27. Ibid.

28. Sisters' Survey, Materials Sent to Major Superiors, UND: CNEA 14.

29. "Disintegration and Reintegration, report on the study made within the Congregation of Notre Dame de Namur with some sociological interpretation," KASKI, The Hague, August 1972, Dr. C. Spruit, Introduction, 10, 13–15. The report was issued from an institute, KASKI, that conducted research for the Catholic Church in the Netherlands. Located in The Hague, province of Kaski, it accepted

projects such as this study for the purpose of testifying to the strength of witness given by religious life (Dr. W. J. J. Kusters, Director, Preface, 2, UND: CNEA 16).

30. Adapted from Neal, "Implications," 5–7, CMSW Report, Textual copies. Neal's words are quoted.

31. "Implications," 18, 20, CMSW Annual Assembly.

32. Interview, Summer 2000.

33. Records of the Community Secretary.

34. Dante Alighieri, *The Divine Comedy*, Canto 33, ll. 143–455, vol. 2, Purgatory, trans. Mark Musa (New York: The Penguin Classics, 1985).

4. Untold Stories

1. According to some archival records, the total membership at the time was 986; the apparent discrepancy may be due to differences in the time of recording and inclusion of novitiate members in the latter count.

2. Former Sisters, Community Secretary's records; Former Candidates, ASCL.

3. The minimal return for validity of surveys is 17 percent.

4. Conversation with Sister Mary Seraphine Sheehan, Summer 2001.

5. "Implications of the Sisters' Survey for Structural Renewal," CMSW Annual Assembly Proceedings 1967, 10, UND: CLCW 10/12.

6. Former Sisters, ASCL; Former Sisters, Community Secretary's records.

7. The percentage of response from those who left in decades of rising and falling departures reveals a slightly higher response from the earlier half of the trend. Of the 132 who departed during the twelve years between 1958 and 1969, when numbers peaked, 23.5 percent responded to the survey. Of the 157 who left in the next decade, 1970–1979, 20.4 percent responded. From the fifteen years following, 1980–1995, when departures had slowed to an annual average of 3.8, the response fell to 14 percent. This *may* suggest that those who left in the 60s and 70s had stronger motivation to clarify their experience to others as well as to themselves.

8. Survey 1. All quotations are cited with permission from responses to this survey.

9. Survey 1: Kathleen Eraerts Stark, Mercedes A. Leonard Doherty, Marcella A. Tshum, Patty Hughes Cole (Sr. Jean Pierre), Mary Isabelle Hardesty Rolewicz (Sr. Ann Michael), and Lucille B. Canjar Stanaway.

10. Survey 1: Charlotte Dillon-Moran, Frances Granattan, Eleanor Olguin.

11. Direct service to the poor was a tradition of the Community from its beginnings. The individual sister participated insofar as time and energy allowed, given the duties of her assigned mission. With changes in mission assignment policy, personal discernment of ministry brought individual choices of full-time direct service to those in material need.

12. Conversation with Sister Mildred Marie Irwin, Summer 2000.

5. Unfolding of a Drama

1. LaFeber et al., *The American Century*, 428–505 passim.

2. Hennesey, *American Catholics*, 307–21 passim. These and other conflicting realities affected indirectly the stability of Catholic education. Due to a complex mix of causes, enrollment in Catholic schools fell from 5.6 million in 1965 to less than 3.2 million in 1980. In the same period, the number of Catholic grade schools fell from 10,879 to 8,149; the number of secondary schools, from 2,413 to 1,527; and the number of colleges and universities, from 309 to 239 (p. 323).

3. After an extended exchange inspired by conviction and deep feeling about the role of the individual person in community, a sister responded with an appeal for faith in one another "through hearing the sincerity and concern for truth that underlie a sister's words..., through hearing what a sister is actually saying, not what we have previously decided she is saying..., through hearing the Spirit speaking where even two are gathered in His name (Letter from Sister Marie de Paul Combo, *Perspective*, Dec. 10, 1967).

4. Committee on Election of Chapter Delegates; letters of Mother Leo Frances to the sisters, Apr. 19 and Aug. 22, 1967, Circular Letters, ASCL.

5. Sisters under temporary vows had diminished in number since 1962 by 17 percent, a 10 percent greater loss than that of the previous six years. Professed sisters who had left during the same period totaled a shocking seventy, forty-one under temporary vows, twenty-nine under perpetual vows. The number of postulants seeking admittance since 1962 had plunged by nearly three-fourths and novices by more than two-thirds (Community Secretary's records).

6. *Special Chapter Letters*, June 18 and 20, 1968, Chapter of 1968–1969 file, ASCL. The unprecedented publication of Chapter Letters was a sign of the continuing involvement and intense interest of the sisters in the processes of renewal and of the Community's commitment to open communication of its progress. A report on daily Chapter meetings was written by Sister Mary Ernestine Whitmore, distributed across the campus, and mailed throughout the Community. In response to readers' requests, the weekly letter was published every other day throughout the first Chapter session. Sisters Kathleen Eraerts and Carol Hinds followed suit for the second session in the summer of 1969.

7. *Special Chapter Letter*, July 14, 1968.

8. Position Paper and statistics from Community Questionnaire, April 1968, Chapter of 1968–1969 file, ASCL. Issues and figures that follow derive from this source.

9. Quoted phrases are from questions posed by the position paper.

10. Issues of governance were discussed in *Perspective*, Jan. 13, 1968.

11. Sister Mary Claudelle (Joan Sue) Miller's paper on values and functions of religious attire appeared in *Perspective*, Feb. 8, 1968.

12. *Special Chapter Letter*, July 24, 1969.

13. *Special Chapter Letters*, July 3, 12, and 24, 1969. In discussion of renewal in governance structures, a possible expansion of the General Council and re-ordering

of its responsibilities had been suggested. In view of the increasing demand on the Generalate's time for necessary travel and major decisions regarding the Community's institutions, half the Council might take on administrative tasks, the other half be personally responsible throughout the year for the individual sister's welfare and local community's needs. Regional authority for the latter role, with regular meetings of the whole Council, would facilitate the arrangement (Sister Mary Lenore Martin, "S.C.L. Aggiornamento," *Relay*, Summer 1968, pp. 18–19).

14. *Special Chapter Letter*, June 28, 1968; *In Touch*, Dec. 10, 1968. This was an interim newsletter begun between Chapter sessions. The new Formation Committee included Sister Mary Seraphine Sheehan, Community councilor; Sisters Gregory (Eileen) Sheehy, Mary Incarnata (Anne) Callahan, and later Leo Therese (Mary Lou) Mendel, formation directors; Sister Mary Clarence (Madelon) Burns, vocation director; Sister Mary Louise Sullivan, college representative; and Sister Rose Dominic Gabisch, personnel consultant. Sisters from apostolates served in a consultant capacity.

15. *Perspective*, July 17, 1968, and see *Special Chapter Letter*, June 23, 1969, for samples of the fifty-five assumptions.

16. *Special Chapter Letter*, July 26, 1968; Advisory Board Minutes, Oct. 5, 1968, ASCL. The board included apostolate representatives, members of the Renewal Committee and the Constitutions Committee, formation directors, and the president of the college, who was chair of the Formation Committee.

17. Renewal and Experimentation, 1966–1969 file, ASCL. In proposing any project of renewal, sisters were asked to identify the problem to be addressed, state a hypothesis in support of the proposed action, and clarify its purpose, method, or procedure as well as means of evaluating results.

18. *Special Chapter Letter*, Dec. 18, 1968.

19. *Relay*, Winter 1968–69, pp. 1–5.

20. *Relay*, Summer 1968, pp. 20–29.

21. Sister Mary Lenore Martin, "A School and a School," *Relay*, Winter 1968–69, pp. 12–18.

22. *Relay*, Spring 1968, pp. 1–3.

23. *Relay*, Spring 1968, pp. 2–5, 9–14.

24. *Perspective*, June 20, 1969.

25. Report to Chapter, 1968–1969 file; Education Apostolate Study–1968 folder, Education file, ASCL.

26. *Special Chapter Letter*, June 23, 1969.

27. *Special Chapter Letter*, July 12, 1969.

28. *Special Chapter Letters*, July 3 and 12, 1969.

29. *Special Chapter Letters*, June 28, 1968; July 8 and 10, 1969. Notes from an address on the vows by canonical consultant Father Thomas Swift, SJ, were published in the July 22 Chapter Letter.

30. *Special Chapter Letter*, July 10, 1969.

31. *Special Chapter Letter*, July 15, 1969.

32. Area Superiors file, ASCL.

33. Chapter Minutes, Regional Coordinators; *Special Chapter Letter*, July 19, 1969.
34. Personnel Board file; Renewal and Experimentation Board file, ASCL.
35. *Special Chapter Letter*, July 24, 1969.
36. Story from Janice Steiger.
37. Conversation with Sister Maureen Craig, Spring 2001.

6. Experimentation: An Interval of Learning

1. Chronicles, ASCL; conversations, Fall 2002.
2. Conversation, Spring 2001.
3. The study was conducted by Sisters Mary Kevin Hollow and Rose Dominic Gabisch at the request of Mother Leo Frances Ryan. Statistics and statements that follow come from examination of responses to the survey.
4. Studies of Withdrawals, 1968–1972, ASCL.
5. Sr. Margaret Mary Modde, OSF, student, the Catholic University of America, and Dr. John P. Koval, De Paul University, "Phase I of Research Project on Women Who Have Left Religious Communities," Proceedings of NSVC symposium, August 1974, National Sisters Vocation Conference–Liaison 1967–1981, UND: CLCW 6/11. Sister Margaret Mary and Dr. Koval presented a report, "Women Who Have Left Religious Communities: A Study in Role Stress," at the 1974 annual meeting of the Society for General Systems Research in New York. Statistics of their research included the little-known contrast in sheer numbers of women and men who had committed themselves to a celibate life in service of Church and Christian community. In their peak years of 1966 and 1967 there were approximately 180,000 women and 60,000 men, a 3-to-1 ratio. But women led the men as well in the number of departures from religious or clerical life after those peak years by a ratio of 4 to 1, that is, a 21 percent loss of women religious as opposed to a 5.6 percent loss of priests. Further, an 81 percent decrease in the number of women entering religious life contrasted with a 55.5 percent decrease in the number of seminarians—losses that prompted serious investigations from the late 1960s forward. The survey of women religious was mailed to 2,302 former sisters whose names were supplied in total confidentiality by major superiors of congregational members of LCWR, by board members of NSVC, and by former sisters themselves (pp. 1–2).
6. Modde and Koval, "Women Who Have Left Religious Communities: A Study in Role Stress," 3–6, 7.
7. Ibid., 13–16, 18–19, 22.
8. Regional Coordinators file, ASCL. Facts from this file as recorded were checked with former coordinators Sisters Marie de Paul and Edna Hunthausen.
9. Conversations with Sisters Regina DeCoursey and Marie de Paul Combo, Fall 2003.
10. Regional Coordinators file.

11. Conversations with Sisters Marie Madeleine, Mary Elizabeth Strecker, Maureen Craig, Fall 2002.
12. Conversation with Sister Maureen Craig, Fall 2002.
13. Conversation with Sister Marie de Paul Combo, Fall 2003.
14. Conversation with Sister Edna Hunthausen, Summer 2003.
15. Ibid.
16. Placement Policies file, ASCL.
17. Evaluation Survey, Regional Coordinators' file.
18. Evaluation Forms, Placement Policies file.
19. Formation file, ASCL.
20. Tertianship file, ASCL.
21. Comment from Sister Maureen Kehoe, A Survey of Community Members, November 2001.
22. National Conference of Major Superiors, 1972, LCWR file, ASCL.
23. Sister Marie de Paul Combo, personal account required for application to Institute of Spirituality, Personal file, ASCL.
24. Sister John Mary (Maureen) Craig, "A Part of It All," *Relay*, Summer 1966.
25. Government Commission, 64–73 passim, Community Study, 1967, ASCL.
26. Conversation with Sister Marie Madeleine, Fall 2002.

7. Drama of Renewal, Continued

1. Mother Leo Frances's message to Eleventh General Chapter, June 28, 1973, pp. 6–9, ASCL.
2. Taken from *Chapter Newsletter*, vol. 1, no. 1 (1973).
3. *Chapter Newsletter*, vol. 1, no. 2 (1973).
4. Ibid.
5. Report of Commission on Community, Minutes of General Chapter, July 2, 1973. One sister's rejection of changes in sisters' garb became well known because of her relationship to many as their former mistress of novices. Her rebuffs on their visits to the Mother House were sharp. When she came to realize the pain she had caused, her response was profound. For years before she died, she sought out those sisters or wrote to those at a distance to express her sorrow. Many were moved by the depth of her pain.
6. Relevant here is Dr. C. Spruit's explanation of reorganization or synthesis, in the KASKI Institute's report. See chapter 3, page 60, and page 518, note 29, above.
7. *Chapter Newsletter*, vol, 1, no. 2 (1973).
8. Ibid.
9. Ibid.
10. Report of Commission on Community, Minutes of General Chapter, July 11 and 12, 1973.
11. Report of Commission on Spirituality, Minutes of the General Chapter, July 11 and 12, 1973.

12. Report of Commission on Call to Mission, Minutes of the General Chapter, July 11 and 12, 1973.
13. Ibid.
14. Report of Commission on Governance, Minutes of the General Chapter, July 11 and 12, 1973.
15. Ibid.
16. Mother Leo Frances to sisters, July 19, 1973, Circular Letters 1970–1973, ASCL.
17. Apostolate Consultants' Reports, Eleventh General Chapter, 1973–1974.
18. Variation in statistics recorded in the Education file depend on differences in time between recording data from the study and gathering data for the report to Chapter.
19. Mother General's Report to the Eleventh General Chapter, July 1974.
20. *Chapter News Briefs*, July 11, 1974, vol. 1, no. 1. The Chapter newsletter summarized day-to-day progress on proposals. It was edited that summer by Sisters Kathleen Coman, Mary Cecilia Carig, and Virginia Bartolac. Sister Mary Jo Coyle was photographer; Sister Joseph Eileen Shea, secretary in the Chapter sessions; and Sister Marie Loretta Modricin, printer.
21. Minutes of Eleventh General Chapter, 1974; *Chapter News Briefs*, vol. 1, nos. 4 and 5, 1974.
22. *Chapter News Briefs*, vol. 1, no. 2, 1974.
23. *Chapter News Briefs*, vol. 1, no. 3, 1974.
24. *Chapter News Briefs*, vol. 1, no. 5, 1974.
25. *Chapter News Briefs*, vol. 1, no. 3, 1974.

8. Getting from Here to There

1. Conversation with Sister Mary Seraphine Sheehan, Summer 2001; free responses to Survey 2, the first unsigned, the second from Sister Mary Arthel Cline. Conducted in 2002, the survey asked for reflection on the impact of renewal on the Community and its members. Chapter 22 includes analysis of responses to its seven comprehensive questions and eighty-six items.
2. Statistics from Apostolate Study, February 1975, ASCL.
3. "Another Look," Future Directions of SCL Ministries, Apostolate Study 75II, ASCL.
4. Sisters of Charity of Leavenworth Apostolate Study 75II Opinionnaire, ASCL.
5. Ibid.
6. Ibid.
7. Report of Elementary Education, Apostolate Study 75II, ASCL.
8. Future Directions of Sisters of Charity of Leavenworth Ministries, Community Council Response to Personnel Board Recommendations of November 15, 1975, Apostolate Study.
9. Report of Elementary Education.

10. Report of Secondary School Apostolate, Apostolate Study.
11. Community Council Response, Apostolate Study.
12. Future Directions for SCL Ministry file, Apostolate Study.
13. Report of Special Services, Apostolate Study.
14. Report of Social Services; Community Council Response, Apostolate Study.
15. Pastoral Ministry–Religious Education Apostolates; Community Council Response, Apostolate Study.
16. Report of Health Care Apostolate, Apostolate Study.
17. Report of Mount St. Joseph's Home under Health Care Apostolate.
18. Health Care report.
19. The elementary education group had argued from the same principle in their recommendation for fewer and better schools. But it pointed them in a contrary direction. A higher percentage of sisters committed to revitalizing their professional life and cultivating leadership, and willing to sacrifice and risk could renew the face of a school. One sister's words were quoted: "Ultimately the value of a school ... depends upon the dynamism of the faculty.... Any school could survive now given the right staffing." To 85 percent of elementary education respondents, "right staffing" meant 25 to 50 percent sisters. Number crunching was in order.
20. Opinionnaire, Apostolate Study.
21. Ibid.
22. Future Directions, Council Response, General Recommendations, Apostolate Study.
23. Accounts of what today is called mentoring from administrators fortunate enough to have had the experience confirm in fact the contrast between an inadequate academic program and the unimposing, unconscious modeling that some women in administration exemplify.
24. The organizing committee—Sisters Mary Lenore Martin, chairperson, Lynn Casey, Judy Jackson, Maurita Postlewait, and Mary Kathleen Stefani—launched the triduum, July 2–4, with Morning Praise and flag raising, then celebration of Eucharist. More than 600 sisters participated in full voice (Bicentennial file, ASCL).
25. Sister Nadine Foley, OP, "Ministry and Leadership of Women Religious in the Church Today," Bicentennial file.
26. Sister Kathleen Wood, SCL, "Mother Xavier's Charism," Bicentennial file.
27. Sister Marie de Paul Combo, "Hunger for Freedom and Justice I," Bicentennial file.
28. Sister Frances Russell, "Hunger for Freedom and Justice II," Bicentennial file.
29. Sister Mary Lenore Martin, "The SCLs in the American Catholic Tradition," Bicentennial file.
30. Sister Mary Janet McGilley, "Hope and the Vision of Things To Come," Bicentennial file.
31. Sister Mary Kevin Hollow, "On Gathering," Bicentennial file.
32. Survey 2; conversations with sisters; Mother Mary Ancilla Spoor, Personal file, ASCL.

9. A Heritage of Care: Children and the Aging

1. "Ye Olden Days now Golden Days," 1908, Golden Jubilee publication, pp. 46–47; Notes on St. Vincent's Home, Leavenworth, Kansas, from a citation in longhand on the first page of a Register at the Home, probably 1885, Saint Vincent's Home (SVH) file, ASCL; Candy Ruff, *Lifestyles* editor, "Christmas at orphanage was a time of joy," *Leavenworth Times*, n.d., Newspaper Articles, History file, Immaculate Conception–St. Joseph (IC-SJ) parish office, Leavenworth, Georgia Scanlon, secretary.

2. Miege to Urbain Miege [his brother in France], Jan. 14, 1967 in J. Garin, *Biographical Notices of Mgr. J.B. Miege, First Vicar Apostolic of Kansas*, Moutiers, [France],1886, cited in *History of Sisters of Charity of Leavenworth*, vol. 1, pp. 111–13 (Sister Mary Buckner's *History* in manuscript before publication, no longer available, SVH file, ASCL; Gilmore, *Come North*, 126–27). The sisters sewed and mended articles of clothing, linens, and bedding for the early decades of the orphanage's history. Later such items were contributed by members of a sewing circle, St. Vincent's Guild, organized in 1906 by Mrs. Thomas Walsh and others, including Ellen Farrell and Mrs. Al Dempsy [sic] (account by Ella V. Carroll; *Catholic Advance*, May 23, 1931, SVH file).

3. Notes, St. Vincent's Home, SVH file, ASCL; *Leavenworth Times*, n.d., History file, IC-SJ parish office.

4. Christopher Huot, "History of the African-American Catholic Church, Leavenworth, Kansas," paper for Historical Methods, Sister Kathleen Mary Connelly, Feb. 28, 1999, ASCL; Candy Ruff, "Facing Hardships," *Leavenworth Times Lifestyles*, Apr. 17, 1988, History file, IC-SJ parish office.

5. Huot, "History"; Oblate Sisters of Providence file, File A, ASCL; Ruff, "Facing Hardships."

6. Profiles of twelve Oblate Sisters buried in Mount Olivet, Archives of the University of Saint Mary (hereafter cited as AUSM); Huot, "History." Mother Baptista Roberts, who joined the first four sisters in 1888, spent fifty years among the black people of Leavenworth. Born in Baltimore she had been, as a child, a slave in the home of John Carroll of Carrollton. She died at St. John Hospital in 1938. Msgr. Joseph Shorter, friend of the sisters and their orphans and pastor of Holy Epiphany, is buried in Mount Olivet as well.

7. Huot, "History."

8. Sister Julia Gilmore, SCL, *We Came North* (St. Meinrad, IN: Abbey Press, 1961), 222; MS, "That Finer Charity," 219; Report, Sister Alice Clare Hill, 1940, SVH file, ASCL. In the report by Sister Alice Clare, administrator of the Home in the 1930s and 1940s, she stressed that no child had contracted a contagious disease in four years. Manners at table included serving one's companions and eating a portion of everything prepared.

9. Gilmore, "That Finer Charity," 219. An inquiry sheet from Sister Julia Gilmore to Sister Rose Vincent Staten cites 3,032 for the years between 1866 and 1955 (SVH file, ASCL).

10. Year of the Child, 1979; Catholic Charities News Letter, Mar. 1968, SVH file, ASCL.

11. Notes from Sister Frances Russell, January 2006.

12. Report on St. Vincent's Home in meeting with Generalate, June 1971, SVH file, ASCL; notes from Sister Frances Russell.

13. Minutes of Community Council meeting, 1971; SVH file; House History, St. Vincent's Home, Topeka, ASCL.

14. *Eastern Kansas Register*, Oct. 18, 1974, SVH file; Sister Rita Marie Anderson, "We're Home!" *Relay*, February 1970, ASCL; notes from Sister Frances Russell.

15. Notes from Sister Frances Russell.

16. *Independent Record*, Mar. 6, 1997; History, St. Joseph's Home folder, Helena, MT, St. Joseph's Home file; St. Ann Infant Home, 1915–1935 folder, St. Joseph's Home, Helena, MT file; Fitzgerald, Syllabus, 208–9; Gilmore, *We Came North*, 367–68. (The two files are distinct.)

17. Sister Mary Seraphine Sheehan, "St. Joseph's Home—Helena, Montana," History folder, Helena, MT, St. Joseph's Home file. *Montana Register* for Nov. 17 numbers 115 children and fifteen nuns as passengers on the buses.

18. An unidentified newspaper account of September 1951 describes the children's daily schedule at Holy Child Nursery, maintained at St. John Hospital, Helena (Holy Child Nursery folder, St. Joseph's Home, Helena, MT file).

19. Notes from Sister Angela Berry, superior of the home, March 1941, History folder, Helena, MT, St. Joseph's Home file. Another record in the file, dated 1941 and revised by Sister Angela, gives the number as sixty-nine.

20. Sheehan, "St. Joseph's Home," History folder, Helena, MT, St. Joseph's Home file; Quarterly Report, Department of Public Welfare, Division of Child Welfare Services, Jan. 1, 1965, History, St. Joseph's Home folder, St. Joseph's Home, Helena, MT file. Sister Mary Seraphine's account numbers sixteen Cuban children in 1962, increasing to thirty-three within the school year and to fifty-three in August, 1963. Departures left figures in flux.

21. General Home History folder; Fitzgerald, Syllabus, 201–2, ASCL.

22. St. Ann's Infant Home, Denver, and Holy Child Nursery folders; Sister Mary Amata Murtha to Sister Leo Gonzaga Erbacher, Mar. 12, 1938; Sister Mary Bertha Carig, "Review of All Years of St. Vincent's Home Since Its Foundation, February 21, 1960," St. Vincent's Home History (SVHH) file; Sister Veronica Toner's account, n.d., SVHH file, ASCL.

23. Home History, SVHH file; conversation with Sister Daniel Stefani, Fall 2003. The staff included Sisters Mary Carmella Neuman, Margaret Jerome Murphy, Mary Eugenia Floersch, and Mary Agnesia O'Sullivan. Child care workers were Sisters Michael Joseph (Ann) Moylan, Del Patrick Manion, Mary Gerald (Roberta) Furey, and Jean Patrice (Jacquelyn) Krueger (Sisters Stephen Ann [Virginia] Bartolac and Jean Patrice Krueger, "The Denver Boys," *Relay*, Winter 1966–67, ASCL).

24. "The Denver Boys."

25. Ibid.; conversations with Sister Daniel, Fall 2003, and with Sisters LaVonne Guidoni and Josephine Bustos, August 2004.

26. Conversation with Sister Daniel; Home History, *Spectrum*, May 1976, Clippings folder, SVHH file; Sister Virginia Bartolac, "Sugar 'n Spice," *Relay*, June 1971, ASCL.

27. "St. Vincent's Home—a Changed Program for the '70's," *Catch-Up*, Community Forum newsletter, n.d., ASCL.

28. *Catch-Up*, Winter 1979, ASCL.

29. Sisters who worked at the Home told the stories. After Sister Joseph Cecilia (Mary Ann) Gausz's brief term in the early 1950s, Sister Mary Ursula Dailey was superior from 1955 to 1961, when Sister Daniel succeeded her as administrator (Home Missions, ASCL).

30. *Vision*, vol. 1, March 1992; *Denver Catholic Register*, July 14, 1993, Home History, SVHH file, ASCL.

31. *Rocky Mountain News*, July 6, 1993; *Vision*, vol. 3, October 1993; *Denver Catholic Register*, July 5, 1995, Home History, SVHH file.

32. *Billings Gazette*, Sept. 10, 2003; newspaper accounts and notes posted near Ross Hall Chapel at the Mother House the day before Sister Daniel's funeral, Home History, SVHH file.

33. Sisters Virginia Marie Eraerts and Marie Elizabeth Corkle, "At Mount St. Joseph's Home"; *Relay*, Fall 1965; Sister Regina DeCoursey, "A Liberated Woman," *Relay*, December 1970; Mount St. Joseph's Home file, ASCL.

34. "A Liberated Woman."

35. Apostolate Study, 1975, ASCL.

36. *Kansas City Kansan*, Jan. 12, 1999, Personal file, Sister Mary Adolph Schuele, ASCL. St. Margaret's Hospital had been vacated in 1976 when Providence–St. Margaret's Hospital was relocated from central Kansas City, Kansas, to western Wyandotte County. (See details of the merger in chap. 14.)

37. *The Leaven*, May 1, 1992, and Jan. 20, 1995, Sister Mary Adolph Schuele, Personal file, ASCL; conversations with Sister Mary Adolph and Mary Kenneth, Fall 2005. Administration of St. Joseph Nursing Care Center came under the archdiocesan Catholic Housing Service Inc. (Sister Mary Kevin Hollow to the sisters, Mar. 17, 1977, Circular Letters).

38. *The Leaven*, Dec. 17, 2004; *Kansas City Kansan*, Jan. 17, 1999, Sister Mary Adolph, Personal file.

39. Talara file, ASCL.

40. *The Leaven*, Oct. 21, 1983, Chalaco y Chulucanas folder, Chalaco file, ASCL.

41. Chalaco Project folder, Chalaco file; conversations with Agnes Robin, Josie and Peter Plummer, Maura and Bob Shaw, Angela and John Maguire, and Anna Browning, Birmingham, England, Spring 1998. A production crew works from Anna Browning's home, where all spare space is filled with boxes of carefully ordered materials, used and new, some of it donated by local companies. The group meets weekly for prayer, planning, and conversation. In 2004 Agnes Robin, entrepreneur of the Birmingham project, died at age 103. The next year, Anna Browning turned 85.

42. Chalaco y Chulucanas folder, Chalaco file, ASCL; conversation with Sister Rose Dolores Hoffelmeyer, Fall 2005.

10. The Care of Teaching

1. The number is calculated from consulting Mission Files of the earliest schools and the Community secretary's files of members living and deceased. In either record, ministry information is lacking for 219 names. The percentage derives from the number of known teachers within the number whose record is complete.

2. Hospitals and Schools file, ASCL. Whether a school closed or was staffed by another religious community was the decision of the diocese that owned it, depending on the resources of the parish that maintained it.

3. Review of Elementary School Personnel, Education Apostolate Study–1968 folder, Education file, ASCL. Of the total, twenty-two had moved into other apostolates; thirty had withdrawn from the Community.

4. Elementary School Reports, Sister Bernadette Helfert, 1975–1980, ASCL.

5. According to reports for the Education Apostolate Study, enrollments in schools staffed by the Community were plunging from 1968 to 1972. A decrease of 11 percent was recorded for the years between 1975 and 1980 (Education Study, 1968, and Apostolate Report for Elementary Education, 1980, ASCL).

6. Constitutions of the Sisters of Charity of Leavenworth.

7. Conversations with Rolland Dessert, December 2003.

8. "Re-Vision: Educators take a long look at the schools…," *Relay*, August 1969, ASCL.

9. Sister Mary Seraphine Sheehan's compilation of assignments in the dioceses and archdioceses served by the Community, dated c. 1971; Education file, ASCL.

10. "The SCL's in the Land of ABC's and the 3 R's" and "Social Studies Trends Studied," *Relay*, Fall 1965 and September 1971; "Religion Program Brings Christian Life to Class," *Relay*, Winter 1966–67, ASCL.

11. Sister Regina Joseph Malmstrom, "School Receives Aid Under Title I," *Relay*, Winter 1966–67; Sisters Rosalie Curtin and Mary Jo McDonald, "Changing School"; and Sisters Jean Martin Dawson and Ann McGuire, "One at a Time—Together," *Relay*, March 1971, ASCL.

12. Sister Virginia Marie Eraerts, "Criticism and Challenge," *Relay*, Winter 1966–67.

13. Sister Anna Mary Lawrence, Personal file; video of Sister Anna Mary relating her experiences, 2002, Videotape file, ASCL.

14. Conversation with Sister Virginia Flanick, Winter 2004.

15. *We've Come This Far by Faith*, Our Lady of Perpetual Help Parish 1924–1999.

16. Instead of issuing grades, her faculty made individual evaluations at parent-teacher conferences. Special help with study skills complemented classroom teaching.

A fifth of the students were not of the Catholic faith and a third received welfare assistance. Tuition on a sliding scale ranged from $6 to $165 a year (Sister Anna Totta, "Because we put up a lot of fuss and bother," *Relay*, March 1973, ASCL; conversation with Sister Mary Timothy Hoban, Spring 2004).

17. *Kansas City Kansan*, May 29, 1970, Our Lady and St. Rose of Lima School file; Sister Mary Donald Gore, "Focus: A Glimpse of the Inner City," *Relay*, September 1971; *Eastern Kansas Register*, Nov. 19, 1976, ASCL.

18. *Blessed Sacrament News*, Sept. 1, 1974; Case Statement for School Year 1989–1990; *Kansas City Star*, June 6, 1991, Blessed Sacrament School, Kansas City, KS file, ASCL; conversation with Sister Mary Geraldine Yelich, February 2004; brochure, Blessed Sacrament Parish Ninetieth Anniversary Celebration, 1899–1989.

19. Sisters of Charity of Leavenworth at Blessed Sacrament School, Kansas City, MO, 1916–1982; memorial booklet, Blessed Sacrament Legacy; *Kansas City Star*, Feb. 25, 1973, Blessed Sacrament School, Kansas City, MO file, ASCL.

20. Brochure of Blessed Sacrament Church, 1909–1991; St. Louis School file, 1952–1981, ASCL; *Catholic KEY*, Oct. 20, 1974; *Connecting*, Oct. 16, 1980; *Catholic KEY*, Mar. 9, 1980, and Mar. 22, 1981, St. Martin de Porres School file, ASCL.

21. St. Martin de Porres School file, ASCL; conversation with Sister Mary Helen McInerney, Spring 2004.

22. St. Augustine School file, 1979–1980, ASCL.

23. History and Letters folder, St. Charles Borromeo School file, ASCL; conversation with Sister Kathleen Coman, Fall 2003.

24. *KEY to the News*, Kansas City–St. Joseph Archdiocese, May 6, 1973; Four Area Editions, Feb. 28, 1973; Annual Report 1975–1976, St. Patrick's, North Kansas City School file, ASCL.

25. Notes from Sister Julia Golkoski, April 2004; School Missions, Missouri, ASCL. The four parishes were St. Louis, St. James, St. Therese Little Flower, and St. Monica's.

26. *Topeka State Journal*, Dec. 26, 1961 and Feb. 4, 1977; *Eastern Kansas Register*, Feb. 10, 1978, Holy Name School file, ASCL. Holy Name received unexpected notoriety when one of its seventh-graders made her way up the ladder to the National Spelling Champion title and was received by Rosalyn Carter on the White House lawn. Peg, the student, was the daughter of Liz McCarthy, Saint Mary alumna, and her husband Jerry (*Topeka State Journal*, June, n.d.).

27. Conversation with Sister Mary Corita Conlan, Winter 2004.

28. *Guadalupe Communique* April-May-June 1998; *The Leaven*, Apr. 29, 1988; *Capital-Journal*, n.d., Our Lady of Guadalupe School file, ASCL.

29. *Capital-Journal*, n.d.

30. Conversation with Sister Perpetua McGrath, Winter 2004; St. Patrick's School, Hornif, Kansas file, ASCL.

31. *Kansas City Kansan*, Aug. 24, 1979, and Apr. 20, 1991, History folder, St. Peter's Cathedral School, Kansas City, Kansas file; School Missions, Kansas, ASCL.

32. St. Ann's School file, ASCL.

33. Visitation School file, ASCL.

34. Father Charles F. Kelly, pastor of St. Daniel's, commended the school at the farewell reception for the six sisters in June, 1985 (Reception and Philosophy folders, St. Daniel the Prophet School file, ASCL; conversations with Sisters Vincent Clare McDonald and Patricia Smith, Spring 2004).

35. Sister Mary Josephine Engelhardt, "At Annunciation School and Convent...," *Relay*, June 1973, Annunciation School files, ASCL.

36. Conversations with Sister Jean Anne Panisko, Winter 2004, and Sister LaVonne Guidoni, August 2004; *Vision* newsletter, January 1996 and 1997, Mount St. Vincent's Home file, ASCL.

37. Hospitals and Schools, ASCL; Sister Mary Seraphine Sheehan's compilation; School Missions, Colorado, ASCL; Daily News by e-mail, Community Secretary, Jan. 23, 2006. Throughout the 1970s and into the 1980s, six sisters staffed St. Bernadette's. Sister Jean Martin Dawson was the last principal; Sisters Agnes Eileen Dunn and Mary Elaine Murphy were the last teachers in 1983. Into the 1990s, five or six sisters were assigned to St. Therese.

38. Comparable commitments were those that helped to build and equip the Kate Fratt Memorial School in Billings and the new Immaculate Conception School in Leavenworth financed in 1965 through the trust fund established by May Hannon Whitaker (Xavier Schools file, ASCL).

39. House History 1958–1999; Margaret Williams, "A Brief History of Holy Name School," 1974; *Sheridan Press*, Oct. 29, 1999; *Wyoming Catholic Register*, October 1992, September 1994, History folder, Holy Name School, Sheridan, Wyoming file, ASCL; School Missions, Wyoming, ASCL.

40. *Laramie Daily Boomerang*, May 18, 1998, House History 1951–1998, St. Laurence School, Laramie, Wyoming file, ASCL. When U.S. Senator Alan Simpson visited the school in 1983, the students plied him with questions. He later remarked that he had never before received such good spontaneous questions from secondary school students. Their teacher was Sister Kathleen Mary Connelly; Sister Katherine Mary Westhues was principal (House History, 1983–1984, St. Laurence School, Laramie, Wyoming file, ASCL).

41. Facts recorded by Sister Mary Eugenia Floersch, St. Cyril and Methodius School, Rock Springs, Wyoming file; House History, 1952–1970, Our Lady of Sorrows School, ASCL.

42. *Wyoming Register*, Oct. 11, 1978, Rock Springs Catholic School file, ASCL.

43. *Rock Springs Daily Rocket-Miner*, Mar. 8, 1968, Rock Springs Catholic School file, ASCL.

44. Record of Closed Missions, Montana, ASCL; Sister Mary Kevin Hollow, "The Helena Story," *Relay*, August 1969, ASCL; conversations with Sisters Anita Sullivan and Roberta O'Leary, February 2004.

45. Conversations with Sister Mary Kathleen Stefani, Sister Anita Sullivan, and Sister Roberta O'Leary, February 2004.

46. Conversations with Sisters Roberta O'Leary and Mary Jane Schmitz, Fall 2004; Montana Schools files, ASCL. On her retirement as principal after seventeen years of service in the schools, Sister Roberta took on the job of leading Butte Central

Futures Incentives, designed by the BC Schools Foundation to unite the business community of Butte in support of the Catholic schools.

47. Schools and Hospitals file, ASCL; conversation with Sister Mary Ann Bartolac, February 2004.

48. Observations and Reflections, Sister Bernadette Helfert, Mar. 8, 1980, ASCL.

49. Bulletins, Sister Mary Baptista Ward, 1940, Schools file, ASCL. The supervisors' suggestions were sometimes unpredictable. Points for discussion of character during religion period included Knute Rockne's ideals and advice from Babe Ruth.

50. *Sister Mary Baptista and Sister Mary Afra*, collection by Sister Jean Dawson, 2003.

51. Conversation with Sister Perpetua McGrath, Fall 2005.

52. Conversations with Sister Agnes Mary Brickley, Fall 2003. In 1969 Sister Agnes Mary was named education consultant for both elementary and secondary schools.

53. Elementary Education, Apostolate Reports, 1980; Mission Assignments, Elementary Schools, ASCL.

54. House History, Immaculate Conception Convent, 1977–1981, 1983–1984; School Missions, Kansas, ASCL; conversations with Sister Anita Sullivan, Spring 2004, and Katherine Franchett, Winter 2005. Lamar (Bud) Weaver, chair of central planning, and Anne and Frank Hesse, members of the sub-committee on unification, led an executive committee of seven pastors, director of the diocesan school office Blake Mulvaney, and school council members Bill Ault and James Murphy. Sister Mary Serena Sheehy, general councilor, and Sister Bernadette Helfert, elementary school coordinator, represented the Community (*Eastern Kansas Register*, Feb. 2, 1979, and *The Leader*, May 31, 1979, Xavier Schools file, ASCL).

55. The Xavier Schools enrolled 476 but just 382 from the parishes; a total enrollment of 454 was needed for financial stability. Immaculata enrolled 197 in total but only 161 from the parishes; 225 were needed for stability. Students in the system from Fort Leavenworth families numbered as many as 100 in a given year; other numbers varied as well. Sponsorships to aid families in need of tuition assistance and a grants program for teachers' study were necessary additions to the budget. Goals set for income sources were 50 percent from parents, 35 percent from parish subsidies, and 10 percent from development. The aim for Educational Foundation funds was one million dollars (Summary of Study by Leavenworth Catholic School Board, 1982–1984, Xavier Schools file, Box 1, ASCL).

56. *Wyandotte/Leavenworth Kansas City Star*, Nov. 6, 1997; *Leavenworth Times*, July 11, July 23, and Sept. 3, 2000; *Connections*, Nov. 27, 2001, Xavier Schools file, Box 1, ASCL; conversation with Rolland Dessert, Winter 2003.

57. *Eastern Montana Catholic Register*, Dec. 3, 1954; House History 1987–1988, Holy Rosary School file; Elementary Education, Apostolate Reports, 1980, ASCL.

58. *Billings Gazette*, Jan. 13, 1987, Billings Catholic Schools file, ASCL. The transition plan included bus transportation and child care; numbers already waited for the pre-school to open.

59. Sisters Katherine Franchett, Elizabeth Youngs, and Jean Martin Dawson, Personal files, ASCL.

11. Teaching an Investment

1. Blake Mulvaney came to Ward High School in 1957 as its fifth lay teacher and succeeded Father Ray Davern as principal in 1971. In 1984 Archbishop Ignatius Strecker asked him to serve as regional administrator of the archdiocesan schools with emphasis on new institutions. He became president of St. Thomas Aquinas High School in 1988 with Sister Kathleen Condry, OSU, principal (Conversation with Blake Mulvaney, February 2004).
2. Sister Mary Seraphine Sheehan, "History of SCL Secondary Schools," talk given to SCL Secondary School Sisters, June 10, 1985, ASCL.
3. Ibid.
4. St. Vincent's Academy, Helena, Montana file; Closed Missions, Montana, ASCL. Administrators during the 1950s and 1960s included Sisters Mary Zoe Ahern, Josephine Mitchell, Agnes Clare Moylan, Rose Teresa McHale, Ann Teresa Conroy, Ann Patrice Harrington, and Mary Cecilia Carig.
5. *Montana Standard*, Aug. 6, 1950, and Apr. 22, 1951; *Western Montana Register*, Mar. 10 and 24, 1957; June 6 and 22, Aug. 31, 1958; May 3, 1959; House History report, 1958–1959; Reports, Clippings and Correspondence, Girls Central High School file, ASCL.
6. *Montana Standard*, June 5, 1961 and August 1964; Reports to Mother General, September 1960 and June 1961; House Histories, 1962–1965; *Montana Catholic Register*, Aug. 18, 1967; Proposals for coordinated school system, 1968, Girls Central file, ASCL.
7. Closed Missions, Montana, ASCL; conversation with Sister Mary Kathleen Stefani, Winter 2004.
8. Financial Report to Pastors, 1967–68, Butte Central file, ASCL.
9. Ward High School file, ASCL; conversation with Margaret Fay, Winter 2004. Rita Dwight and Dottie Jean Allen were the first African American students enrolled at Ward.
10. Scholarships and Awards reports, Faculty Publications, 1960–69, House Histories, Ward High School Convent,1958–1970; *Eastern Kansas Register*, May 22, 1959, May 1, 1964, Feb. 9 and May 31, 1968; *Kansas City Kansan*, Oct. 30, 1964, Ward High School file; Sister Susan Rieke, "for WARD march! with Sister Mary Constantia," *Relay*, June 1972, ASCL.
11. Desegregation of Kansas City schools was causing more than the usual shifts in population. A unique change on the Kansas side of the river was the opening of Sumner Academy to offer the finest education to African American students. Its attraction of topflight teachers and students and consistent record of achievement was accompanied by decline in enrollments at four public schools and a substantial movement of families south to Johnson County (Newspaper Clippings folder; Report from

the Principal, President's letter, May 1979, History, Ward High School file, ASCL; conversation with Blake Mulvaney, February 2004).

12. Fact Sheet, 1982–83, Ward High School file, ASCL.

13. *bishop ward after-ward*, Autumn 1984; Blake Mulvaney, President, 1984–85, 1987; *The Leaven*, Mar. 19, 1989, and Apr. 13, 1990, Sister Rita McGinnis, Personal file, ASCL. In 1990 Sister Rita was named a member of the Principals Academy of the National Catholic Education Association, an honor awarded to outstanding school principals.

14. History, Immaculata High School (IHS) file, ASCL.

15. *I-High News*, 1960–1963; *The I-High News* magazine, January 1964, IHS file, ASCL.

16. History, IHS file; conversation with Sister Mary Jo Coyle, Winter 2004.

17. History, IHS file; conversation with Sister Ann Barton, Winter 2004.

18. History, IHS file; conversation with Sister Rita Smith, Winter 2004.

19. *St. Mary Star*, May 24, 1945, History, Immaculate Conception High School, St. Mary's, Kansas file, ASCL. Sister Mary Patrice McInerney had been principal of Immaculate Conception but was not part of the negotiating team and left no document; it had been "a gentleman's agreement." The president of the school board had urged the merger and Bishop Paul C. Schulte consented to it, provided the sisters were to teach in the Catholic high school classrooms. The sisters' salaries of $4,500 each were used to defray the parish's cost of providing for all sisters teaching in both grade and high schools. No church-state difficulties developed. In 1948 the combined schools graduated thirty-seven.

20. The sisters' stipend increased during the fifteen years after the consolidation but not sufficiently to meet expenses. In a letter dated Oct. 23, 1959, Mother Mary Ancilla thanks Mrs. Harold E. Ryan and Mrs. George H. Marstall for readying the convent for the sisters (account of the merger by Sister Rose Dominic Gabisch, Aug. 12, 1959, and notes, Nov. 7 and 20, 1959, and Mar. 14, 1961, History, Immaculate Conception High School, St. Mary's, Kansas file, ASCL).

21. Principals of the 1950s were Sisters Mary Dolorine Eakes, Ann Teresa Conroy, and Joseph Mary Schwieder.

22. Annunciation High School account by Sister Leo Gonzaga Erbacher, Mar. 22, 1940; *Denver Catholic Register*, Apr. 19, 1956, May 16, 1957, Feb. 11 and May 26, 1960, Mar. 2, 1961; Recognitions Report, 1959–1960, Annunciation High School file, ASCL.

23. *Denver Catholic Register*, Dec. 17, 1964, and Nov. 24, 1966; *The Cardinal*, Mar. 1966, Annumciation High School file, ASCL. After the school's entry into the National Forensics League, Annunciation students had competed in more than five thousand interscholastic debates and public programs. One of the smallest schools in the League, it had captured seventeen degrees of distinction and sixty-five degrees of excellence.

24. "Annunciation High School's 43 Years End in Phase-Out," *Relay*, Summer 1968; *Denver Catholic Register*, Jan. 25, 1968, Annunciation High School file, ASCL.

25. History folder; *Eastern Kansas Register*, Apr. 7, 1967, Clippings folder, Hayden High School (HHS) file, ASCL.

26. *Capilolite*, 1962–1964, HHS file.

27. *Capitol-Journal*, n.d., Clippings folder, HHS file

28. *Eastern Kansas Register*, Nov. 12, 1975; Archbishop Ignatius Strecker, June 20, 1980, Miscellaneous folder, HHS file.

29. Mission Assignments, Kansas, ASCL.

30. Individuals set records: George Selovsky, twenty-nine years as coach, sponsor, and principal; Gerald Rohr, twenty years as teacher and counselor; Margaret Borgren, English teacher for nineteen years (*Pacemaker*, November 1981 and September 1983, Miscellaneous folder; North Central Self-Study, Hayden High School, Nov. 15–17, 1981–1982, History, HHS file).

31. The number of graduates comes from the Missions record for Montana in the Community Treasurer's office. A publication records twenty-five (History, Billings Central Catholic High School [BCCHS] file, ASCL).

32. With the highest score in an exam on homemaking attitudes, Maureen Hall, who entered the Community after graduation, was eligible for the Betty Crocker "Homemaker of Tomorrow" contest (*Centralrama*, January 1960; Piess quoted in October 1959 edition).

33. *Centralrama*, 1959–1961, Publications, 1945–1980, BCCHS file, ASCL.

34. A letter from Sister Mary Lenore to Mother Leo Frances written in January of 1966 indicates how tentative at the time was the prospect of Irish teachers. On a visit to Ireland, Bishop William J. Condon had invited Sisters of Mercy to come to Montana (History, BCCHS file, ASCL; *Catholic Directory*, 1954).

35. *Billings Gazette*, Nov. 29, 1972; "Historical Review of BCCHS, 1975," Clippings and Programs; *The Rampage*, May 27, 1980, Publications, BCCHS file, ASCL.

36. *Hogan Citizen*, Feb. 28, 1955, Publications; Minimum Essentials for Written English, Vocations from Bishop Hogan High School, Miscellaneous, Bishop Hogan High School (BHHS) file; Sister Mary Seraphine's History of Secondary Schools, ASCL.

37. *Rampage*, 1963–1968, Publications, BHHS file. Both Billings Central and Hogan named a publication for their athletic teams, the Rams. Academic achievements were many. Thirty-six participants took "Lucifer at Large," a modern morality play, to the National Catholic Theatre Conference and a junior Thespian, Donna Kieffer, won the coveted Medallion of St. Genesius. Sodality Prefect Sue Miller was elected the most representative senior girl.

38. Sister Mary Denise Sternitzke, Report on Study of Hogan, 1977, BHHS file, ASCL.

39. Conversation with Sister Ann Barton, Winter 2004; conversation with Alvin Brooks, Fall 2005. Three Brooks daughters were Hogan students at the time; two grandsons and a great-granddaughter graduated in subsequent years.

40. Sister Victoria Perkins, Personal file, ASCL.

41. Report on questionnaire, May 1977, BHHS file, ASCL.

42. *Kansas City Star*, Aug. 2, 1987; *Catholic Key*, Oct. 22, 1989; Sept. 9, 1990; Mar. 31, 1991, Sister Barbara Aldrich, Personal file, ASCL.

43. Conversations with Sisters Vickie Perkins and Katherine Franchett, Spring 2004. Among benefits of the partnership to Rockhurst students and to Hoganites—80 percent of them minority students and 40 percent of them Catholic—was the Distinguished Program/Project award of the Association of Jesuit Colleges and Universities.

44. History of Sacred Heart School, <http://www.sacredheart.esu6.org/general/ghistory.htm>; Schools folder, Nebraska file, ASCL. Sister Mary Zoe was principal until 1947, followed by Sister Patricia Eeraerts; Sisters Mary Eugene Francis, Mary Columba Connaughton, and Mary Ellenice Colvin in the 1950s; Sisters Ann Teresa Conroy and Marie Carmel Dunning in the 1960s and into the 1970s; and Sisters Mary Hilaria Phipps and Mary Denise Sternitzke in the 1970s and 1980s. Sister Mary Paulette Fitzgerald was the last Sister of Charity to serve the people of Falls City.

45. Sacred Heart High School, Falls City, Schools folder, Nebraska file; Sister M. Hilaria Phipps, "Mini school produces MIGHTY results in Falls City," *Relay*, Spring 1968, ASCL.

46. History; *Falls City Journal*, May 25, 1983; Parish bulletin, June 2, 1991, Schools, Nebraska file, ASCL.

47. A year before Pius X opened, the Community sent two sisters to a secondary school staffed by members of several religious communities. Sisters Margaret Delores Green and Marie Aquina (Mary Beth) Kelly joined the faculty of Central Catholic High School, Oklahoma City, renamed for Bishop Eugene McGuinness in 1958. The former Sister Mary Edwarda Caffrey and Sister Regina DeCoursey were appointed to the school before the Community withdrew in 1959.

48. History folder; *The Sartonian*, 1957, 1959; *Perspective*, a Guidebook..., 1960, St. Pius X High School file, ASCL.

49. *Perspective, The Sartonian*, 1971–1973.

50. History, St. Pius X High School file.

51. Conversation with Sister Rita Smith, Winter 2004.

52. Conversations with Sister Sharon Verbeck and Mary Lenore Martin, Fall 2005; *The Key*, Sept. 26, 1903.

53. Conversation with Sister Maureen Craig, Winter 2003.

54. From "Volcanoes and Fireworks," Sister Susan Rieke, *From the Tower: Poems from Saint Mary College*, 1996.

55. Conversation Sister Susan Rieke, Winter 2003.

56. By 1977, Saint Mary College had conferred the baccalaureate degree on 427 Sisters of Charity and the master of science degree in education on seventy-six. Almost twenty years later, the bachelor's degree had been awarded to 691 Sisters of Charity and 313 sisters of other communities. Ninety-eight Sisters of Charity had earned the master's degree in education (Professional Study Status Report, December 1977, Education file, ASCL; Registrar's Annual Reports, University of Saint Mary).

57. Responses to the 2005 national survey of U.S. Catholics reveal that Catholic high school education for the Vatican II and post–Vatican II generations contributed

significantly to their advance to higher education, to their earnings, and to their commitment to the Catholic Church in its core teachings and their life of faith (Mary L. Gautier, "Does Catholic Education Make a Difference?" Survey of U.S. Catholics, *National Catholic Reporter*, Sept. 30, 2005).

58. Community Director's Report to Chapter, 1980; Former Sisters' file, Community Secretary's office.

59. In 1986 an interview of several sisters by a newspaper reporter in Billings, Montana, reflected something of this deep change. Asked whether young women were entering the Community to succeed them in their ministries, these Sisters of Charity explained that fear of lifelong commitment was a block to a possible religious vocation not apparent fifteen years ago. They spoke of other fears—of far-reaching nuclear destruction or of missing countless options. The sisters called it a culture in transition. Kim Larsen, the reporter, interviewed Sisters Mary Lou Mendel, Ellen Dore, Mary Ann Petrich, Dolores Erman, and Marian Berry (*Billings Gazette*, Apr. 9, 1986, Holy Rosary School file, 1952–86, ASCL).

12. The Maturing of a College

1. Saint Mary College catalogs, 1933–36, 1939–53, 1963–65, 1969–71, 1990–92; University of Saint Mary 2003–2004 Undergraduate Catalog; conversation with Sister Diane Steele, president of the University of Saint Mary.

2. Saint Mary College catalog, 1980–81, ASCL.

3. Graduate Division file, Saint Mary College, ASCL; Saint Mary College (SMC) Data 1970s, p. 6, AUSM; Registrar's Reports; *The Taper*, Sept. 18, 1966; Professional Studies Status Report, December 1977, ASCL.

4. SMC Data 1960s, pp. 1–30 passim, AUSM; *The Taper*, May 10, 1966.

5. Site plan, St. Joseph Dining Hall, courtesy of Pete Zink, building project manager, and Mike Logan, assistant director of facilities; *The Taper*, Oct. 25, Nov. 9, 1962, and May 27, 1963. Maurice Carroll, of Saint Louis, father of then Sister Mary Mauricita, had designed Berchmans, the Mother House, and Miege and Maria Hall. He conceived of St. Joseph's octagonal structure of stone and glass as a modern contrast to the buildings that surrounded it. The spacious dining room's adaptability to various college functions proved almost limitless.

6. *The Taper*, Oct. 25, 1962; Oct. 3, 1963; SMC Data 1960s, pp. 17, 19, 21, AUSM.

7. President's News Briefs 1960 and SMC Data 1960s, pp. 15–17, 27, AUSM; *The Taper*, Nov. 29, 1962; Jan. 21 and Feb. 11,1963; Oct. 13, 1964; Sept. 24, 1965; conversations with Molly Sirridge, Institutional Development Officer, and e-mail from Maureen Burke Emrich, March 2004. Sister Mary Paul died in April 1962. The memorial scholarship was a gift of W. D. Leitch, MD, of Denver.

Sister faculty of the decade included Sisters Marie Janelle Kreuger, philosophy; Marion Clare (Barbara) Sellers, classics; Mary Mauricita (Suzanne) Carroll, Mary Adelaide (Alice) Grellner, and Mary Leonilla (Marie) Brinkman, English; Mary Denise

Sternitzke, mathematics; Bernadette Marie Teasdale, education; and Jean Patrick Meeker, nursing education. Staff in the 1960s included Sister Anthony Marie (Regina) Dietchman and Doris Blockburger, successive directors of housekeeping; Sisters Rose Marie Desch and Mary Aloysia (Catherine) Palmer, registrar's office; lay women Etha Linda Linehardt and Louise Everhardy, library; Rose Otto Fish and Florence Trudelle, student services; and Sister Ann Modesta Mulholland, bookstore (Saint Mary College Faculty and Staff, 1923–1994, ASCL).

    8. SMC Data 1960s, pp. 3–8 passim; *The Taper*, Feb. 11, Oct. 18, and Nov. 8, 1963; April 29, 1964; Mar. 30, Aug. 28, and Sept. 29, 1965; Dec. 9, 1966.

    9. *The Taper*, Oct. 13, 1964.

    10. *The Taper*, Oct. 13, 1964, and Oct. 31, 1964.

    11. SMC Data 1960s, pp. 12, 14, 16. Among the President's Council's early members were Dr. Lawrence Blades and Dr. J. Anthony Burzle of the University of Kansas, James E. Burke, Maurice Carroll, Senator Mike Mansfield, Ray H. Miller, mayor of Leavenworth; Lt. Gov. James DeCoursey, Mary Goetz Ryan, Col. Jo Zach Miller III, Kansas University Chancellor Clark Wescoe, Robert O'Brien, of MGM; Martha Peterson, Stephen J. Maronick, and Dr. Bernard Hall, chief psychiatrist at the Menninger Foundation. George Lehr and Joe Burke were council chairmen in succeeding decades. First chairpersons of the Women's Associates were Mrs. Walter Lambert and Mrs. Bert Collard.

    Council members in the 1980s included Donald Biggs, Homer Davis, Robert Aaron, Ivan J. Meyer, Clyde Graeber, Harley Russell, Bernard Ruysser, Mary Ryan, Virginia Greenlease, J. E. Dunn Jr., Ruth Snyder, John McGilley, Dan and Joan Hauserman, Richard P. Ryan, William Shea, John DeLine, Dan Duncan, Richard W. Miller, Dr. and Mrs. C. Kermit Phelps, Mary Alice and Kevin Murphy, Gretchen Poston, Ernest Renfro Jr., Dorothy Ritter, Robert Rudin, Dr. James Hayes, and R. Crosby Kemper (SMC Data 1980s, pp. 4, 72).

    12. PNB 1970–71; SMC Data 1980s, pp. 2, 36.

    13. Conversation with Sister Mary Vincentia Maronick, July 2003. In 1981 Sister became director of planned giving in the development office. She did that job until 1996. James Crim, husband of Winifred Coman Crim, class of 1951, and vice president of International Investors Inc., inspired the first "Saint Mary Story" on video (PNB 1970–71; *The Taper*, Sept. 21, 1974).

    14. SMC Data 1970s, pp. 9, 12, 14; PNB 1970–71, AUSM; *The Taper*, Mar. 25, 1966.

    15. Data, pp. 7–8, 1–2; Special Collections, DePaul Library, USM; conversation with Penny Lonergan, head librarian; *The Taper*, Jan. 30, 1970.

    16. Conversation with Michael Novak, Winter 2004; PNB 1970–71; SMC Data 1970s, pp. 4–5, 28.

    17. PNB 1970–72; SMC Data 1970–71, AUSM.

    18. PNB 1970–71 and Data, pp. 3, 6, 8, 14; notes from Sister Barbara Sellers and Michael Novak. Additional new faculty in the 1970s who served many years in the college included Sister Mary Suzanne Braun, music; Sister Patricia Eggert Waters, modern languages; James Murphy, political science; Sister Carmen Echevarria, art; and Sister Mary Carol Conroy, nursing education. Department

chairs were Sisters Carol Hinds, English; Gregory Sheehy, education; and Constance Phelps, sociology. Sister Bernadine Hon was artist-in-residence until her death in 1980.

Staff of long service included Sister Margaret Petty, Evening/Weekend program, main campus; Ralph Langley, plant manager; Dolly Wamsley and Sister Eileen Whitman, library; Lee James, LCF coordinator; Angela Hurst Lavery and Sister Mary Jacinta Teets, financial aid; Sisters Maureen Kauffman, business office; Irene Skeehan, admissions; and Monica Coz, auditor. Housekeepers of twenty-five to thirty years were Ella Mae Treat, Marilyn McClure, and Roberta West (SMC Data 1970s, pp. 3, 6; PNB 1970–71; *The Taper*, Sept. 18, 1976; Saint Mary College Faculty and Staff, 1923–1994, ASCL).

19. PNB 1970–71; Data 1970s, pp. 11–12.
20. Conversation with Sister Mary Lenore Martin, Fall 2003.
21. SMC Data 1970s, pp. 8, 12; PNB 1970–72; conversation with Sister Barbara Sellers, March 2004; *The Taper*, Dec. 9, 1976, May 5, 1977, Feb. 26, 1981.
22. PNB 1971–72, 1973–74; Data 1970s, p. 23; 1980s, p. 54; *The Taper*, May 16, 1973.
23. Data 1970s, pp.1, 3–10, 15; *The Taper*, May 5, 1977; Oct. 5, 1978; Mar. 13, 1980; Feb. 26, 1981; conversation with Sister Anne Callahan, March 2004.
24. Conversation with Sister Kathleen Wood, March 2004. Father Lee had been sent as a young man by his parents to a seminary in the States during China's Cultural Revolution. He was able to visit his home village once before his parents died. Unable to travel farther than Taiwan in his final illness, he returned to Saint Mary to die and was buried in Mount Olivet Cemetery. During his final years of teaching, he served as chaplain to the sisters in Ross Hall infirmary.
25. PNB 1970–71; SMC Data 1970s, pp. 2, 17.
26. PNB 1970–71; Data 1970s, pp. 11–12, 21. Among the earliest Council members were Marguerite Strange and Mary Archer.
27. PNB 1969–73; Data, 1970s, pp. 3–4, 15, AUSM; conversations with faculty and staff. The Beacon of Hope choir from Lansing State Penitentiary performed on campus for the first time in December 1970, in grateful response to a donation of the Sisters of Charity of Leavenworth to their prison chapel.
28. PNB 1970–71; Data 1970s, pp. 1, 9, 19; 1980s, pp. 1, 8, AUSM; *The Taper*, Jan. 28, 1972. Additional faculty of the 1980s included Lelia Walters, education; Janet Lowenstein, physical education; Sister Kathleen Mary Connelly, history; Victor Meyer, computer science; and Sister Susan Wood, theology and French. Additional newcomers to the staff were Sheila Pedigo, director of Student Services; Minda Whiteside, Wanda Owen, and Patricia Zink, registrar's office; Judy Wiedower, financial aid; Joy Kozak, library; Sue Suwalsky, development; Carolyn Zimmerman, public relations; Bruce Appel, KSP program; Brian Barnett and Shirley Rockwell, maintenance; and Dale Baustian, Pearl Garvey, Lavern Frederick, and Judith Zielinski, housekeeping (SMC Faculty and Staff, 1923–1994, ASCL).
29. PNB 1970–71; SMC Data 1960s, p. 1; 1970s, pp. 2, 13; 1980s, p. 68; Sisters Joann Serafin and Virginia Bartolac, "Dr. Phelps Puts People First," *Relay*, November 1969; *The Taper*, Jan. 28, 1972; Nov. 15, 1979.

30. SMC Data, 1970s, pp. 2, 25, 30.

31. Data 1970s, pp. 3–4; Sister Mary Lenore Martin, Personal file, ASCL. During a yearlong observance of the bicentennial of the United States Constitution, Sister Mary Lenore was named a STAR scholar in a state-wide program sponsored by the Kansas Committee for the Humanities.

32. Data 1970s, pp. 3–4, 12, 18; 1980s, pp. 5, 22–76 passim; PNB 1970–71.

33. Conversation with Father John Stitz, Summer 2002.

34. Data 1970s, pp. 13–15.

35. Letters re Professional Activities folder, Sister Formation folder, Social Concerns folder; Sister Rose Dominic Gabisch, Personal file, ASCL. *The Taper*, Sept. 27, 1979.

36. Father John Stitz, Oct. 23, 1997, Biographical folder; Personal file, Sister Mary Louise Sullivan, ASCL; *The Taper*, Nov. 24, 1959.

37. Sister Mary Mark Orr, Mexico folder, Personal file, ASCL; SMC Data 1980s, pp. 9–10; *The Taper*, Sept. 26, 1972.

38. *Saint Mary Go Round*, 1985; Sister Marie Therese Bride, Personal file, ASCL.

39. *Leavenworth Times*, Feb. 27, 1981; Notes for Special Archival Project, LCWR, Feb. 1, 1980; Sister Mary Ernestine Whitmore, Personal file, ASCL. Sister Mary Janet's words are from the Memorial Mass and Fall Convocation, 1968 (Sister Frances Therese Shea, Personal file, ASCL).

40. PNB 1972–73, 1973–74; *The Taper*, May 16, 1973.

41. *Prison Programs Information, 1994–1995*, compiled by Sister Edward Mary Brown; SMC Data 1970s, pp. 6–7, 17, 22–28, 39; 1980s, pp. 7, 20, 53, 62, 83; PNB 1971–72; *The Taper*, Sept. 23, 1976, Mar. 17, 1977, Sept. 9, 1979; *Relay*, December 1973, ASCL.

42. SMC Data 1980s, pp. 36, 63, 66, 86. Kitty Bronec directed OutFront for twelve years before and after Donna Schmidt Simons (Conversation with Kitty Bronec, February 2006).

43. Board of Control Minutes, Nov. 13, 1974; SMC Data 1970s, pp. 7, 14, 17; 1980s, pp. 28, 38, 40, 42; PNB 1972–73, AUSM; *The Taper*, Jan. 28, 1972. Under the tuition grant, an average grant of $300 went to some 1,200 Kansas students annually, won by demonstrating need.

44. *The Taper*, Sept. 29, 1975; Dec. 9, 1976.

45. SMC Data 1970s, p. 17; PNB 1971–72, 1972–73, 1973–74, AUSM; *The Taper*, Sept. 26, 1973; Apr. 16, 1974.

46. SMC Data 1980s, pp. 3, 36, 7, 79–81, 83, 85; *The Taper*, Sept. 27, 1979. Sisters Barbara Kushan and Mary Erwin Baker extended the training of students and faculty to sisters residing in the Mother House.

47. SMC Data 1980s, pp. 4, 23; President's Budget Message 1981–82.

48. The initial Campaign for Saint Mary, 1979–1981, was led by Chairman Joseph Burke and Virginia Greenlease of the President's Council. National co-chairs of its second phase, "A Living Legacy," were Mary Alice and Kevin Murphy. Major gift organizers for Leavenworth were Ivan Meyer and Robert Aaron; for Kansas City,

NOTES   541

John McGilley and James Burke. From 1981 to 1983, Harry Briscoe, vice chairman of the President's Council, led the Heritage Campaign to exceed its goal. Alumnae Association officers who took leadership roles were Patricia Eggert Waters, Patricia Connor Naime, Annabel Crawford Willcott, Jane Flick Distler, and Martha Miller Roult. Development consultants from early years through the campaign were Ed Hall, Robert Rudin, and Tom Tompkins (SMC Data 1980s, pp. 23, 31, 33, 45, 62, 72; Campaign brochures, 1979–1984).

49. Community director and chair of the board, Sister Mary Kathleen Stefani, Sept. 12, 1987; SMC Data 1980s, pp. 61–62, 73, 78, 87.

50. SMC Data 1980s, pp. 62–63, 72.

51. SMC Data 1980s, pp. 75–77, 82–83.

52. Preface to the Budget Message for 1989–90, 7; The Legacy Celebration, Saint Mary College, Oct. 2, 1980, SMC Data 1980s.

13. A Heritage of Healing

1. Story from Sister Dorothy Henscheid.

2. "Hearts at High Altitude" and "From Winter 1878 to Spring 1972 SCLs serve Leadville," *Relay*, Winter 1964–65 and Spring 1972, ASCL.

3. Sister Mary Francine Stubbs, "Comments on factors which led to decision to discontinue operation of hospital," St. Ann's Hospital file; letter of Sister Macrina Ryan to president of Catholic Charities and pastors of Helena, Mar. 14, 1973; "Recollections of St. John's Hospital, 1973"; *Independent Record*, Dec. 6, 1970, St. John's Hospital, Helena file; St. Anthony's Hospital file, ASCL.

4. Sister Mary Carol Conroy, SCL, BSNE, *The Historical Development of the Health Care Ministry of the Sisters of Charity of Leavenworth* (Manhattan, KS: Kansas State University, 1984), 90, 93–94.

5. By that time, the nation's 178 hospitals in 1873 had multiplied to more than 2,500. The Catholic Hospital Association was founded in 1914 (*Historical Development*, 95, 98–100, 107–11).

6. Health Services Corporation file; Sister Cornelia Donnelly, Personal file, ASCL; *Historical Development*, 116–17.

7. Sister Maureen Craig, *The Golden Promise, Saint John's Hospital and Health Center, 1942–1992* (Santa Monica, CA: Saint John's Hospital and Health Center, 1992), 48.

8. *The Golden Promise*, 19–20.

9. Account by Sister Zita Marie Cotter, 1970, Sister Ann Raymond Downey, Personal file, ASCL.

10. *Los Angeles Times*, Apr. 16, 1951, Clippings, Sister Ann Raymond Downey, Personal file. Sister Ann Raymond's gift of team-building had been particularly evident in the dedication in 1951 of the seven-story south wing of Saint John's. The local medical staff contributed $100,000 to the total cost of the addition; Irene Dunne, founder and president of the hospital's guild, spoke at the ceremony.

11. Sister Kathleen Keenan, Personal file; *Kansas City Kansan*, n.d., Clippings, Providence Hospital file, ASCL.

12. *New York Times*, May 10, 1959, Sister Kathleen Keenan, Personal file. Sister Kathleen reported for the Center's first year more than 80 percent occupancy, good use of the family-centered maternity care unit, more than 16,600 outpatients, and a two-year accreditation by Joint Commission (Providence–St. Margaret Health Center file, ASCL).

13. Presentation of Distinguished Service Award for 1970 by president of Medical Care and Research Foundation, Sister Mary Asella Delaney, Personal file, ASCL.

14. *Historical Development*, 123–30.

15. Jack Gaskie, *Rocky Mountain News*, Apr. 10, 1960, Sister Mary Asella Delaney, Personal file, ASCL.

16. *Rocky Mountain News*, Dec. 22, 1963, Sister Mary Asella, Personal file, ASCL.

17. Conversation with Sister Mary Andrew Talle, Fall 2003.

18. *Historical Development*, 124–26. While new technologies and treatments developed as a result of crisis situations in World War II, hospitals sought exemplary physicians, hired degreed nurses, and created specialized staffs for sophisticated equipment. Medicare and Medicaid increased hospital counts even as strict regulation limited hospital stays. Non-profit hospitals' immunity from litigation was eliminated state by state as insurance companies protected litigants from personal confrontation.

19. "Management Manifesto," Medical Staff Assemblies file, ASCL.

20. Ibid. The program of the first assembly included presentations by the executive assistant director of the American College of Surgeons, a vice president of the American Medical Association, and the executive director of the Catholic Hospital Association.

21. Mother Leo Frances Ryan to the sisters, Oct. 2, 1973, accompanying Cresap, McCormick and Paget Report, and Mar. 21, 1974, History folder, Sisters of Charity of Leavenworth Health Services Corporation file, ASCL.

22. Therese Horvat, *God's Healing Love Made Present 1972–1997* (Sisters of Charity Health Services Corporation, 1997), pp. 16–17, Health Care System file, ASCL.

23. History folder, Health Care System file, ASCL.

24. Sister Mary Dennis Shea, Personal file, ASCL.

25. Sister Mildred Marie Irwin, Personal file; *God's Healing Love*, 19.

26. Letter from William Murray, president of the Health Services System, Nov. 7, 2003, Health Care System file, ASCL.

27. As a member of the American College of Hospital Executives, Sister Mary David was assigned lifetime status (Biography folder, Personal file, ASCL).

28. Conversations with Sister Macrina Ryan and Margaret Anne Kearns, Winter 2004.

29. Booklet, c. 1980, Philosophy, Structure, Purpose folder, Sisters of Charity of Leavenworth Health Services Corporation file, ASCL; *God's Healing Love*, 20–21, 23.

30. List of Sisters of Charity Schools of Nursing; Chronology, Colorado and Kansas, recorded by Sister Cornelia Donnelly, Schools of Nursing file, ASCL; conversation with Sister Rose Orchard, Winter 2003.

31. Saint Mary College Nursing Program folder, Schools of Nursing file; St. Joseph's Hospital, Colorado, SCL Schools of Nursing file, ASCL. Sister Rose Victor Felscheim, RN, BNE, was the first chairperson of the college's nursing department. During her term she was elected vice president of the Missouri-Kansas Catholic Hospital Conference.

32. Sister Eugene Teresa McCarthy, "History of the Department of Nursing within Carroll College;" *Montana Catholic Register*, Feb. 4, 1966; Sister Mary Clementine (Rosalie) Mahoney, St. James Community Hospital folder, Montana SCL Schools of Nursing file; Sister Mary Jerome Kelly, Personal file, ASCL. The first Sister of Charity to hold the master's degree in nursing education, Sister Eugene Teresa McCarthy became head of Carroll's department of nursing in 1948; she was succeeded by Sister Mary Jerome Kelly.

33. *Nursing in Montana*, Montana Nurses' Association, 1961, pp. 33, 47, 53, Montana SCL Schools of Nursing file; Sister Marie Kelly's record of directors, Schools of Nursing file, ASCL.

34. Note from Sister Mary Louise Sullivan, academic dean, in St. Joseph's Hospital folder, Colorado SCL Schools of Nursing file; *Historical Development*, 209–10, 216–26 passim; *Relay*, Spring 1968, ASCL.

35. Saint Mary College Nursing Program folder, Schools of Nursing file, ASCL.

36. History, St. John Hospital (SJH) file, ASCL. Administrators of the 1950s and early 1960s were Sisters Mary Thaddea McCarthy, Mary Leocadia Johanning, Mary Own Horner, and Mary Aurelia Henry. Quotation from *Saint John Hospital Celebrating 140 Years 1864–2004. The Mission Continues, 2004* (Catherine Rice, Marketing and Volunteer Services, Providence Health).

37. History, SJH file; conversation with Sister Mary Francine Stubbs. Administrators of St. John for brief terms in the 1970s and 1980s were Sisters Michael Marie O'Leary and Concetta Mock.

38. Don Biggs was elected president of the board; St. John's administrator, Sister Ann Marita Loosen, vice president; Ed Reilly Jr., secretary; and Norman Nolop, treasurer. Other members were Robert Davis and Ambrose Dempsey; Sister Mary Francine Stubbs, former administrator; Sisters Mildred Irwin and Macrina Ryan of the Health Care System; Community councilor Sister Mary Liguori Horvat, and Sister Marie Celeste Bride (*A Tradition of Service... 125 Years, St. John Hospital, 1864–1989*, Clippings folder, St. John Hospital file, ASCL).

39. Sister Ann Marita Loosen, Personal file; *Hill Highlights* 1983, 1984, SJH file; *A Tradition of Service*.

40. *Leavenworth Times*, June 6, 1989, Clippings folder; Dorothy Stock's agenda for Task Force on 125th Anniversary celebration, Anniversary folder; *Hill Highlights* 1988, SJH file; *A Tradition of Service*.

41. History folder, Health Services System, St. John Hospital, Leavenworth; *Leavenworth Times*, June 6, 1989, Clippings folder, SJH file; *A Tradition of Service*.

42. Conversations with Sisters Mary Andrew Talle and Ann Marita Loosen, Fall 2004.

43. Sister Mary Clementine (Rosalie) Mahoney, Personal file; Proposal Regarding Health Care for the Poor to SCL/HSC, April 6, 1984; Proposal, July 1985, Clinics file, ASCL.

44. Leavenworth County census records, 1980, Clinics file, ASCL.

45. *Leavenworth Times*, Mar. 16 and Oct. 19, 1986, Clinics file, ASCL; conversation with Sister Mary Jo Downey, Spring 2005.

46. *St. Vincent Clinic 1991 Newsletter*; *Kansas City Star*, May 24, 1990; *The Leaven*, Nov. 17, 1995, Duchesne folder, Caritas Clinics Inc. file, ASCL.

47. *1991 Newsletter*; RESPONSE, June 1993; Board of Directors Meeting, Feb. 27, 1993; *Kansas City Kansan*, May 12, 1993, Duchesne folder, Caritas Clinics Inc. file; A $25,000 grant from the Hall Family Foundation paid for insulated windows in Duchesne Clinic replacing those installed in St. Anthony's School in 1907.

48. *Topeka Metro-News*, Dec.13, 1989; brochure, Marian Clinic, Clinics file, ASCL.

49. Marian Clinic press release, Summer 1998; *Topeka Capitol-Journal*, July 19, 1998, and Feb. 23, 2002; brochure, Marian Clinic file, ASCL.

50. *Intercom*, St. Francis Hospital and Medical Center, Apr. 6, 1995, and Nov. 9, 1995; *The Leaven*, Oct. 27, 1995; *Topeka Capitol-Journal*, Feb. 9, 1996, and Feb. 23, 2002, St. Martin de Porres Clinic folder, Clinics file, ASCL.

51. *Daily Sentinel*, Dec. 9, 1987; *Marillog*, Fall 1989 and Winter 1990; *Marillac News*, Fall 2000, Marillac Clinic folder, Clinics file, ASCL.

52. *Chronicle of Catholic Life*, August 1988; History folder, Marillac Clinic Inc. file, St. Mary's Hospital and Regional Health Center Archives.

53. Information from Sister Michel Pantenberg, Fall 2005.

14. Expanding Frontiers of Healing

1. Dave Fishell, *Towers of Healing: The First 125 Years of Denver's Saint Joseph Hospital* (Denver, CO: Saint Joseph Hospital Foundation, 1999), 18–190, passim; *Rocky Mountain News*, Dec. 22, 1963, St. Joseph's Hospital file, ASCL. Designed by Robert Irwin, Denver architect, the pair of rounded twelve-story structures of steel and glass flanked a tall lighted cross overlooking the hospital's main entrance. A comprehensive pediatrics floor with an adjacent outdoor play area was the contribution of the hospital's long-time patron, Margery Buell. The Sacred Heart Chapel that tops one tower was the gift of Ella Mullen Weckbaugh, who had provided the Catherine Mullen Nurses' home and school built in the 1930s (*Rocky Mountain News*, May 1, 1964, Dedication folder, Sacred Heart Chapel file, St. Joseph's Hospital Archives [SJHA]). In 1997, Lutheran Medical Center renamed itself Exempla Healthcare and entered into an agreement with SCL/Health Services Corporation to manage St. Joseph's Hospital.

2. Narrative for grant application, 1961, St. Joseph's Hospital file, ASCL; Gilmore, *We Came North*, 383–84. Remarks at 100th Anniversary of Medical

Education, Nov. 13, 1992; Residency Centennial Celebration, 1893–1993, Centennial file; "Surgery Education," June 1992, *Medical Staffletter* series, SJHA. Under Dr. Marion McDowell, director of Medical Education for twenty years, and Dr. Robert Gibbons, director of Internal Medicine, the residency in surgery alone grew to be the largest private training program in eight mountain states.

3. Conversations with Sister Mary Aloys Powell and Dr. William Rainer, Summer 2004.

4. Conversation with Sister Mary Andrew Talle, Winter 2003.

5. Notes on Clinics, SJHA; "Mission of Saint Joseph Hospital for the Care of the Aging," July 1985, Family Practice Center file, SJHA.

6. Conversation with Sister Mary Andrew, Winter 2003. Dr. Holyoke fell to his death Aug. 14, 1981, when he was the last man on a rope of climbers ascending Crestone Peak in the Sangre de Cristo mountain range. At the top of that mountain, 14,000 feet high, the doctor had added St. Joseph's Hospital to the plaque of inscriptions.

7. *Celebrating 120 Years of Service*, special edition of *Denver Post*, n.d., 1993, St. Joseph's Hospital file, ASCL.

8. Letter of Understanding to Sister Mary Andrew from Carl E. Berner Jr., Vice President and Regional Manager, Kaiser Foundation Health Plan of Colorado, Jan. 10, 1974, Kaiser Permanente file, SJHA.

9. Women's Pavilion file, SJHA. The coordinator of the Women's Pavilion was Patricia Moore, assisted by Joan Greland-Goldstein, RN, and education coordinator Lori Londrat.

10. History, Health Services System, St. Joseph's Hospital; Strategic Plan 1980–1985 Summary; *Celebrating 120 Years of Service*, St. Joseph's Hospital file, ASCL.

11. Sister Mary Andrew Talle, Personal file, ASCL; Fishell, *Towers of Healing*, 189–95 passim; conversation with Atwill Gilman, Summer 2004.

12. *Denver Business World*, Aug. 10, 1981; Middle States Economic Council *Bulletin*, March 1986; *Denver Catholic Register*, May 10, 1976; *Towerscope*, November 1977, News Clippings folder; Sister Mary Andrew Talle, Personal file, ASCL. When St. Joseph's was one of the health centers reviewed for the NBC documentary, "Medicine in America," aired in 1978, Sister was interviewed as the hospital's administrator.

13. The award came from the Samaritan Institute, a national network of interfaith counseling centers (*Denver Post*, Sept. 3, 1994; Programs, Awards and Recognitions file, SJHA).

14. *St. James Hospital 1881–1981*, Centennial booklet, St. James Community Hospital (SJCH) file, ASCL.

15. Sister Mary Seraphine, March 1980, SJCH file, ASCL.

16. Centennial booklet; *Butte Daily Sentinel*, May 13, 1965, Centennial folder, SJCH file, ASCL; Paula J. McGarvey, "St. James marks 125 years," <http://www.MontanaStandard.com>, accessed 11/10/2006.

17. Sister Mary Bridget Mullen, "In the Beginning…there was Alpha," *Relay*, May 1970, ASCL.

18. The administrator was Sister Mary Clarice Lousberg (*Montana Standard*, n.d. and Aug. 24, 1978, Sister Mary Clarice Lousberg, Personal file, ASCL).

19. Centennial booklet, SJCH file; History, Health Services System; Apostolate Study 1975, ASCL.

20. *Montana Standard*, Aug. 18, 1985, and July 4, 1986, Sister Mary Serena Sheehy, Personal file, ASCL.

21. Dave Fishell, *A Spirit of Charity, 1896–1996, St. Mary's Hospital, Celebrating a Century of Caring*, 79, 86; *Daily Sentinel*, n.d. 1969, St. Mary's Hospital and Regional Medical Center Archives (SMH&RMCA); Centennial wall exhibit. Major support in fund-raising came from chairman Robb Ranney, the Goodwin Foundation, and Walter Walker, editor of the *Sentinel*, who declared St. Mary's to be a community hospital. An auxiliary, first organized in 1955 by Mrs. Tom Truesdell and Marietta Benge, volunteered thousands of hours and dollars.

22. Wall exhibit; editorial, *Daily Sentinel*, Dec. 11, 1958, and Feb. 1959; *Morning Sun*, Feb. 5, 1959, SMH&RMCA; *Spirit of Charity*, 94, 97, 99 ff.

23. St. Mary's Hospital file; Sister Anne Karen Martinez, "Ask the Lord To Send Laborers for the Harvest," *SCL Relay*, December 1970, ASCL; *Daily Sentinel*, Aug. 25, 1968; Sept. 23, 1981; n.d., Mar. 5 and 6, 1984; Nov. 1, 1986, SMH&RMCA; wall exhibit; conversations with Sisters Marianna Bauder and Michel Pantenberg, Summer 2004.

24. For years Sabina organized volunteers to pick fruits and vegetables from the orchards and gardens of Grand Junction. Donations from farmers and ranchers were shipped to the Catholic orphanages, hospitals, and convents of Pueblo and Denver. In 1963 she was elected president of the National Council of Catholic Women; in 1967 she received the Colorado Woman of Achievement Award (conversations with sisters missioned to Grand Junction).

25. Conversation with Sister Michel, Summer 2004; *Daily Sentinel*, May 1967; Apr. 1968; Nov. 27, 1973; *The Chimes*, Supplement to *Daily Centinel*, May 1969, SMH&RMCA. Herbert Bacon and DeeDee Mayer, civic leaders in Grand Junction, co-chaired fund raising in the 60s during the administrations of Sisters Mary Aloys Powell and Zita Marie Cotter. Immediate needs were met with the first cobalt therapy on the Western Slope and intensive cardiac care; a blood bank served more than twenty hospitals.

26. St. Mary's Hospital file, ASCL; brochure, *Project Critical Care*; *Daily Sentinel*, Nov. 27, 1973, and Dedication edition; *Colorado Business*, September and November 1981, SMH&RMCA.

27. History, Health Services System, St. Mary's Hospital, ASCL; brochure, *Project Critical Care*; *Daily Sentinel*, n.d.; Aug. 31 and Nov. 18, 1980; June 11 and July 2, 1985; Karen Fishell, quoted in *Daily Sentinel*, Nov. 14, 1985, SMH&RHCA.

28. Strategic Plan 1988–90; *Daily Sentinel*, n.d. and Nov. 1, 1988; History, Marillac Clinic Inc., SMH&RMCA; conversation with Sister Marianna Bauder, Summer 2004.

29. Brochure, Project Critical Care, *Daily Sentinel*, Mar. 11 and 18, Oct. 7, 1990, SMH&RHCA.

30. "History, Saint Vincent's Hospital, Billings, Montana;" Sister Mary Paul Fitzgerald, "Some Contributions to the Midland Empire by St. Vincent's Hospital, Billings, Montana," Aug. 15, 1959, St. Vincent Healthcare (SVHC) file, ASCL. From different perspectives the residence at St. Vincent's of Crow Chief Plenty Coups in 1923 and of Ernest Hemingway in 1930 were significant events. Crow braves spent a night on the front lawn of the old hospital awaiting the outcome of their chief's cataract surgery. For Hemingway, the seven weeks he spent after surgery for a broken arm ultimately produced a story. The sister nurse and baseball fan who visited him, Sister Florence Cloonan, and a rented radio were title characters in "The Nun, the Gambler, and the Radio" (Sue Hart, SCLA, *The Call To Care, 1898–1998*, 11–15, 24–44 passim, 51–52).

31. "History" and Fitzgerald, "Some Contributions." Those who founded the Hospital Auxiliary included Mrs. Ralph Studer, Mrs. Louis Allard, and Julia Morledge (*Call to Care*, 81). In a move ahead of common practice in sisters' hospitals, Sister Cornelia hired a lay administrative assistant, Robert Layng, who succeeded to Sister Leo Catherine's office. In a letter of 1959 addressed to Sister Mary Paul Fitzgerald, who had requested his views, Layng laid out the advantages he saw in a lay administrator's role in a hospital operated by a religious congregation: learned concepts and practices of business efficiency, skill in making public contacts and maintaining lines of communication, "hard-headed attitudes" needed for custodianship of funds and property, and experience in administering complex institutions. The advantages were those sought in the sisters' establishing lay advisory boards for the hospitals and in the Community's assigning administrators to formal study. Whether or not women religious could manage an institution with the business acumen Layng described was a question to be resolved by their performance.

32. Sister Alice Marie Schwieder, Personal file, ASCL; *Call to Care*, 99, 105–7, 110.

33. Brochure, SVHC file; *Billings Gazette*, May 3, 1974, Sister Michel Pantenberg, Personal file, ASCL; *Call to Care*, 108–9. Hundreds of flights were made in safety, but one flight of August 31, 1980, remains in the memory of St. Vincent's family. In a helicopter crash caused by a severe mountain storm, a mother and her eleven-month old infant and Flight Nurse Alean Brassey Hartford lost their lives. Memorial services continued throughout the following week (Notice of hospital-wide service, Sept. 4, 1980, SVHC file, ASCL).

34. 1984–1985 Long-Range Strategic Plan, 1985 Annual Report; *Developments in Health Care Planning, Design and Construction*, n.d., SVHC file; Sister Michel Pantenberg, Personal file, ASCL; *Call to Care*, 110–11, 119–21.

35. History, Health Services System, St. Vincent's Hospital, ASCL.

36. History, St. Francis Hospital file; St. Francis Hospital House Histories, 1957, ASCL; <Stormontvail.org/aboutus/history.html>; Donald A. Chubb Jr., "Christ's Hospital" and W. Merrill Mills, MD, and Milo G. Sloo, MD, "Jane C. Stormont Hospital and Training School," *A Century of the Healing Arts, 1850–1950* (Shawnee County Historical Society Reprint, 1989, John W. Ripley, ed.); conversation with Harry Briscoe, retired district manager, Santa Fe Railroad, Topeka, Kansas.

37. Conversation with Sister Mary Andrew Talle, Winter 2004.

38. History, St. Francis Hospital and Medical Center file, ASCL.
39. Ibid; *Relay*, Spring 1968; House Histories, 1966, ASCL.
40. History, St. Francis Hospital and Medical Center file; House Histories, 1968–1969, ASCL.
41. *Topeka Daily Capital*, Mar. 10, 1970; History, St. Francis Hospital and Medical Center file; Virginia Bartolac, "St. Francis, Tomorrow's Hospital Today," *Relay*, Mar. 1971, ASCL.
42. History, St. Francis Hospital and Medical Center file, ASCL. The convener, Harry Briscoe, was convinced that such a meeting would clarify common purposes, identify causes of problems, and improve subsequent communication.
43. History, St. Francis Hospital and Medical Center file, ASCL.
44. Ibid. Three Topeka hospitals and the Veterans Administration Medical Center collaborated in various ways to serve Topeka and seven surrounding towns, a base of 4,200,000 residents. Fifty-five percent of them lived outside Shawnee County.
45. History, Health Services System, St. Francis Hospital; Sister Ann Marita Loosen, Personal file, ASCL.
46. Origin of Providence Hospital, manuscript by Sister Gabriella Connell, Providence Hospital file, ASCL; notes of conversation between Mother Mary Berchmans Canaan and Sister Mary Paul Fitzgerald, Sept. 5, 1945.
47. Brochure, Diamond Jubilee folder, Providence Hospital file, ASCL.
48. *Hospital Progress*, June 1977; research paper by John Grattendick, University of Kansas School of Architectural and Urban Design, 1987, Providence–St. Margaret Health Center file; Sister Susan Rieke, "New Medical Complex," *Relay*, March 1971; Sister Kathleen Keenan, Personal file, ASCL.
49. *Kansas City Kansan*, n.d.; Supplement to *Basehor Sentinel, Edwardsville Chieftan, The* [Lansing] *Leader,* and *Wyandotte West*, Clippings; Jubilee Brochure, Providence–St. Margaret file, ASCL.
50. *The Kansan*, Dec. 27, 1977; *Good News Progress*, 1978, Clippings, Jubilee Brochure, Providence–St. Margaret file, ASCL.
51. Brochure, Diamond Jubilee folder, Providence Hospital file, ASCL; conversations with Sister Ann Marita Loosen and Mary Andrew Talle, Fall 2004.
52. History, Saint John's Hospital file, Saint John's Hospital and Health Center Archives (SJH&HCA). See also Sister Julia Gilmore's *Saint John's and Its People*, a Silver Jubilee publication, 1967. The group of executives gathered in 1948 by Hernando Courtwright, president of the Beverly Hills Hotel, learned what Sister Ann Raymond, the administrator, had in mind—something like $2,300,000 for necessary major expansion of Santa Monica's new hospital. Kay Keyser and Louis B. Mayer enlisted sixty other MGM producers, writers, directors, and stars to support Saint John's. Benefits that included movie premieres, dinner dances, and a Ringling Brothers circus along with the Community's second loan for $950,000 made possible the dedication in 1953 of the Veterans Memorial north wing (History and Post-Graduate Assembly files, SJH&HCA).
53. Jubilee 1942–1992; Saint John's Hospital Guild and Irene Dunne Guild files, SJH&HCA. Sister Ann Raymond's proposal for an auxiliary to sponsor activities in support of the maternity and pediatrics units drew the enthusiastic action of

NOTES 549

women who gave personal service and organized special events for years to come. Irene Dunne Griffin proved such an effective first president of this Hospital Guild that her suggestion of a Men's Committee to support and extend the women's work was welcome (Jubilee 1942–1992; Saint John's Hospital Guild and Irene Dunne Guild files, SJH&HCA).

54. Clinics file; Dental, Eye, Muscular Dystrophy, Pacemaker, Speech & Hearing files, SJH&HCA.

55. Ross Center and Mental Health Services files, SJH&HCA; Craig, *The Golden Promise*, 76.

56. Michael Burke Foundation file; Heart Institute file, SJH&HCA; John P. Kelley, Director, Public Relations, "Saint John's, Santa Monica: Twenty-five years of care, compassion, and progress," *Relay*, Fall 1968, ASCL. During his eight-year term as director in the 1970s, Stephen Berens, MD, started up the cardiac rehabilitation and wellness program. Thanks to pioneer work by surgeons like Rodney Smith, MD, and James McEachen, MD, the medical school of the University of California in Los Angeles used Saint John's as a research base. Howard Cohen, MD, director of the catheterization laboratory, was a pioneer in alternative procedures for cardiac patients (Craig, *The Golden Promise*, 28–29).

57. Nuclear Medicine and Critical Care files, SJH&HCA.

58. Hope Guild and Cerebral Palsy files, SJH&HCA; Craig, *The Golden Promise*, 48–49, 178.

59. Child Study Center file, SJH&HCA; Sisters M. Serena Sheehy, M. Caritas Kroetch, Josepha Porter, "Kennedy Child Study Center," *Relay*, Spring 1965, ASCL. The professional staff included pediatricians, psychologists and psychiatrists, therapists, social workers, and educators. Sister Marie James Simms first administered the Center; as it grew, Sisters Ann Marita Loosen and John Baptist O'Neill directed children and adult services respectively. To honor Della Hawley, mother of Mrs. Hilton, the Conrad Hilton Foundation made a million-dollar birthday gift to the Center, a welcoming courtyard. As a volunteer, Mrs. Hawley had served for twenty years with Sisters Jean Stewart, Lucy Walter, and Lynn Casey, the Center's new administrator.

60. Venice Clinics file, SJH&HCA.

61. *The Tidings*, May 21, 1965, Sister Rita Louise Cunningham, Personal file; Cleft Palate and Native Sons of the American West files, SJH&HCA; Craig, *The Golden Promise*, 110–11.

62. Radiology, South Wing, and Cancer Center files, SJH&HCA.

63. Orthopedics and Medical Staff files, SJH&HCA.

64. Chemical Dependency Center file, SJH&HCA. Sister Ann Marita Loosen was administrator in charge of children's care and Sister John Baptist (Kathryn) O'Neill was supervisor of adult services for the Chemical Dependency Center.

65. Saint John's Health Center Foundation file, SJH&HCA; Craig, *The Golden Promise*, 24. Glen McDaniel first chaired the Foundation; Robert Campion, J. Howard Edgerton, John Anderson, William Smith, and James Hesburgh were chairmen in succeeding years.

66. *Los Angeles Times*, April 1979, Sister Marie Madeleine Shonka, Personal file, ASCL.

67. Ambulatory Care Center file, SJH&HCA; announcement of Senior Health and Peer Counseling Center Humanitarian Award, Sister Marie Madeleine Shonka, Personal file. Entry to the facility was a cul-de-sac given by the Corwin Denneys; Mariana Hermann provided for décor of the interior. The Center offered a pain management program, a wellness center, and free preventive physical and mental health services to senior citizens, all of which became common in health centers within two decades.

68. News release, Mar. 26, 1981, Sister Alice Marie Schwieder, Personal file; *Modern Healthcare*, July 29, 1988, Harold N. Samuels, Western States Development Director, June 11, 1987, to Sister Marie Madeleine Shonka, Personal file; Sisters of Charity Health Services System and Saint John's Hospital and Health Center files, ASCL.

69. *California Hospitals* journal, n.d., Sister Marie Madeleine, Personal file.

70. Caritas Award information, 1992, SJH&HCA; Circles of Excellence; Craig, *The Golden Promise*, chap. 2.

71. Account of DePaul Hospital by Sister Catherine Lebhart, 1989. An essay by Suzanne Pattno names Mrs. W. H. McInerney and Mrs. John (Ruth) Loomis as officers of the volunteer members of the Guild. In 1989 she records more than $400,000 donated for medical equipment over thirty-seven years (History folder, DePaul Hospital file, ASCL).

72. *Wyoming State Tribune*, June 4, 1964, *Wyoming Eagle*, Mar. 29, 1956, and May 16, 1958; History, DePaul Hospital file; Sister Alice Marie Schwieder, Personal file, ASCL.

73. Sister Rita Louise Cunningham and Sister Kathleen Keenan, Personal files, ASCL.

74. Sister Michael Marie O'Leary, Personal file, ASCL.

75. *Wyoming Tribune-Eagle*, Mar. 27, 1983; *Wyoming State Tribune*, Sept. 28, 1985; *Wyoming Eagle*, Mar. 1, 1988; Sister Mary Clarice Lousberg, Personal file, ASCL. Appointed a Fellow in the American College of Health Care Executives, Sister Mary Clarice was Regent for Montana and Wyoming. A fellowship supported travel to Finland, the Soviet Union, and China. Chair of the board of the Wyoming Hospital Association, she was appointed to the Board of Certification of Needs Review by the governor of Wyoming and coordinator of health affairs for the Diocese of Cheyenne.

76. Sister Mary Francine Stubbs, Personal file; DePaul Hospital, History folder, Health Services System file, ASCL.

77. Letter dated Feb. 18, 1985, History, DePaul Hospital file, ASCL.

15. Ministry in a Post–Vatican II World

1. Mission, Norm 1.1, *Directory of the Sisters of Charity of Leavenworth*, ASCL.

2. Mother General's Report to Tenth General Chapter, 1968; Community Director's Report to Thirteenth General Chapter, 1986, ASCL.

3. Mother Leo Frances Ryan to members, Nov. 1972, Circular Letters file; Leadership Conference of Women Religious file, ASCL.

4. "Bishops, Major Superiors Discuss Common Concerns," *Relay*, March 1972, ASCL.

5. "Happiness Is Having a Teacher" and "Youths Share in Tutoring Program," *Relay*, Spring and Fall 1968, ASCL.

6. Confraternity of Christian Education file, ASCL; conversation with Sister Mary Pauline Degan, Fall 2003.

7. Sisters Lorraine Nicely and Patricia Toy, "Adults Assume Active Role in Butte Plan"; Sister Theresa Lackamp, "Questions People Ask," *Relay*, May 1970, ASCL.

8. "It's Happening in Billings," *Relay*, May 1970, ASCL.

9. "Catechesis Program," *Relay*, Fall 1964, ASCL.

10. Sister Anna Totta, "Olive Branch: New growth from SCL 'family tree,'" *Relay*, February 1970, ASCL; copy for *Voices of Charity*, Winter 2006 issue.

11. Sister Regina DeCoursey, "Parish Associates," *Relay*, June 1971; Sister Alice Marie Shea, "Team Ministry in Rural Kansas," *Relay*, December 1972, ASCL.

12. Sisters Judith A. Hayes and Lillian Grieshaber, "New Friends Among Senior Citizens," *Relay*, November 1969, ASCL.

13. Sister M. Bridget Mullen, "Uprooting and Transplanting," *Relay*, December 1971, ASCL; conversation with Sister Agnes Eileen Dunn, Winter 2004.

14. Conversations with Sisters Ann Winnifred McGarry and Paula Marie Tweet, August 2003, and Sister Mary Pat Lenahan, Winter 2004.

15. Sisters Margaret Marie Mitchell and Jeanne Marie Jette, Personal files, ASCL.

16. *Relay*, Fall 1964 and March 1971, ASCL.

17. Conversations with Sisters Rosalie Curtin and Lillian McGuire, Spring and Summer 2003. Parishes served by the team were St. Therese, St. Louis, St. Augustine, and St. Joseph. After Vatican II, RCIA was first adopted widely in France and Africa. Translation into English in 1972 introduced it into midwestern parishes implementing renewal.

18. Conversations with Sisters Eileen Sheehy and Bonnie Bachle, Summer 2004.

19. Sister Letitia Lenherr, Personal file, ASCL; conversation with Sister Therese Steiner, Summer 2004; Re-markings, *Voices of Charity*, June 2006.

20. Conversation with Sister Mary Jo McDonald, August 2003.

21. Conversation with Sister Irene Skeehan, Spring 2004; *The Catholic Key*, Summer 1991; Sister Maureen Hall, Personal file, ASCL. Sister Irene had been campus minister at the University of Missouri in Kansas City, the only woman in that office in the metro area at the time (*Union News*, December 1978; Sister Irene Skeehan, Personal file).

22. *Relay*, March 1971; Sister Perpetua McGrath, Personal file, ASCL.

23. Sisters Mary Jo Coyle, Mary Ellen Beyhan, and Barbara Kushan, Personal files, ASCL.

24. Sister Mary Catherine Daugherty, Personal file, ASCL.
25. Conversation with Sister Margaret Hogan, Summer 2003.
26. Sister Jane Hays, Personal file, ASCL.
27. Conversation with Sister Bernadette Marie, Summer 2004. Thomas Keating's *Open Mind, Open Heart* trilogy and retreat conferences are resources for the center. Sister coordinates the Colorado unit in Denver, a training center for religious and lay leaders in the ancient Benedictine method known as *Lectio Divina*. It has evolved into what is now known as centering prayer.
28. *Golden Jubilarians 1950–2000*; *Eastern Kansas Register*, Mar. 25, 1977; Wichita Diocesan paper, n.n., n.d., 1995, Sister Carmen Echevarria, Personal file, ASCL.
29. Sister David Marie (Gloria) Solomon, "Credo for a Prayer House," Sept. 27, 1979, General Chapter 1980 file, ASCL.
30. Sisters Mary Annette Bohrer and Paula Day, "Where Next?" *Relay*, Spring 1968, ASCL.
31. Conversation with Sister Nancy Svetlic, Summer 2004.
32. Conversation with Sister Kathryn O'Neill, Summer 2003.
33. Sister Virginia Bartolac, "Sisters bring health care into homes," *Relay*, March 1974, ASCL.
34. Conversations with Sisters Jean William Lockett, Summer 2004 and 2005.
35. Notes from Sister Mary Georgette Groh; conversations with Sisters Patricia Field and Mary Depner, Summer 2003; Sister Pat Connolly, Fall 2005.
36. Sister Mary Joan Eble, personal file, ASCL.
37. Conversation with Sister Mary Francine Stubbs; Sister Bernice Himmelberg, "Pastoral Care at Saint John's, Santa Monica," *Relay*, March 1974, ASCL.
38. *Vision*, National Association of Catholic Chaplains, November/December 2003, Sister Rose Carmel McKenna, Personal file, ASCL.

16. Mission Unlimited

1. *Catholic Key*, Apr. 16, 1995, quoting Sister Marie de Paul Combo; conversation with Sister Frances Russell, Summer 2004; *project NOTES*, n.d., quoting Sister Kevin Marie Flynn; "Ministry to the Poor," undated vocation story by Sister Margarita Padilla.
2. Apostolate Reports of 1985 in preparation for Thirteenth General Chapter, ASCL.
3. Conversation with Sister Mary Lyons, Summer 2004; *Denver Catholic Register*, Dec. 23, 1992, Sister Mary Lucy Downey, Personal file, ASCL. First place in HUD's Fair Housing Awards was assigned to the projects in the early 1990s.
4. Conversation with Marie de Lourdes and Owen Marie Falk, Summer 2004.
5. *Denver Catholic Register*, Dec. 23, 1992, Sister Mary Lucy Downey, Personal file, ASCL.

6. Sister James Mary Killoy, "Prison Apostolate," *Relay*, Summer 1965; "Saint Mary Commitment to Involvement," *Relay*, June 1972, ASCL.

7. Sister Darlyne Kern, Personal file, ASCL.

8. Personal account; *The Leaven*, Oct. 26, 1984, Sister Dolores Brinkel, Personal file, ASCL.

9. *Connecting*, July 10, 1997; *Kansas City Times*, Dec. 3, 1970; *The Examiner*, Sept. 14, 1976, and Dec. 12, 1980, Sister Margaret Mary Driscoll, Personal file, ASCL.

10. *The Leaven*, Mar. 4, 1988; *Catholic Charities* newsletter, Spring 1989 and Summer 1990, Sister Margaret Mary Driscoll, Personal file. Sisters educated for such work learned the value of training and internship for others who volunteered for social services or advocacy.

11. Conversation with Sister Margaret Groh, Fall 2006; Community Secretary's records.

12. Conversation with Sister Mary Helen McInerney, Spring 2004; Community Secretary's records.

13. *Catholic Key*, June 13, 1999, Sister Virginia Bartolac, Personal file, ASCL. Sister Mary Ann Bartolac is a marriage case advocate for the diocese in Johnson County, KS.

14. Sister Mary Cele Breen, Personal file, ASCL. Sisters Mary Ellen Burns and Lillian McGuire in turn succeeded as coordinators of the training program.

15. Conversation with Sister Eileen Hurley, Summer 2004.

16. *Catholic Key*, May 3, 1992, and Aug. 13, 1993; *Montana Catholic*, Sept. 8, 1995, and June 20, 1997; "Crossing the Threshold to the Third Millennium," Diocese of Helena, Ecumenical Reconciliation Service, June 4, 1997; *Connections*, program of Helena diocese, Carroll College, Oct. 8–9, 1999, Sister Rita McGinnis, Personal file, ASCL.

17. Conversation with Sister Lynn Casey, July 2006; *The Harvest*, April 2003; *Voices of Charity*, April 2006.

18. *The Harvest*, November 2001, Sister Jean Martin Dawson, Personal file, ASCL.

19. *Catholic Key*, Nov. 17 and Dec. 8, 1991; Aug. 22, 1993; *Kansas City, Kansas Business Journal*, Oct. 9–15, 1992, Sister Vickie Perkins, Personal file, ASCL.

20. Conversations with Sister Michel Pantenberg, Summer 2004; House History, Spokane, Washington, 1990–91.

21. *Montana Catholic Register*, May 2, 1962; *The Tablet*, Dec. 5, 1974; *Westmont Word*, May 2, 1984; *Leavenworth Times*, May 22, 1990, Sister Mary Sarah Fasenmeyer, Personal file, ASCL.

22. Conversation with Sister Susan Wood, Summer 2004; Personal file, ASCL.

23. Personal record; remarks by Sister Sue Miller at presentation of Sister Rosalie Mahoney Award, 2001; account for Jubilee by Sister Mary Janet McGilley, Sister Margarita Padilla, Personal file, ASCL.

24. Article by Sister Margarita in newsletter, n.n., n.d.; *Connecting*, Feb. 17, 1994, Sister Margarita Padilla, Personal file, ASCL.

25. Personal record; *Connecting*, Nov. 19, 1981; *Rocky Mountain News*, Nov. 12, 1981, quoting *Anchorage Times*, Oct. 23, 1981; *Denver Catholic Register*, Nov. 11, 1981, Sister Mary Ermin Lambrecht, Personal file, ASCL.

26. Sister Agnes Therese Weir, "2 SCL's go north to Blackfoot Indians," *Relay*, March 1974; Sisters Mary Paulette Fitzgerald and Vera Schwaubauer, "A Summer in the Third World," *Relay*, September 1971, ASCL; conversation with Sister Edna Hunthausen, Summer 2004; Sister Therese Klepac, Personal file, ASCL.

27. Personal record and House Histories for 1983, 1984–85, 1987–88, and 1990–91; brochure on the Pine Ridge Reservation, Sister Mary Hilaria Phipps, Personal file, ASCL. On a committee of the American Indian Science and Engineering Society (AISES), Sister Mary Hilaria helped edit a book of activities for science teachers and coordinated a teacher-training workshop. An acquaintance and part-time colleague in the AISES projects was Phillip J. Stevens, founder of an engineering firm on the West Coast and great-grandson of the Sioux warrior, Standing Bear, who fought at the battle of Little Bighorn. Red Cloud, chief of an Oglala band of Teton Lakota Indians, was one of the Sioux chiefs who in 1868 escorted Father De Smet into Wyoming in search of Sitting Bull. In 1877, after loss of the Black Hills and Powder River country by tribes of the Great Sioux Reservation, six agencies were carved out of Dakota land, some 35,000 square miles. Pine Ridge was the first of them. In 1889, in violation of the Fort Laramie Treaty that had established the Reservation in 1868, its nine million acres were opened to settlement, except for six reservations, including Pine Ridge (*Insight*, Oct. 8, 1988; Dee Brown, *Bury My Heart at Wounded Knee, An Indian History of the American West* [New York: Henry Holt and Company, 1970], 416–17, 428–31).

28. Conversations with Sisters Mary Frances Kirkpatrick and Dolores Erman, Summer 2004.

29. Sister Ruth Barron, Personal file, ASCL; conversation with Sister Claire Scherr, Summer 2004, and materials from St. Anthony's Mission.

30. Sister Marie Bernard Martin, Personal file, ASCL.

31. GSP *project NOTES*, n.d.; *Kansas City Star*, February 1991; *Sisters Today*, September 1998; *Extension Magazine*, October 2001, Sister Kevin Marie Flynn, Personal file, ASCL.

32. *Los Angeles Times*, Mar. 19, 1982; *The Leaven*, Jan. 17, 1992, Sister Lucy Walter, Personal file, ASCL; conversation with Sister Lucy, Fall 2005.

33. Personal account and letters; brochure of Llamba, 1962; *Kansas City Star*, Dec. 17, 1981, Sister Mary Jo Downey, Personal file, ASCL.

34. Conversation with Sister Ann Margaret Noonan, Spring 2004.

35. Psychodynamic Account; nomination for Network's Woman of Justice award; *The Leaven*, Apr. 13, 1984; Donnelly College newspaper, January-February, 1986; *The Leaven*, Apr. 26, 1985; *Kansas City Times*, n.d. and Mar. 18, 1988; *Catholic Key*, Apr. 16, 1995, Sister Marie de Paul Combo, Personal file, ASCL.

36. Program, Catholic Charities Annual Meeting, May 22, 1992; *Network Connection*, March-April 1997, Sister Marie de Paul Combo, Personal file, ASCL.

17. "The beginning and the end of our coming together..."

1. The group included Sisters Mary Janet McGilley, Marie Aquina (Mary Elizabeth) Kelly, Mary Margaret Shea, Mary Serena Sheehy, and Mary Jude Redle.

2. The second group included Sisters Mary Serena Sheehy, Susan Rieke, Gabriella Connell, Margaret Mary Driscoll, Judith Jackson, and Kathleen Wood. Sister Susan, free in summers, accepted the task of examining canon law referring to religious life (Preparation for General Chapter of 1980; *Chapter News Notes*, July 3, 1980, ASCL; conversation with Sister Susan Rieke, Fall 2004).

3. Report to General Chapter, 1980, ASCL.

4. *Chapter News Notes*, June 28 and 29, 1980, ASCL.

5. *Chapter News Notes*, July 1, 1980. Sister Constance added a principle that implied in its scope the work of Chapters to come: "If the Community wants its *aggiornamento* to be real, it must introduce into its structures a principle of permanent evolution. Twelve years ago, we began a 'conversion' journey. As we have responded and struggled to discover new patterns of governing our lives, we have raised significant questions concerning every aspect of our life and work. Perhaps, in the final analysis, the raising of these questions is the most far-reaching result of the changes, for these questions are enduring human issues and the answers have serious implications for the entire Church and for society."

6. *Chapter News Notes*, July 2, 1980.

7. *Chapter News Notes*, July 3 and 7, 1980; Chapter Enactments, General Chapter, 1980, ASCL.

8. *Chapter News Notes*, July 7, 1980; Chapter Enactments, General Chapter, 1980, ASCL.

9. Chapter Enactments; *Chapter News Notes*, July 10, 1980. A pre-Chapter survey studied by the delegates revealed that the Sisters of Charity affirmed the traditional religious vows but did not agree on their meaning. That poverty for many implied simplicity of life and social justice did not erase ambiguities regarding the use of cars, mounting travel, and inequities in practices of the common life. Not all enjoyed a healthy range of friendships in living a celibate life in community. Some confusion of collegiality with independence and some misunderstanding of the demands of accountability stood in the way of consensus about the meaning of religious obedience.

10. Chapter Enactments; *Chapter News Notes*, July 9 and 10, 1980.

11. Chapter Enactments.

12. Notes from Sister Regina Deitchman, Community Survey 2001. The first candidate was received in 1981.

13. *Chapter News Notes*, July 15, 1980; Chapter Enactments.

14. Chapter Enactments, *Chapter News Notes*, July 16, 1980.

15. Election, General Chapter, 1980, ASCL.

16. A team of three sisters similar in background, age, and attitudes analyzed individually each of ten documents and compared their findings to arrive at a 90 percent

similarity. The documents were grouped according to the size of communities, ranging in membership from two hundred or fewer to fifteen hundred or more. After evaluating fifty documents, a team was given ten randomly selected for recoding and checking for consistency with original scoring ("Analysis of Chapter Decrees of Religious Orders of Women in the United States," with Specific Data for Sisters of Charity of Leavenworth, UND: CNEA Box 26, Reports to Congregations, Contemporary Survey).

17. "Analysis of Chapter Decrees."
18. Ibid.
19. Ibid.
20. Marie Augusta Neal, "The Sisters' Survey, 1980: A Report," *Probe* X:5 (May/June 1981): 1–2, UND: CNEA 40/13, Sisters' Survey Reports; Neal, "Sisters' Survey 1980–National Profile," 1, UND: CLCW 86/01, Sisters' Survey 1979–1984. Conclusions came from responses of a random sample of sisters from thirty-one congregations selected by invitation and by the range of their responses on religious belief scales tested as an indication of renewal. The 1980 survey linked its several hundred items with those of the 1967 survey to ensure valid comparisons for purposes of evaluating growth.
21. Neal, "The Sisters' Survey, 1980: A Report," 2–5; Neal, "Sisters' Survey 1980–National Profile," 2–3, 11.
22. Neal, "Sisters' Survey 1980–National Profile," 15.
23. Neal, "The Sisters' Survey, 1980: A Report," 7.
24. Members of the Personnel Board were appointed representatives of seven apostolic groups and five chosen at large.
25. "Assumption Statement," Long Range Planning Committee, General Chapter 1980 file, ASCL. No source is given for the assumptions as they appeared in the committee's document.
26. Quotation from "Chicago Declaration of Christian Concern," Chicago, December 1977, <http://www.CatholicLaborOrganization/NCLInitiative@yahoo.com>. Communication from Sister Kathleen Coman and Personnel Board Members, Sept. 13, 1984, General Chapter 1980 file.

18. Seeking a Common Voice

1. Sisters' Forum 1974, 1978, 1979, Local and General Forums file, 1972–82, ASCL.
2. Sisters' Forum, 1979.
3. Sisters' Forum, 1980.
4. General Forums 1981 and 1982, General Forum Proposals, Local and General Forums file.
5. General Forum 1983, Local and General Forums 1983–92.
6. Ibid.

NOTES 557

7. Leavenworth County Statistical Information, United States Census Bureau; Social Services from SRS, Indigent Assistance Statistical Information, Social Rehabilitation Services, General Forum1984. In April, a collective response calling for an end to the development and deployment of a nuclear weapons system and for action by the U.S. government to reduce nuclear weapons arsenals was published by sisters missioned in southeast Kansas City, Missouri. Twenty-seven sisters signed the published document.

8. General Forum 1984.

9. General Forums 1985 and 1986.

10. Report to General Chapter, 1986; Sister Mary Kevin to Community, Dec. 9, 1983, Circular Letters file; Sister Linda Roth, Feb. 23, 1983, Vocation Office file, ASCL. Sister Rosalie responded to requests from Formation directors across the country for workshops in the program.

11. Introduction to Social Analysis and Theological Reflection, 1982 and 1983 folders, Social Justice, 1979—file, ASCL. Sister Amata Miller, IHM, and Michael J. Schultheis, SJ, Center of Concern, conducted the sessions, referring to Pope Paul VI's letters of the 1970s, "Faith That Does Justice" and "Call to Action."

12. On the Feast of the Annunciation, 1982, the Mother House and college communities gathered for the Eucharist. Designed by Sister Mary Teresita, OP, blood sister of Sister Marie Kelly, the enlarged sanctuary space included a reredos portraying Mary receiving the angel Gabriel's message. In the eucharistic chapel, windows of antique blown glass depicted wheat and landforms characteristic of the territory that had brought the sisters westward.

13. The first liturgy committee included Sisters Catherine Laboure Conway, Mary Julianne O'Flannigan, Macrina Ryan, and Anne Callahan. Sister Mary Loretta Beier was named director of retreats and prayer programs (Sister Mary Kevin to the sisters, May 19, 1983, Circular Letters file, ASCL).

14. Circular letters, Apr. 22 and Aug. 15, 1983.

15. Report of Communications Director to General Chapter, 1986, ASCL.

16. Report of Personnel Board.

17. Sisters of Charity of Leavenworth Long Range Plan, August 1984; Report of Communications Director to General Chapter, 1986, ASCL.

18. *Leavenworth Times*, July 1, 3, and 7, 125th Celebration file, ASCL.

19. Personal record; *The Leaven*, Mar. 2, 1979, Sister Charlotte Swain, Personal file, ASCL; conversation with Sister Lucille Harrington, November 2004.

20. Journal, July 16, 1982, Personal file, ASCL.

21. Talk by Sister Lucille Harrington, Nov. 9, 1984, Sister Charlotte Swain, Personal file, ASCL.

22. Letter of Pope John Paul II to Bishops of the United States, Apr. 3, 1983, with sections from "Essential Elements in the Church's Teaching on Religious Life," General Forum 1984.

23. Yves Congar, "How Christian is the Christian Church?" *Listening/Current Studies in Dialog*, Spring 1967. In his analysis, Congar quoted the thirteenth-century

Cistercian Bernard of Clairvaux and echoed German theologians who resisted Hitler.

19. Seeking a Common Vision

1. Community Director's Report, Thirteenth General Chapter, 1986 file, ASCL.
2. Apostolate Reports, General Chapter 1986 file.
3. One example of such ideas was a proposal developed by a group of principals and consultants during the first months of 1985 (Sister Mary Kevin to Sister Helen Forge, Jan. 23, 1985, ASCL).
4. Chapter Enactments; *Chapter News*, June 12–18, General Chapter 1986 file. Published in 1986, the booklet, "Initial and On-Going Formation, an RCIA Model," guided the commission and formation team. Sister Rosalie Curtin, its author, was invited by formation directors in several religious communities to discuss the model's implementation.
5. *Chapter News*, June 12.
6. *Chapter News*, June 18.
7. Constitutions of the Sisters of Charity of Leavenworth, Nov. 11, 1983, Mission, 5; Community, 10.
8. Survey of Community Members, February 2002 (hereafter cited as Survey 2), Question 1.
9. Survey 2; conversation with Sister Mary Seraphine Sheehan, September 2002.
10. Affiliate Program of the Sisters of Charity of Leavenworth, Pilot Year 1987–88, Associate Membership Program, March 1989; Sister Mary Kathleen Stefani to Community, July 11, 1990, Circular Letters file, ASCL; Noreen Walter to Associates, May 19, 1993, Associate Program 1979–1997 file, ASCL.
11. Sister Mary Kathleen to Community, Nov. 16, 1987, Circular Letters file, ASCL; communication from Sister Marie de Paul to Community, Nov. 18, 1987, Social Justice Network file, ASCL.
12. Notes, Formation Program folder, Latin American file, ASCL.
13. The Formation Team included Sisters Kevin Marie Flynn and Kathleen Wood, director of temporary vow sisters (Chapter Reports, Fourteenth Community Chapter, June 1992, ASCL).
14. Communications file, ASCL; Chapter Reports.
15. Rainbow Reflections, July 1989 file, ASCL.
16. Sister Bernadette Helfert, "The Vocation and Mission of the Laity"; Sister Rosalie Mahoney, "Human Needs: Present and Future"; Sister Sue Miller, "SCL Presence Is the Heart of the Matter"; and Sister Rosalie Curtin, "Evangelization: Who Needs to Hear the Good News?" (Rainbow Reflections). Remarks of others further clarified the claim about Sisters of Charity of Leavenworth. They had a ca-

pacity to look "forward and backward at the right times." This enabled them "to assess needs as lay people see them" and "to feed that information into diocesan planning."

17. Sandra M. Schneiders, IHM, *New Wineskins: Re-imagining Religious Life Today* (New York/Mahwah, NJ: Paulist Press, 1986), 1–2.

18. John J. Fialka, in *Sisters: Catholic Nuns and the Making of America* (New York: St. Martin's Press, 2003), sought reasons for the diminishing number of sisters in Catholic institutions and their general invisibility in the Church. In his review of the book, Kenneth L. Woodward registered the hunch that the sisters "did themselves in" by abandoning the common life and traditional ministries and opting for relative independence ("Change of Habit," *New York Times Book Review*, Feb. 16, 2003). He concluded that reading Fialka might be a way of reminding contemporary sisters of what they had lost.

20. Re-envisioning the Charism

1. For statistics, see LaFeber et al., *The American Century*, 570–71, 578–85.

2. United States Conference of Catholic Bishops website; *American Catholic Studies Newsletter*, Spring 2004.

3. See Peter Steinfels, *A People Adrift* (New York: Simon & Schuster, 2003), 46–47.

4. John R. Quinn, "The Exercise of the Primacy: Facing the Cost of Christian Unity," lecture given at Oxford, June 29, 1996, printed in *Commonweal*, July 12, 1996.

5. In more expansive statements, the transformative elements were enunciated by the Leadership Conference of Women Religious and the Conference of Major Superiors of Men in their Joint Assembly of 1989.

6. The councilor was Sister Bernadette Helfert.

7. *Trends in Community Living...a Comparison of 1986 and 1991*, For Your Reflection packet, Preparation for Chapter of 1992 file, ASCL.

8. *Statistical Trends* and *Reports from Community Committees*, For Your Reflection packet, Preparation for Chapter of 1992 file, ASCL. According to a report of membership in women's religious communities in the United States, the Sisters of Charity of Leavenworth had a lower percentage of members under forty than the national average and a higher percentage over ninety. They had, however, a relatively lower percentage between seventy and ninety; a much higher percentage between sixty and seventy; and a slightly higher percentage between forty and sixty.

9. *Theological Reflection Days*, June 1992, General Chapter 1992 file, ASCL.

10. *Chapter Newsletter*, Chapter 1992 file.

11. The trio of writers was Sisters Mary Cele Breen, Mary Janet McGilley, and Rita McGinnis.

12. *Chapter Newsletter*, Chapter 1992 file.

13. Chapter 1992 file; *Leavenworth Times*, n.d., News Clippings folder, Mount St. Vincent's file, ASCL.

14. *Rocky Mountain News*, July 6, 1993; *Vision*, Mount Saint Vincent's Home, October 1993, including reprint from *Denver Catholic Register*.

15. Strategic Direction Plan 1993–96 folder; *God's Healing Love*, 24–25, Health Services Corporation (HSC) file, ASCL.

16. After formal study in systematic theology, Sister Charlotte gained experience in pastoral ministry, in mission integration for archdiocesan schools, and in the new Exempla Healthcare in Denver before she returned to the SCL/Health System half-time in the office of Sponsorship and Mission. She developed mission modules for use with front line staff, makes presentations for health care systems, and teaches medical ethics, contemporary moral issues, and doctrine in pastoral and university settings.

17. *SCL/HSC Newsletter* 6/94–12/95 folder, HSC file.

18. *Montana Register*, June 1993, News Clippings folder, St. James Community Hospital (SJCH) file, ASCL.

19. *Montana Catholic*, May 5, 1986; Oct. 30, 1992; Nov. 26, 1993; *Montana Register*, June 1993; *Montana Standard*, Dec. 2, 1990; June 8, 1991; n.d., News Clippings folder, SJCH file, ASCL.

20. *Billings Gazette*, Jan. 23, 1988, and June 25, 1990, News Clippings folder; *Healthful Tips* folder; Spring 1990, *In Touch* folder, St. Vincent's Hospital and Health Center (SVH&HC) file, ASCL. During two weeks, with almost a hundred volunteers from the Christian Medical and Dental Society, Sallie Arellano learned of Central America's radical needs. From St. Vincent's, three surgeons and their wives were the first of a group of doctors, nurses, and anesthesiologists who began to travel annually with equipment for training and treatment of native villagers at Cholutica Hospital.

21. Conversation with Sister Bernadette Helfert, August 2003; *Billings Gazette*, Oct. 18, 1998, Centennial folder, SVH&HC file, ASCL.

22. Chronologically ordered files, St. Mary's Hospital Archives; Sister Lynn Casey to Sister Charlotte White, Nov. 2, 1992, Personal files, ASCL; conversation with Sister Lynn Casey, September 2002. St. Mary's multifaceted rural networks on the Western Slope brought Sister Lynn invitations to Gov. Roy Raemer's Health Advisory Board and subsequently to the national Governor's Conference in Washington, DC.

23. *Daily Sentinel*, Jan. 27, 2003, Collaborative Care file, St. Mary's Health Center Archives. An article about the research was published in *Families, Systems and Health*, vol. 20, no. 4, 2002. The Consortium included Colorado West Mental Health, St. Mary's Psychiatric Center, and Marillac Clinic.

24. The Ave Maria Clinic was an outpatient facility originally sponsored in 1939 by three midtown Catholic hospitals to serve the uninsured. Catholic Charities and later Mile High United Way assisted the operation. In the 1960s, St. Joseph's outpatient department, where the clinic functioned, also served medical, obstetrical, and

surgical patients regardless of ability to pay. In 1974 Ave Maria's services were absorbed into Caritas Clinic relocated in an enlarged outpatient department in St. Joseph's Midtown Medical building (Ave Maria Clinic file, St. Joseph Hospital Archives).

25. Conversation with Sister Mary Aloys Powell, August 2004; *Denver Catholic Register*, Nov. 10, 1993; *Mission Services Newsletter*, January/February and November/December 1995; Sister Mary Walter Swann, Personal file, SJHA. By 1995, teams of physicians and nurses were traveling to Ecuador in summer and fall months to a clinic for Indians and mestizos. A doctor and lawyer carried supplies to Tanzania for the Kilimanjaro Children's hospital.

26. *Celebrating 120 Years of Service* folder, SJHA; *Rocky Mountain News*, Feb. 26, 1995, and *Denver Post*, Nov. 16, 1995, Other Hospitals file; *Denver Business Journal*, Sept. 9–15, 1994, Kaiser Permanente file; *Rocky Mountain News*, Mar. 21, 1996; press release, Nov. 22, 1996; Letter of Resignation, Sister Marianna Bauder to employees and physicians, June 30, 1997, Integration file, SJHA.

27. Brochures for Winter 1989 and Winter 1991, St. Francis Hospital and Medical Center (SFH&MC) file, ASCL. The director of pastoral care, Sister Mary Francine Stubbs, brought team services to grieving families and patients in hospice care.

28. Brochure, Summer 1993, SFH&MC file, ASCL.

29. *Pulseline*, Apr. 21, 1989; 125th Anniversary folder; *Leavenworth Times Anniversary Edition*, June 6, 1989; *Hill Highlights*, Dec. 1988, St. John Hospital file, ASCL.

30. *Center Signal*, May 1991, Providence–St. Margaret Medical Center (PSMMC) file, ASCL.

31. *Center Signal*, August, September, November 1991; January, April, December, 1992; January, February, March, 1993; Diamond Jubilee program, Nov. 19, 1996; *News*, Jan. 24, 1997, PSMMC file.

32. Annual Reports, 1988, 1990–1993, Saint John's Health Center (SJHC) file, ASCL; Craig, *The Golden Promise*; and Saint John's Health Center Archives.

33. Sister Marie Madeleine Shonka to SCL/HSC Hospital Presidents, Jan. 17; to Sister Mary Kathleen and all Sisters at the Mother House, Jan. 18; to All of Saint John's Friends and Supporters, Jan. 28, 1994; fax report, Sister Marie Damian to Sister Mary Julie, Jan. 21, 1994, Earthquake folder, SJHC file, ASCL.

34. Sister Marie Madeleine to Saint John's Friends and Supporters, Feb. 25; to Sister Mary Kathleen and Sisters, May 25, 1994, Earthquake folder, SJHC file, ASCL.

35. *Outlook*, Santa Monica, Oct. 3, 1994, Earthquake folder, SJHC file, ASCL.

36. *Outlook*, Feb. 18; *Los Angeles Times*, Feb. 21, Aug. 9, and n.d., 1994, Earthquake folder, SJHC file, ASCL.

37. SMC Data 1980s, pp. 63, 72.

38. *President's News Briefs*, 1988–90, 1991–93, Saint Mary College Archives; *Saint Mary-Go-Round*, 1994, Saint Mary College (SMC) file, ASCL; Sister Mary

Mercita Jackson, Personal file, ASCL; conversations with Penny Lonergan and Kevin Montgomery, Winter 2006.

39. Press release, Nov. 3, 1993; *Saint Mary Go Round* Fall 1993, Presidential Search file, 1993, SMC file, ASCL.

21. Crossing Borders

1. Sister Mary Andrew Talle conducted the study and directed its implementation.

2. 1992–1996 Mid-Term Report to the Community, Summer 1996, Converging Paths file, ASCL.

3. Chronicles, 1990–1995, 1995–2000, ASCL; 1992–1996 Mid-Term Report.

4. The Federation maintains an office in the United Nations as a non-governmental organization holding consultative status with the Economic and Social Council; the sister assigned collaborates with other NGOs, especially of the Vincentian family, to influence global initiatives and decision-making. In its geographical region each member congregation participates in projects of advocacy for the rights of the poor and of education to global issues of human rights and socio-economic justice. Member congregations are located in Emmitsburg, Maryland; Nazareth, Kentucky; Charleston, South Carolina; New York City; Cincinnati and Bedford, Ohio; Saint John and Moncton, New Brunswick; Halifax, Nova Scotia; Convent Station, New Jersey; Greensburg and Pittsburgh, Pennsylvania; and Leavenworth, Kansas.

5. Chronicles, 1995–2000, ASCL; conversation with Sisters Nancy Bauman and Mary Beth Minges, Winter 2005.

6. In July 1994, Sisters Joan Kilker and Paula Rose Jauernig opened St. Peter Claver clinic in Quito to offer basic health care service and health education to the indigent people there. A group of physicians and health care workers at St. Joseph Hospital in Denver supported their work and provided Spanish lessons for volunteers to Ecuador.

7. Chronicles, 1995–2000; Mid-term Report, Come North Project, Reflection ...Before Our Paths Converge, Come North Projects file, ASCL.

8. Heritage Room records, Mother House; 1996 Converging Paths Directory. Two objects of particular interest were Mother Xavier's small handmade writing table and a harp given to the sisters by friends in Nashville and transported by wagon and riverboat to Leavenworth. Sister Helen Forge, Community secretary, compiled the record. A new Directory of Community Members photographed during the gathering included living sisters in all their diversity of age, origin, condition, and culture. A candlelight pilgrimage to Mount Olivet Cemetery on the second day of Converging Paths honored lives that represented 140 years of mission on the North and South American Continents.

9. Chronicles, 1995–2000; Mid-term Report, Converging Paths file; conversation with Therese Horvat, Spring 2005.

10. Fifteenth General Chapter 1998, ASCL.

11. Sister Mary John Mananzan, OSB, "Challenge to Women Religious in the Third Millenium," Chapter 1998 file. In the Philippines, sisters found common cause with workers, women, and children caught in an oppressive regime. Forced to rethink the principles of theology they lived by, they realized that taking Jesus seriously implied radical Christianity. Structural analysis of a society where 2 percent controlled 75 percent of the land and capital and 80 percent of the people were controlled by the economic system showed that radical change was needed. On-the-ground analysis of a global market economy that prioritized profit above social and ethical concerns threatened loss of supports for a people's culture.

12. Report to Chapter, General Chapter 1998 file, ASCL.

13. Councilors' Reports and Report of the Director of Missions.

14. Report on Mount St. Vincent's Home.

15. Saint Mary College Report to General Chapter.

16. Community Secretary's report to SCL Health Services, 1997; Sisters of Charity of Leavenworth Health Services Corporation Report to the Community Director, Chapter 1998 file; Chronicles, 1995–2000; 1992–1996 Mid-term Report, Converging Paths file, ASCL.

17. Transfer of Sponsorship agreement and Sister Mary Kathleen's remarks at public ceremony, Apr. 1, 1997; *SCLHSC Newsletter*, Holy Rosary Hospital file, ASCL; conversation with Sister Marie Damian Glatt, Winter 2005.

18. Ongoing Formation Team Report, Chapter 1998 file.

19. Associate Program Report, Associate Program 1979–1997 file, ASCL; conversation with Sister Noreen Walter, Winter 2005. In 1995 the Associate director issued the first *SCLA Connection*, a newsletter printed by Johnny Johnston, Leavenworth Associate with his wife Annie. Sister Susan Rieke edited the newsletter in its early years before Associate Mary Rau took on the editing responsibilities.

20. Social Justice Executive Committee Report, Chapter 1998 file.

21. Initial Formation, North America, and Vocation Ministry Report, Chapter 1998 file; *SCL Spirit*, July 2001; conversation with Sisters Nancy Bauman and Mary Beth Minges, Winter 2005.

22. Chronicles, 1995–2000; Vocation Committee file, ASCL; conversation with Sister Noreen Walter, Winter 2005.

23. Communications Steering Committee Report, Chapter 1998 file.

24. *Chapter 15*, newsletter, June 1998, Chapter 1998 file.

25. Survey 2, Question 1.

26. Community, Norm 12, Constitution of the Sisters of Charity of Leavenworth.

27. Among others, see Sandra M. Schneiders, "Congregational Leadership and Spirituality in the Postmodern Era," *Review for Religious* (January–February 1998); Ada Maria Isasi-Diaz, *Mujerista Theology* (Maryknoll, NY: Orbis Books, 1996); Miriam D. Ukeritis, CSJ, "What has happened since the FORUS study gave religious life 10 years to make life-saving changes?" *Horizon* (Fall 2001): 9–14; Sister Marie Augusta Neal, SNDdeNamur, "A Report on the National Profile of the Third

Sisters' Survey," Emmanuel College, Boston, July 1991, rev. Feb. 20, 1992, CNEA: UNDA. For early accounts of experience in developing countries and its theological implications, see Paulo Freire, *Pedagogy of the Oppressed* (New York: Continuum, 1997); Johannes Metz, *Theology of the World*, trans. William Glen Doyel (New York: Herder & Herder, 1971).

22. Jubilee: "Year of Favor from the Lord"

1. Exod 20:8, Lev 25:2, Isa 61:1–2, Luke 4:16–18; notes on Jubilee Themes: Sabbath and Fallow Land, Sabbath Time folder, Chapter 1998 Committees file, ASCL.

2. Chaplains folder, Clergy file; Sister Sue Miller to the sisters, Oct. 1, 1998, Circular Letters file, ASCL; telephone conversation with archivist Sister Marie Louise Krenner, OSB, Abbey of St. Benedict, Atchison, Kansas.

3. Sabbath Time and Global Mission folders, Chapter 1998 Committees file.

4. Partnership folder, Chapter 1998 Committees file; *SCL Spirit*, July 2000, February and June 2001, June 2002, In the Spirit of Charity file, ASCL.

5. Sister Sue Retherford, coordinator of teacher training in the Kansas City–St. Joseph Diocese for ten years, designed and implemented the program.

6. Immersion Experience folder, Chapter 1998 Committees file.

7. Theology Update folder, Ongoing Formation Team Report, Chapter 1998 Committees file; *Spirit*, July 2001, ASCL.

8. Communications folder, Chapter 1998 Committees file. Sister Rita McGinnis, Rick Hite, chair of the information technology program at the University of Saint Mary, and Rebekah Kite, former SCL communications director, developed the website. Sister Mary Erwin Baker, retired mathematics and education professor at USM, mastered photo editing, scripting programs, and layout software in order to maintain the website. Julie Cogley, communications director, provided the material (*Spirit*, November 2000 and December 2001).

9. Summary of three-day consultation of the Bishops' Committee on Women in Society and in the Church, Diocese of Great Falls–Billings, Montana; *Spirit*, April 2001; conversation with Sister Eileen Hurley, Feb. 15, 2005. Participants also urged study of canon law to determine precisely what roles are open or closed to the non-ordained. They voiced hope for regional consultations similar to the ground-breaking sessions they had just experienced.

10. Leadership Meeting 2001, Charity Federation file, ASCL; *Spirit*, May 2001.

11. Ada Maria Isasi-Diaz, keynote address and program, In the Spirit of Charity file, ASCL.

12. *Sisters of Charity Federation*, Office of NGO Representative, June 2001, Charity Federation file, ASCL.

13. Sister Roberta O'Leary hosted the evening performance. Sister Maureen Hall led Sunday morning's reflection.

NOTES 565

14. SCL Family Reunion folder; *Spirit*, July 2001, Red Carpet file, ASCL. Sister Mary Lenore Martin chaired the Jubilee Committee.

15. Survey 2.

16. Ibid., Question 2.

17. Ibid., Question 3.

18. Interestingly, two of the six respondents who ranked women's poverty first, second, or third for its significant effect on Community were women who ministered directly and consistently to the poor in South America and on the Mexican border. Ages of the six at entry to the Community ranged from seventeen to twenty-seven.

19. Survey 2, Question 4.

20. Ibid., Question 5.

21. Ibid., Question 6.

22. Ibid., Question 7.

23. Ibid., Question 1.

24. Survey 3 of Associates, colleagues, and friends, May 2002, analysis of demographic data.

25. Survey 3, Question 2.

26. Ibid., Question 3.

27. Ibid., Question 1.

28. Ibid., Question 4.

29. Ibid., Question 5.

30. Ibid., Questions 1–5 passim.

31. *Tertullian of Carthage, Selected Writings, 197–200*, The Apology, 197, *The Apologetical Works of Tertullian*, trans. Sister Emily Joseph Daly, CSJ (New York: Fathers of the Church Inc., 1950), 10, 198–202, in *Readings in Church History*, vol. 1, ed. Colman J. Barry, OSB (Westminster, MD: Newman Press, 1960), 57.

23. Motto for Community: "Choose Life"

1. *SCL Spirit*, September 2001 and June 2002.

2. "Significant Moments in LCWR History;" *Update*, October 2003; press release, Jan. 29, 2003; notes, LCWR file, ASCL; *SCL Spirit*, May 2002, September/October 2002 and 2003.

3. Blood Sisters file; Membership Record; Retirement Task Force, 1974, 1991— file; *SCL Spirit*, January 2001, ASCL. An increased nursing staff, enlargement of the physical therapy area, and educational workshops on health issues served both Mother House and Ross Hall sisters.

4. Sister Ann Dolores Muckenthaler, Personal file, ASCL.

5. Harvest Time Committee's Interviews on Aging, Retirement Study 1991–1999, ASCL.

6. Philosophy of Aging of the Sisters of Charity of Leavenworth, Retirement Study 1991–1999, ASCL.

7. *SCL Spirit*, November 2000, February 2001, and May 2002. Sisters Charlotte White and Sharon Smith were delegates from the Community's Vocation Network.

8. *"Who Are the Sisters of Charity?"* The original brochure was revised in 2002 by the Vocation Office.

9. Sister Sue Miller to the Community, Mar. 25, 2002, Circular Letters file. Quotation from the e-mail sent by Hermana Susana, Mar. 25, 2002.

10. Program materials, Alpha and Omega file, ASCL; *SCL Spirit*, September/October 2002 and January/February 2003.

11. *SCL Spirit*, Special Anniversary Issue; *The Leaven*, Dec. 26, 2003, Latin American file, ASCL.

12. Conversation with Hermanas Julia Huiman Ipanaque, Maria de los Melagros Orozco, Esther Vilela Gutierrez, Summer 2003.

13. Latin American file.

14. Sister Mary Jo Coyle to sisters regarding Christmas in October, n.d. 2002 and Dec. 2, 2003, e-mails from Community Secretary; *SCL Spirit*, February 2001. Sister Mary Jo's spare time during terms of teaching in the community college system was given to repair of homes and other services for elderly, incapacitated, or uninsured homeowners. In 1998 Sister Mary Jo joined ten other Sisters of Charity for construction work on the All Women's House in Kansas City. She served on the Habitat Board and on the construction committee.

15. *The Leaven*, Apr. 22, 1988; *Connecting*, Nov. 6, 1997; *SCL Spirit*, January/February 2003; *Kansas City Star*, Aug. 11, 2004.

16. Chronicles, 1997, ASCL; *Leavenworth Times*, n.d., 1997 and Feb. 27, 2005; *Kansas City Star*, n.d., 1997, Personal file, Sister Jane Albert Mehrens, ASCL; *Voices of Charity*, June 2005.

17. Sister Janet Cashman, Personal file, ASCL.

18. *Leavenworth Times*, Mar. 18, 2001, Sister Rosella Mary Hehn, Personal file, ASCL.

19. *SCL Spirit*, July/August and September/October 2003; presentation by Sister Paula Rose Jauernig, Mother House, Feb. 28, 2005.

20. Report of SCL Social Justice Executive Committee, General Chapter 1998 file; resource sheet for Pentecost Prayer in the Twenty-first Century, "Toward a New Paradigm of Peacemaking," Social Justice Committee file; *SCL Spirit*, July and November/December 2002 and July/August 2003. An Associate Advisory Council began to meet regularly with the Associate director and wrote a mission and vision statement guiding plans for future projects.

21. Geraldine Anthony, SC, *Vision of Service: Celebrating the Sisters of Charity* (Kansas City, MO: Sheed & Ward, 1997); *Kansas City Star*, Aug. 12, 1999; *Leavenworth Times*, July 7, 2000, Sister Therese Bangert, Personal file, ASCL.

22. Each of the meeting rooms was named for a saint who figured in the Community's traditions of special devotion and patronage of homes and hospitals. Marillac's first guests were the parish staff of Our Lady of Guadalupe Church, Topeka.

NOTES 567

23. History, Marillac Center file, ASCL; *SCL Spirit*, March/April 2003; conversations with Sisters Noreen Walter and Mary Loretta Beier, February 2005.

24. Blessing and Open House, O'Shea Conference Center, Feb. 29, 2004.

25. Xavier Community file; *SCL Spirit*, November 2000 and April 2001; *Lawrence Journal-World*, Oct. 11, 2003 and *Menuha Moments*, July 2001, Sister Ann Loendorf, Personal file, ASCL. Sisters Mary Beth Minges, Sue Retherford, and Barbara Schrader opened the Kansas City Xavier House.

26. Conversation with Sister Frances Marie Grady, Winter 2005; Living Waters brochure, 2005.

27. Conversation with Sister Dominique Long, Winter 2005.

28. Archdiocesan Housing Senior and Family Communities, 2003 Annual Report. To serve low-income families and aging residents of Wyandotte County, Sister Charles Marie Beeby was employed in the Mercy Sisters' Catholic Housing enterprise in Kansas City, Kansas.

29. Message and photos from Sister Amy Willcott, Feb.16, 2005; *SCL Spirit*, May/June 2003; Sisters of Charity of Leavenworth website, Mar. 8, 2005.

30. *Denver Catholic Register*, Apr. 4, 2001; Oct. 16 and Nov. 6, 2002, Mount St. Vincent's Home file, ASCL; conversations with Sisters Roberta Furey and Elizabeth Adams, August 2004.

31. Conversation with Sister Michael Dolores Allegri, August 2004.

32. Conversation with Sister Margaret Mary Driscoll, Summer 2005; brochure, St. Joseph Adoption Ministry; notes from Sister Marie Noel Bruch, Winter 2006.

33. *125 Years: The History of Mount Saint Vincent Home for Children*, p. 12; *SCL Spirit*, May 2001; conversation with Sister Mary Rachel Flynn, Fall 2005.

34. *Spiritual Writings* of Louise de Marillac, ed. Sister Joan Pytlik, DC, Vincentian Awareness Series [6 of 12], Congregation of the Mission.

35. Demographic data from Survey 4, Community Ministries, Fall 2002; Community Secretary's records.

36. Survey 4, Question 2.

37. Ibid., Question 3.

38. Ibid., Questions 2 and 3.

39. Ibid., Question 4.

40. Ibid., Question 5.

41. Ibid., Question 6.

24. Teaching: A Heritage Firm and at Risk

1. Newsletter, Xavier Schools file; *Connecting*, Feb. 22, 2002, *Connecting* file, ASCL.

2. *Connecting*, Feb. 22, 2002.

3. *Leavenworth Times*, June 30, 2003; *The Leaven*, Apr. 4, 2003, Xavier Schools file.

4. *Connecting*, Nov. 6, 1997; Distinguished Graduate Award, Jan. 2, 2005.

Three of the Laramie group were the last to serve at St. Laurence O'Toole: Sisters Elizabeth Skalicky, Ann Lucia Apodaca, and Sharon Parr.

5. Conversation with Sister Katherine Franchett, February 2005.

6. Conversation with Sister Elizabeth Youngs, February 2005.

7. Tradition of Excellence Campaign, 1999–2000; Butte Central Catholic Schools Annual Report 2001–2002, Butte Elementary and Junior High file, ASCL.

8. Conversation with Sister Jean Martin Dawson, March 2005.

9. Central City School Fund files; conversation with Sister Barbara Schrader, March 2005.

10. Conversations with Blake Mulvaney, Spring 2004 and Sister Victoria Perkins, March 2005. Monsignor Gardner's educational leadership was far-reaching. He had been a founding member of the Kansas Association of Non-Public Schools and president of the board of the Secondary School Department of the National Education Association.

11. Record of School Openings and Closings, ASCL; *Kansas City Star*, Mar. 6, 2005.

12. Conversation with Sister Bernadette Helfert, March 2005. Of the sixty-seven elementary schools staffed by the Community for more than a few years since 1867, thirty-eight remained open in 2005, ten of them merged or consolidated and operated by lay administrators, faculty, and staff (list compiled up to 1971 from Sister Mary Buckner's history, Chronicles, House Histories, and letters, 1957–1963, by Sister Mary Seraphine Sheehan before she retired. It was completed March 4, 2005, ASCL).

13. John Paul II's *Ad Lumina* Address, "Catholic Education: Relating Freedom and Moral Truth," *Origins*, June 18, 1998, p. 77.

14. U.S. Bishops, "Sharing Catholic Social Teaching: Challenges and Directions," *Origins*, July 2, 1998, pp. 103–4.

15. Sister Bernadette Helfert's Christmas letter, 1994, St. Gabriel's Parish, Chinook, Montana, Personal file, ASCL.

16. *The Key*, Dec. 4, 1988, *Kansas City Star*, Dec. 13, 1990; Nov. 18, 1995, Sister Bernadette Helfert, Personal file, ASCL.

17. Conversation with Sister Margarita Padilla, Fall 2004; *Connecting*, Feb. 17, 1994; Office of Religious Education, Archdiocese of Omaha, Apr. 20, 2004, Sister Margarita Padilla, Personal file, ASCL.

18. Fr. Ed Hislop, homily, Twentieth Sunday in Ordinary Time, Aug. 16/17, 2003.

19. Sister Mary Jo Quinn, SCL, "Story of a Renovation: Saint Mary Catholic Community, Helena, Montana," *E&A, Environment & Art Letter*, February 2003.

20. Conversation with Sister Rita McGinnis, March 2005, and correspondence, Dec. 19, 2005; *Montana Catholic*, June 17, 2005, Sister Rita McGinnis, Personal file, ASCL.

21. Financial Aid records; President's Update, Sept. 9, 2004.

22. In 2001 department chairs and faculty of long standing included Sisters Frances Juiliano and Mary Pat Lenahan, Hattie Gilmore, and Mary Matzeder, edu-

cation; Sisters Susan Rieke and Barbara Sellers, language and literature; Sister Kathleen Wood and Robert Schimoler, theology and philosophy; George Steger and Sister Kathleen Mary Connelly, history and political science; Nancy King, Terry Brungardt, and David Greene, behavioral science; William Krusemark, Van Ibsen, Susan Nelson, and Freda Proctor, fine arts; Les Rubenstein, business; Jean Emerson, Marian Van Vleet, and Sisters Mary Erwin Baker and Susan Chase, sciences and mathematics; and Yvonne Mauton, modern languages.

Sister Margaret Petty coordinated adult evening/weekend programs. Penny Lonergan directed De Paul Library with Sister Madonna Fink as reference librarian. Wanda Owen, associate registrar, was joined by transcript analyst Annette Dye. Kevin Montgomery became AS400 specialist in the Computer Center. Judy Wiedower, financial aid officer, served as pro tem admissions director. Veteran support staff included Linda Quinley, Donna Bagby, Deena Huffman, Marleen Clark, and Shirley Rockwell.

Grants and faculty appointments took some to other campuses. Sister Marie Paula Hardy guided the education faculty at Spalding University in Nazareth, Kentucky, through the accreditation process required by the National Association of Teacher Education (*SCL Spirit*, Jubilee 2000; conversations with faculty members and staff).

23. *Aspire*, 2002–2003 Annual Report.

24. *Aspire*, Winter 2004.

25. Conversation with George Steger, March 2005. New and returning faculty in 2005 who assisted the curriculum renewal led by the academic dean were Julie Bowen, Joy Raser, and Sister Rosemary Kolich, English; Freda Proctor, music; Rick Hite, chair of information technology; Janet Lowenstein, physical education; Brian Hughes and Sister Rosalie Curtin, theology and pastoral ministry; Randy Scott, chair of history, political science, and global studies; Rick Silvey, chair of mathematics and science; Danielle Trebus, theatre; Leo Rycken and Press Barnhill, business; Patti Carnahan, Nancy Murphy, and Gretchen Wilbur, education.

Staff members in the new century included Laura Davis, head of marketing, with Rachael Johnson, Bryan Schrepel, and Jackie Goldsmith on staff; Kevin Gantt, head of computer services; Carole Gonzales and Kathi Rohr, institutional advancement; and Laura Ng, head of the learning center.

26. The thirteen-volume set, twenty years in the making, was the gift of Leavenworth County surveyor Cameron Howell and his mother, Frances G. Lopata, of Little Rock, Arkansas (*Aspire*, Fall 2004; conversation with Penelope Lonergan). A station on the Underground Railroad in the local AME church, Fort Leavenworth's role on the frontier, Lewis and Clark's voyage, Lincoln's visits, and innumerable antebellum and Victorian homes were only a few of the sources for students' research.

27. News releases, marketing office, University of Saint Mary, Feb. 7 and Mar. 8, 2005.

28. Conversations with Sister Diane Steele and Karen Fernengle, RN, PhD, March 2005; *Aspire*, Winter 2005–2006.

29. *Aspire*, Spring 2004; *Inspire*, University of Saint Mary Service Learning office, Spring 2005; *Neighborhood News, Kansas City Star*, Apr. 20, 2005; conversation with Sharon and Tony Albers, Spring 2005.

30. President's Update, Sept. 9, 2004; letter from Sisters and Associates at Bishop Ward High School, Jan. 25, 2005; Summit Scholars brochure.

31. Conversation with Kitty Bronec, Winter 2005.

32. *Aspire*, Summer 2005.

33. Investigative series published from 2002 to 2005 in *Los Angeles Times*; *Aspire*, Fall 2004; conversation with Francine Orr, Fall 2005.

34. *Aspire*, Fall 2005.

35. Conversations with Tammy and Tim Stalker, Fall 2005 and Winter 2006.

36. *Aspire*, Summer 2005.

37. Program, installation of Judith Vogelsang, MD, Honorary Consul for Croatia, Kansas City, Kansas and Missouri, Oct. 1, 2005.

38. Conversation with Charles DiLeonardo, November 2005.

39. Matriculation Ceremony and Mass of Convocation, University of Saint Mary, Aug. 19 and Sept. 17, 2005.

40. News release, marketing office, University of Saint Mary, Feb. 7 and Mar. 8, 2005. Students and a few faculty came from Somalia and Gambia, Hawaii and the Philippines, Australia and Malaysia, Vietnam and Taiwan, India and Pakistan, Armenia and Finland, Germany and Scotland, Brazil, Canada, and thirty-five states of the Union.

25. Health Care in New Hands

1. Conversation with William Murray, February 2005.

2. *Sponsorship, Resources for Sponsors*, The Catholic Health Association of the United States, 2005.

3. Biographical record, Sister Mildred Marie Irwin, Personal file, ASCL.

4. Sister Mary Julie Casey, Personal file, ASCL.

5. Conversation with Sister Macrina Ryan, Winter 2004; letter from William M. Murray, Feb. 28, 2005, Sister Macrina Ryan, Personal file, ASCL.

6. Conversation with William Murray, Sister Macrina Ryan, Personal file, ASCL.

7. Sister Marie Damian Glatt, Personal file, ASCL. On her retirement from the presidency of the SCL/Health System, Sister Marie Damian was a visiting scholar at St. Louis University in the doctoral program in ethics before joining the Providence Health System as vice president for mission integration.

8. Conversation with Sister Judith Jackson, August 2005.

9. Conversations with Sisters Bernadette Helfert and Jean Casey, August 2003.

10. Ministry Formation Plan draft document, June 24, 2003 and Principles of Ministry Formation document, July 10, 2002, created by Sister Jean Casey.

11. Conversation with Sister Mary Agnes Hogan, August 2003.

12. Conversation with Sister Joy Duff, August 2003; *Mission Milestones 2004*; *In Touch*, August 1998, St. James Hospital file, ASCL.

13. "SCLHS translates SCL mission through Health Assembly," *SCL Spirit*, June 2002. Ann Zimmerman was coordinator of the event; Sisters Rita McGinnis, Maureen Hall, and Gloria Solomon developed the rituals of the assembly.

14. Staff members who contributed to the application were David Miller, RN, director of respiratory care; Roz Lewis, RN, director of the New Life Center; Paula Ellis, RN, director of the recovery center; Mickey Bradshaw, director of purchasing; and Don Abdallah, director of cancer medicine (Stakeholder References, 2004 International Spirit at Work Award, St. Francis Health Center, Topeka, Kansas).

15. Text of application for International Spirit at Work award; conversation with Sister Loretto Marie Colwell, Summer 2005.

16. Conversation with Sister Loretto Marie Colwell, Summer 2005.

17. St. Mary's Hospital and Medical Center Archives; conversations with Robert Ladenburger and Sister Michel Pantenburg, Summer 2003.

18. Conversation with Tish Wells Starbuck, Summer 2003; *Mission Milestones 2004*, Sisters of Charity Health System file, ASCL.

19. Conversations with Leslie Hirsch and Martin Helldorfer, Summer 2003; *Exempla Physician Pulse* and *ESJH On Site*, August 2004.

20. Conversations with Barbara Wertz and Carl Unrein, August 2004.

21. SCL Health System Sponsorship and Mission Integration Annual Report 2004, SCL/Health System (SCLHS) file, ASCL.

22. Ibid.; conversation with Sister Catrina Bones, Fall 2005.

23. SCLHS Sponsorship Report, Fifteenth General Chapter, 2004; "Building a future of healing and hope," program of the Blessing Ceremony, Saint Vincent Clinic, Dec. 14, 2004, Caritas Clinics file, ASCL.

24. "Response," Annual Report Newsletter of Caritas Clinics Inc., Summer 2004, Caritas Clinics file, ASCL; *Mission Milestones 2004*, SCLHS file, ASCL.

25. *Mission Milestones* and *FY 2000 Community Benefit Report*, SCLHS file.

26. *FY 2000 Community Benefit Report*.

27. *SCL Spirit*, August 2000; *Tower Talk*, March 2000; Saint Joseph Hospital Foundation Annual Reports 2001 and 2002; *Mission Milestones 2004*; *ESJH OnSite* newsletter, July and August 2004, St. Joseph Hospital file, ASCL.

28. *Mission Milestones 2004*.

29. Ibid.

30. Ibid.

31. Contributors included Janet Salmonson, MD, and Louise West, MSW, Saint John's, Santa Monica; Sisters Mary Walter Swann and Ann Schumacher, MD, Exempla St. Joseph, Denver; Frank Flanner, MD, Helen Flanner, St. John, Leavenworth; Carol Sharp, SCLHS office; Mark Hayden, executive director, and Lisa McLean, RN, St. James, Butte; and Shelley White, RN, St. Vincent, Billings.

32. *Leadership Notes*, Summer 2003.

33. Affiliation Ceremony, December 1998; press release, Apr. 6, 2001; Sister Catrina Bones, vice president for mission integration, Mar. 4, 2002; press release,

July 8, 2003, Bethany Medical Center file, ASCL; conversation with James Paquette, Winter 2006.

34. Conversations with Sisters Judith Jackson and Loretto Marie Colwell, Summer 2005; MIRROR on SCLHS, Sponsorship and Mission Integration Annual Report 2004, SCLHS file, ASCL.

35. William J. Cox, "Nurturing the Ministry's Soul," *Health Progress*, September-October 2004. <http;//www.chausa.org>.

36. Conversation with James Paquette, Winter 2005.

37. Ibid.

38. William M. Murray to SCLHS, Jan. 31, 2005; Sister Ann Marita Loosen, Personal file, ASCL.

39. James T. Paquette, CEO, Providence Health, and Greg Madsen, administrator, St. John Hospital, Jan. 19, 2005, Providence Health Center file, ASCL; conversation with Greg Madsen, Summer 2006.

40. Conversation with Sister Loretto Marie Colwell, Summer 2005; *Mission Milestones 2004*; *Capital-Journal*, n.d.; *Metro News*, Sept. 17, 2004, St. Francis Health Center file, ASCL.

41. Conversation with Michelle Hood, August 2003.

42. *2002 Report to the Community* and *Art of Survival, Healing in Life*, SVHC file, ASCL. In 2004 St. Vincent's Foundation made the first Michel Award to Laura May and Herb Bacon, two of the hospital's major supporters and patrons.

43. Conversation with James Kiser, August 2003. Raymond Berger was the labor relations specialist (*Mission Milestones 2004*, SCLHS file, ASCL).

44. *Diocesan News*, May 20, 2005, News Clippings folder, St. James Hospital file, ASCL; *HeartBeat*, St. James Healthcare Cardiology Services; *Mission Milestones 2004*; *MontanaStandard.com*, Nov. 10, 2006.

45. *Mission Milestones*, 2004.

46. Century Program folder; *Daily Sentinel*, Feb. 15, 2001, St. Mary's Regional Health Center file, ASCL.

47. *Healthcare Investment Report 2002*; *Saint Joseph Hospital Foundation Annual Report 2003*, St. Joseph Hospital Foundation Archives; conversation with Leslie Hirsch, August 2004.

48. *Campaign for Saint John's: Creating the Future*, Capital Campaign Newsletter, Winter 2001.

49. *Saint John's Health Center: Creating an Exceptional Place for Health and Healing*; *Caritas Magazine*, Summer and Fall 2002.

50. *Creating an Exceptional Place*; conversations with Bruce Lamoureux and David Blake, Spring 2005; conversation with Jerry Epstein, August 2005.

51. <http://www.saintjohns.news>, August 2005; <http://www.sjhc.professional practice>.

52. *Catholic Health World*, February 15, 2005; *CareQuest*, July and October 2005.

53. Conversations with William Murray, March and October 2005.

26. Emerging Frontiers

1. John R. Quinn, "Exercise of Primacy," *Commonweal*, July 12, 1996.
2. Constance Phelps, SCL, "Some Reflections on Peace." <http://www.lcwr.org/lcwrannualassembly/2004assembly/presaddress2004>.
3. Regional meeting at Providence Hospital and Health Center, Feb. 20–21, 2003.
4. Notes from Circle Reports, Chapter Materials.
5. Report to Chapter, 2004.
6. Notes from Chapter, 2004.
7. Recommendations from Chapter table conversation.
8. Chapter Statement, 2004.
9. Sister Sue Miller's comments, Wisdom Gatherings, January 2005.
10. Community Director to Community, Aug. 30, Sept. 24, Nov. 2, 2004; Sister Linda Roth to sisters, September 2004; Sisters of Charity of Leavenworth website.
11. In 1965 Sister Rose Vincentia Tomlin offered to Mother Leo Frances a detailed recommendation inspired by the Vatican II Constitution on the Sacred Liturgy for the sisters' training in liturgical music, beginning from postulancy through novitiate and juniorate. Each novitiate group was trained by Sister Rose Matthew Sillers in Gregorian chant. Sister Rose Vincentia directed the *schola* and choir. She urged training for music teachers to include emphasis on distinct areas of instrumental, vocal, and direction (Personal file, ASCL).

In her introduction of the Charity Notes, Sister Mary Lenore Martin told of discovering in the Community archives what appeared to be an original piano exercise composed by Mother Mary Vincent Kearney in her teaching days.

12. Unpublished manuscript, *Miege*, letters of the bishop edited by Sister Mary Paul Fitzgerald.
13. Community Secretary's records.
14. *Voices of Charity*, June 2005. Regular features and columns included "Heart of the Matter," named by Sister Judith Jackson; "Leaven Words," Sister Marie de Paul; and "Re-markings," Sister Rita Smith.
15. Sister Janet Cashman, Personal file, ASCL; "Beyond All Borders," *Voices of Charity*, June 2006.
16. Community Secretary's records; conversations with Sister Mary Beth Minges and Peg Johnson, August 2005.
17. Conversation with Sister Sharon Smith, August 2005. By 2006, Associates numbered 175, with 28 in the process of applying.
18. Catholic Education Special Edition, *National Catholic Reporter*, Mar. 25, 2005. <http://www.cristoreynetwork.org/about/FAQ.htm>.
19. Notes from Sister Vickie Perkins, director, and Community Secretary's office; Cristo Rey Kansas City brochure.
20. Vigil Service, July 31, 2005.

21. Edward Hays, *Prayers for the Domestic Church* (Leavenworth: Forest of Peace Publishing Inc., 1979), 194.

22. Profession of Perpetual Vows, Sister Victoria Ann Lichtenauer, Annunciation Chapel, Aug. 7, 2005.

23. Elizabeth A. Johnson, *Friends of God and Prophets* (New York: Continuum, 1999).

24. John Allen, Catholic News Service article, *National Catholic Reporter*, Sept. 2, 2005.

25. The retreat director was Tom Nelson, CM, June 2005.

26. <http://www.onlinecatholics.com.au>, <WeBelieve1@comcast.net>, "Australian priests speak out on the Eucharist," *We Believe! A Newsletter for Roman Catholic Liturgical Reform*, May 2005, p. 5.

Epilogue

1. John Paul II, "The Mother of the Redeemer," encyclical letter, *Redemptoris Mater* (U.S. Catholic Conference, May 25, 1987); Vatican Doctrinal Congregation, "Letter on the Collaboration of Men and Women," *Origins*, Aug. 26, 2004, pp. 169–76.

Appendix

LIVING SISTERS OF CHARITY OF LEAVENWORTH, 1955–2005

Name	First Vows
S. Deidy Rosario Abad Pulache	3/25/2001
S. Nery Lourdes Abad Pulache	3/25/1997
S. Elizabeth Adams	8/19/2001
S. Barbara Aldrich	8/24/1961
S. Michael Delores Allegri	9/3/1964
S. Regina Marie Allgaier	6/28/1938
S. Rita Marie Anderson	8/15/1950
S. Mary Jo Anzik	1/11/1968
S. Ann Lucia Apodaca	9/3/1964
S. Mary Rosenda Arkfeld	8/15/1951
S. Kathy Atkins	8/15/1974
S. Bonnie Ann Bachle	9/2/1962
S. Mary Erwin Baker	2/22/1955
S. Therese Bangert	8/15/1965
S. Angela Rose Barbieri	8/22/1957
S. Mary Ann Bartolac	8/22/1954
S. Virginia Bartolac	9/3/1964
S. Ann Barton	8/22/1953
S. Marianna Bauder	9/2/1963
S. Nancy Bauman	9/2/1962
S. Charles Marie Beeby	8/15/1950
S. Mary Loretta Beier	8/15/1948
S. Erica Frances Berg	8/6/2005

S. Mary Ellen Beyhan	8/15/1948
S. Michael Blossom	3/4/1943
S. Catrina Ann Bones	1/8/1970
S. Mary Cecile Breen	8/22/1956
S. Mary Lucilla Brekel	3/2/1942
S. Agnes Mary Brickley	6/18/1939
S. Dolores Ann Brinkel	8/22/1955
S. Marie Brinkman	8/15/1950
S. Helen Bristow	9/2/1963
S. Veronica Marie Brost	6/17/1934
S. Marie Noel Bruch	8/15/1950
S. Anne Marie Burke	8/15/1952
S. Josephine Bustos	8/15/1951
S. Anne Callahan	8/15/1950
S. Melissa Camardo	8/19/2001
S. Patricia Canty	8/24/1961
S. Mary Cecilia Carig	3/2/1940
S. Donna Lynn Casey	8/22/1958
S. Dorothy Jean Casey	8/22/1959
S. Janet Cashman	1/11/1968
S. Rose Marie Catudal	8/15/1948
S. Susan Chase	9/2/1963
S. Helen Cheeney	8/22/1957
S. Catherine Marie Chmidling	6/18/1935
S. Mary Arthel Cline	8/22/1959
S. Mary Carlo Colibraro	8/22/1955
S. Loretto Marie Colwell	8/24/1960
S. Marie de Paul Combo	8/15/1950
S. Mary Corita Conlan	2/15/1951
S. Kathleen Mary Connelly	8/15/1982
S. Mary Rebecca Conner	8/15/1948
S. Patricia Connolly	8/22/1953

S. Susana Córdova Castillo	3/25/1985
S. Mary Jo Coyle	8/22/1957
S. Maureen Craig	2/22/1955
S. Rosalie Curtin	2/22/1953
S. Marjorie Cushing	8/22/1958
S. Marie Kathleen Daugherty	8/15/1975
S. Jean Martin Dawson	8/22/1956
S. Linda Dean	8/24/1961
S. Mary Edwin DeCoursey	3/4/1943
S. Regina DeCoursey	3/6/1944
S. Ann Cecile DeDonder	7/19/1941
S. Lucille Degenhart	8/15/1950
S. Regina Deitchman	8/15/1948
S. Carol Depner	9/2/1963
S. Mary Depner	9/8/1949
S. Georgeanne Desch	3/5/1941
S. Mary Julitta Doerhoff	8/15/1951
S. Liduvina Domínguez Córdova	3/25/1994
S. Frances Cecilia Domme	6/18/1935
S. Ann Donovan	8/22/1955
S. Ellen Dore	8/15/1952
S. Mary Jo Downey	8/22/1956
S. Margaret Mary Driscoll	2/15/1949
S. Mary Rosaleen Driscoll	8/15/1949
S. Joy Duff	5/30/1971
S. Agnes Eileen Dunn	3/2/1940
S. Marie Carmel Dunning	8/22/1953
S. Mary Georgia Dwyer	8/15/1947
S. Ann Louise Eble	1/4/1945
S. Mary Joan Eble	8/15/1952
S. Carmen Echevarria	8/15/1952
S. Maria Edwards	8/15/1948

S. Regina Erbacher	8/15/1949
S. Elizabeth Marie Ereth	6/18/1935
S. Mary Rose Erickson	3/11/1936
S. Dolores Erman	8/15/1950
S. Marie de Lourdes Falk	2/15/1949
S. Owen Marie Falk	3/2/1941
S. Mary Sarah Fasenmyer	3/2/1941
S. Marjorie Feuerborn	8/24/1960
S. Loretta Fick	8/22/1956
S. Margaret Finch	1/11/1967
S. Madonna Fink	8/22/1954
S. Virginia Flanick	3/2/1940
S. Kevin Marie Flynn	9/8/1949
S. Mary Rachel Flynn	8/22/1957
S. Helen Forge	8/15/1947
S. Katherine Franchett	8/22/1959
S. Mark Friday	8/22/1954
S. Mary Vincent Fritton	3/6/1945
S. Jane Ellen Furey	2/22/1954
S. Roberta Furey	8/22/1955
S. Mary Clare Gappa	8/22/1958
S. Ann Victoria Garcia	9/2/1962
S. Marie Damian Glatt	8/15/1951
S. Carolyn A. Gloege	9/24/1995
S. Julia Golkoski	8/22/1955
S. Jennifer Gordon	8/29/2004
S. Frances Marie Grady	2/19/1956
S. Regina Ann Green	10/7/1954
S. Lillian Grieshaber	2/15/1949
S. Marie Helen Grieshaber	8/22/1953
S. Catherine Rose Grimm	8/15/1949
S. Mary Alberta Grimm	8/15/1949

S. Marguerite Grogman	8/22/1958
S. Margaret Groh	8/15/1945
S. Mary Georgette Groh	8/15/1951
S. LaVonne Guidoni	8/15/1952
S. Karen Guth	9/3/1964
S. Felicitas Hagest	6/18/1939
S. Maureen Hall	9/2/1963
S. Agnes Virginia Hamm	6/28/1938
S. Irene Hanley	8/15/1952
S. Dorothy Hanly	6/17/1933
S. Marie Paula Hardy	6/20/1945
S. Lucille Harrington	8/15/1951
S. Dorothy Harvat	2/15/1948
S. Judy Hayes	8/24/1960
S. Mary Elise Hayes	4/5/1943
S. Eileen Haynes	8/15/1979
S. Jane Hays	8/15/1948
S. Rosella Mary Hehn	8/22/1955
S. Ruth Ann Hehn	9/2/1962
S. Bernadette Helfert	8/22/1959
S. Dorothy Henscheid	8/22/1953
S. Kathleen Marie Henscheid	8/22/1957
S. Donna Jean Henson	8/24/1961
S. Jean Highberger	8/15/1951
S. Pamela Hinkle	1/8/1970
S. Mary Timothy Hoban	8/15/1948
S. Rose Dolores Hoffelmeyer	8/15/1950
S. Margaret Hogan	8/22/1957
S. Mary Agnes Hogan	8/22/1959
S. Mary Kevin Hollow	3/4/1943
S. Mary Laura Huddleston	8/15/1949
S. Julia Huiman Ipanaque	3/25/1994

S. Edna Hunthausen	2/15/1951
S. Diane Hurley	8/22/1957
S. Eileen Hurley	9/2/1962
S. Jane Jackson	9/2/1962
S. Judith Jackson	8/15/1965
S. Virginia Jakobe	9/2/1962
S. Paula Rose Jauernig	9/2/1963
S. Jeanne Marie Jette	9/15/1948
S. Patricia Marie Johannsen	1/10/1969
S. Eileen Marie Johnson	8/15/1965
S. Margaret Ellen Johnson	1/11/1968
S. Mary Patricia Johnson	1/11/1968
S. Andrea Johnston	3/6/1944
S. Frances Juiliano	9/2/1962
S. Mary Kamperschroer	8/24/1961
S. Helen Keane	8/15/1952
S. Maureen Kehoe	1/11/1967
S. Marie Kelly	8/15/1948
S. Mary Elizabeth Kelly	8/15/1948
S. Susanna Kennedy	8/22/1959
S. Darlyne Kern	8/15/1947
S. Mary Patricia Kielty	2/21/1957
S. Mary Frances Kirkpatrick	8/15/1951
S. Mary Agnes Klein	3/2/1941
S. Agnes Ann Kneib	8/15/1951
S. Celine Kobe	1/9/1942
S. Rosemary Kolich	8/11/1985
S. Paulette Krick	8/15/1974
S. Barbara Kushan	9/2/1963
S. Ann Louis LaLonde	8/15/1950
S. Mary Lillian Landauer	12/19/1942
S. Delia Ann Lawless	8/22/1958

S. Catherine Louise Lebhart	6/18/1939
S. Lorraine Leist	8/15/1947
S. Mary Patricia Lenahan	1/11/1968
S. Letitia Lenherr	8/22/1954
S. Mary Cecilia Lenherr	8/15/1948
S. Victoria Ann Lichtenauer	8/29/1999
S. Jean Lind	10/26/1954
S. Regina Mary Link	8/22/1956
S. Jean Lockett	1/11/1967
S. Ann Loendorf	1/10/1969
S. Dominique Long	8/15/1952
S. Ann Marita Loosen	8/15/1952
S. Mary Clarice Lousberg	8/15/1951
S. Mary Loretto Lyons	8/15/1981
S. Genevieve Macan	3/6/1945
S. Elena Mack	1/10/1969
S. Lillian Maguire	8/22/1955
S. Mary Vincentia Maronick	8/15/1947
S. Marie Bernard Martin	2/24/1960
S. Mary Lenore Martin	8/15/1949
S. John Vianney Martinez	8/22/1956
S. Mary Jo McDonald	9/2/1962
S. Vincent Clare McDonald	8/15/1950
S. Ann Winifred McGarry	3/2/1940
S. Rita McGinnis	1/11/1968
S. Irene McGrath	3/10/1946
S. Perpetua McGrath	3/2/1942
S. Ann McGuire	2/19/1961
S. Mary Helen McInerney	3/4/1943
S. Audrey Meanor	8/15/1950
S. Jane Albert Mehrens	8/22/1957
S. Mary Lou Mendel	8/22/1954

S. Mary Kenneth Messina	8/22/1955
S. Joan Sue Miller	8/22/1958
S. Mary Beth Minges	8/11/1985
S. Margaret Marie Mitchell	8/15/1948
S. Concepta Mock	9/25/1945
S. Marie Loretta Modrcin	1/10/1969
S. Marie Michael Mollis	8/22/1956
S. Ann Moylan	8/22/1959
S. Mary Bridget Mullen	8/15/1948
S. Mary Patricia Murry	8/22/1959
S. Susan Marie Newland	1/11/1968
S. Catherine Nichol	3/10/1946
S. Mary Julianne O'Flannigan	2/19/1961
S. Mary Sheila O'Flannigan	8/15/1947
S. Roberta O'Leary	9/2/1963
S. Kathryn O'Neill	12/19/1942
S. Sheila O'Neill	8/15/1952
S. Mary O'Rourke	8/15/1949
S. Rose Orchard	3/2/1940
S. Mary Donalda Orleans	3/2/1941
S. Rita Orleans	6/20/1945
S. María de los M.Orozco Olaya	3/15/1989
S. Margarita Padilla	8/22/1959
S. Jean Anne Panisko	9/2/1963
S. Michel Pantenburg	8/15/1947
S. Peter Parry	8/15/1951
S. Victoria Perkins	8/24/1961
S. Rose Anthony Perko	2/22/1955
S. Mary Monica Peterson	8/15/1949
S. Margaret Pfennigs	3/2/1940
S. Constance Phelps	8/24/1961
S. Mary Hilaria Phipps	3/10/1946

S. Mary Aloys Powell	2/15/1948
S. Susan Pryor	8/15/1952
S. Mary Jo Quinn	8/15/1974
S. Margaret Quirk	5/30/1971
S. Charlene Race	8/22/1956
S. Genitha Helen Regan	8/22/1958
S. Ruth Reischman	8/22/1953
S. Blanche Marie Remington	3/10/1946
S. Suzanne Retherford	9/2/1962
S. Mary Helen Richstatter	3/6/1945
S. Susan Rieke	1/11/1967
S. Dorothy Marie Rilinger	8/22/1956
S. Jean Marian Rilinger	1/11/1967
S. Linda Suzanne Roth	1/11/1968
S. Laura Rumiche Morales	3/15/1992
S. Frances Russell	8/15/1951
S. Lin Marie Sayatovic	8/15/1980
S. Clara Scherr	8/22/1959
S. Mary Jane Schmitz	8/15/1954
S. Barbara Schrader	8/12/1990
S. Mary Eleanor Schram	8/15/1947
S. Mary Adolph Schuele	8/6/1932
S. Ann Schumacher	8/2/1997
S. Barbara Sellers	8/22/1959
S. Eileen Sheehy	8/15/1948
S. Marie Madeleine Shonka	2/15/1950
S. Mary Siefken	8/22/1957
S. Rose Cecilia Sillers	6/28/1938
S. Jo Anne Sistrunk	8/15/1979
S. Elizabeth Skalicky	9/3/1964
S. Irene Skeehan	2/15/1951
S. Mary Lex Smith	9/2/1962

S. Rita Smith	8/24/1960
S. Sharon Smith	8/15/1977
S. Gloria Solomon	8/22/1955
S. Diane Steele	8/10/1986
S. Mary Kathleen Stefani	8/15/1947
S. Madonna Stehno	8/15/1949
S. Janice Steiger	8/22/1959
S. Therese Marie Steiner	8/24/1961
S. Mary Clarita Sternitzke	2/15/1950
S. Mary Denise Sternitzke	3/2/1942
S. Phyllis Stowell	1/11/1967
S. Mary Elizabeth Strecker	8/15/1952
S. Mary Francine Stubbs	8/15/1949
S. Anita Sullivan	8/22/1953
S. Patricia Sullivan	8/15/1947
S. Nancy Svetlecic	8/10/1986
S. Mary Walter Swann	8/15/1947
S. Anne Joseph Swiderski	3/12/1937
S. Mary Andrew Talle	3/19/1945
S. Mary Josepha Talle	8/15/1948
S. Celine Taskan	8/15/1951
S. Sheila Taylor	8/15/1976
S. Bernadette Marie Teasdale	8/22/1957
S. Mary Ann Theisen	1/11/1967
S. Helen Mary Thill	8/15/1951
S. Mary Antoinette Thomas	9/25/1945
S. Clorinda Timaná Martinez	3/15/1989
S. Patricia Toeckes	8/24/1960
S. Mary Marcianna Trujillo	8/15/1951
S. Paula Marie Tweet	8/22/1957
S. Mary Sharon Verbeck	8/15/1948
S. Esther Vilela Gutiérrez	3/25/1990

S. Mary Patricia Walsh	6/24/1943
S. Lucy Walter	1/11/1968
S. Noreen Walter	8/15/1973
S. Renee Washut	1/11/1967
S. Kathleen Waterman	8/15/1951
S. Carol Wells	9/2/1962
S. Anita Marie Westhues	2/15/1949
S. Katherine Mary Westhues	8/22/1955
S. Michael Mary Whelan	8/15/1949
S. Charlotte Marie White	9/2/1962
S. Mary Barbara Wieseler	1/8/1970
S. Amy Willcott	8/10/1986
S. Joan Williams	8/24/1961
S. Mary Willoughby	8/15/1948
S. Jean Winkler	9/17/1947
S. Mary Marcella Winninghoff	8/22/1953
S. Mary Rita Winter	8/15/1948
S. Kathleen Wood	8/22/1959
S. Susan Wood	1/10/1969
S. Mary Geraldine Yelich	8/15/1951
S. Susan Yerkich	8/15/1965
S. Marie Benedict Young	2/15/1952
S. Elizabeth Youngs	8/15/1976
S. Jeanne Marie Zeugin	6/18/1935
S. Therese Zimmerman	8/15/1952

DECEASED SISTERS OF CHARITY OF LEAVENWORTH, 1955–2005

Name	First Vows	Death Date
S. Mary Kostka Cody	7/19/1898	2/6/1955
S. Mary Celestine O'Shea	7/19/1898	2/10/1955
S. Mary Lorian Degan	2/4/1911	2/27/1955
S. Othelia Hurni	10/30/1904	3/10/1955
S. Mary Teresa Roades	12/8/1911	7/9/1955
S. Mary Amelia Quinn	12/21/1890	7/30/1955
S. Mary Natalia McGurk	11/1/1909	8/12/1955
S. Mary de Chantal Gleason	12/29/1900	9/19/1955
S. Mary Domitilla Breen	7/19/1898	10/14/1955
S. Mary Gelasia Mundy	5/12/1906	11/20/1955
S. Mary Agnes Bauer	8/15/1909	2/26/1956
S. Mary Sienna Cullen	7/2/1911	3/7/1956
S. Charles Francis Robertson	6/18/1938	8/5/1956
S. Mary Defrosa Skelley	3/25/1887	9/4/1956
S. Rose of Lima Robinson	1/13/1902	9/7/1956
S. Petronilla Barbaz	12/21/1890	9/29/1956
S. Mary Ida Murphy	8/15/1892	10/25/1956
S. Mary Anthony Mueller	1/01/1893	11/6/1956
Mother Mary Berchmans Cannan	7/19/1891	11/19/1956
S. Mary Gabriella Coll	4/5/1948	12/21/1956
S. Blandina Travis	9/29/1885	2/11/1957
S. Ann Elizabeth Shea	4/20/1924	5/14/1957
S. Mary Genevieve Buckley	7/19/1898	6/2/1957
S. Mary Dympna Brosnan	5/24/1905	8/21/1957
S. Mary Rufina Jullien	5/04/1879	9/30/1957
S. Mary Madelberte Lehane	7/2/1900	10/9/1957
S. Mary Anacleta Flynn	2/02/1884	11/4/1957
S. Marian Kelly	1/01/1895	1/1/1958
S. Mary Grace Wright	3/25/1907	2/9/1958

APPENDIX

S. Martina Donahy	5/26/1881	3/13/1958
S. Mary Sylvia O'Leary	7/2/1906	4/14/1958
Mother Mary Francesca O'Shea	10/28/1898	5/19/1958
S. Mary Aidan Rochford	7/2/1906	8/10/1958
S. Helen Smith	12/25/1895	8/10/1958
S. Mary Syra Keiley	7/19/1894	9/8/1958
S. Evarista O'Mahony	10/30/1904	9/8/1958
S. Ignatia Burke	9/6/1915	10/22/1958
S. Mary Zoe Ahern	7/19/1904	11/11/1958
S. Hyacintha Marksman	2/16/1901	3/16/1959
S. Anna Marie McDonald	7/19/1898	3/16/1959
S. Mary Demetria O'Neill	7/2/1906	4/9/1959
S. Mary Enda Harmon	4/15/1918	5/3/1959
S. Florence Louise Cosgrove	9/6/1915	6/9/1959
S. Mary Carmelita Harmon	7/18/1898	4/7/1960
S. Ann Catherine Hogan	1/23/1910	5/30/1960
S. Mary Noel Fobes	8/22/1955	6/7/1960
S. Mary Bertha Carig	12/18/1924	6/14/1960
S. Mary Paula Keville	7/2/1900	7/28/1960
S. Mary Finbarr McCarthy	11/16/1902	8/24/1960
S. Mary Macaria Carroll	7/2/1906	8/31/1960
S. Mary Prudentia Cunneen	7/19/1904	9/26/1960
S. Mary Ignatia Marksman	3/25/1889	10/7/1960
S. Mary Patrick McInerney	9/6/1915	11/8/1960
S. Mary Theodota Cosgrove	8/15/1906	12/18/1960
S. Mary Verena Curtin	7/2/1906	1/8/1961
S. Mary Melita Walsh	5/1/1908	3/30/1961
S. Mary Mercedes Brady	12/29/1900	6/22/1961
S. Crescentia Sack	6/27/1926	7/27/1961
S. Mary Seraphia McGinty	2/23/1903	8/30/1961
S. Agnes Stella Sullivan	12/25/1909	10/20/1961
S. Ada O'Neill	8/2/1902	10/24/1961

S. Mary Ethna McInerney	3/17/1906	11/29/1961
S. Marina Good	7/19/1917	12/9/1961
S. Mary Vida Hayes	1/06/1899	12/15/1961
S. Beatricia Rashford	3/17/1906	1/21/1962
S. Rose Mary Berry	8/15/1890	3/8/1962
S. Mary Paul Fitzgerald	6/17/1927	4/16/1962
S. Mary Blanche Connolly	1/6/1899	5/8/1962
S. Mary Eudocia Kramer	12/26/1910	6/7/1962
S. Mary Faber McGeehan	3/25/1908	9/14/1962
S. Ann Bernardine Martin	7/10/1907	10/9/1962
S. Catharine Conlon	12/25/1899	10/24/1962
S. Mary Alice Sullivan	5/01/1897	12/1/1962
S. Mary Leontia Gleeson	7/19/1898	1/17/1963
S. Mary Angelita Ventura	3/2/1942	3/10/1963
S. Agnes Teresa Spiller	4/6/1902	3/26/1963
S. Mary Patrice McInerney	3/17/1913	7/4/1963
S. Helen Therese O'Leary	7/19/1934	9/3/1963
S. Mary Anacaria O'Sullivan	2/11/1899	9/11/1963
S. Teresa Joseph Latham	9/20/1910	9/30/1963
S. Mary Raphael Brosnan	7/19/1898	10/11/1963
S. Mary Ferdinand Eisenbeis	9/6/1915	12/7/1963
S. Mary Consolata Moore	8/15/1906	12/9/1963
S. Mary Maurice Coughlin	3/25/1916	7/29/1964
S. Marietta Lynch	1/6/1904	9/28/1964
S. Mary Corona Harrington	4/6/1902	1/3/1965
S. Mary Bernard Knipscheer	11/01/1887	1/24/1965
S. Mary Edith Bessette	2/18/1902	3/26/1965
S. Mary Brigida Cunneen	7/19/1898	4/14/1965
S. Theresa Fagan	3/25/1918	4/23/1965
S. Mary Joseph Flynn	8/24/1888	5/24/1965
S. Mary Gerard Downs	3/25/1908	5/26/1965
S. Mary Philomena Otis	4/5/1921	6/29/1965

S. Annette Daily	1/13/1902	7/23/1965
S. Mary Rosine Yerger	8/15/1922	10/10/1965
S. Mary Christina Curran	1/06/1899	11/2/1965
S. Mary Ellen Lennemann	9/1/1915	11/7/1965
S. Jane de Chantal Heffron	12/8/1922	12/24/1965
S. Mary Leocadia Johanning	7/7/1931	1/17/1966
S. Anthony Aubert	3/25/1918	3/5/1966
S. Mary Eulalia Butler	7/19/1898	4/19/1966
S. Mary Victoria McCormick	8/15/1923	6/25/1966
S. Mary Bonita Johnson	12/8/1904	7/4/1966
S. Mary Alacoque Sheerin	5/6/1922	7/5/1966
S. Mary Lidwina Gaida	7/1/1917	8/4/1966
S. Margaret Anne McGuirk	6/17/1929	8/27/1966
S. Mary Agatha McGranahan	1/21/1906	10/7/1966
S. Mary Vivina Fitzgerald	11/1/1931	12/13/1966
S. Mary Benedict Caples	5/1/1907	12/24/1966
S. Mary Ephrem Shanahan	9/8/1906	12/25/1966
S. Mary Alodia Crowe	3/25/1908	1/3/1967
S. Mary Perpetua Quigley	10/28/1897	2/4/1967
S. Joseph Hafner	8/15/1909	3/4/1967
S. Mary Pelagia McCaffery	7/19/1914	3/16/1967
S. Magdalen Ford	8/22/1954	3/31/1967
S. Mary Bernice Mulcahy	8/15/1908	5/21/1967
S. Mary Giovanni Giacomini	11/1/1912	6/5/1967
S. Mary Paschal McCann	7/2/1908	7/8/1967
S. Mary Virginia Hoyez	3/25/1908	8/28/1967
S. Mary Bernadette Dalton	2/13/1905	10/7/1967
S. Mary Jeannette McAuliffe	4/11/1909	11/5/1967
S. Mary Cordis Maier	8/15/1948	11/20/1967
S. Mary Michael Carroll	6/3/1910	11/29/1967
S. Mary Esther O'Connor	7/2/1906	12/27/1967
S. Mary Philippa Rock	3/25/1911	1/4/1968

S. Mary Damian Harnett	12/26/1910	2/27/1968
S. Mary Euphrasia Maguire	12/20/1928	4/4/1968
S. Mary Germaine Kramer	7/2/1908	4/6/1968
S. Mary Gervase Fagan	7/19/1918	6/3/1968
S. Mary Martha Murphy	2/11/1913	6/6/1968
S. Mary Teresina Gokey	7/2/1900	6/18/1968
S. Rose Alexius McLaughlin	9/25/1934	6/30/1968
S. Eugenia Donnelly	5/2/1926	7/12/1968
S. Frances Therese Shea	6/17/1933	7/14/1968
S. Mary Charitina Cody	6/13/1901	8/19/1968
S. Agnes Marie Horner	3/9/1928	8/24/1968
S. Mary Hortense Kelly	2/18/1922	9/8/1968
S. Francis de Sales Moore	8/15/1906	9/16/1968
S. Mary Jovita Hecht	6/27/1937	10/4/1968
S. Mary Ambrose Dorrian	3/26/1919	10/16/1968
S. Mary Catherine Floersch	3/26/1919	11/7/1968
S. Mary Regina Schauf	5/12/1899	12/8/1968
S. Mary Lewine McMahon	1/6/1904	12/9/1968
S. Mary Dolores Delaney	7/2/1906	1/1/1969
S. Mary Hilda Hughes	8/15/1898	2/3/1969
S. Mary Rachel Rausch	12/26/1925	6/5/1969
S. Mary Lavinia Stewart	3/25/1908	8/17/1969
S. Leo Gonzaga Erbacher	9/20/1915	12/5/1969
S. Mary Alicia Glick	7/19/1924	1/8/1970
S. Mary Augusta Curran	1/06/1899	1/9/1970
S. Margaret Jerome Murphy	7/7/1936	1/24/1970
S. Francis Xavier Erbacher	9/29/1912	2/2/1970
S. Mary Augustine Quinn	8/18/1927	2/2/1970
S. Mary Lucia Whelan	2/11/1899	2/28/1970
S. Mary Nathaniel Reilly	12/25/1922	3/3/1970
S. Mary Leonarda Gerspach	7/2/1902	4/25/1970
S. Mary Charles Weiss	7/19/1921	5/19/1970

S. Vincent de Paul Paul	7/19/1894	5/20/1970
S. Mary Bertrand Finnerty	9/29/1918	6/22/1970
S. Mary Carmel Brennan	8/15/1915	6/25/1970
S. Mary Dolorosa O'Flaherty	11/21/1910	6/28/1970
S. Francis Borgia Galvin	6/17/1934	7/8/1970
S. Mary Loyola Burns	8/15/1927	7/9/1970
S. Mary Austin Moran	11/27/1912	9/3/1970
S. Dorothea Thiel	10/20/1912	11/12/1970
S. Mary Corde Gleason	1/14/1906	12/7/1970
S. Mary Dominic Matthews	9/15/1922	12/15/1970
S. Mary Remi Gokey	12/25/1908	12/19/1970
S. Mary Joanna Kinsella	7/2/1906	1/23/1971
S. Mary Richard Becker	2/15/1917	2/11/1971
S. Mary Ita O'Brien	7/19/1898	2/16/1971
S. Agnes de Sales Aldridge	2/11/1913	5/23/1971
S. Margaret Clare Herron	7/4/1910	7/26/1971
S. Mary Luke Gaffney	4/24/1910	8/3/1971
S. Mary Donata Smith	3/24/1910	8/3/1971
S. Mary Odelia Ambrose	3/25/1899	10/8/1971
S. Mary Ellenice Colvin	1/18/1924	10/8/1971
S. Mary Annunciata O'Brien	11/1/1906	12/3/1971
S. Agnes Regina McCarthy	12/26/1910	2/3/1972
S. Mary Inez Keltus	7/13/1909	3/18/1972
S. Mary Charlotte Reynolds	7/1/1917	4/20/1972
S. Mary Patrick Harmon	11/1/1909	4/22/1972
S. John Marie Pithoud	5/1/1930	7/23/1972
S. Ann Gertrude O'Connor	12/26/1910	8/14/1972
S. Mary Eustelle Howard	4/22/1933	8/17/1972
S. Marie Owen	12/8/1906	8/30/1972
S. Mary Thaddea McCarthy	7/2/1906	9/18/1972
S. Mary Roberta Fitzgerald	6/17/1933	10/1/1972
S. Rose Veronica Jellik	3/16/1930	10/17/1972

S. Margaret O'Connor	8/15/1952	11/15/1972
S. Mary Francis Derben	11/1/1906	12/1/1972
S. Mary Wilhelmina Berger	7/13/1909	12/6/1972
S. Mary Leonard Higgins	3/25/1913	12/8/1972
S. Mary Senan McInerney	8/22/1921	2/9/1973
S. Mary Rosalita Smith	7/19/1904	3/20/1973
S. Mary Cosmas Kennedy	2/2/1908	5/16/1973
S. Mary Sylvester McGowan	5/5/1921	6/4/1973
S. Mary Florena Cunneen	7/19/1904	8/8/1973
S. Mary Sebastian Delapp	1/13/1926	1/26/1974
S. Mary Diomede Sack	7/31/1916	4/15/1974
S. Margaret Therese Beauchamp	2/2/1974	4/17/1974
S. Rose Agnes Nadeau	3/26/1919	6/17/1974
S. Ann Thomas McCormick	7/31/1916	7/11/1974
S. Mary Bernarda Klein	2/15/1917	8/1/1974
S. Anne Serene Butler	9/8/1934	9/18/1974
S. Mary Waltrude Schneider	10/20/1901	9/27/1974
S. Mary Frederic Higgins	7/31/1916	11/16/1974
S. Loretto Connell	3/25/1924	4/1/1975
S. Elizabeth Ryan	1/3/1919	5/4/1975
S. Mary Albia Quinn	7/2/1906	7/19/1975
S. Mary Leo McNamara	6/19/1903	7/28/1975
S. Agnes Joseph Walker	8/22/1923	10/6/1975
S. Mary Elizabeth Nolan	8/15/1915	10/20/1975
S. Mary Emilda Gleason	12/25/1911	3/21/1976
S. Mary Anysia McHugh	7/2/1906	3/30/1976
S. Rita Louise Cunningham	6/18/1935	4/7/1976
S. Rose Etzel	5/1/1928	5/14/1976
S. Veronica Ragan	3/9/1932	5/27/1976
S. Rose Dorothy Waidele	12/29/1918	5/28/1976
S. Rose McNulty	12/26/1919	6/13/1976
S. Margaret Ambrose McGowan	6/20/1936	6/24/1976

S. Mary Oswald Erb	3/25/1912	10/14/1976
Mother Mary Ancilla Spoor	2/15/1931	11/8/1976
S. Antonia McDonagh	2/25/1912	12/8/1976
S. Mary Lea McCormack	7/2/1906	1/5/1977
S. Rose Ellen O'Neil	6/27/1926	1/11/1977
S. Mary Eustatia Cantwell	11/1/1906	1/15/1977
S. Brenda Boyle	6/27/1937	2/25/1977
S. Mary Georgina Degan	8/15/1915	5/1/1977
S. Mary Alphonsine Ryan	1/3/1919	5/2/1977
S. Frances Antonia Fasenmyer	3/25/1912	5/6/1977
S. Mary Gilberta Nash	7/2/1906	9/11/1977
S. Rose Matthew Sillers	2/19/1924	9/28/1977
S. Mary Benedicta Gasperich	6/17/1929	10/10/1977
S. Elizabeth Anzicek	8/15/1950	10/11/1977
S. Matilda McInnes	9/1/1915	11/9/1977
S. Mary Asella Delaney	11/27/1912	12/10/1977
S. Mary Bonaventure Ihlefeld	12/14/1927	2/14/1978
S. Mary Valentina Harmon	7/2/1906	4/21/1978
S. Mary Clara Hughes	12/18/1902	4/23/1978
S. Alice Clare Hill	3/9/1925	5/10/1978
S. Mary Clare Reilly	12/29/1918	5/31/1978
S. Mary Aquinas Haas	3/8/1933	7/18/1978
S. Grace Marie Gibson	8/15/1920	7/27/1978
S. Mary Martin Scanlan	9/6/1915	9/6/1978
S. Rose Gertrude Gardner Hamilton	7/7/1931	9/15/1978
S. Catherine Lorraine Reilly	6/17/1933	9/29/1978
S. Mary Hildegarde Eberwein	8/15/1925	10/19/1978
S. Mary Emile Gamba	4/4/1920	10/25/1978
S. Mary Agnesia O'Sullivan	8/15/1907	11/28/1978
S. Mary Cornelius Gleason	8/15/1948	12/22/1978
S. Julia Gilmore	3/26/1919	1/7/1979
S. Mary Clement O'Neil	6/11/1924	2/20/1979

S. Mary Athanasia Hogan	10/10/1924	2/26/1979
S. Anne Leo Cooney	3/26/1919	3/30/1979
S. Louis Marie O'Leary	3/25/1914	5/6/1979
S. Mary Vincenta Giacomini	10/4/1914	12/4/1979
S. Mary Margaret Shea	8/15/1947	12/24/1979
S. Mary Alexine Hollenback	7/19/1930	1/21/1980
S. Mary Alberta McEvoy	3/9/1928	1/25/1980
S. Mary Margaret Coughlin	3/8/1933	5/25/1980
S. Mary Hedwig Herzog	3/25/1908	6/1/1980
S. Frances Clare Harrington	3/25/1916	6/5/1980
S. Ann Raphael Mahoney	6/18/1939	11/5/1980
S. Mary Baptista Ward	7/2/1906	12/7/1980
S. Eulalia Uhlrich	3/9/1932	12/22/1980
S. Mary Bernardine Hon	12/18/1924	12/27/1980
S. Mary George Wanstrath	8/15/1929	1/8/1981
S. Ann Francis Creal	9/25/1923	1/31/1981
S. Mary Ernestine Whitmore	4/19/1923	2/22/1981
S. Agnes Cecilia Fennelly	6/9/1921	2/25/1981
S. Rose Margaret Lee	6/17/1933	5/3/1981
S. Mary Catherine Palmer	8/15/1951	6/8/1981
S. Joan Marie Erbacher	4/15/1918	8/10/1981
S. Mary Ermin Lambrecht	8/15/1950	11/5/1981
S. Ann Regina Van Zele	12/26/1923	1/13/1982
S. Mary Flora (Hickey) Lewis	5/11/1913	1/24/1982
S. Mary Stephen Conway	8/5/1933	2/9/1982
S. Mary Victor Whitman	8/15/1927	3/3/1982
S. Ann Veronica Gleason	2/19/1923	3/9/1982
S. Mary Stella Seaman	12/28/1929	5/26/1982
S. Bernard Connell	5/10/1923	8/12/1982
S. Mary Odile Bohrer	3/9/1925	9/5/1982
S. Alexandrine Dowling	9/6/1915	10/12/1982
S. Ann Gabriel Callan	10/4/1914	12/8/1982

S. Margaret Alacoque Crowley	3/25/1916	12/8/1982
S. Mary Mark Orr	6/27/1926	12/23/1982
S. Mary Boniface Lynch	3/25/1912	1/17/1983
S. Anne Anderson	8/6/1934	2/27/1983
S. Mary Dominica Niland	2/2/1917	3/7/1983
S. Theodora Merrick	12/25/1922	7/1/1983
S. Mary Ruth Mangan	4/4/1920	8/3/1983
S. Rose Elizabeth McFadden	3/2/1942	8/18/1983
S. Mary Vincentine Gripkey	6/17/1929	8/29/1983
S. Josephine Mitchell	5/3/1914	10/7/1983
S. Mary Chrysostom Knox	7/19/1916	10/23/1983
S. Catherine Ann McCormack	3/10/1946	2/16/1984
S. Mary Aquin Fischer	6/28/1938	3/8/1984
S. Mary Linus Harrington	9/29/1912	3/25/1984
S. Rose Dominic Gabisch	6/19/1925	4/23/1984
S. Ignatius Loyola Ryan	7/19/1937	6/4/1984
S. Mary Dolorine Eakes	6/25/1931	6/5/1984
S. Helen Joseph Gillespie	3/8/1933	9/22/1984
S. Charlotte Swain	2/15/1949	9/27/1984
S. Agnes Eugenia Finn	3/9/1934	11/11/1984
S. Rose Bernard Renyer	2/16/1932	11/24/1984
S. Marianna DeTarr	4/12/1914	3/30/1985
S. Kathleen Connors	5/2/1926	3/31/1985
S. Mary Eileen Whitman	6/19/1925	4/27/1985
S. Rose Michael O'Connor	3/9/1928	5/24/1985
S. Helen McDevitt	8/15/1950	6/8/1985
S. Helena Fisher	2/7/1920	7/22/1985
S. Cornelia Donnelly	4/20/1919	9/9/1985
S. Mary Daniel Foxworthy	10/10/1924	11/9/1985
S. Anne Clarice Tibbetts	6/19/1925	3/14/1986
S. Adrienne Mitchell	3/4/1943	7/15/1986
S. Xavier Andree	8/16/1940	7/27/1986

S. Eleonora Baldessari	6/27/1926	7/31/1986
S. Mary Cyprian Friedman	8/15/1915	9/28/1986
S. Angela Marie Doman	6/8/1930	10/16/1986
S. Mary Ursula Dailey	10/22/1930	11/10/1986
S. Mary Madeleine Hefner	12/29/1918	12/3/1986
S. James Marie Taney	6/27/1937	1/1/1987
S. Francis Regis Verschelden	12/25/1921	3/8/1987
S. Mary Audrey Neugebauer	7/19/1926	3/27/1987
S. Marie Celeste Bride	3/2/1942	5/25/1987
S. Mary Aurita Donovan	6/18/1935	7/22/1987
S. Mary Irene Lally	12/8/1917	8/11/1987
S. Frances Floersch	3/26/1919	8/28/1987
S. Mary Raymond Hanratty	3/25/1915	9/20/1987
S. Ann Modesta Mulholland	6/17/1934	11/11/1987
S. Mary Anita Doleshal	6/27/1937	12/3/1987
S. Mary Eunice Murphy	2/14/1926	12/28/1987
S. Mary Catherine Carter	8/15/1950	1/19/1988
S. Mary de Lourdes Schuelle	1/21/1918	2/25/1988
S. Margaret Angela O'Rourke	3/8/1927	7/4/1988
S. Ann Virginia Petty	6/18/1935	7/15/1988
S. Mary Afra White	11/1/1914	8/1/1988
Mother Leo Frances Ryan	6/17/1928	8/11/1988
S. Mary Edmunda Pratt	6/27/1937	11/11/1988
S. Mary Angela Welsh	12/14/1927	2/1/1989
S. Mary Anselm Towle	6/20/1929	2/19/1989
S. Mary Concetta Mock	8/22/1956	4/28/1989
S. Evangelista Wiss	12/18/1915	6/23/1989
S. Bernice Himmelberg	2/15/1951	8/5/1989
S. Mary Ann Wheaton	8/15/1951	10/9/1989
S. Mary Columba Connaughton	6/8/1930	2/8/1990
S. Cecilia Marie Desch	7/2/1932	7/30/1990
S. Mary Owen Horner	6/28/1938	9/9/1990

S. Rose Teresa McHale	2/17/1921	12/9/1990
S. Eugene Teresa McCarthy	6/18/1935	3/31/1991
S. Ann Teresa Conroy	3/16/1930	4/15/1991
S. Kathleen Anderson	10/14/1932	4/22/1991
S. Jean Marie Reilly	12/8/1931	5/29/1991
S. Mary Winifred O'Donnell	12/8/1933	8/6/1991
S. Vincentia McDermott	6/18/1935	1/22/1992
S. Kathleen Keenan	6/19/1940	1/23/1992
S. Laura Gutierrez	1/11/1967	4/10/1992
S. Ellen Marie Gibb	1/7/1936	5/9/1992
S. Rosalie Mahoney	3/4/1943	6/20/1992
S. Mary Serena Sheehy	3/4/1943	7/2/1992
S. Mary Theodosia Roth	6/2/1927	7/10/1992
S. Patricia Eeraerts	6/17/1927	8/14/1992
S. Jane Frances Bauman	7/19/1926	10/21/1992
S. Margaret Dolores Green	3/2/1940	10/24/1992
S. Mary Jane Wilson	2/14/1926	10/28/1992
S. Laurentia Sullivan	3/26/1919	11/30/1992
S. Mary Lucy Downey	2/22/1954	12/20/1992
S. Zita Marie Cotter	3/3/1942	12/27/1992
S. Mary Josephine Engelhardt	3/4/1950	12/29/1992
S. Margaret Frances Robertson	3/12/1937	2/4/1993
S. Mary de Paul Downey	6/27/1937	3/6/1993
S. Jomary Schwieder	6/28/1938	4/22/1993
S. Mary Immaculata Desmond	3/25/1916	7/6/1993
S. Mary Nadine Feuerborn	8/22/1953	8/27/1993
S. Jean Stewart	8/15/1947	9/1/1993
S. Mary Judith Flynn	1/21/1918	10/18/1993
S. Mary Lawrence Sullivan	6/17/1928	11/5/1993
S. Agnes Rita O'Neill	6/8/1930	11/9/1993
S. Mary Suzanne Braun	2/15/1949	11/24/1993
S. Mary Eugene Francis	6/17/1934	11/25/1993

S. Mary Ann Gausz	6/17/1934	12/30/1993
S. Mary Regis McEnroe	2/16/1932	1/1/1994
S. Mary Mercita Jackson	12/19/1940	1/4/1994
S. Elizabeth Ann West	6/15/1932	1/8/1994
S. Mary Aurelia Henry	6/17/1927	1/12/1994
S. Clare Mary Hayes	3/16/1930	1/21/1994
S. Rose Vincent Staten	10/30/1927	1/29/1994
S. Mary Romana Hirschfeld	8/15/1927	3/3/1994
S. Mary Constantia Towle	6/17/1928	3/10/1994
S. Teresa Marie McCaffrey	6/25/1931	4/1/1994
S. Ann William Mountain	6/18/1935	6/10/1994
S. Therese Klepac	8/24/1961	7/10/1994
S. John Gabriel Cahill	6/28/1938	8/28/1994
S. Mary Baptist Franklin	10/30/1927	9/22/1994
S. Louise Vosen	12/26/1925	11/14/1994
S. Agnes Clare Moylan	3/25/1922	1/11/1995
S. Mary Gregory Dusselier	6/17/1933	2/2/1995
S. Mary Edmund Gray	6/17/1933	3/22/1995
S. Mary Alma Humm	2/22/1953	4/22/1995
S. Walter Marie Coyne	2/19/1956	8/19/1995
S. Alice Higbee	2/15/1952	10/8/1995
S. Ann Loretta Carney	2/16/1933	11/29/1995
S. Ann Raymond Downey	4/5/1921	12/2/1995
S. Frances Edward Bauman	6/20/1936	2/1/1996
S. Mary Borromeo Brose	6/17/1928	2/13/1996
S. Agnes Vincent Bauman	2/17/1921	4/12/1996
S. Ann Patrick Callahan	8/22/1954	6/12/1996
S. Mary Hubert Gockel	2/22/1954	7/22/1996
S. Alice Therese Dorsey	6/27/1937	7/23/1996
S. Marian Berry	6/19/1940	7/29/1996
S. Joseph Louise Gallagher	6/20/1936	12/14/1996
S. Barbara Ann Kaberlein	2/16/1933	12/15/1996

Name	Born	Died
S. Therese Deplazes	6/17/1927	12/28/1996
S. Ann Vincent Roth	12/14/1927	12/28/1996
S. Charlotte Marie Howell	6/15/1932	1/22/1997
S. Mary Carmella Neuman	3/2/1940	4/7/1997
S. Mary Camilla Montgomery	8/18/1927	6/16/1997
S. Mary Jude Redle	7/19/1934	7/23/1997
S. Alice Vincent Downey	6/25/1931	8/20/1997
S. Frances Joseph Whitman	7/19/1930	9/1/1997
S. Mary Cornelia Haffey	6/17/1928	10/11/1997
S. Mary Louise Sullivan	12/8/1931	10/21/1997
S. Mary Carlotta Flynn	8/15/1922	11/3/1997
S. Mary Coletta Michaud	6/27/1937	3/21/1998
S. Agnes Steiner	6/18/1935	5/10/1998
S. Mary Thomasine O'Connor	6/28/1938	7/8/1998
S. Vivian Podrebarac	2/15/1952	9/2/1998
S. Mary Conrad Ihlefeld	6/18/1935	9/22/1998
S. Dolores Hall	8/15/1947	10/14/1998
S. Thomas Aquinas O'Connor	3/9/1931	10/23/1998
S. Mary Lucian Winter	3/16/1930	11/14/1998
S. Mary Irmina Scheetz	12/25/1922	12/4/1998
S. Mary Antonia Talle	3/6/1945	12/14/1998
S. Mary Jacinta Teets	2/15/1950	12/14/1998
S. Anna Rose Hanne	8/15/1950	1/3/1999
S. Mary James Harrington	6/17/1928	1/19/1999
S. Mary Veronica O'Toole	3/2/1942	4/7/1999
S. Marguerite Koch	3/2/1942	8/8/1999
S. Ann Patrice Harrington	9/20/1933	8/10/1999
S. Marcellina Telgmann	8/15/1928	8/31/1999
S. Michael Marie O'Leary	8/15/1947	10/18/1999
S. Mary Florentia Schouten	6/25/1931	10/20/1999
S. Mary Harrington	3/9/1925	10/31/1999
S. Michael Therese Magrath	8/22/1956	12/3/1999

S. Catherine Hartman	6/18/1935	1/9/2000
S. Rose Marie Desch	6/17/1934	3/21/2000
S. Mary Madeleva Ditmars	8/15/1949	3/27/2000
S. Frances Catherine Curran	3/16/1930	6/12/2000
S. Agnes Celine Dooley	12/8/1930	9/11/2000
S. Mary Valeria Monnig	7/7/1931	10/3/2000
S. Gabriella Connell	3/2/1940	12/20/2000
S. Rose Linus Manley	7/19/1941	12/25/2000
S. Maureen Kauffman	6/20/1929	12/26/2000
S. Maura Thompson	6/17/1934	1/12/2001
S. Mary de Sales DeLange	3/4/1943	2/11/2001
S. Mary Corine Pohle	6/18/1935	4/3/2001
S. Mary Paulette Fitzgerald	3/10/1946	4/17/2001
S. Ann Perpetua Swiderski	6/18/1935	6/5/2001
S. Genevieve Tebedo	12/8/1916	6/21/2001
S. George Towle	6/18/1935	8/20/2001
S. Ann Lorraine Repp	6/19/1940	9/6/2001
S. Mary Liguori Horvat	6/17/1934	10/4/2001
S. Antonella Gonzales	9/2/1963	11/15/2001
S. Jean Bernadette Baldessari	2/17/1946	11/28/2001
S. Charles McGowan	9/17/1953	12/3/2001
S. Agnes Klein	2/15/1952	12/11/2001
S. Mary Dolorita Flynn	6/18/1935	12/24/2001
S. Mary Clare Meek	3/2/1941	2/11/2002
S. Joan Therese Cunningham	6/17/1934	2/19/2002
S. Mary Jerome Kelly	6/18/1935	3/17/2002
S. Ruth Barron	6/20/1950	4/18/2002
S. Frances Eileen Donnelly	3/10/1935	5/27/2002
S. Jean Carmel Guth	3/6/1945	6/3/2002
S. Rose Paul Tetyak	6/17/1934	6/24/2002
S. Herman Joseph Koch	6/20/1936	8/26/2002
S. Rose Anne Colvin	6/28/1938	10/15/2002

S. Mary Thomas O'Flannigan	3/10/1946	11/21/2002
S. Rose Tomlin	6/15/1932	12/6/2002
S. Mary Carol Conroy	2/19/1961	12/8/2002
S. Mary Magdalen Merrick	6/25/1931	1/16/2003
S. Mary Gertrude Glotzbach	8/15/1951	1/27/2003
S. Edward Mary Brown	8/22/1954	2/15/2003
S. Mary Seraphine Sheehan	6/8/1930	2/23/2003
S. Noreen Kerscher	6/17/1934	3/23/2003
S. Marie Ann Bertels	8/22/1955	3/28/2003
S. Joan Allard	3/4/1943	4/7/2003
S. Agnes Ellen Smith	6/15/1932	5/5/2003
S. Mary Peter Brost	6/17/1929	5/9/2003
S. Margaret Mary Sajbel	7/19/1927	7/22/2003
S. Mary Elaine Murphy	1/9/1942	7/25/2003
S. Daniel Stefani	3/6/1944	9/8/2003
S. Mary Janet McGilley	2/15/1948	9/13/2003
S. Ruth Anne Desch	6/28/1938	10/15/2003
S. Mildred Marie Irwin	6/17/1933	10/22/2003
S. Rose Celine Siebers	6/18/1935	10/30/2003
S. Rose Carmel McKenna	6/20/1936	11/3/2003
S. Joan Kilker	8/22/1955	11/20/2003
S. Anna Mary Lawrence	3/2/1942	11/26/2003
S. Catherine Labouré Conway	6/27/1937	2/11/2004
S. Mary Julie Casey	2/19/1956	2/18/2004
S. Mary Ellenita Uhlrich	3/10/1935	3/13/2004
S. Mary Pauline Degan	6/18/1935	4/12/2004
S. Francetta O'Donnell	3/11/1936	4/20/2004
S. Patricia Field	9/2/1962	4/25/2004
S. Margaret Petty	8/22/1953	4/29/2004
S. Madelon Burns	3/2/1941	5/27/2004
S. Maurita Postlewait	8/6/1934	8/5/2004
S. Ann Dolores Muckenthaler	3/9/1928	9/6/2004

S. Mary Catherine Daugherty	3/4/1943	9/22/2004
S. Ann Jeannette Mathias	3/9/1934	10/26/2004
S. Barbara McCauley	8/22/1953	10/26/2004
S. Kathleen Coman	8/15/1948	12/11/2004
S. Monica Coz	8/15/1951	12/20/2004
S. Clarice Marie Heaney	2/15/1951	1/22/2005
S. Macrina Ryan	2/15/1952	2/6/2005
S. Mary Eugenia Floersch	3/2/1941	3/24/2005
S. Rose Anita Young	12/19/1942	4/26/2005
S. Alice Marie Schwieder	12/19/1940	5/20/2005
S. John Regis Lesser	6/18/1935	7/7/2005
S. Leo Marie Cooper	8/15/1951	7/19/2005
S. Mary Brost	6/17/1934	7/23/2005
S. Maureen Writt	3/9/1932	7/26/2005
S. Mary Hugh Dearborn	9/17/1953	8/5/2005
S. Agnes Lobeck	3/2/1940	9/5/2005
S. Mary Raymunda Painter	3/4/1943	10/15/2005
S. Ann McGloin	9/17/1947	10/18/2005
S. Sally Virginia Watson	6/28/1938	11/2/2005
S. Marie Therese Bride	6/27/1937	12/13/2005
S. Ann Margaret Noonan	6/18/1935	12/23/2005

INDEX

Academy, St. Mary's. *See* St. Mary's Academy
Anniversary—125th, 349, 350–51
Annunciation Chapel, 398–99
Annunciation High School, Denver, Colorado, 208–9
Apostolate Study—1975, 98, 136, 138–41, 153–54, 158
area superiors, 38, 100
Associates, 77, 335, 364–65, 396, 412, 416, 438, 496, 500

Berchmans, Mother Mary, 6, 22
Berchmans Hall, 225–26, 244
Bethany, Kansas City, Kansas, 473
Between Alpha and Omega, 419
Bicentennial, national, 155
Billings Central High School, Billings, Montana, 211–13
Bishop Hogan High School, Kansas City, Missouri, 213–16
Butte Central High School, Butte, Montana, 202–3

campus ministry, 288
CareQuest, 481–82
Casey, Sister Mary Julie, 255, 332, 335, 464
centennial, Community, 3, 8, 20, 22, 24
chaplains, 118, 401–2
Charity Federation. *See* Federation of Charity
Charity Notes, 494, 496
child care, 3–4, 7–8, 159, 177, 439, 441

children's homes
   Guardian Angel Orphanage, Leavenworth, Kansas, 160
   Holy Child Nursery, Denver, Colorado, 168
   Mount St. Vincent's Home, Denver, Colorado, 39–40, 149, 168–72, 349, 438–41
   St. Ann Infant Home, Helena and Deer Lodge, Montana, 167
   St. Joseph's Home, Helena, Montana, 39, 166–68
   St. Vincent's Home, Leavenworth, Kansas, 4, 30–31, 160–62
   St. Vincent's Home, Topeka, Kansas, 149, 162–65, 440
Clifford, Brother Peter, FSC, 386–87
Cristo Rey Kansas City, 495, 501, 504
clinics
   Caritas Clinic, Denver, Colorado, 268
   Caritas Clinics, Inc., Leavenworth and Kansas City, Kansas, 262–63
   Duchesne Clinic, Kansas City, Kansas, 262, 389, 472
   Marian Clinic, Topeka, Kansas, 263–64, 472
   Marillac Clinic, Grand Junction, Colorado, 265–66, 472
   Martin de Porres Dental Clinic, Topeka, Kansas, 264
   Saint Vincent Clinic, Leavenworth, Kansas, 261, 472, 508
   Venice Family Clinic, Santa Monica, California, 284
clinical pastoral ministry, 308

Combo, Sister Marie de Paul, 156, 327–28, 365
Come North project. *See* Converging Paths
communications
  audit, 495
  Chapter Newsletter, 332
  committee, 397, 403
  Connecting, 77, 301
  Mother House Moments and letters, 26–27
  Perspective, 86
  Relay, 95–96
  SCL Newsletter, 26
  Voices of Charity, 491
Community Chapters
  1956 and 1962, 19, 21, 29–30
  1968–1969: Advisory Board, 94; Apostolate Directors, 94–95, 115, 132; election, 86–87; Reports to Chapter, 96–97, 98
  1973–1974: Active Reconciliation, 132; Commission on Community, 123–28, 132, 135–6; Commission on Governance, 130–31, 132, 135; Commission on Mission, 129–30, 132, 136; Commission on Spirituality, 128–29; election, 136–37; Reports to Chapter, 132–34
  1980: election, 335–36; Reports to Chapter, 331–33
  1986: Chapter Statement, 361–62; election, 360–61; Reports to Chapter, 357–59
  1992: Chapter Statement, 376; election, 375–77; Reports to Chapter, 373–74
  1998: Chapter Statement, 397–98; election, 392, 399; Reports to Chapter, 392–97
  2004: Chapter Statement, 490–91, 506, 508; Community Director's address, 988–89; election, 491–94; Reports to Chapter, 488–94
Community Constitutions
  Congregation for Religious review, 330, 349
  LCWR evaluation, 335–38
  revisions, 48, 53, 99–100, 101–2, 329–31
Conferences, national
  Conference of Major Superiors of Women (CMSW), 21, 42, 93
  Leadership Conference of Women Religious (LCWR), ix, 117–18, 291, 485, 495
  National Congress of Religious, 1951, 42
  National Congress of Major Superiors, 117–18
  National Sisters Vocation Conference, ix, 387
  Notre Dame Institute of Spirituality, 2, 42
Confraternity of Christian Doctrine, 20, 33–34, 46, 292–93
Congregation for Religious, 6, 18–19, 34, 41, 86–87, 117–18, 291
Converging Paths, 390–92
Cresap, McCormick, and Paget, 98, 253

degree completion programs, 228, 232–33, 241
Delaney, Sister Mary Asella, 251–52
Denver Archdiocese Housing, 311–12
DePaul Hospital, Cheyenne, Wyoming, 286–87
De Paul Library, 230–31, 237, 239–40, 244, 387, 458
Donnelly, Sister Cornelia, 249–50, 253
Downey, Sister Ann Raymond, 250

education
  certification, 7

INDEX 605

evaluation, 6–7, 23, 116, 142–44, 182
ministry, 133–34, 145–48, 178, 183–84, 200–202, 219–21, 445–47, 452–53, 462–63
Professional Education Board, 134
supervision, 27, 183, 195–96
El Centro, 389, 432, 502
elementary schools
consolidation, 184, 186, 187–88, 191–92, 197–99, 446
Kansas, 184–86, 188–90
Missouri, 186–87
West and Far West, 40, 191–95, 446–47
Exempla Saint Joseph Hospital, Denver, Colorado, 23, 168, 267–69, 381–82, 470–71, 432, 479–80
Federation of Charity, 365, 389, 404–5, 434, 495
Fitzgerald, Sister Mary Paul, 3, 4, 22, 225
formation, 37, 92–93, 116–17, 134, 340, 348, 367, 397, 427–28
See also Sister Formation Movement
Forums
  general, 135–36, 331, 335, 344–46
  local, 335, 344–46, 347
Founders Day, 24
Gabisch, Sister Rose Dominic, 22, 31, 47, 179, 223, 239
Girls Central High School, Butte, Montana, 202
Häring, Bernard, CSCR, 122–23, 125
Harvest Committee, 426–27
Hayden High School, Topeka, Kansas, 209–11
health care, 7, 149, 150–52, 247–48, 288, 304–5, 325, 433
higher education, 300–301, 318–19

Hinds, Carol, 244, 386
Hispanic ministry, 319–21
Hollow, Sister Mary Kevin, 87, 136–37, 157, 224, 330, 335, 363–66
Holy Rosary Healthcare, Miles City, Montana, 395–96, 472–73, 478
home health care, 261, 305–7, 307–8
Horvat, Sister Mary Liguori, 25, 47–53, 176
Immaculata High School, Leavenworth, Kansas, 206–8
Immaculate Conception–St. Joseph parish, Leavenworth, Kansas, 150th anniversary, 495–96
In the Spirit of Charity gathering, 404–5
incorporation
  hospitals, 259–60, 264, 474
Mount St. Vincent's Home, 377
Saint Mary College, 386
Institute for Superiors, 22
Irwin, Sister Mildred Marie, 254, 255, 283, 465
John XXIII, 24, 31, 42–43, 70, 76, 85, 507
John Paul II, 172, 354, 371, 372, 373, 377, 402, 452, 484, 485, 505, 510
Jubilee 2000, 401–5
Juneteenth celebration, 161
Keenan, Sister Kathleen, 250–51
Kelly, Sister Mary Elizabeth, 237
Kennedy Child Study Center/Child and Family Development Center, 283–89

Latin America
Director of Missions for, 335
formation programs in, 335, 365, 428
fortieth anniversary of community service in, 428

INDEX

Latin American missions
  Bolivia, 33, 335, 352
  Ecuador, 390, 393–94
  Guatemala, 335
  Peru, 31–32, 335, 393–94
lay boards
  hospitals, 27, 36, 474
  Mount St. Vincent's Home, 377
  Saint Mary College, 386
Leadership Conference of Women Religious (LCWR), ix, 117–18, 291, 425, 434, 485, 495
Liturgy Committee, 349
long-range planning, 427
Louise de Marillac, 61, 86, 118–19, 266, 435
Macowski, Father Richard, OFM, 394–95
Mahoney, Sister Rosalie 260–61
Maria Hall, 30, 225
Marian Mother's Guild, 21
Marillac Center, 434–36
Martha and Mary's Way, 436
McGilley, Sister Mary Janet, 31, 33, 156, 223, 227–28, 229–30, 245–46, 457
McGilley Field House, 458
Mead Hall, 244
Medical Staff Assembly, 33, 252
Medicare, 260, 278–79, 283, 499
Menuha House, 389, 436
Miege, John Baptist, SJ, 3, 5, 24, 496
Miege Hall, 30, 225
migrant ministry, 31, 297
Miller, Sister Sue, 241, 249, 360, 376, 415–16, 430–36, 494, 496
Ministry Development office, 388, 440, 499
mission integration/lay ministry formation, 378, 466–71, 474
Mother House
  Mission Statement, 436
  renovation, 434–35
  Ross Hall, 33, 348, 426
  Special Services, 148
Mother Xavier. *See* Ross, Mother Xavier
  Mother's Loan Library, 19
  Mount St. Joseph's Home, Kansas City, Kansas, 8, 150, 173–75
Murphy, Arthur M., 224, 228
Native American ministry, 261, 321–23, 451–52
nursing degree programs, 257–58
nursing schools, 256–57
O'Shea, Mother Mary Francesca, 2, 18
Our Lady of Perpetual Help, Falls City, Nebraska, 248
OutFront, 242
Partnerships with the Poor, 402, 488
pastoral ministry
  diocesan and archdiocesan, 315–18, 403–5, 454–55
  parish, 134, 149, 296, 298–300, 308, 316, 423, 453–54
Paul VI, 28, 42–43, 57, 85, 507
Personnel Board, 101, 135, 139–40, 152–53, 331, 335, 342, 350
  See also Placement Policy
Peru
  Chalaco, 175–77
  Chuschi, 496
  Piura, 496, 504
  Talara, 132
Phelps, C. Kermit, 237, 333
Phelps, Sister Constance, 244, 332, 394, 424–25, 485
physical therapy, 307
Pius XII, 2, 21, 24, 28, 41
Placement Policy, 115–16, 346, 350
prayer and spiritual life ministries, 301–4, 318, 324, 437

INDEX 607

prison ministry, 34, 228, 243, 312-14, 341-42
Providence Medical Center, Kansas City, Kansas, 36, 260, 280-82, 381-82, 474-75
Rainbow Reflection Days, 366-68
Red Carpet Reunion, 72, 77, 405
Regional Coordinators, 100-101, 109-15
regional meetings, 406, 487, 494-95
Reid, James, 394
religious education, 20, 33-34, 52, 134, 150, 292-95
renewal
community life and ministry, 47-53, 86, 94-95, 102-3, 117-18, 152-55, 309-10, 327-28, 361-63, 484-86, 498-99
Renewal and Experimentation Board, 92, 95, 101
Vatican II documents, 42, 47, 65-67, 79, 92, 98, 103-4, 582
See also Community Chapters
retirement fund, 135, 499
Rite of Christian Initiation for Adults (RCIA), 297-98
Ross, Mother Xavier, 1, 3-4, 15, 155, 159, 404, 496
Ross Hall. *See* Mother House, Ross Hall
Ryan, Mother Leo Frances, 21, 24, 30, 34-36, 120-22, 253, 364
Ryan, Sister Macrina, 256, 335, 465-66
Ryan Center, 386

Sacred Heart High School, Falls City, Nebraska, 217
Saint John Hospital, Leavenworth, Kansas, 4, 27, 31, 258-60, 261, 282, 383, 475
Saint John's Health Center, Santa Monica, California, 7, 21, 27, 33, 282-86, 384-86, 444, 480-81

Saint Mary College/University of Saint Mary
academic programs, 8, 27, 224-26, 230-33, 234-35, 243-44, 457
Ancilla Center, 226-27
athletic programs, 230, 244-45, 394-95
campus ministry, 235, 238
College Community Cultural co-education, 244
Council, 236, 234-40, 496
faculty, 224, 230-34, 235-38, 239-40, 496
foreign student exchange, 233, 235
Global Studies Institute, 458, 502
Graduate Division, 179, 223
master's degrees, 41, 223-24, 386, 456, 460-62
mission, 222-23, 455, 457
nursing degree program, 338, 458-59
OutFront, 242
prison programs, 228, 241-43, 386
public programs, 225, 233-38, 459
service learning, 459-60
Student Life, 226, 231-32, 243-44
St. Ann's Hospital, Anaconda, Montana, 248
St. Anthony's Hospital, Las Vegas, New Mexico, 40, 248-49
St. Francis Health Center, Topeka, Kansas, 263, 277-80, 382-83, 468-69, 476
St. James Healthcare, Butte, Montana, 27, 269-71, 379-80, 477-78
St. John's Hospital, Helena, Montana, 7, 248
St. Joseph's Dining Hall, 30, 225, 227
St. Joseph's Hospital, Deer Lodge, Montana, 248
St. Mary's Academy, 2, 4, 200, 223
St. Mary's Hall, 223, 244
St. Mary's High School, St. Mary's, Kansas, 208

INDEX 809

Sturz, Father John, 61, 238, 387, 503
Sullivan, Sister Mary Louise, 22, 239
surveys, national
　National Catholic Education
　　Association, 24
　Conference of Major Superiors of
　　Women (CMSW), 43-47, 49,
　　59-60, 63-64, 79, 89
　Leadership Conference of Women
　　Religious (LCWR), 291
　National Sisters' Vocation
　　Conference, 108, 109
surveys, Community
　Apostolate, 141-45, 150-51, 349-50
　former sisters, 63-80
　friends and colleagues, 416-22
　ministries, 441-44
　pre-Chapter, 1968 and 1973, 38-39,
　　87, 88-92, 105-7
　regional coordinators, 115-16
　sisters, 139, 405-15
Swain, Sister Charlotte, 352-54

tertianship, 18
Theology Update task force, 403, 488
tutoring, 291-92

Van Hoose, Sandra, 242, 456
Vatican II, ix, 10, 18, 34, 85, 118, 180,
　342, 348, 407-8, 485-86
Vincent de Paul, 9, 118-19, 128, 155,
　266, 290, 365
Vincentian charism, 93, 130, 238, 368,
　437, 510
vocation ministry, 365-66, 388, 427
vows ceremony, 18, 501

Ward, Sister Mary Baptista, 195-96
Ward High School, Kansas City,
　Kansas, 203-6, 220

Xavier Hall, 223, 244
Xavier Houses, 389, 436
Xavier Theater, 234

SCL Health Services
　Corporation/SCL Health
　System, 253-56, 260-61, 289-90,
　379, 395, 422, 464, 482, 505
Shea, Sister Mary Margaret, 254-55
Sheehan, Sister Mary Seraphine, 104,
　137-38, 270
Sister Formation Movement, 24-26,
　37, 41, 47, 179
social encyclicals, 42-43, 228, 336
Social Justice Network, 347, 388, 405
Social Justice Office, 327, 344, 347,
　365, 396, 434
Social Security, 2, 135
social service ministries
　adoption services, 440
　Catholic Social Services, 440
　counseling, 314
　Emergency Assistance Center, 326
　foster care, 439-40
　Foster Grandparents, 277
　housing ministry, 311-12, 431-33
　L'Arche, 324-25, 437-38
　Mother-to-Mother ministry, 389
　service to the poor, 34, 325-27
　special education, 295-96
　sponsorship, institutional, 377, 464-65
Spoor, Mother Mary Ancilla, 18-19,
　24, 157-58, 238-39, 252
Steele, Sister Diane, 223, 456
Stefani, Sister Mary Kathleen, 335-36,
　360-61, 388, 392-93, 398, 434

St. Mary's Hospital and Medical
　Center, Grand Junction,
　Colorado, 272-75, 381, 469-70,
　478-79
St. Pius X High School, Kansas City,
　Missouri, 217-19
St. Vincent Center, Piura, Peru, 496
St. Vincent Healthcare, Billings,
　Montana, 8, 21, 36, 275-76,
　380-81, 467, 472, 476-77
St. Vincent's Hospital, Leadville,
　Montana, 248